MW00780501

The 1931 Manuscript

of

An Objective Impartial Criticism of the Life of Man or Beelzebub's Tales to His Grandson

Edited by Robin Bloor

KARNAK PRESS

Austin, Texas

The 1931 Manuscript of Beelzebub's Tales to His Grandson

ISBN 978-0-9789791-9-5

Printed in the United States of America

The cover design is based on a photograph of an Armenian carpet

KARNAK PRESS

Introduction

The book, authored by G. I. Gurdjieff and published in 1950 under the title: ***An Objectively Impartial Criticism of the Life of Man or Beelzebub's Tales To His Grandson***, requires no improvement. It is, in the view of this book's editor, Gurdjieff's meticulously prepared and fully complete literary masterpiece—an objective work of art.

Why then publish this earlier version?

The 1931 Manuscript was the first complete draft in a series of author's drafts that led up to the eventual publication of his masterpiece in 1950. It has a particular historical importance. It is the last draft of ***The Tales****[*] that Alfred Orage worked on, and it is the only other version of ***The Tales*** which Gurdjieff sanctioned for publication prior to his death, albeit privately in a limited edition.

The Historical Context

The 1931 Manuscript was, strange though it may now seem, the first book related to the Gurdjieff Work to be published. Gurdjieff's ***Herald of Coming Good***, which might be thought of as occupying that position, was not published until 1933.

The record suggests that just 100 mimeographed copies were made of the manuscript and that they were sold for $10.00 each. Alfred Orage organized their publication, in an effort to raise funds for Gurdjieff. Prior to its publication, from 1926 to 1930, Orage held group meetings that studied and discussed some of the draft chapters of ***The Tales***. Concurrently, he was editing and refining the text of ***The Tales*** in collaboration with Gurdjieff.

* For the sake of brevity, we adopted the convention of referring to ***An Objectively Impartial Criticism of the Life of Man or Beelzebub's Tales To His Grandson*** as ***The Tales*** throughout this book.

Notes on those meetings that Orage held were published, in edited form, by C. S. Nott in his book ***Teachings of Gurdjieff: A Pupil's Journey.*** They were also recently published by Book Studio, in a more complete form, in a book entitled ***Orage's Commentary on Gurdjieff's "Beelzebub's Tales To His Grandson."*** This latter book publishes the notes taken at those meetings by Lawrence Morris and Sherman Manchester.

Students of The Work who read either book could be forgiven for assuming that the comments made during those meetings relate to the 1950 published version of ***The Tales***, but they do not. Neither do they necessarily refer to the text of ***The 1931 Manuscript*** published here, since Orage will at times have been working from earlier versions of the text.

In any event, when Orage published the limited edition of ***The 1931 Manuscript,*** there was a group of his close pupils who were familiar with some of the text of ***The Tales*** and had discussed its literary form with Orage. No doubt these were the primary audience for ***The 1931 Manuscript***, which at the price of $10 was expensive indeed ($10 in 1931 was roughly equivalent to $140 now).

It was not until 1927 that Gurdjieff organized public readings from draft chapters of his book. His motivation for organizing such readings was to observe the reaction of audiences to his work. We can only guess at what Gurdjieff was able to know from watching audience reactions to such readings, but it is clear that this was how he measured whether ***The Tales*** was having the "objective impact" that he intended. And in 1927, it wasn't.

He explains this clearly in ***Life Is Real, Only Then When 'I Am'***:

> ". . . when, after working for almost three years with unimaginable difficulties and being ready to die happily, I certainly and clearly understood, without doubt, that, of these writings of mine, people who did

> not know me personally could understand absolutely nothing."

So it was that in the subsequent three years, in collaboration with Orage, he revised the book completely. As far as we know there is no remaining record of that first "incorrect" draft, and there is scant evidence of what it contains. There is, however, this trace, as reported in ***To Fathom The Gist: Volume 2 The Arch-absurd***:

> It is also clear from this record that significant changes were indeed made. A clear example of this can be found in the notes of a meeting held on January 31st, 1927, which reads:
>
> "The Archangel Psycharchy decided in view of this foreseen necessity to set off to secure permission from His Endlessness."
>
> We find this quite startling. Clearly, in the earlier version of The Tales, Gurdjieff named this Archangel Psycharchy. This is Archangel Sakaki, who led the commission of Angels and Archangels sent to the solar system Ors to investigate the collision of the comet Kondoor with Earth.
>
> The etymology of the name Psycharchy suggests "rule by the psyche" or "rule by the mind." In Greek mythology, the Goddess Psyche (meaning "soul" or "breath of life") consorts with Eros (meaning "sexual love" or "desire").

The note about Psycharchy is published in ***Orage's Commentary on Gurdjieff's Beelzebub's Tales to His Grandson: New York Talks 1926-1930***.

So ***The 1931 Manuscript*** is the product of the years of effort from 1927 to 1931 to rewrite ***The Tales***. It is the version of ***The Tales*** that Gurdjieff refers to in ***Herald of Coming Good***, when he writes:

> "Since then, during all those years, until today, I occupied myself exclusively with writing, and often, on account of new plans which suggested themselves in the course of my meditations, I changed the text, as well as the outward form, of what was already written, and only last year did I finally adopt the text and the final form in which my writings will be published."

While, in 1931, Gurdjieff may have been reasonably satisfied with what he had produced, with the help of his literary team (Orage, Jean Toomer, Jane Heap, Bernard Metz, Olga de Hartmann, Lily Galumnian Chaverdian and others), his editing activity was in fact far from over. In the years between 1931 and 1949 Gurdjieff continued to have chapters from ***The Tales*** read out to groups of his pupils and to public audiences, and he continued to make changes to the book.

In those intervening years an extensive amount of new text was added and the original text was changed, usually in minor ways, but occasionally in very significant ways. ***The 1931 Manuscript*** is approximately 290,000 words in length, just 80 percent of the length of the eventual book which is roughly 360,000 words long. This difference in length is accounted for by the following factors:

- Gurdjieff made minor additions of detail to the text.
- In places Gurdjieff simply made the text more verbose and hence more difficult to comprehend.
- In some parts of the book he added new tales or embellished tales that were already there, adding significant further details.
- In a few places he restructured the main flow of the book. In particular it is clear that chapters 39, *The Holy Planet Purgatory* and 40, *Heptaparaparshinokh* were significantly

changed, with some text moving from chapter 40 to 39. Ultimately he lengthened both chapters. He also restructured chapters 44, 45 and 46, changing their order and adding text.

Gurdjieff removed very little text from *The 1931 Manuscript*, although there were a few pages that almost duplicated earlier content that he did remove.

The Virtues of The 1931 Manuscript

Readers who enjoy reading *The Tales* will most likely enjoy reading *The 1931 Manuscript.* Irrespective of the differences between the two, the text bears the mark of Gurdjieff. It is permeated with his rhythm and style. In some chapters the text is very similar to that of the 1950 publication, but in many other chapters it is distinctly different. And when reading those chapters you often get the impression that you are reading a book by Gurdjieff that you have not met with before. The subject matter may be familiar but the text is "entirely new."

Our experience suggests that *The 1931 Manuscript* has a very similar impact on the reader as the 1950 publication, when read in the first or second way that Gurdjieff recommends—that is:

> "at least as you have already become mechanized to read all your contemporary books and newspapers" (the first way)

and:

> "as if you were reading aloud to another person" (the second way).

The third mode of reading that Gurdjieff recommends to the reader, is to:

> "try and fathom the gist of my writings."

Our experience suggests that you will find ***The 1931 Manuscript*** very useful indeed for this effort. It provides you with a valid alternative version of the text. Both versions are unquestionably legitimate in the sense that they were completed and approved by Gurdjieff. Nevertheless, when read carefully on a word by word basis, they give different perspectives of meaning. If you discover any real contradiction between the two texts, there is no difficulty at all in resolving it, since the 1950 publication is undoubtedly the master version. However, that is rarely what you find. The more common outcome of reading both versions is that Gurdjieff's intended meaning seems to emerge more clearly.

We suspect that a very simple psychological mechanism comes into play here. When we have but one version of a particular sentence or paragraph, we may attach a slightly distorted meaning to it, simply by virtue of what Gurdjieff calls "mentation by form." However when we have two versions of the text the likelihood of such inner distortion is reduced or even eliminated.

In summary, then, there are two main reasons why someone might choose to read ***The 1931 Manuscript***.

- For the sheer joy of reading unfamiliar text written by Gurdjieff
- As part of an effort to "try and fathom the gist" of ***The Tales***.

Editing the Manuscript

Our initial editing work on ***The 1931 Manuscript*** was not done for the sake of publication. The goal was to produce a "cleaned" version of the text that was "easy to read and study." That work was carried out sporadically over about a year. The decision to publish the manuscript engendered a more detailed and precise editing effort. Taking these two efforts together, we describe below how the editing was done, explaining the motivation for our editing and typographical choices:

- The original 1931 manuscript was typed manually and bore all the characteristics of a typed document. It bore a typewriter font and there was no paragraph formatting at all. In publishing it, we naturally provided a publishing level of presentation. We adopted the same font choice (Garamond) and formatting as that of the 1950 publication of ***The Tales***, although we chose a slightly larger page size and font size.

- ***The 1931 Manuscript*** was clearly created and distributed in great haste. It exhibited many simple typos that would have been detected in a single edit pass by a competent copy editor. For example, one encountered the word "end" when "and" was intended, or the word "vary" where "very" was intended. Such errors are not difficult to spot and they are simple to correct. However, because we regarded every word in the text as important (every word was chosen by Gurdjieff), even in situations where the "mistake" seemed obvious, the editing process needed to be meticulous. So, where possible, for every error detected, the text was compared to the text of the 1950 publication. When the texts differed widely, we pondered the meaning and used our "common sense."

- Aside from typos there were also spelling errors, although surprisingly few—perhaps a testament to the diligence of the typists who worked on the manuscript.

- The spelling standard adopted in the original was UK English rather than American English. This is not surprising, of course, and probably only of little importance. Nevertheless, because this book is being published in the US, we adopted American spelling standards: labor for labour, center for centre, realize for realise, and so on. Similarly we imposed American punctuation standards.

- Gurdjieff's many invented words (neologisms) and names are particularly troublesome in the original manuscript. Many of them are spelt differently to the way they are spelt in the 1950 publication. We could have simply left them as they were, but to do so would have confused readers who are familiar with the 1950 text—probably the vast majority. Confusion would be particularly likely with frequently appearing words like Triamazikamno (sometimes rendered as Triamonia in the manuscript and sometimes not) and Heptaparaparshinokh (sometimes rendered as Eftologodiksis). In short, which word to use had not been standardized, so there were variances from chapter to chapter. To make matters worse, there was a particularly large number of typos among these words. As a consequence, in every instance we adopted the spelling used in the 1950 publication.

- While we decided that the standardization of the neologisms would make life easier for the reader, we were keen to provide a full record of the changes made, for the sake of those who might wish to study the differences between the two version of the book in every detail. Consequently, we also included a complete list of all such changes among the various indexes we provide.

- The punctuation of ***The Tales*** is very complex in some parts of the book. This is particularly the case with quotation marks. The original 1931 manuscript was not well punctuated in this respect. We edited it to conform with the punctuation in the 1950 publication. The standard adopted is as follows: When Beelzebub speaks his words are wrapped in quotation marks. When his words stretch over multiple paragraphs, the opening quotation marks are given at the start of each paragraph, but the closing ones are given only at the end of the final paragraph of his words. It becomes more complex when Beelzebub reports conversations he has had. When he reports what someone says, we get quotation marks within quotation marks. In such cases the normal convention of alternating double quotation marks with single quotation marks is used. This becomes even more complex, as happens once or twice, when Beelzebub reports someone speaking who, in turn, is reporting someone speaking.

- Gurdjieff also employs the typographical style of using quotes for emphasis. For example, he wrote "they therefore kept on demanding what they call 'money' from the ordinary beings of their community," suggesting that the reader play close attention to the word "money." There are differences in Gurdjieff's choice of when to use quotation marks for emphasis in this way between the two texts. In such circumstances we have left the 1931 text as it was.

- Gurdjieff's use of full capitalization was different between the manuscript and the 1950 publication. In the 1950 publication all direct mentions of God (the Absolute) are fully capitalized and very few other words or phrases are. In the 1931 manuscript there was no consistency in the use of full capitalization. We chose to follow the 1950 publication identically in its use of full capitalization for mentions of God.

- Gurdjieff also sometimes capitalizes the initial letter of a word. He uses such capitalization, in our view, to distinguish nuances of the meaning of that particular word. So, for example, we should assign a slightly different meaning when he writes "Reason" than when he writes "reason."

There are significant differences between the manuscript and the 1950 publication. We decided not to make any changes.

- Gurdjieff makes frequent use of the hyphenation of several words together. In doing so he is adopting the convention of indicating to the reader that all the words should be run together to create a single concept. There are individual instances where Gurdjieff chose to change his use of hyphenation between the manuscript and the 1950 publication. Where this was the case we have not made any changes, leaving Gurdjieff's initial choice intact.

In summary, as regards the "word-by-word" edit of the manuscript, the policy was to leave the original as it was in most respects. We made changes where we believed that the text was in error and we made changes to conform to American English and American punctuation. We changed the use of full capitalization and we standardized the spelling of the neologisms to conform to the 1950 publication.

Changes Made To The Text

There were some defects in the manuscript that clearly needed to be fixed that required more than simple editing. In its original form, in a few places, the reader would encounter confusing disconnects in the flow of the text. In each instance of this we made changes that eliminated the problem.

In the text we have identified each such alteration by providing a footnote, explaining what was done at the point that the change was made, so that the reader can form his own judgement as to whether the change made was justified. We describe here each of the defects and what we did to address them:

- In the manuscript Chapter 35, *A Change in the Appointed Course of the Falling of the Trans-space Ship* Karnak was missing entirely. In the 1950 publication this is a short chapter consisting of just less than three pages. We decided to address this defect by taking the chapter verbatim from the 1950 publication and inserting it.

- In Chapter 40, *Heptaparaparshinokh* on page 646 the list of 42 substances that are "active elements of opium" was missing completely, although the text surrounding the list was almost identical to the 1950 publication. We took the list from the 1950 publication and simply added it in.

- In the manuscript, Chapters 36 and 37 are run together under the common title of *Just A Wee Bit More About The Germans, And France or (Germany and Paris).* No change to the text was necessary to separate the two chapters, but it was necessary to insert the chapter title *France* for Chapter 37.

- A similar but more complicated situation arose with Chapters 44, 45 and 46 which were identified as separate chapters but were not separated out. The original common title was: *Electricity, Justice, Form & Sequence Or (Good And Evil).* In the combined chapter, the text that made up *Form & Sequence* was so interwoven with the text that described *Justice*, that we chose not to try to separate them, preferring to leave them as they were. Far too much "surgery" would have been required for us to feel comfortable making such a change.

- We we were able to and did separate out the chapter on *Electricity* (Chapter 46 in the manuscript). However, the text of this chapter terminated abruptly and was clearly incomplete. In the 1950 publication from that point in the text there are a further six pages. We added those six pages from the 1950 publication into the manuscript.

- Chapter 44 (*Form and Sequence*) of the manuscript begins with the words "After this moving event." However the previous chapter does not end with a "moving event." By referring to the 1950 publication we identified the corresponding point in the text and found what we believe the manuscript was referring to. As a consequence, we added two paragraphs from the 1950 publication at the end of the previous chapter to provide continuity.

- The reader should take note that in ***The 1931 Manuscript***, the three chapters, 44, 45 and 46 are in a different order to their order in the 1950 publication.

- An odd anomaly of the original manuscript was that the chapter titles provided at the start of the manuscript did not match the chapter titles as they occurred in the text. We decided therefore to replace the original contents list with one that matched the text, as we believed that it would be less confusing to the reader. We print the list of contents in its original inaccurate form in the Appendix to this book.

On only one occasion did we decide that it was necessary to entirely remove any text from the manuscript. We removed almost two pages of text that occurred, disjointedly, at the end of Chapter 34 *Russia.* These pages duplicated content from earlier in that chapter, so they seemed superfluous. Nevertheless, for the sake of completeness we reproduce those pages in the Appendix, at the end of the book.

The Indexes

On page 991, following the Appendix, we provide a series of indexes to the whole book. These six indexes are intended primarily for use by those who wish to study the manuscript in detail rather than just to read it.

The final index, which we title the ***Word Index*** is similar to the standard kind of index that one often finds at the end of a text book. It may be useful to readers to use it in the fashion of such an index, or perhaps a concordance, to find out where a particular character (personage) term or idea can be found in the text.

The other indexes we included are:

- **Substitutions.** This gives the pages where we made word substitutions to the original text so that Gurdjieff's neologisms and invented names of characters and places would conform with the 1950 publication.
- **Lists.** This index highlights every instance in the text where Gurdjieff provides a list of items.
- **Quotes.** This indexes every instance in the text where Gurdjieff quotes proverbs or pithy sayings.
- **Phrases.** This indexes hyphenated phrases.
- **References to God.** This index includes all references to God, both reverential references and mundane references.

An Original Copy of the 1931 Manuscript

Some readers may wish to own a copy of the original manuscript. If so, we advise them to contact ***By The Way Books*** (ByTheWayBooks.com), which current sells loosely bound paper copies of the original 1931 manuscript.

G. GURDJIEFF

An Objective Impartial Criticism of the Life of Man

or

Beelzebub's Tales to his Grandson

Contents

BOOK ONE

CONTENTS

BOOK ONE

CHAPTER I

WARNING (Instead of a Preface)

EVERYWHERE on the Earth, before beginning anything new, it is customary first of all, to pronounce aloud, or, at least mentally, the following words understandable by every contemporary even quite illiterate person—namely:

"In the name of the Father and of His Son and in the name of that Holy Ghost who, if not understood by all ordinary mortals, is, at any rate, understood and beyond all doubt known by our priests and theologians.

That is why I also, setting out on this for me new venture, namely, authorship, begin with these same words and even pronounce them aloud very distinctly and with the proper intonation, with the intonation, of course, arising from the data crystallized in my common presence in the course of my life, those data, which, in general, engender in a man's Being, a quality of intonation manifest of the impulses of "faith," "doubt," "superstition" and so on.

"In the name of the Father and of the Son and of the Holy Ghost, Amen."

Having begun in this way, I ought to be quite assured and to be able to count without any essence anxiety, upon everything further now gliding along, as is said, "on-oil-to-an-Italian-hurdy-gurdy-accompaniment."

I shall begin by placing my own hand—though somewhat injured through a misfortune which recently befell me, yet nevertheless indeed my own—upon my heart, of course also my own, and frankly confess that, for myself, I have not the slightest wish to write; but unfortunately for me, I am constrained to do so by surrounding circumstances, not dependent on my individuality, which have either arisen accidentally, or perhaps have been intentionally created by an outside force, and which constrain me to write not just "so-so" but "weighty-fat-tomes."

And so I begin. But how?

Just in this case, experienced people, "who-know-what's-what," always talk about "being-on-three-horns-of-a-dilemma."

Hurrah! Eureka!

Most of the books I have chanced to read in my life have begun with a preface.

So, I, too, shall begin with something of the kind.

I say "of-the-kind" because in the process of my life, I have so far in general done absolutely everything not as other similar biped beings do, so that, in writing now, I must also begin not as any writer would.

In the present instance, instead of the required conventional preface, I shall begin quite simply with a Warning.

Beginning with a Warning will not only not be contrary to those of my already thoroughly fixed principles which have now become, as it were, natural inherencies, but from my point of view—ensuing from the totality of those aims upon which I intend to base my proposed writings—it will be more honest, of course, in the objective sense.

Professional writers usually begin such introductions with an address to the reader full of all kinds of "sugary," magniloquently bombastic what are called "blown-up-phrases."

Just in this alone, I shall follow their example and also begin with an address, but, of course, not with a very, as is said, "mellifluous" one, as they usually do.

Thus . . .

My dear, highly honored and very patient Sirs, and my highly respected, charming, and of course impartial ladies! Forgive me; I have omitted the most important—and my "in-no-wise-hysterical" Ladies!

I have the honor to inform you that although, with the help of my patron saints and by the permission of the local authorities, and also of course of my "merciless-domestic-tyrant"—a personality, that is, inevitably present in every contemporary household, who has automatically acquired power owing only to the abnormally established conditions of contemporary ordinary life—I am now about to write books, nevertheless, I have not only never during the whole of my life written either books or various what are called "informative-articles," but also never even a letter in which the rules of what is called "bon-ton-grammaticality," prevalent in contemporary civilization, should be observed; and having, in consequence of this, no practice at all in so to say "automatic-twaddle," therefore although I have now to become a writer, I am now in respect of all the accepted rules and procedures of professional writers and also in respect of what is called the "literary-language-of-the-intelligentsia" a complete as is said "booby," or as certain contemporary so-styled "well-read" people would call me, "an-ignoramus-on-the-zigzag-plane-squared"—in consequence of all which, I am not going to write at all like the "Patented-professional-writers," to whose form of writing you are undoubtedly already well accustomed; and I must add that of course in you also, an ideally well working automatism has already been acquired and permanently fixed for perceiving as well as for as is said "digesting," thanks to which "blessing" no individual effort whatsoever is ever required of you.

I particularly warn you about the latter, namely, what I have called the "literary-language-of-the-intelligentsia."

Concerning this language it must be said that although I too was taught it in my childhood, and some of my elders who were preparing me for responsible life even constantly compelled me to "learn-by-rote" the multitude of various nuances which compose this "contemporary delight," yet unfortunately—in this case obviously for you—nothing of all I then learnt by rote stuck, and nothing now survives for my writing activities.

And according to the very minute investigations and elucidations of a meteorologist very well known at the present time on the continent of Europe, with whom I chanced to become what is called "bosom-friends" owing to frequent meetings in the nocturnal restaurants of Montmartre, it was not assimilated for the reason that even in my childhood my instinct already contained a certain, as he defined it, "something" which did not permit my Being to absorb this contemporary high-wisdom, and also because, owing to various fortuitous surrounding conditions of my later life, I neither automatically nor semiconsciously, nor even at times, I confess, on principle, that is to say, consciously, employed that language for intercourse with others.

As a result of all this, esteemed buyer of my writings, though I now intend to become a professional writer, yet having, as you see, none of the mentioned "automatic experience" for it, I am already willy-nilly compelled to disregard—and if you like, I again confess, I will even, as if intentionally disregard—that language and write in the ordinary simple everyday language established by life, without any so-to-say "grammarian wiseacrings."

But the pot is not yet full. For I have not yet decided the most important item of all—in which language to write.

Although I have began to write in Russian, nevertheless as the wisest of the wise, Mullah Nassr Eddin* would say, in that language "you-cannot-go-far."

I recalled this saying from among the many "infallible" and "indisputable" sayings of that, in my opinion, universal teacher, the wisest of all the terrestrial sages, one whom

* Mullah Nassr Eddin, or as he is also called, Hodja Nassr Eddin, is, it seems, little known in Europe and America, but he is very well known in all the countries of the continent of Asia. This legendary personage corresponds somewhat to the German Till Eulenspiegel. Numerous tales popular in the East, akin to wise sayings, are ascribed to this Nassr Eddin; and various witticisms, some of long standing and others newly arisen, still continue to be ascribed to him also.

I particularly esteem, and one who, again, of course, in my opinion, ought to be esteemed and respected by everybody without exception—Mullah Nassr Eddin—and I have set it down at this point in my Warning, because of my proposed subsequent writings I intend often to touch upon philological questions also.

The said Russian language is, it cannot be denied, very good. I even like it, but . . . only for swapping anecdotes in the cooling room of that "Hamman" of mine, which I especially constructed on a spot in that place which by the Will of Fate has become my refuge, like a second "native-land."

The Russian language is like the English, which language is also very good . . . for discussing on the easy sofas of what are called "smoking-rooms," the topic of "Australian-frozen-meat" or, sometimes, the "Indian question."

Both these languages are like the dish which is called in Moscow "Solianka," into which everything goes, dear buyer of my wiseacring, except just you and me.

I think I might as well say here also that although the surrounding circumstances and conditions of my life during both my preparatory age and also my maturity have been such that I have had to speak, read and write in many languages, yet circumstances have so fallen out that in recent years I have had practice mostly in Russian and in Armenian.

I can now write in either of these languages with ease, but to my pained regret, the niceties of philosophical questions cannot be expressed in Russian, while, to the misfortune to all contemporary Armenians, although this is possible in Armenian, it has now become quite impossible to employ that language for contemporary questions.

In my early youth, when I first became interested in and was much absorbed in philological questions, I preferred the Armenian language above all others I spoke.

This language was then my favorite chiefly because it was

original and had nothing in common with the neighboring languages, of which there is today an innumerable host.

All of its tonalities were peculiar to it alone, and according to my understanding then, based of course, as is characteristic of young people who have not yet tasted the "delights-of-life," upon the impulses of "self-imagining," "self-enthusing," "self-puffing-up" and so on, it responded perfectly to the psyche of the people composing that nation.

But I have witnessed during the last thirty or forty years, such a change in that language, that instead of an original independent language, there has resulted and now exists—although similarly original and independent—what might be defined as a "kind-of-motley-pot-pourri-of-languages," the totality of whose consonances, falling on the ear of a more or less conscious listener, rings just like the tones of Turkish, Persian, Kurd, French and Russian words, together with various other completely "indigestible" inarticulate noises.

As for my native language, namely, the Greek which I spoke in childhood, and as might be said, the "taste-of-the-automatic-associative-power-of-which" I still retain, I could now, I dare say, express anything I wish in it, but I cannot employ it for writing, for the following for me very serious reasons.

For must not someone transcribe my writings and translate them into the language I desire? And who can do this?

Even the most learned-philologist of modern Greek would understand simply nothing of what I should write in the native language I assimilated in childhood, because my dear compatriots being also inflamed with the wish at all costs to be like the representatives of contemporary civilization also in their conversation have, as a consequence, in the mentioned flow of time, treated my dear native language just as the Armenians, anxious to become Russian intelligentsia, have treated theirs.

That Greek language, the spirit and essence of which were transmitted to me by heredity, and the language now spoken by contemporary Greeks, are as much alike, as, according to the expression of Mullah Nassr Eddin, "a-nail-is-like-a-requiem."

What is to be done?

Eh . . . Eh . . . Ekh! Never mind, esteemed buyer of my writings.

If only there be plenty of French "Armagnac" and "Khaizarian-bastourma"—I shall find a way out of even this difficult situation.

I am an old hand at this!

During the period of the process of my life, I have so many times got into difficult situations and out of them, that this has for me become almost a matter of habit.

In the present case, I shall meanwhile write partly in Russian and partly, where it is necessary, so to say, to "philosophize," in Armenian, the more readily because there are people near to me and always at hand who "cerebrate" more or less in both languages, and I entertain the hope that they will be able to transcribe and translate from these languages fairly well for me.

But, of course, whatever language I use, you must know that I shall always disregard the aforesaid "bon-ton-language."

Why from my earliest childhood I have always disliked this "language-of-the-intelligentsia" I do not know—apparently simply because at the moment of my appearance here below there was being played in our neighbor's house a "phonograph" and at the same time the "midwife" had in her mouth a lozenge dipped in cocaine.

While still a youth, I felt that the whole of my, as the ancient Theosophists called it, "planetary-body," and moreover—why I don't know—chiefly with the right-half, and in later years—particularly when I became a "teacher-of-dancing" and came in contact with people of different "types"—I became gradually convinced of it also with my what is called "mind,"—that the so-styled "grammar" of any language is compiled by people who not only in respect of knowledge of the given language are those biped "somethings" which His Uniqueness Mullah Nassr Eddin characterizes by the words "all-they-can-do-is-to-wrangle-with-pigs-about-the-quality-of-oranges," but, who furthermore, have not even any approximate representation of the screamingly obvious fact that during the preparatory age there is required in the brain-functioning of every creature, and, of man, of course, also, a particular and definite property, the automatic actualization and manifestation of which the ancient Korkolans called the "law-of-association," and that the process of the mentation of every "life," including the "life" of man, proceeds exclusively in accordance with this law.

From the very beginning on the Earth it has become usual that every man who, so to say, "devotes-himself-to-the-field-of-a-conscious-thinker" should be well informed while still in the early years of his responsible existence, that man has in general two kinds of mentation; one kind, by thoughts, for the expression of which, subjective words, possessing always a relative sense, are employed; and another kind, proper to man as well as to all animals, called by those same ancient Korkolans "mentation-by-form."

The second kind of mentation, by which, strictly speaking, the exact sense of all writing must also be perceived, is formed in dependence upon the conditions of geographical locality, climate, time and, in general, upon the whole environment in which the arising of the given man has proceeded and in which his existence has flowed up to maturity.

Accordingly, in the brains of people of different geographical localities, different races and different conditions, there are formed about one and the same thing or idea, a number of quite independent forms, which in their association evoke in a being some sensation or other which in turn conditions a picturing, and which picturings in their turn are expressed by this, that or the other word that serves for their outer expression.

That is why each word, for the same thing or idea, almost always acquires for people of varying geographical locality and race, entirely different so to say "inner-content."

In other words, suppose that in the common presence of some given man who has arisen and been formed in any given locality, a certain "form" has been crystallized from the results of specific local influences and impressions, and that this form evokes in him by association the sensation of a definite "inner-content" and consequently of a definite image or notion, and he should then employ for the expression of this image or notion some word which has eventually become habitual and subjective to him, then, the hearer of that word—in whose being, owing to the quite other conditions of his arising and formation, there has been crystallized concerning the given word, quite another form of data for the mentioned "inner-content"—will in consequence always perceive and inevitably understand that same word in quite another sense.

This fact, by the way, can with attentive and impartial observation be very clearly constated when one is present at an exchange of opinions between persons belonging to different nations.

And so, esteemed buyer of my writings, I warn you that I am going to write not as "professional-writers" usually write, but quite otherwise. So before embarking on the reading of my further "wiseacrings," first reflect seriously, and only then undertake it. Maybe your hearing and other perceptive organs are already so thoroughly automatized to the "literary-language-of-the-intelligentsia," that the reading of these writings of mine might affect you frightfully cacophonously, as a result of which you might lose your . . . you know what? . . . your relish for your favorite dish.

I consider it my duty to say, that thanks to oft-repeated past experiences, I am already quite as convinced with my whole being of this possibility ensuing from my language or rather from the form of my mentation, as a "thoroughbred-donkey" is convinced of the right and justice of his obstinacy.

Now that I have given you warning of the most important thing, I am already tranquil about everything further, because if any misunderstanding should arise on account of my writings, you alone will be entirely to blame, and my own conscience will be as clear as the Ex-Kaiser Wilhelm's.

In all probability you are now thinking that, as a novice in writing, I am obviously trying to be eccentric, in the hope of becoming famous and thereby rich. And of course you also think that I am a young man with a pleasing exterior and, as some express it, "suspicious-interior."

If you indeed think so, then you are mightily mistaken.

First of all, I am not young. I have already lived so much that I have been through even more than one mill in my life; and secondly, I am not trying to be eccentric nor do I intend to make my career or to plant myself in this profession—a profession which, I must add, in my opinion provides many opportunities for candidates d.i.r.e.c.t. . . . for "Hell," assuming of course, that such people can in general by their Being perfect themselves to that extent—for the reason that knowing nothing whatsoever themselves, they write all kinds of "claptrap," and acquiring authority thereby, they become, of course unconsciously, what are called "automatically-working-factors" for the diminution of the without this already sufficiently diminished psyche of those around them.

And as regards my personal career, then thanks to all forces high and low and, if you like, even right and left, I have actualized it long ago, and have already long been standing on "firm-feet," and maybe on very good feet; and moreover, I am certain that their strength is sufficient for many more years, in spite of all my past and future enemies.

But enough of trifling, old fellow, one must write.

Yes . . . I think you might as well be told also about an idea which has only arisen in my brain, and namely, specially to request the printers, to whom I shall give my first book, to print this warning on the opening pages so that anybody may read it before cutting the pages of the book itself, whereupon, on learning that it is not written in the "language-of-the-intelligentsia," he may if he likes, without wasting words with the bookseller, return it and get his money back, which perhaps he has earned by the sweat of his brow.

While writing and cogitating how to explain this idea to Mr. Printer, there arose unsought in this madcap brain of mine, another idea quite disadvantageous for me personally, namely, the idea to be sure to assign a definite sum of money for the misunderstandings which may arise when the uncut books are returned to the bookseller.

The disadvantage to myself in this idea which has spontaneously arisen in my madcap brain consists chiefly in this; that I shall be forced to take this money from a fund, dependent solely on my own will, free from the advice or disagreement of others, misbegotten busybodies, always around me, and, namely, from what is called my "Crayfish-fund."

Now that I happen to be speaking of this fund of mine, which depends solely on my independent will, objective justice demands that I should not fail, first of all, to praise and extol with an impulse of great affection and sentiment the names of the noble "Uncle Sam" and "John Bull," and then, with an impulse of gratitude, to remark that during several years, genuine sprigs of those names I have just extolled, who for various objective merits have become worthy to rank as "Crayfish-idiots," have hitherto always punctually and even with unction kept supplied and so far still supply this solitary hearth of my, so to say, hopes and expectations.

It must be allowed that by reducing the number of my so to say "crayfish-parasites," who have become indispensable assistants in what has lately become, as it were, a necessity for my recreation, I ought to be able also to provide that sum of money from this fund, but owing to that specific and moreover terrible disease, always chronic and, lately, on the increase among the poor and wretched money-changers, which disease has become well known on the Earth under the description of being "hell-bent," not even such a self-deprivation can save me, because on account of this terrible disease, it has already now become extremely difficult for me to make both ends meet.

Eh . . . Ekh! . . . unfortunate me, hapless victim of a combination of planetary influences at the moment of my appearance here below!

This time also it is already beyond doubt—as it has happened to me many a time before my arrival in Europe—that on account of this altruistic intention which spontaneously arose in me, all the rest of the parts of my entire whole will once again "totally-unexpectedly" be made the "scapegoats."

It has always been so; no sooner does an idea arise in my madcap brain, but it inexorably compels the whole of me to carry it out at any cost, as for instance in the present case, to assign without fail the said sum of money, when, in fact, I have none, nor are there in sight any likely "fat-sheep-for-shearing."

The data engendering just this feature of my character, on account of which on all occasions, all kinds of factors for the formation of diverse for me personally "indigestible-consequences" always arise, were crystallized in my common presence from an impression perceived by me in my early youth, thanks to a story I heard about what happened to a certain

"Transcaucasian Kurd."

Of course I must not fail to confess here, that it was only recently that I made clear to my pure Reason when precisely these data for my psyche were formed in me and all the details of their crystallization—that is to say, it was only after I had forced myself to spend a certain time punctiliously following all the indications of the Yogis and after I had later thoroughly studied from all sides that perfectly bewitching branch of "contemporary science" now existing everywhere under the name of "Psycho-analysis."

These specific data together with other similar data which constitute and manifest my present individuality, and which had in their formation decidedly nothing issuing from my essence and which were crystallized in my common presence owing only to various fortuitous surrounding conditions of my life, not only became thereafter, for the whole of me for the rest of my life, almost the dominant what is called "initiating-factor" in the begetting of always the same "indigestible consequences," but also, during their, as the learned psychiatrists would say, "gravity-center-functioning," which proceeds in general under the influence of a corresponding association, they evoke in me almost every time the experiencings called in ancient Indian philosophy "commiseration-with-impartial-affection."

Thanks to this feature of my character, on account of which especially in recent years, I find myself already quite incapable of refraining from actualizing in practice every idea, however personally disadvantageous to me, so in this case also, the whole of my common presence will be inexorably compelled to follow this solicitous procedure, merely in order to caution you, just you a person wholly alien to me, against falling a victim to cunning through the effect upon you of the usual "honeyed-words" of the bookseller; I repeat that I do this in spite of the fact that this measure, as you see for yourselves will mean a considerable loss for me personally.

To fret about it now and to think up some measure less detrimental for me, it is already too late.

So it pleases Fate.

But meanwhile, I think it will not be useless and may perhaps be productive for me as well as instructive for you, if I relate to you somewhat in detail the story of what happened to the mentioned Transcaucasian Kurd.

And it may be productive for me and instructive for you because I have already categorically decided to make use in my proposed writings of the very "Tzimus" of this story also for the actualization of the aims I have in view.

This Transcaucasian Kurd once set out from his village on some business or other to town, and there in the market he saw in a fruiterer's shop, a handsomely arranged display of all kinds of fruit.

In this display he noticed one fruit, very beautiful in both color and form, and its appearance so took his fancy and he so longed to try it, that, in spite of his having scarcely any money, he decided that he couldn't not buy at least just one of these fruits, and try it.

With intense eagerness and with an audacity not common to him, he entered the shop and pointing with his horny finger at the fruit which had taken his fancy, he asked the shopkeeper its price.

The shopkeeper replied that a pound of the fruit would cost "six-groschen."

Finding that this price was not at all high, our Kurd decided to buy a whole pound.

Having finished his business in town, he set off for home the same day.

Walking at sunset over the hills and dales, and perceiving the exterior visibility of those enchanting scenes of the bosom of Great Nature, the common mother, and there inhaling a pure air uncontaminated by the usual exhalations of industrial towns, our Kurd quite naturally suddenly felt a wish to gratify himself with some ordinary food also; so sitting down by the side of the road he took from his provision-bag some bread and fruit he had brought that had looked so good to him and began to eat.

But . . . oh horror! . . . very soon, everything inside him began to burn.

But in spite of this he kept on eating.

And this hapless biped creature of our planet kept on eating only thanks to that same particular human inherency which I first mentioned, and which was just what I had in view when I began to relate the present story, and the sense and meaning of which moreover you will, I am sure soon grasp—of course, according to the degree of your resourcefulness—during the reading of any subsequent chapter of my writings, assuming, of course, that you take the risk and read further, or, it may perhaps be that you will even already "smell" something at the end of this warning of mine.

Meanwhile I boldly or, if you like, impudently, take it upon myself in advance to advise you to absorb with, as might be said, an "intensive-mobilization" of all your perceptive organs, the information elaborating the rest of this story, in order that the crystallization in you of the new impression may proceed normally and not in the manner in which it has already become habitual for this to proceed, that is to say, as the great sage Mullah Nassr Eddin defines and expresses it:

"One part is used up for one's own welfare, and that only for today, while all the rest going in at one ear, is exhausted in the process of trying to get out at the other."

Well then, just at the moment when our Kurd was overwhelmed by all the unusual sensations proceeding within him from this strange repast on the bosom of Nature, there came along the same road a fellow-villager of his, once reputed by those who knew him to be very clever and experienced; and seeing that the whole face of our Kurd was aflame, that his eyes were streaming with tears, and that in spite of this, as if intent upon the fulfilment of his most important duty, he was eating real "red-pepper-pods," he said to him:

"What are you doing, you jackass! You'll be burnt alive! Stop eating that extraordinary and, for your nature, unaccustomed product."

But our Kurd replied:

"No, not for anything on Earth will I stop. Didn't I pay my last 'six-groschen' for them? Even if my soul leaves my body, I shall go on eating."

Whereupon our resolute Kurd—it must, of course, be assumed that he was such—did not stop, but continued eating the "red-pepper-pods."

After what you have just perceived, esteemed buyer of my writings, I hope—of course only faintly—that there may already be arising in your mentation a corresponding association which should, as a result, bring about as it happens sometimes to some people, what you call an understanding, and that in the present case you will understand just why I, well knowing and having many a time commiserated with this human inherency—whose inevitable manifestation takes the form that if anybody pays money for something he is bound to use it to the end—was seized with the idea, to take every possible measure in order that you, my "neighbor"—in the event that you should prove to be already accustomed to reading books, though of any kind yet nevertheless only those written exclusively in the mentioned "language-of-the-intelligentsia"—having already paid money for my writings and learning only afterwards that they are not written in the usual easily and comfortably read language, should not be compelled, as a consequence of the said human inherency, to read my writings through to the end at all costs, as our poor

Transcaucasian Kurd was compelled to continue eating what he had taken a fancy to from its appearance alone—that "not-to-be-joked-with" noble "red-pepper."

For the purpose of avoiding any misunderstanding through this inherency in man, I wish that this warning of mine may be printed in the said manner, so that everyone can read it through without cutting the pages of the book itself.

Otherwise I am very much afraid that the bookseller may, in that case also, try to make a profit for himself and decline to take back a book whose pages had once been cut.

I have no doubt of this possibility, and I fully expect such unconscionableness on their part.

And the data for the engendering of my certainty as to their unconscionableness were acquired in me just when, while I was a professional "Indian-fakir," I happened to become familiar also with, among other things the various aspects of the psyche of contemporary booksellers and particularly with that of their clerks when palming off books on their buyers, and now, having become, since the misfortune which befell me, by nature just, in the maximum degree, I cannot help repeating, that is to say, I cannot help again warning you and even imploringly advising you before beginning to cut the pages of my first book, to read through very attentively and even more than once this Warning of mine.

But in case you decide and notwithstanding this Warning of mine, should wish to become acquainted with the further contents of my "wiseacrings," then there is already nothing else left for me to do but to wish you with all my genuine soul an excellent appetite, and that you may "digest" all that you may read not only for your own health, but also for the health of all those near to you.

I say with my "genuine-soul" because it is a habit of mine to refer often to what is called my "English-soul"; but why it is a habit of mine, I suggest that you puzzle out for yourself, assuming, of course, that there is or should arise in you any curiosity to learn how easily the very highest and most particularly beloved of our ALL-MAINTAINING CREATOR may unconsciously be taken for the very lowest in man.

The plan and sequence of my intended expositions I have already composed in my "swollen" head, but into what form they will mould themselves upon paper, I frankly confess that I myself do not know with my consciousness, though with the total result of the functioning of my instinct I already definitely feel that on the whole it will all mould itself into "something" so to say "hot," and will have an effect on the common presence of every reader like that which the "red-pepper-pods" had on the poor Transcaucasian Kurd.

Thanks to the data crystallized in me which long ago became the main lever of my individuality, and about which I wish just now to inform you, I shall of course touch in my proposed writings upon questions not only of the everyday life of people, already so to say regularized on the Earth—an everyday life, it must be said, contracted—of course only in my opinion—to the point of wretchedness—but I shall also touch upon questions from which there must inevitably arise unusual sensations and uncommon picturings in all your separate relatively independent parts, which parts the ancient sages characterized as "falsely-ascribing-initiative-to-themselves"; namely, in your thoughts, your feelings, and simply in your body. The process of the beneficent Armagnac proceeding at the present moment in my common presence bids me confess to you and warn you that owing to the aforementioned data, the whole of my common presence, in the present period of my life, namely, just when from causes not dependent on me, I have now to become a professional writer, is already such that even with the whole of my mental categorical decision and desire, and with the help of all my separately spiritualized and independent parts—those educated of themselves as well as those educated intentionally by my own will, just that will of mine which flows from and is based exclusively only on my Pure Reason—which parts constitute in me as well as in you this common presence of mine—I cannot do otherwise than as the most exalted great terrestrial sage Mullah Nassr Eddin would say, "tangle-and-entangle" the whole of you, or as he also sometimes says, "put-you-in-galoshes," in full face of the fact that I am counting on your help, or rather on your money, which I shall receive thanks to your purchase of writings; for the full possibility of accomplishing even with a "flourish," my self-imposed and perhaps from your point of view, purely egoistic aim.

And now, my dear, as yet only candidate for my, so to say, future "voluntary-slaves," listen attentively and try your hardest without letting any thing escape you, to transubstantiate in your common presence the information concerning the arising of the original cause and also of those two events whose effects on the whole of me, having become by the Will of Fate, as contemporary scientists and pious pastors would say, "vivifying," served as factors for the accomplished crystallization in my common presence, of just those specific data on account of which, it may be said, firstly, that I am now an "exceptional-monster" among the many millions of animals similar to me, and secondly, that since in the present period of my existence I must become a professional writer, I am compelled to employ this new profession of mine, at whatever cost, as our esteemed Mullah Nassr Eddin has expressed it, to "tangle-and-entangle" all your, as you call them, "images" and "notions" you have until now acquired, which though they are your own attainments, are nevertheless, even in your frank opinion, "very-suspicious."

And so, my dear and precious future "voluntary-slave."

When I was still only as is said, a "chubby-mite," my dear, now deceased grandmother—may she attain the Kingdom of

Heaven—was still living and was a hundred and some years old.

When she was dying, my mother, as was then the custom, took me to her bedside, and as I kissed her right hand, my dear now deceased grandmother placed her dying left hand on my head and in a low voice but very distinctly and even a little imperatively said:

"Eldest of my grandsons!

Listen and always remember my strict injunction to you.

In life never do as others do.

Either do nothing—just go to school—or do something that nobody else does."

Whereupon, she immediately, without hesitation, and with a perceptible impulse of contempt and with commendable self-cognizance, gave her soul directly into the hands of His Truthfulness the Archangel Gabriel.

I think it will interest you and even perhaps be instructive, to know that all this then made so powerful an impression on me, that I suddenly could not hear those similar around me; and when we left the room where the mortal "planetary-body" of the cause of the cause of my arising lay, I very quietly, without attracting attention, stole away to the pit where the bran for our pigs was stored, and lay there without food or drink in a tempest of whirling and confused thoughts—of which, fortunately for me, I had then in my childish brain still only a very limited number—right until the return from the cemetery of my mother, whose weeping, on finding me gone and after searching for me in vain, recalled me to myself, and I emerged from the pit as if in a state of somnambulism, and, flustered, ran to her and as is said "clung-fast" to her skirts.

Though many times in later years, and somehow or other always during the days we call "Shrove-tide," I have seriously thought and tried to make clear to myself exactly why this event made so strong an impression on me, I have not succeeded to this day.

Perhaps it was only because the room in which occurred this sacred scene, which was to be significant for the whole of my life, was full of the scent of incense from what is called "Old-Athos."

Whatever it may have been, the fact remains a fact.

During the days following this event, nothing particular could have proceeded in my general state, or I should now have remembered it, unless it was perhaps the fact that during these days I walked more often than usual with my feet in the air, that is to say, on my hands.

My first act of obvious discordance with the manifestations of others, occurred exactly on the fortieth day after the death of my dear grandmother, when all our family, our relatives, and all those by whom my dear grandmother, who was loved by everybody, had been held in esteem, gathered in the cemetery according to custom, to perform over her mortal body, reposing in what seemed to me a not very cosy grave, what is called the "requiem-service." Suddenly without any rhyme or reason, instead of observing the conventional what is called "bon-ton-etiquette," that is to say, standing as if overwhelmed, with an expression of grief on one's face and even if possible with tears in one's eyes, I started skipping around the grave as if dancing, and sang:

"Let her with the saints repose Now that she's turned up her toes . . . "

And just from this it began, that in my common presence a "something" arose which in respect of any kind of so to say "aping," that is the imitation of the ordinary automatized manifestations of those around me—always and in everything engendered what I should now call an "irresistible urge" to do not as others do.

At that age, of course, I did all this as yet unconsciously, that is to say, my what you call "reasonable-consciousness" did not then participate in all these manifestations of mine.

At that age these acts of mine were like the following:

If for example when learning to catch a ball with the right hand, my brother, sisters, and the neighbor's children who came to play with us, threw the ball into the air, I, with the same purpose, would first bounce the ball on the ground, and only on the rebound would I catch it, and then just with the thumb and middle finger of the left hand.

Or if all the other children sledded down hill head first, I would try to do it, and moreover as expertly as possible, as the children then called it, "backside-first."

Or if we children were given various kinds of what are called "Abaranian pastries," then all the other children would first of all lick them, evidently to try their taste before putting them into their mouths; but I . . . would first sniff it and sometimes even put it to my ear and listen intently with the definite instinctive intention of discovering whether there might be in this exterior form some inner peculiarity that would disclose itself, and so on and so forth.

Time passed. From a "chubby-mite" I changed into what in called a "young-rascal."

Just at the end of this age, namely, the age in which one is sometimes called a "candidate-for-a-young-man-of-pleasing-appearance-and-dubious-content," the first of the mentioned two events occurred, the effect of which enabled the essence of my dear grandmother's behest to take foot in as yet my nature alone.

And this fell out in the following way.

With a number of other young rascals like myself, I was once setting snares for pigeons on the roof of a neighbor's house.

One of the boys, who was watching me closely, said:

"I think the snicker of horsehair ought to be so arranged

that the pigeon's big toe never gets caught in it, because, as our zoology teacher recently explained to me, during movement it is just in that toe that the pigeon's greatest strength is concentrated, and it might therefore easily, of course, break the noose."

Another boy, leaning just opposite me, from whose mouth by the way, whenever he spoke, saliva always splashed abundantly in all directions—sneezed at this remark of the first boy and delivered himself, with a copious quantity of saliva, of the following words:

"Shut your trap, you Hottentot bastard, you abortion, just like your teacher!"

"Suppose its true that the greatest physical force of the pigeon is concentrated in that toe, then all the more, all we've got to see is that just that toe will be snickeled."

"Only then will there be any sense for our aim—that is, for the catching of these also unfortunate pigeon creatures—in that brain-particularity proper to all possessors of that soft and "slippery something," namely, in that particularity which, when a little disharmony occurs in it, or so to say "confusion" arises, enables the center of gravity of the whole functioning in which that particularity plays a very small part to pass temporarily to another place and this at times yields surprising results ridiculous to the point of absurdity."

He "discharged" the last word with such a shower of saliva, that it was as if my face was exposed to the action of the "pulverizer" invented by the Germans for dyeing material with aniline dyes.

This was more than I could endure, and without changing my squatting position, I flung myself at him, and my head, charging him with full force in the pit of his stomach, immediately laid him out and made him lose what is called "consciousness."

Curious and exceedingly peculiar is the coincidence of accidental life-circumstances, that this dexterity should have been thoroughly taught me only a few days before this event by a Greek priest from Turkey who, persecuted by the Turks for his political convictions, had been compelled to flee from there, and having arrived in our town had been hired by my parents as a teacher for me of the new Greek language. It must be said that he longed to get to the island of Crete and there manifest himself as befits a true patriot.

On beholding the effect of my skill, I was, I must confess, extremely frightened, because, knowing nothing of any such reaction from a blow in that place, I quite thought I had killed him.

But another boy, his cousin, seeing this, without a moment's pause, and obviously overcome with the feeling called "consanguinity" immediately leapt at me and with a full swing struck me in the face with his fist.

This blow struck sparks from my eyes and at the same time my mouth became as full as if it had been stuffed with the porridge for the artificial fattening of a thousand chickens.

After a little time when both these sensations had died down within me and blood began to ooze out of my mouth, I then actually discovered that in my mouth was some foreign substance and when I pulled it out with my finger, it turned out to be nothing less than a tooth of large dimensions and strange form.

By this time the boy who had been prostrate had recovered and was standing up; and seeing me staring at this extraordinary tooth, he and all the other boys swarmed round me as if nothing had happened and gazed at it with me with utter curiosity and in a strange silence.

This tooth had seven fangs and at the end of each of them realistically stood a drop of blood, and through each drop there shone clearly, definitely, and separately, all the seven aspects of the white ray.

After this silence, rare among us "young-rascals," the usual hubbub broke out again, and in this clatter it was decided to go at once to the barber, a specialist in extracting teeth and to ask him just why this tooth was like that.

So we all climbed down from the roof and went off to the barber's.

And I, as the "hero-of-the-day" stalked at the head of them all.

The barber, after a casual glance, simply pronounced it a "wisdom-tooth."

From the whole totality of the effect of this event—which became significant for the rest of my life and in the process of which my poor "wisdom-tooth" had become so to say the "exemplary victim"—not only did the essence of my dear grandmother's injunction become definitely instilled into my nature, but also because I did not go to a "qualified-dentist" to have the former cavity of this tooth of mine treated—which as a matter of fact I could not, because our home was too far from any contemporary centers of culture—there began to ooze chronically from this cavity a "something" which had the property of engendering an interest and a tendency to seek out the causes of everything suspicious—as this was made clear to me only recently according to a very minute what is called "psycho-physiological-analysis" made by an occultist well known on the continent of Europe—there was acquired in me an irresistible-urge to become a specialist in the investigation of every kind of "suspicious-phenomenon" which happened to come my way.

After this event, with this inherency now rooted in my nature, I began, again of course with the cooperation of our All-Common Master the Merciless Heropass, that is, the "flow-of-time," to grow up into the mentioned young man.

I think that it may be significant for you to know also that according to my later, personal, detailed investigations, none of the results of my manifestations at that age corresponding to the injunction of my deceased grandmother had up to that time any specific effect on what are called the present "corns" of various degree of those around me, only because in my opinion my own so to say "reasonable-consciousness" had not yet begun to participate in these actions of mine.

Furthermore, it must be confessed that even then, although this reasonable-consciousness of mine had not yet begun to participate in these manifestations, I endeavored nevertheless, with an instinctive consciousness of my duty, to perform everything very honorably, without giving way to all my various weaknesses, both those acquired and those transmitted by heredity also.

The second of the mentioned vivifying factors, this time for the complete fusion of my dear grandmother's injunction—may she attain the kingdom of Heaven—with all the data constituting my general individuality, was the totality of impressions received from information I chanced to perceive concerning the story that happened here among us on the Earth, of the arising of that "principle-of-living" which, as it turned out according to data elucidated by Mr. Alan Kardek during an "absolutely secret" spiritualistic séance, subsequently became a "principle" everywhere among beings similar to ourselves arising and existing on all the other planets of our Great Universe as well.

The formulation in words of this now "All-Universal-principle-of-living" is as follows:

"If-you-decide-to-go-on-the-spree-then-go-the-whole-hog-including-the-postage."

As this "principle-of-living" now already universally accepted arose on that same planet on which you too arose and on which, moreover, you exist almost on a bed of roses, and frequently dance the fox-trot, I consider I have no right to withhold from you the information approximately elucidating certain details of the arising of just that universally general fact.

Well then, when I was once actualizing in practice just that specificity of mine, which had already become also an inherency in the whole of my common presence, namely, the investigation of suspicious phenomena, and I was investigating also Russian legends and sayings, I happened—whether accidentally or as a result of some objective law-conformable successiveness I don't know—to learn among other things the following:

Once upon a time, a certain Russian, who in external appearance was to those around him a simple merchant, had to go from his provincial town on some business or other to the second capital of Russia, the city of Moscow, and his son, furthermore, his favorite one, asked him to bring him a certain book.

When this truly great merchant, the unconscious author of the "all-universal-principle-of-living," arrived in Moscow, he together with a friend of his became—as used to be and is still usual there—as is said "blind drunk" on genuine "Russian-vodka."

And when these two inhabitants of this most great contemporary grouping had drunk the proper number of glasses of this Russian "blessing," and according to long custom were discussing what is called "public-education," our merchant suddenly remembered by association his dear son's commission and decided to set off to a bookshop at once with his friend—who, it must be said, had become his friend chiefly by the common tie of the said Russian "blessing"—in order to buy the book.

In the shop, the merchant, looking through the book he had asked for and which the clerk handed him, asked its price. On being told by the assistant that the book was sixty kopecks and noticing that the price marked on the cover of the book was only forty-five kopeks, our merchant first began pondering in a strange manner unusual for him, and afterwards, making a certain movement with his shoulders, straightening himself up and throwing out his chest like an officer of the guards when he as is said "becomes-stiff-as-a-poker," he very quietly but with an intonation in his voice expressing great authority, said after a little pause:

"But it is marked here forty-five kopeks, why do you ask sixty?"

Thereupon the assistant, putting on, as is said the "plasto-oleaginous"expression proper to all shop assistants, replied that the book indeed cost only forty-five kopeks, but had to be sold at sixty because fifteen kopeks were added for the postage.

Upon this, the Russian merchant—pardon me, the most great author of one of the universal "principles-of-living"—fixing his gaze on the ceiling, again cogitated this time seriously perplexed, when, suddenly turning to his friend, he delivered himself of the first verbal information of the very essence of that principle defining an indubitable so to say objective truth.

And he then uttered it to his friend as follows:

"Never mind, old dear! We'll take the book. What's it matter, we're on the spree today, and 'if-you-go-on-the-spree-then-go-the-whole-hog-including-the-postage.'"

As for me, esteemed buyer of my writings, as soon as I had elucidated this to myself, something very strange, that I never experienced before or since, immediately began and for a rather long time continued to proceed in me; it was as if all kinds of so to say "general-postraces" for what are called "peshkash" or, as they call them here in Europe, "great-stakes" began to proceed in me between all the various-sourced associations and experiences usually proceeding in me, and at the same time, without any rhyme or reason, an intense almost intolerable itching broke out over the whole region of my vertebral column, and an also intolerable colic in the very center of my what is called "solar plexus." After a time all this suddenly quieted down of its own accord, and when I, that is to say, that uncertain something of mine which in olden times one crank—called by those around him, as we also now call such persons, a scientist—defined as "a-certain-relative-arising-depending-on-the-quality-of-the-functioning-of-thought-feeling-and-organic-automatism"—and which a certain famous Arabian Mal-el-Lel, another ancient scientist, formulated in a definition which was borrowed and repeated in another way by the no less famous Greek scientist Xenophon, as "the-result-of-the-totality-of-consciousness-and-unconsciousness-and-instinct"—well then, when this same "I" directed my confused attention within myself, that is, within the whole of me, I then very clearly constated that the whole substantial result of what I had just made clear with my consciousness about the said "principle-of-living" had, without any residue, fused with the data already crystallized in me long before from the results of my dear grandmother's injunction, and this "I" of mine then very definitely sensed, and, with an impulse of submission simultaneously arising in me, cognized the fact, grievous for me, that from that moment on, I should willy-nilly have to manifest myself always and in everything without exception according to these data which had formed in me and which arose under the influence of three external accidental causes having nothing in common with one another, namely, owing firstly to the arbitrary injunction of a person who had become without any desire whatsoever on my part, the passive cause of the cause of my arising; secondly, through some rascal having knocked out a tooth of mine, chiefly on account of somebody else's "slobbering"; and thirdly, thanks to the verbal formulation issuing from the drunken lips of a personality quite strange to me who existed on the Earth under the name of a "Russian-merchant."

That is why "I" and all the heterogeneous sources of the common presence of this "I" of mine, began from that time on, not only, as before, automatically and only occasionally semiconsciously, to actualize manifestations different from those of other surrounding similar biped beings arising and existing on the same planet as I, but to do so from then on consistently and consciously.

Formerly, that is to say, until my elucidation of the arising of this "principle-of-living" through the lips of the Russian merchant immortalized through objective glory, if indeed I did do everything not as others did, my manifestations were not yet patently thrust before the eyes of my fellow-countrymen around me, but from the moment when to my increased misfortune I made all this clear to myself, not only did I do everything without exception intentionally, and not only was everything also done intentionally through me in accordance with the injunction of my deceased grandmother, but I began carrying out all these actions of mine to the utmost possible limits; and from the very beginning the practice was acquired in me and now continues, on beginning anything new and also at any change—of course, on a large scale—always to utter silently or aloud:

"If-I-decide-to-go-on-the-spree-then-go-the-whole-hog-including-the-postage."

And now that owing to circumstances and causes not dependent on me, I happen to be writing books, I am compelled to do so in accordance with that same principle, also.

In the present case I shall begin not by following the practice of all writers, established from the remote past down to the present, of taking as the theme of their various "wiseacrings" events which have, as it were, taken place or are taking place on the Earth, but I shall for my writings take instead the scale of events of the whole World. Thus in the present case also, if "you take, then take"!—that is to say "If-I-decide-to-go-on-the-spree-then-go-the-whole-hog-including-the-postage."

Within the scale of the Earth, any writer can write, but I am not any writer!

Can I confine myself merely to this in the objective sense "paltry-Earth" of ours? Is it for nothing, firstly, that I am the grandson of my dear grandmother, and is it for nothing secondly that that intensive transformation then took place in me for the assimilation without residue of the now already All-universal-principle-of-living?

Please, however, do not worry my dear future and to me very necessary "voluntary-slave . . . " I shall of course also write of the Earth, but with such an impartial attitude and on such a correspondent objective scale that the planet itself and also everything on it may take that position which, in fact, according even to your own sane logic, they do and must occupy in our Great Universe.

Likewise as regards the various what are called "heroes," I intend in these writings of mine to present types not like those which in general the writers of all epochs on the Earth have extolled and still extol, that is to say, like the Toms, Dicks or Harrys who arise by a misunderstanding and who fail to acquire during the process of their formation up to what is called "responsible-existence" anything at all which is proper to a human-being and not merely to an animal to have, and who during the whole of their responsible existence progressively develop in themselves to their last breath only those various "charms" called "lasciviousness," "mawkishness," "amorousness," "maliciousness," "chicken-heartedness," "enviousness," and so on in the same strain.

I intend, as is said, to "create" personages in my writings whom everybody must, whether he will or not, sense with his whole Being as something real, and about whom in every reader, even though he has never encountered such "typenesses," data must inevitably be crystallized for the conclusion that they are indeed "something" and not merely "tails-of-donkeys."

About two weeks ago, while I was mentally drafting the summary sketch of these proposed writings of mine, I categorically decided to make what is called my chief hero . . . do you know whom? . . . Beelzebub himself—even in spite of the fact that this choice of mine might from the very beginning evoke in the mentation of most of my readers an association of so to say "moral-contortions."

But do you know what, reader?

If, in spite of this Warning, you decide to risk familiarizing yourself with my writings and, perceiving them with an impulse of impartiality, will try to understand the essence of my subsequent expoundings, then in view of the fact that a contact of mutual trust must necessarily be established between you and me, I must now frankly confess to you about the associations which have arisen within me and which as a result have precipitated in the corresponding sphere of my individuality the data engendering the deliberate so to say cunning, which has prompted the whole of me to select as the chief hero for my writings just such a type as is presented before your inner eyes by this same Mr. Beelzebub.

My cunning in selecting Mr. Beelzebub as my principal hero is that I expect personal profit for myself from it, on the assumption that if I show him this attention, He will of course without fail—as I for myself am certain with the whole of my left fundament—wish to express his gratitude by helping me with all the means available to Him, in these proposed writings of mine.

Although Beelzebub is made, as is said, "of-a-different-cloth," nevertheless, since He also can think, and besides—as I long ago learned from the treatise of the famous Catholic Monk, Brother Foolon—also has a curled tail, then I conclude, according to the sane-logic formed in my consciousness also owing to education and the reading of contemporary books—that he also must of course possess a good share of vanity and will therefore find it extremely difficult not to help one who is going to advertise His name.

It is not for nothing that our renowned and incomparable Mullah Nassr Eddin frequently says:

"Without-greasing-palms-not-only-is-it-impossible-to-live-anywhere-but-even-to-breathe."

And another also terrestrial sage named Till Eulenspiegel has expressed the same in the following words:

"If-you-don't-grease-the-wheels-the-cart-won't-go."

In accordance with the sayings just quoted, the veracity of which is plain to every contemporary person, I have decided to "grease-the-palm" precisely of Mr. Beelzebub, who, as everyone understands, has means and knowledge, as is said, "enough-and-to-spare" for everything.

All joking, even philosophical joking aside, this Warning of mine has in truth turned out to be rather lengthy.

But this does not matter, I think . . .

It will be no great calamity if you spend an extra twenty or thirty minutes of your time reading it, after I, who in every respect am rather badly "battered," have spent almost two weeks writing it.

The more so, as you—and in this it seems I am not mistaken—value your time and everything else, according to the wise saying of, as always, that same All-Common teacher Mullah Nassr Eddin, which consists in the following words:

"It's-all-the-same-everything-under-the-sun-is-nonsense-and-ha-ha-if-only-the-process-of-digestion-goes-fairly-well-and-the-functioning-of-the-essence-of-our-actual-existence-never-misses-fire."

So good night . . . although morning is already here.

It is already late morning; yet to lie in bed and sleep when normal people have by the sweat of their brow honestly earnt and eaten their breakfast, has already lately become fixed in my mode of living.

And so, I shall try to fall asleep; and you . . . continue to think your usual morning thoughts, probably of the following kind: precisely how many francs must be left just for today for housekeeping; because yesterday one of the members of your family ventured not to consider you and rudely stepped on just that "corn" of yours which already long ago chose its place of existence on the fourth toe of your left foot.

If one has recourse to the priceless definitions of our great Teacher, Teacher above all Teachers, Mullah Nassr Eddin, in this situation in which I, doing nothing, intend to go carefree to bed, while at the same time advising you to think well and honestly to apportion the said francs, he would say:

"Today, for the whole day, I pass . . . and you . . . stir water in a bucket till it is thick."

Just now on concluding, I asked one of those always "hanging-about" me, to read me aloud straight through all that I have written in this first chapter, and thereupon my "I"—of course with the participation of all the results of the data crystallized in my common presence during my past years, which give, by the way, also knowledge and understanding of the psyche of the surrounding diversely-typed fertilizers of such "Nature's-blessings" as wheat, potatoes, horseradish and other similar products which our poor hapless Earth yields with great difficulty—constated and cognized with anxiety that in the common presence of every reader without exception belonging to any of the three sexes, there must inevitably thanks to this chapter alone, arise a "something" engendering so to say "unfriendliness" towards me.

To tell the truth, it is not this which now chiefly worries me, but the fact that at the end of his reading, I also constated that I had manifested myself in this writing contrary to one of the fundamental commandments of that All-Common teacher whom I particularly esteem, Mullah Nassr Eddin, which he formulates in the words:

"Never-stir-up-a-hornets'-nest."

As regards the first qualms that arose in me, they immediately ceased when I remembered an ancient Russian proverb, the truth of which I have many times experienced and verified, and which says:

"Time-grinds-every-grain."

But my agitation from cognizing my negligence in obeying the always irrefragably sound advice of Mullah Nassr Eddin, not only now seriously troubles me, but I experience now, at an accelerating tempo, an impulse of "Remorse-of-Conscience"; and furthermore, after I understood this, a very strange process began and at the present moment continues in both of my recently acquired "souls," which manifests itself in the form of an unusual itching, the result of which evokes and produces an almost intolerable pain in the region a little below the right half of my, already without this, over-exercised "Solar Plexus."

Wait! Wait! . . . This process, it seems, is beginning to slow down, and I am now completely certain that it will cease entirely because, remembering another fragment of life-wisdom, I immediately reflected that if I indeed acted against the advice of the highly esteemed Mullah Nassr Eddin, I, however, acted unintentionally, according to the principle of that extremely sympathetic—though not well known everywhere on the Earth, yet memorable to all who have once met him—that nugget, Karapet.

I think, patient reader, that now that this Preface of mine has turned out to be so long, it will not matter if I spin it out a little more—lead where it may—to tell about this Karapet also.

Twenty or twenty-five years ago, the Tiflis railway station

had a "steam-whistle."

It was blown every morning to awaken the railway-workers and station-hands, and as the Tiflis station stood on a hill, this whistle was heard almost all over the town, and woke up not only the railway-workers, but the inhabitants of the town of Tiflis itself.

The Tiflis local government, as I recall it, had even had, as was then the custom, what is called a "long-drawn-out-correspondence" with the railway authorities about the disturbance of the morning sleep of the peaceful citizens.

To release the steam into this whistle every morning was the job of this same Karapet, who was employed in the station.

So when this Tiflis Karapet would come in the morning to the rope with which he released the steam for the whistle, he would before taking hold of the rope, wave his hand in all directions and solemnly, like a Mohammedan Mullah from a minaret, loudly cry:

"Your mother is a . . . , your father is a . . . , your grandfather is more than a . . . , may your eyes, ears, nose, spleen, corns . . . " and so on; in short, he pronounced in various keys all the curses he knew, and not until he had done so, would he pull the rope.

Having heard of him and of this custom of his, I visited him one evening after the day's work, with a small Boordook of "Kahketeenian-wine," and after performing the local what is called "Toasting-ritual" I asked him, of course in a suitable form and also according to the local "amenities" for relationship, why he did this.

He frankly answered as follows:

"You see . . . everybody who hears the whistle disturbing his sweet slumbers, will undoubtedly curse me, as the cause of this hellish row, 'by-everything-under-the-sun.'

"One morning when I had not had enough sleep myself,

thanks to a christening at the neighbor's, and I was on my way to release the steam, I reflected upon this and decided to curse them all in advance, so that however much all those, as might be said, 'who-lie-in-the-realm-of-idiotism,' that is between sleep and waking, might afterwards curse me—it would have no effect on me."

Now, this is indeed already enough.

This warning of mine must be signed.

He who . . .

Stop! Old fellow! With a signature there must be no joking. Otherwise the same will be done to you as was done to you once before in one of the Empires of Central Europe, when you were made to pay ten years' rent for a house you occupied for only three months in all, merely because you had set your hand to a paper undertaking to renew the contract for the house each year.

Of course after this and still other instances from life experience, I must, in any comparable case, in respect of my own signature, be scrupulously careful.

Very well then. He who in early youth was called the "Black-Greek"; in middle age, the "Turkestan-Tiger"; and now, not just anybody, but the genuine "Monsieur" or "Mister Gurdjieff," or the nephew of "Prince Mukransky," or finally, just a "Teacher-of-Dancing."

CHAPTER II

Introduction: Why Beelzebub Was In Our Solar System

IT WAS in the year 223 after the creation of the World, by objective time-calculation, or, as it would be said here on the Earth, in the year 1921 after the Birth of Christ.

Through the Universe flew the ship "*Karnak*" of the "trans-space" communication.

It flew from the spaces "Assooparatsata," that is, from the spaces of the "Milky Way," from the planet "Karatas" to the solar system "Pandetznokh," the sun of which is also called the "Pole Star."

On the said "trans-space ship" was Beelzebub with his kinsmen and near attendants.

He was on his way to the planet "Revozvradendr" for a certain conference in which he had consented to take part, at the request of his friends of long-standing.

Only the remembrance of these old friendships had constrained him to accept this invitation since he was no longer young, and so long a journey, and the contingencies attached to it presented by no means an easy task for one of his years.

Only a little before this journey, Beelzebub had returned home to the planet "Karatas" where he had received his arising, and far from which, on account of circumstances independent of his essence, he had passed many years of his existence in conditions not proper to his nature.

This many-yeared existence, unsuited to him, and the perceptions unusual for his nature, connected with it, and the experiences, inappropriate to his essence, had not failed to leave on his general "presence" a perceptible mark.

In addition, time itself had already aged him, and in the said unusual conditions of existence had brought Beelzebub, just that Beelzebub who had had so exceptionally strong, fiery, and splendid a youth, to an unusual old age also.

Long, long before, when Beelzebub was still existing at home on the planet "Karatas," he had been taken, owing to his exceptionally resourceful intelligence, into service on the "Sun Absolute," where our LORD SOVEREIGN ENDLESSNESS had the fundamental place of HIS dwelling; and there Beelzebub among others like himself, was attached as an attendant upon HIS ENDLESSNESS.

It was just then that, owing to the as yet unformed reason due to his youth, and owing to his callow and therefore still fiery mentation with unequally flowing associations, that is, owing to a mentation based as is natural to beings who have not yet become finally responsible on a narrow understanding, Beelzebub saw in the government of the World something which seemed to him "illogical," and having found support amongst comrades, beings like himself not yet formed, interfered in what was none of his business.

Thanks to the fury and force of Beelzebub's nature, his intervention together with that of his comrades, then soon captured all minds and the effect was almost to bring the central kingdom of the Megalocosmos into revolution.

Having learned of this, HIS ENDLESSNESS, in spite of his All-lovingness and All-forgivingness, was constrained to exile Beelzebub with his comrades to one of the remote corners of the Universe, namely, to the solar system "Ors," whose inhabitants call it simply the "solar system," and HE assigned as the place for their existence one of the planets of that solar system, namely, "Mars," with the privilege of existing on other planets also, although of the same solar system only.

Among these exiles, besides the said comrades of Beelzebub, were a number of those who merely sympathized with him, and also the attendants and subordinates both of Beelzebub and of his comrades.

All, with their households, arrived at this remote place and there in a short time on the planet "Mars" a whole colony was formed of three-centered beings from various planets of the central part of our Great Universe.

All this population, incongruous with the said planet, accommodated itself little by little to its new dwelling place and many of them even found one or another occupation for shortening the long years of their exile.

They found occupations either on this same planet "Mars" or upon the neighboring planets, namely, on those planets that had been almost neglected on account of their remoteness from the center and the poverty of all their formations.

As the years rolled by, many, either voluntarily or in response to needs of a general character, migrated gradually from the planet "Mars" to other planets, but Beelzebub himself, together with his near attendants, remained to exist on the planet "Mars," where he organized his existence more or less tolerably.

One of his chief occupations was the arranging of an "observatory" on the planet "Mars" for the observation of remote points of the Universe and the conditions of existence of beings on neighboring planets; and this observatory of his, it may be remarked, afterwards became well known and even famous everywhere in the Universe.

Although the solar system "Ors" had been neglected owing to its remoteness from the center, and to many other reasons, nevertheless our LORD SOVEREIGN had sent HIS Messengers from time to time to the planets of this system, to regulate, more or less, the being-existence of the three-brained beings arising on them for the coordination of the process of their existence with the general World Harmony.

And thus, to a certain planet of this solar system, namely, the planet "Earth" as such a Messenger from our ENDLESSNESS there was once sent, a certain Jesus Christ, and as Beelzebub had then fulfilled a certain need in connection with his mission, when the said Messenger returned again to the

"Sun Absolute," he ardently besought HIS ENDLESSNESS to pardon this once young and fiery but now aged Beelzebub.

In view of this request of Jesus Christ and also of the modest and cognoscent existence of Beelzebub himself, our MAKER CREATOR pardoned him and gave him permission to return to the place of his arising.

And that is why Beelzebub, after a long absence, happened now to be again in the center of the Universe.

His influence and authority had not only not diminished during his exile, but, on the contrary, were much increased, since all about him were clearly aware that, thanks to his prolonged existence in the unusual conditions mentioned, his knowledge and experience must inevitably have become both wider and deeper.

And so, when events of great importance happened to occur on one of the planets of the solar system "Pandetznokh," Beelzebub's old friends at once decided to intrude upon him and to invite him to the conference concerning them.

It was as a result of this that Beelzebub was now making the long journey on the ship "*Karnak*," from the planet "Karatas" to the planet "Revozvradendr."

On this big spaceship "*Karnak*," there were as passengers the kinsmen and attendants of Beelzebub and also many beings who served on the ship itself.

During the period to which this tale of ours refers, all the passengers were occupied either with their duties, or they simply actualized what is called "active-being-mentation."

Amongst all the passengers aboard the ship was conspicuous a very handsome boy; he was always near Beelzebub himself.

This was Hassein, the son of the favorite son of Beelzebub, Tooloof.

After his return home from exile, Beelzebub had seen this grandson of his, Hassein, for the first time, and appreciating his good heart and also owing to what are called "family ties," he immediately took a liking to him.

And as the time chanced to coincide with the time when the reason of little Hassein needed to be developed, Beelzebub having a great deal of free time there undertook himself the education of his grandson, and from that time on took Hassein everywhere about with him.

That is why Hassein also was accompanying Beelzebub on this long journey and was among the number around him.

And Hassein, on his side, so loved his grandfather that he would not stir a step without him and he eagerly absorbed everything that his grandfather either said or taught.

At the time indicated, Beelzebub with Hassein and his devoted old servant Ahoon, who always accompanied him everywhere, were seated on the highest "Kasnik," that is, on the upper deck of the ship "*Karnak*" under the "Kalnokranonis," somewhat resembling what we should call a large "glass-bell," and talking there among themselves while observing the boundless space.

Beelzebub was just then describing the peculiarities of the nature of the planet called "Venus."

During the conversation it was reported to Beelzebub that the captain of their ship wished to speak with him and to this request Beelzebub agreed.

CHAPTER III

The Reason Of The Delay In The Falling Of The "Karnak"

THE CAPTAIN soon afterwards entered and, having performed before Beelzebub all the ceremonies appropriate to Beelzebub's position, said:

"Your Right Reverence, allow me to ask you your authoritative opinion upon an inevitable eventuality that lies in the line of our course, which will hinder our smooth falling by the shortest route.

"The case is, that if we follow our intended course, then our ship, after two 'Kilpreno*', will pass through the solar system 'Vuanik.'

"But just through where our ship must pass, there also must pass, about a 'Kilpreno' before, the great comet belonging to that solar system named 'Sakoor' or, as it is sometimes called, the 'Madcap.'

"So if we keep on our arranged course, we must inevitably traverse the space through which the comet will have passed.

"Moreover, Your Right Reverence knows that this 'Madcap' comet always leaves in its track a great deal of 'Zilnotrago†,' which on entering the 'planetary body' of a being, disorganizes most of its functions until all the 'Zilnotrago' is dispersed from it.

"I thought at first," continued the captain, "to avoid the 'Zilnotrago' by steering the ship around these spheres. But a long detour would then be necessary which would greatly lengthen the time of our passage.

"On the other hand, to wait somewhere until the 'Zilnotrago' disperses will take still longer.

* The word 'Kilpreno' in the language of Beelzebub means a period of time equal approximately to the duration of the flow of time which we call an 'hour.'

† The word 'Zilnotrago' is the name of a special gas similar to what we call 'cyanic acid.'

"In view of the sharp distinction in the alternatives before us I cannot decide now by myself what to do and so I have ventured to trouble you, Your Right Reverence, for your competent advice."

The captain having finished speaking, Beelzebub thought a little and then said as follows:

"Really I do not know how to advise you, my dear captain. Ah, yes . . . in that solar system where I existed for a long time, there is a planet called 'Earth.' On that planet 'Earth' very peculiar three-centered beings arose and still continue to arise. And among the beings of a continent of that planet called 'Asia' there arose and existed a very wise three-brained being whom they called there 'Mullah Nassr Eddin*.'

"For each and every peculiar situation, whether great or small in the existence of the beings there, this same terrestrial sage, Mullah Nassr Eddin, had an apt and pointed saying.

"As all his sayings were full of the sense of truth for existence there, I also always used them in order to have a comfortable existence among the beings of that planet.

"In the given case also, my dear Captain, I intend to profit by one of his wise sayings.

"In such a situation as has befallen us he would probably say:

"You cannot jump over your knees and it's absurd to try to kiss your own elbow.

"Now I also say the same to you and add: There is nothing to be done; when an event is foreseen, coming from forces

* Mullah Nassr Eddin or, as he is otherwise called, Hodja Nassr Eddin, is, it seems, little known in Europe and America. He is very well known, however, in all the countries of the continent Asia. This legendary personality is like the Russian "Kusma Prutkoff," the American "Uncle Sam," or the English "John Bull." To this Mullah Nassr Eddin are ascribed numerous popular tales of the East, akin to sayings of the wisdom of daily life. They also now continue to ascribe to him various witticisms recalled from long ago as well as those newly made.

immeasurably superior to us, one must submit.

"The question is only this: which of the two alternatives you mentioned should be chosen, namely, to wait somewhere or to make a roundabout 'detour.'

"You say that to make a detour will greatly lengthen our journey, but that waiting will take still longer.

"Good, my dear captain. Suppose we should make the detour and even save a little time by it, what do you think? Is the wear and tear and working of the parts of our ship's machinery worthwhile for the sake of getting to the end of our journey a little sooner?

"If such a detour involves even trifling damage to our ship, then in my opinion we ought to prefer your second suggestion, that is, to stop somewhere until the path is cleared of the noxious 'Zilnotrago,' thereby at least saving our ship useless damage.

"And the period of this unforeseen delay we will try to fill with something useful for us all.

"For instance, it would give me personally great pleasure to talk with you about contemporary ships in general and our ship in particular.

"Very many new things, as yet quite unknown to me, have been done in this field during my absence from these places.

"I can cite this as an example, that in my time these big trans-space ships were so complicated and cumbersome that almost half their power was spent in carrying the necessary materials to make their locomotion possible.

"But these contemporary ships in their simplicity and the freedom on them are just embodiments of 'Bliss-stokirno.'

"There is such a simplicity upon them for beings and such a freedom in respect of all being-manifestations that you could frequently forget that you were not on one of the planets.

"So, my dear captain, I should very much like to know how this blessing was brought about and how the contemporary ships work.

"And now go and make all the arrangements necessary for the needed stopping. And then, when you are quite free, come to me again and we will pass the time of our unavoidable delay in conversation useful for all of us.

When the captain had gone, Hassein suddenly sprang to his feet and began to dance and clap his hands and shout:

"Oh, I'm glad, I'm glad, I'm glad for this!"

Beelzebub looked with affection at these manifestations of his favorite, but old Ahoon could not restrain himself and, shaking his head reproachfully, called the boy—half to himself—a "growing egoist."

Hearing what Ahoon called him Hassein stopped in front of him, looked at him mischievously and said:

"Don't be angry with me, old Ahoon. The reason of my joy is not egoism but only the happy chance coincidence for me. You heard, didn't you? My dear grandfather decided not only just to make a stop but he also promised the captain to talk with him.

"And this you know, that the talks of my dear grandfather always bring out tales of places where he has been, and you know also how well he relates them and that from these tales so much new and interesting information becomes crystallized in our 'presences.'

"Where is the egoism? He has himself of his own free will, having weighed with his wise reason all the circumstances of this unforeseen event, decided to make a stop which evidently doesn't upset his intended plans very much.

"It seems to me that my dear grandfather has no need to hurry; everything necessary for his rest and comfort is present on the '*Karnak*' and here also are many who love him and whom he loves.

"Don't you remember he said recently, 'We must not oppose forces higher than our own,' and added that not only one must not oppose but even submit and receive all their results with reverence, at the same time praising and glorifying the wonderful and providential works of our LORD CREATOR.

"I am not glad because of the misadventure but because an unforeseen event issuing from above has occurred, owing to which we shall be able to listen once more to the tales of my dear grandfather.

"Is it my fault that the circumstances are by chance most desirable and happy for me?

"No, dear Ahoon, not only ought I not to be blamed but I should be joined in rendering gratitude to the source of all beneficent results which arise."

All this time Beelzebub listened attentively and with a smile to the chatter of his favorite and when he had finished said:

"You are right, dear Hassein, and for being right I shall tell you, even before the captain's arrival, anything you like."

Upon hearing this, the boy at once ran and sat at the feet of Beelzebub and after thinking a little said:

"My dear grandfather, you have told me so much about the solar system where you spent so many years that I could now perhaps even continue logically to describe the details of the nature of this peculiar corner of our Universe.

"But I am now curious to know whether there dwell three-brained beings on the planets of that solar system and whether higher 'being-bodies' are coated in them.

"Please tell me now just about this, dear grandfather," concluded Hassein, looking affectionately up at Beelzebub.

"Yes," replied Beelzebub, "on almost all the planets of that solar system also, three-brained beings dwell and in almost all of them higher being-bodies can be coated.

"Higher being-bodies or, as on some planets of that solar system they are called, souls only do not arise in the three-brained beings breeding on those planets, before reaching which, the emanations of our most holy 'Sun Absolute' owing to repeated refractions, gradually lose the fullness of their strength and eventually cease to contain the vivific power for coating the higher being-bodies.

"Certainly, my boy, on each separate planet of that solar system also, the 'planetary' bodies of the three-brained beings are coated and take an exterior in conformity with the nature of the given planet, and are adapted in their detail to the surrounding nature.

"For instance, on that planet on which all we exiles had been ordered to exist, namely, the planet Mars, the three-brained beings are coated with planetary bodies having the form . . . how shall I tell you, a form like a 'karoona,' that is to say, they have a long broad trunk, amply provided with fat, and heads with enormous protruding and shining eyes. On the back of this enormous 'planetary-body' of theirs are two large wings, and on the under side two comparatively small feet but having very strong claws.

"Almost the whole strength of this enormous 'planetary body' is adapted by Nature for the transforming of energy for their eyes and wings.

"As a result, the three-brained beings breeding on that planet can see freely everywhere whatever the 'Kal-da-zakh-tee' and they can also move, not only over the planet itself but also in its atmosphere and some of them occasionally even manage to travel beyond its limits.

"The three-brained beings breeding on another planet, a little below the planet 'Mars,' owing to the intense cold there, are covered with thick soft wool.

"The external form of these three-centered beings is like that of a 'Toosook,' that is, it somewhat resembles a 'double-sphere,' the upper sphere serving to contain the principal organs of the whole planetary body, and the other, the lower sphere, for the transformation of food.

"There are three apertures in the upper sphere, one in front opening outwards; two serve for sight and the third for hearing.

"The other, the lower sphere, had only two apertures: one is in front for taking in food and the other at the back for the elimination from the organism of the residue.

"To the lower sphere are also attached two very strong sinewy feet, and on each of these is a growth that serves the purpose of fingers with us.

"There is still another planet, a quite small one, bearing the name 'Moon,' in that solar system, my dear boy.

"During its motion this peculiar little planet often approached very near to our planet 'Mars' and sometimes during whole 'Kilprenos' I took great pleasure in observing through the 'Teskooano' in my observatory the process of existence of the three-brained beings upon it.

"Although the beings of this planet have very frail 'planetary bodies,' they have, on the other hand, a very 'strong spirit,' owing to which they all possess an extraordinary perseverance and capacity for work.

"In exterior form they resemble what are called large ants; and, like these, are always bustling about, working both on and within their planet.

"The results of their ceaseless activity are already now plainly visible.

"I once happened to notice that during two of our years they 'tunneled,' so to speak, the whole of their planet.

"They were compelled to undertake this task on account of the abnormal local climatic conditions which are due to the fact that this planet arose unexpectedly, and the regulation of its climatic harmony was therefore not prearranged by the Higher Powers.

"The 'climate' of this planet is really 'mad,' and in its variability it could give points to the most highly strung hysterical woman existing on another of the planets of that same solar system of which I shall also tell you.

"Sometimes there are such frosts on that 'Moon' that everything is frozen through and through, and it becomes impossible for the beings to breathe in the open atmosphere; and then suddenly it becomes so hot there that an 'egg' can be cooked in its atmosphere in a jiffy.

"For only two short periods on that peculiar planet, namely, before and after its complete revolution about its neighbor—another planet nearby—the weather is so glorious that for several rotations the whole planet is in blossom and yields the various products for their first being-food greatly in excess of their general need for their existence in that peculiar intraplanetary kingdom which they have arranged and where they are protected from all the vagaries of that 'mad' climate which unharmoniously changes the state of the planet's atmosphere.

"Nearest to that small planet is another, a large planet, which also occasionally approaches quite close to the planet 'Mars' and is called 'Earth.'

"The said 'Moon' is just a part of this 'Earth' and the latter must now constantly maintain the Moon's existence.

"On the just mentioned planet 'Earth,' three-brained beings also are formed; and they also contain all the data for coating higher-being-bodies in themselves.

"But in 'strength of spirit' they do not begin to compare with the beings breeding on the little planet before mentioned.

"The external coatings of the three-brained beings of that planet 'Earth' closely resemble our own only, first of all, their skin is a little slimier than ours, and then, secondly they have no tail, and their heads are without horns. What is worst about them is their feet, namely, they have no hoofs; it is true for protection against external influences they have invented what they call 'boots' but this invention is of very little use to them.

"Not only is their external form imperfect, but even their reason is quite 'uniquely strange.'

"Their 'being-reason,' owing to very many causes about which also I may tell you sometime, has gradually degenerated, and, at the present time is very very strange and exceedingly peculiar."

Beelzebub would have said still more, but the captain of the ship entering at that moment, Beelzebub, after promising the boy to tell him about the beings of the planet 'Earth' on another occasion, began to talk to the captain.

Beelzebub asked the captain to tell him, first, who he was, how long he had been captain, and how he liked his work, and afterwards to explain some of the details of the contemporary cosmic ships.

Thereupon the captain said:

"Your Right Reverence, I was destined by my father, as soon as I approached the age of a responsible being, for this career in the service of our ENDLESS CREATOR.

"Starting with the lowest positions on the trans-space ships, I ultimately merited to perform the duties of captain, and it is now eight years that I have been captain on the long distance ships.

"This last post of mine, namely, that of captain of the ship '*Karnak*' I took, strictly speaking, in succession to my father, when after his long years of blameless service to HIS ENDLESSNESS in the performance of the duties of captain from almost the very beginning of the World-Building, he was promoted to the post of the Ruler of the solar system 'Kalman.'

"In short," continued the captain, "I began my service just then when Your Right Reverence was departing for the place of your exile.

"I was still only a 'sweeper' on the long distance ships of that period.

"Yes . . . a long, long time has passed by.

"Everything has undergone change and is changed since then; only OUR LORD AND SOVEREIGN remains unchanged. The blessings of 'Amenzano' upon HIS UNCHANGEABLENESS throughout Eternity!

"You, Your Right Reverence, have condescended to remark very justly that former 'ships' were very inconvenient and cumbersome.

"Yes, they were then, indeed, very complicated and cumbersome. I also remember them very well. There is an enormous difference between the ships of that time and the ships now.

"In my youth all these ships both for trans-system and for trans-planetary communication were still run on the cosmic substance 'Elekilpomagtistzen,' which is the totality of the separate parts of the omnipresent active element Okidanokh in a certain proportion and is found chiefly in the atmosphere surrounding planets.

"And it was to obtain this substance that just those numerous materials were necessary which the former ships had to carry.

"But after your flight from these parts these ships did not remain in use long, having soon thereafter been replaced by ships of the system of Saint Venoma."

CHAPTER IV

The Law of Falling

THE CAPTAIN continued: "This happened in the year 185 by objective time-calculation.

"Saint Venoma had been taken for his merits from the planet 'Soort' to the holy planet 'Purgatory' where, after he had familiarized himself with his new surroundings and new duties, he gave all his free time to his favorite work.

"And his favorite work was to seek what new phenomena could be found in various combinations of phenomena already existing according to law.

"And some time later, in the course of these occupations, this Saint Venoma constated for the first time in cosmic laws what later became a famous discovery, which discovery he himself first called the 'Law of Falling.'

"This cosmic law which he then discovered, Saint Venoma himself formulated thus:

"Everything existing in the World falls to the bottom. And the bottom for any part of the Universe is its nearest 'stability,' and this said 'stability' is the place or the point upon which all the lines of forces arriving from all directions converge.

"'These points of 'stability' are the centers of all the suns and all the planets of our 'Universe.' They are just the lowest points of those regions of space upon which forces from all directions of the given part of the 'Universe' definitely tend and where they are concentrated. In these points there is also concentrated the equilibrium which enables suns and planets to maintain their position.'

"In this formulation of his, Saint Venoma said further that everything, when dropped in space wherever it may be, tends to fall on one or another sun, or on one or another planet according to that sun or planet to which the given part of the space belongs where the object is dropped, each sun or planet being for the sphere in question the 'stability' or bottom.

"Starting from this, Saint Venoma reasoned in his further researches as follows:

"'If this is so, may it not therefore be possible to employ this cosmic particularity for the locomotion we need between the spaces of the Universe?'

"And from then on, he worked in this direction.

"His further saintly labors showed that, although in principle this was generally possible, yet for this purpose it was impossible to employ fully this 'Law of Falling' discovered for the first time by him. And it was impossible owing solely to the atmosphere around most of the cosmic concentrations, which atmosphere would prove an obstacle to the straight falling of the object dropped in space.

"Having constated this, Saint Venoma then devoted his whole attention to discovering some means of overcoming the said atmospheric resistance for ships constructed on the principle of falling.

"After three 'Looniases,' Saint Venoma found such a possible means also and later on when the building of a suitable special construction had been completed under his direction, he began his practical trials.

"This special construction had the appearance of a large enclosure all the walls of which were made of a special material something like glass.

"Then to every side of that large enclosure were fitted things like 'shutters' of a material impervious to the rays of the cosmic substance 'Elekilpomagtistzen,' and these shutters, although hermetically fitted to the walls of the said enclosure, could yet freely slide in every direction.

"Within that enclosure was placed a special 'battery,' developing and giving this same substance 'Elekilpomagtistzen.'

"I myself, Your Right Reverence, was present at the first trial made by Saint Venoma according to the principles he had found.

"The whole secret lay in this, that when the rays of 'Elekilpomagtistzen' were made to pass through this special glass, then everything within the space they reached, usually composing the atmosphere itself of the planet, such as 'air,' every kind of 'gas,' 'fog' and so on, was destroyed. This part of space became indeed absolutely empty and had neither resistance nor pressure, so that if even an infant-being pushed this enormous structure, it would be moved forward as easily as a feather.

"To the outer sides of this peculiar structure there were attached appliances similar to wings, which were set in motion by means of this same substance 'Elekilpomagtistzen' and served to give the impetus to move all this enormous construction in the required direction. The results of these experiments having been approved and blessed by the Commission of Inspection under the presidency of Archangel Adossia, the construction of a big ship based on these principles was begun.

"The ship was soon ready and commissioned for service. And little by little in a short time only ships of this type were used on all the lines of trans-system communication.

"Although later, Your Right Reverence, the inconveniences also of this system gradually became more and more apparent, nevertheless it continued to displace all the systems that had existed before.

"It cannot be gainsaid that although the ships constructed on this system were ideal in atmosphereless spaces, and moved there almost with the speed of the rays 'Etzikolnianakhnian' issuing from a planet, yet when nearing some sun or planet, it became real torture for the beings directing them, as a great deal of complicated maneuvering was necessary.

"The need for this maneuvering was due to the same 'Law of Falling.'

"And this was because when the ship came into the medium of the atmosphere of some sun or planet by which it had to pass, it immediately began to fall towards that sun or planet, and, as I have already stated, very much care and considerable knowledge were needed to prevent the ship from falling out of its course.

"While the ships were passing near any sun or planet whatsoever, their speed of locomotion had sometimes to be reduced by some hundreds of times below the usual rate.

"It was particularly difficult to steer them in those spheres where there was a great aggregation of 'comets.'

"That is why great demands were then made upon the beings who had to direct these ships, and they were prepared for these duties by beings with very high reason.

"But, in spite of the said drawbacks of the system of Saint Venoma, it gradually, as I have already stated, displaced all the previous systems.

"And the ships of this system of Saint Venoma had already existed for twenty three years when it was first rumored that the Angel Hariton had invented a new type of ship for trans-system and trans-planetary communication.

CHAPTER V

The System of Archangel Hariton

AND INDEED soon after this rumor, practical experiments open to all, again under the superintendence of the Great Archangel Adossia, were made with this new and later very famous invention.

"This new system was unanimously acknowledged to be the best, and very soon it was adopted for general-Universal-service and thereafter gradually all the previous systems were entirely superseded.

"That system of the Great Angel, today Archangel Hariton is in use everywhere at the present day.

"The ship on which we are now flying also belongs to this system and its construction is similar to that of all the ships built on the system of the Angel Hariton.

"This system is not very complicated.

"The whole of this great invention consists of only a single 'cylinder' shaped like an ordinary barrel.

"The secret of this cylinder lies in the disposition of the materials of which its inner side is made.

"These materials are arranged in certain order and isolated each from the other by means of 'Amber.' They have such a property that if any cosmic gaseous substance whatever enters into the space which they enclose, whether it be 'atmosphere,' 'air,' 'ether' or any other 'totality' of homogeneous cosmic elements, then, owing to the mentioned disposition of materials within the cylinder, it immediately expands.

"The bottom of this cylinder-barrel is hermetically sealed, but its lid, although it can be closely shut, yet is so arranged on hinges that, at a pressure from within, it can be opened and shut again.

"So, Your Right Reverence, if this cylinder-barrel is filled with atmosphere, air or any other such substance, then from the action of the walls of this peculiar cylinder-barrel, these substances expand to such an extent that the interior becomes too small to hold them.

"Striving to find an outlet from this, for them, constricted interior, they naturally press also against the lid of the cylinder-barrel, thanks to the said hinges the lid opens and, having allowed these expanded substances to escape, immediately closes again. And as in general, Nature abhors a vacuum, simultaneously with the release of the expanded gaseous substances, the cylinder-barrel is again filled with fresh substances from outside, with which in their turn the same proceeds as before and so on without end.

"Thus the substances are always being changed, and the lid of the cylinder-barrel alternately opens and shuts.

"To this same lid there is fixed a very simple lever which moves with the movement of the lid, and in turn sets in motion certain also very simple 'cog-wheels' which again in their turn revolve the fans attached to the sides and stern of the ship itself.

"Thus, Your Right Reverence, in spaces where there is no resistance, contemporary ships like ours simply fall toward the nearest 'stability'; but in spaces where there are any cosmic substances which offer resistance, these substances, whatever their density, with the aid of this cylinder enable the ship to move in any desired direction.

"It is interesting to remark that the denser the substance in any given part of the Universe, the better and more strongly the charging and discharging of this cylinder-barrel proceed and in consequence, of course, the force of the movement of the levers is also changed.

"But nevertheless, I repeat, a sphere without atmosphere, that is, a space containing only World-Etherokrilno, is for contemporary ships also the best, because in such a sphere there is no resistance at all, and the 'Law of Falling' can therefore be fully employed in it without any assistance from the work of the cylinder.

"Further than this, the contemporary ships are also good, because they contain such possibilities that in substanceless spaces an impetus can be given to them in any direction, and they can fall just where desired which was not possible for ships of the system of Saint Venoma without complicated manipulations.

"In short, Your Right Reverence, the convenience and simplicity of the contemporary ships are beyond comparison with former ships, which were often both very complicated, and at the same time, had none of the possibilities of the ships we use now."

CHAPTER VI

Perpetual Motion

"WAIT! . . . WAIT!" Beelzebub interrupted the captain, "This that you have just told us must surely be just that flimsy idea, which the strange three-brained beings breeding on the planet Earth call 'Perpetual Motion,' and on account of which at one period very many of them there went as they themselves say quite 'mad,' and many even quite perished.

"It happened that somebody once there on that ill-starred planet in some way or other got into his head, as they say, the crazy notion that he could create a 'mechanism' that would work forever without needing any material from outside.

"This notion so took everybody's fancy that most of the queer fellows of that peculiar planet thought about it and tried to realize this miracle in practice.

"How many of them paid for this flimsy idea with their material and spiritual welfare which they had acquired previously with great difficulty!

"And everyone wished for one or another reason absolutely to invent what, in their opinion, was this 'trifle.'

"External circumstances permitting, many took up the invention of this 'Perpetual Motion' without any inner data for such work; some from reliance upon their 'knowledge,' others upon 'luck' but most of them just from their already fulfilled psychopathy.

"In short, the invention of 'Perpetual Motion' was, as they say, the 'rage,' and everyone of these freaks was expected to be interested in this question.

"I was once in one of the towns there where 'models' of every kind, and innumerable 'descriptions' of proposed 'mechanisms' for this 'Perpetual Motion' were assembled.

"What, what only was not there! . . . what 'ingenious' and complicated machines did I not see there . . . In any single one of the 'mechanisms' I saw, there must have been more ideas and 'wiseacrings' than in all the laws of the World-creation and World-existence.

"I noted at the time that in these innumerable models and descriptions of proposed mechanisms, the idea of using what is called the 'force of weight' predominated. And the idea of employing the 'force of weight' they explained thus: a very complicated mechanism was to lift 'some' weight and this latter was then to fall and by its fall set the whole mechanism in motion, which motion would again lift this weight and so on and so on.

"The result of it all was, that thousands were shut up in 'lunatic asylums'; thousands more, having made this idea their dream, already either began to fail to fulfil even those being duties of theirs which had somehow or other in the course of many years been established there, or did them already quite atrociously.

"I don't know how it all would have ended if some quite demented being there already with one foot in the grave, such a one as they themselves call an 'old codger' and who had previously acquired somehow a certain authority, had not 'proved' by 'calculations' known only to himself that it was absolutely impossible to invent 'Perpetual Motion.'

"Now after your explanation, I can well understand how the cylinder of the system of Archangel Hariton works. It is the very thing of which these unfortunates dreamed there.

"Indeed, of the cylinder of the system of Archangel Hariton, it can be safely said that, with atmosphere alone given, it will work perpetually without needing the expenditure of any outside materials.

"And since the World without planets and hence without atmospheres cannot exist, then it follows that as long as the World exists and, in consequence, atmospheres, the cylinder-barrels invented by the great Archangel Hariton will always work.

"Now one question occurs to me personally just about the material from which this cylinder-barrel is made.

"I very much wish, my dear captain, that you would roughly tell me what materials it is made of and how long they can last," asked Beelzebub.

To this question of Beelzebub's the captain replied as follows:

"Although this cylinder-barrel does not last forever, it can certainly last a very long time.

"Its chief part is made of 'amber' with 'Platinum' hoops, and the interior panels of the walls are made of 'coal,' 'copper' and 'ivory,' and a very strong mastic unaffectable either by 'paischakir,' or by 'tainolair,' or by 'saliakooriapa,' or even by the radiations of cosmic concentrations.

"But the other parts," the captain continued, "both the exterior 'levers' and the 'cog-wheels,' must certainly be renewed from time to time, for although they are made of the strongest metal, yet long use will wear them out.

"And concerning the body of the ship itself, its long existence can certainly not be guaranteed."

The captain intended to say still more, but at that moment a sound like the vibrations of a long minor chord of a far off orchestra of wind instruments resounded through the ship.

With an apology the captain rose to leave, explaining as he did so, that he must be needed on very important business, since everybody knew that he was with his Right Reverence and would not venture to trouble the ears of his Right Reverence for anything trifling.

CHAPTER VII

Becoming Aware Of Genuine Being-Duty

AFTER the captain had gone, Beelzebub glanced at his grandson and, noticing his unusual state, asked him solicitously and with some anxiety:

"What is the matter, my dear boy? What are you thinking so deeply about?"

Looking up at his grandfather with eyes full of sorrow Hassein said thoughtfully:

"I don't know what is the matter with me, my dear grandfather, but your talk with the captain of the ship has brought my thinking to some exceedingly melancholy thoughts.

"Things about which I have never before thought are now a-thinking in me.

"It has gradually become very clear to my consciousness during your talk that in the Universe of our ENDLESSNESS everything has not always been such as I now see and understand.

"Formerly, for instance, I should never have admitted such thoughts to associate in me, as that this ship on which we are now flying has not always been as it is at this moment.

"Only now have I come very clearly to understand that everything we have at the present time and everything we use—in a word, all the contemporary amenities and everything necessary for our comfort and welfare—have not always existed and did not appear so easily.

"It seems that certain beings in the past have during very long periods labored and suffered very much and for this endured a great deal, which perhaps they even need not have endured.

"They labored and suffered only that we might now have all this and use it for our welfare.

"And all this they did, either consciously or unconsciously, just for us, that is, just for beings quite unknown and absolutely indifferent to them.

"And now not only do we not thank them, but we even do not know a thing about them, but we take it all as in the natural order, and neither ponder nor trouble ourselves about the question at all.

"I, for instance, have already existed so many years in the Universe, yet the thought has never even entered my head, that perhaps there was a time when everything I see and have did not exist, and that everything was not born with me like my nose.

"And so, my dear and kind grandfather . . . Now, owing to your conversation with the captain, having gradually become aware of all this with all my 'presence,' there has arisen in me, side by side with this, the need to make clear to my reason just this, namely, why I personally have all the comforts which I now use, and what obligations I am under for them?

"It is just because of this that at the present time, there just proceeds in me a 'process-of-remorse.'"

Having said this, Hassein drooped his head and became silent; and Beelzebub, looking at him affectionately, began to speak as follows:

"I advise you, my dear Hassein, not to put such questions to yourself yet. Be patient meanwhile.

"Only when the proper period of your existence arrives for your becoming aware of such an essence-question, and you actively think about it, will you understand what you must do far it in return.

"Your present age does not yet oblige you to pay for your existence.

"The time of your present age is given you not in which to pay for your existence, but for preparing yourself for the future, for the obligations becoming to a responsible three-brained being.

"So in the meantime exist as you exist. Only do not forget one thing and that is, very often with the consciousness you already have, persuade the unconscious parts of your general 'presence' that if these unconscious parts hinder their whole presence, then this whole presence when it becomes a responsible cosmic individuum will be unable to pay for its existence as it should, and in consequence unable to be a good servant to our COMMON ENDLESS CREATOR.

"I repeat, once more, my dear boy, try in the meantime not to think about these questions, about which it is still early far you at your age to think.

"Everything in its proper time!

"Now ask me what you like and I will reply. As the captain has not returned by now, he must be occupied there with his duties and will not be coming back so soon."

CHAPTER VIII

The Impudent Brat Hassein, The Grandson Of Beelzebub, Dares To Call Us 'Slugs'

HASSEIN immediately sat down at Beelzebub's feet and coaxingly said:

"Tell me anything you like, dear grandfather. Anything you tell me will be the greatest joy for me, only because it is just you who relate it.

"No," objected Beelzebub, "You yourself ask what interests you most of all. It will give me at the present moment much pleasure to tell you just about whatever you particularly wish to know."

"Dear and kind grandfather, tell me then something about those . . . how? . . . those . . . I forget . . . yes . . . about 'slugs.'"

"What, about what 'slugs'?" asked Beelzebub, not having understood the boy's question.

"Don't you remember, grandfather, that a little while ago, when you spoke about the three-centered beings breeding on various planets of that solar system where you existed for such a long time, you happened to say, that on one planet . . . I forget how you called it . . . on this very planet three-centered beings exist who are on the whole like us, but whose skin is a little slimier than ours."

"Ah . . . " laughed Beelzebub, "you surely are asking about those beings who breed on the planet "Earth" and who call themselves 'men.'"

"Yes! Grandfather, yes! . . . just about these 'men-beings,' relate a little more in detail. I wish to know more about them," concluded Hassein.

Then Beelzebub said; "I could tell you a great deal about them for I often visited that planet and existed among them and even made friends with many of those terrestrial three-brained beings.

"Indeed, you will find it very interesting to know more about these beings, for they are very peculiar.

"There are many things among them which you would not see among any other beings of any planet of our Universe.

"I know them very well for even their arising and their existence and self-perfecting during many, very many, centuries by their time-calculation have occurred before my eyes.

"And not only their own arising occurred before my eyes, but also even the completed formation of the planet itself on which they arise and exist.

"When we first arrived on this solar system and settled on the planet 'Mars," nothing yet existed on this planet 'Earth,' which had not even yet had time to cool completely after its concentration.

"Quite from the beginning, this same planet has been the cause of many serious troubles to our ENDLESSNESS.

"If you wish I will tell you first of all about the events of general cosmic character connected with this planet which were the cause of the said cares of our ENDLESSNESS.

"Yes, my dear grandfather, tell me first about this. It will surely be quite as interesting as anything you relate."

CHAPTER IX

The Cause Of The Genesis Of The Moon

BEELZEBUB began his tale as follows:

"After we arrived on the planet 'Mars,' where we were directed to exist, we began slowly to settle down there.

"We were still fully absorbed in the bustle of organizing everything externally necessary for a more or less tolerable existence amidst that Nature absolutely foreign to us, when suddenly, on one of the very busiest days, the whole planet 'Mars' was shaken, and a little later such a 'stupefying-odor' arose, that we thought at first that everything in the Universe had been mixed with something 'unmentionable.'

"Only after a considerable time had passed and when the said odor had disappeared did we recover and gradually make out what had happened.

"We understood that the cause of this terrible phenomenon was just that same planet 'Earth' which from time to time approached very near to our planet 'Mars' and which therefore we could observe very clearly, sometimes even without a 'Teskooano.'

"For reasons we could not yet comprehend, this planet, it transpired, had 'burst,' and two fragments separated from it had flown off into space.

"I have already told you, that this solar system had then only recently been formed and was not yet 'blended' completely with what is called 'The-Harmony-of-Reciprocal-Maintenance-of-all-Cosmic-Concentrations.'

"It was subsequently learned that in accordance with this said "General-Cosmic-Harmony-of-Reciprocal-Maintenance-of-all-Cosmic-Concentrations,' a comet of what is called 'vast orbit' still existing and named the comet 'Kondoor' had, also, to function in this system.

"And just that comet, although it was then already concentrated, was making its full appointed path for only the first time.

"As certain competent sacred Individuums also later explained confidentially to us, the line of the path of the said comet had to cross the line on which the path of that planet 'Earth' also lay; but as a result of the erroneous calculations of a certain sacred Individuum concerned with the affairs of World-building and World-maintenance, the time of passing through the point of intersection of the lines of the paths of both of these concentrations coincided, and owing to this error the planet 'Earth' and the comet 'Kondoor' collided, and collided so violently that from this shock, as I have already told you, two large fragments were broken off from the planet 'Earth' and flew into space.

"This shock entailed such serious consequences because on account of the recent arising of this planet, the atmosphere which usually serves us a buffer in such cases, had not yet had time to be completely formed upon it.

"So, my boy, our ENDLESSNESS was also immediately informed of this general cosmic misfortune.

"In consequence of this report, a whole commission under the direction of the Most Great Archangel Sakaki, consisting of Angels and Archangels, specialists in the affairs of World-building and World-maintenance, was immediately sent from the Most Holy Sun Absolute to that solar system 'Ors.'

"The Most High Commission arrived on our planet 'Mars,' it being the nearest to the planet 'Earth,' and from this planet of ours began its investigations.

"The sacred members of this Most High Commission at once quieted us by saying that the apprehended danger of a catastrophe on a great cosmic scale had already passed.

"And the Arch-engineer Archangel Algamatant was good enough to explain to us personally that in all probability what had happened was as follows: "The broken off fragments of that planet 'Earth' had lost the momentum they received from the shock, before they had reached the limit of that part of the space which is the sphere of this planet, and hence according to the 'Law of Falling,' these fragments had begun to fall back towards their fundamental piece.

"But they could no longer fall upon their fundamental piece, because in the meantime they had come under the cosmic law called 'Law-of-Catching-Up' and were entirely subject to its influence, and they would therefore now make regular elliptic orbits around their fundamental piece, just as the fundamental piece, namely, the planet 'Earth,' made and makes its orbit ground its sun 'Ors.'

"And so it will continue until some fresh unforeseen catastrophe on a large scale changes it one way or another.

"Glory to the event' . . . concluded his Pantamensurability. The harmonious general-system-movement was not destroyed by all this, and the peaceful existence of that system 'Ors' was soon again reestablished.

"But nevertheless, my boy, this Most High Commission, having then calculated all the given facts at that time, and also all that might happen in the future, came to the conclusion that although the fragments of the planet 'Earth' might maintain themselves for the time being in their existing positions, yet in the future in view of certain so-called 'Tastartoonarian' transpositions conjectured by the Commission, they might leave their position and bring about a large number of irreparable calamities both for this system 'Ors' and for other neighboring solar systems.

"The Most High Commission therefore decided to take certain measures beforehand to anticipate this eventuality.

"And they agreed that the best measure in the given case would be that the fundamental piece, namely, the planet 'Earth' should send constantly the sacred vibrations 'Askokin' to its separated fragments for their maintenance.

"This sacred substance can be formed on planets only when both fundamental cosmic laws operating in them, the sacred 'Heptaparaparshinokh' and the sacred 'Triamazikamno' function, as it is said, 'Ilnosoparno,' that is to say, when the said sacred cosmic laws in the given cosmic concentration are refracted and manifest on its Surface as well, independently—of course independently within certain limits only.

"And so, my boy.

"Seeing that such a cosmic actualization was possible only with the sanction of HIS ENDLESSNESS, the Great Archangel Sakaki, accompanied by several other sacred members of that Most High Commission, set off immediately to HIS ENDLESSNESS to beg Him to give the said consent.

"And afterwards when the said sacred Individuums had obtained the sanction of HIS ENDLESSNESS for the actualization of the 'Ilnosoparnian' process on this planet also, and when this process was actualized under the direction of the same Great Archangel Sakaki, then from that time on on that planet also, just as on many others, there began to arise the 'Corresponding,' owing to which the said separated fragments exist until now without constituting a menace for a catastrophe on a great scale.

"Of these two fragments the larger was named 'Loonderperzo' and the smaller 'Anulios'; and the ordinary three-brained beings who afterwards arose on this planet also called them at first by these names; but the beings of later times called them differently at different periods, and the three-brained beings of the latest period there call the larger fragment 'Moon,' but the name of the smaller has been gradually forgotten.

"As for the beings there now, not only have they no name for this smaller fragment at all, but they do not even suspect its existence.

"It is interesting to notice here that the beings of a continent on that planet called 'Atlantis,' which afterwards perished, still knew of this second fragment of their planet and also called it 'Anulios,' but the beings of the last period of the same continent in whom the consequences of the properties of the organ Kundabuffer were crystallized and became part of their general presence, called it also 'Kimespai,' the meaning of which for them was 'One-That-Never-Allows-One-To-Sleep-In-Peace.'

"Contemporary three-brained beings of this peculiar planet are unaware of this former fragment of their planet, chiefly because its comparatively small size and the remoteness of the place of its movement, make it quite invisible to their sight, and also because no 'grandmother' ever told them that once upon a time such a small satellite of their planet was known.

"And if any of them should by chance see it through their good, but nevertheless children's toy, called a telescope, he would pay no attention to it, mistaking it simply for a big as they call it aerolite.

"The contemporary beings will probably never see it again since it has become a property of their nature to see only unreality.

"They must be given their due; during recent centuries they have indeed artistically mechanized themselves to see nothing real.

"So, my boy, owing to all the aforesaid, there first arose on this planet 'Earth' also, as they should, what are called 'Similarities of the Whole,' or, as they are also called, 'Microcosmoses'; and, further, there were forced from these 'Microcosmoses' what are called 'Oduristolnian' and 'Polormedekhtic' vegetations.

"Still further, as it also usually proceeds, various forms of what are called 'Tetartocosmoses' of all three-brained systems also began to group themselves from the same 'Microcosmoses.'

"And among these latter there then first arose just those biped 'Tetartocosmoses' whom you a while ago called 'slugs.'

"About how and why upon planets where the fundamental sacred laws become 'Ilnosoparnian' there arise the 'Similarities of the Whole,' and about what factors contribute to the formation of one or another as they are called 'Systems of Being-Brains,' and concerning also all the laws of World-creation and World-existence in general I will specially explain to you some other time.

"But meanwhile know that these three-brained beings who interest you, arising on the planet 'Earth,' contained those same possibilities for perfecting the function of acquiring being-reason which possibilities all other forms of 'Tetartocosmoses' arising throughout the whole Universe.

"But afterwards, just during the period that they also were gradually being spiritualized by what is called being-instinct, as it proceeds on other similar planets of our great Universe, just then, unfortunately for them, there befell that misfortune which was unforeseen from Above and which was so deplorable for them."

CHAPTER X

Why 'Men' Are Not Men

BEELZEBUB sighed deeply and continued to speak as follows:

"After the actualizing on this planet of the 'Ilnosoparnian' process, one year by objective time calculation passed.

"In the course of this period there had gradually been established on this planet also, the corresponding processes of the involution and evolution of everything arisen there.

"Naturally also, there began gradually to be crystallized in the three-brained beings there also, the corresponding function for their acquisition of objective reasoning.

"In short, on this planet also everything was then already following the usual order.

"And therefore, my boy, there perhaps would not have been all the subsequent eccentricities associated with the three-brained beings arising on that ill-starred planet, if, at the end of a year, the Most High Commission under the supreme direction of the same Archangel Sakaki had not again gone there.

"This second descent thereto of the Most High Commission was due to this, that in spite of the measures they had taken of which I have just told you, complete assurance of the impossibility of any unwelcome surprise in the future had not crystallized in the Reasons of a majority of its sacred members and they then wished to verify on the spot the results of the measures they had taken.

"It was just during this second descent that the Most High Commission decided if only for their peace of mind, to actualize in any event still certain other special measures, among which was that measure also whose consequences have been not only gradually transformed into a stupendous terror for the three-brained beings arising on this ill-starred planet themselves, but which have also become, so to say, a festering ulcer even for the whole of the great Universe.

"You must know that by the time of this second descent of the Most High Commission, there had already been gradually engendered in them—as is proper to three-brained beings—what is called 'mechanical instinct.'

"The sacred members of this Most High Commission thereupon then reasoned that if the said mechanical instinct in these biped three-brained beings of that planet should develop towards the attainment of objective Reason—as usually is the case everywhere among three-brained beings—then it might happen that they would prematurely grasp the real cause of their arising and existence and make a good deal of trouble; it might happen that having understood the reason for their arising, namely, that by their existence they should maintain the separated fragments of their planet, and being convinced of this their slavery to circumstances utterly foreign to them, they would protest against continuing their existence and destroy themselves on principle.

"So, my boy, in view of this the Most High Commission then decided among other things provisionally to introject into the three-brained beings there such a special property that, firstly, they might perceive reality upside down and, secondly, that every repeated impression from outside should be a contributory factor in evoking in them sensations of 'pleasure' and 'satisfaction.'

"Thereupon, indeed, with the help of the Chief-Common-Universal-Arch-Physico-Chemist Angel Looisos, who also was among the members of this High Commission, they made grow in a special way in the three-brained beings there, at the base of their spinal column, 'something' which would enable the said properties to arise in them.

"And this 'something' they then first called the 'Organ Kundabuffer.'

"And having then made this organ grow in their 'presence' and practically assured themselves that it would work, the Most High Commission consisting of sacred Individuums headed by Archangel Sakaki, were content and returned to the center with a good conscience, while there on the planet which interests you, the action of this astonishing and exceedingly ingenious invention bloomed and blossomed from the very first day, as the wise Mullah Nassr Eddin would say— 'Like the trumpets of Jericho in full blast.'

"Now in order that you may have at least an approximate understanding of the results of the properties of the organ devised and actualized by the incomparable Angel Looisos— blessed be His Name forever!—you must assuredly know about certain manifestations of the three-brained beings of that planet, both during the period when this organ Kundabuffer existed in their 'presence' and during later periods when although this astonishing organ and its properties were destroyed in them, nevertheless owing to many causes, the consequences of its properties began to be crystallized in their 'presence.'

"But I shall explain this to you later

"You must note that the descent to that planet of that Most High Commission occurred there for the third time three years later, but this time it was under the supreme direction of the Most Great Archseraph-Sevohtartra, because the Most Great Archangel Sakaki had in the meantime been raised to be the divine Individuum he even now is, namely, one of the four All-Quarters-Maintainers of the whole Universe.

"It was just on this third descent there, when owing to the thorough investigations of the sacred members of this third Most High Commission it was elucidated that for the maintenance of the existence of those said separated fragments, there was no longer any need to continue in force the measures that had previously been deliberately undertaken; that, in consequence, among other measures taken with the help of the same Arch-Chemist-Physicist Angel Looisos, there was also destroyed in the 'presence' of the three-brained beings there, the said organ Kundabuffer with all its astonishing properties. But now let us return to the tale I began.

"Then listen . . . when our confusion caused by the catastrophe that had occurred and that had menaced that whole solar system had calmed down, we slowly, after the unexpected interruption, resumed the settlement of our new place on the planet 'Mars.'

"Little by little we all of us became familiar with the Nature there and adapted ourselves to the existing conditions there.

"As I have already said, many of us settled on the planet 'Mars,' and others, by the ship '*Occasion*' which had been put at the disposal of the beings of our tribe for interplanetary communication, either went or prepared to go to exist on some other planet of the same solar system.

"But with my kinsmen and some of my near attendants, I remained to exist on that planet 'Mars.'

"Yes, I must note that by the time to which my tale refers, my first 'Teskooano,' which I had had constructed on the planet 'Mars,' had already been set up in my observatory, and I was just then devoting myself entirely to the further organization and development of my observatory for the more detailed observation of the remote concentrations of our great Universe and of the planets of this Solar System. Among the objects of my observations then was this planet 'Earth' also.

"Time went on.

"The process of existence on this planet also was gradually established and it seemed, from all appearances, that the process of existence there was proceeding just as on all other planets.

"But by close observation, firstly, it could be clearly seen that the numbers of these three-brained beings increased, and, secondly, it was possible to observe some very strange occasional manifestation of theirs; they did something from time to time that was never done by three-brained beings on any other planet, namely, they would suddenly without any reason begin destroying each other's existence.

"This destruction of each other's existence, especially in masses, sometimes proceeded there not in one region only but in several at once, and would last not just one 'dionosk,' but many 'dionosks' and sometimes even for whole 'onakra.'

"It became also perceptible that from time to time, as a result of this horrible process of theirs, their numbers rapidly diminished; but on the other hand, during other periods when there was a respite from such processes, their numbers noticeably increased.

"We gradually got used to this peculiarity of theirs also, and explained it to ourselves, that for certain higher considerations these properties also must have been deliberately given to the organ Kundabuffer by the Most High Commission; in other words, seeing the fecundity of these biped beings we presumed that it had been done for a reason, because large numbers of them were needed and the planet itself was not big enough.

"Had it not been for these strange peculiarities of theirs, then it would have entered nobody's head that there was anything 'fishy' about that planet.

"During the period to which what has been said refers, I had time to visit most of the planets of that solar system, both populated and unpopulated.

"I personally liked best of all the three-centered beings breeding on the planet bearing the name 'Saturn'; their appearance is quite unlike ours; but they resemble the large bird called the 'raven.'

"It is interesting to remark, by the way, that for some reason or other, the form of the bird-being raven breeds not only on almost all the planets of this solar system, but also on most of those other planets of the whole of the great Universe upon which beings of various brain-systems arise and are coated with planetary bodies of different forms.

"These bird-beings ravens of that planet 'Saturn' have verbal intercourse among themselves just as we have.

"It can be compared to the singing of our best singers when with all their being they sing in a minor key.

"And as for their mutual relations, they . . . I don't even know how to describe them—they can be understood only by existing among them and by personal experience.

"All that can be said is that these bird-beings have hearts like those of the angels nearest OUR ENDLESS MAKER AND CREATOR.

"They exist strictly according to the ninth commandment of our CREATOR, namely: Represent another's as your own, and be so related.

"I will certainly tell you more in detail sometime later about those three-brained beings who arise and exist on the planet 'Saturn' and whose external coating is like that of the 'raven,' since one of my real friends during the whole of the period of my exile in that solar system was a being of just that planet who had the exterior coating of a 'raven' and whose name was 'Harharkh.'"

CHAPTER XI

A Piquant Trait Of The Peculiarity Of Man's Psyche

LET US talk again about those three-brained beings arising and existing on the planet Earth who have most interested you and whom you call 'slugs.'

"I shall begin by saying how glad I am that you are a long way from those three-centered beings whom you call 'slugs' and they are never likely to hear of it.

"Do you know, you poor thing—a mere chit of a boy who has not yet become aware of himself—what they, and particularly the contemporary beings there, would do to you if they should hear how you referred to them?

"What they would do to you if you were there, or if they should get hold of you—I'm seized with horror as I even mention it.

"At best they would so thrash you that as our Mullah Nassr Eddin there says: 'You wouldn't recover your senses before the next crop of birches.'

"In any case, I advise you that, whenever you start anything new, you should always bless and beseech Fate always to kindly watch out that beings of the planet Earth never suspect that just you, my beloved and only grandson, dared to call them 'slugs.'

"You must know that during the time of my observation of them from the planet Mars and during the periods of my existence among them, I studied the psyche of these strange three-brained beings very thoroughly, and I already know very well what they would do to anybody who dared to nickname them so.

"Although it was only in boyish naïveté that you called them this, the three-brained beings of that peculiar planet, especially the contemporary ones, do not deal in such refinements.

"Who it was, why it was, in what circumstances it was—it's all the same! They were called by a name which they consider insulting—and that's quite enough.

"Discrimination is for most minds there simply, as they express it, 'pouring from the empty into the empty.'

"Be that as it may, you were, in any case, extremely rash to call the three-brained beings breeding on the planet Earth by such an offensive word; firstly, because you have made me anxious for you, and secondly, you have laid yourself up trouble for the future.

"The position is this: although, as I have already told you, being a long way off, they may be unable to get at you to punish you personally, yet nevertheless, if they should by remote chance learn even at twentieth hand how you insulted them, then you can certainly already be assured of their real 'anathema,' the dimensions of which will depend on the subject of interest at the given moment.

"Perhaps it is worth while describing to you how the beings of the Earth would behave if they happened to learn that you insulted them in this way. This description may serve as a very good example for the elucidation of the strange psyche of these three-brained beings who interest you.

"Provoked by such an event, namely, your insulting them, if everything was rather 'dull' with them at the given moment, owing to the absence of any other similar absurd interest, they would arrange somewhere in a place previously chosen what is called a 'solemn council' consisting of people previously invited, all, of course, dressed in special costumes for such occasions.

"For their 'solemn council' they would first select what is called a 'president' from among themselves and only then would they proceed with their 'trial.'

"To begin with, they would, as they say there, 'try you minutely,' and not only you, but your father, your grandfather, and perhaps even back to Adam.

"If they should then decide—certainly of course by a majority of votes—that you are guilty, they would sentence you according to a code of laws collated from former similar 'puppet plays' by beings called 'old fossils.'

"But if they should happen, by a 'majority of votes,' to find nothing criminal in your conduct at all—though this very seldom occurs among them—then this whole 'trial' of theirs, set out on paper in detail and signed by the whole lot of them would be dispatched . . . you think into the wastepaper basket . . . Not on your life . . . to appointed specialists, in the given instance, to what is called the 'Holy Synod' or 'Hierarchy' where the same procedure would again be repeated—only in this case you would be 'tried' by 'important' beings there.

"Only at the very end of this real 'pouring from the empty into the empty' would they come to the vital point, namely, that they couldn't get hold of the accused.

"Yes, but it is just at that point that the rub comes for you personally . . . namely, that when they are quite certain beyond all doubt, that they can't get hold of you, they will, then, unanimously decide neither more nor less than, as I have already said, to 'anathematize' you.

"And do you know what that is and how it is done?

"No?

"Then listen and shudder.

"The most 'important' beings will ordain that in all their appointed establishments called 'churches,' 'chapels,' 'Synagogues,' 'town-halls' and so on, special officials shall on special occasions with appointed ceremonies wish for you in their thoughts something like the following:

"That you should lose your horns, or that your hair should turn grey, or that the food in your stomach should become coffin-nails, or that your future wife's tongue should be three times its size, or that whenever you take a bite of your pet pie, it should taste like 'soap,' and so on and so forth in the same strain.

"Do you now understand to what dangers you exposed yourself when you called these remote three-brained freaks 'slugs'?"

Having finished thus, Beelzebub looked with a smile on his favorite.

CHAPTER XII

The First "Growl"

A LITTLE later Beelzebub spoke as follows:

"A story I have just recalled connected with the 'anathema' I have just mentioned may provide very useful material for beginning to comprehend the strangeness of the psyche of the three-brained beings of that planet which has pleased you; and, furthermore, the story may reassure you a little and give you hope that if these peculiar terrestrial beings should chance to learn that you had insulted them and should 'anathematize' you, then perhaps after all something not so very 'bad' might come of it for you.

"The story I am going to tell you occurred quite recently amongst contemporary three-brained beings there.

"And it arose there from the following events:

"In one of those large communities, there peaceably existed an ordinary being who was by profession what is there called a 'writer.'

"Here you must know that, in previous ages, you might still occasionally run across beings of that profession who still invented and wrote something really by themselves; but in these later epochs the 'writers' among the beings there, particularly among contemporary beings, were of the kind that only plagiarize ideas from many already existing books, and make a 'new book' by fitting them together.

"As a rule, they prefer books which have reached them from their remote ancestors.

"It must further be particularly remarked that the books written by contemporary 'writers' there, are, taken all together, the principal cause that the Reasoning of the rest of the three-brained beings there becomes progressively what the venerable Mullah Nassr Eddin calls 'stuff and nonsense.'

"And so, my boy!

"The contemporary 'writer' of whom I began to speak, was just a 'writer' like all the rest there, and nothing particular in himself.

"Once when he had finished some book or other, he began to think what he should write about next, and with this in view, he decided to look for some new 'idea' or other in the books contained in what is called a 'library,' such as every writer there is bound to have.

"As he was looking, a book called the 'Gospels' happened to fall into his hands.

"The 'Gospels' is the name given there to a book written some time ago by a certain Matthew, Mark, Luke and John about Jesus Christ, a Messenger from our ENDLESSNESS to that planet.

"This book is widely circulated among the three-centered beings there, who, nominally, exist according to the indications of this Messenger.

"This book having chanced to fall into this writer's hands, the thought suddenly entered his head, 'Why shouldn't I also make a "Gospel"?'

"From the investigations I happened to make for quite different aims of mine, it seems that he then deliberated further in the following way:

"'I'm no worse than those ancient barbarians, John, Luke, Matthew and Mark!

"'And, at least, I am more cultured than they ever were; and I can write a much better 'Gospel' for my contemporaries.

"'And very decidedly it is necessary to write just a 'Gospel,' because the wealthiest people now existing—those called 'English' and 'American'—have a weakness for this book and the exchange rate of their pounds and dollars is 'not half bad' just now.

"No sooner thought than begun!

"And from that very day he 'wiseacred' away at his new 'Gospel.'

"It was just when he had finished it, however, and given it to the printers, only then it was that all the further events associated with this new 'Gospel' of his began.

"At any other time, nothing perhaps would have happened and this new 'Gospel' of his would simply have slipped into its niche in the libraries of the bibliophiles there, among the piles of other books expounding similar 'truths.'

"But fortunately or unfortunately for this writer, it happened that certain 'power-possessing' beings of that great community where he too existed had just had rotten luck at what is called 'roulette' and 'baccarat,' and they therefore kept on demanding what they call 'money' from the ordinary beings of their community, whereupon, thanks to these demands for money, inordinate for that time, the ordinary beings of that community at length began to wake from their usual torpor and to 'sit up.'

"Seeing this, the 'power-possessing' beings who remained at home, became alarmed and took corresponding 'measures.'

"And among the 'measures' they took was also the immediate destruction from the face of their planet of everything 'new' in their native land that could possibly keep the ordinary beings of their community from resuming their hibernation.

"It was just at this time that the aforementioned 'Gospels' of this writer appeared.

"In the contents of this new 'Gospel' also, the 'power-possessing' beings found something which to their understanding might also keep ordinary beings of their community from hibernating again; and they therefore decided almost immediately to 'bump off' both the writer himself and his 'Gospel,' and especially because they had now become quite expert in 'bumping off' such native agitators as did not mind their own business.

"But for certain reasons, they couldn't treat this writer like that, and so they became much agitated and considered along time what they should do.

"Some proposed that he should just be confined there where breed many 'rats' and 'lice'; others proposed to send him to 'where Makkar had never driven his calves,' that is, very far away, indeed; and so on and so forth; but in the end, they decided to anathematize this writer together with his 'Gospel' publicly and punctiliously according to all the rules, and with the self-same 'anathema' with which no doubt they would also anathematize you, if they learned how you had insulted them.

"And so, my boy; the strangeness of the psyche of the contemporary three-brained beings of this peculiar planet was revealed in the given instance in this, that when this writer and his 'Gospel' had been publicly anathematized with this 'anathema,' the result for him was as the highly esteemed Mullah Nassr Eddin once again says: 'simply roses, roses.'

"What further occurred was as follows:

"The ordinary beings of the said community, seeing the fuss made about this writer by the power-possessing beings, became very greatly interested in him and greedily bought and read, not only this new 'Gospel' of his, but also all the books he had written before.

"Whereupon, as usually happens with the three-centered beings breeding on this peculiar planet, all their other interests gradually died down and the beings of the said community all talked and thought only of this writer.

"And, as it also happens there—when some praised him extravagantly, others spoke against him; and the result of these discussions and conversations was that the numbers interested in him grew not only among the beings of his own community, but among the beings of other communities also.

"And this occurred because some of the power-possessing

beings of this community, usually with pockets full of money, still continued in their turn to go to other communities where 'roulette' and 'baccarat' proceeded, and, carrying on their discussions there concerning this writer, they gladly infected beings of other communities also with this affair.

"In short, owing to the strangeness of their psyche, it has gradually come about there that even at the present time, when the cause of the anathematizing of this writer has already long been forgotten, and even his 'Gospel' has been forgotten also, his name is still known almost everywhere as that of a 'very good writer.'

"Anything he writes now, they all seize upon and regard an indisputable truths.

"Everybody looks upon his writings with the same veneration with which the ancient Kalkians listened to the predictions of their sacred 'Pythias.'

"It is very interesting to notice here, that if you ask any being you like there about this writer, everybody would know him and, of course, speak of him as 'great.'

"But if you were then to ask them what he wrote, it would turn out that most of them—if, of course, they confessed the truth—had never even read a single one of his books.

"All the same they would discuss him, and of course, splutteringly insist that he was a being with an 'extraordinary mind' and phenomenally acquainted with the psyche of the beings dwelling on the planet Earth."

CHAPTER XIII

In Man's Reason, Fantasy May Be Perceived As Reality

"MY DEAR and kind grandfather," exclaimed Hassein "be so kind as to explain to me, if only roughly, why they there are such that they take the ephemeral for reality?"

To this question of his grandson, Beelzebub replied thus:

"It was only during later periods that the three-brained beings of the planet 'Earth' began to have this particularity of their psyche.

"Just that particularity arose in the beings there, only because their chief part, which was formed in them as in all three-brained beings, gradually allowed other parts of their total 'presence' to perceive new impressions without what is called 'being-Partkdolgduty,' but just merely as, in general, such impressions are perceived by the separate independent localizations existing under the name of being-centers present in the three-brained beings; or, as I should in their language say, they believe everything anybody says, and not solely that which they themselves could cognize with their own sane deliberation.

"In general, any new understanding in these strange beings becomes crystallized only if you say about somebody or something just what John Smith says, and then if only John Brown says the same, the hearer is now quite persuaded that it is just so and couldn't possibly be otherwise.

"Thanks merely to this particularity of their psyche and to the fact that the said writer was much spoken about in the said manner, most of the beings there at the present time are now persuaded that he is indeed a very great psychologist and has an incomparable knowledge of the psyche of the beings of his planet.

"But, as a matter of fact, when I was on that planet for the last time and, having heard of the said writer, once went myself specially to see him, on quite another matter, he seemed to me to be not only like all the other contemporary writers there, that is to say, extremely limited, and also as our dear Mullah Nassr Eddin would say: 'seeing no further than his nose,' but as regards any knowledge of the real psyche of the beings of that planet in real conditions, he might safely be called 'totally illiterate.'

"I repeat that the story of this writer is a very characteristic example of the extent to which, in these three-brained beings who please you, particularly in the contemporary ones, the realization of the 'being-Partkdolgduty' is absent and how—as in general it is proper to the three-brained beings—their own subjective being-convictions formed by their own logical deliberations are never crystallized in them but only those are crystallized which depend exclusively only upon what others say about the given question.

"It was only because they failed to realize the 'being-Partkdolgduty,' which realization alone enables a being to become aware of genuine-reality, that they saw in the said writer some perfection or other that was not there.

"This strange trait of their general psyche, namely, of being satisfied with just what John Smith or John Brown says, without trying to know more, became rooted in them already long ago, and now they no longer strive at all to know anything cognizable only by their own active deliberation.

"And it must be said concerning all this, that neither the organ Kundabuffer is to blame, which their ancestors had, nor its consequences, which owing to a mistake on the part of certain sacred Individuums, were crystallized in their ancestors and later began to pass as an inheritance, from generation to generation.

"But they themselves are personally to blame for it, and just on that account of the abnormal conditions of external ordinary being-existence which they themselves have gradually established, and which gradually have formed in their general 'presence' just what has now become that inner 'Evil God' called 'Self Calming.'

"But you yourself, later on, will well understand when I shall have given you, as I have already promised, more information about that planet which pleases you.

"In any case, I strongly advise you to be very careful in the future in your references to the three-brained beings of that planet not to offend them in any way; otherwise, as they also say there, 'With what may the Devil not joke,' and they might find out some crime or other of yours and 'lay you by the heels'—to use another of their expressions.

"And as for the given case, there is no harm in recalling again one of the wise sentences of our dear Mullah Nassr Eddin who says:

"'Struth! What only may not happen in the world! A flea might swallow an elephant!'"

Beelzebub intended to say something still more, but at that moment a ship's servant entered and approached and handed him an 'etherogram' in his name. When Beelzebub had finished listening to the contents of the said 'etherogram' and the ship's servant had gone, Hassein turned to Beelzebub again with the following words:

"Dear Grandfather, please go on talking about the three-centered beings arising and existing on that interesting planet called 'Earth.'"

Beelzebub having looked at his grandson, again with a particular smile, and having made a very strange gesture with his head, continued to speak as follows:

CHAPTER XIV

The Beginnings Of Perspectives Promising Nothing Very Cheerful

I MUST first tell you that the three-brained beings on that planet also had in the beginning a 'presence' similar to that possessed in general by all what are called 'Keschapmartnian' three-centered beings arising on all the corresponding planets of the whole of our great Universe; and they also had the same, as it is called, 'duration of existence' as other three-brained beings.

"All the various changes in their 'presence' occurred for the most part after the second misfortune to this planet during which misfortune the principal continent of that ill-starred planet then existing under the name 'Atlantis' entered within the planet itself.

"And from that time forward, as, little by little they created for their existence every possible kind of condition of external being-existence, thanks to which the quality of their radiations went steadily from bad to worse, Great Nature was compelled gradually to regenerate their general 'presence' by means of various compromises and changes in order to regulate the quality of the vibrations which they radiated and which were chiefly required for the preservation of the well-being of the former parts of that planet.

"For the same reason, Great Nature gradually increased the numbers there, with the result that at the present time they are breeding on all the lands formed on the planet.

"The exterior forms of their planetary bodies are all much alike and, of course, in respect of size and in their subjective particularities they are each coated, just as we are, in accordance with the reflection of heredity, the conditions at the moment of conception and with the rest of the factors that serve in general as the causes for the arising and formation of every being.

"They differ also among themselves in the color of their skin and in the conformation of the hair arising on them, and these latter particularities are also determined in each of their 'presences' just as they are everywhere else, by the effects of that part of the planetary surface where the given beings arise and where they are formed up to the age of a responsible being, or, as they say, until they become 'adult.'

"As regards their general psyche itself and its fundamental traits, no matter upon what part of the surface of their planet they arise, these traits in all of them have precisely the same particularities, among them being also that property of the three-brained beings there, thanks to which on that strange planet alone in the whole of the Universe does that horrible process occur among three-brained beings which is called the 'process of the destruction of the existence of each other,' or, as it is called on that ill-starred planet, 'war.'

"Besides this chief particularity of their common psyche, there are completely crystallized in them, regardless of where they may arise and exist, and there unfailingly become a part of their general 'presence,' functions which exist there under the names, 'egoism,' 'self-love,' 'vanity,' 'pride,' 'self-conceit,' 'credulity,' 'suggestibility,' and many other properties quite abnormal and quite unbecoming to the essence of any three-brained beings whatsoever.

"Of the just named abnormal being-particularities, that particularity of their psyche, the most terrible for them personally, is called 'suggestibility.'

"About this extremely strange and singular psychic particularity I shall especially tell you some time."

Having said this Beelzebub became thoughtful and this time for longer than usual and then he resumed to his grandson as follows:

"I see that the three-brained beings arising and existing on the peculiar planet called 'Earth' interest you very much, and as, during our voyage on the ship '*Karnak*' we shall have to talk about many things just to pass away the time, I will tell you all I can just about these three-brained beings.

"I think it will be best for your clear understanding of the strangeness of the psyche of the three-brained beings arising on the planet 'Earth' if I relate to you my personal descents to that planet in their order and the events which occurred there during these descents of mine and of which I was myself a witness.

"But I personally visited the surface of the planet 'Earth' only six times and each of these personal visits of mine was brought about by a different set of circumstances.

"I shall begin with my first descent."

CHAPTER XV

The First Descent Of Beelzebub Upon The Earth

UPON THAT planet Earth," Beelzebub began to relate, "I descended for the first time on account of a young being of our tribe who had had the misfortune to become deeply involved with a three-brained being there, as a consequence of which he had got himself mixed up in a very stupid affair.

"There once came to my house on the planet Mars a number of beings of our tribe, also dwelling there on Mars, with the following request:

"They told me that one of their young kinsmen, 350 Martian years before, had migrated to exist on the planet Earth, and that a very disagreeable incident for all of us, his kinsmen, had recently occurred to him there.

"They told me further:

"'We, his kinsmen, both those existing there on the planet Earth and those existing here on the planet Mars, intended at first to deal with the unpleasant incident ourselves, with our own resources. But notwithstanding all our efforts and the measures we have adopted we have been unable so far to accomplish anything.

"'And being now finally convinced that we are unable to settle this unpleasant affair by ourselves independently, we venture to trouble you, Your Right Reverence, and urgently beseech you to be so kind as not to withhold from us your wise advice how we may find a way out of our unhappy situation.'

"They told me further in detail in what the misfortune which had befallen them consisted.

"From all they told me I saw that the incident was disagreeable not only for this young being's kinsmen, but that it might also prove disagreeable for the beings of all our tribe.

"So I could not help deciding at once to undertake to help them to settle this difficulty of theirs.

"At first I tried to help them while remaining on the planet Mars, but when I became certain that it would be impossible to do anything effective from the planet Mars, I decided to descend to the planet Earth and there, on the spot, to find some way out. The next day after this decision of mine I took with me everything necessary which I had 'at hand' and flew there on the ship '*Occasion*.'

"I may remind you that the ship '*Occasion*' was the ship on which all the beings of our tribe were transported to that solar system and as I have already told you, it was left there for the use of the beings of our tribe for the purpose of interplanetary communication.

"The permanent port of this ship was on the planet Mars; and its supreme direction had been given me from Above.

"Thus it was on this same ship '*Occasion*' that I made my first descent to the planet Earth.

"Our ship landed on this first visit of mine, on the shores of just that continent which during the second catastrophe to this planet, disappeared entirely from its surface.

"This continent was called 'Atlantis' and most of the three-brained beings and likewise most of the beings of our tribe then existed only upon it.

"Having descended, I went straight from the ship '*Occasion*' to the city named 'Samlios,' situated on the said continent, where that unfortunate being of our tribe, who was the cause of this descent of mine, had the place of his existence.

"The city 'Samlios' was then a very large city, and was the capital of the largest community then on the planet Earth.

"In this same city the head of this large community existed who was called 'King Appolis.'

"And it was with just this same 'King Appolis' that our young inexperienced countryman had become involved.

"And it was in this city of 'Samlios' itself that I learned all the details of this affair.

"I learned, namely, that before this incident our unfortunate countryman had for some reason been on friendly terms with this King Appolis, and was often at his house.

"As it transpired, our young countryman once, in the course of conversation, during a visit to the house of King Appolis, made a 'wager' which was just the cause of all that followed.

"You must first of all know that both the community of which King Appolis was the head, and the city of Samlios where he existed were at that period the greatest and richest of all the communities and cities then existing on the Earth.

"For the upkeep of all this wealth and grandeur King Appolis certainly needed both a great deal of what is called 'money' and a great deal of labor from the ordinary beings of that community.

"It is necessary to premise just here that at the period of my first descent in person onto this planet, the organ Kundabuffer was no longer in three-brained beings who interest you.

"And it was only in some of the three-brained beings there that various consequences of the properties of that for them maleficent organ had already begun to be crystallized.

"In the period to which this tale of mine refers, one of the consequences of the properties of this organ which had already become thoroughly crystallized in a number of beings there, was that consequence of the property which, while the organ Kundabuffer itself was still functioning in them had enabled them very easily and without any 'remorse-of-conscience' not to carry out voluntarily any duties taken upon themselves or given them by a superior. But every duty they fulfilled was fulfilled only from the fear and apprehension of 'threats' and 'menaces' from outside.

"It was in just this same consequence of this property already thoroughly crystallized in some beings of that period there, that the cause of this whole incident lay.

"And so, my boy, this is how it was. King Appolis who had been extremely conscientious in respect of the duties he had taken upon himself for the maintenance of the greatness of the community entrusted to him had spared neither his own labor nor wealth, and at the same time he demanded the same from all the beings of his community.

"But, as I have already said, the mentioned consequences of the organ Kundabuffer having by that time been thoroughly crystallized in certain of his subjects, he had to employ every possible kind of 'threat' and 'menace' in order to extract from everybody all that was required for the greatness of the community entrusted to him.

"His methods were so varied and at the same time so reasonable that even those subjects-beings in whom the said consequences had already been crystallized could not help respecting him, although they added to his name, of course behind his back, the nickname 'Arch-cunning.'

"And so, my boy, these means by which King Appolis then obtained what was necessary from his subjects for the maintenance of the greatness of the community entrusted to him seemed to our young countryman, for some reason or other, unjust, and, as it was said, he often became very indignant and restless whenever he happened to hear of some new device of King Appolis for getting what was necessary.

"And once, while talking with the King himself, our naive young countryman could not restrain himself, but expressed to his face his indignation and his views of this 'unconscionable' conduct of King Appolis towards his subjects.

"Not only did King Appolis not fly into a temper, as usually happens on the planet Earth when somebody pokes his nose where he has no business, nor did he pitch him out by the scruff of his neck, but he even talked it over with him and discussed the reasons for his 'severity.'

"They talked a great deal and the result of the whole of their conversation was precisely a 'wager,' that is to say, they made an agreement and set it down on paper, and each of them signed it with his own blood.

"Among other things there was included in this agreement that for the obtaining from his subjects of all that was necessary King Appolis should be obliged to employ thereafter only those measures and means which should be indicated by our countryman.

"And in the event that all the subjects should fail to contribute all that which according to custom was required, then our countryman would become responsible for everything, and he pledged himself to procure for the treasury of King Appolis as much as was necessary for the maintenance and further aggrandizement of the capital and of the whole community.

"And so, my boy, King Appolis did indeed, already from the following day fulfil very honorably the obligation which according to the agreement he had assumed; and he conducted the whole government of the country exactly according to the indications of our young countryman. The results of a government of this kind, however, very soon proved to be quite the opposite of those expected by our simpleton.

"The subjects of that community—principally, of course, those in whom the said consequences of the properties of the organ Kundabuffer had already been crystallized—not only ceased to pay into King Appolis' treasury what was required, but they even began gradually snatching back what had been put in before.

"As our countryman had undertaken to contribute what was needed, and furthermore, had signed his undertaking with his blood—and you know, don't you, what the voluntary undertaking of an obligation, especially when signed with his blood, means to one of our tribe—he had of course soon to begin making up to the treasury all that was short.

"He first put in everything he had himself, and afterwards everything he could get from his nearests, dwelling also there on the planet Earth. And when he had drained dry his nearests there, he addressed himself for assistance to his nearests dwelling on the planet Mars.

"But soon on the planet Mars also everything ran dry and still the treasury of the city of Samlios demanded more and again more; nor was the end of its needs in sight.

"It was just then that all the kinsmen of this countryman of ours became alarmed and thereupon they decided to address themselves to me with the request to help them out of their plight.

"So, my boy, when we arrived in the said city I was met by all the beings of our tribe, both old and young, who had remained on that planet.

"In the evening of the same day a general meeting was called to confer together to find some way out of the situation that had arisen.

"To this conference of ours there was also invited King Appolis himself with whom our elder countrymen had already previously had many talks on this matter with this aim in view.

"At this first general conference of ours, King Appolis, addressing himself to all, said as follows:

"'Impartial friends!

"'I personally am deeply sorry for what has occurred and what has brought about so many troubles for those assembled here; and I am distressed in all my being that it is beyond my power to extricate you from your prospective difficulties.'

"'You must know, indeed' King Appolis continued, 'that the machinery of the government of my community which has been wound up and organized during many centuries, is at the present time already radically changed; and to revert to the old order is already impossible without serious consequences, namely, without those consequences which must doubtless evoke the indignation of the majority of my subjects. The present situation is such that I alone am not able to abolish what has been created without provoking the mentioned serious consequences, and I therefore beg you all in the name of Justice to help me deal with it.'

"'Still further,' he then added, 'I bitterly reproach myself in the presence of you all, because I also am greatly to blame for all these misfortunes.'

"'And I am to blame because I ought to have foreseen what has occurred, since I have existed in these conditions longer than my opponent and your kinsman, namely, he with whom I made the agreement known to you.'

"'To tell the truth it was unpardonable of me to risk entering into such conditions with a being who, although he may be of much higher reason than I, is, nevertheless, not so practiced in such affairs as I am.'

"'Once more I beg all of you, and Your Reverence in particular, to forgive me and to help me out of this sad plight, and enable me to find some issue from the situation that has been created.'

"'With things as they now are, I can at present do only what you will indicate.'"

"After King Appolis had left, we decided the same evening to select from among ourselves several experienced elderly beings who should weigh together, that same night, all the data and draw up a rough plan for further action.

"The rest of us then departed on the understanding that we should assemble the ensuing evening at the same place; but to this second conference of ours King Appolis was not invited.

"When we assembled the next day, one of the elder beings elected the night before, first reported as follows:

"'We pondered and deliberated the whole night upon all the details of this lamentable event, and as a result we have unanimously come to the conclusion first of all that there is no way out but to revert to the former conditions of government.

"'Further, we all, and also unanimously, agree that to return to the former order of government must indeed inevitably provoke a revolt of the citizens of the community, and, of course, that there will certainly follow all those consequences of revolt which have already became inevitable in such circumstances during recent times on Earth.

"'And of course, as it has also become usual here, many of those called 'power-possessing' beings of this community will suffer terribly, even possibly to the degree of their complete destruction; and above all, it seemed impossible that King Appolis could escape such a fate.

"'Thereafter we deliberated in order, if possible, to devise some means of diverting the said unhappy consequences at least from King Appolis himself.

"'And we had every wish to devise such a means because at our general conference yesterday evening King Appolis himself was very frank and friendly towards us, and we should all be extremely sorry if he himself should suffer.

"'During our further prolonged deliberations we came to the conclusion that it would be possible to divert the blow from King Appolis only if during the said revolt the exhibition of the fury of the rebellious beings of this community were directed not against the King himself but against those around him, that is, those who are there called his 'administration.'

"'But then the question arose among us, would those near the King be willing to take upon themselves the consequences of all this?'

"And we came to the categorical conclusion that they certainly would not agree, because they would assuredly consider that the King himself had been alone to blame for it all, and that therefore he himself should pay for it.

"'Having come to all these aforesaid conclusions we finally also unanimously decided as follows:

"'In order at least to save King Appolis from what is inevitably expected, we must with the consent of the King himself replace all the beings in this community who now hold responsible posts, by beings of our tribe, and each of these latter, during the climax of this 'psychosis' of the masses must take upon himself a share of the consequences anticipated.'"

"When this elected being of ours had finished his report, our opinion was quickly formed; and a unanimous resolution was carried to do just as the elder beings of our tribe had advised.

"And thereupon we first sent one of our elder beings to King Appolis to put our plan before him, to which the latter agreed, once more repeating his promise, namely, that he would do everything according to our directions.

"We then decided to delay no longer and from the following day to begin to replace all the officials by our own.

"But after two days it turned out that there were not sufficient beings of or tribe dwelling on the planet Earth to replace all the officials of that community; and we therefore immediately sent the '*Occasion*' back to the planet Mars for our beings there.

"And meanwhile King Appolis guided by two of our elder beings, began under different pretexts replacing various officials by our beings, at first in the capital of Samlios itself.

"And when several days later our ship '*Occasion*' arrived from the planet Mars with beings of our tribe, similar replacements were made in the provinces also, and soon everywhere in that community what are called the responsible posts were filled by the beings of our tribe.

"And when all had been changed in this way, King Appolis, always under the guidance of these elder beings of ours, began the restoration of the former code of regulations for the administration of the community.

"Almost from the very first days of the restoration of the old code, the effects upon the general psyche of the beings of that community in whom the consequences of the mentioned property of the maleficent organ Kundabuffer had already been thoroughly crystallized, began as it was expected, to manifest themselves.

"Thus the expected discontent grew thereupon from day to day, until one day, not long after, there occurred just that which has ever since been definitely proper to be present in the presence of the three-brained beings there of all ensuing periods, and that is, to produce from time to time the process which they themselves nowadays call 'revolution.'

"And during their 'revolution' of that time, as it has also become proper there to these three-brained phenomena of our Great Universe, they destroyed a great deal of the property which they had accumulated during centuries, much of what is called the 'knowledge' which their kind attained during centuries also was destroyed and lost forever, and the existences of those other beings similar to themselves who had already chanced upon the means of freeing themselves from the consequences of the properties of the organ Kundabuffer, were also destroyed.

"It is extremely interesting to notice here one exceedingly astonishing and incomprehensible fact.

"And that is that during their later 'revolutions' of this kind, almost all the three-brained beings there or at least the overwhelming majority who begin to fall into such a 'psychosis,' always destroy for some reason or other, the existence of just such other beings like themselves, as have for some reason or other, chanced to find themselves more or less on the track of the means of becoming free from the crystallization in themselves of the consequences of the properties of that maleficent organ Kundabuffer which unfortunately their ancestors possessed.

"So, my boy, while the process of this 'revolution' of theirs was running its course, King Appolis himself existed in one of his what are called suburban palaces of the city of Samlios.

"Nobody laid a finger on him, because our beings had arranged by their propaganda that the whole blame should be placed not upon King Appolis but upon those surrounding him, that is as they are called his administration.

"Moreover, the beings who had fallen into the said 'psychosis' even 'suffered grief' and really pitied their king saying that it was because their 'poor King' had been surrounded by such unconscionable and ungrateful subordinates that these undesirable revolutions had occurred.

"And when the revolutionary psychosis had quite died down, King Appolis returned to the city of Samlios and again with the help of our elder beings, gradually began replacing our countrymen either by those of his old subordinates who were still alive, or by selecting absolutely new ones from among his other subjects.

"And when the earlier policy of King Appolis towards his subjects had been reestablished, then the citizens of this community resumed filling the treasury with 'money' as usual and carrying out the directions of their King, and the affairs of the community settled again into the former already established tempo.

"As for our naive, unfortunate countryman who was the cause of it all, it was so painful to him that he would no longer remain upon that planet that had proved so disastrous for him, but he returned with us to the planet Mars.

"And later on he became there an even excellent bailiff for all the beings of our tribe."

CHAPTER XVI

The Relative Understanding Of Time

AFTER a short pause Beelzebub continued thus:

"Before telling you more about the three-brained beings who please you, breeding on the planet 'Earth,' I think that for a clear conspectus of the strangeness of their psyche and, in general, for a better understanding of everything concerning the peculiarity of that planet, it is indispensably necessary for you to have, first of all, an accurate conception of their time-calculation and of how the being-sensation of what is called the 'process-of-the-flow-of-Time' in the 'presence' of the three-brained beings of that planet has gradually undergone change and of how this process now flows in the 'presence' of the contemporary three-brained beings there.

"It must be made clear to you because only then can you have a clear view and understanding, both of those events there which I have already related and those I have still to relate.

"You must first know that for the definition of Time, the three-brained beings of that planet, just as we do, take the year as the fundamental unit of their Time-calculation, and also just as we do, they define the duration of their year by the time of a certain movement of their planet in relation to another definite cosmic concentration; namely, they take that period in the course of which their planet, during its movement—that is, during the process of 'Falling' and 'Catching Up'—makes what is called its 'Krentonalnian' revolution in relation to its sun.

"It is similar to our reckoning of a year for our planet 'Karatas,' which is the period of time between one nearest approach of the Sun 'Samos' to the Sun 'Selos' and its next similar approach.

"A hundred of such years of theirs, the beings of the 'Earth' call a 'century.'

"And they divide this 'year' into twelve parts and each part they call a 'month.'

"For the definition of the duration of this 'month' of theirs, they take the time of the complete period during which that larger fragment—which was separated from their planet and which they now call 'Moon'—makes, owing to the same cosmic law of 'Falling' and 'Catching Up,' its full 'Krentonalnian' revolution in relation to their planet.

"It must be noticed that the twelve 'Krentonalnian' revolutions of the said 'Moon' do not correspond exactly to a single 'Krentonalnian' revolution of their planet round its sun and therefore they have made some compromise or other when calculating these 'months' of theirs so that in the sum-total these may correspond more or less to reality.

"Further, they divide these 'months' of theirs into thirty 'diurnities,' or, as they usually say, 'days.'

"And a 'diurnity' they reckon as that period of time during which their planet makes its appointed rotation during the operation of the said cosmic laws.

"Bear in mind, by the way, that they also call it 'day'—when in the atmosphere of their planet—just as in general upon all the other planets on which, as I have already told you, the cosmic process called 'Ilnosoparnian' is actualized—that 'Trogoautoegocratic' process which we call 'Kshtatsavacht' periodically proceeds; and they also call this cosmic phenomenon 'daylight.'

"And concerning the other process, the opposite one, namely, that which we call 'Kldatzacht,' they call it 'night' or speak of it as 'the dark.'

"And thus the three-brained beings breeding on the planet 'Earth' call the greatest period of the flowing of Time a 'century,' and this century of theirs consists of one hundred years.

"A 'year' has 'twelve months.'

"A 'month' has an average of thirty 'diurnities.'

"Further they divide their 'diurnity' into twenty-four 'hours' and an 'hour' they divide into sixty 'minutes.'

"And a 'minute' in its turn they divide into sixty 'seconds.'

"But as you are aware in general, my boy, of the altogether exceptional peculiarity of this same cosmic phenomenon Time, you must first be told that genuine objective Science formulates this cosmic phenomenon thus:

"Time in itself does not in general exist; there is only the totality of the results arising from the cosmic phenomena of every kind present in the given place.

"Time in itself no being can either understand by reason, or sense by any outer or inner being-function. It cannot even be sensed by any gradation of instinct which arises and is generally present in every kind of more or less independent cosmic concentration.

"It is possible to judge Time only if one compares some or other of the real cosmic phenomena which proceed in the same place and in the same conditions where Time is being ascertained and investigated.

"It is necessary to notice that in the Great Universe all phenomena in general without exception wherever they arise and manifest, are simply successively lawful fractions of some whole phenomenon which receives its prime arising on the Most Holy Sun Absolute.

"And owing to all this, all cosmic phenomena wherever they proceed, receive a 'sense of objectivity.'

"And these successively lawful fractions are actualized in every respect, and even in the sense of their evolution and involution, very strictly according to the chief cosmic law, the sacred 'Heptaparaparshinokh.'

"Only Time alone has no 'sense of objectivity,' because it is not the consequence of the functioning of any definite cosmic phenomenon; and as it does not issue from anything, but blends always with everything, and becomes predominantly independent; therefore, alone in all the Universe, it can be called and lauded as the 'Ideal Unique Subjective Phenomenon.'

"Thus, my boy, uniquely Time alone, or, as it is sometimes called, the 'Heropass,' has no source from which its arising should depend, but like Divine Love alone flows always, as I have already told you, independently by itself, and blends proportionately with all the phenomena present in the given place and in the given arisings of Our Great Universe.

"Again I tell you, you will be able clearly to understand all that I have just told you only when I shall, as I have already promised you, specially explain to you sometime later all about the fundamental laws of World-creation and World-existence.

"Meanwhile only remember this also, that since Time has no source of its arising and cannot like all other cosmic phenomena in every cosmic sphere establish its exact 'presence,' the already mentioned objective Science has therefore for its investigations a standard unit, similar to that used for an exact definition of the density and quality—in the sense of the vivifyingness of their vibrations—of all cosmic substances in general, present in each and every place and in every sphere of our Great Universe.

"And for the definition of Time this standard unit has from long ago been reckoned as the moment of what is called the sacred 'Egokoolnatsnarnian-sensation,' which 'Egokoolnatsnarnian-sensation' always appears in the Most Holy Sun Absolute whenever the vision of our ENDLESS UNI-BEING is directed into space and touches their 'presence' immediately.

"Such a standard unit is established in Objective Science as a means to exact definition and to the comparison both of the difference between the gradations of the processes of the subjective sensations of separate conscious Individuums, and also of what are called 'differing tempos' among various objective cosmic phenomena which are manifested in various spheres of our Great Universe and which actualize all cosmic arisings both large and small.

"The chief particularity of the process of the flow of Time in the 'presence' of cosmic arisings of various scales consists in this, that all of them perceive it in the same way and in the same sequence.

"In order that you may meanwhile have, if only an approximate conspectus of what I have just said, let us take as an example the process of the flow of Time proceeding in any drop of water contained in that decanter standing there on the table.

"Every drop of water in that decanter represents in itself also a whole independent World, namely a World of 'Microcosmoses.'

"In that little world also, exactly as in other cosmoses, there arise and exist relatively independent infinitesimal 'individuums' or 'beings.'

"For the beings of that infinitesimal World also, Time flows in the same sequence in which the flow of Time is sensed by all individuums in all other cosmoses; these infinitesimal beings also, like the beings of cosmoses of other 'scales' have their experiences of a definite duration for all their perceptions and manifestations; and also, like them, sense the flow of Time by the comparing of the duration of the phenomena around them.

"Exactly like the beings of other cosmoses, they are born grow up and unite and separate for what are called 'sex results'; they also fall sick and suffer, and finally, like everything existing in which Objective Reason has not been conceived, they are, as such, destroyed forever.

"For the whole process of the existence of these infinitesimal beings of this smallest World also, Time of definite proportionate duration is also required, and this duration just as in other Worlds also flows from all the surrounding phenomena which are manifested in the given 'cosmic scale.'

"For them also, Time of definite length is required for the processes of their arising and formation as well as for various events in the process of their existence down to their complete final destruction.

"In the whole course of the process of existence of the beings of this drop of water also, corresponding sequential definite, as they are called, 'stages' of the flow of Time are also required.

"A definite time is required for their joys and their sorrows and, in short, for every other kind of indispensable being-experiencings, down to what are called 'runs-of-bad-luck,' and even to the 'periods of thirst for self perfection.'

"I repeat, among them, too, the process of the flow of Time has its harmonious succession also, and this succession flows from the totality of all the phenomena surrounding them.

"By all the aforementioned cosmic individuums and by the already definitely formed, as they are called, 'instinctivized' units, the duration of the process of the flow of Time is generally perceived and sensed in the same way, but with only this difference, namely, that which in final sum depends on the difference in the 'presence' and states at the given moment of these said cosmic arisings.

"It must be noticed, however, my boy, that though for separate individuums existing in any independent cosmic unit, their definition of the flow of time is not objective in the general sense, yet nevertheless for them themselves it acquires a 'sense of objectivity' because it is perceived by them according to the completeness of their own 'presence.'

"The same drop of water which we have taken as an example can serve for a clearer understanding of this thought of mine.

"Although, in the sense of general Universal Objectivity, the Whole period of the process of the flow of Time in that same drop of water, is for the whole of it subjective, yet for the beings existing in it—that is, in the drop of water itself—the said given flow of time is already perceived by them as objective.

"For the clarification of this, the beings called 'Hypochondriacs' can serve who exist among those three-brained beings of the planet Earth who please you.

"To these terrestrial 'hypochondriacs' it seems very often that time flows infinitely slowly and long, and, as they express themselves, 'it drags marvelously tediously.'

"So exactly in the same way, it might also sometimes seem to some of the infinitesimal beings existing in that drop of water—assuming of course, that there happens to be such hypochondriacs among them—that Time drags very slowly and 'marvelously tediously.'

"But actually from the point of view of the sensation of the duration of Time by your favorites of the planet Earth, the whole length of the existence of the beings, the Microcosmoses, is only a few of their 'minutes' and sometimes even only a few of their 'seconds.'

"Now in order that you may still better understand Time and its peculiarities, we may as well compare your age with the corresponding age of a being existing on that planet Earth.

"For this comparing of ours also, we must take the same standard unit of Time, which as I have already told you, Objective Science employs for such calculations.

"Bear in mind first of all that according to what also you will learn when I shall specially explain to you later the fundamental laws of World-creation and World-existence, it is also established by the same Objective Science that in general all normal three-brained beings, and amongst them certainly even the beings arising on our planet 'Karatas,' sense the sacred 'Egokoolnatsnarnian' action for the definition of Time forty-nine times more slowly than the same sacred action is sensed by the sacred Individuums dwelling on the Most Holy Sun Absolute.

"Consequently the process of the flow of Time for the three-brained beings of our 'Karatas' flows forty-nine times more quickly than on the Sun Absolute, and in this manner it should flow for the beings breeding on the planet Earth also.

"But, nevertheless, it is also further calculated that in the period of Time during which the Sun 'Samos' actualizes its most near approach to the Sun 'Selos'—which period of the flow of Time is considered a 'year' for the planet 'Karatas'—then during this period of the flow of Time the planet Earth actualizes in relation to its Sun 'Ors' three hundred and eighty-nine of its 'Krentonalnian' revolutions.

"As a deduction from this then, our 'year,' according to the conventionally objective Time-calculation, is three hundred and eighty-nine times longer than the period of time which your favorites consider and call their 'year.'

"It may not be without interest for you to know, that all these calculations were explained to me partly by the Great Arch-Engineer of the Universe, His Measurability Archangel Algamatant.

"May he be perfected unto the Sacred Anklad! . . .

"He explained this to me just when he had come to the planet Mars as one of the sacred members of the third Most Great Commission, on account of the first great misfortune to the planet Earth; and the captain of the trans-space ship 'Omnipresent,' with whom I had several friendly talks during that journey also explained it in part to me during my journey home.

"Now concerning this it must be noticed that you, as a three-brained being who arose on the planet 'Karatas,' are at the present time still only a boy of twelve years, and in the sense of Being and Reason, you are exactly the same boy of twelve, not yet formed and not yet cognizant of himself, which being-age all the three-brained beings arising on the planet Earth also experience during the process of their growing to the being of a responsible being.

"All the 'features' of the whole of your psyche—what are called your 'character,' 'temperament,' 'inclinations' and, in short, all the particularities of your psyche which are manifested exteriorly are exactly the same as those of a still immature and pliant three-brained being there of the age of twelve years.

"And thus on the basis of all that has been said, it happens that, although according to our Time-calculation you are still only the same boy of twelve who is also there on the planet Earth and who is not yet formed and not yet cognizant of himself, yet according to their subjective understanding and their being-sensations of the flow of Time, you have already existed, according to their Time-calculation, not twelve years but all of four thousand six hundred and sixty-eight years.

"In all the aforesaid you will have in this connection material for the clarification of certain of those factors which later became the causes that the average normal duration of their existence began gradually to be shortened and has now already become in the objective sense almost 'nothing.'

"Strictly speaking, for this gradual contraction of the average length of the existence of the three-brained beings of that ill-starred planet, not one cause but many and very varied causes have finally brought the whole of the duration of their existence to 'nothing.'

"And among these many and varied causes the first and the chief one is of course that Nature herself had to adapt herself correspondingly to change gradually their 'presence' to that which they now have.

"And concerning all the other various causes, Justice demands that I should first of all emphasize that on that ill-starred planet these many other causes might never have arisen had that first cause not occurred there from which, at least in my opinion, all the rest of the causes chiefly arose, though of course very gradually.

"Concerning all this you will understand in the course of further talks of mine about these three-brained beings, and meanwhile I will tell you only of the first and chief cause, namely, why and how great Nature herself was compelled to take stock of their 'presence' and to form it into such a new 'presence.'

"You must first be told that there exist in the Universe generally two kinds or two 'principles' of the duration of being-existence.

"The first kind or first 'principle' of 'being-existence' which is called 'Fulasnitamnian' is proper to the existence of all three-brained beings arising on any planet of our great Universe, and the fundamental aim and sense of the existence of these beings is that there must proceed through them the transmutation of cosmic substances necessary for what is called the 'common-cosmic-Trogoautoegocratic-process.'

"And it is according to the second principle of being-existence that all one-brained and two-brained beings in general exist wherever they may arise . . .

"And the sense and aim of the existence of these beings also, consists in this, that there are transmuted through them the cosmic substances required not for purposes of a common cosmic character, but only for that solar system, or even only for that planet alone, in which and upon which these one-brained and two-brained beings arise.

"In any case for the further elucidation of the strangeness of the psyche of those three-brained beings who please you, you must know this also, that in the beginning, after the organ 'Kundabuffer' with all its properties had been removed from their 'presence,' the duration of their existence was according to the 'Fulasnitamnian' principle, that is to say, they also were obliged to exist until there was coated in them and completely perfected by Reason what is called the body 'Kesdjan,' or, as they themselves later began to name this being-part of theirs—of which, by the way, contemporary beings know only by hearsay—the 'Astral body.'

"And so, my boy, when afterwards for reasons of which you will learn in the course of my further tales, they began to exist already too abnormally—that is to say, entirely unbecomingly to three-brained beings—and having on the one hand in consequence of this ceased to emanate the vibrations needed by Nature for the maintenance of the separated fragments of their planet, and on the other hand, having begun on account of the chief peculiarity of their strange psyche to destroy beings of other forms of their planet, thereby diminishing gradually the number of sources necessary for the same purpose, it was just then that Nature herself was compelled gradually to actualize the 'presence' of these three-brained beings according to the second principle, namely, the principle 'Itoklanoz,' that is, in the same way in which Nature actualizes one-brained and two-brained beings in order that the equilibrium, in quality and quantity of necessary vibrations, should be attained.

"And concerning the significance of the principle 'Itoklanoz' I shall also specially explain it to you sometime.

"And meanwhile remember that although the fundamental motives for the diminution of the duration of the existence of the three-brained beings of this planet were from causes not depending on them, yet nevertheless, subsequently the main grounds for all the sad results were and particularly now continue to be the abnormal conditions of external ordinary being-existence established by them themselves, owing to which, down to the present time, the duration of their existence continues to become shorter and shorter, and is already contracted to such a degree that, at the present time, the difference between the duration of the process of the existence of the three-brained beings of other planets in the whole of the Universe and the duration of the process of the existence of the three-brained beings of the planet Earth has become similar to the difference between the real duration of their existence and the duration of the existence of the infinitesimal beings in that drop of water we took as an example.

"You understand now, my boy, that even the Most Great Heropass or Time has also been compelled to actualize such plain absurdities in the 'presence' of these unfortunate three-brained beings arising and existing on this ill-starred planet Earth.

"And owing to all I have just explained to you, you can put yourself in the position and understand the although merciless yet always and in everything, just Heropass."

Having said these last words Beelzebub became silent; and when he again spoke to his grandson he said with a heavy sigh:

"Eh . . . my dear boy!

"Afterwards when I shall have told you more about the three-brained beings of that ill-starred planet Earth you will yourself understand and have your own opinion about everything.

"You yourself will very well understand that although the fundamental causes of the whole chaos that now reigns on that ill-starred planet Earth were certain 'oversights' coming from Above on the part of various sacred Individuums, yet nevertheless that the chief causes for the developing of further ills are only those abnormal conditions of ordinary being-existence which they themselves gradually established and which they continue to establish down to the present time.

"In any case, my dear boy, when you learn more about

these favorites of yours, not only, I repeat, will you clearly see that the duration of the existence of these unfortunates has gradually become so pitiably small in comparison with that normal duration of existence which has already long ago been established as a Law for the three-centered beings of every kind of the whole of our Universe; but you will also understand that in these unfortunates for the same reasons, there began gradually to disappear and at the present time are quite absent in them, any normal being-sensations whatever concerning any cosmic phenomenon.

"Although the beings of that ill-starred planet had their rising according to conventionally objective Time-reckoning already many tens of years ago, not only have they not as yet any being-sensation of cosmic phenomena such as is proper to all three-centered beings of the whole of our Universe, but in the reasonings of these unfortunates there is not even an approximate notion of the genuine causes of these phenomena.

"They have not an approximately correct conception even of those cosmic phenomena that occur on their own planet round about them."

CHAPTER XVII

The Arch-Absurd: In The Opinion Of Beelzebub, Our Sun, It Appears, Neither Lights Nor Heats

IN ORDER, my dear Hassein, that you may meanwhile have a fair representation also of just how far that function called 'instinctive-feeling-of-reality,' which is proper to every three-brained being of the whole of our Great Universe, is already completely lacking in the 'presence' of the three-centered beings breeding on the planet 'Earth' and especially in those of the most recent periods, it will be enough to begin with, I think, if I explain to you only about this—how they understand and explain to themselves the causes why there periodically proceed on their planet those cosmic phenomena which they call 'daylight,' 'darkness,' 'heat,' 'cold,' and so on.

"All, without exception, of the three-brained beings of that planet who have attained the age of a responsible being, and even those many and various 'wiseacrings' existing there which they call 'sciences,' are categorically certain that all the said phenomena arrive on their planet, so to say, absolutely-ready-made, directly from their own Sun . . . and . . . no more hokey-pokey about it!

"What is most peculiar, in this case, is that absolutely no doubt whatever concerning this persuasion of theirs has ever as yet crept into a single one of them.

"Not only has no single one of them, having a Reason which, though strange has nevertheless some resemblance to sane logic, ever yet doubted the causes of the said phenomena, but not a single one of them has manifested, concerning these cosmic phenomena, even that strange special property of their common psyche which also has become proper to the three-brained beings of that planet alone, and which is called 'to fantasy.'"

Having said these last words, Beelzebub, after a little while, with a bitter smile, continued to talk as follows:

"You, for instance, have the normal 'presence' of a three-brained being; and within your 'presence' an intentionally externally 'grown' Oskiano, or, as they say there on the 'Earth,' 'education,' which is founded on a morality based solely on the commandments and indications of the UNI-BEING HIMSELF and the Most Holy Individuums nearest Him. And yet, if you should chance to be there among them, you would be unable to prevent the process in yourself of the 'being-Nerhitrogool,' that is, the process, which, again there on the 'Earth' is called 'choking-with-mirth'; in other words, you could not restrain yourself from such laughter, if only it were to come about that they should suddenly clearly sense, in some way or another, and understand without any doubt whatever, that to their planet from their Sun itself, not only does nothing of any such thing as 'light,' 'darkness,' 'heat,' and so on, come, but that their supposed source of heat and light is itself almost always freezing with cold like the hairless dog of our highly esteemed Mullah Nassr Eddin.

"In reality, this surface of their 'Source of Heat,' like that of all the ordinary suns of our great Universe in general, is perhaps more covered with ice than the surface of what they call their North Pole.

"Surely this 'hearth of heat' itself would like to borrow, if only a little heat, from some other source of cosmic substances, rather than send a part of its own heat to any planet whatever, and especially to that planet which, although it belongs to its system, yet in consequence of the splitting off from it of a whole side became a 'lopsided-monstrosity' and is now already the occasion of 'offensive shame' for that system 'Ors.'

"But you yourself, my boy, do you know in general how and why in the atmosphere of certain planets during Trogoautoegocratic processes, there proceed those 'Kshtatsavacht,' 'Kldatzacht,' 'Tainolair,' 'Paischakir,' and other such phenomena, which, your favorites call 'daylight,' 'darkness,' 'cold,' 'heat' and so on?" Beelzebub asked Hassein.

"If you don't clearly understand, I shall explain this also to you a little.

"Although I have promised to explain to you later in every detail all the fundamental laws of World-creation and World-maintenance, yet the necessity has here arisen, to touch upon, if only briefly, the questions concerning these cosmic laws, without waiting for that special talk I promised.

"And this is necessary in order that you may be able better to take in all that we are now talking about, and also in order that what I have already told you may be transubstantiated in you in the right way.

"It is necessary to say, first of all, that everything in the Universe, both the intentionally created and the later automatically arisen, exists and is maintained exclusively on the basis of what is called the common-cosmic-Trogoautoegocratic-process.

"This Most Great common-cosmic-Trogoautoegocratic-process was actualized by our ENDLESS UNI-BEING when there already existed Our Most Great and Most Holy Sun Absolute, on which our ALL-GRACIOUS ENDLESS CREATOR had and still has the fundamental place of His existence.

"This system, which maintains everything arisen and existing, was actualized by our ENDLESS CREATOR in order that there might proceed in the Universe what is called the 'exchange of substances' or the 'Reciprocal-feeding' of everything that exists, and thereby that the merciless 'Heropass' might not exert its maleficent influence upon the Sun Absolute.

"This same Most Great 'common-cosmic-Trogoautoegocratic-process' is actualized always and in everything on the basis of the two fundamental cosmic laws, the first of which is called the fundamental first-order sacred Heptaparaparshinokh, and the second the fundamental first-order sacred Triamazikamno.

"Owing to these two fundamental sacred cosmic laws, there first arise from the substance called 'Etherokrilno,' under certain conditions, what are called crystallizations; and from these crystallizations, but later, and also under certain conditions, there are formed various large and small more or less independent cosmic definite formations.

"It is just within and upon these cosmic 'definite formations' that the processes of what are called the involution and evolution of both the already formed concentrations and of the said crystallizations take place—of course also according to the two said fundamental sacred laws; and all the results obtained from these processes both in atmospheres and also, further, by means of these atmospheres themselves, blend and go for the actualizing of the said 'exchange of matters' for the purposes of the Most Great common-cosmic Trogoautoegocrat.

"Etherokrilno is that prime-source substance with which the whole Universe is filled and which is the basis for the arising and maintenance of everything that exists.

"Not only is this Etherokrilno the foundation of the arising of, without exception, all cosmic concentrations, both large and small; but also all cosmic phenomena in general proceed, during any transformation both within the same fundamental cosmic substance and from the process of the involution and evolution of various crystallizations—or, as your favorites say, from those active elements—which have obtained and still continue to obtain their prime arising from this same fundamental prime-source cosmic substance.

"Bear in mind here, that it is just because of this that the mentioned Objective Science says that 'Everything in the Universe without exception is material.'

"You must also know, further, that only one cosmic crystallization, existing under the name 'Omnipresent Okidanokh,' although it also is crystallized from Etherokrilno, owes its prime arising to the three Holy sources of the sacred Theomertmalogos, that is, to the emanation of the Most Holy Sun Absolute.

"Everywhere in the Universe this 'Omnipresent Okidanokh' or omnipresent active element, takes part in the formation of all both great and small arisings, and is in general the fundamental cause of most of the cosmic phenomena and, in particular, of the phenomena proceeding in the atmospheres.

"In order that you may be able to understand, at least approximately, concerning this 'Omnipresent Okidanokh' also, I must tell you first of all that the second fundamental cosmic law—the sacred Triamazikamno—consists of three independent forces, that is to say, this sacred law manifests in everything without exception and everywhere in the Universe, in three separate independent aspects.

"And these its three aspects exist in the Universe under the following denominations:

The first, under the denomination, the Holy Affirming.
The second, the Holy Denying.
The third, the Holy Reconciling.

"And this is also why, concerning this sacred law and its three independent forces, the said Objective Science has the following among its other formulations specially concerning this sacred law:

"'A law which always flows into a consequence and thereby becomes the cause of further consequences, and always functions by three independent and absolutely opposite characteristic manifestations concealed within it in invisible and nonsensible properties.'

"Our sacred Theomertmalogos also, that is, the prime emanation of our Most Holy Sun Absolute, acquires just this same legitimacy at its prime arising; and during its farther actualizations gives results in accordance with it.

"And so, my boy, the 'Omnipresent Okidanokh' receives its prime arising already in space, outside of the Most Holy Sun Absolute itself, from the blending into one, of these three independent forces, and during its further involutions, it is correspondingly changed in respect of what is called the 'Vivifyingness of Vibrations' just according to its passage through what are called the 'Stopinders' or 'gravitational centers' of the fundamental 'common-cosmic sacred Heptaparaparshinokh.'

"I repeat, among the number of other already definite cosmic crystallizations, the 'Omnipresent Okidanokh' unfailingly always participates in both large and small cosmic formations, wherever and under whatever external surrounding conditions they may arise in the Universe.

"This 'common cosmic unique crystallization' or 'active element' has several peculiarities proper to this element alone, and it is chiefly owing to these, its proper peculiarities, that the majority of cosmic phenomena proceed, including, among other things, the said phenomena that take place in the atmospheres of certain planets.

"Of these proper peculiarities of the 'Omnipresent Active Element' there are several, but it is enough for the theme of our talk if we become acquainted with just two of them.

"The first peculiarity is this, that when a new cosmic unit is being concentrated, then the 'Omnipresent Active Element' does not blend in such a new arising, as a whole, nor is it transformed as a whole in one definite corresponding place—as happens with every other cosmic crystallization in all the said cosmic forms—but immediately on entering any cosmic unit as a whole, there at once occurs in it what is called 'Djartklom,' that is, it scatters into the three fundamental sources from which it received its prime arising, and only then do these its sources, each separately, give the beginning for an independent concentration of three separate corresponding formations within the given cosmic unit. And in this way, the 'Omnipresent Active Element' actualizes, at the outset, in every such new arising, the sources for the possible manifestation of its own also sacred law of Triamazikamno.

"It must not fail to be noticed also, that in every cosmic formation the said separated sources, both for the perception and further utilization of this peculiar property of the 'Omnipresent Active Element' for the purpose of the corresponding actualizing, exist and continue to be able to function as long as the given cosmic unit exists.

"And only after the said cosmic unit has been completely destroyed do these holy sources of the sacred Triamazikamno, localized in the 'Omnipresent Active Element Okidanokh,' reblend and are again transformed into 'Okidanokh,' but having now another quality of the 'Vivifyingness of Vibrations.'

"Concerning the second peculiarity of the 'Omnipresent Okidanokh,' equally proper to it alone, and which it is also necessary for us to elucidate just now for the given theme of our talk you will be able to understand about that, only if you know something concerning one fundamental cosmic second-order law existing in the Universe under the denomination of the 'Sacred Aieioiuoa.'

"And this cosmic law consists in this, that there proceeds within every arising large and small, when in immediate touch with the emanations either of the Sun Absolute itself or of any other Sun, what is called 'Remorse'; that is, such a process, when every part that has arisen from the results of any one Holy Source of the sacred Triamazikamno, revolts, as it were, and criticizes the former unbecoming perceptions and contemporary manifestations of another part of its whole—a part obtained from the results of another Holy Source of the same fundamental sacred Cosmic law Triamazikamno.

"And this sacred process 'Aieioiuoa' or 'Remorse' always proceeds within the 'Omnipresent Active Element Okidanokh' also.

"The peculiarity of this latter during this sacred process consists in this, that while the direct action either of the sacred Theomertmalogos or the emanation of any other ordinary Sun is round about the whole of its 'presence,' this 'active element' scatters into its three prime parts which then exist almost independently, and when the said immediate action ceases these parts blend again and then again exist as a whole.

"Here it will do no harm, I think, to tell you, by the way, an interesting fact concerning the strangeness of the psyche of the ordinary three-brained beings of that planet that pleases you, which occurred in the history of their existence and concerns what they call the 'scientific speculations.'

"And that is, that during the period of my many-centuried observation and study of their psyche I had occasion to ascertain several times that although science appeared among them almost from the very beginning of their arising—and, it may here be said, periodically, like everything else there, rose to a more or less high degree of perfection—yet, though during these periods and others, many millions of three-brained beings called there 'scientists' must have arisen and been again destroyed, yet—with the single exception of a certain Chinaman named Choon-Kil-Tez, about whom I shall tell you later in detail—not once has the thought entered the head of a single 'scientist' there that between these two cosmic phenomena which they call 'emanation' and 'radiation' there is any difference whatever.

"Not a single one of those 'sorry scientists' has ever thought that the difference between these two cosmic processes is just about the same as that which the highly esteemed Mullah Nassr Eddin once expressed in the following words:

"'They are as much alike as the beard of the famous English Shakespeare and French Armagnac, no less famous.'

"For the further clarification of the phenomena taking

place in the atmospheres, and concerning the 'Omnipresent Active Element' in general, you must know and remember this also, that during the periods when, owing to the sacred process 'Aieioiuoa,' there proceeds 'Djartklom' in the 'Okidanokh,' then there is temporarily released from it the proportion of the pure—that is, absolutely unblended—Etherokrilno which unfailingly enters into all cosmic forms and there serves, as it were, for connecting all the active elements; and afterwards when its three fundamental parts reunite, then the said proportion of Etherokrilno is reestablished.

"It is necessary to touch also, though again only briefly, on another question, namely, what effect the Omnipresent Active Element Okidanokh has upon the common 'presence' of beings of every kind, and what are the cosmic results actualized owing to it.

"It is chiefly necessary to touch upon this question because you will then have still another very striking and illuminating fact for the better understanding of the difference between the various brain-systems of beings, namely, the systems called one-brained, two-brained, and three-brained.

"Know first that, in general, every such cosmic formation called 'brain' receives its formation from those crystallizations for whose arising according to the sacred Triamazikamno the Affirming source is one or other corresponding holy force of the fundamental sacred Triamazikamno localized in the 'Omnipresent Okidanokh.' And the further actualizings of the same holy forces proceed in the 'presence' of the beings just through these three localizations.

"Sometime in the future I will specially explain to you about the process itself of the arising of these corresponding being-brains in the 'presence' of a being; but meanwhile let us talk, though not in detail, about this, namely, what results the 'Omnipresent Okidanokh' actualizes by means of these being-brains.

"The Omnipresent Active Element Okidanokh enters into the 'presence' of beings through all the three kinds of being-food.

"And this proceeds because, as I have already told you, this same 'Okidanokh' obligatorily participates in the formation of products of every kind which serve the purpose of all three being-feedings and is always contained in the actuality of these products.

"And so, my boy, the chief peculiarity of the 'Omnipresent Okidanokh consists, in the given case, in this, that the process of Djartklom proceeds in it, in the 'presence' itself of every being also, but not from being in touch with the emanations of large cosmic concentrations, but as factors, there are either the results of the conscious processes of Partkdolgduty on the part of the beings themselves—about which processes I shall also explain to you in detail later—or that process of Great Nature herself which exists in the Universe under the name 'Kerkoolnonarnian actualization,' by which is meant the 'Obtaining-the-Necessary-Sum-Total-of-Vibrations-by-Adaptation.'

"This process proceeds in beings absolutely without the participation of their consciousness.

"In both cases when Okidanokh enters into the 'presence' of a being, and the process of Djartklom proceeds in it, then each of its fundamental parts blends with those perceptions contained in the being at that moment which correspond with it according to what is called 'Kindred-Vibrations,' and then is further concentrated upon the corresponding localization, that is, upon the corresponding brain.

"And just such blendings are called 'Being-Impulsakri.'

"It is necessary to notice further that these localizations or brains in beings serve not only as apparatuses for the transformation of corresponding cosmic substances for the purposes of the Most Great Common Cosmic Trogoautoegocrat, but also as the means for beings whereby their conscious self-perfecting is possible.

"Just this latter aim depends upon the quality of the 'presence' of the Being-Impulsakri concentrated, or, as it is otherwise said, deposited, upon the said corresponding being-brains.

"Concerning the qualities of Being-Impulsakri, there is among the direct commandments of OUR ENDLESS ALL EMBRACING even a special commandment, which is very strictly carried out by all the three-brained beings of our Great Universe, and which is expressed in the following words:

"'Always guard against such perceptions as may impair the purity of your brains.'

"The possibility of a personal self-perfecting by the three-brained beings exists because three such centers of three such being-brains are localized in their common 'presence,' upon which afterwards, when the process of Djartklom proceeds in the Omnipresent Okidanokh the three holy sources of the sacred Triamazikamno are deposited and acquire the possibility for their further, this time, independent actualizings.

"Just in this is the point, that the beings having this three-brained system can, by the conscious and intentional fulfilling of Being-Partkdolgduty, utilize from this process of Djartklom in the Omnipresent Okidanokh, its three holy sources for their own 'presence,' and lead this their 'presence' to what is called the 'Sekronoolanzaknian state'; that is to say, they can become such Individuums as have their own sacred law of Triamazikamno and thereby the possibility of consciously perceiving and coating in their common 'presence' all that 'Holy' which, incidentally, also aids the actualizing of the functioning of Objective or Divine Reason in these cosmic units.

"But the great terror of it, my boy, lies just in this, that although in those three-brained beings who have interested you, breeding on the planet 'Earth,' there arise and are present in them, up to the time of their complete destruction, these three independent localizations or three being-brains, through which are transformed and go for the further corresponding actualizations separately all the three holy sources of the sacred Triamazikamno, which they might also utilize for their own self-perfecting—yet, chiefly on account of the irregular conditions of ordinary being-existence established by them themselves, these possibilities beat their wings in vain.

"It is interesting to note that the said being-brains are found in the same parts of the planetary body of these three-brained beings arising on the planet 'Earth' as in us, namely:

"The brain assigned by Great Nature for the concentration and further actualizing of the first holy force of the sacred Triamazikamno, denominated the Holy Affirming, is localized and found in their head.

"The second brain, which transforms and crystallizes the second holy force of the sacred Triamazikamno, namely, the Holy Denying, is placed in their common 'presences,' also as in us, along the whole of their back in what is called the 'spinal column.'

"But as regards the place of concentration and source for the future manifestation of the third holy force of the sacred Triamazikamno, namely, the Holy Reconciling, the exterior form of this being-brain in the three-brained beings there, bears no resemblance whatever to ours.

"It must be remarked that in the earliest three-brained beings there, this said being-brain was localized in the same part of their planetary body as in us, and had an exterior form exactly similar to our own; but for many reasons which you will be able to work out for yourself during the course of my further talks, Great Nature was compelled little by little to regenerate it and to give it the form which this brain now has in the contemporary beings.

"This being-brain in the contemporary three-brained beings there is not localized in a common mass, as it properly is in the 'presence' of all the other three-brained beings of our Great Universe, but in them it is localized in parts, according to what is called 'Specific Functioning,' and each such part is localized in a different place of their whole planetary body.

"But although, in its exterior form, this being-center of theirs has now such variously placed concentrations, nevertheless all its separate functionings have corresponding connections among themselves, so that the sum-total of these scattered parts can function exactly as in general it is proper for it to function.

"They themselves call these separate localizations in their common 'presence' 'nerve-nodes.'

"It is interesting to notice that most of the separated parts of this being-brain are localized in them just in that place of their planetary body where a normal being-brain should be, namely, in the region of their breast, and the mass of these 'nerve-nodes' contained in their breast they call the 'Solar Plexus.'

"And so, my boy; in the 'presence' of each of these favorites of yours also, there proceeds the process of Djartklom in the Omnipresent Okidanokh; in them also, all its three holy sources are blended independently with other cosmic crystallizations, and go for the corresponding actualizations, but because, owing chiefly to the already mentioned abnormal conditions of being-existence gradually established by them themselves, they have completely ceased to fulfill the Being-Partkdolgduty—then, as a consequence of this, of all those three holy sources of everything existing, with the exception of the denying force alone, no other is transubstantiated for their own 'presence.'

"The crystallizations arising in their 'presence' from the first and from the third holy sources go almost entirely for the service only of the common cosmic Trogoautoegocratic process, while for the coating of their own 'presence' there only serve the crystallizations of the second part of the Omnipresent Okidanokh, namely, of the Holy Denying; and hence it is that the majority of them remain with a 'presence' consisting of the planetary body alone, and thus they are for themselves destroyed forever.

"As regards all the peculiarities proper to the omnipresent everywhere-penetrating Active Element Okidanokh alone, and also as regards the further results which these peculiarities actualize, you will have a complete representation of them only after I have sometime explained to you, as I have already promised I would in more or less detail, about the fundamental laws of World-creation and World-maintenance.

"But meanwhile I will tell you about some elucidating experiments which were concerned with this Omnipresent cosmic crystallization and at which I was personally present.

"But I must tell you that I was an eyewitness of these said elucidating experiments, not on that planet 'Earth' which pleases you, nor did your favorites make them, but on the planet 'Saturn' where just that three-brained being performed them who during almost the whole period of my exile within that Solar System was my real friend, and about whom I recently promised to tell you a little more in detail."

CHAPTER XVIII

The Arch-preposterous

BEELZEBUB continued further thus:

"The following served as the cause of my first meeting with that three-centered being who subsequently became my essence-friend, and through whom I saw the said experiments with the Omnipresent Okidanokh.

"That you may have a better understanding concerning the events of this tale of mine, you must first know this also—that at the beginning of my exile in that solar system, by certain correspondent essence-friends of mine, who had not taken part in those events from which had also issued the causes of my exile in that solar system, that sacred process concerning my personality had also been enacted which exists in the Universe under the name of the 'Sacred Vznooshlitzval,' that is to say there was implanted in the 'presence' of those three-brained beings concerning my personality by means of other sacred cosmic processes called 'Askalnooazar,' that certain 'isness' which objective science defines by the conception 'Other-Self-Trust.'

"So, just after my arrival in that solar system Ors, when I began visiting its various planets and first descended upon the surface of the planet Saturn, it turned out in connection with the aforesaid, that one of the beings who had undergone the sacred action of 'Vznooshlitzval' regarding my person, was also what is called there the Harahrahroohry himself of all the three-centered beings arising and existing on the planet Saturn.

"On the planet Saturn a being is called the Harahrahroohry who is the sole head over all the other beings on that planet.

"Similar head-beings exist also on all the other planets upon which three-brained beings breed; they are differently named on different planets; and upon your planet Earth such a head is called a 'king.'

"The only difference is that while everywhere else, even on all the other planets of the same system, there is one such king for the whole of the given planet, on your peculiar planet Earth there is one such king for every accidentally segregated group of these favorites of yours and sometimes even several.

"So...

"When I first descended on the surface of the planet Saturn and mingled with the three-centered beings there, it chanced that I had occasion the next day to meet the Harahrahroohry himself of the planet Saturn; and during what is called our 'Exchange-of-Subjective-Opinions' he invited me to make his own Harhoory, that is, his own palace, the fundamental place of my existence during the whole of my stay on their planet.

"And this I did.

"So, my boy, when we were once talking, simply according to the flow of what is called 'being-associative-mentation,' and happened to touch on the question, among other things, of the strange results realized in the manifestations of the particularities of the Omnipresent Okidanokh, it was just then that the venerable Harahrahroohry of the planet Saturn first mentioned that one of his learned-being subjects, by name Harharkh, had recently devised for the elucidation of many of the previously unexplained properties of that cosmic substance, an exceedingly interesting contrivance which is called a 'Rhaharahr,' the chief demonstrating part of which he called the Hrhaharhtzaha.

"And further, he offered to make if I wished, the necessary arrangements for showing me all these new inventions and for giving me every possible explanation of them.

"The result of it all was that the following day, escorted by one of that venerable Harahrahroohry's court, I went to the place of existence of that Gornahoor Harharkh and there it was that I first saw those novel elucidatory experiments with the Omnipresent Okidanokh.

"Gornahoor Harharkh, who afterwards, as I have already told you, became my essence-friend, was then considered one of the foremost scientists among the ordinary three-brained beings of the whole Universe, and his ascertainments of all kinds as well as the elucidatory apparatuses he invented, were everywhere spread, and other learned beings on the various planets were more and more using them.

"Here it will do no harm to remark that I also, thanks only to his learning, had later in my observatory on the planet Mars that Teskooano which, when it was finally established, enabled my 'sight' to perceive, or, as it is said, to 'approach the visibility' of remote cosmic concentrations, seven million two hundred and eighty-five times.

"Strictly speaking, it was owing to just this Teskooano that my observatory was afterwards considered one of the best artifacts of its kind in the whole Universe; and, most important of all, it was by means of this Teskooano that I myself thereafter could, even while staying at home that is, on the planet Mars—relatively easily see and observe the processes of existence occurring on the surfaces of those parts of the other planets of that solar system which in accordance with what is called the 'Common-system-harmonious-movement' could be perceived by 'being-sight' at the given moment.

"When Gornahoor Harharkh was informed who we were and why we had come, he approached us and forthwith very amiably began his explanations:

"Before repeating his explanations I think it not inadvisable to warn you once and for all that all my conversations with various three-centered beings arising and existing on various planets of that system, where I was obliged to exist for the 'sins of my youth,' as, for instance, in the present case, the conversation with this Gornahoor Harharkh which I am now just about to relate to you as we travel on the spaceship '*Kar-*

nak'—all proceeded in verbal dialects you have never heard, and in some cases whose consonance is utterly unassimilable by the normal being-functions assigned for this purpose.

"So, my boy, in view of all this I shall not repeat these talks word for word, but will give you only their 'sense' in our 'common speech,' continuing of course to employ those terms and 'specific names' of every kind, or rather those consonants produced by what are called the 'being-vocal-chords' which are used by your favorites of the planet Earth and which have now become for you, owing to the continued repetition during my former tales about them, habitual and easily perceived.

"Yes . . . it must be noticed here that the word Gornahoor is used by the three-brained beings of the planet Saturn in courtesy; they pronounce it before the name of one whom they are addressing.

"It is the same with your favorites on the planet Earth. They also have invented the addition to the name of every other person the word 'mister' or sometimes a whole meaningless phrase expressing such conception as our honorable Mullah Nassr Eddin has the following sentence for:

"And namely, he says:

"'All the same, there is more reality in it than in the wiseacrings of an expert in monkey-business.'

"So, my boy . . .

"When this subsequent essence friend of mine Gornahoor Harharkh, was informed of what was required of him, he invited us by a sign to approach one of the separate special appliances of the whole he had created and which was named by him, as it later turned out, the Hrhaharhtzaha.

"When we were nearer the said special and very strange construction, he said, pointing to it with a particular feather of his right wing:

"'Just this special appliance is the principal part of the whole of my new invention; and it is just in this that the results are brought out and shown of almost all the peculiarities of the Omnipresent World-substance "Okidanokh."'

"And then, pointing to all the other separate appliances also present in the 'khrh,' he added:

"'I succeeded in the obtaining extremely important elucidations concerning the omnipresent and everywhere penetrating Okidanokh because, thanks to all these separate special appliances of my invention, it became possible, first to obtain all the three fundamental parts of the Omnipresent Okidanokh from every kind of sur- and intraplanetary process, and artificially to blend them into a whole, and secondly, also artificially, afterwards to dissociate them for the purpose of elucidating the specific properties of each part separately in its manifestations.'

"Having said this, he again pointed to the Hrhaharhtzaha and added that by means of the elucidating apparatus, not only can any ordinary being clearly understand the details of the properties of the three absolutely independent, and in their manifestations, uniquely different parts of the whole 'Unique Active Element,' whose peculiarities are the chief cause of everything existing in the Universe, but furthermore, that any ordinary being can become categorically convinced that results of every kind, normally obtained from the processes occurring through this Omnipresent World-substance, can never be perceived by beings or sensed by them; but only those results of the said processes can be perceived by certain being functions, which proceed, for one reason or other, abnormally on account of causes coming from outside and due either to conscious sources or to accidental mechanical results.

"The part of Gornahoor Harharkh's new invention which he himself called the Hrhaharhtzaha and regarded as the most important, was in appearance very much like the 'tirzikiano' or, as your favorites would say, a 'huge electric-lamp.'

"The interior of this special structure was rather like a smallish room with a door that could be hermetically closed.

"The walls of this peculiar construction were made of a certain transparent stuff which looked like what on your planet is called 'glass.'

"As I learned later, the chief particularity of this said transparent stuff consisted in this, that although by means of the organ of sight, beings could perceive through it the visibility of cosmic concentrations of every kind, the stuff nevertheless admitted no passage through it, from within or from without, of any rays arising from any causes whatsoever.

"As I looked at this part or this said astonishing being-invention, I could clearly distinguish through its transparent walls that inside, in the middle, stood something like a table and two chairs. Above the table hung what is called an 'electric lamp,' and underneath were three somethings exactly alike and each resembling the 'Momonodooar.'

"Upon and around the table, stood or lay several different apparatuses and instruments previously unknown to me.

"It subsequently also proved that the said objects contained in this Hrhaharhtzaha as well as everything we had later to put on were made of special materials invented by the same Gornahoor Harharkh.

"However, as regards these materials also, I shall explain it a little more in detail at the proper point in the course of my further explanations concerning Gornahoor Harharkh.

"And meanwhile bear in mind that in the enormous Khrh or workshop of Gornahoor Harharkh there stood, besides the already mentioned Hrhaharhtzaha, several other large independent appliances, and, among them, two quite special called 'Lifechakan' which Gornahoor Harharkh himself called 'Krhrrhihirhi.'

"It is interesting to note that your favorites also have something like this 'Lifechakan' or 'Krhrrhihirhi,' and they name such an apparatus a 'Dynamo.'

"There also stood there separately another independent large contrivance which as it afterwards appeared, was a special 'Soloohnorahoona' of a special construction, or as your favorites would say, a 'pump-of-complex-construction-for-exhausting-atmosphere-to-the-point-of-an-absolute-vacuum.'

"While I was looking over all this with surprise, Gornahoor Harharkh himself approached the said pump of a special construction and with his left wing moved one of its parts, owing to which a certain mechanism began to work in the pump. He then approached us again, and pointing with the same special feather of his right wing to the largest Lifechakan or Krhrrhihirhi or, finally, dynamo, continued his explanations.

"And namely, he said that by means of this special appliance there are first 'drawn' separately from the atmosphere or from any intra- or sur-planetary formation, all the three independent parts of the Omnipresent active element Okidanokh present in them, and only afterwards, when in a certain way, these separate independent parts are artificially reblended in the Krhrrhihirhi into a single whole, Okidanokh, now in its usual state, flows and is collected there—in that 'container'—saying which, he again with the same special feather pointed to something very much like what is called a 'Generator.'

"'And then from there,' he said, 'Okidanokh flows here into another Krhrrhihirhi or Dynamo where it undergoes the process of "Djartklom," and each of its separate parts is concentrated—look!—in those other "containers"'—and this time he pointed to what resembled "accumulators"—'and only then do I take from the containers of the second order, by means of various artificial appliances, each active part of Okidanokh separately for my elucidatory experiments.'

"'I will first demonstrate to you,' he continued, 'one of the results occurring when, for one reason or other, one of the active parts of the Omnipresent Okidanokh is absent during the process of their striving to be reblended into a whole.

"'At the present moment this special construction contains a space which is indeed a vacuum; obtained it must be said, only owing firstly to the special construction of the suction pump and to the materials of special quality of which the instruments are made, which alone make experiments possible in an absolute vacuum, and secondly, to the property and rigidity of the staff of which the walls of this part of my new invention are made.'

"Having said this, he shifted still another lever and again continued:

"'Owing to this present shifting of one of the levers, that process has begun in this vacuum whereby in the separate parts of the Omnipresent Okidanokh there proceeds what is called the 'striving-to-be-reblended-into-a-whole.'

"'But because, intentionally by an 'able-Reason'—in the present case by myself—there is artificially excluded from the said process the participation of that part of Okidanokh existing under the name of 'Parijrahatnatioose,' the said process proceeds there just now between only two of its parts, namely, between those two independent parts which science names, the one Anodnatious, and the second Cathodnatious. And on account of all this, instead of the obligatory lawful results of the said process, that non-lawful result is then actualized which exists under the denomination of 'the-result-of-the-process-of-mutual-destruction-of-two-opposite-forces,' or as ordinary beings express it, 'the-cause-of-artificial-light.'

"'Proceeding there at the given moment, that is to say, in this vacuum, the "striving-to-be-reblended-into-a-whole" of two active parts of the Omnipresent Okidanokh has a force, as calculated by Objective Science, of what is called 3,040,000 "volts" and this force is indicated by the needle—look!—of that special appliance.'

"He pointed to a 'something' very much like the apparatus existing also on your planet and there called a 'voltmeter' and said as follows:

"'One of the advantages of this new invention of mine for the demonstration of the given phenomenon consists in this, that in spite of the unusual power of the process of the 'force-of-striving' now proceeding there, nevertheless the, as they are called, 'Salnichizinooarnian-momentum-vibrations' which, by the way, the majority of beings consider also to be 'rays,' and which ought to be obtained and to issue from this process . . . do not issue out of the place of their arising, that is, out of this artificial-construction in which just the particularities of the Omnipresent Okidanokh are elucidated.

"'And in order that beings outside this part of my invention may nevertheless also have the possibility of elucidating the force of the given process, I purposely made the composition of the stuff, of the wall in one place such that it has the property of permitting the passage through itself of the said "Salnichizinooarnian-momentum-vibrations" or "rays."'

"Having said this, he approached nearer to the Hrhaharhtzaha and pressed a certain button. The result was that the whole of the enormous Khrh or 'workshop' was suddenly so strongly lit up that our organs of sight temporarily ceased to function and only after a considerable time had passed could we with great difficulty raise our eyelids and contrive to look around us.

"When we had recovered and Gornahoor Harharkh had shifted still another lever, the result of which was that the whole surrounding space was restored to its former usual appearance, he first, with his customary angel-voice, again drew our attention to the 'voltmeter' the needle of which indicated the same figure constantly, and then continued thus:

"'You see that although the process of the clash of two opposite integral parts of the Omnipresent Okidanokh of the same power of 'force-of-striving' still continues, and the part of the surface of the construction which has the property of admitting the passage of the said 'rays' is still open, yet, in spite of all this, the phenomenon which ordinary beings define by the phrase, 'the causes of artificial light' is no longer there.

"'And this phenomenon is no longer there only because of this, that by the final shifting of a certain lever, I introduced into the process of the clash of two integral parts of Okidanokh a current of the third independent integral part of Okidanokh which began to blend proportionately with its other two parts, owing to which the result derived from this kind of blending of the three integral parts of the Omnipresent Okidanokh, unlike the process of the non-lawful blending of its two parts, cannot be perceived by any of the functions of beings.

"After all these explanations of his, Gornahoor Harharkh then invited me to venture to enter with him into that demonstrating part itself of the whole of his new invention, in order that I might become, there within, an eyewitness of many particular manifestations of the Omnipresent and everything-penetrating active element.

"Of course without thinking long about it, I decided at once and gave him my consent.

"And I decided at once chiefly because I expected to obtain thereby for my being a changeless and imperishable 'objective-essence-satisfaction.'

"When this future essence-friend of mine had my consent, he at once gave the necessary order to one of his assistants.

"It appeared that for the realization of this, various preparations had first to be made.

"Namely, his assistants first of all put on both myself and Gornahoor Harharkh some special very heavy costumes resembling those which your favorites call 'diving-suits,' but with many small heads of what are called 'bolts' projecting.

"And when these extremely peculiar costumes had been put on us, his assistants screwed up the heads of these bolts in a certain order.

"On the inner side of these said 'diving-suits,' and at the ends of the said bolts, there were, it appeared, special plates which pressed against parts of our planetary body in a certain way.

"It later also became quite clear to me why this was necessary, namely, that there might not occur to our planetary bodies what is called 'Taranooranura' or, as it might otherwise be said, in order that our planetary bodies should not fall to pieces as usually occurs to sur—and intraplanetary formations of every kind when they happen to find themselves in a vacuum.

"In addition to these special costumes, they placed on our heads a 'something' also resembling what are called 'diver's helmets,' but with very complicated, as they are called, 'connectors' projecting from them.

"One of these 'connectors' was called the 'Harhrinhrarh,' which meant 'supporter-of-the-pulsation,' and was a long thing like a rubber tube, one end of which, by means of complicated appliances on the helmet itself, was hermetically attached to the corresponding place of the helmet for the breathing organs, while the other end, after we had already entered that strange Hrhaharhtzaha, was screwed to an apparatus, there present, which was connected in its turn with the space, the presence of which corresponded to the second being-food.

"Between myself and Gornahoor Harharkh a special connector also led, through which we could easily communicate with each other while we were inside the Hrhaharhtzaha, from which the atmosphere was pumped out to make a vacuum.

"One end of this connector also, by means of appliances present on the helmets, was fitted in a certain way to what are called my organs of 'hearing' and 'speech,' and the other end to the same organs of Gornahoor Harharkh.

"Thus, by means of this connector between myself and my subsequent essence-friend, there was set up, as again your favorites would say, a peculiar 'telephone.'

"Without this artificial appliance we could not communicate with each other in any way, and chiefly because Gornahoor Harharkh was at that time still a being with a presence perfected only up to the state called the 'sacred Inkozarno'; and a being with such a presence not only cannot manifest himself in a vacuum, but he cannot even exist in it, even though the products of all the three being-foods should be artificially introduced into him in such a space.

"But the strangest and, as it is said, most 'cunningly ingenious' of all the 'connectors' present for various purposes on those strange diving-suits and helmets, were the connectors created by that great scientist Gornahoor Harharkh to enable the organ of sight of ordinary beings to perceive the visibility of surrounding objects of all kinds in 'absolutely empty space.'

"One end of this astonishing connector was fitted in a certain way, also by means of appliances present on the helmets, to our 'temples,' while to other end was joined to what is called the 'Amskomoutator,' which in its turn was joined in a certain way by means of what are called 'wires,' to all the objects within the Hrhaharhtzaha as well as with those outside, namely, with those objects whose visibility was needed during the experiments.

"It is very interesting to notice here, that to each end of that artificial appliance—a creation almost incredible for an ordinary three-reason-being-Reason—in their turn, two independent connectors also of wire were led, through which what are called special magnetic currents flowed from outside.

"As it was afterwards explained to me in detail, these connectors and the said special magnetic currents had, it seems, been created by that truly great scientist Gornahoor Harharkh in order that, in the case of learned three-centered beings not perfected even to the Sacred Inkozarno, thanks to one property of the 'magnetic current,' their own presence might be 'reflected' for their own essence; and thanks to another property of the 'magnetic current' there might be 'reflected' the presence of the mentioned objects; and so that thereby the perception of the reality of the said objects might be realized by their imperfect organs of being-sight also, in a vacuum containing none of those factors or those results of various cosmic concentrations which have received such vibrations, from the realization of which alone, the functioning of any being-organ whatsoever is possible.

"Having fitted upon us the said very heavy artificial appliances for enabling beings to exist in a sphere not proper to them, the assistants of this then still great all-universal scientist Gornahoor Harharkh, with the help once again of special appliances, carried us into the Hrhaharhtzaha itself; and having screwed up all the free ends of the artificial-connectors projecting from us to the corresponding apparatuses present in the Hrhaharhtzaha itself, went out, hermetically closing behind them the only way by which it was still possible, if at all, to have any communication with what is called the 'From-everything-one-representing-World.'

"When we were alone in the Hrhaharhtzaha itself, Gornahoor Harharkh after shifting one of the so-called 'contacts' present in that strange artifact said:

'The work of the 'pump' has already begun and soon it will have pumped out all without exception of the results present here of those cosmic processes whatever they may be, the totality of whose results is the basis and significance, as well as the process itself, of the maintenance of the existence of everything existing in the whole of this 'From-everything-one-representing-World.'

"And he added in a half sarcastic tone: 'Soon we shall be absolutely isolated from everything existing and functioning in the whole of the Universe; but, on the other hand, owing firstly to my new invention, and secondly, to the knowledge we have previously obtained for ourselves, we have not only now the possibility of returning to the said world, to become again a particle of all that exists, but also we shall soon be worthy to become non-participating eyewitnesses of certain of those World-laws, which for ordinary uninitiated three-centered beings are what they call the great inscrutable mysteries of Nature, but which in reality are only natural and very simple 'one-from-the-other-automatically-flowing-results.'

"While he was speaking, one could feel that this pump, that is, another and also very important part of the whole of this new invention, was perfectly realizing the work assigned to it by the being-Reason.

"To enable you to represent and understand better the excellencies of this part also of the whole of this new invention of Gornahoor Harharkh, I must not fail to tell you also about the following:

"Although I personally, as a three-brained being also, on account solely of certain quite particular reasons had had occasion many times before to be in atmosphereless spaces and had had to exist, sometimes for a long time, by means of the Sacred 'Kreemboolazoomara' alone; although from frequent repetition a habit had been acquired in my presence of moving from one sphere to another gradually and almost without feeling any inconvenience from the change of the presence of the sacred being-food, occurring with the charge of the presences of cosmic substances undergoing transformation and which are always around both large and small cosmic concentrations; although the causes themselves of my arising and the subsequent process of my being-existence were arranged in an entirely special way, in consequence of which the various being-functions contained within my general presence had perforce gradually become also special—nevertheless in spite of it all, the pumping out of the atmosphere by the said pump proceeded then with such force, that such sensations were impressed on the separate parts of the whole of my presence, that even today I can very clearly experience the process of the flow of my then state and relate it to you almost in detail.

"This extremely strange state began in me shortly after Gornahoor Harharkh had spoken in a half-sarcastic tone about our prospective situation.

"First, in all my three 'being-centers,' namely, in the three centers usually localized in the presence of every three-centered being, which exist under the names of the centers of Thinking, Feeling and Moving, in each of them separately and independently I had very definite impressions, in a very strange and unusual way, that there was taking place in separate parts of my whole planetary body an independent process of the sacred Rascooarno, and that the cosmic crystallizations composing their 'presence' were again dissolved into the 'void.'

"At first, what is called my 'initiative-of-ascertaining' proceeded in the usual way, that is, according to what is called the 'center-of-gravity-of-associative-experiencing'; but, later, as my said 'initiative-of-ascertaining' of everything proceeding in me gradually and almost imperceptibly became the function of my essence alone, my essence not only became the unique all-embracing initiator of everything proceeding in me, but everything, without exception, of that which newly proceeded, began to be perceived by and fixed in my essence alone.

"From the moment that my essence began to perceive impressions directly and to ascertain independently that from what was proceeding, there was being entirely destroyed, as it were, in my general presence, first, the parts of my planetary body, and then, little by little, the localizations of the 'second' and 'third' being-centers also—at the same time, the ascertainment was definitely made that the functioning of these latter centers passed gradually to my 'thinking-center' and became proper to it, with the consequence that the thinking-center, with the increasing intensity of its functioning, finally became the 'unique-powerful-perceiver' of everything realized outside of itself, and the autonomous initiator of the ascertaining of everything proceeding in the whole of my presence as well as outside of it.

"While this strange and still rationally incomprehensible being-experiencing was proceeding in me, Gornahoor Harharkh himself was occupied in shifting certain 'levers' and 'contacts' present in great numbers at the edges of the table at which we were placed.

"An incident which happened to Gornahoor Harharkh himself changed all this being-experiencing, and in my general presence the usual 'inner-being-experiencing' was resumed.

"The following is what happened:

"Gornahoor Harharkh with all those unusual heavy appliances which had been put on him as well, suddenly found himself at a certain height above the chair, where he began to wriggle, as our dear Mullah Nassr Eddin says, 'like a puppy in a well.'

"As it afterwards proved, my friend Gornahoor Harharkh had made a mistake during the shifting of the mentioned levers and contacts, and had made certain parts of his planetary body more tense than was necessary. As a consequence, his presence together with everything on him, having received a shock and afterwards the momentum given by the shock, and thanks to the 'tempo' proceeding in his presence from taking in the 'second being food' and to the absence of any resistance in that absolutely empty space, he began to drift, or, as I have already said, to wriggle like a 'puppy in a well.'"

Having said this with a smile, Beelzebub became silent; a little later he made a very strange gesture with his left hand, and with an intonation not proper to his voice, he continued thus:

"While I am gradually recalling and telling you about all this concerning the events of a period of my existence now long since past, the wish arises in me to wake an admission frankly to you—just to you, to one of those my direct heirs who must inevitably become the resultant of all my deeds during the periods of the process of my past being-existence; and namely, I wish to confess to you frankly that just while I was inside that principal demonstrating part of that novel invention of my subsequent essence-friend Gornahoor Harharkh—even although my essence itself, with the participation of the subordinate parts of my presence subject to it alone, had independently decided to take part in those scientific elucidatory experiments with the demonstrating part of the new invention of Gornahoor Harharkh, and I had entered into this demonstrating part without the least compulsion from outside—nevertheless, in spite of all I have said, my essence allowed to creep into my being and to be developed side by side with the said strange experiencings, a criminally egoistic anxiety for the safety of my common personal existence.

"All the same, my boy, in order that you may not at this moment grieve too much, I see no harm in adding that this happened in me then both for the first and the last time during all the periods of my being-existence.

"It is better, however, not to touch on questions that concern only our family exclusively.

"Let us return to the tale I began concerning the Omnipresent Okidanokh and my essence-friend Gornahoor Harharkh, who, I must say, though once everywhere considered among ordinary three-brained beings as a 'great-scientist,' is now, though he still continues to exist, not only not considered as even great, but thanks to his own result, that is to say, to his own son, is what our dear Mullah Nassr Eddin would call a 'has-been,' or, as he sometimes says in such cases, 'He is now sitting in old American galoshes.'

"So, while thus wriggling, Gornahoor Harharkh with great difficulty and only by means of a special and very complicated maneuver which he made, managed finally to get his planetary body, burdened with the various unusual heavy appliances, down on to the chair again; and this time he fixed it all with the aid of special screws which were on the chair for that purpose; and when we were both more or less arranged and communication was possible between us by means of the said artificial-connectors, he first drew my attention to those apparatuses hanging over the table which I told you were very much like the 'Momonodooar.'

"On close inspection all these were alike in appearance and resembled three identical 'sockets.'

"From the end of each of these sockets 'carbon candles' projected, such as are usually to be found in the apparatuses which your favorites call 'electric-arc-lamps.'

"Having drawn my attention to these three socket-like Momonodooar, he said:

"'Each of these externally similar apparatuses has a direct connection with these 'containers' of the second order, which I pointed out to you, while we were still outside, in which each of the active parts of Okidanokh, after the artificial Djartklom, collects into a general mass.

"'I have adapted these three independent apparatuses in such a way that here in this vacuum, we can obtain from those second-order "containers," which I also pointed out to you, as much as you like for the required experiment, of every active part of Okidanokh in a pure state, and also we can at will change the 'force-of-the-striving-to-be-blended-again-into-a-whole,' which is acquired in them and is proper to them in the degree of density of the concentration of the mass.

"'And here within the vacuum, I will just show you the same non-lawful phenomenon which we recently observed while we were outside the place of its origin. And namely, I will again demonstrate to you this World phenomenon which occurs when after some lawful Djartklom, the separate parts of the whole Okidanokh meet in a space outside of some lawful arising, and without the participation of one part, "strive-to-be-reblended-into-a-whole."'

"Having said this, he first closed that part of the surface of the Hrhaharhtzaha whose stuff had the property of admitting 'rays' to pass through it and then he shifted two 'contacts' and pressed a certain button, from the pressing of which the small plate lying on that table, also composed of a certain special mastic, automatically moved towards the mentioned 'carbon candles'; and then having again drawn my attention to the 'ammeter' and the 'voltmeter' he added:

"'I have again admitted the confluence of parts of the Okidanokh, namely the Anodnatious and the Cathodnatious of equal "force-of-striving-to-be-reblended."'

"When I looked at the 'ammeter' and the 'voltmeter' and saw indeed that their needles moved and stopped on the same figures I had noticed the first time while we there still outside the Hrhaharhtzaha, I was greatly surprised, because in spite of the indications of the needles and the reminder of Gornahoor Harharkh himself, I had neither noticed nor sensed any charge in the degree of my perception of the visibility of the surrounding objects.

"So without waiting for his further explanations, I asked him:

"'But why is there no result from such non-lawful "striving-to-be-reblended-into-a-whole" of the parts of the Okidanokh?'

"Before replying to this question, he turned off the only

lamp which worked from a special magnetic current. My astonishment increased still more, because in spite of the darkness which instantly ensued, it could clearly be seen through the walls of the Hrhaharhtzaha, that the needles of the Ammeter and Voltmeter still stood in their former places.

"Only After I had somehow got accustomed to such a surprising ascertainment, Gornahoor Harharkh said:

"'I have already told you that the composition of the stuff of which the walls of this artifact in which we are at this moment are made, possesses the property of not allowing vibrations arising from any sources whatever to pass through it, with the exception of certain vibrations arising from concentrations nearby; and furthermore, these vibrations can be perceived by the organs of sight only of three-brained beings, and even then only, of course, of normal beings.

"'Further, according to the law called "Heteratogetar," the "Salnichizinooarnian-momentum-vibrations" or "rays" acquire the property of acting on the organs of perception of beings only after they have passed a limit defined by science in the following formula, "the-result-of-the-manifestation-is-proportionate-to-the-force-of-striving-received-from-the-shock."'

"'So because the given process of the clash of the two parts of the Okidanokh has the strength of high power, the result of the clash is manifested much further than the place of its arising.'

"'Now Look!'

"Having said this, he pressed some other button, and suddenly the whole interior of the Hrhaharhtzaha was filled with the same blinding light which, as I have told you, I experienced when I was outside the Hrhaharhtzaha.

"It appeared that the said light was obtained because by pressing this last button, Gornahoor Harharkh had again opened that part of the wall of the Hrhaharhtzaha which had the property of permitting rays to pass through itself.

"As he explained further, the light was only a consequence of the result of the 'striving-to-be-reblended-into-a-whole' of the parts of Okidanokh proceeding in that entirely empty space within the Hrhaharhtzaha and owing to what is called 'reflection,' it is manifested back to the place of its arising.

"After this he continued as follows:

"'I will now demonstrate to you how and by what combinations of the process of "Djartklom" and "striving-to-be-reblended-into-a-whole" of the active parts of Okidanokh there arise in planets, from what are called the "minerals" which compose their interior presence, definite formations of varying densities, as for instance, "mineraloids," "gases," "metalloids," "metals," and so on; and how these latter are afterwards gradually transformed owing to the same factors one into another, and how thereby the vibrations flowing from these transformations form just that "totality of vibrations" which gives the planets themselves the possibility of stability in the process called the "Common-system-harmonious-motion."'

"'For the demonstration I propose, I must obtain the necessary materials as I always do, from outside; and these materials my people will give me by means of appliances which I have prearranged.'

"It is interesting to remark that at the same time that he was speaking, he was tapping with his left foot on a certain 'something' very much like what your favorites call the famous Morse transmission apparatus—famous, of course, only to the planet Earth.

"And a little later there slowly ascended from the lower part of the Hrhaharhtzaha a small 'something' like a box, also with the transparent walls, within which, as it proved later, were certain 'minerals,' 'metalloids,' 'metals,' and various 'gases' in liquid and solid states.

"Then with the aid of various appliances already present on one side of the table, he with complicated manipulation first took out from the 'box' some, what is called 'red Copper' and placed it on the mentioned plate, and then said:

"'This metal is a definite intraplanetary crystallization and is one of the densities required for the said stability. It is a formation from preceding processes of the action of the parts of the Omnipresent Okidanokh and at the given moment I wish to allow the subsequent transformations of this metal to be produced artificially and acceleratedly by means of the particularities of the same factors.

"'I wish to assist artificially the evolution and involution of its elements towards a greater density or, on the other hand, towards their transformation back to their primal state.

"'To make the picture of the further elucidatory experiments clearer to you, I find I must inform you, even if only briefly, of my first personal scientific conclusions concerning the evidence of the causes and conditions from and under which there proceeds in the planets themselves the crystallizing of separate parts of the Okidanokh in these or the other mentioned definite formations.

"'Evidently, first of all, from some non-lawful "Djartklom" of the Omnipresent Okidanokh contained also in the presence of every planet, its separate parts are localized in the medium of that part of the presence of the planet, that is to say, in just that mineral which was just then properly in that place where the said non-lawful Djartklom occurred.

"'So, if what is called the "vibration-of-the-density-of-the-element" of the said medium has an "affinity-of-vibration" with the said active part of the Omnipresent Okidanokh, then according to the World-Law called "Symmetric-entering," this active part blends with the presence of the said medium and becomes an inseparable part of it. And from that moment the given parts of the Omnipresent Okidanokh begin, together with the said elements of the said medium, to represent the corresponding densities required in planets, namely, various kinds of metalloids or even metals, as for instance, the metal I have placed in this sphere, and in which there will proceed artificially at this moment, at my wish, the action of "striving-to-be-reblended-into-a-whole" of the parts of the Okidanokh, and which metal, as I have already said, exists under the name of "red copper."

"'And further, having arisen in the planets in this way, the said various metalloids and metals then begin, as it is generally proper to arisings of every kind in which Okidanokh or any of its active elements participates, and according to the common universal law called the "Reciprocal-feeding-of-everything-existing," to radiate from their presence the results of their inner "Interchange-of-matters." And as is proper to radiations of every kind issuing from sur—and intraplanetary formations that have acquired in their vibration the property of Okidanokh or of its active parts, and which reside in what is called the 'center-of-gravity' of each such said formation, the radiations of these metalloids and metals possess properties almost similar to the properties of Okidanokh itself or of one or another of its active parts.

"'When the said masses of different densities that have thus arisen in planets under normal surrounding conditions proceed to radiate from their presences the vibrations required for the said World-Law—the "Reciprocal-feeding-of-everything-existing"—then, among these vibrations of various properties, there is established on the basis of the World-Law "Troemedekhfe," a "contact-of-reciprocal-action."

"'And the result of just this contact is the chief factor in the gradual change of the various densities in planets.

"'My observations over many years have almost fully persuaded me that it is owing only to this said contact and its results that there is realized the "Stability-of-harmonious-equilibrium-of-planets."

"'The element of the metal "red copper" which I have

placed in this sphere where I anticipate my artificial realization of the action of the active parts of the Okidanokh, has at this moment what is called a "specific density," reckoning from the unit of density of the sacred element "Theomertmalogos," of 444; that is to say, the atom of this metal is 444 times more dense, and as much less vivifying, than the atom of the sacred Theomertmalogos.

"'Now see in what order its artificially accelerated transformations will proceed.'

"Having said this, he first fixed before my organ of sight the automatically, moving 'Teskooano,' and then switched on and off various 'contacts' in a certain sequence; and he explained to me as follows as I looked through the Teskooano:

"'At this moment I admit the "confluence" of all three parts of Okidanokh into the sphere containing this metal; and because all three parts have the same "density" and, hence, the same "force-of-striving," they reblend into a whole in this sphere, without changing anything in the presence of the metal; and the Omnipresent Okidanokh thus obtained flows through a special connection in its usual state out of the Hrhaharhtzaha and is reconcentrated in the first container which you have already seen.

"'Now look:

"'I deliberately increase the "force-of-striving" of one only of the active parts of the Okidanokh for example, I increase the force called Cathodnatious. In consequence of this, you see that the elements composing the presence of that "red copper" begin to involve towards the quality of the substances that compose the usual presence of planets.'

"As he explained this, he at the same time switched on and off various contacts in a certain sequence.

"Although, my boy, I then looked very attentively at everything proceeding, and everything I saw was impressed in my essence 'Pestolnootiarly,' that is, indelibly—all the same, not even with my best wish could I now describe to you in words a hundredth part of what then proceeded in that small fragment of a definite intraplanetary formation.

"And I will not try to put into words for you what I then saw because, also, I have just thought of a possibility of soon actually showing it all to you when you also can be an eyewitness of so strange and astonishing a cosmic process.

"But I will tell you meanwhile that there proceeded in that fragment of 'red copper' something rather like those terrifying pictures which I occasionally observed from Mars through my Teskooano among your favorites on the planet Earth.

"I said 'rather like' because what occasionally proceeded among your favorites had a visibility only possible of observation at its beginning, whereas in the fragment of 'red copper,' the visibility was continuous to the final completion of transformation.

"A rough parallel can be drawn between the occasional proceedings on your planet and the proceedings in that small fragment of copper, if you imagine yourself high up and looking down an a large public square, where thousands of your favorites, under the most intense form of their chief psychosis, are destroying each other's existence by every means they have invented, that in their places there immediately appear what are called their 'corpses,' which 'corpses' on account of the outrages done to them by those who were not yet destroyed, change color very perceptibly, with the consequence that the general visibility of the surface of the said square is gradually changed.

"Then, my boy, this subsequent essence-friend of mine, Gornahoor Harharkh, by means of switching on and off the confluences of the three active parts of Okidanokh and changing their forces of striving, also changed the density of the elements of the said metal and thereby transformed the 'red copper' into all the other also definite intraplanetary 'metals' of lower or higher degree of vivifyingness.

"And here, for the elucidation of the strangeness of the psyche of the three-brained beings who please you, it is very important and interesting to note that while Gornahoor Harharkh was artificially and deliberately, with the aid of his new invention, producing the evolution and involution of the density and vivifyingness of the elements of 'red copper,' I noticed very clearly that this metal was once transformed upon the said plate into just that same definite metal about which the 'sorry savants' of your planet have been 'wiseacring' during nearly the whole time of their arising and existence, in the hope of transforming other metals into this metal—thereby constantly leading astray their already sufficiently erring brethren.

"This metal is called there—'gold.'

"Gold is no other than the metal we call 'Przarhalavr' whose 'specific weight,' reckoning from the element of the sacred Theomertmalogos, is 1439; that is to say, its active element is three and a fraction times less vivifying than the element of the metal 'red copper.'

"Why I suddenly decided not to try to explain to you in detail in words all that then took place in the fragment of the said 'red copper,' in view of my suggestion of the possibility of soon practically showing you in definite intraplanetary formations the processes of various combinations of the manifestations of the active parts of Okidanokh, was because I suddenly remembered the all-gracious promise given me by our All-Quarters-Maintainer, the Most Great Arch-Cherub, Peshtvogner.

"And this all-gracious promise was given me, as soon as I had returned from exile and had to present myself first of all to His All-Quarters-Maintainer, the Arch-Cherub Peshtvogner, and had prostrated myself to produce before him what is called the 'Essence-Sacred-Aliamizoornakalu.'

"This I had to do on account of the same sins of my youth. And I was obliged to do so because, when I was pardoned by HIS ENDLESS UNI-BEING, and allowed to returned to my native land, certain sacred Individuums decided to demand of me, in order to provide for any eventuality, to produce over my essence, this sacred process, so that I might not manifest myself, as in the days of my youth, and that the same might not thereby occur again in the reasons of the majority of the Individuums dwelling here at the center of the Great Universe.

"You probably do not know yet what the Sacred Aliamizoornakalu over an essence means? I will explain it to you in detail some time; but meanwhile I shall simply use the words of our dear Mullah Nassr Eddin who explains this process as 'giving-one's-word-of-honour-not-to-meddle-in-the-affairs-of-the-authorities.'

"Briefly, when presenting myself to his All-Quarters-Maintainer, he was good enough to ask me, among other things, whether I had taken with me all the being productions which had interested me and which I had collected from various planets of that solar system in which I had existed during my exile.

"I replied that I had taken almost everything, except those cumbersome apparatuses which my friend Gornahoor Harharkh had constructed for me on the planet Mars.

"He at once promised to give orders that everything I should indicate should be taken at the first opportunity on the next trip of the spaceship *Omnipresent*.

"That is why, my boy, I hope that everything necessary will be brought to our planet Karatas, and that when we return there, you will be able to see with your own eyes, and I shall be able to explain practically everything in detail.

"And meanwhile, during our traveling here on the spaceship *Karnak*, I will as I have already promised you, tell you in their order about my descents there to your planet, and also about the causes of what is called my 'appearance there in person.'"

CHAPTER XIX

Beelzebub's Tale about His Second Descent on the Planet Earth

BEELZEBUB began thus:

"I descended upon your planet Earth for the second time, only eleven of their centuries after my first descent upon it.

"It was shortly after my first descent on to the surface of that planet that the second serious catastrophe just occurred to it; but this catastrophe was local in character and did not threaten disaster on a large cosmic scale.

"During the second serious catastrophe to that planet, the continent Atlantis, together with other large and small terra-firmas also, which had been the largest continent and the chief place of the being-existence of the three-brained beings of that planet during the period of my first descent, was engulfed within the planet both with all the three-brained beings existing upon it, and with almost everything they had attained and acquired during their many preceding centuries.

"In their place there then emerged from within the planet, other terra-firmas which formed other continents and islands, most of which still exist until now.

"It was just on the said continent of Atlantis that the city of Samlios was situated, where existed—do you remember? I once told you—-our young countryman on whose account my first, as it is called, 'personal-descent' took place.

"During the mentioned second great disaster to that planet, many of the three-brained beings who please you, survived, owing to a great variety of accidents and their now already excessively multiplied posterity just descended from them.

"By the time of my second 'personal-descent,' they had already multiplied so greatly, that they were breeding again upon almost all the newly formed terra-firmas.

"And as regards the question, namely what legitimately derived causes resulted in this excessive multiplication of theirs, you will also understand in the course of my further tales.

"There is no harm, I think, in noticing here, in connection with this terrestrial catastrophe, something about the three-brained beings of our own tribe, namely, why all the beings of our tribe, existing on that planet during the mentioned catastrophe to it, escaped the inevitable what is called 'Apocalyptic end.'

"They escaped it, for the following reasons:

"I told you once, in the course of our previous talks, that the greater number of the beings of our tribe who had chosen this planet of yours as their place of existence, existed during my first descent chiefly on the continent of Atlantis.

"It appears that a year before the said catastrophe, our, as she is called, 'Party-Pythoness' there, when prophesying, had required that we should all leave the continent of Atlantis and migrate to another small continent not very far away, where we should exist on that definite part of its surface which she indicated.

"This small continent was then called 'Grabontzi' and the part the 'Pythoness' indicated did indeed escape the terrifying perturbation which then occurred to all the other parts of the general 'presence' of that ill-starred planet.

"In consequence of the said 'perturbation' this small continent 'Grabontzi,' which exists until now under the denomination of 'Africa' became even much larger, because other terra-firmas emerging from the water spaces of the planet were added to it.

"So, my boy, the 'Party-Pythoness' there was able to warn those beings of our tribe, who had been obliged to exist on that planet, and thereby to save them, as I have already told you, from the inevitable 'Apocalyptic fate,' only owing to one special being-property which I must say, in this connection, can be acquired by beings only intentionally, by means of what is called 'Being-Partkdolg-duty,' about which I will tell you later.

"I descended personally to the surface of that planet for the second time for reasons that arose from the following events.

"Once, while on the planet Mars, we received an etherogram from the center announcing the impending reappearance there on the planet Mars of certain most High Sacred Individuums; and indeed, within half a Martian year, a number of Archangels, Angels, Cherubim and Seraphim did appear there, most of whom had been members of that most great Commission, which had already appeared on our planet Mars during the first great catastrophe to that planet of yours.

"Among these most High Sacred Individuums there was again His Conformity, the Angel—now already an Archangel—Looisos, of whom, do you remember, I recently told you that during the first great catastrophe to the planet Earth he had been one of the chief regulators in the matter of averting the consequences of that general cosmic misfortune.

"So, my boy! The day following this second appearance of the mentioned Sacred Individuums, His Conformity, escorted by one of the Seraphim, His second assistant, made His appearance in my house.

"After Te Deums with His Conformity and after certain inquiries of mine concerning the Great Center, His Conformity then condescended to tell me among other things that after the collision of the comet Kondoor with the planet Earth, He, or other responsible cosmic Individuums, superintending the affairs of 'Harmonious-World-Existence,' had frequently descended to this Solar System to take stock of the actualizing of those measures they had put into operation for averting the consequences of that general cosmic accident.

"'And we descended,' His Conformity continued, 'because although we had then put into effect every possible measure and had assured everybody that everything would be quite all right, we ourselves nevertheless were not perfectly convinced that no unexpectedness might not occur there unforeseen.

"'Our apprehensions were partly realized, but, by Good Luck, not in a serious form, that is, on a general cosmic scale, since this new catastrophe affected only the planet Earth itself.

"'This second catastrophe to the planet Earth,' continued His Conformity, 'occurred owing to the following:

"'When during the first disaster two considerable fragments had been separated from this planet, then for certain reasons, the so-called "center of gravity" of the whole of its "presence" had no time to shift immediately into its corresponding new place, with the result that right until the second catastrophe, that planet had existed with an erratic "center of gravity," owing to which, its motion during that time being not "equally harmonious," there often occurred both within and upon it a number of commotions and considerable displacements.

"'But when the "center of gravity" of the planet recently finally shifted into its true center, it was then that the said second catastrophe just occurred.

"'But now,' added His Conformity with a shade of self-satisfaction, 'the existence of this planet will run already quite normally in Conformity with the common cosmic harmony.

"'This second catastrophe to the planet Earth has finally quite quieted and convinced us also that a catastrophe on a great scale cannot again occur on account of that planet.

"'Not only has this planet itself now reacquired a normal movement in the general cosmic balance, but its two detached fragments also, as I have already told you, of the now called "Moon" and "Anulios" have also reacquired a normal movement and have become, although small, yet independent 'Kofensharnian,' that is, additional planets of that solar system Ors.'

"Having thought a little, His Conformity then told me:

"'Your Reverence, I have appeared to you just for the purpose of discussing the future welfare of the large fragment of that planet which exists at the present time under the denomination of Moon.

"'This fragment,' His Conformity continued, 'has not only become an independent planet, but there has now begun on it a process of the formation of an atmosphere, necessary for every planet, which serves for the realization of the most great common cosmic Trogoautoegocrat.

"'So, Your Reverence, the regular process of the formation of the said atmosphere on this small, unforeseenly arisen planet, is just now being hindered by an undesirable circumstance caused by the three-brained beings, arisen and existing on the planet Earth.

"'Concerning what I have just said, I decided to apply myself to you, Your Reverence, and to ask you to consent to take upon yourself, in the name of the UNI-BEING CREATOR, the task of trying to spare us the necessity of resorting to some extreme sacred processes, unbecoming to be used for any three-centered being whatsoever, and to remove this undesirable phenomenon, in some ordinary way through their own "being-reason" contained in their "presence."'

"And in his extended detailed explanations, His Conformity then said among other things further, that after the second catastrophe to the Earth, the chance surviving biped three-brained beings had again multiplied, and that now, the whole process of their being-existence was concentrated on another, newly formed, also large continent called 'Ashhark.'

"Three independent large groups had just been formed on this same large continent 'Ashhark,' the first of which existed in the locality then called 'Tikliamish,' the second in the place called 'Maralpleicie,' and the third in the still existing locality then called 'Gemchania.'

"'The matter is,' continued His Conformity, 'that in the

general psyche of the beings, belonging to all those three independent groups, certain peculiar "Havatvernoni" have been formed, that is, certain psychic strivings, the totality of the process of which they themselves have named "Religion."

"'Although these "Havatvernoni" or "Religions" have nothing in common with each other, yet, nevertheless there is very widely spread among the beings of all three groups in these peculiar religions of theirs the same custom called among them "Sacrificial-Offerings."

"'And this custom of theirs is founded on the notion, recognized by their strange reason alone, that if they destroy the existence of beings of other forms in honor of their gods and idols, these gods and idols would find it very agreeable, and always in everything unfailingly help and assist them in the realization of their various fantastic and absurd whims.

"'This custom is at present so widely spread there, and the destruction of the existence of beings of various forms for this maleficent purpose has reached such dimensions there, that already there is a surplus of the "Sacred Askokin" required from the planet Earth for its former parts, that is to say, a surplus of those vibrations which arise during the sacred process of "Rascooarno" with beings of every exterior form, arising and existing on that planet, from which the said sacred cosmic arising is required.

"'For the normal formation of the atmosphere of the newly arisen planet "Moon," the said surplus of the "Sacred Askokin" has already begun seriously to hinder the regular exchange of matters between the planet Moon itself and its atmosphere, and the fear has already arisen that its atmosphere may be formed irregularly on account of this and later become an obstacle to the harmonious movement of the whole Ors system, and perhaps again give rise to the menace of a catastrophe on a general cosmic scale.

"'So, Your Reverence, my request to you consists in this,

as I have already told you, that you should consent, since you are in the habit of often visiting various planets of that solar system, to undertake the task of descending on the planet Earth specially, and of trying there on the spot to instill into the consciousness of these strange three-brained beings some idea of the senselessness of this notion of theirs.'

"Having said a few more words His Conformity ascended and having risen sufficiently high, he added in a loud voice already from on high: 'Thereby, Your Reverence, you will be rendering a great service to our ENDLESS UNI-BEING.'

"After these sacred Individuums had left the planet Mars, I decided at whatever cost to carry out the said task, and if only by this explicit aid to our UNIQUE-BURDEN-BEARING ENDLESSNESS, to be worthy to become a particle, but already an independent one, of everything existing in the Great Universe.

"So, my boy, imbued with this, I flew the next day for the second time to your planet Earth on the same ship *Occasion*.

"This time our ship *Occasion* alighted on the sea called there in that period of the flow of time, 'Kolhidious.' This sea was also a new formation that had been caused by the perturbation during the second great disaster to that planet of yours.

"The said sea was situated on the north-west of that newly formed large continent Ashhark, which at that period was already the chief center of the existence of the three-brained beings there.

"The other shores of this sea were composed of those newly emerged terra-firmas which had become attached to the continent 'Ashhark,' and which all together were first called 'Frianktzanarali,' but a little later 'Kolhidshissi.'

"It must be remarked that both the said sea and the enumerated terra-firmas exist until now, but naturally they now already have other names; namely the continent Ashhark is now called 'Asia,' the sea 'Kolhidious,' the 'Caspian' sea, and all the 'Frianktzanarali' together exist now under the name 'Caucasus.'

"The *Occasion*' alighted on this sea 'Kolhidious' or 'Caspian' Sea, furthermore, because this sea was the most convenient, both for mooring our *Occasion*, and for my further travels.

"And it was very convenient for my further travels because from its Eastern side a large river flowed into it, which watered almost the whole country of 'Tikliamish,' and just on the banks of which there stood the capital of that country, the city 'Koorkalai.'

"As the greatest center of the existence of those favorites of yours was then the country 'Tikliamish,' I decided to go there first.

"Here there is no harm in noticing that although the mentioned large river then called 'Oksoseria' also still exists, yet it no longer flows into the present Caspian Sea. After a minor planet-quake at almost about the middle of its course, it turned to the right and flowed into one of the hollows on the surface of the continent Ashhark, where it gradually formed a small sea, still existing and called the 'Aral Sea'; but the old bed of the former half of that large river, now already called the 'Amu Darya' can be seen by close observation even at the present time.

"During the period of this second personal descent of mine, the country Tikliamish was considered to be and indeed was the richest and most prosperous of all the terra-firmas, good for the ordinary being-existence then existing on that planet.

"But when a third great catastrophe occurred to that ill-starred planet, this then most prosperous country on the surface of your planet, along with other more or less prosperous terra-firmas, was covered by 'Kashmanoon,' or, as they say, by 'Sands.'

"For long periods after this third catastrophe, this country

Tikliamish was simply called 'bare desert.' At present its parts have various names; and its former principal part is called 'Karakoom,' that is, 'Black Sands.'

"On this same continent during that period there also dwelt the second, equally quite independent group of three-brained beings on your planet. And that part of the continent Ashhark was then called 'The Country Maralpleicie.'

"When this second group later on also had a central point of their existence which they called the 'City Gob,' the whole country was for a long time called 'Goblandia.'

"This locality also was afterwards covered by 'Kashmanoon,' and at present the former principal part of this also once flourishing country is called simply 'The Gobi Desert.'

"And as for the third group of the three-brained beings then of the planet Earth, this also quite independent group had the place of its existence on the South-Eastern side of the continent Ashhark, in the direction opposite to Tikliamish, quite on the other side of those abnormal projections of the continent Ashhark which also were formed during the second perturbation to this ill-starred planet.

"Just that region of the existence of this third group was then called, as have already told you, 'Gemchania.'

"The name of this locality also changed many times afterwards and the whole of this terra-firma region of the surface of the planet Earth exists at the present time under the name of 'Hindustan' or 'India.'

"It is quite necessary to notice also, that at that period, that is, during this second 'Personal descent' of mine on the surface of your planet there was present and already thoroughly crystallized in all these three-brained beings who please you, belonging to each of the three enumerated independent groups, in place of that function called 'the need-to-strive-to-be-perfected,' which should be in every three-brained being, a very strange, also a 'need to strive,' but towards this, that all the other beings of their planet should call and consider their country as the 'Culture-center' for the whole planet.

"This strange 'need to strive' was then present in all three-centered beings of your planet and was for each of them, as it were, the principal sense and aim of his existence. And in consequence, among the beings of these three independent groups at that period, bitter struggles, both material and psychic, were constantly proceeding for the attainments of the mentioned aim.

"And so, my boy.

"We then set off from the sea 'Kolhidious,' or as it is now called, 'Caspian Sea,' on 'Selchans,' that is to say, on rafts of a special kind, up the river 'Oksoseria,' or as it is now called, the 'Amu Darya.' We sailed for fifteen Earth-days and finally arrived at the capital of the beings of the first Asiatic group.

"On arriving there and after arranging the place of our permanent existence there, I first began visiting the 'Kaltaani' of the city 'Koorkalai,' that is, those establishments there which later, there on the continent Ashhark, came to be called 'Chaihana,' 'Ashhana,' 'Caravansary,' and so on, and which the contemporary beings there, especially those breeding on the continent called 'Europe,' call 'Cafes,' 'Restaurants,' 'Clubs,' 'Dance-halls,' 'Assembly-rooms' and so on.

"I began visiting just these establishments of theirs first because there, on the planet Earth, at present, just as formerly, nowhere else so well as in just such gatherings of theirs is it possible to observe and study the specific peculiarities of the psyche of the beings of the locality; which was just what I needed for clearing up for myself their real inner essence-attitude to the custom of sacrifice and to enable me more readily and more easily to draw up a plan of action for the attainment of that aim for which I had made that second 'Personal-stay' of mine there.

"During my wanderings around the 'Kaltaani' there I met

a number of beings, among whom was one whom I happened to meet rather often.

"This three-brained being there, whom I chanced to meet frequently, belonged to the profession of 'priest' and was called 'Abdil.'

"As, my boy, almost all my personal activities during that second descent of mine were connected with the external circumstances of this priest Abdil, and as I was obliged to have during this descent of mine a great deal of trouble on his account, I shall tell you more or less in detail about this three-brained being there; and, moreover, you will at the same time understand from these tales about him what, namely, were the results I then attained for my aim of uprooting from the strange psyche of your favorites the need to destroy the existence of beings of other forms for the 'appeasing' and 'pleasing' of their Gods and revered idols.

"Although this terrestrial being, who afterward became for me like one of my intimates, was not a priest of the highest rank, yet he was familiar with all the details of the teaching of the religion then dominant in the whole country Tikliamish; and he also knew the psyche of the followers of that religion, particularly, of course, the psyche of the beings belonging to his 'flock' for whom he was a 'priest.'

"Soon after we had become on good terms with each other, I discovered that in the Being of this priest Abdil, owing to very many external circumstances, among which there were also heredity and the conditions under which he had been prepared for a responsible being, the function called 'conscience' which ought to be present in every three-centered being was not yet quite atrophied in him, so that after he had cognized with his reason certain cosmic truths I explained to him, he immediately acquired in his 'presence' towards the beings around him, similar to him, almost that attitude which is proper to be present in all normal three-brained beings of the whole Universe; that is to say, he became as it is also said there, 'compassionate,' and 'sympathetic' towards the beings surrounding him.

"Before telling you more about this priest Abdil, I must clear up for your reason, that there, that is on the continent of Ashhark, the mentioned cruel custom of 'sacrificial offerings' was, as it is said, at its 'height' at that time, and the destruction of various 'one-brained' and 'two-brained' weak beings proceeded everywhere in incalculable numbers.

"At that period, if anybody had occasion in any house to appeal to one or other of their imaginary Gods, or fantastic 'Saints,' they invariably promised, that in the event of good fortune, they would destroy in honor of their Gods and Saints the existence of some or other being, or of several at once. And if by chance good fortune befell them, then they fulfilled their promise with the utmost veneration, while, if it were otherwise, then they multiplied their slaughters in order eventually to win the favor of their said imaginary patron.

"With the same aim, these favorites of yours of that period even divided the beings of all other forms into 'clean' and 'unclean.'

"'Unclean' they called those forms of being, the destruction of whose existence was not pleasing, as it were, to their Gods, and 'clean'—those beings the destruction of whose existence, was, as it were, extremely agreeable to those various imaginary idols whom they revered.

"These sacrifices they made not only in their own houses, nor only as private beings, but they were made by whole groups, and sometimes even, in public. There even existed then special places for slaughterings of this kind; these were situated mostly near buildings in memory of something or somebody, chiefly of 'Saints'—naturally, of course, of the 'Saints' they themselves had elevated to 'Sainthood.'

"Several such special public places, where the destruction of the beings of different exterior forms was carried out, then existed in the country of Tikliamish; and among them was then one most celebrated, situated on a small mountain, whence, as it were, a certain thaumaturgist Aliman had once upon a time been 'taken' alive up to 'some' Heaven.

"In that place, just as in others like it, especially at defined times of year, an innumerable number of beings called 'oxen,' 'sheep,' 'doves' and so on were destroyed, and even beings similar to themselves.

"In the latter case, the strong usually sacrificed the less strong, as, for instance, a father his son, a husband his wife, an elder brother his younger brother and so on. But for the most part, 'sacrifices' were offered up of 'slaves,' who then as now were usually what are called 'captives'; that is, beings of a conquered community, or beings of that caste, which, according to the law of what is called 'Solioonensius,' had at the given period a lesser value in respect of their chief particularity, namely, when their needful tendency to mutual destruction there is more intensely manifested in their 'presence.'

"The custom of pleasing their Gods by destroying the existence of other beings is followed there, on your planet, until now, only not on the same scale upon which this same abominable custom was practiced by your favorites then, on the continent Ashhark.

"So, my boy, during the early days of my stay in the town 'Koorkalai,' I often talked on various subjects with this mentioned friend of mine, the priest Abdil, though, of course, I never spoke with him about such questions as might reveal my real nature.

"Like almost all the three-brained beings of your planet during all my descents he also took me for a being of his own planet and looked upon me as very learned and as an authority on the psyche of beings similar to himself.

"During our earliest meetings, whenever we chanced to

speak about other beings similar to himself, his responsiveness and experiencings about them touched me deeply, but when my Reason cleared up definitively that the function of 'conscience,' fundamental for three-centered beings, which had passed to his 'presence' by heredity had not yet become quite atrophied in him, then there began gradually from that moment to arise—and in the end to be crystallized in my 'presence'—a 'really-functioning-needful-striving' towards him as towards an intimate of my own nature.

"Thereafter, he also, according to the cosmic law 'every-cause-gives-birth-to-a-corresponding-result,' naturally began to have towards me 'Silnooyegordpana,' as your favorites say there, a 'feeling-of-other-self-trust.'

"So, my boy.

"No sooner was this clearly ascertained in my reason, than the idea just then occurred to me to realize through this first Earth-friend of mine, the task, on account of which this second 'Personal descent' of mine had been made.

"I therefore intentionally directed all our conversations towards the question of the custom of sacrifice-offering.

"Although, my boy, a very considerable 'flow of time' has passed since I talked with that Earth friend of mine, I could, perhaps, now recall word for word and repeat one of our talks then.

"I particularly wish to recall and repeat just that talk of ours which was our last, and which served as a starting point of all further sad events which brought the existence, though only the planetary existence, of this Earth friend of mine, to a painful end, nevertheless to the beginning of the possibility of an external universal existence.

"This last talk took place in his house.

"I explained to him already openly at that time the utter absurdity and stupidity of this custom of sacrifice offerings.

"I said to him as follows:

"'Good . . .

"'You have a religion, a faith in something! It is excellent to have faith in something, no matter in what; and even if you don't exactly know in whom or in what, nor can represent to yourself the significance and possibilities of what you believe—to have a faith, whether consciously or even quite unconsciously, is very necessary and desirable for every being.

"'And it is desirable because, owing to faith and to faith alone, there appears in the being, an intensity of being-self-consciousness necessary for every being, and the valuation of personal being-hood, as of a particle of the All existing in the Universe.

"'But what has the existence of another being, which you destroy, to do with this, and, above all, one whose existence you destroy in the name of its CREATOR?

"'That life, for the CREATOR both of its and of your life, is just the same as yours.

"'Thanks to your psychic strength and cunning, namely, to those functions, proper to you, which our same COMMON CREATOR has granted you for the perfecting of your reason, you profit by the psychic weakness of other beings and destroy their existence.

"'Do you understand, you wretch, what—in an objective sense—an indeed evil deed you commit in this?

"'Firstly—by destroying the existence of other beings, you reduce for yourself the number of factors in that totality of results which alone can form the necessary conditions for the self-perfection of beings similar to yourself.

"'And secondly, you thereby definitely diminish or completely destroy the hopes of our COMMON FATHER CREATOR, based on those possibilities which have been put into you, yourself, as a three-brained being and upon which He counts, as a help for Him later.

"'The patent senselessness of such a terrible being action is clear already merely in this, that you imagine that by destroying the existence of other beings you do something pleasing just to that ONE who has intentionally created those beings also.

"'Can it be that even the thought has never entered you head, that if our COMMON FATHER CREATOR has created that same life also, then he probably did so for some definite purpose?

"'Think, I told him further, think a little, not as you have been accustomed to think during the whole of your existence, like a "Khorassanian donkey," but think a little honestly and sincerely, as it is proper to think, for a "God-like being" as you call yourself.

"'When GOD created you and these beings, whose existence you destroy, could our CREATOR then have written on the foreheads of certain of His creatures, that they were to be destroyed in His honor and glory?

"'Anybody, if he thinks seriously and sincerely about it, even an idiot from "Albion's Isles," can understand that this could never be.

"'It was invented by men only, by men who call themselves "God-like," but only not by Him, who created men and these other beings of different form whom men destroy, as it were, for His pleasure and satisfaction.

"'For Him there is no difference between the 'life' of man and the 'life' of beings of any other form.

"'Man is "life," and the beings of other exterior forms are "life."

"'It is most wisely foreseen by Him, that Nature should adapt the difference of exterior form of beings in accordance with those conditions and circumstances, under which the process of existence of this or the other form of 'life' is designed to flow.

"'Take yourself as an example; with these your internal and

external organs, could you go and jump into the water and swim like a fish?

"'Of course not, because you have neither the 'gills' 'fins,' nor 'tail' a fish has, that is, "the life" for which it is designed to exist in that sphere which is the "water."

"'If it occurred to you to go and jump into the water, you would at once choke and drop to the bottom for the meal of those same fishes, who, in that sphere, appropriate for them, would naturally be infinitely stronger than you.

"'In a similar situation are the fishes themselves.

"'Could one of them come now to us, and sit with us at this table and drink in our "company" the "Green tea" we are now drinking?

"'Also, of course not! Because it has not the appropriate organs for manifestations of this kind.

"'It was created for the water and both its internal and external organs are adapted for the manifestations required in the water. It can manifest itself effectively and successfully, and fulfill the purpose of its existence, predesigned by the CREATOR, only in the sphere appropriate to it.

"'In exactly the same way, your external and all your internal organs are also created by our COMMON CREATOR in a corresponding manner. You are given legs to walk, you are given hands to prepare and take the necessary food; your nose and the organs connected with it are so adapted that you may perceive and transform in yourself those World-substances by means of which there are coated in the three-brained beings, similar to yourself there, both the higher being-bodies, on one of which the hope of our COMMON ALL-EMBRACING CREATOR is placed for help in His needs, for the purpose of realizations foreseen by him for the good of everything existing.

"'In short, the corresponding principle is foreseen and given to Nature by our COMMON CREATOR, so that it might coat and adapt all your internal and external organs, in accordance with that sphere, in which the process of the existence of such a brain-system as yours is preordained to flow.

"'A very good example for the clarification of this is your "own donkey" standing tied up in your stable.

"'Even as regards this "own donkey" of yours, you abuse the possibilities given you by our COMMON CREATOR, since if this donkey now stands under slavish compulsion there in your stable, it does so only because it is created two-brained; and this again is because just such an organization of the whole of its "presence" is necessary for the common cosmic existence upon planets.

"'And therefore, there is absent from the "presence" of your donkey, according to law, the possibility of "logical mentation," and consequently, according to law, he must be what you call "senseless"—"stupid."

"'And although you are created both for this and for still another purpose also, namely, as a "field of hope" for the hopes for the future of our COMMON ALL-GRACIOUS CREATOR —that is to say, you are created with the possibilities of coating in your "presence" that "Higher Sacred" for the possible arising of which the whole of our now existing World was just created; yet in spite of the said possibilities given to you, that is to say, in spite of your having been created three-brained with the possibilities of a "logic-mentation," you do not use this sacred property of yours for the purpose for which it was designed, but you manifest it as "cunning" towards His other creations, as, for instance, towards your "own donkey."

"'Apart from the possibilities present in you of consciously coating in your "presence" the mentioned "Higher Sacred," this donkey of yours is of the same value for the common cosmic process, and consequently for our COMMON CREATOR, as you yourself, since each of you is designed for some definite purpose, and these separate definite purposes, in their totality, just realize the sense of everything existing.

"'The difference between you and your "own donkey" is merely in the form and quality of functioning of the internal and external organization in your general "presence."

"'For instance, you have two legs only, whereas the donkey has as many as four, any one of which, moreover, is infinitely stronger than yours.

"'Can you, for instance, carry on those two weak legs of yours as much as that donkey can?

"'Certainly not, because your legs are given you only for carrying yourself and the little that is necessary for the normal existence of a three-brained being as foreseen by Nature.

"'Such a distribution of forces and strength which at first sight appears a piece of injustice on the part of a MOST JUST CREATOR through great Nature, is made simply because the surplus of cosmic substance foreseeingly given you to use by the CREATOR and by Nature for the purpose of your personal perfection, is not given to your donkey; but in place of this, great Nature herself transforms the same surplus of cosmic substances in your donkey's "presence" for the forces and strength of certain of its organs, only for its present existence, but of course without the personal cognition of the donkey itself; thus enabling it to manifest the said strength more and better than you.

"'And these differently-powered manifestations of beings of diverse forms realize in their totality, just those exterior conditions in which alone there is possible for those similar to you—that is, for three-brained beings—the conscious perfecting of the "germ of Reason" placed in their "presence," to the necessary gradation of the pure Objective Reason.

"'I repeat, all beings, of all brain systems, without exception, large and small, arisen and existing on the Earth or within the Earth or in the water or in the air are all equally necessary—for our COMMON CREATOR—for the general harmony of the existence of everything existing.

"'And as all the enumerated forms of beings actualize in their common totality the form of process required by our CREATOR, for the existence of everything existing, the essences of all beings are equally valuable and dear to Him.

"'For our COMMON CREATOR all beings are only parts of the existence of a whole essence, spiritualized by Himself.

"'But what do we see here now?

"'One form of beings created by Him, namely, that form of being just in whose 'presence' He has placed all His hope for the future welfare of everything existing, taking advantage of their privileges, lord it over other forms and destroy their existence indiscriminately, and, what is more, they do this, as it were, "in His name."

"'The horror of it is that although these phenomenal anti-God actions take place here in every house and on every square, nevertheless it never enters one of these wretches' heads to think that these beings whose existence I or we are now destroying, are equally dear to that ONE, Who has created them, and that if He created these other forms of beings as well as ourselves, it must have been also for some purpose.

"Having said all this to my friend, the priest Abdil, I said further:

"'And what is most distressing is that the very man who destroys the existence of other beings, in honor of his honored idols, does so with all his heart, and in the complete persuasion that he is doing a "good" deed.

"'I am quite sure, that if one of them should become aware, that in destroying another's existence, he is not only committing a crime against the true GOD and every genuine Saint, but even causing thereby sorrow and grief in their essence that there exist in the great Universe God-like being-monsters who can manifest towards other creations of our COMMON CREATOR so heartlessly and pitilessly; if, I repeat, any of them should become conscious of this, then certainly not one among them, could with all his heart, ever again destroy the existence of beings of other forms for sacrificial offering.

"'Then perhaps on the Earth also, would begin to run the 18th personal commandment of our COMMON CREATOR, which declares: "Love every breathing thing."

"'This offering to God of sacrifices by destroying the existence of His other creations is just the same as if somebody from the street should now break into your house and wantonly destroy all the "goods" there, which have taken you years to collect, and cost you years of labor and suffering.

"'Think, and once more, think sincerely, and represent to yourself what I have just said, and answer: would you like it and thank the impudent thief who broke into your house?

"'Certainly not!! . . . A thousand times not!!!!!

"'On the contrary, your whole being would be indignant and would wish to punish this thief, and with every ounce of your psyche, you would try to find a means of revenge.

"'In all probability, you would now reply, that although it is indeed so . . . however, I am only a man . . .

"'That is true, you are only a man. It is good that GOD is GOD and is not so vindictive and base as man.

"'Certainly he will not punish you nor will He revenge Himself upon you, as you would punish the mentioned robber who destroyed the property and goods it had taken you years to collect.

"'There is no question about it, GOD forgives everything—this has even become a law in the World.

"'But HIS creations—men in this given case—must not abuse this all-gracious and everywhere penetrating Goodness of HIS; they must not only care for, but even maintain all HE has created.

"'Here on Earth, however, men have even divided beings of all other forms—into the "clean" and the "unclean."

"'Tell me what led them, when they made that division?

"'Why, for instance, is a sheep "clean" and a lion "unclean"? Are they not equal beings?

"'This was also invented by men . . . And why have they invented this, and made this division? Simply because a sheep is a very weak being and moreover, stupid, so that they can do just what they like with it.

"'But men call the lion "unclean" simply because they can't do what they like with it.

"'A lion is cleverer and, above all, stronger than they.

"'A lion will not only not allow itself to be destroyed, but will not even permit men to come near it. If any man should once venture to approach it, then this "Mister Lion" would give him such a smack on the sconce that our valiant's life would at once take wings where the Russian Makar has not yet driven his flocks.

"'No . . . a lion is "unclean" simply because men are afraid of it.

"'It is a hundred times higher and stronger than they; a sheep is "clean" merely because it is much weaker than they and moreover—I repeat—much more stupid.

"'Every being according to its nature and to the gradation of its reason attained by its ancestors and passed to it by heredity, occupies its definite place among beings of other forms.

"'A good example for clarifying what I have just said is the difference between the already definitely crystallized "presences" of the psyche of your dog and cat.

"'If you pet a dog a little and get it used to anything you please, it will become obedient and affectionate to the point of humiliation.

"'It will run after you and cut every sort of caper before you just to tickle your fancy.

"'You can be familiar with it, you can beat it, you can aggravate it; it will never turn on you, but will always humiliate itself still more before you.

"'But try the same on your cat.

"'What do you think? Will it respond to your indignities as your dog did, and cut the same humble capers for your amusement? Not much . . .

"'Even if the cat is not strong enough to retaliate at once, it will remember this attitude of yours against you for a long time, and one day or another, it will get its own back.

"'For instance, it has often happened that a cat has torn the throat of a man while he was asleep. I can quite believe it, knowing what may have been the cat's reasons for it.

"'No, the cat will stick up for itself, it knows its value, it is proud; and this merely because it is a cat and its nature is on that gradation of Reason where according to the merits of its ancestors it just should be.

"'In any case, no being, and no man, should be angry with a cat for this.

"'Is it its fault that it is a cat, and that owing to the merits of its ancestors, its "presence" occupies such a gradation of "self-consciousness"?

"'It must neither be despised for this, nor beaten nor maltreated; on the contrary one must give it its due, as one occupying a higher degree on the ladder of the evolution of "self-consciousness."

"By the way, my dear Hassein, keep in mind that concerning the reciprocal relations of beings, a former famous prophet from the planet 'Desagroanskrad,' the great 'Arhoonilo,' now already the assistant of the chief investigator of the whole Universe in respect of the details of Objective Morality—once said:

"'If by his Reason a being is higher than you, you must bow before him and try to imitate him; but if he is lower than you, you must be just with him, because you once occupied the same place according to the scared Measure of gradation of Reason of our CREATOR and ALL-MAINTAINER.'

"So, my dear boy, this particular conversation with that Earth friend of mine produced such a strong impression on him, that for two days thereafter he did nothing but think about it.

"And, briefly, the final outcome of it all was this, that this priest Abdil eventually became conscious and felt about the custom of 'sacrifice' almost as it is proper to feel in reality.

"Several days after this conversation of ours, there occurred one of the two large religious festivals of the whole of Tikliamish, called 'Zadik'; and in the temple where my friend Abdil was the chief priest, instead of delivering the usual address after the temple ceremony, he suddenly began speaking about 'sacrificial-offerings.'

"I chanced to be also in that large temple that day and was among the number of those who heard his sermon.

"Although the theme of his sermon, both for such an occasion and for such a place, was unusual, it shocked nobody, because the priest Abdil spoke extraordinarily well and beautifully.

"Indeed he spoke so well and so sincerely, and cited in his beautiful speech so many persuasive and picturesque examples that as he spoke many of the beings of 'Koorkalai' present there, even began sobbing bitterly.

"What he said produced so strong an impression on all his flock, that although his sermon lasted, instead of the customary, half an hour or an hour, until the next day, nevertheless even when it was over, nobody wanted to leave and everybody stood for a long time as if spellbound.

"Thereafter fragments from his sermon began to be spread among those who had not personally heard it.

"It is interesting to notice, that it was the custom then, for priests to exist simply on the gifts of their parishioners; this priest Abdil had also been in the habit of receiving from the parishioners every kind of product for his ordinary existence—gifts of the roast and boiled 'corpses' of beings of various exterior forms, for instance, 'chickens,' 'sheep,' 'geese,' and so on. But, after this famous sermon of his nobody brought him any of these customary gifts; they brought or sent him only fruits, flowers, handiwork, and so on.

"The day following his sermon, this Earth friend of mine, at once found himself what is called the 'fashionable priest' for all the citizens of the town 'Koorkalai'; and not only was the temple where he officiated always crammed with beings of the town 'Koorkalai,' but he was also in demand to speak in other temples.

"Such sermons concerning Sacrificial offerings he delivered many times, and every time the number of his admirers grew and grew, so that he became popular not only among the beings of the town 'Koorkalai,' but also of the whole of Tikliamish.

"How it would all have ended I do not know, if the whole priesthood, that is, men-beings of the same profession as my friend, had not become alarmed and anxious on account of his popularity, and had not opposed everything he preached.

"These colleagues of his were obviously afraid, that if the custom of 'sacrifice' should disappear, their own excellent incomes would go with it, and that their authority would first totter and finally shake all to nothing.

"As day by day the number of this priest Abdil's enemies thereupon increased, fresh slanders and innuendoes appeared, designed to lower or destroy his popularity and significance.

"His colleagues began delivering addresses in their temples, conclusively proving the opposite of all that the priest Abdil had said in his sermon.

"At last it came to the point that the priesthood already began paying various beings with 'Hasnamuss' properties to plan and carry out every kind of outrage upon this poor Abdil; and in fact, these earth nullities with the properties mentioned, came to such a point, that they even tried on several occasions to destroy his existence by sprinkling poison on the various edible gifts brought to him.

"Notwithstanding all this, the number of sincere admirers of his preaching also daily increased.

"Finally, the whole corporation of the priesthood could stand it no longer and on a sad day for my friend, a general ecumenical trial was held, which lasted four days.

"By the sentence of this general ecumenical trial, this Earth friend of mine was not only absolutely excommunicated from the priesthood, but at the same council, his colleagues also organized his further prosecution.

"Little by little, all this, of course, had a strong effect upon the psyche of ordinary beings, so that even those around him, who had formerly esteemed him, then also began gradually avoiding him and repeating every kind of calumny about him. Those who only a day before had been sending him flowers and various other gifts and almost worshipping him, owing to the constant gossip, even they also soon became his bitter enemies. It was as if he had not only injured them personally, but had cut the throats of and slaughtered all their kith and kin.

"Such is the psyche of the beings of that peculiar planet. In short, thanks to his sincere goodwill to those around him, this good friend of mine underwent a great deal. But even this might have been nothing, if the climax of baseness on the part of the colleagues of my friend and his other Earth 'god-like' beings around him had not put the lid on it; namely, they killed him.

"And this occurred in the following way:

"My friend had no relatives at all in the city 'Koorkalai,' having been born in some distant place.

"And as for the hundreds of servants and other ordinary

terrestrial ciphers who surrounded him when he was important, they of course trickled away from him during this period, since my friend was important no longer.

"Towards the end there remained with him only one very old being who had been with him for a very long time.

"To tell the truth, this old man had remained with him only on account of that old age which, owing to the abnormal being-existence most of the beings there reach, that is to say, on account of his complete uselessness for anything required under the conditions of being-existence there.

"Having no other place to go to, he did not desert my friend, but stayed to exist with him even during the time when he had lost his importance and during his persecution.

"This same old man on going into my friend's room one sad morning saw that he had been killed and that his planetary body had been hacked to pieces.

"Knowing that I was friends with him, he at once ran to me to tell me about it.

"I have already told you, that I had begun to love him as one of my nearest, so that when I learned about this terrible event, there almost occurred in my whole 'presence' a 'Skinikoonartzino,' that is to say, the connection between my separate being-centers was almost shattered.

"But during the day I felt afraid that the same or some similar unconscionable beings like them might commit further outrages on the parts of my friend's planetary body, so I decided at least to prevent the possibility of this fear being realized.

"I therefore, unbeknown to anybody else, immediately hired several suitable beings for a great sum of money and had his planetary body removed and placed temporarily in my 'Selchan,' that is, on my raft which was moored not far away on the river 'Oksoseria.' I had not disposed of it because I had it in mind to sail on it from there to the Sea Kolhidious to our ship '*Occasion.*'

"This sad end of my friend's existence did not prevent his preachings and persuasions about the cessation of sacrifices having a strong effect upon many, even upon very many.

"And indeed, the quantity of such slaughterings began very perceptibly to diminish and one could see that with time even if the custom were not abolished completely, at least it would be considerably mitigated.

"And that was enough for me for the time being. As there was no reason for me to stay there any longer, I decided to return immediately to the Sea 'Kolhidious' and there to consider what further to do with the planetary body of my friend.

"When I arrived on our ship '*Occasion*,' an etherogram from Mars awaited me in which I was informed of the arrival there of still another party of beings from the planet Karatas, and that my earliest return there was desired.

"Thanks to this etherogram a very strange notion came into my mind, namely, I thought that instead of disposing of the planetary body of my friend on the Planet Earth, I might take it with me and return it to the 'presence' of the planet Mars.

"I decided to carry out this idea of mine as I was afraid that my friend's enemies who hated him might make a search for his planetary body, and if they should chance to learn where it had been returned to the 'presence' of that planet, or as your favorites say—'buried,' then doubtless they would find it and perpetrate some or other atrocity upon it.

"Soon from the Sea Kolhidious I indeed ascended to the planet Mars on the ship '*Occasion.*'

"Already there on the planet Mars, our beings and several kind Martians, having learned of the events which had taken place on the planet Earth, paid due respect to the planetary body I had taken with me.

"They 'buried' him with the ceremonies customary on the

planet Mars, and over the spot they erected a suitable construction.

"Anyhow, this was the first and surely it will be the last, as your favorites call it 'grave' for a being of the planet Earth, on this at once so near and so far, and, for the terrestrial beings, quite inaccessible planet Mars.

"I learned afterwards that this story reached His All-Quarters-Maintainer Most Great Archangel 'Setrenotzinarco,' the All-Quarters-Maintainer of that part of the Universe to which that system Ors also belongs, and that He manifested His pleasure by giving to whom it was proper a command concerning the soul of this terrestrial friend of mine.

"On the planet Mars I was indeed awaited by several newly arrived beings of our tribe from the planet Karatas. Incidentally, among them was also your grandmother, who, according to the indications of the chief Zirlikners of the planet Karatas, had been assigned to me as a passive half for the continuance of my line."

CHAPTER XX

The Third Flight of Beelzebub to the Planet Earth

AFTER a brief pause Beelzebub continued to speak further thus . . . He said:

"This time I remained at home, that is, on the planet Mars, only a short while, just long enough to see and talk with the newly arrived, and to give certain directions of a general tribal character.

"Having disposed of the said affairs, I descended again to your planet with the intention of continuing the pursuit of my aim, that is, the uprooting from among these strange three-centered beings, of their horrible custom of doing good as it were, by destroying the existence of beings of other brain-systems than their own.

"On this third descent of mine to the planet Earth our ship *Occasion* landed not on the Sea 'Kolhidious,' which, in contemporary times is there called the Caspian Sea, but on the Sea, called at that period, the 'Sea of Beneficence.'

"We decided to land on this sea, because I proposed to visit this time the capital of the beings of the second group of the continent Ashhark, then named the 'City Gob,' which was situated on the south eastern shore of that sea.

"At that time, the 'City Gob' also was a considerable city, and it was well known over the whole planet as a place that produced the best fabrics and the best as they are called 'precious ornaments.'

"The 'City Gob' was situated on both banks of the mouth of a large river called the 'Keria-chi' which flowed into the Sea of Beneficence and which had its rise in the eastern heights of this country.

"Into this Sea of Beneficence, on its western side, still another large river called the 'Naria-chi' flowed.

"And it was just in the valleys of these two large rivers

that the beings of the second group of the continent Ashhark mainly existed.

"If you wish, my dear boy, I will also tell you a little of the history of the rise of this group of beings of the continent Ashhark," Beelzebub asked Hassein.

"Yes, Grandfather, yes . . . I shall listen to you with great interest and great gratitude," replied his Grandson.

Then Beelzebub began thus:

"A very long time before that period there to which my present tale relates, namely, long before that second great catastrophe to that ill-starred planet, and while the continent Atlantis was still existing and flourishing, a certain one of the ordinary three-centered beings of that continent 'invented,' as my latest detailed investigation and researches cleared up, that the powdered horn of a being of a particular exterior form, then called a 'Pirmaral' was very effective against what they called 'diseases' of every kind; and his 'invention' afterwards was widely spread by various 'freaks' there on your planet, and also there was gradually crystallized in the reason of the ordinary beings there, an ephemeral governing factor, of which factor, I must here say, there is just formed in the whole of the 'presence' of every one of your favorites, especially of the contemporary ones, the Reasonability of what is called their 'waking existence,' and which factor is the chief cause of frequent change in the convictions forming in them.

"Owing just to this factor, crystallized in the presences of the three-brained beings of your planet of that period, it became the rule that anyone, as they say, falling ill of this or that disease, should invariably be given this powdered horn to swallow.

"It is not without interest to remark that 'Pirmarals' breed there at the present time also; but, since contemporary beings look upon them merely as one of the species of being they call collectively 'deer,' they have no special name for them.

"So, my boy, as the beings of the continent Atlantis destroyed very many beings of that form for the sake of these horns, very soon they became extinct.

"A number of the beings of that continent who had by this time already made a profession of such hunting, then went hunting for these beings on other continents and islands.

"This hunting being very difficult, because for the capture of these deer a host of these hunter-beings was required, these professional hunters always took their whole families with them for assistance.

"It happened once that several of these hunter families, having joined together, set off for hunting the 'Pirmaral-beings' to a very remote continent then called 'Iranan' though later, after having been changed, owing to the second catastrophe, it was called 'the continent Ashhark.'

"This was just the continent which you contemporary favorites now call Asia.

"For my further tales concerning these three-brained beings, who please you, it will be very useful for you I think, if I emphasize here that on account of various disturbances during the second terrestrial catastrophe, several parts of the continent 'Iranan' entered within the planet, and there emerged in their place, and attached themselves to it other terra-firma, whereby the continent was considerably changed and became almost the equal in size of the continent Atlantis, before the catastrophe.

"So, my boy, this said group of hunters while once with their families pursuing a herd of these 'Pirmarals,' came unawares upon the shores of the water-space that afterwards was called the Sea of Beneficence.

"Both the sea itself and its rich and fertile shores so greatly delighted this group of hunters that they had no wish to return to the continent Atlantis, but from that time on they remained to exist there.

"That country was indeed so excellent in those days and so 'Sooptaninalnian' for ordinary being-existence, that no being who could think at all could help liking it.

"On that terra-firma part of the surface of your planet, not only at this period did there exist among others, multitudes of the 'two-brained' beings of the said exterior form, namely, 'Pirmaral,' but around this water-space multitudes of various kinds of 'fruit trees' were also formed, whose fruit then still served for your favorites as the principal product of their 'first-being-food.'

"There bred there then, also, so many of the one-brained and two-brained-beings which your favorites call 'birds,' that when they flew in a drove, it became, as your favorites say, 'quite dark.'

"The water-space situated in the middle of that country and then named the Sea of Beneficence, so abounded with fish, that they could almost be taken, as they also say, with bare hands.

"As for the soil both of the shores of the Sea of Beneficence and of the valleys of the two large rivers flowing into it, any part of it could be adapted for growing anything you like.

"In short, both the climate of this country and everything else so delighted the hunters and their families, that not one of them, as I have already said, had any desire to return to the continent Atlantis, and from that time on they remained there, and were soon adapted to everything and existing and multiplying as it is said, 'like a merry-go-round.'

"At this place in my tale I must tell you about an extraordinary coincidence of events, which later had great consequences both for the first beings of this second group and for their remotest descendants.

"It seems, that at the time when the said hunters from the continent Atlantis reached the Sea of Beneficence and decided to settle there for good, there was already existing on the shores of the same sea a being from the continent Atlantis and a very important one for those times, who was a member there of a 'learned society,' the like of which there has never again been on that planet Earth and probably never will be.

"This 'learned society' existed then under the name of 'Akhaldan.'

"And this 'Akhaldan' member had gone there to the shores of the Sea of Beneficence for the following reason: "Just before the second great catastrophe those genuine learned beings then existing on the continent Atlantis who had organized that truly great learned society there, once became aware that something very serious was about to happen in nature, and they set themselves to observe very carefully all the natural phenomena occurring on their continent; but however hard they tried, they could in no way find out what precisely it was that was impending.

"A little later on and with the same object, they sent numbers of their members to other continents and islands, in order, if possible, by means of these common observations, to be able perhaps to learn what awaited them.

"The members who were so sent were to observe not only nature on the planet Earth, but also every kind, as they expressed themselves there, of 'celestial' phenomenon.

"One of their members, namely, the mentioned important being, had chosen as a place for his observations the continent Iranan and having migrated there with his servants, had settled on the shores of just the said water-space later called the Sea of Beneficence.

"It was just this same learned member of the society Akhaldan who once chanced to meet certain of the mentioned hunters on the shores of the said Sea of Beneficence, and having learned that they also had come from the continent Atlantis, he was naturally very glad and began to associate with them.

"And when, shortly afterwards, the continent Atlantis was engulfed in the planet and this learned Akhaldan member had no longer any place to return to, he remained to exist with these hunters in that future 'Maralpleicie.'

"A little later this group of hunters chose this learned being, because of his greater reason, to be their chief, and still later . . . this member of the great society Akhaldan married the daughter of one of the hunters, by name 'Rimala,' and afterwards shared fully in the lives of the founders of the beings of that second group of the continent Iranan, or, as it is called at the present time, 'Asia.'

"A long time passed.

"The beings of this place on the planet Earth were also born and again destroyed; and the general level of the psyche of this group of Earth-beings was also naturally changed thereby, now for the better, now for the worse.

"Multiplying, these beings spread gradually over this country widely and ever more widely, although always preferring just the shores of the Sea of Beneficence and the valleys of the two said large rivers flowing into it.

"Only much later a place of common existence was formed on the south eastern shore of the sea; and this place they called the 'City Gob.' This city just became the chief place of existence for the head of this second group of beings of the continent Ashhark, whom they called a 'king.'

"The duties of this king became hereditary here also; and this inheritance began with the first chosen chief, who was just the said member of the learned society Akhaldan.

"At the time to which the tale I began refers, the king for the beings of that second group was already the grandson of his grandson. His name was 'Konuzion.'

"My latest detailed investigations and researches showed that there had been put into operation by that same King Konuzion exceedingly wise and most beneficent measures for uprooting a 'shocking' evil which had arisen among the beings, who by Fate, had become his subjects. And these said most wise and beneficent measures he had actualized for the following reason.

"This same King Konuzion once constated that the beings of his community were becoming less and less capable of work, and that hitherto unknown crimes, robberies and violence were on the increase among them, and many other such things as had never occurred before, or, if they had occurred, had formerly been quite exceptional.

"These constatations both surprised and at the same time grieved King Konuzion, who after thinking deeply about it, decided to find out the causes of the said sorry state of affairs.

"After long observations he finally cleared up for himself that the cause of the phenomenon lay in a new habit of the beings of his community, namely, their habit of chewing the seeds of a plant then called 'Gulgulian.' This surplanetary formation also arises on the planet Earth at the present time, and those of your favorites who consider themselves 'educated' call it 'Papaveroon,' but the ordinary among them simply call it the 'poppy.'

"Here it must without fail be noticed that the beings of Maralpleicie then developed a passion for chewing the seeds of the mentioned surplanetary formation, and these seeds were necessarily gathered at a certain moment of what is called 'ripeness.'

"In the course of his further close observations and impartial researches the King Konuzion clearly understood that these seeds contained 'something' that could completely change for the time being, all the established habits of the psyche of those beings who introduced it into themselves, with the result that they saw, understood, felt, sensed and acted quite otherwise than they were previously accustomed to see, sense, act and so on.

"For instance, a crow would appear to them to be a peacock; a vessel of water—a sea; a harsh clatter—music; good will they would take for enmity; insults for love; and so on and so forth.

"When King Konuzion became clearly convinced of all this, he immediately dispatched everywhere numbers of those intimate subjected beings devoted to him, strictly to command in his name all beings of his community to cease the chewing of the seeds of the mentioned plant; he also arranged for the punishment and fine of those beings who should disobey this order of his.

"Thanks to these measures of his, the use of the said seeds for chewing showed signs of diminishing in the country of Maralpleicie.

"But it soon afterwards turned out that the number of those who chewed had diminished only apparently; in reality, they were more than before.

"Having understood this, the wise King Konuzion thereupon resolved to punish still more severely those who should continue chewing; and at the same time he strengthened both the surveillance or his subjects and also the strictness of the enforcement of the punishment of the guilty.

"And he himself began going everywhere in the city Gob itself, personally examining the guilty and impressing them by various punishments both physical and moral.

"In spite of it all, however, the desired result was not obtained; the number of those who chewed continued to increase in the city Gob itself; and the returns from other places also in the territories subject to him, correspondingly increased daily.

"It was shown, moreover, that the number of those who chewed had increased still more, because many of the three-brained beings who had never chewed before, then began chewing out of what is called 'curiosity,' which is one of the peculiarities of the psyche of the three-brained beings of that planet that pleases you; curiosity, namely, to try the effects of those seeds whose chewing was forbidden and pushed by the king with such insistence and relentless severity.

"I must emphasize here that though that said particularity of their psyche was crystallized in your favorites immediately after the perishing of the continent Atlantis, yet in none of the beings of former epochs did it function so blatantly as it does now in the contemporary three-brained beings there; they have more of it perhaps, than there are hairs on a 'Toosook.'

"So, my boy . . .

"When the wise King Konuzion became finally quite convinced that by the described measures it was impossible to uproot the passion for chewing the seeds of 'Gulgulian,' and saw that the only result of his measures was the death of several who were punished, he abandoned all the measures he had previously taken and again pondered on the search for some other real means for destroying this evil, lamentable for his community.

"As I learned much later—and I learned it through a very ancient surviving monument—the great King Konuzion then returned to his chamber and for eighteen days neither ate nor drank but only very seriously thought and thought.

"You must notice here, in any case, that those latest researches of mine showed that King Konuzion was then, particularly anxious to find a means of uprooting this evil, also because all the affairs of his community were going from bad to worse.

"The beings who abandoned themselves to this passion almost ceased to work; what is called the money revenue, entirely ceased flowing into the communal treasury; and the ultimate ruin of the community seemed to be inevitable.

"Finally the wise king decided to deal with this evil indirectly, namely, by playing on the weaknesses in the psyche of the beings of his community; and he then first invented for that purpose that which later existed under the denomination 'Religion.' Namely, he invented and formulated a certain what is called 'religious doctrine' adapted to the psyche of the beings then; and this invention of his he spread broadcast among his subjects by every means at his disposal.

"In this first of 'religions doctrines' on the planet Earth, it was said, among other things, that far from our continent Ashhark was a large island where existed our 'Mister God.'

"I must tell you that in those days not one of the ordinary beings was as yet aware that besides their planet Earth still other cosmic concentrations existed.

"The beings of the planet Earth of those days were even certain that the scarcely visible 'white points' far away in space were nothing more than the pattern on the veil of the 'world'; that is to say, just of their planet; since in their notions then the 'whole world' consisted, as I have said, of their planet only.

"They were also convinced that this veil was supported like a canopy on special pillars, whose ends rested on their planet.

"In that ingeniously strange 'religious doctrine' of the wise King Konuzion it was said, that 'Mister God' had intentionally attached to our souls these organs and limbs we now have to protect us against our surroundings, and to enable us efficiently and profitably to serve both himself personally and the 'souls' already taken to that island of His.

"At our death, our soul is liberated from these specially attached organs and limbs and becoming what it should really be, is just then immediately taken to this island of His, where our 'Mister God' according to how our soul has existed with the added parts here, on our continent Ashhark, there assigns to it an appropriate place for its further existence.

"If the soul has honestly and conscientiously fulfilled its duties, 'Mister God' leaves it, for its further existence, on his island; but the soul that here on the continent Ashhark has loafed or has discharged its duties idly and negligently, that has in short, existed only for the gratification of the desires of the parts attached to it, or, finally, that has not kept his commandments—such a soul our 'Mister God' sends for its further existence to a neighboring island of smaller size.

"Here, on the continent Ashhark, exist many 'Spirits' attendant upon Him, who walk among us in 'caps of darkness,' thanks to which they can constantly watch us and either inform our 'Mister God' of all our doings or report them to Him on the day of 'Judgment.'

"We cannot by any means conceal from them, either any of our doings, or any of our thoughts either.

"It was still further said that just like our continent Ashhark, all the other continents and islands of the 'world' were created by our 'Mister God' and now exist as I have said, only to serve Him and the deserving 'souls' already dwelling on His island.

"The continents and islands of the 'world' are all places, as it were, of preparation, and storehouses for everything necessary for this island of His.

"That island on which 'Mister God' Himself and the deserving souls exist is called 'Paradise,' and existence thereon is just 'Roses, Roses.'

"All its rivers are of milk, their banks of honey; nobody needs to work or toil there; everything necessary for a happy, carefree, and blissful existence is there, because everything demanded is supplied there from our own and the other continents and islands of the 'world' in superabundance.

"This island 'Paradise' is full of young and lovely women, collected from all the peoples and races of the world; and each of them belongs for the asking to the 'soul' that fancies her.

"In certain public squares of that superb island mountains of various articles of adornment are always kept, from the most brilliant diamonds to the deepest turquoise; and every 'soul' can take anything he likes, also without the least hindrance.

"In other public squares of that beatific island are piled huge mountains of sweetmeats specially prepared with essence of 'poppy' and 'hemp'; and every soul may take as much as he pleases at any time of the day or night.

"There are no diseases there; and, of course, none of those 'lice' or 'flies' that give us all no peace here, and blight our whole existence.

"The other island, that rather small island, to which our 'Mister God' sends for their further existence the souls whose temporary physical parts have been idle here, have loafed and failed to exist according to His commandments, is called 'Hell.'

"All the rivers of this island are of burning pitch; the whole air stinks like a skunk at bay, swarms of horrible beings blow police whistles in every square; and all the 'furniture,' 'carpets,' 'beds' and so on there present, are made of fine needles with their points sticking out.

"To every soul on this island a single very salted cake is given once a day; and there is not a drop of drinking water there. Still many other things also are there of the kind, that the beings of Earth would not only wish not to encounter, but not even to imagine.

"When I first came to the country of Maralpleicie, all the three-brained beings of that country were followers of the 'religion' based on the just mentioned ingenious 'religious-doctrine,' and this 'religion' was then at its zenith.

"To the inventor himself of this ingenious 'religious-doctrine,' namely, the wise King Konuzion, the sacred 'Rascooarno' had long before occurred, that is to say, he had 'died' already long previously.

"But owing once again to the strangeness of the psyche of your favorites, his invention had naturally taken such deep hold there, that not a single being in the whole country of Maralpleicie then doubted the truth of its peculiar tenets.

"Here also in the City Gob, from the first day of my arrival, I began visiting the 'Kaltaani'—or, as they were now called, 'Chaihana.'

"It must be noticed that although there also, in the country Maralpleicie, the custom of sacrificing was flourishing at that period, it was not on the large scale on which it had flourished in the country Tikliamish.

"There in the City Gob I began deliberately looking for a suitable being, in order to make friends with him, as I had in the city Koorkalai.

"And indeed I soon found such a friend here also, but this time he was not a 'priest' by profession.

"My friend here turned out to be the proprietor of a large 'Chaihana'; and although I became, as it is said there, on very good terms with him, nevertheless I never felt that strange 'tie' with him which my essence had experienced toward the priest Abdil in the city Koorkalai.

"Although I had already existed a whole month in the City Gob, I had neither decided upon nor undertaken anything practical for my aim. I simply wandered about the City Gob, visiting first the various 'Chaihana,' and only later the 'Chaihana' of my new friend there.

"During this time I became familiar with the manners and customs of this second group and also with the niceties of their religion; and in the course of a month I decided to attain my aim here also, through their religion.

"After careful pondering I decided to add something 'to the 'religious-doctrine' existing there, and like the wise King Konuzion, I counted on being able to spread this addition of mine effectively among them.

"Just then I invented as follows: that those spirits with the 'cap of darkness' who, as it was said, in that great religion, observe our deeds and thoughts, to report them later to our 'Mister God,' are none other than just those beings of other forms, which exist among us.

"It is they who watch us and report everything to our 'Mister God.'

"But we people, not only fail to pay them proper honor and respect, but we even destroy their existence, both for our food and as sacrifices.

"I particularly emphasized in my preaching that not only ought we not to destroy the existence of the beings of other forms in honor of 'Mister God,' but that an the contrary, we ought to try to earn their favor and to beseech them not to report to 'Mister God' at least those petty evil acts of ours which we involuntarily do.

"And this addition of mine I began to spread by every possible means, of course, very cautiously.

"At first, I spread this invention of mine through my said new friend there, the proprietor of the 'Chaihana.'

"I must tell you that his 'Chaihana' was almost the largest in the whole City Gob; and it was very famous for a certain reddish liquid of which the beings of the planet Earth are very fond.

"So there were always a great many customers there, and it was open day and night.

"Not only the residents of the city itself went there, but also all the visitors from the whole of Maralpleicie.

"I soon became quite expert in talking with and persuading both single customers and also any company of them present in the 'Chaihana.'

"My new friend himself, the proprietor of the 'Chaihana' was so deeply impressed by my invention, that he didn't know what to do with himself for remorse for his past.

"He was in constant distress and bitterly deplored his previous contemptuous attitude and his treatment of the various beings of other forms.

"Becoming day by day a more enthusiastic preacher of my invention, he thereby helped to spread it not only in his own 'Chaihana,' but he even began of his own accord visiting other 'Chaihana' in the City Gob, in order to spread the truth which had so impressed him.

"He preached in the market places, and several times made special visits to the holy places, of which there then already were many in the outskirts of the City Gob. They also had been established in honor of somebody or in memory of something or other.

"It is very interesting to remark here that the information that serves on the planet Earth for the rise of a holy place is usually due to certain Earth beings called 'Humbugs.'

"This disease of 'Humbugging' also is very widely spread there.

"On the planet Earth, consciously and unconsciously, they lie.

"And they consciously lie there when there is some personal material advantage to be got by lying; and, unconsciously they lie there when they fall ill of the disease called 'hysteria.'

"In addition to the proprietor of the 'Chaihana' there in the City Gob, I was very soon unconsciously assisted by still a number of other beings, who, like the proprietor of the 'Chaihana,' had in the meanwhile become ardent supporters of my invention; and soon, all the beings of that second group of Asiatic beings were spreading this invention of mine and persuading each other of it as an indubitable truth that had been suddenly revealed.

"The result of it all was, that there in that country of Maralpleicie, not only indeed were 'sacrifices' diminished, but they even began giving unprecedentedly good treatment to the beings of other forms.

"Such comic farces very soon began there that though I

was myself the author of the invention, I nevertheless found it very hard not to laugh.

"Such comic farces, for instance, as the following, began: a highly respectable and wealthy merchant of the City Gob would be riding in the morning on his own donkey to his own shop; on the way a motley crowd of beings drag this respectable merchant off his ass and maul him thoroughly because he has dared to ride upon it; whereupon the said crowd, with profound bows, escort the ass on which the merchant had been riding, wherever it chooses to go.

"Or, what is called a 'woodcutter,' with his own oxen, is hauling wood to market from the forest to the town.

"A mob of citizens drag him also off his cart and after mauling him, very tenderly unyoke the oxen and escort them where they wish to go.

"And if the cart should be met in a part of the city where it might hold up the traffic, the mob of citizens itself would drag the cart to the market and leave it there to its fate.

"Thanks to this invention of mine, very soon various quite new customs were created in the City Gob.

"So, for instance, the custom was established there of placing troughs in all the squares and public places and at the cross-roads of the town, where every morning, every resident of the City Gob could throw his choicest morsels of food for dogs and other stray beings of various forms; at 'sunrise,' of throwing into the Sea of Beneficence every kind of food for the beings called 'fishes.'

"But most peculiar of all was the custom of paying attention to the voices of beings of various forms.

"As soon as they heard the voice of a being of any form, they began immediately to praise the names of their gods and to invite their blessing.

"It might be the crowing of a cock or the barking of a dog, or the mewing of a cat, or the squeal of an ape, or so on . . . it always brought them to attention.

"Here it is interesting to notice that for some reason or other they always raised their heads on these occasions and looked upwards, even though, according to the teachings of their religion, their god and his assistants were supposed to exist on the same level with themselves, and not where they directed their eyes and prayers.

"It was extremely interesting at these moments to watch their faces."

"Pardon me, Your Right Reverence," at that moment interrupted Beelzebub's old devoted servant Ahoon who had also been listening with great interest to his tales.

"Do you remember, Your Right Reverence, how many times, we ourselves, in that same City Gob had to flop down on its streets during the cries of beings of different forms?"

To this remark Beelzebub said:

"Certainly I remember, dear Ahoon.

"How could I forget such comic impressions.

"You must know," he then continued, turning to Hassein again, "that the beings of the planet Earth are inconceivably prone and touchy, and if someone does not share their views or agree to do as they do, or criticizes their manifestations, they are, Oh—very, very indignant and offended.

"If one of them had the power, he would order whoever had dared not to do as he does, or who criticized his conduct, to be immured in the sort of room which is usually infested by innumerable what are called 'rats' and 'lice.'

"And sometimes if he happened to be stronger, and a superior power-holding being with whom he is not on very good terms is not watching him, he will simply maul the offender, as the Russian Sidor once mauled his favorite goat.

"Knowing thoroughly this aspect also of their strange psyche, I had no desire to offend them and to incur their wrath; furthermore, I was always profoundly aware that to outrage anybody's religious feeling is contrary to every morality. When existing among them, therefore, I always tried to do as they did, in order to avoid attracting their attention.

"Here it does no harm to notice that on account of the prevailing abnormal conditions of ordinary existence there, just those beings only indeed among your favorites, the three-brained beings of that strange planet Earth, and especially during recent centuries, become notorious and consequently honored by the rest, who manifest themselves, not as the majority of them do, but somehow or other, more absurdly; and the more absurd their manifestations and the more stupid, mean, and insolent the tricks they perform, the more notorious and famous such beings become, and the greater the number of the beings on the given continent and even on other continents who know them personally or at least by name.

"On the other hand, no honest being, without ridiculous manifestations, will ever become famous among other beings or even barely noticed, however good natured and sensible he may be in himself.

"So, my boy, that about which our Ahoon so mischievously reminded me concerned just that custom, established there in the City Gob, of attaching significance to the voices of beings of various forms and particularly to the voice of what are called 'donkeys,' of which, for some reason or other, there were a great many in the City Gob.

"The beings of all other forms of that planet also manifest themselves by voice, but at a definite time. For instance, the cock cries at midnight, an ape in the morning when it is hungry, and so on, but donkeys there bray whenever it enters their heads, in consequence you may hear the voice of that silly being there at any time of the day or night.

"So, my boy, it was established there in the City Gob that as soon as the sound of the voice of the donkey brayed out, all who heard it had at once to flop down and offer up prayers to their god and to the idols they revered; and these donkeys, I may say, usually have a very loud voice by nature, and their voices carry a long way.

"So, as we walked along the streets of the City Gob and saw the citizens flopping down at the bray of every donkey, we had to flop down too, in order not to be distinguished from the rest; and it was just this comic custom, I see now, that gave our old Ahoon so much relish.

"You noticed, dear Hassein, with what wicked satisfaction our old man, after so many centuries . . . reminded me of that comic situation of mine then?"

Having said this, Beelzebub, smiling, went on with the tale he had begun.

"It is needless to say that there also, in this second culture-center of the three-brained beings of your planet, breeding there on the continent of Ashhark, the destruction of beings of other forms in sacrifice entirely ceased; and, if isolated instances occurred, the beings of that group themselves settled accounts with the offenders without compunction.

"Having thus become convinced that there also, among that second group of beings of the continent Ashhark, I had succeeded so easily in uprooting, for a long time, the custom of 'sacrifices,' I decided to leave; but I had it in mind, in any event, to pay a visit to the nearest large centers also where the beings of the same second group were breeding; and I chose for this purpose the region of the course of the river 'Naria-chi.'

"Soon after this decision, I sailed with Ahoon to the mouth of this river, having become persuaded that there had already passed from the beings of the City Gob to the beings of this group populating these large centers the same new customs and the same notions concerning sacrifices by the destruction of the existence of other beings.

"We arrived at length at a small town called 'Arguenia,' which in those days was considered the most remote town of the country Maralpleicie.

"Here also there existed a fair number of beings of this second Asiatic group; they were engaged in mining what is called 'turquoise' from Nature.

"There in the small town of 'Arguenia' I began, as usual, visiting their various 'Chaihana,' continuing there also my usual procedure.

CHAPTER XXI

The First Visit of Beelzebub to India

BEELZEBUB continued to speak as follows:

"Sitting in a 'Chaihana' in this small town of 'Arguenia,' I once over heard a conversation among several beings seated not far from me.

"They were talking and deciding when and how they should go by caravan to 'Pearl-Land.'

"Having listened to their conversation, I gathered that they intended to go there for the purpose of exchanging their 'turquoises' for what are called 'pearls.'

"I must here, by the way, draw your attention also to the fact that your favorites of former as well as of contemporary epochs liked and still like to wear 'pearls' and also the said 'turquoise,' as well as many other what are called 'precious-trinkets' for the purpose, as they say, of 'adorning' their exteriors. But if you would like to know my opinion, they do so of course, instinctively, in order, if only by this, to offset, so to say, the 'value-of-their-inner-insignificance.'

"At that period to which my present tale refers, the said 'pearls' were a great rarity among the beings of the second Asiatic group and commanded a high price among them. But in the country 'Pearl-Land' there was at the same time a great number of these pearls, and there, on the contrary, they were very cheap, because pearls at that time were exclusively obtained only from the water spaces surrounding that country.

"The mentioned conversation of the beings sitting near me in the 'Chaihana' in the small town 'Arguenia' then at once interested me because at that time I had already had the intention of going to that same 'Pearl-Land' where the three-brained beings of the continent Ashhark of the third group bred.

"And the conversation I then heard at once evoked in my

mentation an association to the effect that it might be better to go to the country 'Pearl-Land' directly from here with this large caravan of these beings, rather than return by the way we had come to the 'Sea of Beneficence,' and from there, by means of the same ship '*Occasion*,' to reach this country.

"Although this journey which in those days was almost impossible for the beings of the Earth would take us a good deal of time, yet I thought that the journey back to the 'Sea of Beneficence' with its unforeseeable contingencies, would perhaps not take much less time.

"This association then arose in my mentation chiefly because I had long before heard a great deal about the rare peculiarities of those parts of the nature of that peculiar planet through which the proposed route of the caravan lay, and in consequence, what is called a 'being-love-of-knowledge' already formed in me, having received a shock for functioning, from all that had been overheard, immediately dictated to my common presence the need to be persuaded of everything personally, directly through my own perceptive organs.

"So, my boy, owing to what I have said, I purposely sat with the conversing beings and joined in their deliberations.

"As a result of it all, we also were then included in the company of their caravan, and two days later we set off together with them.

"I and Ahoon then passed through indeed very unusual places, unusual even for the general nature of this peculiar planet, certain parts of which, by the way, only became so because before that period, this ill-fated planet had already undergone two, what are called 'Transapalnian-perturbations,' almost unprecedented in the Universe.

"From the first day we had to pass exclusively through a region of various 'terra-firma-projections' of unusual forms, which had conglomerations of all kinds of 'intraplanetary-minerals.'

"And only after a month's travel, according to their time-calculation, did our caravan from Arguenia come to places in whose soil the possibility had not yet been quite destroyed, of Nature's forming surplanetary formations and creating corresponding conditions for the arising and existing of various one-brained and two-brained beings.

"After difficulties of every kind we at last, one rainy morning, on ascending a height, suddenly saw on the horizon the outline of a large water-space bordering the edges of the continent Ashhark, which just then was called 'Pearl-Land.'

"And in four days more we came to the chief place of the existence of the beings of that third group, then the city 'Kaimon.'

"Having arranged there the place of our permanent existence, we did nothing else during our first days there but stroll about the streets of the town, observing the specific manifestations of the beings of that third group in the process of their ordinary existence.

"It cannot be helped, my dear Hassein—having told you the history of the arising of the second group of three-brained beings of the continent Ashhark, I must already tell you also the history of the arising of the third group.

"You must indeed tell me, my dear and beloved Grandfather," exclaimed Hassein eagerly; and this time with great reverence, extending his hands upwards, he sincerely said:

"May my dear and kind Grandfather be worthy to be perfected to the degree of the sacred 'Anklad'!"

Without saying anything to this, Beelzebub only smiled and continued to relate as follows:

"The history of the arising of this third group of Asiatic beings begins only a little later than that period when the families of hunters for Pirmarals first came to the shores of the 'Sea-of-Beneficence' from the continent Atlantis and, having settled there, founded the second group of Asiatic beings.

"It was just in those, for your contemporary favorites, infinitely remote days, that is, not long before the second 'Transapalnian-perturbation' occurred to this ill-fated planet, that there had already begun to be crystallized in the presences of the three-centered beings then of the continent Atlantis certain consequences of the properties of the organ Kundabuffer, on account of which the need—among other needs unbecoming to three-brained beings—began to arise in them to wear, as I have already told you, various trinkets as it were for their adornment, and also a kind of famous what is called 'Talisman' which they had invented.

"One of these trinkets, then on the continent Atlantis, just as now on the other continents of the planet Earth, was and is this same 'pearl.'

"The said pearl is formed in one-brained beings which breed in the 'Saliakooriap' also of your planet Earth, that is to say, in that part of it which is called 'Hentralispana,' or, as your favorites might express it, the blood of the planet which is present in the common presence of every planet and which serves the actualizing of the process of the Most Great Common Cosmic Trogoautoegocrat; and this part, there on your planet, is called 'water.'

"This one-brained being in which the said 'pearl' is formed, used to breed in the 'Saliakooriapnian,' or water-areas surrounding the continent Atlantis; but in consequence of the great demand for the said pearl and therefore of the great destruction of these one-brained 'pearl-bearing' beings, there were soon none left near this continent. Thereupon, when those beings there who made the aim and sense of their existence the destruction of these 'pearl-bearing' beings; that is to say, who destroyed their existence only in order to procure that part of their common presence called 'pearl' merely for the gratification of their quite absurd egoism, found no more of these said 'pearl-bearing' beings in the water area nearest to the continent Atlantis, they, that is these 'professionals,' then began to look for them in other water-areas and gradually moved further and further away from their own continent.

"Once during these searches of theirs, their rafts, because of what are called 'Saliakooriapnian displacements,' or as they say, prolonged 'storms,' came unexpectedly upon a place where there proved to be a great number of these pearl-bearing beings; and the place itself was extremely convenient for their destruction.

"These water-areas to which the destroyers of the pearl-bearing beings then chanced to come and where these beings bred in large numbered, were just those water-areas which surround the place then called Pearl-Land and now called 'Hindustan' or 'India.'

"For the first days the mentioned terrestrial professionals of that time who had chanced to arrive there did nothing but gratify to the full their inclinations, which had already become inherent to their presences in respect of the destruction of these one-brained beings of their planet; and it was only later, after they had also by chance found out that almost everything required for ordinary existence arose in abundance on the neighboring terra-firma, that they decided never to return to Atlantis but to settle there for their permanent existence.

"A few of these destroyers of pearl-bearing beings then sailed to the continent Atlantis, and having exchanged their pearls for various articles which were still lacking in the new place, they returned, taking with them their own families as well as the families of those who had remained.

"Later several of these first settlers of this—for the beings then at that time—'new' country, visited their native land from time to time for the purpose of exchanging 'pearls' for articles required by them there; and each time they took back with them a further number of beings, either their relatives or their kinsmen or just laborers indispensable to their big work.

"So, my boy, from that time on, that part also of the surface of the planet Earth became known to all the three-brained beings there under the name of 'Land-of-Beneficence.'

"In this way, before the second great catastrophe to the planet Earth, many beings of the continent Atlantis already existed on this part of the continent Ashhark also, and when that second catastrophe occurred to your planet, then many of the beings who chanced to be saved from the continent Atlantis, chiefly those who already had relatives and kinsmen in that Pearl-Land, also gradually collected there.

"Owing as always to their 'fecundity' they gradually multiplied there and began to populate this part also of the terra-firma surface of their planet, more and more.

"At first they populated there in Pearl-Land only two definite regions, namely, the regions around the mouths of the two large rivers which flowed from the interior of Pearl-Land into the large water-space, just in those places near which many of the mentioned pearl-bearing beings bred.

"But when the population there was greatly increased, they began populating also the interior of that part of the continent Ashhark; but nevertheless their favorite regions continued to be the valleys of the two mentioned rivers.

"Well then, my boy, when I first arrived in Pearl-Land, I decided to attain my aim there also by means of the 'Havatvernoni' existing there, that is, through their 'Religion.'

"But it turned out that amongst the beings of this third group of the continent Ashhark, there were at that time several peculiar 'Havatvernonis' or 'Religions' all based on different, quite independent, what are called 'religious-teachings,' having nothing in common with each other.

"In view of this, I first began seriously studying these 'religious-teachings' existing there, and having in the course of my studies constated that one of them—founded on the teaching of a genuine Messenger of OUR COMMON END-

LESS CREATOR, afterwards called Saint Buddha—had the most followers, I, on becoming acquainted with it, devoted most of my attention to its study.

"Before continuing to tell you merely about the three-brained beings breeding just on that part of the surface of the planet Earth, it is, I think, necessary to remark, even if briefly, that there existed and still exist, ever since the time when the custom of having peculiar being 'Havatvernoni' or 'Religions' began to arise and exist among your favorites, two basic kinds of 'religious teachings.'

"One kind was invented by those three-brained beings there themselves, in whom for some reason or other, there arises the functioning of a psyche proper to Hasnamusses; and the other kind of religious teaching is founded there upon those detailed instructions which have been preached, as it were, by genuine Messengers from Above, who indeed are from time to time sent by certain nearest helpers from our COMMON FATHER, for the purpose of aiding the three-brained beings of your planet in destroying in their presences the crystallized consequences of the properties of the organ Kundabuffer.

"The religion whose followers were then the majority of the beings of the country Pearl-Land and to become acquainted with which I then devoted my attention and about which I find it necessary to tell you a little, arose there in the following way:

"As I later learned, with the multiplication of the three-brained beings of that third group, many beings among them with the properties of Hasnamusses were formed into responsible beings; and when these latter began spreading more than usually maleficent ideas among the beings of that group, there was crystallized in the presences of the majority of three-centered beings of that third group, that special psychic property, which, in its totality, already engendered a factor very hindering to the normal 'exchange-of-substances' actualized by the 'Most Great Common Cosmic Trogoautoegocrat.' Well then, as soon as this lamentable result, also issuing from this planet, was noticed by certain most most Sacred Individuals, it was sanctioned that a corresponding Sacred Individual should be sent there, specially to that group of beings, for the more or less tolerable regulation of their being-existence in accordance with the existence of the whole of that solar system.

"It was just then that the aforementioned Sacred Individual was sent to them who, having been coated with the planetary body of a terrestrial being, was called, as I have said, 'Saint Buddha.'

"The coating of the said Sacred Individual with a planetary body of a terrestrial three-brained being was actualized there several centuries before my first visit to the country 'Pearl-Land.'"

At this point in Beelzebub's tales, Hassein turned to him and said:

"My dear Grandfather, during your tales you have already many times used the expression 'Hasnamuss.' I have until now understood only from the intonation of your voice and from the consonance of this word itself, that by this expression you defined those three-brained beings whom you always set apart from others as if they deserved 'objective-contempt.'

"Be so kind as always and explain to me the real meaning and exact sense of this word."

Whereupon Beelzebub, with a smile inherent to him, said as follows:

"Concerning the 'typicality' of the three-brained beings for whom I have adopted this verbal definition, I will explain it to you at the proper time, but meanwhile know that this word designates every already 'definitized' common presence of a three-brained being, both those consisting only of the single planetary body as well as those whose higher being-bodies are already coated in them, and in which for some reason or other, data have not been crystallized for the Divine impulse of 'Objective-Conscience.'"

Having said only this in defining the word Hasnamuss, Beelzebub continued to speak:

"During my detailed studies of the mentioned religious teaching I also clarified that after this Sacred Individual had become finally coated with the presence of a three-brained being there and had seriously pondered how to fulfill the task that had been laid upon him from Above, he decided to attain this by means of the enlightenment of their Reason.

"Here it must without fail be noticed that by that time there had already been crystallized in the presence of Saint Buddha, as the same detailed researches of mine made clear, a very clear understanding that in the process of its abnormal formation, the Reason of the three-centered beings the planet Earth results in a Reason called 'instincto-terebelnian,' that is, a Reason which functions only from corresponding shocks from without; yet in spite of this, Saint Buddha decided to carry out his task by means of this peculiar Reason of theirs, that is, this Reason peculiar to the three-centered beings there; and therefore, he first of all began informing their peculiar Reason with objective truths of every kind.

"Saint Buddha first assembled many of the chiefs of that group and told them the following:

"'Beings possessing presences similar to that of the ALL CREATOR himself:

"'By certain all-enlightened and all-justly guiding most most sacred final results of the actualization of everything existing in the Universe, my essence has been sent to you to serve as a helping factor in the striving of each of you to free yourselves from the consequences of those abnormal being-properties which, in view of highly important common cosmic needs, were implanted in the presences of your ancestors, and, passing by heredity from generation to generation, have reached you also'!

"Saint Buddha spoke again about this a little more in detail but only to certain beings there initiated by him.

"This second time, as it turned out, he then expressed himself in the following words:

"'Beings with presences for actualizing the hope of our COMMON FATHER.

"'Almost at the beginning of the rise of your race, there occurred in the process of the normal existence of the whole of our solar system, an unforeseen accident which portended serious consequences for everything existing.

"'For the regulation of that common universal mishap there was then required, among other measures, according to the explanations of certain Most High, Most Most Sacred Individuals, a certain change in the functioning of the common presences of your ancestors, namely, there was implanted into their presences a certain organ with special properties, owing to which everything external was perceived by their whole presence, transformed for their own coating, and afterwards manifested, not in accordance with reality.

"'A little later, when the normal existence of your solar system was stabilized and the necessity for certain intentionally created abnormal actualizations had passed, our MOST ALL-GRACIOUS COMMON FATHER did not fail to give the command immediately to annul certain artificial measures among which was the removal from the common presences of your ancestors of the now already superfluous organ Kundabuffer with all its special artificial properties, and this command was immediately executed by corresponding Sacred Individuals, who superintend such cosmic actualizations.

"'After a considerable time had passed, it was suddenly brought to light that although all the properties of the said organ had indeed been removed from the presences of your ancestors by the mentioned Most Sacred Individuals, yet nevertheless, a certain lawfully flowing cosmic result, existing under the name of 'predisposition,' and arising in every more or less independent cosmic presence owing to the repeated action in it of any function, had not been foreseen and destroyed in their presences.

"'And so, it turned out that owing to this 'predisposition' which began to pass by heredity to the succeeding generations, the consequences of many of the properties of the organ Kundabuffer began gradually to be crystallized in their presences.

"'No sooner was this lamentable fact which proceeded in the presences of the three-brained beings breeding on this planet Earth first made clear, than, by the All-Gracious sanction of our COMMON FATHER, a suitable Sacred Individual was immediately sent here, so that, being coated with a presence like your own and having become perfected by Objective Reason under the conditions already established here, he might better explain and show you the way of out-rooting from your presences the already crystallized consequences of the properties of the organ Kundabuffer as well as your inherited predispositions to new crystallizations.

"'During the period when the said Sacred Individual, coated with a presence like your own and who had already attained to the age of a responsible three-centered being similar to yourselves, directly guided the ordinary process of the being-existence of your ancestors, many of them did indeed completely free themselves from the consequences of the properties of the organ Kundabuffer, and either thereby acquired 'Being' personally for themselves or became normal sources for the arising of normal presences of succeeding beings similar to themselves.

"'But in consequence of the fact that before the period of the said Sacred Individual's appearance here, the duration of your existence had, owing to very many firmly fixed abnormal conditions of ordinary existence created by yourselves, already become abnormally short, and therefore the process of the 'Sacred Rascooarno' had also very soon to occur to this Sacred Individual, that is to say, he also had, like you, to die prematurely, then after his death, the former conditions were gradually reestablished there owing on the one hand to the established abnormal conditions of ordinary being-existence and, on the other hand, to that maleficent particularity in your psyche, called 'Wiseacring.'

"'Owing to this said particularity in your psyche, the beings here already of the second generation after the contemporaries of the mentioned Sacred Individual who had been sent from Above, began gradually to change everything he had explained and indicated, and the whole of it was finally completely destroyed.

"'Again and again the same was actualized by the Most Most High Common Cosmic Final Results, and each time the same sterile results were obtained.

"'In this present period of the flow of time, when the abnormal being-existence of the three-brained beings of your planet, particularly of the beings arising and existing on that part of the surface of the Earth which is called Pearl-Land, is already beginning seriously to hinder the normal harmonious existence of the whole of this solar system, my essence is manifested among you from Above, in order that here on the spot, it may, together with your own essences, find ways and means under the conditions already fixed here of freeing your presences from the said consequences now present in them, owing to the absence of foresight on the part of certain Most Saintly Final Cosmic Results.

"'After having said all this, Saint Buddha thereafter, just by means of talks with them, first cleared up for himself and afterwards explained to them how the process of their existence must be conducted and the order in which their positive part should consciously guide the manifestations of their unconscious parts, so that the crystallized consequences of the properties of the organ Kundabuffer and also the inherited predisposition to them might gradually disappear from their common presences.

"As the same detailed researches of mine made clear to me—at that period when the inner psyche of the beings of that part of the surface of the Earth was guided by this genuine Messenger from Above, Saint Buddha, the said, for them very maleficent, consequences indeed again began gradually to disappear from the presences of many of them.

"But to the grief of every Individual with Pure Reason of any gradation whatsoever and to the misfortune of the three-brained beings of all succeeding generations who arise on that planet, the first succeeding generation of the contemporaries of this genuine Messenger from Above, Saint Buddha, already also began, owing once again to that same particularity of their psyche, namely, of wiseacring, which until now is one of the chief results of the conditions of the ordinary being-existence abnormally established there—to wiseacre with all His indications and counsels, and this time to 'superwiseacre' so thoroughly that there reached the beings of the third and fourth generations no more than what our Honorable Mullah Nassr Eddin defines by the words:

"'Only-information-about-its-specific-smell.'

"Little by little they so changed these indications and counsels of His that if their Saintly Author himself should chance to appear there and for some reason or other should wish to make himself acquainted with them, he would not be able even to suspect that these indications and counsels were made by him himself.

"Here I cannot refrain from expressing essence-grief at that strange practice of these favorites of yours there, which in the course of many of their centuries during the process of their ordinary existence has gradually become, as it were, conformable to law.

"And in the given case also the same established and already fixed peculiar practice there served for the modification of all the true indications and exact counsels of Saint Buddha and for the creation thereby of yet another factor for a still greater dilution of their psyche.

"This already long established practice there consists in this, that a small, sometimes an almost trifling, cause, is enough to bring about a change for the worse or even the complete destruction of any and every objectively good outer and inner previously established what is called, 'tempo-of-ordinary-existence.'

"Because, my boy, the clarification of certain details of the arising of such a trivial cause, which served in this instance as a basis for the distortion of all the true explanations and exact indications also of this genuine Messenger from Above, Saint Buddha, may provide you with excellent material for a better sensing and understanding of the strangeness of the psyche of these three-brained beings who have taken your fancy, I shall tell you about this in as great detail as possible and shall explain to you just in what sequence the said practice then arose there which led to the following sad misunderstanding which began to exist there and which is still manifested particularly clearly.

"I must inform you first of the two following facts:

"The first is this: that I cleared up this misunderstanding much later than the period to which my present tale refers; among other things I made it clear to myself only during the period of my sixth descent there, when in connection with a question concerning the Saint Ashiata Shiemash, about whom also I shall soon tell you in detail, it became necessary for me to find out about the activities of that genuine Messenger from Above, Saint Buddha.

"And the second fact is this; that unfortunately the basis of the lamentable misunderstanding was certain authentic words contained in one of the explanations of Saint Buddha himself.

"It turned out, indeed, that Saint Buddha himself had in the course of his explanations to some of his closest initiates, initiated by himself, very definitely expressed himself concerning the means of the possible destruction in their nature of the mentioned consequences of the properties of the organ Kundabuffer transmitted to them by heredity.

"He then, among other things, told them very definitely the following:

"'One of the best means of rendering ineffective the predisposition present in your nature for the crystallization of the consequences of the properties of the organ Kundabuffer is "intentional suffering"; and the greatest "intentional suffering" can be obtained in your presences if you compel yourself to be able to endure the "displeasing manifestations of others towards yourself"!'"

"This explanation of Saint Buddha together with other definite indications of his was spread by his nearest initiates among the ordinary beings there; and after the process of the sacred 'Rascooarno' had occurred to him, it also began to pass from generation to generation.

"So, my boy, when, as I have already told you, those three-centered beings there among the second and third generations of the contemporaries of Saint Buddha in whose psyche, already from the time of the loss of Atlantis, there had been fixed that peculiarity called the 'organic-psychic-need-to-wiseacre' began—unfortunately, for the ordinary three-centered beings of that period and unfortunately also for the beings of all succeeding generations and even for those of the present time—to 'wiseacre' and 'superwiseacre' concerning these counsels of Saint Buddha, then as a result a very definite action became fixed and also began to pass from generation to generation, that this same 'endurance' should without fail be produced in complete solitude.

"Here that strangeness of the psyche of your favorites then manifested itself just as it now manifests itself, in this, that they did not consider and do not consider the obvious fact—obvious, that is, to every more or less sane Reason—that the divine Teacher, Saint Buddha, in advising them to employ that kind of 'endurance' while existing among other beings similar to themselves, in order that by frequently producing in their presences this sacred being-actualization towards the manifestations displeasing to them of other beings similar to themselves, there might thereby be evoked in them what are called those 'Trentroodianos' or, as they themselves would say, those 'psychic-chemical-results,' which, in general, in the presence of every three-centered being form those sacred being-data, which actualize in the common presences of the three-centered beings, one of the three holy forces of the sacred 'being-Triamazikamno'; and this holy force in beings always becomes affirming towards all the denying properties already present in them.

"So, my boy, from that time when the mentioned definite notion had begun to exist, your favorites began leaving those already established conditions of being-existence on account of which the predisposition to the crystallization of the consequences of the properties of the organ Kundabuffer became intense in their presences, and in which conditions, as the Divine Teacher Buddha supposed, the said 'endurance towards others' manifestations displeasing to oneself,' could alone crystallize in their common presences that 'Partkdolgduty' which in general is necessary for all three-centered beings.

"So, for the purpose of this famous 'suffering' of theirs, many of the three-centered beings of that planet of yours, either singly or in groups, that is to say, with others who thought as they did, began from then on to go away from amongst beings similar to themselves.

"They even organized special colonies for this purpose, where although existing together, they nevertheless arranged everything so as to produce this 'endurance' of theirs in solitude.

"It was just then that their famous what are called 'monasteries' came into existence, which exist down to the present time and in which, as it were, certain of your contemporary favorites, as they say, 'save their souls.'

"When I first visited that 'Pearl-Land,' most of the three-brained beings there, as I have already said, were followers of that same religion which was based, as it were, on the exact counsels and indications of Saint Buddha himself, and the faith of everyone of these beings in this religion was unshakably firm.

"At the outset of my investigations into the doctrinal subtleties of that religion there, I had as yet come to no definite decision how exactly to utilize it to attain my aim; but when in the course of my investigations I clarified one very definite comprehending—proper to all the followers of that religion—which arose there again owing to a misunderstanding, from the words that had indeed been spoken by Saint Buddha himself, I then at once decided how just to act there through this peculiar 'Havatvernoni' or 'Religion' of theirs.

"It transpired that in his explanations to them about cosmic truths, Saint Buddha had, among other things, told them also that in general the three-centered beings existing on various planets of our Great Universe—and of course the three-centered beings of the Earth also—were in result nothing else but part of that Most Great Greatness which is the All-embracing of all that exists; and that the foundation of this Most Great Greatness is there Above, for the convenience of the embracing of the essence of everything existing.

"This Most Great Foundation of the All-embracing of everything that exists, constantly emanates throughout the whole of the Universe and coats itself from its particles upon planets—in certain three-centered beings who attain in their common presence the capacity to have their own functioning of both fundamental cosmic laws of the sacred Heptaparaparshinokh and the sacred Triamazikamno—into a definite unit, in which alone Objective Divine Reason acquires the possibility of becoming concentrated and fixed.

"And this had been foreseen and created in this manner by our COMMON CREATOR in order that when these certain parts of the Great All-embracing, already spiritualized by Divine Reason, return and reblend with the great Prime Source of the All-embracing, they should compose that whole which our COMMON ENDLESS UNI-BEING has the hope may just actualize the sense and the striving of all that exists in the whole of the Universe.

"Further it seems Saint Buddha had also told them:

"'You, three-centered beings of the planet Earth, having the possibility of acquiring in yourselves both chief fundamental, universal sacred laws, have the full possibility also of coating yourselves with this most sacred part of the Great All-embracing of everything existing and of perfecting it by the required Divine Reason.'

"'And this Great All-embracing of all that is embraced, is called 'Holy Prana.'"

"This quite definite explanation of Saint Buddha was well understood by his contemporaries and many of them began, as I have already said, to strive with eagerness, first to absorb and to coat in their presences the particle of this Most Great Greatness and afterwards to 'make inherent' to it, Divine Objective Reason.

"But when the second and third generations of the contemporaries of Saint Buddha began 'wiseacring' with his explanations of cosmic truths, they just wiseacred with their peculiar 'Reason' and fixed—for its transmission—a very definite notion to the effect, that that same 'Mister Prana' already begins to be in them immediately upon their arising.

"Thanks to this misunderstanding, the beings of that period and of all subsequent generations, including the contemporary, have imagined and still imagine, that without any being-Partkdolgduty they are already parts of that Most Great Greatness, which Saint Buddha himself had personally very definitely explained.

"So, my boy, as soon as I had made this misunderstanding clear to myself and had clearly constated that the beings of that country Pearl-Land were all, without exception, convinced that they were already particles of 'Mister Prana' himself, I then at once decided to use this misunderstanding, and there also to attain my aim through that religion of theirs.

"Before saying more about this, it must without fail be noticed that, concerning these same explanations of Saint Buddha's, namely, that he, as it were, had said that beings already have in themselves a particle of the Most Great Greatness at their very arising, my personal detailed investigations quite clearly showed me that he never could possibly have said just that.

"And he could not have said it because, as the same detailed investigations of mine have cleared up to me, that when Saint Buddha once happened to be among his devoted disciples in the locality 'Senkoo-ori,' he definitely said:

"'If this most sacred Prana is crystallized in you, consciously or unconsciously on the part of your "I," you must without fail bring the perfecting of the individual Reason of the totality of its most holy atoms to the required gradations; otherwise this most holy coating will, changing various exterior coatings, suffer and languish eternally.'

"Here it is interesting to notice that concerning this they

were warned by still another Saint-Individual, also a genuine Messenger from Above, namely, the Saint Kirmininasha.

"And this Saint and genuine Messenger gave this warning to them in the following words:

"'Blessed is he that hath a soul; blessed also is he that hath none; but grief and sorrow are to him that hath in himself its conception.'

"So, my boy, when I made this clear to myself there in Pearl-Land, I at once decided to use this error of theirs for the accomplishment of my aim.

"There in Pearl-Land also just as in the city Gob, I first 'invented' a detailed addition to the mentioned religious teaching, and afterwards by every possible means I began spreading this invention of mine.

"I began to spread there in Pearl-Land that that 'Most-Sacred-Prana,' about which our Divine Teacher Saint Buddha had explained, is already present not only in people, but in all the other beings that arise and exist on our planet Earth.

"A particle of that fundamental Most Great Great All-embracing, namely, the 'Most-Sacred-Prana,' has already from the very beginning settled in every form of being of every scale, breeding both on the surface of the planet itself and within it, and in the water as well as in the atmosphere.

"I regret to have to say here, my boy, that I was then constrained more than once to emphasize that these words had been uttered by the very lips of Saint Buddha himself.

"These several beings there with whom I had meanwhile established 'friendly' relations and whom without any discussion I first of all persuaded there of that invention, immediately not only completely believed it, but afterwards also very effectually helped me, of course unconsciously, in spreading this new invention of mine.

"Here also these friends of mine always and everywhere very zealously and passionately proved to other beings like themselves, that this was just so and could not possibly be otherwise.

"In short, there in Pearl-Land, owing to this second invention of mine, the desired results were unexpectedly rapidly brought about.

"And there in Pearl-Land, owing simply to my invention, your favorites so greatly changed their essence relations towards the beings of other forms, that they not only ceased to destroy the existence of these beings for their famous 'sacrifices,' but even began very sincerely with the whole of their Being to regard these beings of other forms as beings like themselves.

"If only it had all continued like that, it would have been good; but here as well, just as in the country Maralpleicie, they soon began, as is proper to them, to 'wiseacre' and to manifest all kinds of comical aspects of their 'Havatvernoni.'

"For instance, only a quarter of their year after the commencement of my preaching, strolling down the street of the city Kaimon you could see, almost at every step, beings there walking on what are called 'stilts.'

"And they walked on 'stilts' in order not to risk crushing some insect or other, a 'little being,' as they thought, just like themselves.

"Many of them were afraid to drink water that had not been freshly taken from a spring or stream, because they thought that if the water had been a long time out of the spring or stream, 'little-beings' might have got into it, and without seeing them, they might suddenly swallow these 'poor-little-creatures-like-themselves.'

"Many of them took the precaution to wear what are called 'veils,' lest poor little beings like themselves, found in the air, might chance to enter their mouths or noses, and so on and so forth.

"From that time on there began to arise there in Pearl-

Land, both in the city Kaimon and in its outskirts, various societies whose aim was to protect 'defenseless' beings of various form, both those existing among them and those they called 'wild.'

"Rules existed in all such societies prohibiting not only their destruction for 'sacrifices' but also the use of their planetary bodies for the 'first-being-food.'

"Eh-h-h-h-h-h-kh! . . . my boy.

"Owing once again merely to the strangeness of their psyche, the intentional sufferings and conscious labors of this Sacred Individual Saint Buddha, who had been specially actualized for them with a planetary presence similar to theirs, have hovered ever since and still hover in vain; nor have they yet actualized any lawfully expected real results whatsoever, but have engendered and until now continue to engender only all kinds of 'pseudo-teachings' there, like those existing there in recent times under the names of 'Occultism,' 'Theosophy,' 'Spiritualism,' 'Psychoanalysis,' and so on, which, before as now, are means only for the obscuring of their already, without this, obscured psyche.

"It is needless to say that from the truths indicated by Saint Buddha himself, absolutely nothing has survived and reached the beings of the present time.

"Half of one of the words, however, managed to reach even the contemporary beings of that unparalleled planet.

"And this half of a word reached them in the following way:

"Saint Buddha among other things explained to the beings of Pearl Land, how and to what part of the body of their ancestors the said famous organ Kundabuffer had been attached.

"He told them that the Archangel Looisos had by a special means made this organ grow in their ancestors at the extremity of that brain which in them, just as in you, Nature has placed along their back in what is called the 'spinal-column.'

"Saint Buddha, as I also made clear, then also said that though the properties of this organ had been absolutely destroyed in their ancestors, yet the material formation of this organ had remained at the lower extremities of this brain. And this material formation, being transmitted from generation to generation, had also reached them

"'This material formation,' he said, 'now has no significance whatever in you, and it can be completely destroyed in the course of time, if your being-existence proceeds as is becoming to three-centered beings.'

"It was just when they began 'wiseacring' and inventing various forms of that famous 'suffering' of theirs that they also played then usual 'tricks' with this word.

"Namely, first of all, as the root of the second half of this word chanced to coincide with a word in the language of that time which meant 'Reflection' and as they had also invented a means for destroying this material formation rapidly, and not merely in the course of time as Saint Buddha had told them, they also wiseacred about this word according to the following rumination of their bobtailed Reason. Of course, when this organ is in action, it ought to have in its name, also the root of the word to 'reflect'; now, since we are destroying even its material basis, the name must end with a word whose root means 'former'; and because 'former' in their current language was then pronounced 'lina,' they changed the second half of this word, and instead of 'reflection,' they stuck in the mentioned 'lina,' so that instead of the word Kundabuffer, they obtained the word 'Kundalina.'

"Thus it as that a half of the word Kundabuffer survived, and being transmitted from generation to generation, finally reached your contemporary favorites also, accompanied, of course, by a thousand and one different explanations.

"Even the contemporary 'learned-beings' also have a name

for that part of the spinal-marrow, made up of very abstruse Latin roots.

"The whole of what is called 'Indian-philosophy' now existing there, is based also on this famous 'Kundalina,' and about the word itself there exist thousands of various occult, secret and revealed 'sciences' which explain nothing.

"And as regards the way in which the contemporary terrestrial learned beings of what are called the exact 'sciences' define the significance of this part of the spinal marrow, that my boy, is a profound secret.

"And it became a secret because several centuries ago, this 'explanation' suddenly for no reason whatever, entered the favorite mole of the famous 'Scheherazade' which that incomparable Arabian fantasist chanced to have on the right side of her adorable navel.

"And there this 'learned-explanation' remains perfectly preserved down to the present day.

"When I was quite convinced that I had succeeded so easily in the destruction, perhaps for a long time, of that terrible practice among the beings of that group there in Pearl-Land, I decided to stay there no longer but to return to the 'Sea-of-Beneficence' to our ship '*Occasion*.'

"When we were quite ready to leave that Pearl-Land, the intention suddenly arose in me not to return to the 'Sea-of-Beneficence' by the way we had come, but by another way quite unusual in those days.

"Namely, I decided to return through the locality which was later called 'Tibet.'"

CHAPTER XXII

Beelzebub in Tibet for the First Time

AS THE MODE of travel then planned was still quite uncommon in those days for the three-brained beings there, we could not count on the chance of joining some 'caravan.' So, having to organize my own 'caravan' I began the same day preparing and procuring everything necessary for this purpose.

"I then procured some tens of the quadruped beings called 'horses,' 'mules,' 'asses' and 'Chamianian goats,' and so on, and hired a number of your biped favorites to look after the said beings and to do the semiconscious labor required on the way during this mode of travel.

"Having procured everything necessary, accompanied by Ahoon, I set off.

"This time we passed through places still more peculiar, and still more uncommon parts of the general Nature of that ill-starred planet; and we also encountered this time, or there came within the sphere of our sight, a greater number of the one-brained and two-brained beings of various forms, which are there called 'wild' and which in those days came there from very remote parts of the continent Ashhark for the purpose, as it is said there, of 'hunting.'

"The said 'wild' beings there were at that period particularly 'dangerous' both for the three-brained beings there, and also for those forms of quadruped beings which your favorites, with the 'cunning' proper to them, had already been able to make their slaves, compelling them to work exclusively for the satisfaction of their egoistic needs.

"And the said 'wild beings' were particularly, dangerous then only because there was being crystallized just at that period, in the presence of such 'wild beings,' that special function which arose in them also owing to the abnormally established conditions of being-existence of the three-brained beings there, and about which special function I shall explain to you in detail.

"The places through which our way went this time were at that period almost inaccessible for the three-brained beings then, chiefly on account of such 'wild beings.'

"In those days it was perhaps possible for the three-brained beings to pass through these places only, as they say, during the 'day,' that is to say, when in the atmosphere of their planet there, the process of 'Aieioiuoa' proceeds with the active element 'Okidanokh.'

"And they could pass during the 'day' because during this time of 'Krentonalnian' position of their planet in relation to the rays of their sun almost all the 'wild' terrestrial beings are in the state called 'sleep,' that is to say, in a state of the automatic elaboration in their presence of that energy, which is necessary to their ordinary existence and which elaboration of energy just then proceeds in them; whereas, on the contrary, in the three-centered beings there, the same is elaborated only when the said sacred property is not proceeding in the atmosphere, the period of the diurnity which they call 'night.'

"So, my boy, for the said reason it was possible for your favorites in those days to pass through these places only by 'day.' At night, great vigilance and the use of various artificial shelters were required as a defense against these wild beings, both for themselves and for their 'goods.'

"During the period of the mentioned 'Krentonalnian' position of the planet Earth, these 'wild' beings there are wide awake and take their first being-food; and because, by that time, they had already become accustomed to use for this purpose almost only the planetary bodies of weaker beings of other forms arising on their planet, they were always trying, during that period, to get hold of such a being in order to use his planetary body to satisfy that need of theirs.

"These 'wild' beings, particularly the smallest of them, were already at that time, owing also, of course, to the abnormally established conditions of the ordinary being-existence of the three-brained beings, perfected in point of ruminating and cunning up to the ideal.

"In consequence of this, throughout our whole route, we, and especially our workmen for the semiconscious work, had to be extremely careful and on the watch in order to guard ourselves, our quadruped workers and our supplies.

"A whole 'meeting' of these 'wild' beings would form around our camp at night, that had come there to provide themselves with something suitable for their first food, a gathering rather like an 'assembly' of your favorites during what is called the 'quotation of stock prices' or during their 'election' of representatives to some society or other whose nominal purpose is the joint pursuit of a means to the happy existence of all beings like themselves without distinction of their notorious castes there.

"Although we kept logs burning brightly all night, to scare these 'wild' beings, and although our biped workers, notwithstanding that they were forbidden, destroyed with the help of the so-called poisoned arrows of 'Elnapara,' those beings that came too near our camp, yet not a single night passed upon which what are there called 'tigers,' 'lions' and 'hyenas' did not carry off one or more of our quadruped beings; whose number in consequence diminished daily.

"Although, my boy, this way back to the 'Sea of Beneficence' then took us far longer than the way by which we had come there, all that we then saw and heard during our passage over those places, concerning the strangeness of the psyche of your favorites, fully justified the extra time spent.

"We travelled under these conditions more than a month of their time, and finally we came upon a small settlement of three-brained beings, who, as it appeared later, had only recently migrated there from Gemchania.

"As we afterwards learned, this settlement was called 'Sincratorza'; and when this region was subsequently populated and this same place became the principal center for all the beings of that region, the whole country was called by the same name.

"The name of this place was afterwards changed several times and at present it is called 'Tibet.'

"As we chanced to meet the said beings just as night was coming on, we asked them for, as it is said, a 'night's lodging.'

"And when they gave us permission to pass the night under their shelter we were very glad at the prospect of a night's rest, since, indeed, we were all so exhausted by the constant warfare with these wild beings, that both for ourselves and especially for our biped workers, it was already urgent to pass at least one night in peace.

"In the course of the evening talk, it was made clear that all the beings of this settlement belonged to the sect known then in Gemchania under the name 'The Self-tamers,' which had been formed from among the followers of just that religion which, as I have already told you, purported to be based on the direct instructions of Saint Buddha.

"There is no harm in noticing in this connection that the beings of that planet had still another peculiarity which had long before become proper to them alone; it consists in this, that no sooner does a new common 'Havatvernoni' or 'religion' arise among them, than its followers immediately begin to split up into different parties, each of which very soon creates its own, as it is called, 'sect.'

"The particular strangeness of this peculiarity of theirs consists in this, that those who belong to a sect never call themselves 'sectarians,' the name being considered offensive; they are named 'sectarians' only by these beings who do not belong to the same sect.

"And the adherents of any sect are sectarian for other beings only as long as they have no 'guns' and 'ships'; but as soon as they get hold of a sufficient number of 'guns' and 'ships' their particular sect at once becomes the dominant religion.

"The beings both of this settlement and of many other regions of Gemchania became sectarians, having separated just from the religion, the doctrine of which, as I have already told you, I studied in detail and which later was called 'Buddhism.'

"These sectarians of the Buddhist religion who called themselves the 'Self-tamers' arose owing to the same misconception, which, as I have already told you, they 'wiseacred' and named 'suffering-in-solitude.'

"And those beings with whom we passed the night, had settled so far away from their own people, in order to produce upon themselves the said notorious 'suffering,' without hindrance from others like themselves.

"Because, my boy, everything I learned that night and saw the next day of the followers of that sect, then produced so painful an impression upon me that for very many of their centuries I could never recall it all without what is called 'shuddering,' it was not until already long afterwards that I made perfectly clear to myself all of the causes of the strangeness of the psyche of these favorites of yours. It is for this reason that I wish to tell you all I then saw and learned in greater detail.

"As I then cleared up during the night-talk, even before the migration of the followers of that new sect there of the Buddhist religion, there had been invented by its leaders in Gemchania a 'suffering' of a special form, namely: they had decided to settle somewhere in some inaccessible place where other beings like themselves, not belonging to the sect and not initiated into its 'arcana,' might not prevent them from producing upon themselves this same 'suffering' of special form which they had invented.

"When after long search they finally found this same place to which we also had chanced to come—a place well suited for such a purpose as theirs, they, already solidly organized and materially secured, migrated with great difficulties, together with their families, there to that place almost inaccessible to their ordinary countrymen; and this place they then at first called, as I have already told you, 'Sincratorza.'

"While they were still only settling in this new place, they more or less agreed among themselves; but when they began practically carrying into effect the special form of 'sufferings' they had invented, their families and especially their wives, having learned of what it consisted, protested, and made a great outcry about it, with the result that schism arose among them.

"The said schism had taken place among them shortly before our chance encounter with them.

"Although at that time when we arrived in that 'Sincratorza,' all these migrants from Gemchania still existed there together, yet they had already begun little by little to migrate to other places which they had newly found and which were suitable for an isolated existence.

"For a clear understanding of what follows, you must know about the fundamental cause of the schism among those sectarians.

"It seems that the leaders of that sect, while they were still in Gemchania, had agreed among themselves to leave the beings like themselves, and to stick at nothing in order to attain their deliverance from the consequences of that organ of which the divine Teacher Saint Buddha had spoken.

"Among their conditions the agreement was included that they would exist in a certain way until their final planetary destruction or, as they say, until their death, in order that, as they said, their 'soul' might be cleansed by this special form of existence of alien growths of every kind, due to that organ Kundabuffer which, as Saint Buddha told them, their ancestors had, and, being freed from these consequences, to acquire thereby, the possibility, as the divine Saint Buddha had said, of reblending with the 'All-embracing Holy Prana.'

"But when, as I have already said, they, being settled, set about practically effecting the special form of 'suffering' which they had invented, and their wives, having learned its true nature, protested, then many of them, having fallen under the influence of their wives, declined to carry out the obligations they had undertaken while still in Gemchania, with the result that they just divided into two independent parties.

"Thereafter these sectarians, before called the 'Self-tamers,' began already to be called by various names, namely; those of the 'Self-tamers' who remained faithful to the obligations they had taken upon themselves were called 'Orthodoxhydooraki,' while the rest, who had renounced the certain obligations they had undertaken there in their native country, were called 'Katoshkihydooraki.'

"By the time of our arrival in 'Sincratorza' those of the sectarians who were named 'Orthodoxhydooraki' had their well-organized so-called monastery not very far from their original settling-place, and therein the said special form of 'suffering' was in full process.

"On resuming our journey the next day after a restful night, we passed quite near the monastery of these sectarians of the Buddhist religion of the 'Orthodoxhydooraki' doctrine.

"As we made our usual halt at this time of day, for feeding our quadruped workers, we asked the monks to allow us to make our camp under the covers of their monastery.

"Strange and unusual as it may seem, the beings there bearing the name monks, did not refuse our objectively just request, but at once, without any of the 'swaggering' that had become proper to the monks there of all centuries and of all doctrines, admitted us, whereupon we unexpectedly then entered the very center of that region which, from the very beginning of their arising, the beings of the planet Earth have, from time to time, become very skillful in concealing from the observation and understanding even of Individuums of pure Reason—in the present instance, into the sphere of the arcana of this doctrine. In other words, they had become skillful in 'wiseacring' something and making what they call a 'mystery' of it, and in so thoroughly concealing this mystery of theirs from others by every means, that even beings with pure Reason could not discover it.

"The monastery of this sect 'Orthodoxhydooraki' of the Buddhist religion occupied a large square with a strongly fortified wall around it, that protected everything within both from beings like themselves and from 'wild' beings.

"In the middle of this enormous walled enclosure stood a large, also strongly boarded, construction, which constituted just the main part of the monastery.

"In one half of this large edifice their ordinary being existence was carried on, and in the other, they practiced those special manipulations of theirs which were just the peculiarity of the form of belief of the followers of their sect and which were arcana to the rest.

"Around the outer wall on its inner side stood, in a row, small, strongly boarded sections like cells.

"It was just these same cells that represented the difference between this monastery and other monasteries on the planet Earth in general.

"These sentry box shapes were entirely boarded in on all sides, save that near the bottom was a small opening through which, with great difficulty, a hand could be thrust.

"These strong constructions, of sentry box shape, were for the perpetual immurement of those already deserving beings of that sect whose occupation until the complete destruction of their planetary existence, was a certain manipulation of what they call their emotions and thoughts.

"And it was when the wives of these 'sectarian-self-tamers' learned of this that they just made the said great outcry.

"In the fundamental religious teaching of this sect, there was a complete explanation of how long a time and namely which manipulations it is necessary to produce upon oneself in order to merit being immured in one of those strongly constructed cells, there to receive every diurnity a morsel of bread and a small jug of water.

"On our visit to that enclosure of that terrible monastery, all these monstrous cells were already occupied; and the care of the immured, that is giving them once a diurnity, through the mentioned tiny openings, a morsel of bread and a small jug of water, was discharged with great reverence by the sectarians, who were candidates for that immurement, and who, while waiting their turn, existed in the said building that stood in the middle of the monastery square.

"Your immured favorites did indeed exist in the said monstrous sepulchers until their half-starved motionless existence, full of deprivations, came to an end.

"When the companions of the immured learned of the ceasing to exist of one of their number, his planetary body was removed from the improvised sepulcher and immediately in the place of the self-destroyed being, another similar unfortunate fanatic of that maleficent religious doctrine of theirs was immured, their ranks being filled up by other members of that peculiar sect, dribbling in from Gemchania.

"In Gemchania itself all the adherents of that sect already knew of the existence of that special 'convenient' place for the actualization of the finale of their 'religious doctrine,' purporting to have been based on the exact instructions of the Saint Buddha; and in every big center they even had what are called agents who helped them to get there.

"Having rested and fed our biped and quadruped workers, we left that melancholy place of sacrifices to that same wretched organ which, in the ruminations of certain most high cosmic individuums had for some reason or other, without fail, to be introjected into the presence of the earliest three-brained beings of that ill-starred planet.

"Eh! Eh! Eh!, my boy, we left there, as you can well believe, scarcely with agreeable sensations and happy reflections.

"Continuing our route in the direction of the 'Sea-of-Beneficence,' we again passed through terra-firma of very many different forms, also with conglomerations of intraplanetary minerals, but which had oozed to the surface of the planet from still greater depths.

"Here I must say something about an exceedingly strange thing, which I constated, closely connected with just that part of the surface of your planet which is now called Tibet.

"At that period when I was passing through Tibet for the first time, its elevations were indeed also unusually far above the surface of the Earth, but they did not differ particularly from similar elevations on other continents and on the same continent Ashhark or Asia, of which Tibet was a part.

"But when during my sixth and last personal stay on the planet Earth there, my way again took me through these, for me, extremely memorable places, I just then constated that in the interval of the few tens of their centuries, the whole of that locality had projected so far from the planet that no heights on any of the other continents could even be compared with them.

"For instance, the chief range of that elevated region through which we had then passed, namely, the range of elevations which the beings there call a 'mountain range,' had in the interval projected so far from the planet that some of its peaks are now the loftiest among all the abnormal projections of that vainly-long-suffering-planet. And supposing you could climb them, you could possibly with the aid of a Teskooano, 'see clearly' the center of the opposite side of that peculiar planet.

"When I first constated that strange phenomenon occurring on that remarkably peculiar planet of yours, I at once thought that in all probability it contained the germ for the arising of some subsequent misfortune on a great common cosmic scale, and when I afterwards collected statistics concerning that abnormal phenomenon, this first apprehension of mine very soon more and more grew in me.

"And it grew chiefly, because, in my statistics one item concerning phenomenon there, showed an increase every decade.

"The said item concerning those Tibetan elevations referred just to this, which of the terrestrial, as they are called, 'planetary tremors,' or as they are otherwise called 'earthquakes,' occur to that planet, and when, on account of these excessively lofty elevations.

"Although 'planetary-tremors' or 'earthquakes' frequently occur to that planet of yours from other intraplanetary disharmonies also, that have arisen in consequence of the two already mentioned great Transapalnian-perturbations, the causes of which I shall sometime explain to you, nevertheless most of the planetary-tremors there, and especially during recent centuries, have occurred solely on account of those excessive elevations.

"And they occur because, in consequence of those excessive elevations, the atmosphere also of that planet has acquired and continues to acquire in its presence the same—that is to say, what is called the 'Blastegoklornian-circumference' of the atmosphere of the planet Earth has acquired in certain places and continues to acquire an excessively projecting materialized presence, for what is called the 'reciprocal-blending-of-the-results-of-all-planets-of-the-given-system'; with the result that during the motion of that planet, and in the process of what is called 'common-system-harmony,' its atmosphere at certain times 'hooks on,' as it were, to the atmosphere of other planets or comets of the same system.

"And owing to these 'hookings on,' there occurs in the corresponding places of the general presence of that planet of yours just those said 'planetary tremors' or 'quakes.'

"I must also explain to you that the region of the general presence of the planet where such 'planetary tremors' occur on this account, depends upon the position occupied by the planet itself in the process of the common-system-harmonious-movement, in relation to other concentrations belonging to the same system.

"Be that as it may, if this abnormal growth of the Tibetan mountains continues thus in the future, a great catastrophe on a general cosmic scale is sooner or later inevitable.

"However, when the menace I foresee becomes already evident, no doubt the most high, most sacred cosmic Individuums will, at the proper time, take the proper precautions."

"If you please, if you please, your Right Reverence," Ahoon thus interrupted Beelzebub, and rattled off the following:

"Allow me to report to you, Your Right Reverence, some information which I happened to pick up concerning just that growth of these same Tibetan mountains about which you have deigned to speak.

"Just before our flight from the planet Karatas," continued Ahoon, "I had the pleasure of meeting the Archangel Viloyer, the Governor of our solar system, and His Splendiferousness condescended to recognize me and to speak with me.

"Perhaps you remember, Your Right Reverence, that while we were existing on the planet Zernakoor, His Splendiferousness, Archangel Viloyer, was still an ordinary angel, and used often to drop in to see us.

"So when His Splendiferousness, during our conversation, heard the name of that solar system where we were exiled, he told me that at the last most high and most most sacred reception of final cosmic results who had returned, a certain Individuum, Saint Lama, had had the privilege of personally presenting at the feet of our ENDLESS UNI-BEING, in the presence of all the most high Individuums, a certain petition regarding the abnormal growth of some elevations of some planet—it seems just of that solar system—and having received this request our ALL-GRACIOUS ENDLESSNESS immediately ordered Archangel Looisos to be dispatched to that solar system where, as one familiar with that system, he might there on the spot clarify the causes of the manifestation of the said projections and take appropriate measures.

"That is why His Conformity Archangel Looisos is at the present time hastily winding up his current affairs in order to set off there."

"So, dear Ahoon . . . " commented Beelzebub; and he added, "Thank you for this information . . . Glory be to our CREATOR . . . what you have just said will probably help destroy in my presence the anxiety which arose in me when I first constated the abnormal growth of those said Tibetan mountains, namely, my anxiety for the complete disappearance from the Universe of the precious memory of our Endlessly Revered Wisest of the Wise, Mullah Nassr Eddin."

Having said this and giving his face its usual expression, Beelzebub continued thus:

"Through that region at present called Tibet, we then continued our route, encountering hardships of every kind; and finally we came to the source of the river called the Keria-chi and a few days later, sailing down it to the Sea of Beneficence, we came to our ship *Occasion*.

"Although after this third descent of mine to your planet Earth, I did not go there in person for a considerable time, nevertheless, from time to time, I attentively observed those favorites of yours, through my big 'Teskooano.'

"And I had no reason for a long time to go there personally on account of the following.

"After returning to the planet Mars I soon became interested there in a work which the three-brained beings of the planet Mars were just then carrying out on the surface of their planet.

"Clearly to understand in what work there it was that I became interested, you must know, first of all, that the planet Mars is for the system Ors, to which it belongs, what is called a 'Mdnel-outian-link' in the transformation of cosmic substances, in consequence of which it has, what is called, a 'Keskestasantnian-firm-surface,' that is to say, one half of its surface consists of land-presence and the other of 'Saliakooriapnian' masses; or, as your favorites would say, one half of its land or one continuous continent, and the other half is covered with water.

"So, my boy, as the three-brained beings of the planet Mars use for their first being-food exclusively only 'prosphora'—or as your favorites call it, 'bread'—they, for the purpose of obtaining it, sow on the land half of their planet, what is called 'wheat,' and as this 'wheat' derives the moisture it needs for what is called evolving Djartklom, only from what is called 'dew,' the result is that a grain of wheat there yields only a seventh part of the fulfilled process of the sacred Heptaparaparshinokh, that is to say, what is called 'the yield' of the harvest is only a seventh.

"As this amount of wheat was insufficient for their needs, while to get more of it, they would have to utilize the presence of the planetary 'Saliakooriap,' the three-centered beings there from the very beginning of our arrival there, were always talking of conducting that same 'Saliakooriap' in the requisite quantity, from the opposite side of their planet to that side on which their being-existence proceeded.

"And when several of their years later they finally decided

the question and began making every preparation, they began operations just before my return from the planet Earth, that is to say, they began digging special canals for conducting the 'Saliakooriap.'

"So, my boy, this work thing extremely complicated, the beings of the planet Mars had invented and continued to invent for the work, every kind of machine and appliance . . .

"And as there were very many peculiar and interesting ones among those machines and appliances they invented, I, being always interested in every kind of new invention, was very much taken by the said work of the beings of the planet Mars.

"By the courtesy of the kind Martians, then, I then spent nearly all my time at these works, and that is why during that period I very seldom descended to the other planets of that solar system.

"Only sometimes I flew to the planet Saturn to rest, to Gornahoor Harharkh, who during this time, had already become my real essence-friend, and thanks to whom I had such a marvel as that big Teskooano of mine which, as I have already told you, brought remote visibilities, seven million, two hundred and eighty-five times nearer."

CHAPTER XXIII

The Fourth Personal Sojourn Of Beelzebub On The Planet Earth

BEELZEBUB continued thus:

"I descended for the fourth time to that planet Earth owing to the request of my essence-friend Gornahoor Harharkh.

"I must first of all tell you that after I had met this Gornahoor Harharkh and had become friendly with him, I always, whenever we again met and during our 'subjective-exchange-of-opinions,' shared my impressions with him about the strange psyche of the three-brained beings of that planet of yours.

"And the result of these exchanges of opinion of ours concerning your favorites was that he finally also became interested in them and moreover, to such a degree, that once he even very seriously asked me to keep him always informed, even if only partially, of my observation on them, and thereafter, I sent him, just as I did to your uncle Tooilan, copies of all my brief notes concerning the strange particularities of their psyche.

"And how Gornahoor Harharkh came to be the cause of this descent of mine ensued from the following:

"I have already once told you that after my third personal descent to your planet, I occasionally, just for a rest, ascended only to the planet Saturn to this friend of mine.

"When during these flights I had become convinced of his great learning, the idea once arose in me to invite him to descend on our ship '*Occasion*' to the planet Mars, in order there, on the spot, to help me personally with his knowledge in arranging the details of my observatory which was just then being completed.

"Here I might as well emphasize the fact that if this observatory of mine afterwards became famous and indeed the best among all the artificial constructions of its kind in the whole of the Universe, I am chiefly indebted just to the learning of this same essence friend of mine.

"Well then, when I spoke to Gornahoor Harharkh about this, he, without thinking long about it, agreed, and together we immediately began considering how to carry out our intention.

"The problem was that our route from the planet Saturn to the planet Mars would cross such cosmic spheres as did not correspond to the presence of Gornahoor Harharkh, that is to say, of a being who had as yet the possibilities only for an ordinary planetary existence.

"The result of our deliberations then was that on the following day his chief assistants, under his direction, began to arrange a special compartment in our ship '*Occasion*' itself, and to furnish it with every kind of adaptation and apparatus for generating those substances of which the atmosphere of the planet Saturn consists, and to which Gornahoor Harharkh was adapted by Nature for existence.

"When all these preparations had been completed, we, in one Hrkh-hr-hoo, set out on our journey in the direction of the planet Mars and successfully descended there at my house.

"And there on the planet Mars, which had almost the same atmosphere as the planet Saturn, my essence-friend Gornahoor Harharkh, very soon became acclimatized and existed fairly freely.

"It was just during his stay on Mars that he invented that 'Teskooano' or, as your favorites call it, that 'telescope,' thanks chiefly to which, as I have already said, my observatory afterwards became particularly famous throughout the whole of the Universe.

"The 'Teskooano' he constructed is indeed a marvel of being-Reason, as it increases the visibility of remote cosmic concentrations up to seven million and two hundred and eighty-five times, both during certain processes in cosmic substances proceeding in the atmosphere surrounding almost all the cosmic concentrations, and also during certain processes in the cosmic Etherokrilno of interspatial spheres.

"Thanks to this 'Teskooano' I was sometimes fully able, while seated in my house on Mars, to observe almost everything that proceeded on those parts of the surface of other planets of this Solar System, which in the process of what is called the general-system-movement, were at the given time within the sphere of vision of my observatory.

"Well then, my dear boy, while Gornahoor Harharkh was then staying with me as my guest and we were once observing together the existence of these favorites of yours, a certain fact which we happened to notice was the cause of a very serious exchange of opinions between us concerning the three-centered beings of that peculiar planet of yours.

"The result of this 'exchange-of-opinions' of ours was that I undertook to descend upon the surface of that planet and to bring back a certain number of beings there called apes, in order to carry out certain elucidating experiments with them concerning that fact we had noticed and which had then surprised us. At this point of Beelzebub's tales he was given a 'Leitoochanbros,' that is, a special metal plate on which the text is recorded of an etherogram received from somewhere or other; the addressee has only to hold it to his perceptive hearing organ to hear everything communicated in it. When Beelzebub had in this way heard the contents of the 'Leitoochanbros' handed to him, he turned to his grandson and said:

"You see, my boy, what coincidences occur in our Great Universe.

"The contents of this etherogram just concern your favorites in regard to these terrestrial beings I just mentioned, that is to these 'apes.'

"It has been sent to me from the planet Mars, and among

other things there is communicated in it, that the three-centered beings of the planet Earth are again excited by what is called the 'Ape-question.'

"I must tell you, first of all, that on account of a cause also ensuing from the abnormal being-existence there, an extraordinary factor which became periodically intensified in its functioning was long ago crystallized in the presences of those strange three-brained beings arising and existing on the planet Earth, and every now and then produces in their presences a crescendo-impulse, owing to which, during periods of its action, they wish to find out at all costs, whether it is they who have descended from these apes or whether these same apes have descended from them.

"Judging from the etherogram, this question is, this time, agitating chiefly those biped beings there who breed on the continent called 'America.'

"Although this question always agitates them from time to time, yet every once in a while it becomes there for a long time, as they express it, the 'burning-question-of-the-day.'

"I very well remember that this 'agitation-of-mind' among them concerning the origin of these same apes occurred there for the first time when, as they also like to express it, their 'center-of-culture' was Tikliamish.

"The beginning of that 'agitation-of-mind' there was the wiseacring of a certain 'learned-being' of 'new formation' there named Menitkel.

"This Menitkel then became a learned being, firstly, because his childless aunt was an excellent what is called matchmaker and mixed a great deal with power-possessing beings, and, secondly, because when, by age, he was approaching the 'threshold-of-Being' of a responsible being, he received on his birthday the gift of a book entitled 'Guide-to-etiquette-and-love-letter-writing.' Being materially provided for, and therefore quite free, thanks to an inheritance left him by his uncle, a former pawn-shop proprietor, he, out of boredom, then compiled a massive and erudite work in which he spun out an elaborate theory with every kind of 'logical proof' concerning the origin of these apes, but, of course, with such 'logical-proofs' as could be perceived and crystallized only in the Reasons of those queer ducks who have taken your fancy.

"This Menitkel then 'proved' by his theory that these 'fellow-apes' of theirs had descended neither more nor less than from what are called 'people-run-wild.'

"The other beings of that period, as it had already become proper to them, implicitly believed this 'Auntie's-darling' without any essence-criticism whatever, and so from that time on, this question which then agitated the strange Reason of your favorites, became a subject of discussion and fantasying, and existed up to what is called, the 'seventh-in-turn-great-general-planetary-process-of-reciprocal-destruction.'

"Thanks to this maleficent idea, there was even fixed in the instincts of most of these unfortunates at that period still another abnormal what is called 'dictatory factor,' which began to engender in their common presences the false feeling that these ape-beings were, so to say, sacred; and this abnormal factor for engendering such a sacrilegious impulse, also passing by inheritance from generation to generation, has reached the instincts of very many beings even of the present time.

"This false idea that arose and was fixed there owing to the said 'pawn-shop-progeny,' existed during nearly two of their centuries, and became an inseparable part of the Reason of the majority of them; and only various events proceeding from the mentioned general planetary process of reciprocal destruction which lasted nearly half a century gradually effaced it until it ultimately completely disappeared from their common presences.

"But when what is called their 'cultured-existence' was concentrated on the continent named Europe, and when the time of the maximum intense manifestation of the peculiar illness there, namely, 'to wiseacre,' had come round again, which illness, by the way, had already long before become subject to the fundamental cosmic law of Heptaparaparshinokh, according to which it had, in respect of intensity, to function also with a certain periodicity, then, to the grief of three-brained beings of the whole of the Universe, that 'Ape-question,' namely the question who is descended from which, again arose, and having become crystallized, again became a part of the presence of the abnormal Reason of your favorites.

"The stimulus for the revival there of this 'Ape-question' was this time also a 'learned' being, and of course also 'great,' but 'learned' of quite a 'new formation'—named Darwin.

"And this 'great-learned' being, basing his theory on that same logic of theirs, 'proved' that it was they themselves who were descended from these Mister Apes.

"And as for the objective reality of the theories of both these 'great' terrestrial 'learned-beings,' I am reminded and willy-nilly impelled to utter one of the wise sayings of our esteemed Mullah Nassr Eddin, namely:

"'They both succeeded, though of course not without luck, in finding the authentic god-mother of the incomparable Scheherazade on an old dung-hill.'

"In any case you must know and bear in mind that for many centuries just this question among similar ephemeral questions, provides material for the kind of mentation which is considered among your favorites as the 'highest-manifestation-of-Reason.'

"These favorites of yours would in my opinion get quite a correct answer to this question which always excites them, that is, the question how the apes arose, if they were able in the given case to apply one of those sayings again of our dear Mullah Nassr Eddin, who often used to say:

"'The-cause-of-every-misunderstanding-must-be-sought-only-in-woman.'

"If with that wisdom of his they had attempted the solution of this enigmatic question, then perhaps they would have finally discovered whence and how these countrymen of theirs originated.

"As the question of the genealogy of these apes there, is indeed exceedingly abstruse and unusual, I shall inform your Reason about this also as far as possible from every aspect.

"In fact, neither have they descended from apes nor have apes descended from them, but . . . the cause of the origin of these apes is in this case, just as in every other misunderstanding there, also . . . their women.

"I must tell you first of all that the species of terrestrial ape-beings now arising there under several different exterior forms never existed at all before the second 'Transapalnian-perturbation'; only afterwards did the genealogy of their species begin.

"The cause of this arising of this 'Misconceived' being as well as the causes of all the other events more or less serious in an objective sense, which occur on the surface of that ill-fated planet, are two circumstances totally independent of each other.

"The first of them, as always, was the same want of foresight on the part of certain Most High, Most Very Saintly Cosmic Individuals, and the second was, in the given case, also the same abnormal conditions of ordinary being-existence established by them themselves.

"The point is that when the second 'Transapalnian-perturbation' occurred to that ill-fated planet, then, besides its chief continent Atlantis, many other both large and small terra-firmas entered within the planet, and in their place, new terra-firmas appeared on the surface of the planet.

"These displacements of the parts of the common presence of that ill-fated planet then continued for several days there, with repeated planetary tremors and with such manifestations, that they could not fail to evoke terror in the consciousness and feelings of beings of every kind.

"During that same period many of our three-brained favorites who chanced to survive together with various one-brained and two-brained beings of other forms, unexpectedly struck upon other newly formed terra-firmas in entirely new places unfamiliar to them.

"It was just at this period that many of these strange Keschapmartnian three-brained beings of active and passive sex, or as they say, 'men' and 'women,' were compelled to exist for some years there apart, that is to say, without the opposite sex.

"Before relating how this then further occurred, I must explain to you a little more in detail concerning that sacred substance which is the final result of the evolving transformations of every kind of being-food formed in the presence of every being without distinction of 'brain-system.'

"This sacred substance which arises in the presences of beings of every kind is almost everywhere called 'Exioëhary'; but your favorites on the planet Earth call it 'sperm.'

"Thanks to the all-gracious foresight and command of our COMMON FATHER CREATOR and according to the actualization of Great Nature, this sacred substance arises in the presences of all beings without distinction of brain system and exterior coating, chiefly in order that by its means they might, consciously or automatically, fulfill that part of their being-duty which consists in the continuation of their species; but in the presences of three-brained beings it arises also in order that it might be consciously transformed in their common presences for coating their highest being-bodies for their own Being.

"Before the second 'Transapalnian-perturbation' there, which period of their planet the contemporary three-brained beings define by the words: 'Before-the-loss-of-the-continent-

Atlantis,' when various consequences of the properties of the organ Kundabuffer had already begun to be crystallized in their presences, a being-impulse began to be formed in them which later became predominant.

"This impulse is now called 'pleasure'; and in order to satisfy it they had already begun to exist in a way that is not becoming to three-centered beings, namely, the majority of them gradually adapted the removal for themselves of this same sacred being-substance only for the satisfaction of the said impulse.

"So my boy! On account of the fact that the majority of the three-brained beings of the planet Earth thereafter carried out the process of the removal from themselves of this substance—which is constantly formed in them—not at certain periods normally established by Great Nature for beings in accordance with their organization simply for the purpose of the continuation of their species, and also because the majority of them ceased to utilize it consciously for coating their highest being-bodies, the result was obtained that when not removing it from themselves by ways which had then already become mechanical, they naturally must experience a sensation called 'Sirkliniamen,' or as your favorites there would say, the state defined by the words 'out-of-sorts,' which state is invariably accompanied by what is called 'mechanical-suffering.'

"Remind me at some opportune moment about the said periods fixed by Nature for the normal process of the utilization of 'Exioëhary' by beings of different brain systems for the purpose of the continuation of their species, and I will explain it to you in detail.

"Well then, in consequence of the aforesaid, and also because just like us they are also Keschapmartnian beings, and the normal removal from their presences of this sacred substance which constantly and inevitably arises in them, can proceed exclusively only with the opposite sex when they utilize it for the continuation of the species by means of the sacred process 'Elmooarno,' and also because they were not in the habit of utilizing it for the purpose of coating their higher being-bodies, these chance surviving three-brained beings there—namely, those who had already been existing as it is not becoming for three-brained beings to exist, that is to say, when during several of their years they had existed without beings of the opposite sex—began to turn to various anti-natural means for the removal from themselves of the sacred substance 'Exioëhary' formed in them.

"The beings of the male sex then turned to the anti-natural means called 'Moordoorten' and 'Androperasty,' or as the contemporary beings would say, 'Onanism' and 'Pederasty,' and these anti-natural means fully satisfied them.

"But for the three-brained beings of the passive sex, or, as they are called, 'women,' the said anti-natural methods proved to be not sufficiently satisfying, and so the poor 'women-orphans' of that time, being already then more cunning and inventive than the men there, began to seek out and accustom beings of other forms of the given place to be their 'partners.'

"Well then, it was after these 'partnerships' that those kinds of beings also began to appear in our Great Universe who in themselves are, as our dear Mullah Nassr Eddin would say, 'Neither-one-thing-nor-the-other.'

"Concerning the possibility of this abnormal blending of two different kinds of Exioëharies for the conception and arising of a new planetary body of a being, it is necessary to explain to you also the following: "On the planet Earth, just as on other planets of our Universe where Keschapmartnian three-brained beings breed and exist, that is to say, those three-brained beings the formation of whose Exioëhary for the purpose of creating a new being must obligatorily proceed in the presences of two distinct independent sexes, the fundamental differences between the sacred Exioëharies formed in the presences of the distinct and opposite sexes of Keschapmartnian beings, that is to say, in 'man' and 'woman,' is, that in the Exioëhary formed in the presences of beings of the male sex, there participates the localized sacred 'affirming' or 'positive' force of the sacred Triamazikamno; while for the completed formation of the Exioëhary of the presences of beings of the female sex, there participates the localized sacred 'denying' or 'negative' force of the same sacred law.

"And owing to the same all-gracious foresight and command of our FATHER OF EVERYTHING EXISTING IN THE GREAT UNIVERSE, and according to the actualization of Great Mother Nature, then in certain surrounding conditions and with the participation of the third separately localized holy force of the sacred Triamazikamno, namely, the holy force called 'Reconciling,' the blending of these two Exioëharies arising in the two distinct independent beings, different in kind, just give, owing to the process called 'the-process-of-the-sacred-Elmooarno' proceeding between these beings of opposite sex, the beginning for the arising of a new being.

"And the possibility in the given case of such an abnormal blending of two different kinds of Exioëhary then occurred owing only to a certain cosmic law called the 'affinity-of-the-number-of-the-totality-of-vibrations,' which proceeded owing to the second 'Transapalnian-perturbation' to this ill-fated planet and which then still continued to act for its common presence.

"Concerning this cosmic law just mentioned, it is now absolutely necessary to tell you that it arose and began to exist in the Universe after the fundamental sacred law of Triamazikamno was changed by our CREATOR for the purpose of rendering the Heropass harmless, and after its previously totally independent holy parts had begun to be dependent upon forces coming from outside.

"Moreover you will understand this cosmic law also in all

its aspects when, as I have already promised you, I shall explain to you in detail all the fundamental laws in general of World-Creation and World-Existence.

"Meanwhile, concerning this question, know that in general everywhere on normally existing planets of our Great Universe, the Exioëhary formed in the presence of a three-brained being who has perceptive and transformative organs for localizing the holy affirming part of the sacred Triamazikamno, that is to say, in the presence of a Keschapmartnian being of the male sex, can, on the basis of the just mentioned cosmic law, never be blended with the Exioëhary formed in the presence of a Keschapmartnian two-brained being of the opposite sex.

"At the same time, the Exioëhary formed in a three-brained Keschapmartnian being of the female sex can sometimes—in those cases, when a special combination of the blending of cosmic forces is obtained and the mentioned law comes into effect—be completely blended under certain surrounding conditions with the Exioëhary formed in two-brained Keschapmartnian beings of the male sex, but only as the active factor in such an actualizing process of the fundamental sacred Triamazikamno.

"In short, during the said terrible years on this planet of yours, a result very rare in the Universe was obtained, that is to say, there was obtained the blending of the Exioëharies of two Keschapmartnian beings of different brain systems of opposite sexes; and as a result, there arose the ancestors of these terrestrial sportive beings now called apes, who give your favorites no peace and from time to time agitate their strange Reason.

"But when after the mentioned terrible period there on your planet, when the relatively normal process of ordinary existence was reestablished and your favorites of different sexes again began to find each other and to exist together, then the continuation of their species among the ape-beings was thereafter actualized also among beings similar to themselves.

"And this continuation of their species by these abnormally arisen ape-beings there could be further continued among themselves because the conception for the arising of the first of these abnormal beings had also proceeded on the basis of those same mentioned external conditions, thanks to which the presence of future Keschapmartnian beings of active or of passive sex is generally determined.

"The most interesting result of this already excessively abnormal manifestation of the three-brained beings of your planet is that there now exist very many species of generations of ape-beings differing in exterior form, and each of these varied species bears a very definite resemblance to some form of a two-brained quadruped being still existing there.

"This came about because the blending of the Exioëhary of the Keschapmartnian three-brained beings there of the 'female sex' which served as a beginning for the arising of the ancestors of these apes, then proceeded with the active Exioëhary of these same varied quadruped beings existing there up to the present time.

"And indeed my boy, when during the period of my last personal stay on the planet Earth, I chanced during my travels to meet with the said various independent species of apes, and when by a habit which has become second nature, I also observed them, I constated very definitely that the whole of the inner functioning and what are called the 'automatic-postures' of each separate species of these contemporary apes there, are exactly like those present in the whole of the presence of any normally arisen quadruped being there, and that even what are called their 'facial-features' very definitely resemble those of the said quadrupeds; but on the other hand, that what are called the 'psychic-features' of all the separate species of these apes there are absolutely identical, even down to the details, with those of the psyche of the three-brained beings there of the 'female sex.'"

At this point of his tales, Beelzebub made a long pause and looking at this favorite Hassein, with a smile which very clearly expressed a double meaning, he, continuing to smile, said:

"In the text of the etherogram which I have just received, it is further said that in order this time finally to settle who has descended from which—whether they from the apes or the apes from them—these freaks, your favorites, have even decided to carry out 'scientific-experiments,' and furthermore that several of them have already left for the continent of Africa where many of these apes breed, with the object of bringing back from there the number required for these 'scientific-investigations' of theirs.

"To judge by this etherogram, the beings of the planet Earth who have taken your fancy are again, in their turn, up to their 'extraordinary tricks.'

"From all I have learned about them during my observations, I foresee that this 'scientific-experiment' will, of course, very greatly interest other of your favorites also, and will serve for a time as material to their strange Reason for endless discussion and talks.

"And all this will be quite in the order of things there.

"Concerning the 'scientific-experiment' itself, which they propose to carry out with the apes taken back from Africa, I can with certainly say beforehand, that at any rate the first part of it will without any doubt, succeed wonderfully well.

"And it will succeed wonderfully well, because the apes themselves, as beings of what is called a 'Terbelnian-result' are already, owing to their nature, extremely fond of occupying themselves with 'titillation,' and before the day is out, will no doubt participate in and greatly assist your favorites in this 'scientific experiment' of theirs.

"As for those beings there who are going to carry out this

'scientific-experiment,' and as for any benefit from it for the other three-brained beings there, it can all be pictured if one remembers the profoundly wise saying of our same honorable Mullah Nassr Eddin, in which he says:

"'Happy is that father whose son is even busy with murder and robbery, for he himself will then have no time to get accustomed to occupy himself with "titillation."'

"Yes, my boy, it seems that I have not yet told you why and by whom, since I left the Solar System Ors, I am kept informed by etherograms of the most important events which proceed on various planets of that system, and, of course, also about events proceeding on your planet Earth.

"You remember I told you, that my first personal descent upon the surface of that planet of yours took place on account of one of the young beings of our tribe, who then had no desire to stay there any longer but returned with us to the planet Mars, where he later became a very good chief over all the beings of our tribe existing on that planet, and who is now already the chief over all the beings in general of our tribe who for various reasons still exist on certain planets of that system Ors.

"Well then my boy, when I left that system, I presented my famous observatory to him with everything in it, and in gratitude for this he promised to report every month, according to the time-calculation of the planet Mars, all the more important events occurring on the planets of that system.

"And now this chief keeps me very accurately informed of the most important events proceeding on all the planets on which there is a being-existence; and, knowing my great interest in the three-brained beings breeding on the planet Earth, he does his best, as I now see, to elucidate and send me information concerning all those manifestations of theirs which give me now also the possibility of being constantly informed of the whole process of the ordinary existence of these three-brained beings, even though I find myself already inaccessibly remote even for their featherweight thoughts.

"That chief of our beings remaining there, collects the various information he communicates concerning the three-brained beings of the planet Earth either by means of his own observations of them through the great Teskooano which I left him, or from the reports which, in their turn, are communicated to him by those three-brained beings of our own tribe who chose to exist forever on the planet Earth, and all three of whom have at the present time on the continent of Europe, different substantial independent undertakings indispensable for everyone existing there under the prevailing conditions.

"One of them has in one of the large cities, an 'undertaker's-business'; the second, in another large city, has a bureau for what are called, match-making and divorce; and the third is the proprietor of many offices founded by himself in various cities for what is called, 'money-exchange.'

"However my boy, owing to this etherogram, I have wandered a long way from my original tale.

"Let us go back to our former theme.

"Well then, upon this fourth flight of mine to the planet Earth, our ship '*Occasion*' descended on to the sea called 'Red-Sea.'

"And we descended upon this Sea because it washed the eastern shores of that continent where I wished to go, namely to that continent then called Grabontzi and now called Africa, on which those ape-like beings I needed then bred more than on any other of the terra-firma parts of the surface of that planet of yours; and also because this sea was at that period particularly convenient for the mooring of our ship '*Occasion*'; but what was still more important was that on one of is sides that country was situated which was then called 'Nilia' and is now called Egypt, where those beings of our tribe still existed then, who wished to remain on that planet and with whose help I intended to collect the apes.

"Well then, having descended upon the 'Red-Sea,' we sailed from the ship '*Occasion*' on 'Epodrenekhs' to the shore; and afterwards, on camels we came to that town where our beings existed and which was then the capital of the future Egypt.

"This capital city was then called Thebes.

"On the very first day of my arrival in the city of Thebes, one of the beings of our tribe existing there told me among other things, in the course of our conversation, that the beings of the Earth of that locality had devised a new system for observing other cosmic concentrations from their planet, and that they were then constructing what was required in order to carry it into effect; also, as everybody there said, that the convenience and possibilities of this new system were excellent and until then unparalleled on the Earth.

"And when he had related all he had himself seen with his own eyes, I immediately became greatly interested, because from his description of certain details of this new construction there, it seemed to me that these terrestrial beings had perhaps found a means of overcoming that inconvenience about which I myself had just previously been thinking a great deal while I was completing the construction of my observatory on the planet Mars.

"And so I decided to postpone for a while my first intention of immediately going further south on that continent to collect the apes I needed, and instead, to go first to where the said construction was being made, in order on the spot to become personally acquainted with it from every aspect, and to find out all about it.

"So then, the day following our arrival in the city Thebes, accompanied by one of the beings of our tribe who already had many friends there, and also by the chief constructor of the said construction, and of course by our Ahoon also, I went this time on what is called a 'Choortetev' down the tributary of that great river now called the 'Nile.'

"Near where this river flowed into a large "Saliakooriapnian-area,' those artificial constructions were just being completed of which just one part then interested me.

"The district itself, where the work was being carried on both from this new, what they called 'observatory,' and for several other constructions for the welfare of their being-existence, was then called 'Avazlin' a few years later it came to be called there 'Caironana,' and at the present time it is simply called the 'outskirts-of-Cairo.'

"The mentioned artificial constructions had been begun long before by one of what are called there 'Pharaohs,' the name by which the beings of that region called their kings; and at the time of my fourth flight to the Earth and my first visit to this place, the special constructions he had begun were already being completed by his grandson, also a Pharaoh.

"Although the observatory which interested me was not yet quite finished, nevertheless observations of the exterior visibility of cosmic concentrations could be made from it, and the results issuing from them and the reciprocal action of these results, could be studied.

"Those beings there who were occupied with such observations and studies were called, at that period on the Earth, 'Astrologers.'

"But when afterwards that psychic illness of theirs called 'wiseacring' became finally fixed there, owing to which these specialists of theirs also shriveled and shrunk and became specialists only in giving names to remote cosmic concentrations, they came to be called 'Astronomers.'

"Owing to the fact that for surrounding beings, the difference in the meaning and good sense between those professionals of that time among the three-brained beings who have taken your fancy and those who have now, as it were, the same occupation, might show you, so to say, the 'obviousness-of-the-infallible-deterioration-of-the-degree-of-the-crystallisation' of the data engendering 'sane-logical-mentation' which ought to be present in the common presences of those favorites of yours as three-brained beings, I therefore find it necessary to explain to you and to help you to have an approximate understanding just about this difference, which is also changing for the worse.

"At that period, these terrestrial three-brained beings who are already at responsible age and whom the others named 'Astrologers,' besides making the said observations and investigations of various other cosmic concentrations for the purpose of a greater, as is said, 'detailizing' of that branch of general learning of which they were representatives, fulfilled several further definite essence-obligations taken upon themselves towards surrounding beings similar to themselves.

"One of their fundamental definite obligations was that they, also like our Zirlikners, had to advise all the conjugal pairs of their, as it was then said, 'flock,' about the time and form of the process of the sacred 'Elmooarno' for the purpose of a desirable and corresponding conception of their result, and when such results were actualized, or as they themselves say, 'newly-born,' they had to draw up their 'Oblekioonerish' which is the same as what your contemporary favorites call 'horoscope'; and later, they themselves or their substitutes had—during the whole period of the formation of the newly-born into responsible existence—to guide them and give corresponding indications on the basis of the said 'Oblekioonerish' and also on the basis of cosmic laws constantly explained by them flowing from the actions of the results of other cosmic large concentrations in general during the process of being-existence of beings on all planets.

"These indications of theirs and also their, so to say, 'warning-counsels' proceeded just in the following manner:

"When a function became disharmonized or only began to be disharmonized in the presence of any being of their flock, then the latter applied to the Astrologer of his district, who, on the basis of the said 'Oblekioonerish' made by him, and on the basis of the changes expected, according to his calculations, of the processes proceeding in the atmosphere and ensuing in their turn from the action of the other planets of their solar system, indicated just what they had to do to their own planetary body at which definite periods of the Krentonalnian movements of their planet—as for instance, in which direction to lie, how to breathe, which movements to make in preference, with which types to avoid relations and many things of the same kind.

"In addition to all this, they assigned beings at the seventh year of their existence, likewise on the basis of these 'Oblekioonerishes,' to corresponding mates of the opposite sex for the purpose of fulfilling one of the chief being-duties, that is, the continuation of the race, or as your favorites would say, they assigned 'husbands' and 'wives.'

"Justice must be given to your Favorites of that period, when these 'Astrologers' existed among them they then indeed very strictly followed the counsels of these 'Astrologers' and accomplished their conjugal unions exclusively only according to their indications.

"Therefore at that period they always responded to each other in respect of their conjugal unions according to type, just as the said pairs correspond everywhere on those planets on which Keschapmartnian beings also breed.

"These ancient 'Astrologers' there made these matches successfully because, even if they were very far from the knowledge of many cosmic 'Trogoautoegocratic' truths, yet they at least already very well knew the laws of the influence of the different planets of their solar system on the beings breeding on their own planets, namely—the influence of these planets on a being at the moment of his conception for further formation as well as for his complete acquisition of the Being of a responsible being.

"Having, thanks to the information transmitted to them from generation to generation, a many-centuried practical knowledge, they already knew which type of the passive sex can correspond to which type of the active sex.

"And owing to all of this, the pairs matched according to their indications almost always turned out to be corresponding and not as it proceeds there at the present time, and that is to say, they are now united into conjugal pairs who almost always do not correspond with each other in type, in consequence of which during the continuation of the entire existence of these couples there, about half of their as is said 'inner life' is spent only for what our esteemed Mullah Nassr Eddin expresses in one of his sayings by the following words:

"'What a good husband he is, or what a good wife she is, if the whole of their inner life is not occupied with the constant "nagging" of their other halves.'

"In any case my boy, if these Astrologers had continued to exist there, then surely, thanks to their further practice, the existence of the beings of this unfortunate planet would have by now gradually become such, that at least their family relations would have been a little like the existence of similar beings on other planets of our Great Universe.

"But no, this beneficent practice established in the process of their existence, they also sent, just like all their other good attainments—without even having had time to utilize it properly—'to-the-gluttonous-swine' of our respected Mullah Nassr Eddin.

"And these 'Astrologers,' as usually happens there, also began from the beginning gradually to 'dwindle' and later, entirely, as is said, 'vanished.'

"After the complete abolition among them of the duties

of these Astrologers, others appeared in their places in this same professional sphere, but this time among the 'learned-beings-of-new-formation,' who, as it were, also began to observe and study the results ensuing from various cosmic large concentrations and their influence on the existence of beings of their planet; and their 'studies' consisted only in inventing names for different remote suns and planets meaning nothing to them and existing in milliards in the Universe, and also in measuring, as it were, by a method known to them alone and which was their professional secret, the distance between the cosmic points which they see from their planet through their 'childish-toys' called by them 'telescopes,' they then therefore came to be called, as I have already told you, 'Astronomers.'

"Now my boy that we have spoken also about these contemporary 'ultra-fantasists' from among your favorites, we might as well, imitating the form of mentation and verbal exposition of our dear teacher Mullah Nassr Eddin, also 'illuminatingly' enlighten you about their significance, so esteemed by your favorites.

"First of all, you should know about that ordinary cosmic 'something' actualized just for these same terrestrial types, which is in general always actualized of itself for every cosmic unit and which serves for beings with Objective Reason as what is called an 'issuing-source' for pondering about the explanation of the sense and meaning of any given cosmic 'result.'

"This same 'something' which serves as an 'issuing source' for discovering the significance of these terrestrial contemporary types, is a 'wiseacring-map' named by them themselves—of course unconsciously, the 'map-inventory-of-the-heavenly-spaces.'

"There is no need for us to draw any other logical conclusion from this 'Issuing-source' specially actualized for them; it will be sufficient only to say that the name itself of this map of theirs shows that the designations made on it cannot at all be any other than only relative, because from the surface of their planet, with only these possibilities at their disposal, and breaking their 'esteemed-heads' over the names devised and the calculations of various kinds of measurements, they can see only that sun and those planets, which to their good fortune, do not very quickly change the course of their falling in relation to their own planet, and thus give them the possibility during a long period of time—of course long, comparatively with the shortness of the duration of their own existence—to observe them and as they magniloquently express themselves 'mark-down-their-positions.'

"In any case my boy, however much matters do not go well with the results of the activities of these contemporary representatives of 'learning' among your favorites, please don't get angry with them. If they do not bring any benefit at all to your favorites, they at least do not do them any great harm.

"After all they must be occupied with something!

"It is not for nothing that they wear spectacles of German origin and special smocks sewn in England.

"Let them! Let them be occupied with this! God bless them!

"Like most of the other freaks there who are occupied with, as is said there, 'higher-matters,' they will out of boredom get busy as 'leaders-of-the-struggle-of-five-against-one.'

"And it is known to all that the beings who are occupied with these matters, always radiate from themselves very harmful radiations for beings around them similar to themselves.

"Well enough! Leave these contemporary 'titillators' in peace and let us continue our interrupted definite theme.

"In view of the fact my boy that this 'conscious-ability' expressed in the creation of such an artificial construction unparalleled both before and after this period, of which I was then an eyewitness, was also the result of the attainments of the beings, members of the learned society Akhaldan, which was already formed on the continent of Atlantis before the second large terrestrial catastrophe, I think it will be best, if, before continuing to explain to you further about the mentioned observatory and other constructions erected there for the welfare of being-existence, I should tell you, even though briefly, about the history of the arising there of such an indeed great learned society consisting of ordinary three-brained beings, as this learned society Akhaldan then was on the continent Atlantis.

"It is imperatively necessary to inform you of this because in the course of my further explanations concerning these three-brained beings of the planet Earth who have taken your fancy, I shall in all probability have to refer more than once to that society of learned beings there.

"I must also tell you the history of the arising and existence of that society there on the continent Atlantis, in order that you may have a notion also about this, that if something is attained by three-brained beings there also on your planet, thanks to their 'being-Partkdolgduty,' that is to say, thanks to their conscious labors and intentional sufferings, then these attainments are not only utilized by themselves for the good of their own Being, but also a certain part, of them, as with us, is transmitted by inheritance and becomes the property of their direct descendants.

"Such a lawful result present there, you can see from the fact, that although towards the end of the existence of the continent Atlantis, abnormal conditions of ordinary being-existence had already begun to be established and that after the second great catastrophe they deteriorated at such a rate that they soon finally crushed all the 'potency' to manifest the possibilities present in the presences of every three-brained being, nevertheless their 'attainments-of-learning' passed by inheritance, at least, partially even though mechanically, to their remote direct descendants.

"I must first tell you that I got to know this history, thanks to what are called 'Teleoghinooras,' which are present in the atmosphere also of that planet Earth of yours.

"As you probably do not yet know exactly what a 'Teleoghinoora' is, try to transubstantiate in the corresponding parts of your common presence the information concerning just this cosmic actualization.

"'Teleoghinooras' can be formed from such a quality of being-contemplation which only those three-brained beings have and can actualize, who have coated their higher bodies in their presences and who have brought the perfecting of the Reason of their higher being-part up to the degree of the sacred 'Martfotai.'

"And the sequential series of being-ideas, materialized in this way, concerning any given event, are called 'Korkaptilnian-thought-tapes.'

"It seems that the said 'Korkaptilnian-thought-tapes' concerning the history of the arising of the learned society Akhaldan were, as I found out already much later, deliberately fixed by a certain 'Eternal-Individual,' Asoochilon, now a Saint who became coated in the common presence of a three-brained being named Tetetos who arose on your planet just on the continent of Atlantis and who had existed there four centuries before the second great 'Transapalnian-perturbation.'

"These 'Korkaptilnian-thought-tapes' are never destroyed as long as the given planet exists which is in what is called the 'tempo-of-movement-of-the-prime-arising'; and they are subject to none of those transformations from any cosmic causes whatever to which all other cosmic substances and cosmic crystallizations are periodically subject.

"And however long a time may have already passed, every three-brained being in whose presences there is acquired the ableness to enter into the being-state called 'Soorptakalknian-contemplation' can perceive and cognize the text of these 'Korkaptilnian-thought-tapes.'

"And so my boy, I myself learned about the details of the arising there of the society Akhaldan partly from the text of the just mentioned 'Teleoghinoora' and partly from the many data which I learnt much later, namely when, having become interested also in this highly important factor there, I made my usual detailed investigations.

"According to the text of the mentioned 'Teleoghinoora' and to the data I subsequently learned, it became clear and definitely known to me that this learned society Akhaldan which arose then on the continent Atlantis and which was composed of the three-brained beings of the Earth, was formed seven hundred and thirty-five years before the second 'Transapalnian-perturbation' there.

"It was founded on the initiative of a being there named Belcultassi, who was then able to bring the perfecting of his higher being-part to the Being of a Saint 'Eternal-Individual'; and this higher-part of his now already dwells on the holy planet Purgatory.

"My elucidations of all those inner and outer being-impulses and manifestations which were the cause of this Belcultassi having then founded that truly great society of ordinary three-brained beings—a society which in its time was throughout the whole Universe called 'envied-to-be-imitated'—showed that when this same later Saint Individual Belcultassi was once contemplating, according to the practice of every normal being, and his thoughts were by association concentrated on himself, that is to say, on the sense and aim of his own existence, he suddenly sensed and cognized that the process of the functioning of his whole presence had hitherto proceeded not as it should have proceeded according to sane logic.

"So unexpectedly a constatation shocked him so profoundly that he thereafter devoted the whole of himself only to be able at any cost to unravel it all and understand.

"First of all he decided to attain without delay such a 'potency' as would give him the strength and possibility to be quite sincere with himself, that is to say, to be able to conquer those impulses which had become habitual in the functioning of his common presence from the many varied associations which arose in him and which were started in him by every kind of accidental shock proceeding from without and also by those arising within him, namely, the impulses called 'self-love,' 'pride,' 'vanity' and so on.

"And when after incredible what are called 'organic' and 'psychic' efforts, he attained to this, he then, without any compunction for those being-impulses which had become inherent in his presence, began to think and recall when and what various being-impulses had ever arisen in his presence during the period of his preceding existence and how he had consciously or unconsciously reacted to them.

"Analyzing himself in this manner, he recalled the impulses which evoked in him one or another reaction in his independently-spiritualized parts, that is to say, in his body, his feelings and his thoughts, and what his general essence had become when he reacted to something more or less attentively, and how and when, in consequence of such reactions of his, he had manifested consciously with his 'I' or had acted automatically under the direction only of his instinct.

"Recalling in this way all his former perceptions, experiencings, and manifestations, this bearer of the later Saint Individual Belcultassi just then clearly constated, in consequence, that his external manifestations had no correspondence whatever with either the perceptions or with the impulses definitely formed in him.

"Further, he made the same sincere observations of his of

the impressions proceeding from without and also formed within himself, which were perceived by his common presence; and he made them with always the same exhaustive, conscious verifications of how these impressions were received by his separate spiritualized parts, how on what occasions they were experienced by the whole of his presence and for what manifestations they became impulses.

"These exhaustive conscious observations and impartial constatations finally convinced Belcultassi that something proceeded in his own common presence not as it should have proceeded according to sane being-logic.

"As my subsequent detailed investigations made clear, although Belcultassi had become convinced 'beyond-all-doubt' of the accuracy of his observations on himself, yet he doubted the correctness of his own sensations and understandings and also of the normality of his psychic organization; and he therefore set himself the task of elucidating, first of all, whether he was in general normal while sensing and understanding everything just in this way and not otherwise.

"To carry out this task of his he decided to find out how others sensed and cognized the aforesaid.

"With that aim he began inquiring among his friends and acquaintances to try to find out from them how they sensed it all and how they cognized their former and current perceptions and manifestations, doing this of course, very discreetly in order to avoid touching the mentioned impulses inherent in them of 'self-love,' 'pride' and so on, unbecoming to be present in three-brained beings.

"Thanks to these inquiries Belcultassi was gradually able to evoke sincerity among his friends and acquaintances, and the result proved that all of them sensed and saw themselves just as he did.

"There proved to be, just among these friends and acquaintances of Belcultassi, several serious beings who were not yet entirely slaves to the action of the consequences of the properties of the organ Kundabuffer, and who, having penetrated to the essence of the matter also became very seriously interested in it and began to verify that which proceeded in themselves, and independently to observe those around them.

"Soon after, on the initiative of the same Belcultassi, they began to meet together from time to time, and to share their observations and new constatations.

"After prolonged verifications, observations and impartial constatations this whole group of terrestrial beings also became categorically convinced, just like Belcultassi himself, that they were not as they ought to be.

"Not long after, many others having also the said presences, joined this group of terrestrial beings there.

"And later they founded this society which they named the 'Society-of-Akhaldans.'

"By the word 'Akhaldan,' the following conception was then expressed:

"'The-striving-to-become-aware-of-the-sense-and-aim-of-the-Being-of-beings.'

"From the very beginning of the foundation of this society, Belcultassi himself stood at its head, and the subsequent actions of the beings of this society proceeded under his general guidance.

"For many years there this society existed under the said name, and its member-beings were called 'Akhaldansovors'; but later, when the members of this society, for purposes of a general character, were divided into a number of independent groups, the members belonging to different groups were called differently.

"And the division into groups occurred then for the following reason.

"When they had become finally convinced that there was something undesirable in their presences and had begun to search for means and possibilities of removing it in order to become such as, according to sane logic, they had to be, that is to say, correspondent to the sense and aim of their existence, the elucidation of which, whatever it might cost them, they made the basis of their task, and when they began to actualize in practice this task previously decided upon by their Reason, it very soon became clear that it was imperatively necessary for its fulfillment to have more detailed information in their Reasons concerning various special branches of knowledge.

"But as it proved impossible for each and every one of them to acquire the necessary special knowledge, they divided themselves for convenience into a number of groups, in order that each group might separately study one of these special branches of knowledge required for their common aim.

"Here my boy, you should notice that genuine objective knowledge just then arose there for the first time and began to exist and developed normally up to the time of the second great catastrophe to their planet; also that the growth of the development of its branches then progressed even at an unprecedented rate.

"And in consequence a considerable number of great and small what are called cosmic 'objective-truths' gradually began at that period to become evident also to these three-brained beings who have taken your fancy.

"The learned beings of this great first and probably last terrestrial learned society were then divided into seven independent groups, or as it is otherwise said, 'sections'; and each of these groups or sections received a definite name.

"Members of the first group of the society Akhaldan were called 'Akhaldanfokhsovors,' which meant that the beings belonging to that section studied the presence as well as the reciprocal action of separate parts of their common planet.

"The members of the second section were called 'Akhaldanstrassovers,' and this meant that the beings belonging to that section studied what are called the 'radiations' and their reciprocal action of all the other planets of their solar system.

"Members of the third section were called 'Akhaldanmetrosovors,' which meant beings occupied with the study of that branch of knowledge, which was like that branch of our general knowledge we call 'Silkoornano,' and which partly corresponded to what your contemporary favorites call 'mathematics.'

"The members of the fourth group were called 'Akhaldanpsychosovors,' and by this name those members of the society Akhaldan were then denoted who made their observations of the perceptions, experiencings and manifestations of beings like themselves and verified their observations by statistics.

"Members of the fifth group were called 'Akhaldanharnosovors,' which meant that they were occupied with the study of that branch of knowledge which combined those two branches of contemporary science there, which your favorites called 'chemistry' and 'physics.'

"Members belonging to the sixth section were called 'Akhaldanmistessovors,' that is to say, beings who studied every kind of event arising outside of themselves, actualized consciously from without and also arising by themselves, and in what circumstances which of them are erroneously perceived by beings.

"And as regards the members of the seventh and last group, they were called 'Akhaldangezpoodjnisovors'; these members of the society Akhaldan devoted themselves to the study of those manifestations in the presences of the three-brained beings of their planet which proceeded in them not in consequence of various functionings issuing from different kinds of impulses engendered owing to data already present in them, but from cosmic actions coming from without and not depending upon them themselves.

"The three-brained beings of your planet who then became members of this society did indeed many things in respect of approaching objective knowledge as had never been done there before and probably never will be again.

"And it is impossible not to express regret and to repeat that it was just then, when to the most great misfortune of the three-brained beings there of all later epochs, owing to the incredible being-labors of the member-beings of that great society, the required tempo of work had already been established in respect of conscious discrimination for them themselves and also in respect of their unconscious preparation for the welfare of their descendants, that, in the heat of it all, a number of them constated, as I have already told you, that something serious had to occur to their planet in the near future.

"For the purpose of discovering the nature of the anticipated serious event, they dispersed over the whole planet, and it was shortly afterwards as I have also already told you, that the mentioned second 'Transapalnian-perturbation' occurred to that ill-fated planet of yours.

"Well then my boy, when after this catastrophe, a number of the surviving member-beings of that great learned society gradually came together again, they, having no longer their native country, first settled together with the majority of the other surviving beings in the center of the continent Grabontzi, but later, when they had, on the continent Grabontzi, 'come-to-themselves,' a little after the 'cataclysm-not-according-to-law,' which had occurred, they decided jointly to try to reestablish and perhaps to continue to actualize in practice, all those tasks which had formed the basis of their last society.

"As the manifestations of those abnormal conditions of being-existence of most of the three-brained beings there on the said part of the surface of the continent Grabontzi, which had already been established before the catastrophe, had already begun to 'boil' furiously, these surviving members of the society Akhaldan looked for another place on the same continent for their permanent existence more suitable for this work of theirs which demanded complete separateness.

"Such a suitable place they found in the valley of the large river flowing on the northern side of the said continent, and there indeed they all together migrated with their families in order to continue in isolation the attainment of the tasks set by their society.

"This whole region through which the said large river flowed, they first named 'Sakronakari.'

"But this name was afterwards several times changed and at the present time this region is called 'Egypt,' while the said large river, then called 'Nipilhooatchi,' is now, as I have already said, called the 'Nile.'

"Soon after, certain former members of the learned society Akhaldan settled on this part of the surface of the Planet Earth, all the beings of our tribe then existing on the surface of that planet which has taken your fancy, migrated to the same place.

"And the facts concerning the real relations of the beings of our tribe with that part of your planet and also with the first migration there of the chance surviving former members of the society Akhaldan are as follows:

"I told you once that just before the second 'Transapalnian-perturbation,' our party-Pythoness, while prophesying, insisted that all the beings of our tribe should, without delay, migrate for the continuation of their existence on that planet, to a definite part of the surface of that same continent which is now called Africa.

"This definite part of the surface of the continent which the Pythoness indicated, lay just at the source of the said large river, 'Nipilhooatchi,' where the beings of our tribe existed the whole time the said second 'Transapalnian-perturbation' lasted as well as afterwards when everything had gradually resumed its relatively normal state and when most of the surviving beings had then almost forgotten what had happened and had again formed—just as if nothing had occurred to them—one of their famous 'centers-of-culture' in the very middle of that future Africa. Just at the time when the former members of the society Akhaldan were searching for a suitable place for their permanent existence, and chanced to meet a number of the beings of our tribe, they advised them to migrate to the country further down the said river.

"Our acquaintanceship and our friendly relations with many of the former members of the society Akhaldan, had already been begun on the continent Atlantis almost from the founding of that society.

"Do you remember I told you, that when I descended to that planet for the first time and the beings of our tribe assembled in the city of Samlios with my participation in order together to find a way out of the difficult situation that had been created—well, those general meetings of ours were held just in one of the sections of the principal cathedral of the society Akhaldan; and already, from that time on, good relations were established between many beings of our tribe and certain members of this society.

"And there in that future Egypt whither both had migrated in the said way, the relations of the beings of our tribe with the genuine former members themselves who had chanced to be saved and also with the descendants of other genuine members, remained uninterrupted and continued almost down to the time of the departure of our tribe from your planet.

"Although the hope of the few chance surviving members of the society Akhaldan that they would be able to resume the actualizing of the tasks of their society was not fulfilled, nevertheless, thanks to them alone, there still continued to be present in the presences of several subsequent generations after the loss of Atlantis, the 'instinctive-conviction' concerning the sense of what is there called 'completed-personal-Being.'

"In addition to this, thanks to them, something of what had been attained by the Reason of the three-brained beings there also nevertheless survived when that Reason was still normal in them; and after a while this something began mechanically to be transmitted by inheritance from generation to generation and reached the beings of quite recent periods, even to several beings of contemporary times.

"Among these results of the learned attainments of the members of the society Akhaldan which were transmitted by inheritance, were also, without question, those ingenious and solid 'artificial-constructions' which I saw being erected during this fourth descent of mine to your planet, by the beings of whom I am just going to inform you, who were breeding on that part of the surface of the continent of the present Africa.

"Although the expectations that I had formed from all that our countrymen had told me concerning the mentioned new observatory there, before I had seen it with my own eyes, were not justified, nevertheless the observatory itself and also the other 'artificial-constructions' of the beings then of that region proved to be exceedingly ingenious and provided data for my common presence to become enriched by a great deal of productive information for my consciousness.

"And in order that you may clearly represent to yourself and understand how these various 'artificial constructions' were then erected by the three-brained beings of this region for the welfare of their being-existence, I think it will be enough if I explain to you in as great detail as possible, how the particularity of their ingenious, practical invention was manifested in respect just of their new observatory, on account of which I had decided to visit that region.

"For this purpose I must first of all inform you of two facts connected with the change in the common presences of these three-brained beings who have taken your fancy.

"The first fact is that at the outset, while they still existed normally, that is, as it is in general becoming to all three-brained beings to exist, and while they had what is called 'Olooestesnokhnian-sight,' they also could perceive at a distance proper to be perceived by ordinary three-brained beings, the visibility of all both great and small cosmic concentrations existing beyond them during every process of the Omnipresent Okidanokh proceeding in their atmosphere.

"In addition, those of them who were consciously perfected and had thereby brought the sensibility of the perception of their organ of sight—like three-brained beings everywhere—up to what is called the 'Olooessultratesnokhnian-state,' acquired the possibility of perceiving also the visibility of all these cosmic units situated at the same distance, which arise and have their further existence dependent upon the crystallizations localized directly from the sacred Theomertmalogos, that is to say, upon the emanations of our most holy Sun Absolute.

"And later, when the same constant abnormal conditions of ordinary being-existence were finally established, as a consequence of which Great Nature was compelled, for reasons of which I have already told you, among other limitations, also to remold the functioning of their organ of sight into what is called 'Koritesnokhnian,' that is to say, into the sight proper to the presences of one-brained and two-brained beings, then thereafter they were already able to perceive the visibility, both of their great and small concentrations situated beyond them, only when there proceeded in the Omnipresent active element Okidanokh in the atmosphere of their planet, the sacred process 'Aieioiuoa,' that is, as they themselves say—according to their understanding and their own perceptions—'on-dark-nights.'

"And the second fact, by virtue of the same degeneration

of their sight into a 'Koritesnokhnian' one, is based on that law common to all beings, namely, that the results obtained from every manifestation of the Omnipresent Okidanokh are perceived by the organs of sight only when in immediate contact with those vibrations which are formed in beings and which actualize the functioning of the being-organ for perceiving at the given moment the visibility of cosmic concentrations situated beyond them; that is to say, only when the said results of the manifestation of the Omnipresent Okidanokh take place up to the point beyond which, according to the quality of the given organ for perceiving visibility, what is called the 'momentum-of-the-impulse' dies down; or to put it otherwise, they perceive the visibility of objects only when almost next to them.

"But if these results take place beyond the mentioned limit, then this manifestation does not at all reach those beings in whose presence are organs for the perception of visibility, formed only by the results of the totality of 'Itoklanoz.'

"Here it is very opportune to repeat one of the profound sayings seldom used there, of our Mullah Nassr Eddin, which very nearly defines the given case, that is, this degree of the limitation of the perception of visibility of your contemporary favorites.

"This wise saying of his, seldom used there, consists of the following words:

"'Show me the elephant the blind man has seen, and only then will I believe that you have really seen a fly.'

"Well then, my boy, thanks to that artificial adaptation which I then saw, for the observation of other cosmic concentrations, and which was being constructed in that future Egypt on the initiative issuing from the Reasons of the remote descendants of the member-beings of the learned society Akhaldan, any one of these unfortunate favorites of yours, in spite of the 'Koritesnokhnian-sight' which had long before become inherent to them, nevertheless acquired the potency to perceive freely at any time, as they say, 'of-the-day-and-night,' the visibility of all those remote cosmic concentrations which in the process of the general cosmic harmonious movement, come within the sphere of the horizon of their observation.

"In order to overcome this limitation of their organ of the perception of visibility, they then invented the following:

"Their 'Teskooano' or 'telescope,' the construction of which, it must be here said, passed to them also from their remote ancestors, they did not fix on the surface of their planet, as was usually done there and is still done now—but they placed this 'Teskooano' very deeply within the planet, and they carried out their observations of the cosmic concentrations found beyond the atmosphere of their planet through specially-bored, pipe-like-hollows.

"The observatory I then saw had five of these hollows.

"They began in relation to the horizon, from different places of the surface of the planet occupied by the observatory, but they all met at a small underground common hollow which was something like a cave. From there the specialists, then called 'Astrologers,' made their observations for the purpose of studying, as I have already told you, the visible presences and results of the reciprocal action of other cosmic concentrations belonging both to their own solar system and to other systems of the Great Universe.

"They made these observations of theirs through any of the mentioned hollows which looked out in different directions on to their horizon, depending on the given position of their planet relative to the cosmic concentration observed in the process of the 'common-cosmic-harmonious-movement.'

"I repeat, my boy, that although the chief peculiarity of the observatory constructed there by the three-brained beings of the future Egypt proved not to be new to me, since this principle had also been utilized in my observatory on Mars, with only this difference, that my seven long pipes were fixed not within the planet but on it, nevertheless all their innovations were so interesting in detail that, for any case that might arise, I even made, during my stay there, a detailed sketch of everything I saw, and later even used something of it for my own observatory.

"And concerning the other 'artificial-constructions' there, I shall perhaps tell you about them in detail sometime later, but meanwhile I will only say that all these independent constructions, not then quite finished, were situated not far from the observatory itself, and were intended, as I cleared up during my inspection under the guidance of the constructor who accompanied us and who was a friend of one of our tribe, partly for the same purposes of observing other suns and planets of our Great Universe, and partly for determining and intentionally directing the course of the surrounding atmosphere in order to obtain the 'climate' desired.

"All these 'artificial-constructions' of theirs occupied a fairly large open space of that part of the said region, and were enclosed by a special lattice-work made of the plant then called there 'Zalnakatar.'

"It is extremely interesting to notice here that they erected at the chief entrance of that huge enclosure a rather large—large of course in comparison with the size of their presences—stone statue called 'Sphinx,' which strongly reminded me of the statue I saw on my first personal descent to your planet in the city of Samlios, just opposite the enormous building belonging to the learned society Akhaldan and which was then called the 'chief-cathedral-of-the-society-Akhaldan.'

"The statue I saw in the city of Samlios and which greatly interested me, was the emblem of this Society, and was called 'Conscience.'

"It represented an allegorical being, each part of whose

planetary body was composed of a part of the planetary body of some definite form of being existing there, but of the parts of those beings of various forms in whom, according to the crystallized conceptions of the three-brained beings there, one or another being-function was present in a superlative degree.

"The main mass of the planetary body of the said allegorical being was represented by the 'trunk' of a being there of definite form, called 'Bull.'

"This bull-trunk rested on the four legs of another being existing there, also of a definite form, called 'Lion,' and to that part of the bull-trunk called its 'back,' two large wings were attached similar in appearance to those of a strong bird-being breeding there, called 'Eagle.'

"And on the place where the head should be, there were fixed to the bull-trunk, by means of a piece of 'amber,' two breasts representing in themselves what are called, 'breasts-of-a-virgin.'

"When I became interested on the continent Atlantis in this strange allegorical image, and then enquired about its meaning, one of the learned members of the Great Society of men-beings explained it to me as follows:

"'This allegorical figure is the emblem of the society Akhaldan and serves for all its members as a stimulus constantly to recall and awaken in them the corresponding impulses attributed to this allegorical figure.'

"Further he continued:

"'Each part of this allegorical figure gives to every member of our society in all, three independently associating parts of his common presence, namely, in the body, in the thoughts and in the feelings, a shock for corresponding associations for those separate cognizances which in their totality can alone give us the possibility of gradually getting rid of those undesirable factors present in every one of us, both those transmitted to us by heredity and those acquired by ourselves personally, which gradually engender within us impulses undesirable for us, and as a consequence of which we are not as we might be.

"'This emblem of ours constantly reminds and indicates to us that it is possible to attain freedom from what I have mentioned, only if we compel our common presences always to think, feel and act in corresponding circumstances according to that which is expressed in this emblem of ours.

"'And this emblem of ours is understood by all of us members of the society Akhaldan in the following way:

"'The trunk of this allegorical being, represented by the trunk of a 'bull,' means that the factors crystallized in us and which bring forth in our presences maleficent for us, both those we have inherited and those we have personally acquired, can be regenerated only by indefatigable labors, namely, by such labors as, among the beings of our planet, the bull is particularly capable.

"'That this trunk rests on the legs of a 'Lion' means that the said labors should be performed with that cognizance and feeling of courage and faith in one's 'might,' the property of which 'might' is possessed among all the beings of the Earth in the highest degree by the possessor of these legs—the mighty lion.

"'The wings of the strongest and highest soaring of all birds, the 'Eagle,' attached to the bull-trunk, constantly remind the members of our society that during the said labors and with the mentioned inner psychic properties of self-respect, it is necessary to meditate continually on questions not related to the direct manifestations required for ordinary being-existence.

"'And as regards the strange image of the head of our allegorical being, in the form of the "breasts-of-a-virgin," this expresses that always and in everything during both the inner and outer functionings evoked by one's own consciousness, there should predominate such a "love" as can arise and be present only in the presences of concentrations formed in the lawful parts of every whole responsible being in whom the hopes of our COMMON FATHER are placed.

"'And that the head is fixed to the trunk of the bull with "amber" signifies that the said love should be strictly impartial, that is to say, completely separated from all the other functions proceeding in every whole responsible being.'"

"In order, my boy, that the sense of this latter emblem, put into the material called there 'amber,' may become quite comprehensible to you, I must add that 'amber' is one of those seven planetary formations, in the arising of which the Omnipresent Active Element Okidanokh takes part with all its three separate, independent, sacred parts in equal proportion; and in the process of planetary actualization these intraplanetary and surplanetary formations serve for what is called the 'impeding' of the independent flow of those three localized independent sacred parts.

At this point of his tale Beelzebub made a short pause, as if he were thinking about something, and afterwards continued thus:

"During my narration of what I then saw on a still surviving terra-firma part of the surface of your planet among the three-brained beings there, certain of whom were the direct descendants of members-beings of the truly great learned society Akhaldan there, the result of the manifestations of my being-Reason, owing to various associative recollections of all kinds of impressions of the perceptions of the visibility of the exterior environment of the said region, which became fixed in my common presence, has been that there has been gradually revived in me all the scenes and all the associative flow of thoughts of one of those being-experiencings of mine which occurred during my last stay there, on my visit just to that same contemporary Egypt, when I once sat absorbed in thought at the foot of one of those 'artificial-constructions' that had chanced to survive from that period, and is now already called there, the 'Pyramids.'

"It was just then, that in the general function of my Reason there was also associated among other things, the following:

"Good! . . . If none of the benefits already formerly attained by the Reason of the beings of the continent Atlantis for ordinary being-existence, has become the possession of the contemporary beings of this planet—this might perhaps be logically explained simply because for cosmic causes, not issuing at all from and not depending upon the three-brained beings there, that second great 'cataclysm-not-according-to-law' occurred, during which not only that continent itself perished, but also everything existing on it.

"But this Egypt! . . .

"Its magnificence was still recent . . .

"There is no denying it . . . owing to the third small catastrophe to that ill-fated planet, and also to the fifth, about which I will speak later, this part also of its surface, it is true, suffered, having been covered with sands. Nevertheless, the three-brained beings dwelling there did not perish, but were only scattered over various other parts of the same continent, and consequently, whatever new exterior conditions may have ensued, there should have survived in their presence, it would seem, the crystallized results of the perfected factors, transmitted to them by inheritance for normal 'being-logical-mentation.'

"And so, my boy, being desirous after this distressful 'Alstoozori' of mine, or as your favorites would say, 'sorrowful-reflections,' to clear up for myself the very essence of the causes also of this lamentable fact there, I understood at the end of my minute investigations and became aware with all my Being, that this abnormality there proceeds exclusively owing only to one very remarkable aspect of the chief particularity of their strange psyche, namely, that particularity which has become completely crystallized and an inseparable part of their common presences and which serves as a factor for the periodical arising in them of what is called the 'urgent-need-to-destroy-everything-outside-of-them.'

"The point is that when, during the apogee of the development of such a peculiarity—terrifying to every Reason—of the psyche of the three-brained beings, they began to manifest outside of themselves this phenomenal peculiarity of their common presence, that is to say, when they begin to carry out the process of reciprocal destruction on some part of the surface of their planet, then, at the same time, without any deliberate aim, and even with what is called 'organic-need,' they also destroy everything which chances to come within the sphere of the perception of their organ of sight. At the periods of this 'phenomenal-psychopathic-apogee,' they destroy also all the objects present in the given place and at the given time, which these same beings themselves, between whom this terrifying process proceeds, have intentionally produced as well as the productions which have chanced to survive and to reach them from the beginnings of previous epochs.

"Well then my boy, at the period of this fourth personal sojourn of mine on the surface of your planet, I first arrived in the country now called Egypt, and after having stayed there a few days among the remote descendants of the member-beings of the great learned society Akhaldan, and having become acquainted with certain surviving results of their 'being-Partkdolgduty' for the welfare of their descendants, I, afterwards, accompanied by two of our tribe, went to the southern countries of the same continent, and there, with the help of the local three-brained beings, caught the necessary number of ape beings.

"Having accomplished this, I telepathically signaled our ship '*Occasion*' which descended to us on the first, it must be said, very dark night; and when we had loaded these ape-beings in that special section of the ship '*Occasion*' which had been constructed for Gornahoor Harharkh under his directions, we at once reascended to the planet Mars; and three Martian days later, on the same ship and together with these apes, I ascended to the planet Saturn.

"Though we had previously decided to carry out the experiments with those apes only the following year, when they would have become thoroughly acclimatized and orientated to existence under the new conditions, I ascended then to the planet Saturn so soon because at my last personal meeting with Gornahoor Harharkh, I had promised him to be present at his family solemnity which had soon to take place.

"And this family solemnity of Gornahoor Harharkh's consisted in this, that beings like himself around him, would consecrate the first heir produced by him.

"I promised to attend this family solemnity "Krik-hrakhri' in order to undertake, regarding his recently arisen heir, what is called the 'Atnatoorornian-being-duty.'

"Here it is interesting to remark that the kind of procedure for undertaking this being-duty, took place among the ancient three-brained beings of your planet also, and even reached your contemporary favorites, though these latter, just as in everything else, take only the external form of this serious and important procedure. The beings who undertake, as it were, these duties, are called by your contemporary favorites 'godfathers' and 'godmothers.'

"The heir of Gornahoor Harharkh was then called 'Rakhoorkh.'"

CHAPTER XXIV

Beelzebub's Flight To The Planet Earth For The Fifth Time

BEELZEBUB continued to relate as follows:

"After my fourth stay on the surface of the planet Earth many years again passed.

"During these years I, of course, as before, sometimes observed attentively through my Teskooano the being-existence of these favorites of yours also.

"During this time their numbers considerably increased and they already populated almost all the large and small 'terra-firma-parts' of the surface of this planet of yours, and of course there also continued to proceed among them during the whole of certain periods, their chief particularity, namely, every so often they would destroy each other's existence.

"During this time, that is to say, between my fourth and fifth visits, great changes occurred to the surface of your planet.

"Many changes also occurred there in the concentration of the places of settlement of these favorites of yours. For example, all those 'centers-of-culture' of theirs on the continent Ashhark where I personally was during my previous descents upon the earth, namely, the countries of Tikliamish and Maralpleicie had by the time of my fifth arrival there, ceased altogether to exist.

"The cause of the destruction of the 'centers-of-culture' of theirs and of the changes on the surface of this planet in general, was again a misfortune, the third in number for this ill-starred planet.

"This third misfortune was entirely of a local character and occurred because there had proceeded in its atmosphere during several years unprecedented so-called 'accelerated-displacements-of-the-parts-of-the-atmosphere' or as your favorites there would say, 'great winds.'

"The cause of these abnormal 'displacements' or 'great

winds' at that time was once again those two fragments which had been separated from this planet of yours during the first great calamity, and which afterwards became independent small planets of this solar system. They are now called 'Moon' and 'Anulios.' Strictly speaking, the main cause of this third terrestrial misfortune was only the larger of these separated parts, namely, the Moon; the smaller fragment, 'Anulios,' played no part in it whatever.

"The 'accelerated-displacements' in the earth's atmosphere resulted from this, that when the atmosphere on the small, chance-arisen planet Moon had been finally formed, and the Moon, according to the already mentioned law of 'catching-up,' continued to fall back upon its fundamental mass by the path already then established, and while this newly arisen definite presence of the Moon had not yet acquired its own harmony within the 'Common-system-harmony-of-movements,' then this, so to say, not harmonized on the whole, as it is called 'Osmooalnian friction' just evoked in the atmosphere of the Earth the mentioned 'accelerated-displacements' or 'great winds.' Then by the force of their currents these unprecedented 'great winds' began, as it is said, to 'wear down' the elevated 'terra-firma-parts,' and to fill up the corresponding depressions.

"The two countries of the continent Ashhark upon which chiefly was concentrated the process of existence of the second and third groups of beings of contemporary Asia, that is to say, the fundamental parts of the countries Tikliamish and Maralpleicie, just happened to be also such depressions.

"At the same time sand also filled up certain parts of the country Gemchania as well as that country in the middle of the continent Grabontzi, where, as I have already told you, there was formed after the sinking of Atlantis, what they called the leading 'center-of-culture' for all the three-brained beings there, a country which was at that time the most flourishing part of the surface of this planet of yours, and is already now the desert called 'Sahara.'

"Bear in mind also that during the abnormal winds of that time, besides the countries mentioned, several other inconsiderable terra-firma spaces of the surface of that unhappy planet were also covered by sands.

"It is interesting to note here, that concerning the changes that then occurred in the locale of the permanent existence of the three-centered beings, your contemporary favorites also, by some means or other, learned of it, and having made a label for this as well, this time 'the great migration of races,' they stuck it on what they call their knowledge.

"A number of the 'learned' there now mightily puff and blow to find out why and how it all occurred, so that they can tell everybody else.

"Just now there exist several theories about the matter there, and, although they have nothing in common with each other, and in an objective sense, each is more absurd than the other, nevertheless they are accepted there by what is called 'official knowledge.'

"But in fact the real cause of the migration of the three-centered beings then arose because as soon as the said abrasion began, the beings living on the continent Ashhark, fearing to be buried by the sand, began moving to other, more or less, secure places, and these migrations of the three-brained beings there proceeded in the following order.

"Most of the three-brained beings populating Tikliamish moved to the south of the same continent Ashhark, to the country which was called later 'Persia'; and the rest moved north, and settled in those regions which were afterwards called 'Kirkistcheri.'

"As regards the beings populating the country Maralpleicie, one part wandered eastwards, while the rest, the major part, went west. Having crossed the eastern heights, those who went east settled down on the shores of the large 'salia-kooriapnian-spaces,' and this country was later called 'China.'

"And that part of the beings of Maralpleicie who sought safety by moving to the west, after wandering from place to place, ultimately reached the neighboring continent, later called 'Europe,' while the three-brained beings who then still remained existing in the middle of the continent 'Grabontzi' dispersed over the whole of its surface.

"And so, my boy, this my fifth personal flight to your planet already belongs to the period of time after this said redistribution of the groups of the communities of these favorites of yours. And the reasons of my personal descent there were the following events:

"I must first tell you that the chief peculiarity of the psyche of your favorites, namely, the 'periodic-need-to-destroy-the-existence-of-others-like-oneself,' interested me more and more with every succeeding century of theirs; and side by side with it the craving increased in me to ferret out the exact causes of a particularity so phenomenal in three-brained beings.

"And so, my boy, in order to have more material for elucidating this question that so intensely interested me, I, in the interval between my fourth and fifth stay on the planet Earth, organized through the Teskooano from the planet Mars my observation of the existence of those peculiar three-brained beings in the following way:

"I deliberately kept under observation quite a number of separate beings from among your favorites and during many of their years either I personally, or somebody whom I specially commissioned, observed them attentively, taking pains not, if possible, to miss anything, and to clear up from every aspect every kind of particularity in their manifestations during the processes of their ordinary existence there.

"And I must confess, my boy, that when I happened to be otherwise free I sometimes during whole 'Sinonoums,' or, as your favorites there approximately define the corresponding flow of time, during whole 'hours,' observed with great interest the movements of the three-brained beings there under observation, and tried to explain to myself logically what are called their 'psychic experiencings.'

"And so, during these observations of mine from the planet Mars by means of my Teskooano, that once 'flashed' upon me which just served as the beginning of my further then quite serious study of the psyche of these three-brained beings who please you; namely, it 'flashed' upon me that the length of their existence was, century by century, and even year by year, becoming shorter and shorter, at a very definite and uniform rate.

"Of course, when I first noticed it, I at once took into account not only the chief particularity of their psyche, that is, their periodic reciprocal destruction, but also the innumerable what are called 'illnesses' which exist exclusively only on the planet, the majority of which, by the way, arose and continued to arise owing to the same abnormal external conditions of the ordinary being existence established by them, and which help to make it impossible for them normally to exist up to the sacred Rascooarno.

"When I first noticed this, and as my previous impressions concerning the same began to come back to me, each of the separate independent spiritualized parts of my whole presence become filled with the conviction, and my essence perceived the mentioned 'flash,' that in truth these three-brained beings of your planet had, in the beginning, existed, according to their time calculation, for about twelve centuries, and some of them even, for about fifteen centuries.

"To be able more or less clearly to represent to yourself the rate at which the length of their existence declined during this time, it is enough for you to know that when I left this solar system forever, the maximum length of their existence was already from seventy to ninety of their years.

"And latterly if anybody should exist as long as this, all the rest of the beings of that peculiar planet would already consider that he had existed 'quite decently long,' while if anybody happened to exist a little over a century, he would be exhibited in their museums, and of course all the rest of the beings there would know about him, because his photographs and descriptions of the manner of his existence, even to the enumeration of each of his movements, would constantly be published in all their, what are called 'newspapers.'

"And so, my boy, having suddenly constated such a fact there, as I had no special business on the planet Mars, and it was quite impossible to try to probe this novel peculiarity by means of the Teskooano, I decided to go there myself with the aim of perhaps clearing up for myself, there on the spot, the causes of this also.

"Several Martian days after my resolve I again ascended there on the ship '*Occasion*.' At the time of this fifth personal descent of mine on your planet their 'center-for-the-ingoing-and-outgoing-results-of-the-perfecting-of-the-being-rumination' or as they themselves call it, their 'center-of-culture,' was already the city of Babylon, and it was just there that I decided to go.

"This time our ship '*Occasion*' descended to what is called the 'Persian Gulf,' because we ascertained through the Teskooano before our flight that for my further traveling, that is to say, to get to the town of Babylon, and for the mooring of our ship '*Occasion*' itself, the most convenient place would be that same 'saliakooriapnian-space' of the surface of your planet, now existing there under the name of the 'Persian Gulf.'

"This water space was convenient for my further traveling because the large river on the banks of which the city of Babylon stood, flowed into it, and we proposed to sail up the stream of this river in order to get there.

"During that period of the flow of time this 'Incomparably-majestic' Babylon flourished in every respect. It was a 'center-of-culture' not only for the beings dwelling on the continent Ashhark, but also for all the beings of all those other large and small terra-firmas which were adapted to the needs of the ordinary being existence on that planet.

"At the time of my first arrival there in this 'center-of-culture' of theirs, they were just preparing that . . . which was afterwards the principal cause of the acceleration of the rate of the degeneration of their 'psychic organization,' especially in the sense of the atrophy in them of the instinctive functioning of those three fundamental factors which should exist in the presence of every kind of three-brained being, namely, those factors which give rise to those being-impulses which exist under the names of 'Faith,' 'Hope,' and 'Love.'

"The decline of those being-factors by inheritance from generation to generation has brought it about that instead of a real being-psyche, such as should exist in the presence of every kind of three-brained being, there now already exists in the presence of your contemporary favorites, although a 'real psyche' also, nevertheless one that can be very well defined by the wise sayings of our dear Mullah Nassr Eddin, which consists of the following words:

"'There is everything in it except core, or even kernel.'

"It is absolutely necessary to relate to you in as great detail as possible what occurred during that period in Babylon, since all this information may serve you as valuable material for a better elucidation and transmutation in your reason of all the causes which together have finally given rise to that strange psyche of the three-centered beings, which psyche your contemporary favorites already have, and which has so much interested you.

"I must first tell you that the information concerning the events of that time which I am now about to relate I picked up among those three-centered beings there whom the other beings call 'learned.'

"Here, before going any further, I must dwell a little on the beings there on your planet whom the other beings call 'learned.'

"Even before this fifth stay of mine there, that is to say, before that period when Babylon, as I have told you, flourished in every respect, there became and were regarded as 'learned' by others, not such beings as become and are regarded as learned everywhere in the Universe, and such as at first became learned even on your planet, namely such beings as from the first bring themselves by their conscious labors and intentional sufferings to the ableness to contemplate the details of all that exists, from the point of view of World-arising and World-existence, and owing to which they chiefly perfect their highest body to the corresponding gradation of the sacred measure of objective reason in order that by this means as much about cosmic truths might later be sensed in them as their higher being-body is perfected.

"But they mostly become 'learned,' from the time of what is called the Tikliamishian civilization until now, especially the contemporary ones, who 'learned by rote' as much as possible of every kind of vacuous information such as 'old women' love to report about what was said, as it were, in olden times.

"Note, by the way, that for the definition of the importance of the scientists there, our venerated Mullah Nassr Eddin also has a sentence expressed as follows:

"'Everybody talks as if our learned know that half a hundred is fifty.'

"There on your planet the more of such information one of your favorites mechanically learns by rote—information he himself has never verified and which moreover he has never sensed—the more learned he is thought to be.

"And so, my boy, when we reached the city of Babylon, there were indeed a great many learned beings. Scientific beings were then gathered there from almost the whole of that planet of yours.

"As the reasons for the original congregation of these beings in the city of Babylon at that time are extremely interesting I will tell you also about this a little more in detail. The truth is that most of the scientists of the Earth had been assembled there under the compulsion of a most peculiar Persian King, under whose dominion the city of Babylon was also at that period.

"Thoroughly to understand the fundamental aspects flowing from the total results of the abnormally established conditions of ordinary being-existence there, which gave rise to the said peculiarity of this Persian king, I must first enlighten you in regard to two facts which had long before that been fixed.

"The first fact is this, that from almost the time of the sinking of the continent Atlantis, a particular 'essence property' began gradually to be crystallized and during the later centuries became already finally crystallized in the presence of every one of your favorites there, thanks to which that being-sensation which is called 'happiness-for-one's-being' which is experienced from time to time by every three-brained being from the satisfaction of his inner self-respect, appears in the presence of your favorites exclusively only when they acquire for their own possession a great deal of that popular metal, there called 'gold.'

"A further great misfortune for them arising from this particular 'essence-property' in their general presence consists in this, that the mentioned sensation due to the ownership of the said metal, is also strengthened by the beings surrounding the owner, even if they learn about it only by what is called 'hearsay,' and have not themselves been convinced by personal corresponding perceptions. At the same time it is the established custom there never to consider what kind of being-manifestations one made to become the owner of a great quantity of this metal. But such a being there becomes for all those around him an object which evokes in their presence the functioning of that crystallized consequence of the property of the organ Kundabuffer which is called 'envy.'

"And the second fact consists in this, that when in the presence of your favorites their chief particularity functions 'Crescendantly,' and according to the established custom among different communities of theirs, their process of the reciprocal destruction of each other's existence proceeds, then afterwards when this property only proper to themselves and maleficent for them themselves, has run its course, and they temporarily cease these processes of theirs, then the King of that community in which a greater number of subjects remains unharmed, receiving the title of conqueror, usually takes for himself everything which is possessed by the beings of the conquered community.

"Such a King-conqueror there usually orders his subjects to take from the conquered all their lands, all the young beings of female sex present in the conquered community, and all that which is called 'riches' accumulated by them during centuries.

"And so, my boy, when the subjects of that said peculiar Persian King conquered the beings of another community he ordered them not to take, and even not to touch any of these, but to take with them as what are called 'captives' only all the learned beings present in the conquered community.

"Clearly to represent and transmute in yourself the understanding why in the individuality of that Persian King such a peculiar craze arose and became proper only to him, you must know, that still at the period of the Tikliamishian civilization, there in the town called 'Chiklaral,' a three-brained learned, by name 'Harnahoom,' whose essence later became crystallized into what is called an 'eternal-Hasnamuss-individuum' invented, that any old metal you like abundant in that planet could easily be turned into the rare metal 'gold,' and all that was necessary to know for this, being just one very small 'secret.'

"This maleficent invention of his became widely spread there, and having become crystallized in the presence of the beings of that time, and being transmitted by inheritance from generation to generation, it began to pass to the beings of the subsequent generation as a gradually formed definite maleficent fantastic science there under the name of 'alchemy,' under the name, that is, of just that great science which indeed existed there during those epochs long past, when, in the presence of their ancestors, the consequences of the properties of the organ Kundabuffer had not yet been crystallized and which branch of genuine knowledge might be really necessary and truly advantageous for the three-brained beings there even of contemporary times.

"And as at that period to which my tale relates, this Persian King needed for some or other of his undoubtedly Hasnamussian aims a great deal of this metal, rare on the surface of the Earth, called 'gold,' and as the notion concerning this method that had been invented by the then existing, now 'Hasnamussian individuum,' Harnahoom, had also reached his presence, he was anxious to get gold by so easy a means.

"When this Persian King had finally decided to get gold by 'Alchemy,' he for the first time with all his being realized that he as yet did not know that 'little secret' without which it was absolutely impossible to fulfill this wish of his. So he then pondered how to find out this little 'secret.' The result of his pondering was that he became aware of the following:

"'If the learned already have knowledge of every other kind of "mystery" then to one of them, perhaps, this mystery must also be known.'

"Having finally arrived at such a conclusion, he, with an intensified functioning of 'being-astonishment' at why such a simple idea had never entered his head before, called several of his attendant subjects and ordered them to find out to which of the learned beings of his capital this 'mystery' was known.

"When it was reported to him the following day that not one of the learned beings of the capital knew this 'mystery' he ordered enquiries to be made also of all the learned present among the beings of the whole of his subject-community; and when after several days he again received the same negative reply he once more betook himself to thought, and this time very seriously.

"His serious thinking first led his reason to the understanding that no doubt whatever, one or other of the learned beings of his community was aware of this 'secret' also; but since among beings of that clan the strict keeping of a 'professional' mystery was very strongly developed, nobody, of course, was willing to reveal it.

"The result of his serious thinking was that he became aware that it was not enough merely to question, he must examine the learned beings about this 'Mystery.'

"The same day he gave suitable instructions to his nearest corresponding assistants, and the latter already began to 'examine' after the manner that had already long before been the way of power-possessing beings to 'examine' ordinary beings.

"And when this peculiar Persian King became finally convinced that the learned beings of this community indeed and in truth knew nothing about this mystery, he began to look for learned beings in other communities to whom this mystery might be known.

"As the kings of the other communities were unwilling to offer their learned beings for interrogation he just decided to compel the recalcitrant by force. And from that time on, at the head of numerous hordes in subject on to him, with their help he began to make what are called 'military excursions.'

"This Persian King had many hordes in subjection to him

because at that period, from the region of the surface of this planet of yours where that community was situated and over which he happened to be King, there had been intensified in the presence of the beings even before this time, on the basis of what is called the 'Foreseeing-adaptation' of Great Nature, the, as it is called, 'birth-rate'; and at the given period that which was demanded for the common cosmic Trogoautoegocratic process was being effectuated, that is to say, in order that from this region of the surface of your planet there should issue more of those vibrations arising from the destruction of being-existence."

During this last explanation Hassein interrupted Beelzebub with the following words:

"Dear Grandfather, I do not understand why, for the purpose of the effectuation of this most great cosmic process, the issuing of the required vibrations should depend on any definite region of the surface of the planet."

To this question of his grandson Beelzebub replied as follows:

"As before long I intend to make the special question of those terrifying processes of reciprocal destruction which they call 'wars' the theme of my tales concerning the three-brained beings of the planet Earth, it is better to defer this question of yours also until this special tale, because then, I think, you will understand it well."

Having said this Beelzebub again continued to relate about the Babylonian events.

"When the peculiar Persian King I mentioned began, thanks to the hordes in subjection to him, to conquer the beings of other communities and to seize by force the learned among them, he assigned as a place for their congregation and existence the said city of Babylon to which they were taken in order that this lord of half the then continent of Asia could thereafter freely interrogate them in the hope that one of them perhaps, might happen to know the secret of turning cheap metal into the metal gold.

"With the same aim he even made at that time a special what is called 'campaign' into the country Egypt.

"He then made this special 'campaign' there because the learned beings of all the continents of the planet were assembled there at that period, the opinion being widely spread there that more information for their various 'sciences' was to be got in this 'Egypt' than anywhere else on the planet.

"This Persian King-conqueror then took from Egypt all the learned beings present there, both the native and those who had come from other communities; and among the number were then also several called 'Egyptian Priests,' descendants of just those scientific members of the society Akhaldan who chanced to escape, and who were the first to populate that country.

"When a little later a fresh craze arose in the presence of this peculiar Persian King, just the craze for the process itself of the destruction of the existence of other beings similar to himself, and which thrust out the former craze, he forgot about the learned beings and they began to exist there freely in the city of Babylon awaiting his further directions.

"The neo-learned beings collected in this way there in the city of Babylon from almost the whole of the planet, used often to meet together; and of course, as it is proper to the learned beings of the planet Earth, they began discussing among themselves questions which were either immeasurably beyond their comprehension, or about which they could never elucidate anything useful whatsoever, either for themselves or for ordinary beings there.

"Well, it was just during these meetings and conversations that there arose among them, as it is in general proper to arise among 'learned beings' there what is called a 'burning-question-of-the-day,' a question which in some way or other indeed interested them at that time to, as they say, their very 'marrow.'

"The question which chanced to become the 'burning-question-of-the-day' so vitally touched the whole of everybody's essence that they even climbed down from their, what are called 'pedestals,' and began discussing it not only with the learned like themselves, but with every Tom, Dick and Harry.

"The consequence was that interest in this question gradually spread among all the ordinary three-brained beings then existing in Babylon, and by about the time we reached this Babylon it had become the 'question-of-the-day' for all the beings there.

"Not only did these learned themselves talk and discuss this question, but similar conversations and fierce discussions proceeded like fury among the ordinary beings there also.

"It was talked about and discussed by young and old, both men and women, and even by the Babylonian butchers. They were all, and particularly learned, exceedingly anxious to know about this question.

"Before our arrival there, many of the beings then existing in Babylon had ultimately even lost their reason on account of this question, and many were already candidates for the same—to lose it.

"This 'burning-question-of-the-day' consisted in this, that both the 'neo-learned' and the ordinary beings of the city of Babylon were very anxious to know whether they had a 'soul.'

"Every possible variety of fantastic theory existed in Babylon upon this question; and more and more theories were being freshly cooked up; and every, as it is said there 'catchy theory' had of course its followers.

"Although a whole host of various theories existed there, nevertheless they were one and all based upon only two, but two quite opposite assumptions. One of these was called the 'atheistic' and the other the 'idealistic' or 'dualistic.'

"All the 'dualistic' theories maintained the existence of the 'soul,' and of course its immortality and every possible kind of 'perturbation' to it after the death of the being 'man.'

"And all the 'atheistic' theories maintained just the opposite.

"In short, my boy, when we arrived in the city of Babylon there was then proceeding what is called the 'building-of-the-tower-of-Babel.'"

Having pronounced these latter words Beelzebub became a little thoughtful and then continued as follows:

"Now I wish to explain to you the expression I just used, namely, the 'building-of-the-tower-of-Babel.' This expression is very often used on your planet by the contemporary three-brained beings there also.

"I wish to touch upon this frequently there-used-expression and to elucidate it to you first of all, chiefly because I chanced to be a witness then of all the events which gave rise to it, and secondly because the history of the arising of this expression, and its transmutation in the understanding of the contemporary favorites of yours can very clearly and instructively elucidate to you that, thanks as always to the same abnormally established conditions of ordinary being-existence, no precise information of events there which have indeed occurred to beings of former epochs ever reach the beings of later generations; or if by chance something like this expression does even reach them, then the fantastic reason of your favorites constructs a whole theory on the basis of just one expression such as this, with the result that those baseless 'being-egoplastikoori,' or, as they call them, 'psychic representations,' increase and multiply in their presence from which, also as a result, there has arisen in the universe the strange and unique psyche of three-brained beings which is possessed by every one of your favorites.

"Well then, when we arrived in the city of Babylon, and

with the aim of elucidating the question which had interested me I began mixing with various beings there and making my corresponding observations, then because almost everywhere I ran across only the said learned who had gathered and met there in great numbers, it so fell out that I, associating with them only, began making my observations both by means of them, and in their own individualities.

"Among the number of learned beings whom I met for my mentioned aim there, was also one named Hamolinadir who had also been brought there by compulsion from Egypt.

"Well, between this terrestrial three-brained being Hamolinadir and myself during these meetings of ours, almost the same relations were established which in general are established everywhere between three-brained beings who frequently meet.

"This Hamolinadir was one of those learned there in the total presence of whom the factors for the impulses of a three-brained being which had passed by inheritance were not yet quite atrophied, and moreover it turned out that during his corresponding age the responsible beings around him had prepared him to be also more or less normally responsible.

"It is necessary to notice that many scientific beings of this kind were then in the city of Babylon.

"Although this learned Hamolinadir had his arising and preparation for becoming a responsible being just there in the city of Babylon and descended from the race of beings there called 'Assyrian,' yet he became learned in Egypt where the highest school existing on the Earth at that time was found, and which was called 'Materializing Thought.'

"At the age he was when I first met him, he already had his 'I'—in the sense of rational directing, present in his general presence and which is called 'automatic-psychic-functioning'—of the maximum steadiness for three-centered beings of the planet Earth at that time, in consequence of which during what is called his 'waking-passive-state' he had very definitely expressed being-manifestations, as for instance those called 'self-consciousness,' 'impartiality,' 'sincerity,' 'impressionability,' 'rumination,' and so forth.

"Soon after our arrival in Babylon, I began going with this Hamolinadir to what are called the 'meetings' of the mentioned learned beings, and listening to every possible kind of what they called their 'reports' upon just the question which was then 'the-question-of-the-day,' and which was the reason for the 'agitation-of-mind' of all the Babylonians.

"This friend of mine, Hamolinadir, was also very much excited about the said 'burning-question.'

"He was agitated and perplexed by the fact that both the already existing and the many newly appearing theories upon this question were all, in spite of their entirely opposite proofs, equally convincing and equally veridical.

"He said that those theories in which it was proved that we have a 'soul' were very logically and convincingly expounded; and equally the theories in which quite the contrary was proved were expounded no less logically and convincingly.

"So that you may be able to put yourself in the place of that sympathetic Assyrian, I shall also explain to you that in general on your planet, then in the city of Babylon as also now at the present time, most of the various theories concerning such a question, as they call it, 'of the beyond,' or concerning any other 'elucidation-of-the-details' of any definite thesis whatever, are invented by those three-brained beings there in whom most of the consequences of the properties of the organ Kundabuffer are fulfilledly crystallized, in consequence of which there actively functions in their presence that being-property which they themselves call 'cunning.' Owing to this they gradually and consciously acquire—of course consciously only with the sort of reason which it has already become long ago proper for them alone to possess—and moreover only automatically acquired in their general presence—capacity for 'spotting' the weak points of the psyche of the surrounding beings like themselves; and this capacity is gradually formed in them into data that enable them at times to sense and even to understand the peculiar logic present in the beings surrounding them, and according to these data they invent and propound one of their 'theories' concerning this or that question; and because, as I have already told you, in most of the three-brained beings there, owing to the abnormal conditions of ordinary being-existence established there by them themselves, the being-function called 'instinctively-to-sense-cosmic-truths' gradually atrophies, then, if any one of them happens to devote himself to the detailed study of any one of these 'theories' he is bound, whether he likes it or not, to be persuaded of it with the whole of his presence.

"Well my boy.

"Already seven of their months after our arrival in the city of Babylon I once went with this friend of mine there, Hamolinadir, to what is called a 'general learned conference.'

"This 'general learned conference' had already been convened at that time by the learned beings previously brought there by force; and thus there were at this conference not only the learned forcibly assembled there by the mentioned Persian King, who in the meantime had already got over his craze about the science of 'alchemy,' and forgotten all about it, but many other learned also from other communities who had voluntarily gathered together, as they then said 'for the sake of science.'

"At this 'general learned conference' the reporters spoke by lot.

"My friend, Hamolinadir, having also to report upon some topic, also drew a lot; and it fell to him to speak the fifth in order.

"The reporters who preceded him reported either new

theories they had invented, or they criticized theories already existing and known to everybody.

"At last came the turn of this sympathetic Assyrian.

"He ascended what is called the rostrum, and as he did so some attendants suspended a placard above it on which was indicated the subject of the given reporter's discourse.

"It was the custom at that time to do this.

"The placard announced that the reporter had taken as the theme of his report the 'instability of human reason.'

"Thereupon, this terrestrial friend of mine first expatiated on the kind of structure which in his opinion the human 'head brain' has, and in which cases and in what manner various impressions are perceived by the other brains of man, and how only after definite what is called 'agreement' between all the brains are the total results just impressed on this head brain.

"He spoke calmly at first, but the longer he spoke the more agitated he became, until his voice rose to a shout, and so it was that he criticized the reason present in man.

"Thereupon he also mercilessly criticized his own reason.

"Still continuing to shout, he very logically and convincingly demonstrated the instability and fickleness of man's reason and showed in detail how easy it is to prove and convince this reason of anything you like.

"Although signs of his sobbing could be heard now and then, in the midst of the shouting of this terrestrial friend of mine, Hamolinadir, nevertheless, even while sobbing, he continued to shout. Further he said:

"'To every man, and also of course to me, it's no trouble to prove anything; all it is necessary to know is which shocks and just which associations to arouse in the other human brains, while one or other 'truth' is being proved. It is very easily possible even to prove to man that our whole world and also of course the people in it, are nothing but an illusion, and that the authenticity and reality of the World are only a 'corn,' and moreover the 'corn' growing on the big toe of our left foot. Other than this 'corn,' absolutely nothing exists in the world; everything only seems, and even then only to 'psychopaths squared.'

"At this point in the speech of this sympathetic terrestrial three-brained being, an attendant offered him a bowl of water, and after he had eagerly drunk the water, he continued to speak, but now more calmly.

"He said further:

"'Take myself as an example: I am not an ordinary learned man. I am known by all Babylon and by the people of many other towns as an exceedingly learned and able man.

"'I finished the course of study higher than which has never yet existed on the Earth, and which it is almost impossible will ever exist again.

"'But what has this highest development given to my Reason in respect of that question which, well, already during one or two years, is driving all Babylonians insane? This Reason of mine which has received the highest development, has given me during this general dementia concerning the question of the 'soul' nothing else but 'five Fridays a week.'

"'During this time I have very attentively and seriously followed all the old and newly appearing theories about the 'soul' and there was not a single theory with the author of which I did not inwardly agree, since all of them were very logically and plausibly expounded, and such reason as I have, could not fail to agree with their logic and plausibility.

"'During this time I have even myself written a very lengthy work on this 'Question of the beyond'; and many of those present here have surely become acquainted with this logical thinking of mine and most probably there was none of you but envied this logical mentation of mine.

"'Yet at the same time I now honestly declare to you all

that concerning this 'question of the Beyond' I myself with the whole of the knowledge that has been accumulated in me, am neither more nor less than just an idiot cubed.

"'There is now proceeding among us in the city of Babylon the common public building of a Tower by means of which to ascend to 'heaven' and there to see with one's own eyes what goes on there.

"'This tower is being built of bricks which outwardly all look alike, but which are made of quite different materials.

"'Among these bricks are bricks of iron and wood and also of 'dough' and even of 'eiderdown.'

"'Well, of such bricks, a stupendously enormous tower is being built at the present time right in the center of Babylon, and every more or less conscious person is obliged to bear in mind that sooner or later this tower will certainly fall and crush not only all the people in Babylon, but also everything else that is there.

"'As I personally still wish to live, and have no fancy for being crushed by this Babylonian Tower, I shall therefore now immediately get away from here, leaving you to do as you please . . . '

"These last words he uttered while leaving, and ran off.

"And from that time I never saw that Sympathetic Assyrian again.

"As I later learned, he left the city of Babylon the same day forever, and went to Nineveh, and existed somewhere there to a ripe old age. I also ascertained that this Hamolinadir was never again occupied with 'sciences,' and that he spent his existence only in planting 'choongary' which in contemporary language is called 'maize.'

"Well, my boy, the speech of this Hamolinadir at first made such a deep impression upon the beings there that for almost a month they went about as it is said there, like beings 'down-in-the-mouth.'

"And when they met each other, they could speak of nothing else but only the various passages from his speech which they remembered and repeated.

"They repeated them so often that several of Hamolinadir's phrases spread among the ordinary beings of Babylon and became sayings for ordinary daily existence.

"Some of his phrases even reached contemporary beings of the planet Earth, and among them was also this, namely, the 'Building of the Tower of Babel.'

"And contemporary beings now already quite clearly picture to themselves that once upon a time a certain tower was built in this said city of Babylon to enable beings to ascend to 'God Himself' in their planetary bodies.

"The contemporary beings of the planet Earth also say and are quite persuaded that during the building of this 'Babylonian Tower' a number of 'tongues' were confused.

"Altogether there reached the contemporary beings of the planet Earth a great many such isolated expressions, uttered or fixed by various reasonable beings of former epochs concerning certain details of a complete understanding from the epoch when the 'center-of-culture' was Babylon, and also from other epochs; and your favorites of recent centuries, simply on the basis of these 'scraps,' have with their already quite 'babelish' reason, concocted such 'cock and bull' stories as our Arch-cunning Lucifer might envy.

"Among the many teachings then current in Babylon concerning the 'question of the Beyond,' two had a large number of adherents although these teachings had nothing in common.

"And it was precisely these two teachings which began to pass from generation to generation, and to confuse their being 'sane-mentation,' which had already been confused enough without them.

"Although in the course of their transmission from generation to generation the details of both these teachings underwent change, nevertheless the fundamental ideas contained in them, remained unchanged and have even reached down to contemporary times.

"Of these two teachings which then had many adherents in Babylon one was just the 'dualistic,' and the other the 'atheistic' so that in one of them it was proved that they do contain this 'soul' and in the other, quite the opposite, namely that they contain nothing of the kind.

"It was said in the 'dualistic' or 'idealistic' teaching that within the coarse body of the man-being is a fine and invisible body, and just this latter is the 'soul.'

"This fine body of man is immortal, that is to say, it is never destroyed.

"This 'fine body' or 'soul,' it was said further, must make a corresponding payment for every action of the 'physical body,' whether voluntary or involuntary, and every man already at birth consists of these two bodies, namely the 'physical body' and the 'soul.'

"Further it was said that when a man is born, two invisible spirits immediately perch upon his shoulders.

"On his right shoulder sits a 'spirit of good,' called an 'angel,' and on his left a second spirit, a 'spirit of evil,' called a 'Devil.'

"From the very first day these spirits, the 'spirit of good' and the 'spirit of evil,' record in their ledgers all the manifestations of the man, the spirit sitting on his right shoulder recording all those called his 'good manifestations' or 'good deeds' and the spirit sitting on had left shoulder, the 'evil.'

"Among the duties of these two spirits is that of tempting and compelling a man to do more of those manifestations which are in their respective domains.

"The spirit on the right constantly strives to make the man refrain from doing those actions which are in the domain of the opposite spirit and perform more of those in his own domain.

"And the spirit on the left does the same, but vice versa.

"In this strange teaching it was further said that these two 'spirit rivals' are always at odds with each other and that each strives with might and main that the man should perform more of those actions which are under his charge.

"When the man dies, these spirits leave his 'physical body' on the Earth and take his 'soul' to 'God' who exists somewhere there 'up in Heaven.'

"There in 'Heaven' this 'God' sits surrounded by his devoted Archangels and Angels and in front of him a pair of scales is suspended.

"On each side of the 'scales' 'spirits' stand on duty. On the right stand the spirits who are called 'servants of Paradise' and these are 'Angels'; and on the left stand the 'servants of Hell' and these are 'Devils.'

"The spirits which have sat on the man's shoulders all his life bring his 'soul' after death to 'God,' and 'God' then takes from their hands the 'ledgers' in which the notes have been recorded of all the man's 'doings'; and He places them on the 'pans of the scales.'

"On the right 'pan' He puts the ledger of the 'Angel'—and on the left 'pan' the ledger of the 'Devil'; and according to the 'pan' which falls, 'God' commands the spirits on duty standing on the given side to take this 'soul' into their charge.

"In the charge of the spirits standing on duty on the right is just that place called 'Paradise.'

"It is a place of indescribable beauty and splendiferousness. In that 'Paradise' are magnificent fruits in abundance, endless quantities of fragrant flowers, and enchanting sounds of cherubic songs and seraphic music constantly echo in the air; and many other things were also enumerated whose outer reactions, according to the perceptions and awareness abnormally present in the three-brained beings of that strange planet, are likely to evoke in them, as they say, 'delight,' that is the satisfaction of those needs formed in their general presence which are criminal for three-centered beings to possess, and the totality of which have just ousted from their presence everything, without exception, that was put into it by our COMMON FATHER and which it is imperative for every three-brained being to possess.

"But in charge of the spirits standing on duty on the left of the scales, who, according to this Babylonian teaching are the 'devils,' there is what is called 'Hell.'

"Concerning 'Hell' it was said that it is a place of no vegetation, but it is always unimaginably hot, and without a drop of water.

"Sounds constantly echo in this 'Hell'—of fearful 'cacophony' and infuriatingly offensive 'abuse.'

"Everywhere there are instruments of every conceivable torture from the 'Rack' and the 'Wheel' to instruments for lacerating bodies and mechanically rubbing them with salt, and so on, of the same kind.

"In the Babylonian 'Idealist' teaching it was very minutely explained that in order for his 'soul' to enter this 'Paradise' the man must constantly strive while on Earth to provide most material for the ledger of the spirit 'Angel' sitting on his right shoulder, otherwise a superior amount would be provided for the records of the spirit sitting on the left shoulder, in which case such a man's 'soul' would inevitably go to this most awful 'Hell.'

"Here Hassein could not restrain himself, and suddenly interrupted Beelzebub with the following words:

"And which of their manifestations do they consider good and which bad?"

Beelzebub looked at his grandson with a very strange look, and shaking his head said as follows:

"Concerning this, which being-manifestations are there on your planet considered good and which bad, two independent understandings, having nothing in common with each other, have existed right from the most ancient times up to the present period, having passed from generation to generation.

"The first of these understandings exists there and passes from one generation to another among such three-brained beings there, as those members of the society Akhaldan who were on the continent Atlantis, and such as those who after the second 'Transapalnian-perturbation' several centuries later again became beings, although of another kind, who acquired almost the same in the foundations of their general presence and who were called 'initiates.'

"The first of these understandings exists there under the following formulation:

"Every action of a man is good in the objective sense if it is done according to his conscience, and every action is bad if remorse will afterwards be experienced from it.

"And the second understanding arose there soon after the rational 'invention' of the Great King Konuzion, which invention, passing from generation to generation through ordinary beings there gradually spread over almost the whole planet under the name of 'Morality.'

"Here it will be very interesting to notice a particularity of this 'Morality' which was grafted upon it at the very beginning of its arising and which ultimately became part and parcel of it.

"In what this said particularity of terrestrial 'Morality' just consists, you can easily represent to yourself and understand if I tell you that both within and without it acquired exactly that 'unique-property' which belongs to the beings bearing the name 'chameleon.'

"And the oddity and peculiarity of this said particularity of the 'morality' there, especially of contemporary morality, lies in this—that its functioning automatically depends entirely on the humors of the 'local authorities,' which humors in their turn depend also automatically on the state of the four sources of action existing there, bearing the names of 'mother-in-law,' 'digestion,' 'John Thomas,' and 'Cash.'

"The second Babylonian teaching which then had many followers, and which passing from generation to generation also reached your contemporary favorites, was on the contrary one of the 'atheistic' teachings of that period.

"In this teaching by the terrestrial Hasnamuss candidates of that time, it was flatly stated that there is no God in the world, and moreover no 'soul' in man, and hence that all those talks and discussions about the 'soul' are nothing more than the fancies of sick visionaries.

"It was further maintained that there exists in the World only one special law of mechanics according to which everything that exists passes from one species into another, that is to say, the results which arise from certain preceding causes are gradually transformed and become causes for subsequent results.

"Man is also therefore only a consequence of some preceding cause, and in his turn must as a result serve as a cause of certain consequences.

"Further it was said that even what are called 'supernatural-phenomena' really perceptible to most people are all nothing but these same results flowing out of the mentioned special law of mechanics.

"The full comprehension of this law by the pure reason depends on the gradual impartial, all-round acquaintance with its numerous details which can be revealed to a pure reason in proportion to its development.

"But as regards the reason of man, this is only the sum of all the impressions perceived by him from which there gradually arise in him data for comparisons, deductions, and conclusions.

"As a result of all this, he obtains a greater information concerning every possible kind of similarly repeated fact around him, which facts in their turn serve in the general organization of man as material for forming definite convictions in him. Thus all this reason formed in man is merely his own subjective psyche.

"Whatever had been said in these two 'teachings' about the 'soul,' and whatever maleficent means had been prepared by these scientists assembled there from almost the whole planet, for the gradual transformation of the reason of the beings of their descendants into a veritable 'Mill' of 'Babel,' it would not have been in the objective sense, completely calamitous; but the whole objective terror is concealed in this, that there later resulted from these teachings a great evil, not for their descendants alone, but possibly for everything that exists.

"The fact is that when, owing to their mutual 'wiseacrings' during the mentioned 'agitation of minds' of that time in the city of Babylon, these learned beings acquired in their presences in addition to all they already had, a further mass of new data for Hasnamussian manifestations, and then went to their respective homes, they began everywhere, of course unconsciously, propagating like contagious bacilli, all these notions which together finally and utterly destroyed the last remnants and even the traces of all the results of the holy labors of the very saintly Ashiata Shiemash.

"The remnant, that is to say, of those holy 'consciously suffering' labors which he intentionally performed for the creation, just for the three-centered beings, of such special external conditions of ordinary being-existence in which alone there could gradually disappear from their presence the maleficent consequences of the properties of the organ Kundabuffer, and in their place, there could be gradually acquired those properties proper to be possessed in the presence of every kind of three-brained being, whose whole presence is an exact counterpart of everything in the universe.

"Another result of these divers wiseacrings by these learned beings of the Earth then in the city of Babylon concerning the question of the 'soul' was this: that soon after my fifth personal appearance on the surface of that planet of yours, this, in its turn, 'center-of-culture' of theirs, the incomparable, and indeed Magnificent, Babylon was also, as it is said there, swept away from the face of the Earth to its very foundation.

"Not only was the city of Babylon itself then destroyed, but everything also that had been acquired and accomplished by the beings who had, during many of their centuries, formerly existed there. I must say for the sake of Justice that the prime initiative for the destruction of the holy labors of Ashiata Shiemash, did not spring, however, from these learned of the Earth who were then assembled in the city of Babylon, but from the invention of a 'learned' being very well known there, who, several centuries before these Babylonian events, also existed there on the continent Asia; namely, from the invention of a being named 'Lentrohamsanin' whose higher being part having coated itself into a definite unit, and having perfected itself by its reason up to the required gradation of objective reason, also became one of those three hundred and thirty-five Hasnamuss 'eternal individuums' who now exist on the small planet bearing the name 'Retribution.'

"About this 'Lentrohamsanin' I shall also tell you, since the information concerning him will serve to elucidate for your understanding the strange psyche of those three-brained beings. But I shall tell you about this 'Lentrohamsanin' only when I have finished speaking about the very saintly Ashiata Shiemash, as the information relating to this planet of yours concerning this now already most very saintly Individuum Ashiata Shiemash, is the most important and the most material for your understanding of the peculiarities of the psyche of these three-brained beings who please you and who breed on the planet Earth."

CHAPTER XXV

The Very Saintly Ashiata Shiemash Sent From Above To The Earth

AND SO, my boy!

"Now listen very attentively to the information concerning the most Very Saintly now already Common Cosmic Individuum Ashiata Shiemash, relating to the three-brained beings arising and existing on that planet Earth which has pleased you.

"I have already more than once told you, that by the All-Gracious Command of Our OMNI-LOVING COMMON FATHER ENDLESSNESS, our Cosmic Highest Most Very Saintly Individuums sometimes actualize within the presence of some terrestrial three-brained being or other, a definitized conception of a sacred Individuum, in order that the latter, having become a terrestrial being with such a presence, might there on the spot 'orient himself' and give to the process of their ordinary being-existence, a corresponding new direction, just such a direction that thanks to it perhaps both the already crystallized consequences of the properties of the organ Kundabuffer and the predispositions to such new crystallizations could be removed from their presences.

"Well, namely, already seven centuries before the Babylonian events I have spoken of, there was just actualized in the planetary body of a three-brained being, a definitized conception of a sacred Individuum, named Ashiata Shiemash, who became there in his turn a Messenger from Above, and who is already now one of the Highest Most Very Saintly Common Cosmic Sacred Individuums.

"Ashiata Shiemash had his conception in the planetary body of a boy of a poor family descended from what is called the 'Sumerian Race,' in a small place then called 'Pispascana' and situated not far from Babylon.

"He grew up and became a responsible being partly in this small place and partly in Babylon itself, which was at that time, although not yet magnificent, even already an important city.

"The Very Saintly Ashiata Shiemash was the Unique Messenger from Above to your planet who firstly endeavored by his holy labors to create on that planet conditions in which the existence of its unfortunate beings for a certain time somewhat resembled the existence of the three-brained beings of the other planets of our great Universe on which beings exist with the same possibilities; and secondly, this Saint was the first on that planet Earth, who for the mission preassigned to him refused to employ the ordinary methods established during previous centuries for the three-brained beings of that planet by all the other Messengers sent from above.

"The Very Saintly Ashiata Shiemash taught nothing whatever to the ordinary three-brained beings of the Earth, nor did he preach anything to them, as was done before and after him by all the Messengers sent there from Above with the same aim.

"And in consequence of this, almost none of his teaching in any form passed from his contemporaries even to the third generation of ordinary beings there, not to mention the contemporary ordinary beings there.

"Definite information relating to his Very Saintly activities passed there from the contemporaries of the Very Saintly Ashiata Shiemash to the beings of the following generation, and from generation to generation thereafter through those there called 'Initiated' beings by means of a certain what is called 'Legominism' of his deliberations under the title of: 'The Terror of the Situation.'

"In addition to this, there has survived from the period of his Very Saintly activities and there still exists even until now, what is called a marble tablet on which are graven his 'counsels and commandments' to the beings contemporary with him.

"Even at the present time this surviving tablet serves as the chief holy relic for a small group of initiated beings there, who are called the 'Olbogmek' Brotherhood, and whose place of existence is situated in the middle of the continent Asia.

"The name 'Olbogmek' means, 'There are not different religions, there is only one God.'

"With this 'Legominism' which transmits to the initiated men-beings of the planet Earth of remote generations these deliberations of the Saintly Ashiata Shiemash under the title of 'The Terror of the Situation,' I happened by chance to become acquainted when I was personally on the surface of your planet for the last time.

"This 'Legominism' was of great assistance to me in elucidating certain strange aspects of the psyche of these peculiar beings—just those strange aspects of their psyche which, with all my careful observations of them during tens of centuries, I had previously been unable to understand in any way whatsoever.

"My dear and beloved grandfather, tell me please what the word 'Legominism' means?" Hassein asked.

"This name 'Legominism,'" replied Beelzebub, "is given to one of the means existing there of transmitting from generation to generation information about certain events of long-past ages, through just those three-brained beings who are thought worthy to be and are called 'Initiates.'

"For your better understanding of the said means there, that is of transmitting information to beings of succeeding generations, by means of a 'Legominism,' I must here also tell a little about those beings there, whom other beings called and call 'Initiates.'

"In former times there on the planet Earth, this word was always used in one definite sense only; namely those three-brained beings there were called 'Initiates' who acquired in their presence almost the same objective data sensible to other beings. But during the last two centuries this word has come to be used there already in two senses.

"In one sense it is used for the same purpose as before, that is, those beings there are so named who become initiates, thanks to their personal conscious labors and intentional sufferings, thanks also to which, as I have already told you, they acquire in themselves objective merits sensible to other beings, of any brain system, and which evoke trust and respect.

"In the other sense these beings call each other by this name who belong to what are there called robber gangs, which during the said period greatly multiplied there, and the members of which have as their chief aim to 'steal' from amongst their surroundings only 'essence values.'

"Under the presence of following 'supernatural' or 'Mystic' sciences, these gangs of robbers there are really occupied, and very successfully, with this kind of plunder.

"And so it is any and every full-blown member of such a gang there, that is just called an 'Initiate.'

"There are even 'High Initiates' among them also, and these 'High Initiates,' especially at the present time, are made out of those ordinary 'Initiates' of 'new format,' who during their 'virtuoso' affairs, pass as it is also said there, through 'fire-water-copper-pipes-and-even-through-all-the-roulette-halls-of-Monte-Carlo.'

"Well then, my boy, a 'Legominism' is the name given to the transmission of information about long-past events which have occurred on the planet Earth from initiates to initiates of the first kind, that is, from really meritorious beings, who in their turn, have received the information from similar meritorious beings.

"This means of transmitting information was already invented by beings of the continent Atlantis, and, we must give them their due, this means was indeed very wise and did indeed attain their aim.

"This is the sole means by which information about certain events that proceeded in times long-past has correctly reached the beings of remote later generations.

"As for the information which passed from generation to generation through the ordinary mass of beings of that planet, it either completely disappeared, having been soon forgotten, or there remains of it, as our dear Mullah Nassr Eddin expressed himself, only the 'tail-and-mane-and-food-for-Scheherazade!'

"Hence it is that when a few scraps of information about some event or other do happen to reach the beings of remote later generations and the learned beings of 'new format' there, concoct their hotchpotch out of these scraps, there then occurs a most peculiar and most instructive 'phenomenon,' namely, when the cockroaches there chance to hear what is in this hotchpotch, there immediately enters into their general presence and starts off at full blast, what is called 'the-evil-spirit-of-Saint-Vitus,' which exists there.

"How the contemporary learned beings of the planet Earth concoct their hotchpotch from the scraps of information which reach them, is very well defined by one of the wise sentences of our dear Mullah Nassr Eddin; it consists of the following words: 'A flea exists in the world just for one thing . . . so that when it sneezes, that deluge should occur which our "learned beings" love so much the job of describing.'

"I must tell you that it was always difficult for me when I used to exist amongst your favorites to keep from laughing, as your favorites say, when one or another of the 'learned beings' there delivered a 'lecture' or related to me personally about some past event of which I had myself been an eyewitness.

"These 'lectures' or stories there are crammed with fantasies so absurd that neither our arch-cunning Lucifer nor His staff could invent them if they tried."

CHAPTER XXVI

The Legominism Concerning The Deliberations Of The Very Saintly Ashiata Shiemash, Under The Title Of "The Terror Of The Situation"

THE LEGOMINISM," Beelzebub continued to speak, "through which the deliberations of the Very Saintly Ashiata Shiemash were transmitted, had the following contents:

"It began with the following prayer:

"'In the Name of the causes of my arising, I shall strive always to be just towards every already spiritualized origination, and towards all the originations of the future spiritualized manifestations of OUR COMMON CREATOR, ALMIGHTY AUTOCRAT ENDLESSNESS, Amen.

"'To me, a trifling particle of the whole of the GREAT WHOLE, it was commanded from Above to be coated with the planetary body of a three-centered being of this planet and to assist all other such beings arising and existing upon it, in freeing themselves from the consequences of the properties of that organ which for great and important reasons was actualized in the presences of their ancestors.

"'All the sacred Individuums here before me, especially and intentionally actualized from Above, have always endeavored while striving for the same aim, to accomplish the task laid upon them through one or other of those three sacred paths for self-perfecting, foreordained by OUR ENDLESS CREATOR HIMSELF—namely, through the sacred paths based on the being-impulses called "Faith," "Hope" and "Love."

"'When I reached my seventeenth year, I began as commanded from Above, to prepare my planetary body in order, during my responsible existence, 'to be able to be' impartial.

"'At this period of my self-preparation, I had the intention upon reaching responsible age, of carrying out the task laid upon me through one or other of the said three sacred being-impulses also.

"'But when during this period of my self-preparation, I chanced to meet many beings of almost all 'types' formed and existing here in the city of Babylon, and when during my impartial observations, I constated many traits of their being-manifestations, there crept into me and progressively increased a 'being-doubt' as to the possibilities of saving the three-centered beings of that planet by means of any of these three sacred paths.

"'The different manifestations of the beings I then encountered, which increased my doubts, gradually convinced me that these consequences of the properties of the organ Kundabuffer, having passed by inheritance through a series of generations over a very long period of time, had ultimately so crystallized in their presence, that they now reach contemporary beings already, as it were, as a lawful part of their essence, and hence these crystallized consequences of the properties of the organ Kundabuffer are now, as it were, a 'second nature' within their general presences.

"'So when I finally became a responsible being, I decided that before making my choice among the mentioned three sacred paths, I would bring my planetary body into the state of the sacred 'Ksherknara,' that is, into the state of all-brained-balanced-being-manifestation, and only when already in that state, to choose the path for my further actions.

"'With this aim, I then ascended the mountain "Vezin-iama," where for forty days and nights I knelt on my knees and devoted myself to concentration.

"'A second forty days and nights I neither ate nor drank, but recalled and analyzed all the impressions present in me of all the perceptions I had acquired during my existence here during the period of my self-preparation.

"'A third forty days and nights I knelt on my knees and

also neither ate nor drank, and every half-hour I plucked two hairs from my breast.

"'And only when thereafter, I had finally attained complete freedom from all the bodily and spiritual associations of the impressions of ordinary life, I began to meditate how to be.

"'These meditations of my purified reason then made it categorically clear to me, that to save the contemporary beings by any one of the three sacred paths was already too late.

"'Just these meditations then made it categorically clear to me, that all the genuine functions proper to men being, as they are, proper to all the three-centered beings of Our Great Universe, had already in their remote ancestors degenerated into other functions, namely, into functions included in the number of the properties of the organ Kundabuffer which were very similar to the genuine sacred being-functions of "Faith," "Love" and "Hope."

"'And this degeneration occurred in all probability in consequence of this, that when the organ Kundabuffer had been destroyed in these ancestors and they had also acquired in themselves factors of the genuine sacred being-impulses, the taste of many of the properties of the organ Kundabuffer still remained in them and those properties of the organ Kundabuffer which resembled these three sacred impulses became gradually mixed with the latter, with the result that there were crystallized in their psyche the factors for the impulses "Faith," "Love" and "Hope," which although similar to the genuine, were nevertheless somehow or other utterly exotic.

"'The contemporary three-centered beings here do at times believe, they do love and they do hope, both with their reason and with their feelings, but how they believe, how they love and how they hope—ah, it is exactly in this, that all the eccentricity of these three being-properties lies.

"'They also believe, but this impulse in them functions not independently, as in general it does in all the three-centered beings existing on the various other planets of our Great Universe, upon which beings with the same possibilities breed; but it arises dependently upon these or other factors, which have been formed in their general presence, owing as always to the same consequences of the properties of the organ Kundabuffer; as for instance, the particular properties arising in them which they call "vanity," "self-love," "pride," "self-conceit," and so forth.

"'In consequence of this, the three-brained beings here are for the most part subject just to the perceptions and fixations in their presences of all sorts of 'Sinkrpoosarams' or, as it is expressed here, they 'believe-in-any-old-lie.'

"'It is perfectly easy to convince beings of this planet of anything you like, provided only that during their perceptions of these 'fictions,' there is evoked in them and there proceeds, either consciously from without, or automatically by itself, the functioning of one or another corresponding consequences of the properties of the organ Kundabuffer crystallized in them from among the number of those that formed what is called the 'personality' of the given being; as for instance, "self-love," "pride," "vanity," "swagger," "imagination," "bragging," "arrogance" and so on.

"'From the influence of such actions upon their degenerated reason and upon the localization of the degenerate factors which actualize their being-sensations, not only is there crystallized a false conviction concerning the mentioned fictions, but thereafter in all sincerity and faith, they will even vehemently prove to those around them that it is just so and can in no way be otherwise.

"'In an equally abnormal form, the data were molded in them for evoking the sacred impulse, 'Love.'

"'In the presences of the beings of contemporary times, there also arises and is present in them as much as you please of that strange impulse which they call 'love'; but this strange love of theirs is firstly also the result of certain crystallized consequences of the properties of the same Kundabuffer; and secondly this impulse of theirs arises and manifests itself in the presence of every one of them entirely subjectively—so subjectively and so differently that if ten of them were asked to explain how they sensed this inner impulse of theirs, then all ten of them—if, of course, they for once replied sincerely and frankly confessed their genuine sensations and not those they had read about somewhere or had got from somebody else—then all ten would reply differently and describe ten different sensations.

"'One would explain this sensation in the sexual sense, another in the sense of pity, a third in the sense of desire for submission, a fourth, in common interests regarding outer things, and so on and so forth; but not one of the ten could describe even remotely the sensation of genuine love.

"'And none of them could, because in none of the ordinary men-beings here has there ever been, already for a long time, any sensation of the sacred being-impulse of genuine Love. And without this "taste" they cannot even vaguely describe that most beatific sacred being-impulse in the presence of every three-centered being of the whole Universe, which, in accordance with the divine foresight of Great Nature, forms those data in us from the results of the experiencing of which we can blissfully rest from the meritorious labors actualized by us for the purpose of self-perfection.

"'Here, in these times, if one of these three-brained beings "loves" somebody or other, then he "loves" him either because the latter always encourages and flatters him, or because his nose is much like the nose of that female or male, with whom, thanks to the cosmic law of "polarity" or "type," a relation has been established which has not yet been broken, or finally he "loves" him only because the latter's uncle is in a big way of business and may one day give him a boost, and so on and so forth.

"'But never do men-beings here love with genuine impartial and non-egoistic love.

"'Thanks to this kind of love present in the contemporary beings here, their hereditary predispositions to the crystallizations of the consequences of the properties of the organ Kundabuffer are crystallized at the present time already without hindrance, and finally become fixed in their nature as a lawful part of them.

"'And as regards the third sacred being-impulse, namely, "Hope," its plight in the presences of the three-centered beings here is even worse than with the first two.

"'Such a being-impulse has not only in its distorted form finally adapted itself in them to the whole of their presences, but this maleficent strange "hope" newly formed in them which has taken the place of the being-impulse of the sacred Hope, is now already the principal reason why they can no longer acquire in themselves the data for the functioning of the genuine being-impulses of "Faith," "Love" and "Hope."

"'In consequence of this, and owing to this newly formed abnormal "hope" of theirs they always hope in something; and on this account all those possibilities are constantly being paralyzed in them which arise in them either intentionally from without or accidentally by themselves; and which possibilities could perhaps still destroy in their presences their hereditary predispositions to the crystallization of the consequences of the properties of the organ Kundabuffer.

"'When I returned from the mountain Veziniama to the city Babylon, I continued my observations in order to make it clear whether it was not possible somehow or other to help these unfortunates in some other way.

"'During the period of my year of special observations of every variety of their manifestations and perceptions, I made it categorically clear to myself, that although the data for evoking in their presences the sacred being-impulses of "Faith," "Hope" and "Love" are already quite degenerated in the beings of this planet, nevertheless the factor for producing that being-impulse on which the whole psyche of beings of a three-brained system is in general based, and which impulse exists under the name of "Objective-Conscience" is not yet atrophied in them, and it remains in their presence almost in its primordial state. Thanks to the abnormally established conditions of external ordinary being-existence here, this factor has gradually penetrated and become embedded in that consciousness which is here called "subconsciousness," in consequence of which it takes no part whatever in the functioning of their ordinary consciousness.

"'Well, it was just then that I understood for a surety with all the separate ruminating parts representing the whole of my 'I,' that only if the functioning of this being-factor still surviving in the whole of their presence were to participate in the general functioning of that consciousness of theirs in which they pass their daily, as they here say, "waking-existence," only then would it still be possible to save the contemporary three-brained beings here from the consequences of the properties of that organ which was intentionally introjected into their first ancestors.

"'My further mediations then confirmed for me that this would be possible only if their general being-existence were to flow for a long time under foreseeingly corresponding conditions.

"'When all the above-mentioned was completely transubstantiated in me, I decided to consecrate the whole of myself from that time forward to the creation here of such conditions, that the functioning of the "sacred-conscience" still safely surviving in their subconsciousness, might gradually pass into the functioning of their ordinary consciousness.

"'May the blessing of our ALMIGHTY OMNI-LOVING

COMMON FATHER UNI-BEING ENDLESS CREATOR be upon my decision, Amen!'

"Thus ended the 'Legominism' concerning the deliberations of the Very Saintly Incomparable Ashiata Shiemash, under the title of 'The Terror of the Situation.'

"So, my boy, when, as I have already told you, early in my last personal descent on the surface of your planet, I first became acquainted in detail with this 'Legominism' which I have just repeated, and had at once become interested in the deductions of this later Most High Very Saintly Common Cosmic Individuum Ashiata Shiemash, as there existed neither any other 'Legominism' nor any other sources of information concerning his further Very Saintly activities among these favorites of yours—I then decided to investigate in detail and without fail to make clear to myself, which were the measures he took and how he subsequently actualized them, in order to help these unfortunates to deliver themselves from the consequences of the properties of the organ Kundabuffer which had passed to them by inheritance and were so maleficent for them.

"And so, as one of my chief tasks during this last personal stay of mine there on the surface of your planet, I made a detailed investigation and elucidation of the whole of the further Very Saintly activities there among your favorites, of that great essence-loving now Most High very saintly common-cosmic Individuum Ashiata Shiemash.

"And as regards that 'marble tablet' which by chance has remained intact since the time of the Very Saintly activities of the great Ashiata Shiemash, and now serves there as the principal sacred relic of the brotherhood of the initiated beings there called the 'Olbogmek Brotherhood,' I happened to see and read, during this last stay of mine there, the contents of what was carved on that marble.

"During my subsequent elucidations it proved that later

on, after this Very Saintly Ashiata Shiemash had established there the particular conditions of ordinary being-existence which he had planned, several of these tablets were on his advice and initiative, then set up in corresponding places of many of the large towns, and carved upon them were all kinds of sayings and counsels for corresponding existence.

"But when their big wars later on again began, all these tablets were also destroyed by these strange beings themselves, and only one of them, namely that one now with these brethren, somehow remained intact, as I have already told you, and is now the property of this 'Brotherhood.'

"On this marble still surviving whole were inscriptions concerning the sacred being-impulses called 'Faith,' 'Love' and 'Hope.'

"On this marble there was carved as follows:

Faith, Love and Hope

Faith of consciousness is freedom,
Faith of feeling is weakness,
Faith of body is stupidity.

Love of consciousness evokes the same in response,
Love of feeling evokes the opposite,
Love of body depends on type and polarity.

Hope of consciousness is strength,
Hope of feeling is slavery,
Hope of body is disease.

"Before continuing to tell you more about the activities of the Very Saintly Ashiata Shiemash for the welfare of your favorites, I must I think elucidate to you, a little more in detail, that inner impulse which is called there by your favorites,

'Hope,' and concerning which, the Very Saintly Ashiata Shiemash constated that the case is worse than with the two first ones.

"And the personal observations and investigations I later specially made regarding this said strange impulse present in them, clearly showed me that in truth the data for evoking in their presences this abnormal impulse are most maleficent for themselves.

"Thanks to this abnormal hope of theirs a very singular and most strange disease with its own property of evolving arose and exists among them there even until now—a disease called there 'tomorrow.'

"This strange disease 'tomorrow' brought with it terrible consequences and particularly for those unfortunate three-brained beings there, who chance to learn and to become categorically convinced with the whole of their presence that they contain some very undesirable consequences for the deliverance from which they must make certain efforts, and which efforts moreover they even know just how to make.

"But they too fail to make these required efforts and all on account of that maleficent disease 'tomorrow'; and this is just the maleficent part of all that great terrifying evil, which, owing to various causes great and small, is concentrated in the processes of the ordinary being-existence of these pitiable three-brained beings, since those unfortunate beings there who do by chance learn all about what I have mentioned, postponing from 'tomorrow' until 'tomorrow,' are also deprived of the possibility of ever attaining anything real.

"This strange and for your favorites maleficent disease 'tomorrow' has already become a hindrance for the beings of contemporary times, not only in regard to this, that these favorites of yours have finally lost any possibility of removing from their presences the crystallized consequences of the properties of the organ Kundabuffer, but it has also become a hindrance to most of them in honestly discharging at any rate those being-duties of theirs which have become indispensable in the already established conditions of ordinary being-existence.

"Thanks to the disease 'tomorrow,' the three-brained beings there, particularly the contemporary ones, almost always postpone until 'later' everything that needs to be done at the given moment, being convinced that 'later' they will do better and more.

"On account of the said maleficent disease 'tomorrow,' the majority of those unfortunate beings there who accidentally or owing to a conscious suggestion from without, become aware of their complete nothingness through the reason present in them and begin to sense it with all their separate spiritualized parts, and also chance to learn which and in what way, being-efforts must be made in order that they may become what it is proper for three-brained beings to be—then thanks also to the said maleficent disease of postponing from 'tomorrow' until 'tomorrow' they almost all arrive at the point that on one sorrowful day for themselves, there arise in them and begin to show those forerunners of old age called 'feebleness' and 'infirmity,' which are the inevitable lot of all cosmic formations great and small at the close of their fulfilled being.

"Here I must without fail tell you also about that strange phenomenon which I constated there during my observations and studies of the almost entirely degenerated presence of these favorites of yours; namely, I definitely constated that in many of them, towards the close of their planetary existence, most of the crystallized consequences of the properties of that same organ—which are consequently present in the whole of their presence—begin to decay of their own accord and some of them even entirely disappear, in consequence of which these beings begin to see and sense reality a little more truly.

"In such cases a strong desire appears in the whole of the

presence of such favorites of yours, to work upon themselves, to work as they say, for the 'salvation of their souls.'

"But needless to say, nothing can result from such desires of theirs just on account of this, that it is already too late for them, the time given then for this purpose by Great Nature having already passed; and although they see and feel the necessity of actualizing the required being-efforts, yet for the fulfillment of such desires of theirs, they have now only ineffectual yearnings and the lawful infirmities of old age.

"And so, my boy, my researches and investigations concerning the further activities of the Very Saintly Ashiata Shiemash for the welfare of the three-brained beings arising and existing on this planet of yours eventually made the following clear to me.

"When this great, and in point of Reason, almost incomparable sacred Individuum became finally convinced that the ordinary sacred paths which exist for the purpose of self-perfection for all the three-brained beings of the Universe, were already no longer suitable for the beings of this planet Earth, he then, after his year of now special observations and studies of their psyche, again ascended to that same mountain Veziniama, and during several terrestrial months pondered in which way he could actualize his decision; that is, to save the beings of this planet from those inherited predispositions to the crystallizations of the consequences of the properties of the organ Kundabuffer, by means of those data which remained whole in their subconsciousness for the fundamental sacred being-impulse, Conscience.

"These ponderings of his then first of all finally convinced him, that although it was indeed possible to save them by means of those data which remained in the whole of their presence for bringing forth the sacred being-impulse, nevertheless it would only be possible in the event that the manifestations of that which remained whole in their subconsciousness should without fail participate in the functioning of that consciousness of theirs under the direction of which their daily waking existence flows, and furthermore if this being-impulse were to be manifested through every aspect of this consciousness of theirs over a long period."

CHAPTER XXVII

The Kind Of Organization For Man's Existence Created By The Very Saintly Ashiata Shiemash

BEELZEBUB continued to relate further as follows:

"My further researches and investigations cleared up for me that after the Very Saintly Ashiata Shiemash had pondered on the Mountain Veziniama and formulated in his mind a definite plan for his further Most Saintly activities, he did not again return to the city Babylon but went straight to the capital city Djoolfapal of the country called Kurlandtech, which was situated in the middle of the continent Asia.

"There he first of all established relations with the 'brethren' of the then existing brotherhood 'Tchaftantouri,' a name signifying 'To-Be-or-To-Be-Not,' which had its quarters not far from that city.

"This said brotherhood was founded five of their years before the arrival there of the Very Saintly Ashiata Shiemash, on the initiative of two genuine terrestrial initiates, who had become initiates according to the principals existing, as it is said there, before the Ashiatian epoch.

"The name of one of these two terrestrial three-brained beings of that time, who had become genuine initiates there, was Poundolero and of the other, Sensimiriniko.

"Here it is necessary to notice also that just each of these two terrestrial genuine initiates of that time had already by that time the 'coating' in their general presences of their higher being-parts to the gradation called 'fulfillment,' and they had then time during their further existence to perfect these higher parts of theirs to the required gradation of the Holy Objective Reason, so that their perfected higher being-parts even became worthy to have, and also now have, the place of their further existence on the holy planet Purgatory.

"Concerning these two initiated beings, my further detailed investigations cleared up for me, that when, in all the separate spiritualized parts of the general presence of these two three-brained beings of that period, namely Poundolero and Sensimiriniko, there arose and was continuously sensed the suspicion, which later became a conviction, that owing to some obviously non-lawful causes 'something very undesirable' for them personally had been acquired in their general organization and was functioning there, and at the same time that it was possible for this 'something very undesirable' to be removed from themselves by means of their own possibilities existing in them, they then decided to find other beings like themselves who were striving for this same aim, and together to try to achieve the removal from themselves of this said 'something very undesirable.'

"They soon found beings responding to this aim amongst what were called the monks of places called monasteries, of which there were already many at that period in the environs of the town Djoolfapal.

"And with these monks chosen by them they first founded the mentioned 'brotherhood.'

"And so, after arriving in the town Djoolfapal, the Very Saintly Ashiata Shiemash established corresponding relations with these brethren of the mentioned brotherhood who were already working upon that abnormally proceeding functioning of their psyche which they themselves had constated, and he began enlightening their reason by means of objectively true information, and guiding their being-impulses in such a way that they could sense these truths without the participation either of the abnormally crystallized data already contained in their presences, or of the data newly arising from the results of the exterior perceptions they received from the abnormally established form of ordinary being-existence.

"While enlightening the brethren of the said brotherhood in the mentioned way and discussing his suppositions and intentions with them, the Very Saintly Ashiata Shiemash was occupied at the same time in drawing up what are called the 'rules,' or, as it is said there, 'statutes,' for this brotherhood, which in association with those brethren he initiated, the former brethren of the brotherhood Tchaftantouri, founded in the town Djoolfapal, and which later was called the 'Brotherhood Heechtvori,' signifying 'Only he will be called and will become the Son of God who acquires Conscience in himself.'

"Later, when with the participation of these brethren of the former brotherhood Tchaftantouri, everything had been worked out and organized, the Very Saintly Ashiata Shiemash sent these same brethren to various places and commissioned them under his general guidance to spread the information that in people, namely, in their 'subconsciousness,' there are crystallized and are always present the data manifested from Above for giving birth in them to the divine impulse of genuine conscience, and that only he who acquires such 'ableness' that the activities of these 'data' participate in the functioning of that consciousness of theirs in which they pass their everyday existence, has in the objective sense, the honest right to be called and really to be a genuine Son of our COMMON FATHER CREATOR of all that exists.

"These brethren preached this objective truth at first chiefly among the monks of the mentioned monasteries, many of which, as I have already said, existed in the environs of the town Djoolfapal, and later among the ordinary inhabitants of the town itself.

"The first result of these preachings of theirs was that they selected thirty-five serious and well prepared what are called 'novices' of this first brotherhood 'Heechtvori,' which they founded in the city of Djoolfapal.

"Thereafter, the Very Saintly Ashiata Shiemash while continuing to enlighten the minds of the former brethren of the brotherhood Tchaftantouri, then began with the help of these brethren, enlightening the reason of those thirty-five 'novices' also.

"So it continued during the whole of one of their years; and only after this did some of them from among the brethren of the former brotherhood Tchaftantouri, and from among the thirty-five said 'novices,' gradually prove worthy to become what are called 'All-the-rights-possessing' brethren of this first 'brotherhood-Heechtvori.'

"According to the 'statutes' drawn up by the Very Saintly Ashiata Shiemash, any brother could become an 'All-the-rights-possessing' brother of the 'brotherhood-Heechtvori,' only when, in addition to the other also foreseen definite objective attainments, he could bring himself—in the sense of 'ableness-of-conscious-direction of the functioning of his own psyche'—to the state of knowing how to convince a hundred other beings about self-perfecting, and moreover, so to convince them that each of these others, in their turn, should acquire in themselves what is called the 'required-intensity-of-ableness' to be able to convince and persuade not less than a hundred others, first, that the impulse of being-objective-conscience exists in man, and second, how it must be manifested in order that a man may respond to the real sense and aim of his existence.

"It was those who became worthy to become such an 'All-the-rights-possessing' brother of the 'Brotherhood-Heechtvori,' who were first called by the name 'priest.'

"For your complete elucidation concerning the Very Saintly activities of Ashiata Shiemash, you must also know that afterwards, when all the results of the Very Saintly Labors of the Very Saintly Ashiata Shiemash were destroyed, both this word 'priest' there and also the word 'initiate' about which I have already told you, were used and still continue to be used by your favorites down to the present time in two quite different senses. In one sense, from then until now, this word 'priest' was and is still now commonly used, but only in certain places and for unimportant separate groups of those professionals existing there whom everybody now calls there 'confessors' or 'clergymen.'

"And in the other sense, those beings were called and are still called by this word 'priest,' who, by their pious existence and by the merits of their acts performed for the good of those around them, stand out so much from the rank and file of the ordinary three-brained beings there, that whenever these ordinary beings there have occasion to remember them, there arises and proceeds in their presences the process called 'gratitude.'

"Already during that same period while the Very Saintly Ashiata Shiemash was enlightening the reasons of the brethren of the former brotherhood 'Tchaftantouri,' as well as of the newly collected thirty-five 'novices,' there began to spread among ordinary beings of the city Djoolfapal and it environs, the 'true idea' about this, namely, that in the general presences of man-beings all the data exist for the manifestation of the divine impulse conscience, but that this divine impulse does not take part in their general consciousness; and that it takes no part only because, although their manifestations bring them certain immediate what are called 'quite-late-repaying-satisfactions' and considerable material advantage, nevertheless they thereby gradually atrophy the data put into their presences by Nature for evoking in other beings around them without distinction of 'brain-system,' the objective impulse of Divine Love.

"This true information began to spread, thanks chiefly to that superlatively wise provision of the Very Saintly Ashiata Shiemash that obliged everyone striving to become an 'All-the-rights-possessing' brother of the brotherhood 'Heechtvori' to attain, in addition to all kinds of definite self-merits, the 'ableness' to know how to convince all the three separate spiritualized and associating parts of the total whole of a further hundred three-brained beings there, concerning the divine impulse conscience.

"When the organization of the first brotherhood 'Heechtvori' in the city Djoolfapal had been more or less regulated and was so established that the further work could already be continued independently, by means only of the directions issuing from the Reason then present in the brotherhood, then the Very Saintly Ashiata Shiemash himself selected from among those who had become 'All-the-rights-possessing' brothers of the brotherhood, those who had already sensed the said divine impulse, consciously by their reason and unconsciously by the feelings in their subconsciousness, and who had full confidence that by certain self-efforts this divine being-impulse might become and forever remain an inseparable part of their ordinary consciousness. And those who had sensed and become aware of this divine impulse conscience, and who were called 'first-degree-initiates,' he set apart, and he began to enlighten their Reasons separately concerning these 'objective truths' which before that time were still quite unknown by the three-brained beings.

"It was just these outstanding 'first degree initiated beings' there who were then first called 'Great-Initiates.'

"Here it must be remarked that those principles of Being of the initiated beings there, which later on just came to be called there 'Ashiata's-renewals,' were then renewed by the Very Saintly Ashiata Shiemash.

"Well then, it was to those same 'Great-Initiates' who were first set apart, that the Very Saintly Ashiata Shiemash, now already the Most Very Saintly, then among other things also elucidated in detail what, namely, this being-impulse 'objective conscience' is, and how factors arise for its manifestation in the presences of the three-brained beings. And concerning this he once said as follows:

"'The factors for the being-impulse conscience arise in the presences of the three-brained beings from the localization of the particles of the 'emanation-of-the-sorrow' of our OMNI-LOVING AND LONG-SUFFERING ENDLESS CREATOR; that is why the source of the manifestation of genuine conscience in three-centered beings is sometimes called REPRESENTATIVE OF THE CREATOR.

"'And this sorrow is formed in our ALL MAINTAINING FATHER from the struggle between the joy and the sorrow constantly proceeding in the Universe.'

"And he then also further said:

"'In all without exception of the three-brained beings of the whole of our Universe, among whom are also we men, thanks to these data crystallized in our general presences for the bringing forth in us of the divine impulse conscience, 'the whole of us' and the whole of our essence, are, and must be, already in our foundation, only suffering.

"'And they must be suffering, because the appointed actualizing of the manifestation of such a being-impulse in us can proceed only from the constant struggle of two quite opposite, what are called "Complexes-of-the-functioning" of those two sources which are reciprocally of quite opposite origin; namely, between the processes of the functioning of our planetary body itself and the parallel functionings arising progressively from the coating and perfecting of our higher being-bodies within this planetary body of ours, which functionings in their totality, just actualize every kind of reason in the three-centered beings.

"'In consequence of this, every three-centered being of our great Universe, and also we, men, existing on the Earth, must, owing to the presence in us, also, of the factors for the bringing forth of the divine impulse of "objective conscience," always inevitably struggle with the arising and the proceeding within our general presences of two quite opposite functionings, the results of which are always sensed by us either as "desires" or as "non-desires."

"'And so, he only who consciously assists the process of this inner struggle and consciously assists the "non-desires" to predominate over the "desires"—only he behaves just in accordance with the essence of our COMMON FATHER CREATOR HIMSELF; while he who with his consciousness assists the contrary, only increases His sorrow.'

"Owing to all this, which I have just said, my boy, at that period hardly three years had passed when, on the one hand, all the ordinary beings of the town Djoolfapal and its environs and also of many other countries of the continent Asia, not only already knew that this divine being-impulse of 'genuine conscience' was in them, and that it could take part in the functioning of their ordinary 'waking-consciousness,' also that in all the brotherhoods of the great Prophet Ashiata Shiemash, all the initiates and priests elucidated and indicated how and what had to be done in order that such a divine impulse should take part in the functioning of the mentioned ordinary 'waking-consciousness'—but furthermore, nearly everybody even began to strive and to exert themselves to become priests of the brotherhood 'Heechtvori,' of which many brotherhoods were already founded during that period, functioning almost independently in many other countries of the continent Asia.

"And these nearly independent brotherhoods arose there in the following order:

"When the common work of the brotherhood founded in the town Djoolfapal was finally established, the Very Saintly Ashiata Shiemash began sending the said 'Great-Initiates,' with appropriate instructions, to other countries and towns of the continent Asia, in order to organize similar brotherhoods there also, while he himself remained to exist there in the town of Djoolfapal from where he guided the activities of these helpers of his.

"However it might have been, my boy, it then so turned out, that almost all of your favorites—those strange three-brained beings—also wished and began to strive with all their spiritualized being-parts to have in their ordinary waking-consciousness, the divine genuine objective conscience; with the consequence that most of the beings of Asia at that time began to work upon themselves under the guidance of 'initiates' and 'priests' of the brotherhood 'Heechtvori,' in order to transfer into their ordinary consciousness the results of the data present in their subconsciousness for bringing forth the impulse of genuine divine conscience, and in order to have the possibility, by this means, on the one hand of completely removing from themselves, perhaps forever, the maleficent consequences of the properties of the organ Kundabuffer, both those personally acquired and those passed to them by inheritance; and on the other hand, of consciously taking part in diminishing the sorrow of OUR COMMON ENDLESS FATHER.

"Owing to all this, the question of conscience already began to predominate both in the 'waking-consciousness' state and in the 'passive-instinctive' state among your favorites also, and particularly among those who existed on the continent Asia at that period during the ordinary process of being-existence.

"Even those three-brained beings of that time in whose presences the taste of this divine impulse had not yet been transubstantiated, but who had in their strange peculiar consciousness, proper to them alone, only empty information concerning this being-impulse which could be present in them as well, also exerted themselves to manifest in everything in accordance with this information.

"The total result, however, of everything I have mentioned, was that already within ten terrestrial years, there had disappeared of their own accord those two chief forms of ordinary being-existence abnormally established there, from which chiefly there flow and still continue to flow, most of the maleficent causes whose sum increasingly evokes every possible kind of insignificant factor which opposes obstacles to the establishment of conditions there—if only for a normal being-existence externally—for those favorites of yours.

"And, namely, their numerous communities with various forms of organization for external and even internal existence, or as they themselves express it, 'state organization,' first just ceased to exist, and secondly, in these said numerous communities, there also disappeared, equally just by themselves, those various what are called 'castes' or 'classes' which had long before been established there.

"These two chief maleficent forms of their ordinary existence, namely, their numerous independent communities and the practice of assigning each other to different 'castes,' ceased to exist on account of the following:

"At that period when thanks to the very saintly labors of Ashiata Shiemash the functioning in the presences of the majority of your favorites of the factors which had remained whole in their subconsciousness for the bringing forth of the sacred being-impulse 'conscience,' had begun to take part in the process of that consciousness of theirs under the direction of which it had become proper to them to pass their 'waking-state,' and when, thanks to this, the beings of that period began to exist and to have relations with each other and to take from each other only in accordance with conscience, and when every kind of mutual 'esteem' and 'aggrandizement' began to proceed only in accordance with the personally acquired obvious moral attainments, then, with such mutual relations prevalent among them, the caste distinctions which had formerly existed and which were afterwards reestablished, were, at first, simply dissipated; and in the same way there afterwards gradually began to dissolve and disappear what are called the 'pales of settlement' of their separate independent communities.

"And in my opinion, as you also will surely understand eventually, it was precisely this second of the two mentioned chief abnormally established forms of ordinary being-existence, namely, this assigning of each other to different castes—that has specially become there the basis for the crystallization in the general presences of these unfortunate favorites of yours, of that particular psychic property which, in the whole of the Universe, exists exclusively only in the presences of those three-brained beings.

"This exclusively particular property was formed in them soon after the second Transapalnian-perturbation there, and gradually undergoing development and becoming strengthened in them, was passed from generation to generation by inheritance, until it has now already passed to the contemporary beings as a certain lawful and inseparable part of their general psyche; this particular property of their psyche being called by themselves, 'Egoism.'

"Concerning this exclusively particular property itself of their general psyche, it must assuredly be elucidated to you also, that later during the period of my last personal stay on the surface of this planet of yours, when I became deeply interested in the mentioned 'Legominism' concerning the deliberations of the Very Saintly Ashiata Shiemash entitled the 'Terror of the Situation,' the question arose in me, in the course of my further detailed researches and investigations relating to his subsequent Very Saintly Activities and their results, in which way and why the crystallization of the mentioned factors obtained from the particles of the emanation of the sorrow of OUR COMMON FATHER CREATOR for the actualizing of the divine being-impulse of objective conscience, proceeded in their presences, that is, just in their said 'subconsciousness,' and thus avoided that final degeneration to which all the data placed in them for bringing forth in their presences the other sacred being-impulses, are subject.

"And concerning also this strange anomaly there, one of the numerous wise sentences of our highly esteemed, irreplaceable and honorable Mullah Nassr Eddin, can also be applied.

"In such cases he says:

"'Every real happiness for man can arise exclusively only from some unhappiness—but also real—which he has already experienced.'

"Well, this said particular property of their general psyche, called 'Egoism,' was just gradually formed in them, only because of that mentioned abnormally established form in the process of their ordinary being-existence, namely, the assigning of each other to various 'classes' or 'castes.'

"Some time later, in its appropriate place, during my further tales concerning the three-brained beings existing on the planet Earth, I shall also explain to you in detail how, thanks to those conditions of external being-existence which were established there, you favorites first began assigning each other to various castes, and how, thanks to subsequent similar abnormalities, this same maleficent form of mutual relation then established there, has continued even until now. But meanwhile for my present tale it is necessary for you to know that the basis for the arising in their general presence of the mentioned particular property of their psyche, namely the property of egoism, has also been the reason, owing always to the same abnormal conditions established from the very beginning after the second Transapalnian-perturbation there, that their general psyche has become dual.

"And this happened because on the one hand, various what are called 'Individual-initiatives' began to issue from that localization arising in their presences, which is always predominant during their waking-existence, and which localization is nothing else but only the result of the accidental perceptions of impressions coming from without, brought forth by their abnormal environment, which perceptions in totality are called by them their 'consciousness'; and on the other hand, similar 'Individual-initiatives' also began to issue in them, as it is proper to them, from that normal localization existing in the presences of every kind of being and which they called their 'subconsciousness.'

"And because the mentioned 'Individual-initiatives' issue from such different localizations during their waking existence, each of them, during the process of his daily existence, is, as it were, divided into two independent personalities.

"Here it must be remarked that just this said duality was also the cause, that there was also gradually lost from their presences that impulse necessary to three-brained beings, which is called 'sincerity.'

"Later, the practice of deliberately destroying the just mentioned being-impulse called 'sincerity' even took root among them and, now from the day of their arising, or as they say, from the day of their 'birth,' the three-brained beings there are accustomed by their producers—or, as they say, 'Parents'—to an entirely contrary impulse, namely, 'deceit.'

"To teach and to suggest to their children how to be insincere with others and deceitful in everything, has become so ingrained in the beings of the planet Earth of the present time, that it has even become their conception of their duty towards their children; and just this same they call by the notorious name, 'education.'

"They 'educate' their children to be never able and never to dare to do as the 'conscience' present in them instinctively directs, but only that which is prescribed in the manual of 'Bon-ton,' usually drawn up there just by various candidate 'Hasnamusses.'

"And of course when these children grow up and become responsible beings, they already automatically produce their manifestations and acts just as they were 'educated' during their formation, that is to say, just as they were 'taught,' just as they were 'suggested' and just as they were 'wound up.'

"Thanks to all this, the conscience which might be in the consciousness of the beings of that planet is, from their earliest infancy, gradually driven back within, so that by the time they are grown up the said conscience is already found only in what they call their 'subconsciousness.'

"As a consequence, the functioning of the mentioned data for the bringing forth in their presences of this said divine impulse conscience, gradually ceased long ago to participate in that consciousness of theirs, by means of which their 'waking-existence' flows.

"That is why, my boy, the crystallization in their general presence of the divine manifestation issuing from Above for the 'data' both of this arising and also of this sacred being-impulse in them, proceeds only in their subconsciousness; and as this subconsciousness of theirs has ceased to participate in the process of their ordinary daily existence, that alone is the sole reason why these data have escaped that 'degeneration' to which all the other sacred being-impulses were subjected, namely, the impulses 'Faith,' 'Love' and 'Hope,' which also they ought to have in their presences.

"Furthermore, if for some reason or other the actions of the divine data crystallized in their presences for the said being-impulse should now begin to manifest themselves in them from their subconsciousness and should strive to participate in the functioning of their abnormally formed ordinary 'Consciousness,' no sooner are they aware of it than they at once take measures to avoid it, because it has already become impossible in the conditions already existing there for anyone to exist with the functioning in their presences of this divine impulse of genuine objective conscience.

"From the time when the said 'egoism' had become finally 'inoculated' in the presences of your favorites, this particular being-property became, in its turn, the fundamental auxiliary in the gradual crystallization of the data of their general psyche for the arising of several other already quite exclusively-particular being-impulses now existing there under the names of 'cunning,' 'envy,' 'hate,' 'hypocrisy,' 'contempt,' 'haughtiness,' 'servility,' 'slyness,' 'ambition,' 'double-facedness,' and so on and so forth.

"These exclusively-particular properties of their psyche which I have just named, utterly unbecoming to be possessed by three-brained beings, were already fully crystallized in the presences of the majority of your favorites, and were the inevitable attributes of the psyche of every one of them even before the period of the Very Saintly Ashiata Shiemash; but when there began to be fixed and to flow automatically in the process of their being-existence the new forms of existence intentionally implanted in them by Ashiata Shiemash himself, then these strange properties, previously present in their psyche, entirely disappeared from the presences of most of the three-brained beings there. Later, however, when they themselves destroyed all the results of the Very Saintly Labors of this Essence Loving Ashiata Shiemash, these same psychic properties maleficent for them themselves, gradually again arose anew in all of them, and, for the contemporary three-brained beings there, they are already the foundation of the whole of their essence.

"Well, my boy, when there arose the data in the general presences of your favorites for the bringing forth of this 'Unique-particular' being impulse 'egoism' and of gradually evolving and producing factors flowing from it for other also particular but now secondary strange being-impulses, said 'unique-property' 'egoism' usurped the place of the 'Unique-

All-Autocratic-Ruler' in their general organization, and then not only every manifestation but even what is called the 'desire-for-the-arising' of such a divine being-impulse became a hindrance to the actions of this 'All-Autocratic-Ruler.' And in consequence of this, when eventually your favorites had already, by force of necessity, both consciously and unconsciously always and in everything, prevented its partaking in the functioning of that consciousness of theirs through the control of which it had become proper for them to actualize their waking-existence, the actions of those divine data were gradually, as it were, removed from the functioning of their said 'consciousness.'

"Well, it was only after my detailed researches and investigations had made all the foregoing clear to me, that I understood why there arose and why there still exists that division of themselves there into various 'classes' or 'castes,' which is particularly maleficent for them on account of its consequences.

"My said later 'detailed researches' and investigations very definitely and clearly also showed me that, in that consciousness of theirs, which they call their 'subconsciousness,' even in the case of the beings of the present time, the said data for the acquisition in their presences of this fundamental divine impulse conscience does indeed still continue to be crystallized and, hence to be present during the whole of their existence.

"And, that these data of this divine being-impulse are still crystallized and their manifestations still continue to participate in the process of their being existence, was, apart from what I have already said, further confirmed by this—that I frequently had a good deal of difficulty on account of it, during the periods of my observation of them from the planet Mars.

"The truth is, that through my 'Teskooano' I could freely observe from the planet Mars without any difficulty whatever, the existence proceeding on the surfaces of the other planets of that solar system, but making my observations of the process of the existence proceeding on the surface of your planet was a real misery owing to the special coloration of its atmosphere.

"And this special coloration occurred, as I later ascertained, because there appeared from time to time, in the presence of this atmosphere, large quantities of these crystallizations frequently radiated from the presences of these favorites of yours, owing to that particular inner impulse which they themselves call 'Remorse of Conscience.'

"And this proceeded because in those of them who chance to receive and experience some kind of what is called 'moral shock,' the associations proceeding from their previous impressions almost always become changed and calm, and sometimes even for a time entirely cease in them—associations which, as I have already told you, consist mostly of various kinds of what is called 'rubbish.'

"In consequence, there is then automatically obtained in these three-brained beings there, such a combination of functioning in their general presences, that temporarily frees the data present in their subconsciousness for the manifestation of the divine impulse conscience, and for its participation in the functioning of their ordinary consciousness, with the result that just this said 'Remorse of Conscience' proceeds in them.

"And as this 'Remorse of Conscience' carries with the arising of the mentioned particular crystallizations which issue from them with their other radiations, the result is that the totality of all these radiations occasionally gives the atmosphere of this planet of yours just that particular coloration which hinders the being-organ of sight from penetrating freely through it.

"Here it is necessary to say, that these favorites of yours, particularly the contemporary ones, become ideally expert in not allowing this inner impulse of theirs, called 'Remorse-of-Conscience,' to linger long in their general presence.

"No sooner do they begin to sense the beginning of the functioning in them of such a being-impulse, or even no more than what is called the 'prick' of its arising, than they immediately, as it is said, 'sit on it,' whereupon this impulse not yet quite formed in them, at once 'pipes down.'

"For this 'sitting on' the beginning of any 'Remorse-of-Conscience' in themselves, they have even invented some very efficient special means, which now exist there under the names of 'Alcoholism,' 'Cocainism,' 'Morphinism,' 'Nicotinism,' 'Onanism,' 'Monkism,' 'Athenianism' and others with names also ending in 'ism.'

"Sometime later, on a suitable occasion, I shall explain to you in detail also about those results issuing from the abnormally established conditions of ordinary existence there, which became factors for the arising and permanent existence there of this for them maleficent reciprocal assignment of themselves to various castes.

"I shall without fail explain this to you some time, because the information elucidating their abnormality there, may serve as very good data for your further logical comparisons for the purpose of understanding better the strangeness of the psyche of these three-brained beings who please you.

"Meanwhile listen attentively and transubstantiate in yourself the following: when the mentioned particular psychic property of 'egoism' had been fulfilledly formed in the general presences of these favorites of yours, and later, there had also been formed in them various other secondary also particular being-impulses never present in the presences of any other normal three-brained beings of the whole of our Universe, and which flowed out and now still continue to flow out from this particular psychic property of 'Egoism'—and, furthermore, in consequence of the total absence of the participation of the impulse of sacred conscience in their waking-consciousness—then these three-brained beings arising and existing on the planet Earth, both before the period of the Very Saintly activities of Ashiata Shiemash and also since, have always striven and continue still to strive to arrange their welfare during the process of their ordinary existence, exclusively only for them themselves.

"And as in general, on none of the planets of our Great Universe does there or can there exist enough of everything required for everybody's equal exterior welfare, without distinction of what are called 'objective merits,' the result there is that the prosperity of one is always built on the adversity of many.

"It is just this exclusive regard for their own personal welfare that has gradually crystallized in them the already quite particularly unprecedented and peculiar properties of their psyche which I cited, as for instance, 'cunning,' 'contempt,' 'hate,' 'servility,' 'lying,' 'flattery' and so on, which in their turn, on the one hand are factors for an exterior manifestation unbecoming to three-brained beings, and on the other hand are the causes of the gradual destruction of all those inner possibilities of theirs placed in them by great Nature, of becoming particles of the whole of the 'reasonable whole.'

"At the time when the results of the Very Saintly labors of the Essence Loving Ashiata Shiemash had already begun to blend with the processes of what is called their 'inner' and 'outer' being-existence, and when thanks to this the data for the divine impulse conscience, surviving in their subconsciousness, began gradually to share in the functioning of their 'waking-consciousness,' then the being-existence both personal and reciprocal began to proceed on this planet also, almost as it does on the other planets of our great Universe on which three-brained beings exist.

"These favorites of yours also then began to have relations

towards each other as only towards the manifestations varying in degree of a UNIQUE COMMON CREATOR and to pay respect to each other only according to the merits personally attained by means of 'being-Partkdolgduty,' that is, by means of personal conscious labors and intentional sufferings.

"That is why there just ceased to exist there during that period the said two chief maleficent forms of their ordinary existence, namely, their separate independent communities and the division of themselves in these communities into various 'castes,' or, as is still sometimes said there, into various 'classes.'

"At that time, also, there upon your planet, all the three-brained beings began to consider themselves and those like them merely only as beings bearing in themselves particles of the emanation of the Sorrow of our COMMON FATHER CREATOR.

"And all this then so happened because when the actions of the data of the divine being-impulse began to share in the functioning of their ordinary waking-consciousness, and the three-brained beings began manifesting themselves in relation to each other, solely in accordance with conscience, the consequence was that masters ceased to deprive their slaves of freedom, and various power-possessing beings of their own accord surrendered the rights they had obtained without desert, having become aware by conscience and sensing that they actualized and occupied these rights and offices not for the common welfare but only for the satisfaction of their various personal weaknesses, such, for instance, as 'vanity,' 'self-love,' 'self-calming' and so on.

"Of course, there continued to be all kinds of chiefs, rulers, and 'adviser-specialists' at that period also, just as there are everywhere on all the planets of the Universe on which there breed three-brained beings of varying degrees of self-perfecting arising chiefly from difference of age and from what is called 'essence power,' but they then became such, neither by hereditary right nor by election, as was the case before this blissful 'Ashiatian-epoch' and as again afterwards became and even until now continues to be the case.

"All these chiefs, rulers and advisers then became such by themselves automatically, in accordance with the objective merits they personally acquired, and which were really sensible to all the beings around them.

"And it proceeded in the following way: All the beings of this planet also, then began to work in order to have in their consciousness this divine function of genuine conscience, and for this purpose as everywhere in the Universe, they transubstantiated in themselves what are called the 'being-obligolnian-strivings' and which consist of the following five, namely:

The first striving: to have in their ordinary being-existence everything satisfying for their planetary body.

The second striving: to have a constant and unflagging instinctive need for self-perfection in the sense of Being.

The third: the conscious striving to know ever more and more concerning the laws of World-creation and World-maintenance.

The fourth: the striving to discharge the debt of their arising and their individuality of existence as early and as possible in order afterwards to be free to lighten as much as possible the Sorrow of OUR COMMON FATHER.

And the fifth: the striving always to assist the most rapid perfecting of other beings, both those similar to oneself and those of other forms, up to the degree of the 'sacred Martfotai,' that is, up to the degree of self-individuality.

"At this period when every terrestrial three-centered being began to exist concordantly with these five strivings and work consciously upon himself, many of them, thanks to this, quickly arrived at results of objective attainments perceptible to others.

"Of course, these objective attainments then, as it is said, 'attracted the attention' of all around them who thereupon made those who had attained, stand out from their midst and paid them every kind of respect; they also strove with joy to merit the attention of these outstanding beings and to have for themselves their counsel and advice concerning how they themselves could attain the same perfecting.

"And these outstanding beings themselves of that period in their turn and from their own number, began to make the one most attained stand out, and this outstanding being thereby became mechanically, without either hereditary or other right, the chief of them all. Their directings were spread correspondingly with the occurrence of his recognition as chief, and this recognition included not only the separate neighboring parts of the terra-firma of the surface of your planet, but also even the neighboring continents and islands.

"At that period the counsel and guidance, and in general, every word of these chiefs, became law for all the three-brained beings there; and were fulfilled by them with devotion and joy; not as it had proceeded there before the results obtained by the Very Saintly Labors of Ashiata Shiemash, nor as it again proceeded and still continues since they themselves destroyed the fruits of his Very Saintly Labors.

"Namely, these strange three-brained beings, your favorites, now carry out the various commands and orders of their 'chiefs' and, as they are called 'kings,' only from fear of what are called 'bayonets' and 'lousy cells,' of which there are a great many at the disposition of these chiefs and kings.

"The results of the Very Saintly Labors of Ashiata Shiemash were then also very definitely reflected in respect of that terrible peculiarity of the manifestation of the psyche of your favorites, namely, in their 'needful-tendency-to-the-periodic-destruction-of-each-other's-existence.'

"The process of reciprocal destruction established there

and flowing out from that terrible particularity of their psyche entirely ceased on the continent Asia, and only proceeded occasionally on those large and small terra-firma surfaces of that planet of yours, which were far from the continent of Asia. And this continued there only because owing to their distance, the influence of the 'initiates' and 'priests' could not reach and be transubstantiated in the presences of the beings breeding on these said terra-firmas.

"But the most astonishing and significant result of the Very Saintly labors of Ashiata Shiemash was that at that period not only did the length itself of the existence become a little more normal—that is to say, it began to increase—and also that what they called the 'death rate' itself was also diminished, but at the same time the number of their results manifested for the prolongation of their generation, that is as they say, their 'birth-rate,' diminished at least a fifth.

"Thereby there was even practically demonstrated one of the cosmic laws, namely, what is called 'the law-of-the-equilibration-of-vibrations'—that is, of vibrations arising from the evolutions and involutions of the cosmic substances required for the Most Great Omnicosmic Trogoautoegocrat.

"The said decline in both their 'death-rate' and their 'birth-rate' proceeded because as they approximated to an existence normal for the three-centered beings, they also began to radiate from themselves vibrations responding more closely to the requirements of Great Nature, thanks to which, there was less need in Nature for those vibrations which in general are obtained from the destruction of the existence of beings.

"About this cosmic law 'equilibration-of-vibrations' you will also understand well when at the proper time I shall explain to you in detail, as I have already many times promised you, concerning all the general fundamental cosmic laws.

"It was in just this way, my boy, and in such a sequence that there in that period, thanks to the conscious labors of the

Very Saintly Ashiata Shiemash the said welfare unprecedented for your favorites was gradually created, but to the infinite sadness of all more or less consciously thinking individuums of all gradations of reason, shortly after the departure from this planet of the Very Saintly Ashiata Shiemash, these unfortunates themselves, after the manner that had become in general proper to them before, in respect of every good attainment of their ancestors, totally destroyed it all; and thus it was they destroyed and thus it was they swept away from the surface of their planet all that welfare, so that even the rumor that once upon a time such a bliss existed, on their own planet, failed to reach the contemporary beings there.

"In certain inscriptions which have survived from ancient times and have reached the contemporary beings of that planet, there, is however, some information that there once existed on their planet, what is called a special kind of 'state-organization,' and that at the head of every such state were beings of the highest attainments.

"And on the basis of this information, the contemporary beings have invented just a mere name for this 'state organization'; they call it a 'priest-state-organization' and have done with it.

"But what constituted this 'priest-state-organization,' how it was and why it was . . . ? it's all the same to the contemporary beings of the planet what primitive savages did!

"And now, my boy, hear how these strange three-brained beings who please you, began and finally achieved the complete destruction of all the results obtained from the Very Saintly Labors of the Great Essence Loving now Omnicosmic Most Very Saintly Ashiata Shiemash.

CHAPTER XXVIII

The Chief Culprit Of The Destruction Of All The Very Saintly Labours Of Ashiata Shiemash

YOU REMEMBER that I have already told you that the basis of the initiative for the arising there of the factors which became the causes of the final destruction of the still surviving remains of the beneficent results for the subsequent generations of your favorites of the conscious labors of the Very Saintly Ashiata Shiemash did not issue from the scientific beings who were then assembled from almost the whole of the surface of the Earth, in the city of Babylon, but that these latter—as it had long before become proper to the majority of the terrestrial scientists of 'new format'—were only, like 'carrier-germs,' the unconscious disseminators of every kind of evil, already arisen before them, both for their own and for subsequent generations.

"As the basis for all the further great and small maleficent doings and unconscious maleficent manifestations of the scientific beings of that time, relative to the destruction of even the last remnants of the results, beneficent for the three-brained beings there, that were obtained from the very saintly conscious labors of the Essence Loving Ashiata Shiemash, there served—as my later detailed researches concerning his further very saintly activities made clear to me—the 'invention' of a scientific being, well known there in his time, also belonging to the number of the scientists of 'new format,' named Lentrohamsanin.

"In the presence of this terrestrial three-brained being, the 'highest-being-part' was coated and perfected up to the required gradation of objective reason, and he afterwards became, as I have once already told you, one of the number of those 335 'highest-being-bodies' who are called 'eternal-Hasnamuss-individuums' and who have the place of their further existence in the Universe, on a small planet existing under the name of 'Retribution.'

"Now, strictly speaking, about this terrestrial three-brained being Lentrohamsanin, I would have to fulfill my promise and to explain to you in detail concerning the expression 'Hasnamuss,' but I prefer to do so a little later in the proper place of the sequence of my given tale.

"And so, my boy, the mentioned maleficent 'invention'—or as they themselves, that is, the contemporary terrestrial scientists, name such an invention of a scientist there of 'new format'—'composition' or even a 'creation'—was just actualized, as I have already told you, two or more centuries before the time when, during my fifth stay there, I first reached the city of Babylon, where partly by coercion and partly voluntarily, scientific beings had been assembled from the surface of almost the whole of the planet.

"That maleficent 'invention' of that scientist of former centuries reached the scientific beings of the said Babylonian epoch by means of what is called a 'Kashireitleer,' on which this invention was engrossed by the said learned Lentrohamsanin himself.

"It will do no harm to relate to you a little more in detail the story of the arising of this Lentrohamsanin and also how, owing to which accidental circumstances of his environment, he later became there a 'great scientist' and 'authority' for his contemporary beings of almost the whole surface of your planet.

"This must be explained to you because this story by itself is very characteristic and can moreover serve as a clear indication of what three-brained beings in general there become what are called 'authorities' for other scientists of 'new format' there and hence for all the other unfortunate ordinary beings there.

"The details concerning the conditions of the arising and

subsequent formation of this Lentrohamsanin into a responsible being chanced to become clear to me, by the way, during my investigations of, namely, which aspects taken together of the strange psyche of your favorites had served as the basis for the gradual change and ultimately also for the total destruction of all those beneficent special forms in the process of their being-existence, which had been grafted into that process of theirs by the ideally-foreseeing reason of our now Omnicosmic Most Very Saintly Ashiata Shiemash during the period of his self-preparation to be that which he now is for the whole of the Universe.

"It was then that I learned that this Lentrohamsanin arose, or, as it is said there, 'was born,' on the continent Asia, in the capital of Nievia, the town Kronbookhon.

"The conception of his arising resulted from the blending of two heterogeneous exioëharies formed in two already elderly three-brained Keschapmartnian beings there.

"His 'producers' or, as it is said there, his 'parents,' having chosen as the place for their permanent existence the capital of Nievia, moved there three terrestrial years before the arising of that later Universal Hasnamuss.

"For his elderly and very rich parents he was what is called 'a first-born' for although blendings of their Exioëharies had been many times actualized between them before him, yet, as I found, being deeply engaged in the business of acquiring riches and not wishing to have any hindrance for this, they, in each such instance, had recourse to what is called 'Toosy,' or as your contemporary favorites express themselves, 'abortion.'

"Towards the end of his activities in acquiring riches the source of the active beginning of his origin, or, as it is said there, his 'father,' had several of his own what are called 'Caravans' and he also owned special 'Caravansaries' for the exchange of goods in various cities of this same Nievia.

"And the source of the passive beginning of his origin, that is, his mother, was, at first, of the profession of what is called 'Toosidji,' and afterwards she organized on a small hill what is called a 'Holy place' and published broadcast among other beings information concerning its significance, namely, that beings of the female sex without children would, on visiting this place, acquire the possibility of having them.

"When this couple, in what is called 'the decline of their years' had already become very rich, they moved to Kronbookhon in order to exist there, already only for their own pleasure.

"But soon they felt that without a real result, or as they say there, 'in childlessness,' there cannot be full pleasure, and from that time on, without sparing what is called 'money,' they took every kind of measure in order to obtain such a result.

"They visited, with this object, every kind of 'holy place' existing there for that purpose, of course with the exception of their own 'holy mountain'; and resorted to every kind of what are called 'medical-means,' which purported to assist the blending of heterogeneous exioëharies; and when eventually by chance such a blending was actualized, then there indeed arose, after a certain time, just that long awaited result of theirs, later called Lentrohamsanin.

"From the very first day, the parents were completely wrapped up in what they described as their God-sent 'result' or 'son'; and they spent vast sums on his pleasures and on what is called his 'education.'

"Their ambition was to give this son the best 'upbringing' and 'education' the Earth could provide.

"With this aim, they hired for him various what are called 'tutors' and 'teachers,' both from among those existing in the country Nievia and from various distant lands.

"These latter, that is, these foreign 'tutors' and 'teachers,' they then imported chiefly from the country which at the present time is called 'Egypt.'

"Already by the time this terrestrial what is called 'Papa's and Mama's darling' was approaching the age of a responsible being, he was, as it is said there, very well 'instructed' and 'educated,' that is, he already had in his presence a great deal of dubious information concerning this, that and the other, and could manifest himself automatically accurately conformably with the conditions of being-existence abnormally established there.

"But when he had already reached the age of a responsible being there—although he had indeed a great deal of information, or, as it is called there, 'knowledge'—nevertheless, in regard to this 'information' or 'knowledge' which he had acquired, there was as yet no corresponding Being in him.

"Well, when this said 'Mama's and Papa's darling' became a scientist of 'new-format' there, then because on the one hand there was no Being whatsoever in his presence and on the other hand, because there had already by this time been thoroughly crystallized in him those consequences of the properties of the organ Kundabuffer which exist there under the names of 'vanity,' 'self-love,' 'swagger' and so forth, the ambition arose in him to become a 'famous scientist' not only among the beings of Nievia, but over the whole surface of their planet as well.

"So, with all his presence he dreamed and ruminated how he could attain it

"For many days he then thought very seriously; and finally he decided, first of all, to invent a theory upon a topic which nobody before him had ever discussed, and, secondly, to engross this 'invention' of his upon such a 'Kashireitleer' as nobody had ever before engrossed or would ever be able to in the future either.

"And from that day on he made preparations for the actualizing of that decision of his.

"With the help of many slaves, he first prepared a 'Kashireitleer' such as had never before existed, namely, of a hundred buffalo hides joined together.

"I must tell you that the 'Kashireitleers' were generally made on the planet Earth in those times from one or another part of a single buffalo hide, whereas Lentrohamsanin made his 'Kashireitleer' from a hundred buffalo hides.

"These 'Kashireitleers' were replaced there later by what is called 'Parchment.'

"Well, when this unprecedented 'Kashireitleer' was ready, the future great Lentrohamsanin engrossed upon it concerning a topic which indeed it had occurred to nobody to discuss before—and, in truth, there was no reason why it should.

"Namely, in those 'wiseacrings' of his, he then criticized in every possible way the existing what is called 'Political Organization of Society.'

"This 'Kashireitleer' began thus:

"'Man's greatest happiness consists in depending upon no other personality whatsoever, and in being free from all alien influences whatsoever.'

"Some other time I will explain to you how your favorites, the strange three-brained beings there on the planet Earth, in general understand freedom.

"This subsequent Universal Hasnamuss engrossed further as follows:

"'Undeniably, life under the present state-organization is now far better for us than it used to be; but where then is that real freedom of ours upon which our happiness must depend?

"'Don't we work and labor as much now as during any former state-organization?

"'Haven't we to labor and sweat to get the barley indispensable to enable us to live and not to starve to death like chained dogs?

"'Our lords and masters and pastors are always telling us

about some other sort of world, which is purported to be so much better than here among us on the Earth, and where life is in every respect beatific for the souls of those men who live here on the Earth "worthily."

"'Don't we live here "worthily"?

"'Don't we always labor and sweat for our daily bread?

"'If what all our masters and pastors tell us is true and their own way of living here on the Earth really worthily corresponds to what is required of their souls for the other world, then of course God ought, and even must, in this world also, give more possibilities to them than to us ordinary mortals.

"'If all this, which our masters and pastors tell and try to make us believe, is really true, let them prove it to us ordinary mortals by facts.

"'Let them prove to us by facts at least this—that they can change a pinch of the common sand in which, thanks to our sweat, our daily bread arises, into bread.

"'Let our present masters and pastors do this, and I myself will be the first to run and kneel and kiss their feet.

"'But meanwhile, as this is not so, we ourselves must struggle and we ourselves must strive for our real happiness and for our real freedom from the influence of strange personalities, and also to escape the need to sweat.

"'It is true that for eight months of the year we now have no trouble in obtaining our daily bread; but how do those four summer months go, when we have to spend our sweat to get the barley we need?

"'Only he who sows and mows that barley knows the difficulties of it.

"'For eight months we are free, but from physical labors only, and for this our consciousness, namely, our dearest and highest part, must remain subject night and day to these ephemeral ideas which are always being dinned into us by our pastors and masters.

"'No, enough! Without our present masters and pastors, who have become so without our leave, we ourselves must strive for our real freedom and our real happiness.

"'Only if we act all for each and each for all, can we obtain real freedom and real happiness.

"'To create a happy life for ourselves, we must first destroy all that is old.

"'And we must do so to make room for the new life we shall ourselves create that will give us real freedom and real happiness.

"'Down with dependence on others!

"'We will to be ourselves the masters of our own circumstances; and no longer they should be our masters and rule our lives who do so without our knowledge and without our consent.

"'Our lives must be governed and guided by those whom we ourselves shall elect from our midst, and namely, from amongst those men only who themselves struggle for our daily barley.

"'And these governors and counsellors we must elect from our midst on the basis of equal rights, without distinction of sex or age by universal, direct, equal and open ballot.'

"Thus ended the said famous 'Kashireitleer.'

"When this subsequent Universal Hasnamuss, Lentrohamsanin, had finished engrossing this 'Kashireitleer,' indeed unprecedented there, he arranged an enormous and costly banquet to which he invited all the 'learned' beings from all Nievia, taking upon himself all their traveling expenses; and at the end of this banquet he showed them his 'Kashireitleer.'

"When the 'scientists' then gathered at that free feast from almost the whole Nievia saw that 'Kashireitleer,' indeed unprecedented there, they were at first flabbergasted, and, as it is said there, 'knocked speechless,' and only after a considerable time did they gradually begin looking at each other with dumbfounded glances, and exchanging opinions in whispers.

"Chiefly they asked one another how it was possible that not one of the number of 'scientists' nor one or the ordinary beings had hitherto known or guessed that there in their own country such a scientist with such knowledge existed.

"Suddenly one of them, namely, the oldest among them, who enjoyed the greatest reputation, jumped up on the table like a boy, and in a loud voice and with the intonation which had already long before become proper to the scientists there of 'new format,' and which has also reached the contemporary scientists, pronounced the following:

"'Listen, and all of you be aware that we, the representatives of terrestrial beings assembled here, who have, thanks to our great sciences, already attained independent individuality, have the happiness to be the first to behold with our own eyes the creation of a Messiah of divine consciousness sent to us from Above to reveal "World-truths" to us!

"Thereupon began that usual maleficent what is called 'mutual-inflation,' which had already long been practiced among the scientific beings of 'new format,' and chiefly on account of which no objectively true knowledge ever evolves there as it does everywhere else, even merely from the passage of time itself; but, on the contrary, even the knowledge once already attained there is destroyed; and its keepers themselves are always becoming shallower and shallower.

"That is to say, the rest of the scientists then began shouting and pushing each other in order to get near Lentrohamsanin; and addressing him as their 'long-awaited Messiah' they conveyed to him by their admiring glances what are called their 'tributes of praise.'

"The most interesting thing about it all is this, namely, that the reason why all the other scientists ware so greatly amazed and so freely gave way to what are called their 'scientific whimpers,' lay in a very strange and particularly unconscious need which had been formed in the psyche of the scientists there.

"Namely, thanks as always to the same abnormally established conditions of ordinary existence, the notion had already arisen there long before—and is up until now an inseparable part of the general psyche of each and every one of your favorites—that if anybody is a follower of an already well known and important being, he thereby also becomes, or at least he will seem to be, almost as well known and important himself.

"So it was on the strength of this that all the other scientists of that time, of the country Nievia, immediately manifested themselves approvingly towards this Lentrohamsanin, because he was both very rich and what is most important, already famous.

"Well, my dear boy, when after the said banquet, the scientific beings of Nievia returned home, then they were no sooner there than they began speaking first among their neighbors and later more and more widely, here, there and everywhere, firstly, about that unprecedented Kashireitleer itself, and secondly, already foaming at the mouth, to persuade and convince everybody of the truth of those revelations which that great Lentrohamsanin had engrossed on this 'Kashireitleer.'

"The result of it all was that the ordinary beings both of the town Kronbookhon and of other parts of the country Nievia talked among themselves of nothing but these revelations.

"And gradually, as it also usually happens there, almost everywhere beings became divided into two mutually opposing parties, one of which favored the 'invention' of the subsequent Universal Hasnamuss, and the other the already existing and well fixed forms of being existence.

"Thus it continued during almost a whole terrestrial year, during which time, both the ranks of the contending parties increased and towards each other there grew one of their particular properties called 'hate.'

"And one sorrowful day in the town Kronbookhon itself, there suddenly began among the beings, who already had become followers of one or the other of the two said mutually opposite currents, their process of what is called 'Civil War.'

"'Civil War'—this is the same as 'war'; the difference lies only in this, that in ordinary 'war,' beings of one community destroy the beings of another community, while in a 'civil war,' the process of reciprocal destruction proceeds among beings of one and the same community, as, for example: brother annihilates brother; father–son; uncle–nephew; and so on.

"At the outset, during the four days, while that horrible process was at its height in Kronbookhon, and the attention of the other beings of the country of all Nievia was concentrated on it, everything was still relatively quiet in the other towns, except that here and there, small, what are called, 'skirmishes' occasionally took place; but when at the end of the fourth day, those who were for the 'invention' of Lentrohamsanin, that is, for the scientists, were victorious in Kronbookhon, then, from that time forward, the same process also began at all the large and small points of the whole of the surface of Nievia.

"That widespread horrible process which had nowhere existed before, continued until there already appeared quite powerful 'hordes' of scientists, who, compelling all the surviving beings to acknowledge the ideas of Lentrohamsanin, immediately destroyed everything.

"The result of all I have described was just that all the three-brained beings of Nievia became followers of the 'invention' of Lentrohamsanin and in that community there was established a particular what is called 'Republic.'

"A little later, the community Nievia, being at that period great and what is called 'powerful,' began, as it also usually happens there, 'making war' on the neighboring communities for the purpose of imposing upon them also her new form of 'state-organization.'

"From that time on, my boy, on the then largest continent of your planet, their processes of reciprocal destruction among these strange three-brained beings began to proceed as before; and at the same time gradually were changed and finally were destroyed those various beneficent forms of their ordinary existence which had already been fixed in the process of their ordinary existence, thanks to the ideally foreseeing Reason of our now Most Very Saintly Ashiata Shiemash.

"Thereupon there again arose on the surface of your planet there—only to be destroyed anew and to give place to other arisings—their numerous separate communities with every possible, as it is expressed there, 'form-of-inner-state-organization.'

"Although the direct effect of that maleficent 'invention' of the now universal Hasnamuss Lentrohamsanin was that among your favorites the practice was revived of existing in separate communities and they again resumed their periodic reciprocal destruction, yet within many of these newly arisen independent communities on the continent Asia, beings still continued to conform in their ordinary existence to many of the unprecedentedly-wisely-foreseen-details of the Very Saintly Ashiata Shiemash for their ordinary being-existence, those details which had already been inseparably grafted into, what is called their 'mechanical-daily-life.'

"Well, it was for the final destruction of these said details that still remained in certain communities that the said scientists then assembled in the city of Babylon were just to blame.

"And they were then to blame in this respect also owing to the following:

"When in connection with that notorious question of the Beyond, they organized the 'all-planetary-conference' of all the scientists, there happened to be also among the scientists who went to Babylon on their own accord, the great-grandson of Lentrohamsanin himself, who had also become a scientist.

"And he took with him, there to the city of Babylon, an exact copy of the mentioned Kashireitleer, but made on papyrus, the original of which had been engrossed by his great-grandfather and which he had obtained by inheritance.

"At the very height of the 'frenzy' concerning the 'question-of-the-soul,' during one of the last big general meetings of the 'scientists,' he read aloud the contents of that maleficent 'invention' of his great-grandfather's whereupon, thanks to the strange reason of these 'sorry scientists,' it occurred—as also it had become proper among the scientists of this peculiar planet—that from a question which interested them, they at once passed to quite another, namely, from the 'question-of-the-soul' to the question of what is called 'politics.'

"Thereupon in the city of Babylon meetings and discussions again commenced everywhere concerning the various kinds of 'state-organization' already existing or which ought to be formed anew.

"As the basis of all their discussions they took, of course, the truths indicated in the invention of Lentrohamsanin and contained in what is called the 'Papyrus,' that had been taken there and a copy of which almost every scientist who was then in Babylon carried in his pocket.

"For several months they discussed and argued, and once again, as before, the 'split' into parties; that is to say, all the scientists then in the city of Babylon 'split' into three independent what are called 'sections,' under the following names:

the first—Section of 'Legominists'

the second—Section of 'Neomothists'

the third—Section of 'Paleomothists'

"Each of these sections soon had its adherents from among the ordinary beings there in the city of Babylon; and once again things would certainly have ended also with a 'civil' war, if the Persian King, hearing of it all, had not at once 'cracked' them on their 'scientific noddles.'

"A number of these scientists were executed by him, others were imprisoned with lice, still others were dispatched to places, where even now 'French champagne' could not be taken.

"Finally, certain of those left, who were clearly shown to have been occupied with all this, only because, as it is said there, they were 'obviously mad,' were permitted to return 'to their fatherlands' and those among them who had taken no part whatever in 'politics' were not only also given full liberty to return to their native land, but by the order of the mentioned Persian king, their return to their native land was even accompanied with every kind of what is called 'honor.'

"So, my boy, those Babylonian scientists, who for various reasons survived and were scattered everywhere over the surface of almost the whole of the planet, then just continued wiseacring, as it were, and they took as the basis of their wiseacring—of course, not consciously, but simply mechanically—those two leading questions which had arisen and which had been the 'questions of the day' during the said Babylonian events, namely, the notorious questions concerning the 'soul' of man and the inner-state-organization.

"Well, the net result of these wiseacrings of theirs was that over the whole continent of Asia civil wars again broke out in various communities, and among the communities themselves the processes of mass reciprocal destruction.

"The destruction which thus proceeded of the remnants of the results of the conscious labors of the Very Saintly Ashiata Shiemash, continued on the continent of Asia for about a century and a half; nevertheless there were still in some places preserved and even by momentum were still in some places carried out certain forms that had been created by Ashiata Shiemash for their beneficent being-existence. But when the three-brained beings there, who arose and existed on the neighboring continent, hitherto called Europe, then began taking part in these Asiatic wars and civil wars, and when 'hordes' with the arch-vainglorious Greek called 'Alexander of Macedonia' at their head, were dispatched thence and passed almost everywhere over the continent of Asia, they now finally, as it is said, 'made a clean sweep' of everything from the surface of that ill-starred planet; so clean a sweep that it left not even the trace of the memory that there on the surface of their planet there could once have existed such a 'bliss' specially and intentionally created for their existence by just such a Reason, whose bearer is now one of our seven Most Very Saintly Omni-Cosmic Individuums, without whose participation even our UNI-BEING COMMON FATHER allows Himself to actualize nothing.

"I shall now elucidate rather more in detail concerning what I promised you a little while ago, namely, concerning the expression 'Hasnamuss.'

"In general, those independent individuums are called and defined by the Word 'Hasnamuss' in whom, among a number of other what are called 'Individual-impulses' a certain 'something' obtained from the total presence of every three-brained being arises which participates in what is called their 'fulfilled-formation'; that is to say, which participates in the forming both of the 'planetary-body' itself and of the being and of his two higher being bodies at every stage of the perfecting of these latter.

"This 'something' in these separate cosmic Individuums arises and interblends in the process of crystallization from a certain, what is called 'Naloo-osnian-spectrum-of-impulses.'

"In addition to several very undesirable consequences for the said Individuums themselves, in whom they arise—about which I shall later also explain to you in detail—this said 'something' has still another particularity, namely, that as soon as the action of what is called 'intense-effort' ceases in the presences of the given arisings, it is always perceived and manifested according to some or other part of the mentioned 'Naloo-osnian-spectrum-of-impulses,' as if there were not enough of that something like the first and second being-foods, and it thus helps the totality of the whole given presence to manifest itself 'harmfully-actingly,' both for itself and for other independent Individuums around.

"From the total presence of every kind of three-brained being, there arises four kinds of the mentioned independent 'Hasnamuss Individuums.'

"The first kind arises, when the planetary body of a being becomes such a 'Hasnamuss-Individuum' during its planetary existence.

"The second kind arises when there become 'Hasnamuss-Individuums' with the 'Kesdjan-bodies' of the three-brained beings which are 'fulfilledly' coated in the total presences of the beings, and which acquire in themselves the property of 'Toorinoorino,' that is, they are no longer subject to the property of decomposition in any sphere of that planet on which they arise.

"The third kind of 'Hasnamuss-Individuum' issues from amongst those three-brained beings' in whose presence the highest 'being-body' is already 'fulfilledly' coated and perfected, in the sense of objective reason, up to the corresponding gradation, and who have also acquired in themselves the property 'Toorinoorino' not only as regards the sphere of that planet on which they arise, but also in all the other spheres of the Universe, until that time when there proceeds in the presence of the given Individuum what is called the 'complete-transformation' of this said 'something.'

"The fourth kind of 'Hasnamuss-Individuum' is similar to the third, but with this difference, that for the Hasnamuss of the third kind there is a possibility of at some time obtaining the mentioned transformation, whereas for this fourth kind that possibility is already lost forever. Hence this fourth kind of Hasnamuss is called the 'Eternal-Hasnamuss-Individuum.'

"All the four said independent kinds of 'Hasnamuss-Individuum' who may have their arising in the total presence of any three-brained being, on account of the acquisition and the existence of the said 'something' in their presences, completely lose, firstly, any possibility of crystallizing in themselves the divine data for the arising of the sacred impulse of 'Objective-Conscience'; and secondly, after the sacred process of 'Rascooarno' and pending the elucidation from their presence of the action of the said 'something,' they must inevitably be subject to the corresponding.

"And, namely, in the Hasnamusses of the first kind, that is to say, when the said 'something' is acquired by beings still consisting of only just a 'planetary-body' alone, the decomposition of their planetary body does not proceed according to the general rule. In other words, the ceasing to function of the various kinds of what are called, 'self-sensible impulses' does not simultaneously proceed in their presence with the approach of the sacred 'Rascooarno.'

"But in them the process of the sacred 'Rascooarno' begins still during their planetary existence and proceeds in parts, that is one by one there gradually cease to participate in their total presence the functioning of separate, what are called, 'Complexes' of some of their independent spiritualized 'localizations,' or, as your favorites would say there—in such a being, first, one of his brains with all its appertaining functionings dies, later on, the second dies, and only then does the final death of the being approach.

"This partial death as well as the final 'disintegration-of-the-active-element' of which the given 'planetary body' was formed, proceeds at first more slowly, and secondly, with the complete and inextinguishable action of the said 'self-sensible impulses' still possessed during life.

"The second kind of 'Hasnamuss-Individuum,' namely, such an indeed unfortunate arising, whose 'Kesdjan-body' as a three-brained being becomes such, contains no possibilities of independent self-perfection independently of the planetary coating, or, at least, no possibilities of succeeding in eradicating from his presence what is undesirable and what has not even always been acquired through his own fault.

"And because every planetary formation has a defined duration of existence, and every such 'Kesdjan body' arisen in a three-brained being can be coated in a new exterior only of a one-brained or two-brained system and not in a three-brained one, this said unfortunate cosmic arising, in addition to the said permanent trial, is compelled having had no time to adapt himself to one exterior form—to begin all over again in the form of some one-brained or two-brained being of the given planet with the presence of the permanent impulse of 'Hope.'

"As regards the third kind of 'Hasnamuss-Individuum,' namely, those from amongst the three-brained beings who have perfected themselves up to the 'higher-being-bodies,' their presences are already never subject to decomposition in any sphere of the Universe; nor can any forces from without destroy that 'something' they acquired; but that 'something' can be destroyed in them exclusively by the actions of 'Partkdolgduty' formed in the presences themselves of these cosmic Individuums and which are called 'intentional suffering.'

"Such cosmic arisings, therefore, must inevitably suffer correspondingly, until the time when they shall have succeeded in eradicating this 'something' from their presence.

"For the existence and suffering of these 'Hasnamuss-Individuums' who arise from amongst the 'highest-being-bodies,' there are even intentionally allotted and preserved in the Universe, four small planets situated in various most remote corners of our great Universe.

"One of these four small planets, called 'Retribution,' is specially prepared for the 'eternal-Hasnamuss-Individuums'; and the other three are for the 'highest-being-bodies' of those Hasnamusses in whose presences there is still the possibility of eliminating from themselves at some time or other, the said undesirable 'something.'

"These three small planets exist under the names of:

the first—'Remorse of Conscience'
the second—'Repentance'
the third—'Self-Reproach'

"Here it is interesting to notice that from among the number of all the highest-being-bodies which have been coated and perfected in every kind of exterior form of three-brained beings, there have, so far, reached the planet 'Retribution' from the whole Universe only three hundred and thirty five; and one of them is just the 'highest-being-part' of the said Lentrohamsanin of the planet Earth.

"On that planet 'Retribution' those 'eternal-Hasnamuss-Individuums' must constantly endure those incredible sufferings called 'Inkiranoodel' which are like the sufferings called 'Remorse of Conscience,' but still more terrible, their chief terror being this, that these 'highest-being-bodies' must always undergo those horrible sufferings with the consciousness of complete hopelessness.

"As regards the 'Naloo-osnian-spectrum-of-impulses' which I spoke of, on account of which certain separate cosmic arisings are transformed into Hasnamusses, then, on the basis of the chief cosmic law the sacred Heptaparaparshinokh, this spectrum has the essence to be the source of the 'perception-for-the-bringing-forth' and 'manifestation' of seven heterogeneous, what are called, 'aspects.' And these 'aspects,' if characterized according to the ideas of your favorites and defined in their conversational language, may be called as follows:

(1) Conscious and unconscious depravity of every kind.
(2) Self-satisfaction from leading others astray.
(3) The urge to destroy the existence of other breathing things.
(4) The urge to succeed in never actualizing being-effort.
(5) The wish to conceal one's defects under the cloak of pretence.
(6) Calm self-content in the use of what is not personally deserved.
(7) The striving not to be what one is; and thus never to be aware or to sense one's real place in the Universe; and neither to give to others what is due, nor what corresponds, nor what is, in fact, deserved.

"And so, my boy, from the time that your favorites made a 'clean sweep' from the surface of their planet of every kind of result of the very saintly conscious labors of Ashiata Shiemash, their separate communities gradually arose again in great numbers as before, under those two forms of what is called 'subjective-ordering' which they themselves called 'hereditary monarchy' and 'republic.'

"And in connection with these 'state-organizations' established for these 'inner-subjective-orderings' there again began to exist there, terrors for all the beings of that ill-starred planet."

CHAPTER XXIX

The Fruits Of Former Civilizations And The Blossoms Of The Contemporary

ACCORDING to the stream of association of my tales concerning the three-brained beings breeding on the planet Earth which pleased you, I must not fail now already to explain to you, my boy, a little more about those too powerful communities there, called 'Greeks and Romans,' who made a 'clean sweep' from the surface of that ill-starred planet of even the memory of the results obtained from the most saintly labors of the Essence Loving Ashiata Shiemash.

"I must tell you, first of all, that at that period when on the surface of your planet, namely on the continent of Asia, there was actualized from Above within the presence of a three-brained being there the already definitized sacred conception of our now Omnicosmic Very Saintly Ashiata Shiemash, and later also, during the periods of his very saintly activity and the subsequent gradual destruction by your favorites of all the results obtained from it, there also existed on the neighboring continent, then already called Europe, great numbers of those strange three-brained beings who please you, and who had already long before grouped themselves into various independent communities.

"Among the number of those independent communities, there were during those periods, on the basis of the same cosmic laws which I have once mentioned to you, those two large and, as they say there, 'most powerful' communities—communities, that is to say, well organized and possessing more means for the processes of 'reciprocal destruction'—the 'Greeks' and 'Romans.'

"And about these, from the point of view of your contemporary favorites, 'very ancient' communities, I must furthermore not fail to explain to you and possibly in detail—because not only did they then, as I have already said, make a 'clean sweep' from the face of that unfortunate planet of also the last results beneficial for all the three-brained beings of all subsequent epochs, and even of any traces of the memory of the very saintly labors of the Essence Loving Ashiata Shiemash, but they were also just the cause that there already proceeds real 'nonsense' in the reasons of the contemporary favorites of yours, and that there is completely atrophied in your favorites that 'fundamental-being-impulse' which is the main lever of objective morality and is called 'organic shame.'

"A closer acquaintance with these big groupings of your favorites and with various form of 'bliss' prepared by them and which have passed to the beings of later epochs, will give you a good idea and enable you to understand, exactly how separate independent communities are formed there, and also how a given community, having become powerful quite independently of the beings themselves, takes advantage of the fact and sets about destroying everything already attained by the other 'less powerful' communities, and forcing upon them their own 'new inventions' usually in the most sincere feeling that they truly are just what the others need.

"I must premise, my boy, that my story both of the history of their arising and of everything later that was connected with those ancient communities called 'Greeks' and 'Romans,' is not based on the results of my personal investigations; no, I shall only give you the information about them which I got from one of those beings of our tribe who decided to remain to exist forever on that planet of yours.

"The circumstances were these: In descending to the planet Earth for the sixth and last time, I proposed to attain, at any cost, the final elucidation to myself of all the genuine causes why the psyche of those three-brained beings, which ought to be and might be the psyche of the rest of the three-brained beings of our great Universe, had, on that planet become so phenomenally strange.

"And having, during my investigations repeatedly constated that a fundamental cause of the various abnormalities of the general psyche of the contemporary beings was also what is called the 'civilization,' originating in those two large groups of beings called 'Greeks' and 'Romans,' I was obliged to enquire into certain details about them also.

"But as I was fully occupied at that time with my researches concerning the activities of the Very Saintly Ashiata Shiemash, I handed over the elucidation of the history of the arising of these two independent groupings of your favorites—in respect of, what is called their 'subjective-being-Being'—to that same being of our tribe who, as I have already told you, carries on an Undertaking Business in a large city on the continent of Europe down to the present time.

"From the investigations of this countryman of ours, it seems that long long before the period to which what I told you about the majestic city of Babylon referred, namely, at a time when the process of the existence of those strange beings was proceeding mainly on the continent Asia alone, and when their chief culture center was Tikliamish, on that said continent of Europe, which is now the chief place of existence of your favorites, there were, as yet no definitely organized communities.

"Mainly there then existed on that continent, two brained and one-brained beings called 'wild-quadrupeds' and 'reptiles' but of your favorites, the biped beings, there were then on that continent only a number of small groups, almost as 'wild' as the 'quadrupeds' themselves.

"The occupation of these small groups of biped beings was just the destruction of the 'quadruped' and "reptile' beings—and occasionally also of each other.

"And the numbers of your favorites on that continent Europe only increased when emigrants from Maralpleicie, wandering from one place to another, finally arrived and settled there.

"Towards the close of that period there migrated from Tikliamish to that continent Europe a number of beings of the first Asiatic group who had two quite different professions; namely, some of them were engaged in various marine occupations, and others in what are called there 'cattle-raising' and 'sheep-farming.'

"The cattle-raising families populated chiefly the southern shores of the continent, because those parts were at that time very convenient for the maintenance and grazing of such quadruped beings.

"And that group of terrestrial beings was then called 'Latinaki,' a word that signified 'shepherds.'

"At first these shepherds existed with their families and flocks scattered in different places. But later on their numbers gradually, partly from the immigration of beings from the continent Asia having the same profession as themselves, and partly because they were becoming more and more prolific, for the reason that the Nature of the planet Earth had begun to adapt herself to the deteriorating quality of the vibrations she demanded and that had to be formed from their radiations, by substituting those vibrations which are now already obtained only from the process of their sacred 'Rascooarno,' or, as they say—'from their death.'

"And thus, when thanks to all this, their numbers had considerably increased and external conditions demanded frequent relations between separate families, they formed their first common place, and this common place they called 'Rimk.'

"It was from that group of Asiatic shepherds that the later famous Romans just originated; their name having been taken from the name of their first common place 'Rimk.'

"Those Asiatic beings who were engaged in 'marine occupations,' namely in fishing and in gathering sponges, coral and seaweed, emigrated with their families for the convenience of their profession and settled either on the western shores of their own continent Ashhark or on the southeastern shores of the continent Europe, or on the islands of the Straits which still divide the continents Asia and Europe.

"The beings of those newly-formed groups of three-brained terrestrial beings there then called 'Hellenaki,' a word that meant 'Fishermen.'

"The number of the beings of that group, also, gradually increased owing to the same causes already mentioned respecting the group of shepherds.

"The name of the beings of this second group changed many times and finally they came to be called 'Greeks.'

"And so, my dear boy.

"The beings of just these two groups were one of the chief causes that the Reasons of the contemporary favorites of yours have become mechanical, and that there have become completely atrophied in them the data for engendering the impulse of being-shame.

"The Greeks were the cause why the Reasons of the three-brained beings there began gradually to degenerate and became at last so degenerate that among contemporary beings it is already as our dear Mullah Nassr Eddin says, 'a real nonsense mill.'

"And the Romans were the cause why in the result of successive changes, those factors are never crystallized in the presences of the contemporary three-brained beings there, which in other three-brained beings engender the impulse called 'instinctive-shame'; that is, the being-impulse that maintains what are called——and 'objective morality.'

"Thus it was that those two communities arose there, which afterwards, as it often happens there, became very solid and powerful for a definite period. And the history of their further maleficent 'prepared inheritance' for the beings of subsequent generations is as follows:

"According to the investigations of our countryman, it seems the earliest ancestors of the beings of the community, which was later called 'Greece,' were often obliged, on account of the frequent storms at sea which hindered them in their 'marine occupations,' to seek shelter during the rains and winds, in quiet places, where just from boredom, they played various 'games' which they invented for their distraction

"As it later became clear, these ancient fishermen amused themselves at first with such 'games' as children now play there, but children, it must be noticed, who have not yet started the contemporary schooling—because the children there who do go to school have so much homework to do, consisting chiefly of learning by rote the 'poetry' which various candidate 'Hasnamusses have composed there, that the poor children never have time to play any 'game.'

"Briefly, these poor bored fishermen played at first the ordinary 'children's games' already established there long before; but afterwards when one of them invented a new game called 'Pouring from the empty into the void,' they were all so tickled with it that thereafter, they amused themselves with that alone.

"This game consisted in formulating some question or other, always about some 'fiddle-faddle' or other, that is to say, a question about some deliberate piece of absurdity, and the one to whom the question was addressed had to give as plausible an answer as possible.

"Well, it was just this same game that became the cause of all that happened later.

"It turned out that among those ancient bored fishermen, were a number so 'bright' and 'ingenious' that they got to be expert in inventing, according to the principles of that peculiar 'game,' very long explanations.

"And then one of them discovered how to make what was afterwards called 'parchment' from the skin of the fish called 'shark,' then some of these skillful fellows, just to 'swagger' before their companions, even began engrossing these long explanations of theirs on these fish skins, employing those conventional signs which had been inherited earlier, for another game called 'Mouse-trap.'

"Still a little later, when these bored fishermen had already given place to their descendants, both these engrossed fish-skins and the craze for the said peculiar 'game' passed to the latter by inheritance; and these various new inventions, both their own and their ancestors, they called first by the very high-sounding name—'sciences.'

"And thus in course of time the craze for cooking up these 'sciences' passing from generation to generation, the beings of that group, whose ancestors had been simple Asiatic fishermen, became 'specialists' in inventing every sort of such 'sciences' as these.

"These 'sciences,' moreover, also passed from generation to generation and a number of them have reached the contemporary beings of that planet almost unchanged.

"And hence it is that a good half of what are called the 'Egoplastikoori' arising in the Reason of the contemporary beings of that ill-starred planet, from which, what is called a 'being-world-view' is in general formed in beings—are crystallized just from the 'truths' invented there by those bored fishermen and their subsequent generations.

"Concerning the ancient shepherds, who later formed the great powerful community called 'Rome,' their ancestors also were often forced, on account or bad weather, to put their flocks into sheltered places, and to pass the time together somehow or other.

"Being together, they had 'various talks.' But when everything had been talked out and they felt bored, then one of them suggested that as a relief they should take up the pastime which they then called for the first time 'Cinque contra uno'—i.e. five against one—an occupation which has been preserved to the present time under the same name, among their descendants who continue to arise and to exist there.

"So long as only the beings of the male sex then engaged in that business, everything went 'slowly-and-peacefully,' but when a little later their 'passive halves' also joined in, that is to say, their women, and who at once appreciating it, soon became addicted to it—they just then gradually attained in these 'occupations' such 'finesses' that even if our All-universal Arch-cunning Lucifer should rack his honorable brains, he could not even invent a tithe of the 'turns' these erstwhile shepherds then invented and 'prepared' for the beings of the succeeding generations of that ill-starred planet.

"And so, my boy, when both these independent groupings of terrestrial three-brained beings multiplied and began alluring every variety of those effective 'means,' whose acquisition is the usual aim of all communities there during all periods of their existence, really, the 'means' of reciprocal destruction, they then began carrying out these 'processes' with other independent communities there—for the most part, of course, with the less powerful communities—and occasionally among themselves.

"Here it is extremely interesting to notice that when periods of 'peace' occurred between these two communities there, communities of almost equal strength—in respect of the possession of efficient 'means' for the processes of 'reciprocal destruction'—the beings of both groups, the places of their existence being adjacent, often came into contact and had friendly relations with each other; with the result that little by little they then picked up from each other those specialties which had first been invented by their ancestors and which had become proper to them. In other words, the result of the frequent contact of the beings of those two communities was that the Greek beings, borrowing from the Roman beings all the finesses of sexual 'turns,' began arranging their what are called 'Athenian-nights,' while the Roman beings, having learned from the Greek beings how to cook up 'sciences,' composed their later very famous what is called 'Roman Law.'

"A great deal of time has passed since then. The authors of both those kinds of being manifestation have already long been destroyed, and their descendants who chanced to become 'powerful' have been destroyed also. Yet no . . . the contemporary three-brained beings of that planet spend even with emotion, more than half their existence and being energy acquired somehow or other in unconsciously and sometimes even consciously absorbing and actualizing those two ideals, the initiators of whose arising were the said bored Asiatic 'fishermen' and 'shepherds.'

"And so, my boy, later on, it seems, when both these groupings among your favorites acquired many of the said efficient 'means' for the successful destruction of the existence of beings like themselves, and when they had become practiced in persuading or by the potency of their 'means,' compelling the beings of other countries to exchange their inner convictions for those ideals invented by their ancestors there, then, as I have said, they first conquered the neighboring communities situated on the continent Europe, and afterwards with the help of the hordes they collected during that period, turned towards the continent Asia for the same purpose.

"And there already on the continent Asia, they began spreading that maleficent influence of theirs, first among the beings populating the Western shores of that continent—beings in whom, as I have already said, being-impulses of a more or less normal being-existence had been cultivated for centuries—and afterwards, they gradually began advancing into the interior.

"This advance of theirs into the interior of the continent Asia proceeded very successfully, and their ranks were constantly being increased, chiefly because the scientists who had been in Babylon then continued everywhere on the continent Asia to infect the Reasons of beings with their Hasnamussian political ideas.

"And they were also helped very much by the fact that there were still preserved in the instincts of the Asiatic beings, the results of the influences of the 'initiates' and 'priests,' disciples of the Very Saintly Ashiata Shiemash, who in their preachings had inculcated among other things, one of the chief commandments of Ashiata Shiemash which declared:

"'Do not kill another even when your own life is in danger.'

"Profiting by all this, these former fishermen and shepherds could very easily advance, destroying on the way all those who declined to worship the 'gods' they themselves had finally acquired, that is to say, their fantastic 'sciences' and their phenomenal depravity.

"At first these 'sowers of evil' for all the three-brained beings there of all the succeeding generations arising on the continent Europe, and especially the Greeks, in their movement into the interior of the continent Asia, acted if slowly nevertheless essentially.

"But when sometime later, there appeared and stood at the head of what is called an 'Army,' that 'fulfilledly formed' 'Arch-vainglorious Greek,' the future Hasnamuss Alexander of Macedonia, then from that time on there just began to proceed the said 'clear sweep' of the last remnants of the results of the very saintly intentional labors of our now Common Cosmic Most Very Saintly Ashiata Shiemash, and again there was resumed, as it is said, the 'old, old story.'

"Although every time the place of the center of culture has been changed, among your favorites those strange three-brained beings, and what is called a new 'civilization' has arisen, and each new 'civilization' has brought for the beings of succeeding epochs something both new and maleficent, nevertheless, not one of these numerous 'civilizations' has ever prepared so much evil for the beings of later epochs, including of course the contemporary epoch, as that same infamous Greco-Roman civilization.

"Not to mention the large number of other and minor psychic features, unbecoming to be possessed by three-brained beings, and now existing in the presences of your favorites, that civilization is mainly to blame for the complete disappearance from the presences of the three-brained beings of succeeding generations, and especially of the contemporary beings of the possibilities for crystallizing the data for 'sane-logical-mentation' and for engendering the impulse of 'being-self-shame.'

"Namely, the 'ancient-Greek-fantastic-sciences' served for the complete atrophy of the former, and the 'ancient-Roman-depravity' for the latter.

"In the early period of that Greco-Roman civilization, the said maleficent impulses, which have now become being-impulses, namely, the 'passion-for-inventing-fantastic-sciences' and the 'passion-for-depravity,' was proper to the Greek and Roman beings alone; when, as I have already said, the beings of both these communities chanced afterwards to acquire the said strength and began coming into contact with and influencing the beings of other communities, the beings of many other communities of your unfortunate favorites, gradually began to be infected by these peculiar and unnatural being-impulses.

"This took place, on the one hand, as I have already said, owning to the constant influence of both these communities, and, on the other hand, owing to that peculiarity of their psyche—common to all the three-brained beings of that planet, and already well fixed in it before this which is called there 'imitation.'

"And thus, little by little these 'inventions' of those two ancient communities have brought it about that already, at the present time, the psyche of your favorites, shaky enough already before then—has now become so unhinged in all of them without exception, that both their 'world-outlook' and the whole ordering of their ordinary existence in general, rest and proceed exclusively on the basis of those two said 'inventions' of the beings of that 'Greco-Roman-civilization,' namely, on the bases of fantasying, and of striving-for-sexual-gratification.

"Here it is very interesting to notice that although, as I have already told you, thanks to the inheritance from the ancient Romans the 'organic self-shame'—proper to the three-brained beings—has gradually entirely disappeared from the presences of your favorites, nevertheless there has arisen in them in its place something rather like it. Of this pseudo-being impulse, which they also call 'shame,' there is all you like in the presences of your contemporary favorites, but the data for its bringing forth, just as of all the rest, are quite singular.

"This being-impulse arises in their presence only when they do something which under their abnormally established conditions of ordinary being-existence is not acceptable to be done before others.

"But if nobody sees what they do, then nothing they do—even if in their own consciousness and their own feeling it should be undesirable—engenders any such impulse in them.

"The 'bliss' prepared there by the ancient Romans has in recent times already so penetrated the nature of your favorites breeding on all the continents of that ill-starred planet, that it is even difficult to say which beings of which contemporary communities have inherited most from these 'obliging' Romans.

"But as regards the inheritance passed down from the ancient Greeks, namely, the passion for inventing various fantastic 'sciences,' this passion has not become proper to all the three-brained beings of contemporary time equally, but it has passed down only to certain beings arising among the beings of all the contemporary both large and small communities, breeding on all the terra-firma parts of the surface of that peculiar planet.

"Proportionately, this passion, namely, 'to-invent-fantastic-sciences,' has passed down by heredity from the ancient Greeks mainly to the beings of the contemporary community existing there under the name of 'Germany.'

"The beings of that contemporary Germany can be boldly declared the 'direct-heirs-of-the-ancient-Greek-civilization.' And they can be so declared, because at the present time it is just they chiefly who bring every kind of new 'science' and invention, into contemporary civilization.

"Unfortunately, my boy, the beings of that contemporary community Germany have in many respects, as it is said, gone one better, than the beings of ancient Greece.

"Thanks to the 'sciences' invented by the ancient Greeks, only the being-mentation in other beings was and still continues to be spoiled.

"But in addition to this, the contemporary beings of that community Germany have become very skillful in also inventing such 'sciences,' thanks to which, the said specific disease there of 'wiseacring' has been very widely spread among others of your favorites. And during the process of this disease in them, many of them semiconsciously or even quite automatically, chance to notice some small detail of that common cosmic process which actualizes everything existing, and afterwards, informing others of it, they use it with them for some of their, as they are called, 'new-inventions,' thereby adding to the number of those 'new-means' of which during the last two of their centuries so many have accumulated there, that their total effect has now already become, what is called, the 'resultant-decomposing-force,' in contradistinction to what is called, the 'resultant-creative-force' of Nature.

"And, indeed, my boy, only merely to the 'sciences' 'invented' by the beings of that contemporary Germany, other three-brained beings of your planet, belonging both to that same community and to others, have now acquired the possibility of inventing and they do now almost every day invent here or there some such new invention or 'new means' and, employing them in the process of their existence, they have now already brought it about that poor Nature there—already infected, through no fault of her own, without this—is scarcely able to actualize what are called her 'evolving' and 'involving' processes.

"For your clear representation and better understanding, how, namely, these contemporary direct heirs have surpassed their 'legators,' I would like to explain to you now also about certain 'means' existing there now at the present time and already widely used which owe their existence exclusively to these 'Nature-helping' direct heirs of ancient Greece.

"I will explain to you certain of these means there, now existing and in use everywhere, which have been 'invented' by the beings just of that contemporary community 'Germany.' I should like first to emphasize, by the way, one very odd phenomenon, namely, that these contemporary 'substitutes' for the ancient Greeks give names to their said maleficent 'inventions' which for some reason or other all end in 'ine.'

"As examples of the very many particularly-maleficent 'inventions' of those German beings, let us just take those five of what are called 'chemical-substances,' now existing there under the names of 1) Satkaine, 2) Aniline, 3) Cocaine, 4) Atropine, 5) Alisarine, and which chemical substances are used there at the present time by the beings of all the continents and islands, as our dear Mullah Nassr Eddin says: 'even without moderation.'

"The first of the enumerated means—specially invented by the German beings—namely 'Satkaine' is nothing else but 'Samookoorooazar,' that is to say, one of those seven what are called 'neutralizing gases' which arise and are always present in the general presence of each planet and which take part in the 'accomplishing-crystallization' of every definite surplanetary and interplanetary formation, and which in separated states and always and everywhere, what are called, 'indiscriminate-destroyers-of-the-already-arisen.'

"About this German invention, I once also learned there among other things, that when one of the beings of that community, for reasons I recently described, happened to obtain this gas from some 'surplanetary' and 'Intraplanetary' definite formations, and noticed in the said way its particularity, and told several others about it, then these others—owing to the fact that there was then proceeding in the presences of the beings of their community, consequently in them themselves, what is called 'the-most-intense-experiencing' of the chief peculiarity of the psyche of the three-brained beings of your planet, namely, 'the-urgent-need-to-destroy-the-existence-of-others like themselves'; and indeed, the beings of that community were then quite absorbed in their process of reciprocal destruction with the beings of neighboring communities—these others thereupon at once 'enthusiastically' decided to devote themselves entirely to finding means to employ the special property of that gas for the speedy mass destruction of the existence of the beings of other communities.

"Having begun their practical researches with this in view, one of them soon discovered that if this gas is concentrated in a pure state in such a way that it could be freely liberated in any given space at any given time it could easily be employed for the mentioned aim.

"That was enough, and from that time on, this gas, artificially isolated from the general harmony of the actualization of everything existing, began to be liberated in a certain way into space by all the other ordinary beings of that community during the processes of reciprocal destruction, just when and just where the greatest number of beings of other, as they are called, 'hostile' communities were grouped.

"When this isolated particularly-poisonous cosmic substance is intentionally liberated into the atmosphere under the said conditions, and then, striving to reblend with other corresponding cosmic substances, if it should enter the planetary bodies of three-brained beings nearby, it instantly and completely destroys their existence, or, at best, permanently injures the function of one or other part of their general presence.

"The second of the 'chemical-substances' I enumerated, namely, 'Aniline,' is that chemical coloring substance, by means of which most of those surplanetary formations can be dyed from which the three-brained beings there just make all kinds of such objects as they need in the process of their ordinary being-existence.

"Although thanks to that 'invention' your favorites can now dye any object any color, what the lastingness of the existence of these objects becomes—ah, just there lies their famous Bismarck's 'pet cat.'

"Before ever that maleficent Aniline existed, the objects produced by your favorites for their ordinary existence, such, for instance, as what are called 'carpets,' 'pictures' and various articles of wool, wood and skin, were dyed with simple vegetable dyes, which they had learned during centuries how to obtain, and these just enumerated objects would formerly last from five to ten and even fifteen of their centuries.

"But now, thanks merely to this Aniline, or to dyes of other names into which this same Aniline enters as the basis, there remains of the objects dyed with these new colors, at most after about thirty years, only perhaps the memory of them.

"I must also say that the beings of the contemporary community Germany have been the cause not only that thanks to this maleficent Aniline, the production of all the contemporary beings of this planet are quickly destroyed, but also that productions from ancient times have almost ceased to exist on that ill-starred planet.

"This latter occurred because for various Hasnamussian purposes and not for their notorious, as they call them, 'scientific aims' they collected the surviving ancient productions from all countries and not knowing how to preserve ancient objects, they only hastened their speedy destruction.

"But they used and still use those 'antiques' they collected as 'models' for 'cheap goods' which are everywhere known on that ill-starred planet by the name of 'Ersatz.'

"As for the third of the enumerated chemical substances they 'invented,' namely, Cocaine, that chemical substance not only also is of great assistance to Nature in more rapidly decomposing the planetary formations—in this instance, their own planetary bodies—but this chemical means has an effect on the psyche of the contemporary beings of the planet Earth, surprisingly similar to that which the famous organ Kundabuffer had on the psyche of their ancestors.

"When their ancestors had that invention in themselves of the Great Angel Looisos, then thanks to it, they were always exactly in the same state as the contemporary beings are when they take this German invention called 'Cocaine.'

"I must warn you my boy, of course that even if the action of that German invention was similar to the action of the famous organ Kundabuffer, it happened without any conscious intention on the part of the contemporary beings of the community Germany; the became colleagues of the great Angel Looisos only by chance.

"At the present time almost all the beings who become genuine representatives of contemporary civilization very meticulously and with the greatest delight and tenderness introduce into themselves this 'blessing' of contemporary civilization, of course, always to the glory, as our dear Mullah Nassr Eddin says, of the 'one-eyed-General.'

"The fourth of the enumerated chemical substances, namely, 'Atropine' is also everywhere there in great demand at the present time for a great variety of purposes; but its most common use is for a certain exceedingly odd purpose.

"It seems that, thanks to the same abnormally established conditions there of ordinary being-existence, their organ of sight has acquired the property of regarding the faces of others as good and pleasing, only when they have dark eyes.

"And when this chemical substance, called 'Atropine,' is in a certain way introduced into the eyes of beings, the pupils become dilated and darker; and, because of this, most of them introduce this 'Atropine' into their eyes, in order that their faces may appear good and pleasing to others.

"And, truly, my dear boy, those terrestrial beings who introduce this 'German blessing' into their eyes do have very 'dark eyes' until they are 45.

"I said until 45, because so far there has never been a case there when a being using this means could see and still continue its use, after 45.

"'Alisarine,' the fifth and last of the enumerated inventions, is also everywhere widespread.

"And that 'blessing' of contemporary civilization is used there chiefly by, what are called, 'Confectioners' and such other specialists as prepare for the other beings of that planet most 'tasty' articles for their first food.

"The 'confectioners' and other professionals there who prepare the said tasty articles for the first food of the rest of your favorites use this same German 'sure-fire' composition,

Alisarine, of course unconsciously, for that purpose which has there already finally become the ideal for the whole of the contemporary civilization, the purpose expressed in the language of our honored Mullah Nassr Eddin in the following words: 'As long as everything looks fine and dandy to me, what does it matter if the grass doesn't grow!'

"Anyhow, my boy, those contemporary substitutes for the beings of ancient Greece are already now a great help to poor Nature though only in the process of decomposition with all their practical attainments based on the 'sciences' they have themselves invented.

"It is not for nothing that our dear Mullah Nassr Eddin has the following wise expression: 'Better to pull ten hairs a day out of your mother's head, than not to help Nature.'

"Strictly speaking, the capacity to cook up 'fantastic sciences' and to devise even new methods for ordinary being-existence there, did not pass from the ancient Greeks to the beings of that contemporary community Germany alone; the same capacity was perhaps not less also inherited by the beings of another contemporary community, also an independent one, and also in her turn enjoying dominion.

"The other contemporary community of your favorites is called 'England.'

"There has even passed from ancient Greece to the beings of that second contemporary community, England, and directly to them alone, one of their most maleficent inventions which the beings of that contemporary community has most thoroughly adopted, and now actualize in practice.

"This particularly maleficent 'invention' of theirs, the ancient Greeks called 'Diapharon,' and the contemporary beings call 'Sport.'

"About this contemporary 'sport' there, I shall explain to you in as much detail as possible at the end of my tale; but you must know, in the meanwhile, that though the beings of that community England also now invent large quantities of the various new objects required by your favorites in the process of their ordinary being-existence, nevertheless they do not invent chemical substances like the beings of the contemporary community Germany, no . . . they invent chiefly what are called 'metal-goods.'

"Especially in recent times, they have become expert in inventing and in distributing to the beings existing over the whole of the surface of your planet, vast quantities of every kind of the 'metal-goods' called there locks, razors, mouse-traps, revolvers, scythes, machine-guns, saucepans, hinges, guns, penknives, cartridges, pens, mines, needles and many other things of the same kind.

"And ever since the beings of this contemporary community started inventing these practical objects, the ordinary existence of the three-brained beings of your planet has been, just as our dear Mullah Nassr Eddin say, 'not-life-but-free-jam.'

"The beings of that contemporary community have been the benefactors of the other contemporary beings of your planet, offering them, as they say there, 'philanthropic aid,' especially as regards their first being-duty, namely, the duty of carrying out from time to time the process of 'reciprocal destruction.'

"Thanks to them, the discharge of that being-duty of theirs has gradually become for your contemporary favorites, 'the merest trifle.'

"In the absence of these inventions it used to be exceedingly arduous for these poor favorites of yours to fulfill that being-duty, because they were formerly forced to spend a good deal of sweat in it.

"But, thanks to the adaptations of every 'kind invented by those contemporary beings, it is now as again our esteemed Mullah Nassr Eddin says, 'just roses-roses.'

"The contemporary beings now scarcely need make any effort whatsoever in order to destroy completely the existence of beings like themselves.

"Sometimes sitting quietly in what they call their 'smoke rooms,' they can destroy, just as a pastime, as it were, tens and sometimes even hundreds of others like themselves.

"It will do no harm, I think, to tell you now a little about the still-existing direct descendants of the beings of the mentioned Greek-Roman civilizations also.

"The descendants of the beings of the once 'great' and powerful community Greece there, still continue to exist and also to have their own independent community, but for the other independent communities there, they have at the present time scarcely any significance whatever.

"They already no longer do as their ancestors did there, who were dyed-in-the-wool specialists in cooking up all kinds of 'fantastic sciences'; for if a contemporary Greek did also cook up a new 'science,' the beings of the other communities of the present time would not pay the smallest attention to it.

"And they would pay no attention to it, chiefly because that community has not at the present time enough of what are called 'guns' and 'ships,' to be what is called an authority for other contemporary beings there.

"But though the descendants of the former great Greeks, namely, the Greeks of the present time, have lost the trick of being, what is called a 'fancy-authority' for other three-brained beings there—which has already become proper to their presence—they have now perfectly adapted themselves there on almost all the continents and islands to keeping what are called 'shops,' where without any haste, slowly and gently, they trade in what are called 'sponges,' 'halva,' 'Rahat Lokoum,' 'Turkish delight,' etc., and sometimes 'Persian dried fruits,' never forgetting the dried fish called 'Kefal.'

"And as for the descendants of the famous Romans, although they too still continue to arise and exist, they no longer even carry the name of their ancestors, although they still call the chief place of their community by the consonance 'Rome.'

"The contemporary beings of the community formed by the descendants of those former shepherds, afterwards the great Romans, are called by the other beings there 'Italians.'

"Except for that specific being-impulse which first on that planet the ancient Roman beings crystallized in their presences, and which subsequently spread gradually to all the other three-brained beings of that planet, scarcely anything else had passed by heredity from their ancestors to these beings called Italians.

"The beings of that contemporary community Italy exist at the present time very quietly and peacefully, doing nothing more than unostentatiously inventing ever new forms of their harmless, very innocent, what is called 'macaroni.'

"Nevertheless, there has passed to certain beings of that contemporary Italy, by heredity from their ancestors, one special and very peculiar 'property' called 'giving-pleasure-to-others.'

"Only they manifest this inherited need, that is to say, this 'being-giving-pleasure' not towards beings there like themselves, but to the beings of other forms.

"It must in fairness be said that the said special property came to the beings of various parts of contemporary Italy not from the great Romans alone; this inherited property became more naturalized by their ancestors of considerably later epochs, namely, at the time when they began 'spreading' among other beings both of their own community and of the neighboring weaker communities, the doctrines, already changed for their egoistic purposes, of a certain genuine 'sacred-Messenger-from-Above.'

"At the present time the beings of various parts of contemporary Italy, actualize there this property of 'giving-pleasure-to-others' in the following way:

"The existence of the quadruped beings called 'sheep' and 'goats' whose planetary bodies they also use for their first food—they do not destroy all at once; but in order to give this 'pleasure' they do it 'slowly' and 'gently' over a period of many days; that is to say, one day, they take off one leg, then a few days later, a second leg, and then the third and so on, for as long as the 'sheep' or 'goat' still breathes. And sheep and goats can breathe without the said parts of their general presence for a very long time, because, in the main functions of the 'perceiving' of cosmic substances for the possibility of existing, these parts do not participate, though they do in the functions which actualize those impulses in the beings which give self-sensation.

"After what I have already said, there seems no need to say any more about the descendants of those Romans who were once so 'menacing' and so 'great' for the other communities there.

"Now let us talk about that particularly maleficent 'invention' of the ancient Greeks, which in being actualized there in practice at the present time by the beings of the contemporary community, there called England, and which invention they call 'Sport.'

"Not only have the beings of the contemporary community, England—namely, those beings who chiefly actualize during the process of their ordinary existence this particularly-maleficent invention of the Ancient Greeks—thereby added thanks to its maleficent consequences, one more sure-fire factor, personally for them themselves, for the contraction of the duration of their existence—already trifling enough without that—but also, in addition, that, experiencing in their turn the 'greatness' of their community, which coincides with the present time, that are in consequence authorities for other three-brained beings there; and, furthermore, because they have made the actualizing of the invention in practice their ideal, and its spreading their aim—then in consequence of all this, they, at the present time, by every possible means 'strongly' infect the beings of all other both large and small communities of that ill-starred planet with that invention of theirs. The basis also for that very very serious misconception there was the disappearance from the general presence of those favorites of yours of the possibility of the crystallization in them of those factors from which 'logical-mentation' is actualized in the three-brained beings.

"And in consequence of the absence in them of this 'logical-mentation,' all of them almost without exception, merely because certain candidates for Hasnamuss there have asserted that they could attain something 'good' for themselves by means of this same sport—an assertion they believe with all their presence—have now, in the hope of attaining this same 'something,' given themselves up 'entirely' to that sport.

"None of these unfortunates know and probably never will ruminate that not only is nothing good obtained by them from this magnificent 'sport' of theirs, as I have already told you, solely on its account alone, they still further shorten the duration of their existence which is already sufficiently trifling without this.

"So that you may better represent to yourself and understand why the duration of their existence is being still further diminished on account of this sport, it is here in place to explain to you a little more in detail about what I have already promised you to explain, namely, the difference between the duration of being-existence according to the 'Fulasnitamnian' principle and according to the 'Itoklanoz' principle.

"You remember that when I explained to you how these favorites of yours define the 'flow-of-time,' I said that when the organ Kundabuffer with all its properties was removed from their presences, and they began to have the same duration of existence as all normal three-brained beings arising everywhere in our Universe, that is, according to what is called the 'Fulasnitamnian' principle, they also should then have existed without fail until their 'second-being-body-Kesdjan' had been fulfilledly coated in them and finally perfected by Reason up to the sacred 'Ischmetch.'

"But later, when they began existing in a manner more and more unbecoming for three-brained beings and entirely ceased actualizing in their presences their being 'Partkdolgduty,' foreseen by great Nature, by means of which alone, it is possible for the three-brained beings to acquire in their presences the data for 'coating' their said higher-parts, and when, in consequence of all this, the quality of their radiations failed to respond to the demands of the Most Great Common Cosmic Trogoautoegocratic process—then it was that great Nature was compelled for the purpose of 'equalizing vibrations' gradually to actualize the duration of their existence according to the principle called 'Itoklanoz,' that is, the principle upon which in general and everywhere is actualized the duration of existence of one-brained and two-brained beings that have not the possibilities present in three-brained beings, and are therefore unable to realize in their presences, the said—foreseen by Nature—'Partkdolgduty.'

"According to this principle, both the duration of being-existence and also the whole of the contents of their general presences, are in general acquired from the results arising from the following seven actualizations surrounding them, namely, from:

(1) Heredity in general,

(2) Conditions and environment at the moment of conception,

(3) The combination of the radiations of all the planets of their solar system during their formation in the womb of their

productress,

(4) The degree of being-manifestation of their producers during the period they are attaining the age of responsible being,

(5) The quality of being-existence of beings similar to themselves in their near neighborhood,

(6) The quality of what are called the 'Teleokrimalnichnian' thought-waves formed in the atmosphere surrounding them also during their period of attaining the age of majority—that is, the sincerely manifested good wishes and actions on the part of what are called the 'beings-of-the-same-blood,' and finally—

(7) The quality of what are called the 'being-Egoplastikoori' of the given being himself, that is, his being-effort for the transubstantiation in himself of all the data for obtaining objective Reason.

"The chief particularity of existence according to this principle Itoklanoz, consists in this, that in the presences of beings existing according to it, dependently upon the enumerated seven exterior actualizations, there are crystallized in their being—'localizations'—representing in beings the central place of the sources of actualization of all the separate independent parts of their General presence—or, as your favorites say, in their brains—what are called 'Bobbin-kandelnosts,' that is to say, 'something' that gives in the given localizations or 'brains' a defined quantity of possible associations or 'experiencings.'

"And so, my boy, because these contemporary favorites of yours, these three-brained beings of the planet Earth, already arise only according to the principle 'Itoklanoz,' therefore from the moment of conception up to the age of a responsible three-brained being, there are crystallized in their brains these 'Bobbin-kandelnosts' with well-defined possibilities of actualizing the processes of association.

"For the greater elucidation of this question and for your

better understanding, and also not to waste time on explanations concerning the essence itself and also the forms of functioning of such definite cosmic realizations as these just mentioned 'Bobbin-kandelnosts,' which are lawfully crystallized in the 'localizations' or 'brains' of those beings who exist only on the basis of 'Itoklanoz,' I intend to take as an elucidating example just those 'artificial-Djamtesternokhi' such as your favorites also have and which they call, 'mechanical watches.'

"As you already well know, although such 'artificial-Djamtesternokhi' or 'mechanical-watches' are of different what are called 'systems,' yet they are all constructed or the same principle of 'tension-or-pressure-of-the-unwinding-spring.'

"One system of 'artificial-Djamtesternokhi' or 'mechanical watch' contains a spring, exactly calculated and arranged that the length of the duration of its tension from unwinding may be sufficient for 24 hours; another system has a spring for a week, a third for a month, and so on.

"The 'Bobbin-kandelnost' in the brains of beings existing only according to the principle 'Itoklanoz' corresponds to the spring in 'mechanical-watches' of various systems.

"As the duration of the movement of 'mechanical-watches' depends upon the spring they contain, so the duration of the existence of beings depends exclusively on the 'Bobbin-kandelnost' formed in their brains during their arising and during the process of their further formation.

"As the spring of a watch has a 'winding' of a definite duration only, so these beings also can associate and experience only as much as the possibilities put into them by Nature for experiencing, during the crystallization of those same 'Bobbin-kandelnosts' in their brains.

"They can associate and consequently exist just so much, and neither more nor less.

"As 'mechanical-watches' can act as long as the spring has

what is called 'the-tension-of-winding,' so the beings in whose brains the said 'Bobbin-kandelnosts' are crystallized can experience and consequently exist until these 'Bobbin-kandelnosts' formed in their brains—owing to the mentioned seven external conditions—are used up.

"And so, my boy, because the results of 'Partkdolgduty' were no longer thereafter obtained in the presences of your favorites and the duration of their existence began to depend exclusively on the results of the seven accidentally arranged external conditions I have just enumerated, then thanks to all this, the length of their existence, especially among the contemporary beings, has become of a very different duration.

"At the present time the duration of their existence may be from one of their minutes up to seventy to ninety of their years.

"And so, for all the reasons I have described, however your favorites many exist, whatever measures they may adopt—and even if, as they say, they should 'put-themselves-in-a-glass-case,' as soon as the contents of the 'Bobbin-kandelnost' crystallized in their brains are used up, one or another of their 'brains' immediately ceases to function.

"The difference between 'mechanical-watches' and your contemporary favorites is only that in 'mechanical watches' there is only one spring, while your favorites have three of these independent 'Bobbin-kandelnosts.'

"And these independent Bobbin-kandelnosts having their three independent 'localizations' in three-brained beings generally, have the following names:

"The first—the Bobbin-kandelnost of the 'thinking center,'

"The second—the Bobbin-kandelnost of the 'feeling center,'

"The Third—the Bobbin-kandelnost of the 'moving center.'

"Even that fact which I have recently often repeated,

namely, that the process of the sacred 'Rascooarno' is actualized for these favorites of yours by thirds—or, as they themselves would say—they begin to die in parts—proceeds also from the fact that, arising and being formed only according to the principle of 'Itoklanoz,' they, existing non-harmoniously, unequally use up the contents of these three separate independent brains, namely, 'their Bobbin-kandelnosts,' and hence it is that there frequently occurs to them such a horrible 'dying,' as is not proper to three-brained beings.

"During my stay there among them, I personally very often constated their 'dying-by-thirds.'

"This was possible because, although in the presences of your favorites, especially the contemporary ones, the 'Bobbin-kandelnosts' of one of their brains may be entirely used up, nevertheless the beings themselves would sometimes continue to exist for quite a long time.

"For instance, it often happens there that, owing to their specifically abnormal existence, the contents of one of the 'Bobbin-kandelnosts' are used up in one of them, and if it is of the 'moving-center,' or as they themselves call it, the 'spinal brain,' then although such a contemporary three-brained being there continues to 'think' and to 'feel,' yet he has already lost the possibility of intentionally directing the parts of his planetary body.

"Here it is interesting to notice that when one of your contemporary favorites already partially dies for good in this way, then their contemporary 'Zirlikners'—or, as they are called, 'physicians'—look upon such a death as most certainly a disease, and with every species of the 'wiseacring,' that has become proper to them, they start treating it; and they give these supposed diseases every sort of name consonant with an ancient language utterly unknown to them, called Latin.

"The very widely-spread diseases there with such names are the following: 'Hemiplegia,' 'Paraplegia,' 'Paralysis progressiva,' 'Paralysis-essentialis,' 'tabes-dorsalis,' 'paralysis-agitans,' 'sclerosis-disseminata,' and so on and so forth.

"Such deaths by thirds there on the planet Earth which pleases you, have occurred particularly frequently during the last two centuries, and they occur to those of your favorites, who, thanks either to their profession, or to one of their what are called 'passions,' arising and acquired by the beings belonging to all both large and small communities there, on account of the same abnormally arranged conditions of their ordinary being-existence, have lived out in a greater or smaller degree during their being-existence, the contents of the 'Bobbin-kandelnost' of one or another of their being-brains.

"For instance, a one-third death on account of the Bobbin-kandelnost of the 'moving center' or 'spinal-brain' often occurs there among those terrestrial beings who give themselves up to that occupation which the beings belong to the contemporary community England now practice, and which maleficent occupation they now call there 'Sport.'

"The character of the pernicious consequence of that 'maleficent-occupation' there, you will well understand when I tell you that during my stay there among these favorites of yours, I once prepared a special section of my statistics for elucidating to myself how long those three-brained beings there can exist, who become what are called 'wrestlers' by profession, never once in those statistics of mine, did I notice that any of them had existed longer than forty-nine of their years.

"And a one-third death through the premature using up the 'Bobbin-kandelnost' of the 'feeling-center' occurs for the most part among those terrestrial beings who become by profession, what are called, 'representatives-of-Art.'

"The majority of these terrestrial professionals, especially the contemporary ones, first fall ill with one or another form of what is called 'psychopathy.' Thanks to this, they afterwards in their psychopathy intentionally learn, as they say, to feel; and thereafter repeatedly feeling these abnormal being-impulses they gradually use up the contents of the 'Bobbin-kandelnost' of their 'feeling center' and thus disharmonizing the tempo of their own general presence, bring themselves to that peculiar end which is not often met with even among them there.

"Here, by the way, it is very interesting also to notice that the one-third death through the 'feeling-center' occurs among your favorites also thanks to one very peculiar form of 'psychopathy' called there, 'altruism.'

"And concerning premature partial death through the 'Bobbin-kandelnost' of the 'thinking-center'—the deaths of this kind among your favorites occurs in recent times more and more frequently.

"This kind of death through the being—'thinking-center' occurs there chiefly among those favorites of yours who try to become or have already become scientists of 'new format,' and also among those who during the period of their existence fall ill with the craze for reading what are called 'books' and 'newspapers.'

"The result among those three-brained beings there of reading superfluously and associating only by thoughts, is that the contents of the 'Bobbin-kandelnost' of their 'thinking-center' are exhausted before the contents of the 'Bobbin-kandelnosts' of their other being-centers.

"And so, my boy, all these misfortunes, namely, the contraction of the duration of their existence and also many other consequences, maleficent for them themselves, occur to your favorites exclusively only because they have even until now not yet learned of the existence of the cosmic law called, 'Equalization-of-many-sourced-vibrations.'

"If only such an idea occurred to them, and they were merely to perform their usual wiseacrings with it, perhaps, then, they would get to understand one very simple, as they call it, 'secret.'

"I allow that somebody would be certain to understand this 'secret' because, in the first place, it is simple and obvious, and secondly, because they had discovered it long ago and they even often employ it in what they call their 'practical-use.'

"They even use this simple secret to which I referred, for those 'mechanical-watches' which we took for comparison, as an elucidating example concerning the duration of their existence.

"In all the 'mechanical-watches' of various systems they use this said simple secret for regulating what is called the 'tension' of the said spring for the corresponding part of the general mechanism of the watch; and it is called, it seems, the 'Regulator.'

"By means of this 'regulator' it is possible to make the mechanism of a watch, wound for instance for 24 hours, go a whole month, and on the contrary thanks to this 'regulator' it is possible to make the same winding for 24 hours finish in five minutes.

"In the general presence of every being existing merely on the basis of 'Itoklanoz,' 'something' similar to the 'regulator' in a mechanical-watch is present and is called 'Iransamkeep'; this something means: 'not-to-give-oneself-up-to-those-of-one's-associations-resulting-from-the-functioning-of-only-one-or-other-of-one's-brains.'

"But even if they should understand such a simple secret, it would be all just the same—they still would not make also those being-efforts necessary to it, and quite open even to the contemporary being—and thanks to which by the foresight of Nature, beings in general acquired the possibility of what is called 'harmonious association,' by virtue of which alone energy is created for their active being-existence in the presence of every three-brained being—consequently in them themselves. But at the present time, this energy can already be elaborated in the presences of your favorites, only during their quite unconscious state, that is to say, during what they call 'sleep.' But in your favorites, specially in your contemporary favorites, who exist constantly passively under the direction of only one of the separate spiritualized parts of their general presence, and, in consequence, constantly manifest themselves entirely by their—factors for negative properties also lawfully arising in them, and hence by negative manifestations, only—in them there just proceeds that same unequal using up of the contents of their various 'Bobbin-kandelnosts,' that is to say, the possibilities, placed in them by Nature according to law, of action by one only or by two only of their brains are always experienced, in consequence of which, the contents of one or of two of their 'Bobbin-kandelnosts' are prematurely exhausted; whereupon, just like those 'mechanical-watches' in which the winding is run down or the force of their 'regulator' is weakened, they cease to act.

"Sometime later I shall explain to you in detail not only why when beings existing only according to the principle of 'Itoklanoz' exist by the direction only of one or only of two of their spiritualized sources, and not harmoniously, that is to say, with all three combined, and in agreement—that particular brain of theirs is prematurely used up in them and consequently dies, in which there were superfluous associations, during the period of its existence, but also why, on this account, the other 'Bobbin-kandelnosts' also are used up, even without their own action.

"But you must here know this also, that even on your planet, one still occasionally finds one of your favorites whose duration of planetary existence extends to five of their centuries.

"You will then understand very well, that in the case of certain of your favorites even of recent times who, by some means or other find out and transubstantiate in the right way in their Reason concerning certain details of the law of association proceeding in the separate brains of beings, and also concerning the mutual action of these independent associations, and who exist more or less according to what I have said, then in their case and in consequence of all this, the Bobbin-kandelnosts formed in their separate being-brains are not used up, as they are among the other beings there, but their general presence acquires the possibility of existing much longer than the other three-brained beings there.

"During my stay there for the last time, I myself personally met several of these terrestrial contemporary three-brained beings who were already two, three and even about four of their centuries old. I met them mostly among a small 'brotherhood' of the three-brained beings there, composed of beings from almost all their what are called 'Religions,' and whose permanent place of existence was in the middle of the continent Asia.

"The beings of that brotherhood, it seems, partly elucidated the mentioned laws of association in being-brains for themselves, and in part such information reacted them from ancient times through genuine initiates there.

"As for that same contemporary community, whose beings have become the chief victims of that particularly maleficent invention of the beings of the said ancient civilization, they not only now use it in the process of their own existence but they try to infect 'strongly' the beings of all other communities with this same evil. Moreover, owing to that maleficent 'sport' of theirs, these unfortunates not only still further diminish the duration of their own existence—already trifling without this—but thanks to that action of theirs, they will, in my opinion, eventually entail for their community what quite recently occurred to a large community there named 'Russia.'

"I thought about it during my stay there before my final

departure from that planet.

"And I first began thinking about it when I learned that the 'power-possessing' beings also of that no less great contemporary community, were already utilizing that maleficent means of theirs—'Sport'—for their own Hasnamussian aims, exactly as the power-possessing beings of the community Russia had, for their similar aims, utilized what is called 'the-question-of-Russian-vodka.'

"Just as the power-possessing beings of the community Russia then tried, by every kind of artifice, to instill into the weak wills of the ordinary beings the necessity of the intensive use of the said 'Russian vodka,' so also the 'power-possessing' beings of that community England are now already also maneuvering to intrigue the ordinary beings of their community with this same 'sport' and to urge them to it by every means.

"The apprehensions which then arose in me are already, it seems, being justified.

"And I conclude this from the etherogram I recently received from the planet Mars, in which among other things, it was said, that though there are more than two and a half millions of what are called 'unemployed beings' in that community England yet the power-possessing beings there take no measures concerning this, but Endeavor to spread still more widely among them that same notorious 'sport' of theirs.

"Just as in the large community Russia the contents of all what are called 'newspapers' and 'magazines' used to be always devoted to the question of Russian vodka, so now in that community England, more than half the text of all their evil-sowers is devoted to that notorious 'sport.'"

CHAPTER XXX

Art

AT THIS place of his tales, Beelzebub became silent; then, turning suddenly to his old servant Ahoon, who sat there also listening to him with the same attention as his grandson Hassein, he said:

"What, old man! Are you also listening to me with the same interest as our Hassein? Weren't you yourself personally with me everywhere on that planet Earth and didn't you see with your own eyes and sense for yourself everything about that which I am relating to Hassein?

"Instead of just sitting there open-mouthed at my tales, you also tell our favorite something . . . There is no getting out of it. We have got to tell him all we can about those strange three-brained beings, seeing that they have so intensely interested him.

"Surely you must have been interested in one aspect or another of these queer ducks; well, tell us something just about that aspect."

When Beelzebub had finished speaking, Ahoon, having thought a while, replied:

"After your subtly psychological tales about all these 'unintelligibles,' how can I come in with my tales?"

And then, with an unusual seriousness and preserving the style and even whole expressions of Beelzebub himself, he continued:

"It is, of course . . . How shall I put it? My essence even was often thrown out of balance by those strange three-brained beings, and they, with their 'funny ways' used nearly always to supply an impetus for evoking the being-impulse of amazement, sometimes in one and sometimes in another of my spiritualized parts."

And then addressing Hassein, he said:

"Well, our dear Hassein!

"I will not, like his Right Reverence, relate to you in detail about any particular oddity of the psyche of those three-centered beings of our great Universe who please you. No, I will only remind His Right Reverence of one thing, the cause of which arose just during our fifth stay on the surface of that planet. This one thing, when we were there for the sixth and last time, had already then been formed, and it serves as the chief cause why, in every one of those favorites of yours, from the very first day of their arising until their formation as responsible beings, their ableness of normal being-mentation is step by step distorted and finally transformed almost into a 'Kaltusara.'"

Thereupon, addressing Beelzebub himself, he with a timid look and already in a hesitant tone, continued to speak:

"Don't blame me, your Right Reverence, for venturing to express to you the opinion which has just arisen in me, and which is the outcome of my ruminations on data already perhaps worn too thin for being-mind conclusions.

"While relating to our dear Hassein about all the various reasons that have brought it about that the psyche of the contemporary three-centered beings of the planet Earth who pleased him, has become transformed, as you once deigned to express yourself, already into just a mill for grinding out nonsense, you scarcely even mentioned one factor, perhaps more important than the others, which, during recent centuries, has served as the basis for it.

"I intend to speak about that factor which has already become definitely maleficent for the contemporary beings and at the arising of the cause of which you yourself were present, as I very well remember, during our stay then in Babylon; I mean the factor they themselves call 'Art.'

"If you should vouchsafe in your wisdom to take up that question in detail, then according to my understanding our dear Hassein will have perhaps the choicest material for his better elucidation of all the abnormal strangeness of the psyche of the three-brained beings, who, in most recent times, arise on that planet Earth which has interested him."

Having said this and having with the tip of his tail wiped off the drops of sweat which had formed on his forehead, Ahoon became silent and adopted his usual attentive posture.

With an affectionate glance, Beelzebub looked at him and said:

"Thank you, old man, for reminding me of this. It is true that I have scarcely even mentioned that indeed harmful factor—created also by them themselves for the already final atrophy even of those data for their being-mentation also, which by chance has still survived.

"All the same, old man, though it's true that I have not so far once referred to it, that does not mean that I had not considered it at all. Having still a good deal of time before us during the period of our traveling, I should, in all probability, in the course of my subsequent tales to our common favorite Hassein, have remembered, in its time, about that of which you have reminded me.

"However, perhaps it will be very opportune to speak just now about this contemporary terrestrial 'Art' because, as you said, during our fifth personal stay there, I was really a witness of the events which gave birth to the causes also of this contemporary evil there and which arose, thanks as always, to the same learned beings there who assembled in the city of Babylon from almost the whole of the surface of that ill-starred planet."

Having said this, Beelzebub then turned to Hassein and spoke as follows:

"This same now definite idea there, existing there already under the denomination 'Art' is, at the present time for those unhappy favorites of yours, one of those automatically acting data the totality of which already by itself converts them—that is, beings containing in their presences every kind of possibilities for becoming particles of a part of Divinity—gradually, and though almost imperceptibly yet very surely, into what is called merely 'animated flesh.'

"For the all-round enlightenment of the question about the notorious contemporary terrestrial Art, and for your clear understanding of how it all came about, you must first know about two events that occurred in that same city Babylon during our fifth personal flight to the surface of that planet of yours.

"The first is this: namely, how and why I then came to be a witness of the occurrences which were the basis of the reasons for the existence among the contemporary three-brained beings of the planet Earth of that now definitely maleficent idea called Art; and the second is this; namely, which were the antecedent events that in their turn then served as the origin of the arisings of these reasons.

"Concerning the first, I must say that during our stay then in the city of Babylon, after the events I have already related which occurred always among the same learned terrestrial three-centered beings assembled there from almost the whole planet, that is to say, after they had split into several independent groups and were, as I have already told you, already absorbed in a question of what is called 'politics,' and as I had it in mind at that time to leave Babylon and to continue my observations among the beings of the then already powerful community called Hellas, I decided to learn their conversational language. From then on I chose to visit those places in the city of Babylon and meet those beings there, who would be of most use in my practical study of the conversational languages.

"Once when I was walking in a certain street of the city of Babylon not far from our house, I saw on a large building by which I had already many times passed, what is called an 'Ookazemotra,' or, as it is now called on the Earth, a 'placard,' which had been just put up and which announced that a Club for foreign learned beings, the 'Adherents of the Legominism,' had been newly opened in that building. On the door was a notice to the effect that the enrollment of members of the club was still going on, and that all the reports and scientific discussions would be conducted in the local and Hellenic conversational languages only.

"This interested me very much and I thought at once whether it would not be possible for me to make use of this newly-opened Club for my practice in the Hellenic conversational language.

"So I then enquired of certain beings who were going in or coming out of that building, about the details concerning the Club; and, when, thanks to the explanation of one learned being, with whom, as I chanced to find out, I was already acquainted, I had made it all more or less clear to myself, I then and there decided to become also a member of that Club.

"Without thinking long about it, I entered the building and passing myself off as a foreign learned being, I requested, as an adherent of the Legominism, to be enrolled as a member of the club.

"And I managed this very easily, owing always to the same old acquaintance whom I had met by chance and who, like the others, took me for a learned being like himself.

"And so, my boy, having thus become what is called a 'full member' of that club, I used afterwards to go there regularly and to talk there chiefly with those learned members who were familiar with the Hellenic conversational language which I needed.

"As regards the second thing, this proceeded from the following Babylonian events.

"It must be remarked that among the learned beings of the

planet Earth who were then in Babylon and who were gathered partly by coercion, from almost the whole of the planet, by the mentioned Persian king, and partly voluntarily on account of the already mentioned notorious question of the 'soul,' there were several among the beings brought there by coercion who were not, like the majority, 'the learned of new format,' but who with a sincerity already proceeding from their separate spiritualized parts, strove for High Knowledge only with the aim of self-perfection.

"Owing to their real and sincere strivings, to the corresponding manner of their existence and to their being-acts, these several terrestrial beings had already, before their arrival in Babylon, been considered initiates of the first degree from amongst those terrestrial three-centered beings, worthy to become what are called 'All The Rights Possessing' initiates according to the reformed rules of the Most Saintly Ashiata Shiemash.

"And thus, my boy, when I began going to the said Club, it became quite clear to me, both from the conversations with them and from other data, that these several terrestrial learned beings who sincerely strove to perfect their Reason, had from the beginning kept themselves to themselves in the city of Babylon, and never mixed in any of those affairs with which the general mass of these Babylonian learned beings there of that time very soon became involved.

"These said several learned beings kept themselves apart there, not only in the beginning when all the other learned beings who were then in the city of Babylon first opened a central place for their meetings in the very heart of the city, and when for their better mutual support both materially and morally, they founded there a central Club for all the learned beings of the Earth, but later on, also, when the whole body of learned beings divided into three separate 'sections' and each of these 'sections' had its independent Club in one or another part of the city of Babylon, they identified themselves with none of the said three 'sections.'

"They existed in the suburbs of the city of Babylon and scarcely met any of the learned beings from among the number of the general mass; and it was only several days before my admittance among them as a member of this club that they for the first time united for the purpose of organizing the Club of the 'Adherents of the Legominism.'

"These learned beings about whom I am speaking had all without exception reached the city of Babylon by coercion and they were for the most part from among the number of those learned beings who had been taken by the Persian king from Egypt.

"As I later learned, this uniting of theirs had been brought about by two learned beings who were just from among the number of the said initiates of the first degree.

"One of these two initiated learned beings of the Earth who had his arising amongst, as they are called, the Moors, was named Kanil-El-Norkel. The other learned initiated being was named Pythagoras, and he arose from amongst, as they are called, the Hellenes, just those Hellenes who were afterwards called Greeks.

"These two learned beings, as it later became clear, happened to meet in the city of Babylon and during what is called their 'Ooissapagaoomnian-exchange-of-opinions,' that is, during those conversations the theme of which always refers to the question, which forms of being-existence of the beings of the present time can serve for the welfare of the beings of the future, they clearly constated that in the course of changing generations of beings on the Earth, a very lamentable and melancholy phenomenon occurs, namely, during the processes of reciprocal destruction, that is, during what are called 'wars' and 'popular risings,' invariably a great number of initiated beings of all degrees are for some reason or other destroyed, and, together with them also many Legominisms are forever destroyed, through just which alone up to that time various information about former real events on the Earth had been transmitted and continue to be transmitted from generation to generation.

"When the two mentioned sincere and honest learned beings of the Earth constated, as they then called it, so 'melancholy a phenomenon,' they deliberated a long time about it, and the result of all their deliberations was that they decided to take advantage of the exceptional circumstance, namely, that so many learned beings were together in one city, to confer collectively for the purpose of finding some means for preventing if only this melancholy phenomenon proceeding on the Earth owing to the abnormal conditions of the life of man.

"And it was just for this purpose that they organized that said Club and called it the 'Club of Adherents of Legominism.'

"So many like-thinking beings at once responded to their appeal that two days after my own admission as a member of this club, the enrollment of new members already ceased.

"And on the day when new members ceased to be admitted, the number of those entered amounted to a hundred and thirty-nine learned beings; and it was with this number of members that the club existed until the said Persian king abandoned his former caprice connected with those terrestrial learned beings.

"As I learnt after my entry as a member of that club, what is called a general meeting had been arranged on the very first day of its opening by all the learned beings, at which it was unanimously resolved to hold daily general meetings, at which reports and discussions on just the two following questions were to be made, namely, the measures to be taken by the members of the club on their return home for the collection of all the Legominisms existing in their native lands, and for placing them at the disposal of the learned members of this Club which they had founded; and secondly, what was to be done in order that the Legominisms might be transmitted to remote generations by some other means than through initiates only.

"Before my entry among the members of the club, a great variety of reports and discussions concerning these two mentioned questions had already proceeded at that general meeting of theirs; and on the day of my entry a great deal was said on the question how to obtain the participation in the fundamental task of their club of initiated beings also from among the followers of those so-called 'Ways' which were then called 'Onandjiki,' 'Shamanists,' 'Buddhists' and so on.

"And so, on the third day after my entry among the number of the members of this Club, there was uttered for the first time that same word which has chanced to reach contemporary beings there and which has become one of the potent factors for the final atrophy of all the still surviving data for more or less normal logical being-mentation, namely, the word 'Art.' The word, however, was then used in another sense and its definition referred to quite a different idea and had quite another meaning.

"This term was uttered in the following circumstances: On that day when that word 'Art' was used for the first time, and its real idea and exact meaning were established among the other reporters, there stepped forward a Chaldean learned being very well known in those times, who was called Aksharpanziar and who was also then a member of the Club of the Legominism.

"As the report of that already very aged Chaldean learned being, the great Aksharpanziar, then served as the origin for all the further events connected with this same contemporary Art there, I will try to recall his speech and repeat it to you as nearly as possible word for word.

"He then said as follows:

'The past and especially the last two centuries have shown us that during those inevitable psychoses of the masses, from which wars between states and various popular revolts within states always arise—invariably many of the innocent victims of the popular beastiality are indeed those who, among others, owing to their previous piety and conscious sacrifices are worthy to become initiates, by whose means various Legominisms containing information regarding all kinds of real events which have taken place in the past are transmitted for the conscious beings of succeeding generations.

"'Just such pious men as these, always become such innocent victims of the popular bestiality, only because, in my opinion, being already free within and never wholly identifying themselves, as all the rest do, with all the ordinary interests of those around them, they cannot for that reason, share either in the attractions, pleasures, and sentiments, or in the similarly clearly sincere manifestations of those around them. And because in ordinary times they exist normally and in their relations with those around them are always well-wishing in both their inner and outer manifestations, they acquire in normal periods of everyday life the respect and esteem of those around them; but when the mass of ordinary people fall into the said psychosis and split into their usual two opposing camps, then these latter in their state of bestialized reason during their fighting, begin to entertain morbid suspicions of just those who in normal times have always been unassuming and serious; and then, if it should happen that the attention of those under this psychosis should rest a little longer on these exceptional men, they no longer have any doubt whatever that these said serious and outwardly always quiet men have undoubtedly also in normal times been nothing more nor less than the 'spies' of their present enemies and foes.

"'With their diseased reasons these bestialized men categorically conclude that the previous seriousness and quietness of such men were nothing else but simply what is called 'secrecy' and 'duplicity.'

"'And the sequel of their psychopathic conclusions is, that these bestialized men of one or the other hostile party, without any remorse of conscience whatever, put these serious and quiet men to death.

"'In my opinion, it is what I have just said that has most frequently served as the cause why that very Legominism about events which really took place on the Earth has in the course of its passage from generation to generation also totally disappeared from the face of the Earth.

"'And so, my highly esteemed colleagues, if you wish to know my personal opinion, then I shall sincerely tell you, with all my being, that in spite of all I have said, there is nothing whatever to be done about the transmission of true knowledge to remote generations through corresponding initiates by means of Legominism.

"'Let this means be continued as before, as it has been on the Earth from the dawn of centuries and as this form of transmission by initiates through their 'ableness' to be, was reformed by the great prophet Ashiata Shiemash.

"'If we contemporary men desire at the present time to do something beneficent for men of future times, all we must do is just to add to this already existing means of transmission, some new means or other, flowing from the ways of our contemporary life on the Earth as well as from the many-centuried experience of former generations in accordance with the information that has come down to us.

"'I personally suggest that this transmission to future generations be made through the human, what are called 'Afalkalna,' that is, through various productions of man's hands which have entered into use in people's 'daily life,' and also through the human 'Soldjinoha,' that is, through various forms and ceremonies which have already been established for centuries in the social and family life of people and which automatically pass from generation to generation.

"'Either these human 'Afalkalna' themselves, and in particular those which are made of lasting materials will survive, and, for various reasons go down to men of remote generations, or copies of them will pass from generation to generation, thanks to the property which is rooted in the essence of man—that is, of giving out as their own one or another of the productions of man which have reached them from long past epochs, after having changed it in some minor detail.

"'In regard to the human 'Soldjinoha' as for instance, various 'mysteries,' 'religious ceremonies,' 'family-and-social-customs,' 'religious-and-popular-dances,' and so on, then although they often change in their external form with the flow of time, yet the impulses engendered in man through them and the manifestations of man derived from them always remain the same; and thus by placing the various useful information and true knowledge we have already attained within the inner factors which engender these impulses and these useful manifestations of man, we can fully count on their reaching our very remote descendants, some of whom will decipher them and thereby enable all the rest to utilize them for their good.

"'The question now is only this, namely, by what means can such a transmission through the various human 'Afalkalna' and 'Soldjinoha' as I have described be actualized?

"'I personally suggest that this be done through the Universal Law called the 'Law of Sevenfoldness.'

"'The Law of Sevenfoldness exists on the Earth and will exist forever and in everything.

"'For instance, in accordance with this Law, there are in the white ray seven independent colors; in every definite sound there are seven different independent tones; in every state of man, seven different independent sensations; further, every definite form can be made up of only seven different dimensions; every weight remains at rest on the Earth only thanks to seven 'reciprocal thrusts,' and so on.

"'Well, of the knowledge now existing which we have personally attained or which has reached us from times past, just that knowledge which we shall agree is useful for our remote descendants, most be indicated in some way or other in the said human 'Afalkalna' and 'Soldjinoha' so that it may be perceived in the future by the pure reason of man, by means of this great Universal Law.

"'I repeat that the Law of Sevenfoldness will exist on the Earth as long as the Universe exists, and it will be seen and understood by men in all times as long as human thought shall exist on the Earth, and it can therefore boldly be said that the knowledge indicated in this manner in the mentioned productions will exist also forever on the Earth.

"'And as regards the method itself, that is to say, the mode of transmission through this Law, this, in my opinion, can be actualized in the following way:

"'In all the productions which we shall intentionally create, on the basis of this Law for the purpose of transmitting them to remote generations, we shall designedly introduce certain also lawful inexactitudes, and in these lawful inexactitudes we shall place, by intelligible means, the contents of some or other true knowledge which is already in the possession of men of the present time.

"'In any case, for the interpretation itself, or, as may be said, as the 'key' to those inexactitudes in that great Law, we shall further make in our productions something like a Legominism, and we shall secure its transmission from generation to generation through initiates of a special kind, whom we shall call, initiates of Art.

"'And we shall call them so, because the whole process of such a transmission of knowledge to remote generations through the Law of Sevenfoldness will not be natural but artificial.

"'And so, my highly attained and impartial colleagues' . . .

"It must now be clear to you that if for some reason or another the information useful for our descendants concerning knowledge already attained by men and about past events on the Earth fails to reach them through genuine initiates, then, thanks to these new means of transmission which I have suggested, men of future generations will always be able to reflect upon and to make clear to themselves, if not everything now already existing, then at least those particular fragments of the common knowledge already existing on the Earth, which chance to reach them both through these said productions of the hands of contemporary men and through the various ceremonies already now existing in which, by means of this Great Law of Sevenfoldness we shall now, and with the help of these artificial indications of ours, put what we wish.'"

"With these words the great Aksharpanziar then concluded his report.

"A considerable excitement and noisy discussions followed his speech among all the members of the club of the Adherents of Legominism, and the outcome of it was that then and there they unanimously decided to do as the great Aksharpanziar had suggested.

"A brief interval was then allowed for eating, after which they all assembled again, and the second general meeting of that day continued throughout the night.

"Well, the unanimous decision was then carried, to begin the following day making what are called 'minia-images'—or, as the contemporary three-brained beings call them, 'models'—of various productions; and to try to work out the possible and most suitable means of indication, on the principles laid down by the great Aksharpanziar; and thereafter to bring these 'minia-images' or 'models' of theirs to the Club for exhibition and exposition to the other members.

"In a day or two, many of them already began bringing, in the evenings, the 'minia-images' they had made and showing them with the necessary explanations; and they also began demonstrating every variety of those acts, which beings of that planet had before occasionally performed in the process of their ordinary existence and which also they still manifest up till now.

"Among the number of the models they brought and the various being-manifestations they demonstrated, were combinations of different colors, forms of various constructions, and buildings, the playing on various musical instruments, the singing of every kind of melody, and also the exact representation of various experiencings foreign to them, and so on and so forth.

"For the sake of convenience, the members of the club soon divided themselves into a number of groups, and each seventh part—which they called a 'day'—of that definite period of time which they called a 'week,' they gave over to the demonstration and exposition of their productions in one particular branch of knowledge.

"Here it is interesting to notice that this definite period of the flow of time, namely a 'week,' has always been divided on your planet into seven days; and this division was even made by the beings of the continent Atlantis, who expressed in it that same Law of Sevenfoldness with which they were quite familiar.

"The days of the week were then on the continent Atlantis called as follows:

(1) Adashsikra,
(2) Evosikra,
(3) Cevorksikra,

(4) Midosikra,
(5) Maikosikra,
(6) Lookosikra,
(7) Soniasikra.

"These names were changed there many times and at the present time the beings there already name the days of the week thus:

(1) Monday,
(2) Tuesday,
(3) Wednesday,
(4) Thursday,
(5) Friday,
(6) Saturday,
(7) Sunday.

"And well, as I have already told you, they then devoted each day of the week to the production of one or another specialty either of their hands, or of some other form of consciously designed being-manifestation.

"Namely, Mondays they devoted to the first group, and this day was called the 'day-of-religious-and-civil-ceremonies.'

"Tuesdays were given over to the second group and was called the 'day-of-architecture.'

"Wednesday was called the 'day-of-painting.'

"Thursday, the 'day-of-religious-and-popular-dances.'

"Friday, the 'day-of-sculpture.'

"Saturday, the 'day-of-the-mysteries,' or, as it was also called, the 'day-of-the-theater.'

"Sunday, the 'day-of-music-and-song.'

"On Mondays, namely, on the 'day-of-religious-and-civil-ceremonies,' the learned beings of the first group demonstrated various ceremonies in which the 'fragments-of-knowledge' that had been precariously selected for transmission, were indicated by means of inexactitudes in the Law of Sevenfoldness, chiefly in the inexactitudes of the lawful movements of the participants in the given ceremonies.

"For instance, let us suppose that the leader of the given ceremony—the priest, or according to contemporaries, the clergyman—has to raise his arms towards Heaven.

"This posture of his, infallibly demands, in accordance with the Law of Sevenfoldness, that his feet should normally be placed in a certain position; but these Babylonian learned beings intentionally put the feet of the said leader of the ceremony not as they should be placed in accordance with this Law, but otherwise.

"And in general it was just in all these 'otherwises,' that the learned beings of that group indicated in the movements of the participants in the given religious ceremony, by a conventional what is called 'alphabet,' those ideas which they intended should be transmitted through these ceremonies to the men-beings of their remote descendants.

"On Tuesdays, namely, on the 'day-of-architecture,' the learned beings belonging to the second group, brought various models for such proposed buildings and constructions as could endure a very long time.

"And in this case, they set up these buildings not exactly in accordance with the stability derived from the Law of Sevenfoldness, or, as the beings there were mechanically already accustomed to do, but otherwise.

"For instance, the cupola of a certain construction had, according to all the data, to rest on four columns of a certain thickness and definite strength.

"But they placed this said cupola on only three columns; and the reciprocal thrust, or, as it is also expressed, the 'reciprocal resistance,' derived from the Law of Sevenfoldness for supporting the surplanetary weight, they took not from the columns alone, but also from other unusual combinations derived from the same Law of Sevenfoldness with which the mass of the ordinary beings of that time were also already acquainted; that is to say, they took the required degree of resistance of the columns chiefly from the force of the weight of the cupola itself.

"Or still another example: A certain stone, according to all the established data there, both mechanically from long-centuried practice and also thanks to the fully conscious calculations of certain beings with Reason there, ought infallibly to have its definite firmness corresponding to a certain power of resistance; but this corner-stone they infallibly made and placed so that it did not correspond at all to the mentioned data; but the firmness and power of resistance for the support of the superimposed weight required on the basis of the Law of Sevenfoldness, they took from the setting of the lower stones, which in their turn they did not lay according to the established custom, but again they based their calculations or the manner of laying the still lower stones and so on.

"And it was just in these unusual combinations of the laying of stones, derived from the Law of Sevenfoldness, that they indicated, also by means of a conventional 'alphabet,' the contents of some or other useful information.

"This group of learned members of the club of the 'Adherents of the Legominism' further indicated what they wished in their 'minia-images' or 'models' of proposed constructions by utilizing the Law called 'Daivibrizkar,' that is, the law of the action of the vibrations arising in the atmosphere of enclosed spaces.

"This law, which has utterly failed to reach the contemporary three-brained beings of that planet, was then already quite familiar to the beings there, that is to say, they were already quite aware that the size and form of enclosed spaces and also the volume of the air enclosed in them, influence beings in particular ways.

"Utilizing this law, they indicated their various ideas in the following way: "Let us suppose that according to the character and purposes of some building or other, it is demanded that from the interiors of the given building, in accordance with the Law of Sevenfoldness and with the practice of centuries, definite sensations in a certain lawful sequence must be evoked.

"Then, utilizing the Law of 'Daivibrizkar,' they combined the interiors of these projected in such a way, that the expected sensations were evoked in the beings who entered them, not in the anticipated familiar lawful sequence, but in some other order.

"And it was just these deviations from the lawful sequence of sensations, that they placed whatever they wished in a certain way.

"Wednesdays—the 'day-of-painting'—devoted to the combining of different colors.

"On those days the learned beings of the given group brought for demonstration every kind of object necessary for domestic use made of such colored materials as could last a very long time: namely, they brought 'carpets,' 'fabrics,' 'chinkrooaries,' that is, drawings made in various colors on specially tanned leather capable of lasting many centuries, and things of a similar kind.

"By means of variegated colors of threads, various representations of the nature of their planet and various forms of beings also breeding there were drawn or embroidered on these productions.

"Before continuing to speak about this, namely, in which way those terrestrial learned beings then indicated various fragments of knowledge in their combinations of various colors, one thing bearing on what I am just relating must be noticed—a thing definitely unfortunate for those favorites of yours and which was also obtained in their presences on account of the same abnormal forms of their daily existence established by them themselves.

"First I wish to explain to you also about the gradual change for the worse in the quality of the formation in them of those 'organs-of-perception' which should be formed in the presence of every kind of being, and about the organ which particularly interests us in the given case, the organ for the perception and distinguishing of what is called the 'inter-blending-of-center-of-gravity-vibrations' which reach their planet from the spaces of the Universe.

"I am speaking about what is called the 'General-Total-Vibration-of-all-the-sources-of-the-actualizings,' namely, just about that which the learned being Aksharpanziar, of whom I spoke, called the 'white ray,' and about just those perceptions of impressions from separate blendings of center-of-gravity-vibrations which are distinguished by beings as separate, what are called, 'tonalities-of-color.'

"You must know that at the very beginning of the arising and existence of the three-brained beings of the planet Earth, before the period when the organ Kundabuffer was introjected into them, and later when this organ has totally removed from their presences, and even after the second Transapalnian-catastrophe there almost up to the time of our third personal flight to the surface of that planet, the said organ was actualized in them with what is called a 'sensibility-of-perception,' similar to that which is actualized in the total presences of all ordinary three-brained beings of the whole of our great Universe.

"Formerly, at the periods mentioned, in all the three-brained beings arising on this planet, this organ was formed with the sensibility of perceiving the mentioned blendings of 'separate-center-of-gravity-vibrations' of the 'white-ray' and of distinguishing one third of the quantity of the 'tonalities-of-color' of all the tonalities in general obtained in the presences of the planets as well as in all other greater and smaller cosmic concentrations.

"Objective science has already accurately established that the number of separate interblendings of 'center-of-gravity-vibrations' from the 'General-Total-Vibration,' namely the tonalities, or as your favorites say, 'colors,' is exactly equal to one 'Hooltanpanas,' that is to say, according to the calculations of the terrestrial three-brained beings, of five millions, seven hundred and sixty-four thousand, eight hundred and one tonalities.

"Only a third of this total number of the interblendings or tonalities—minus the one tonality which is accessible only to the perception of OUR ALMIGHTY ENDLESSNESS—that is, one million, nine hundred and twenty-one thousand, and six hundred tonalities, perceived by the beings as 'differences-of-colors'—can be perceived by all the ordinary beings on whatever planet of our great Universe they arise.

"But if the three-brained beings bring the perfecting of their highest part up to fulfillment and at the same time their perceiving organ of visibility acquires the sensibility of what is called 'Olooestesnokhnian-sight,' then they can already distinguish two thirds of the total number of tonalities existing in the Universe, which number, according to terrestrial calculation, amounts to three million, eight hundred and forty-three thousand, and two hundred differences of tonality of color.

"And only those three-brained beings who bring the perfecting of their highest being part up to the state of what is called 'Ischmetch' becomes able to perceive and distinguish all the mentioned number of interblendings and tonalities with the exception of that One tonality which, as I have already told you, is accessible to the perception only of our ALMIGHTY CREATOR.

"Although I intend to explain to you in detail in the future how and why in the presences of the 'Insapalnian-cosmic-concentrations' from the evolving and involving processes of the 'General-Total-Vibration' there is acquired by every kind of definite formation the property of producing various effects upon the mentioned organ of the beings, nevertheless, I do not consider it superfluous to touch upon this question, also, now.

"It is necessary to say, first of all, that according to the fulfilled result of the fundamental cosmic law of the holy Heptaparaparshinokh, that is, that cosmic law which was called by the three-brained beings of the planet Earth of the mentioned Babylonian period 'the Law of Sevenfoldness,' the 'General-Total-Vibration' like all the already 'definitized' cosmic formations, is formed and consists of seven what are called 'complexes-of-results,' or, as it is also sometimes said, of 'seven-classes-of-vibrations' of those cosmic sources, the arising and further action of each of which also arise and depend on seven others, which, in their turn, arise and depend on seven further ones and so forth right up to the first most holy 'unique-seven-propertied-vibration' issuing from the most holy Prime Source; and all together they compose the 'General-Total-Vibration' of all the sources of the actualizings of everything that exists in the whole of the Universe, and thanks to the transformations of these latter, they afterwards actualize in the presences of the cosmic 'Insapalnian concentrations,' the said number of the various 'tonalities-of-color.'

"And as regards the details of the most holy 'unique-seven-propertied-vibrations,' these you will understand only when, as I have already many times promised you, I shall have explained to you in detail in its proper time, concerning all the most great fundamental laws of World-creation and World-maintenance.

"And meanwhile concerning the given case you ought to know that when this said 'Common-Total-Vibration,' that is, what the terrestrial three-brained beings call the 'white ray,' enters with its proper presence into the 'spheres-of-the-possibilities' for its transformation in the presence of an Insapalnian planet, there then proceeds also in it, just as in the case of every already 'definitized' cosmic arising, possessing the possibility of still further actualization, that cosmic process called 'Djartklom,' that is, it itself remains as a presence, but its essence, as it were, disintegrates and produces processes for evolution and involution by the separate 'center-of-gravity-vibrations' of its arising; and these processes are actualized thus: one of the 'center-of-gravity-vibrations' is derived from the others and is transformed into a third, and so on.

"During such transformations, this said 'Common-Total-Vibration,' that is, the 'white ray,' acts with its 'center-of-gravity-vibrations' upon other ordinary processes proceeding nearby in intraplanetary and surplanetary arisings and decompositions, and, on the basis of the 'relativity-of-vibrations,' its 'center-of-gravity-vibrations' dependently upon and in accordance with the surrounding conditions, interblend and become a part of the whole general presence of these said definite intraplanetary or sur-planetary formations, in which the said processes proceed.

"So, my boy, during the periods of my personal descent to the planet Earth which has interested you, at first without any conscious intention on the part of my Reason, and later already quite intentionally, I noticed and finally came to realize definitely the progressive deterioration in all of them of this 'being-organ' also.

"Deteriorating century by century the 'sensibility-of-perception' of that organ also, namely, the organ just by means of which, there chiefly proceeds for the presences of the three-brained beings, what is called the 'automatic-satiation-by-externals,' which just served as the basis for the possibility of natural self-perfecting, had reached such a point that at the time of our fifth stay there, just during the period called by the contemporary beings there, the period of the 'Greatness of Babylon,' that organ of theirs could perceive and distinguish the interblendings of the 'center-of-gravity-vibrations' of the 'white ray,' at most up to the third degree only of what are called its 'sevenfold-strata,' that is, up to only 343 different 'tonalities-of-color.'

"Here it is interesting to note that quite a number of the three-brained beings of the Babylonian epoch themselves already suspected the gradual deterioration of the sensibility of that organ of theirs, and certain of them even founded a new society in Babylon that started a peculiar 'movement' among the painters of that time.

"This peculiar 'movement' of the painters of that time had the following program: 'To-find-and-constate-the-Truth-with-only-the-tonalities-existing-between-white-and-black.'

"And they executed all their pieces already exclusively utilizing only the tonalities derived from the black up to the white color.

"When I got to know of that particular 'movement' of painting there in Babylon, its followers were already using for their productions about 1500 very definite shades of what is called the 'color grey.'

"This new movement in painting there, among the beings who were also striving to learn the truth at least in something, made what is called a 'great stir'; and it was even the basis for the arising of another and still more peculiar 'movement,' this time among what are called the Babylonian 'Nooxhomists,' among just those beings of that time who studied and produced what are called new 'combinations-of-concentrations-of-vibrations' which act in a definite way on the sense of smell of the beings and which produce definite effects in their general psyche, that is to say, among those beings there who made it their aim to find the truth by means of smells.

"So, certain beings who were then crazy just about this, in imitation of the followers of the said branch of painters, founded a similar society also and the motto of their new movement was:

"'To-search-the-truth-in-the-shades-of-smells-obtained-between-the-moment-of-the-action-of-cold-at-freezing-point-and-the-moment-of-the-action-at-warm-decomposition.'

"Like the painters, they also then found between these said two definite smells about seven hundred very definite shades, which they employed in their elucidating experiments.

"I do not know to what these two peculiar 'movements' then in Babylon would have led and where they would have stopped, if a newly appointed chief of the city, still during the time we were there, had not begun prosecuting the followers just of that second new 'movement,' because with their already sufficiently keen sense of smell, they had begun to notice and unwittingly to expose certain of his what are called 'shady-dealings,' with the consequence that he used every sort of means to suppress everything connected not only with that second new 'movement,' but with the first as well.

"As regards that organ of theirs about which we began to speak, namely, the organ for the perception of the visibility of other cosmic arisings which were beyond them, the deterioration of its sensibility, continuing also after the Babylonian period, reached the point that during our last stay on the surface of this planet, your favorites already had the possibility of perceiving and distinguishing instead of the one million nine hundred and twenty one thousand and six hundred 'tonalities-of-color' which they ought to have perceived and distinguished, only the result of the penultimate as it is called 'sevenfold-crystallization-of-the-white-ray,' that is forty-nine tonalities, and even there only some of your favorites had that capacity, while the rest, perhaps the majority, were even deprived of this possibility.

"But what is most interesting in respect of the progressive deterioration of that most important part of their total presence, is the sorry farce that results, namely that those contemporary three-brained beings there, who can still manage to distinguish the mentioned miserable fraction of the total rubber of tonalities—namely, merely forty-nine—look down with superior self-conceit and with an admixture of the impulse of pride, upon those other beings who have lost the capacity to distinguish even this miserable number, as upon beings with an abnormal deficiency in that said organ of theirs; and they call them: diseased, afflicted by what is called 'Daltonism.'

"The last seven interblendings of the center-of-gravity-vibrations of the white ray which, just as now among the contemporary beings there, they then had in Babylon, have the following names:

(1) red
(2) orange
(3) yellow
(4) green
(5) blue
(6) indigo
(7) violet

"Now hear in just which way the learned beings then in Babylon belonging to the group of painters indicated various useful information and fragments of the knowledge they had attained, in the lawful inexactitudes of the great cosmic Law called the 'Law of Sevenfoldness,' by means of the combinations of the mentioned seven independent definite colors and other secondary tonalities derived from them.

"In accordance with that definite property of the 'Common-Total-Vibration,' that is, of the 'white-ray,' during the process of its transformations about which I have just spoken and which was already then familiar to the Babylonian learned painters, namely, that one of its 'center-of-gravity-vibrations' is derived from the others and is transformed into a third and so on—in other words, that said separate colors of the 'white-ray' are always derived one from the other and form a third, as for example, the orange color is obtained from the red, and further the orange color itself passes in its turn into the yellow color, and so on and so forth—then, whenever the Babylonian learned painters wove or embroidered with colored threads or colored their productions, they inserted the distinctions of the tonalities of the colors in the cross lines as well as in the horizontal lines and even in the intersection lines of color, not in the lawful sequence in which this process really proceeds, in accordance with the Law of Sevenfoldness, but otherwise; and in these also lawful 'otherwises' they placed the contents of some or other information or knowledge.

"On Thursdays, namely, the days which the learned beings of this group assigned for 'sacred' and 'popular' dances, there were demonstrated with the necessary explanations every possible form of religious and popular dances, either those already existing which they only modified, or quite new ones which they created.

"And in order that you should have a better view and well understand in which way they indicated what they wished in these dances, you must know that the learned beings of this time had already long been aware that every posture and movement of every being in general, in accordance with the same Law of Sevenfoldness, always consists of seven what are called 'mutually-balanced-tensions,' arising in seven independent parts of their whole, and that each of these seven parts in their turn consists of seven different what are called 'lines-of-movement' and each line has seven what are called 'points-of-dynamic-concentration'; and all this that I have just described, being repeated in the same way and in the same sequence, but always on a diminishing scale, is actualized in the minutest sizes of the total bodies called atoms.

"So during their dances, in the movements lawful in their

accordance with each other, these learned dancers inserted intentional inexactitudes also lawful, and in a certain way in them indicated the information and knowledge which they wished to transmit.

"On Fridays, days devoted to 'sculpture,' the learned beings belonging to this group brought and demonstrated what were then called 'minia-images' and by the contemporaries 'models,' and which were made from material there called 'clay.'

"Those 'minia-images' or 'models' which they brought for exhibition and familiarization represented as a rule separate beings or beings in groups of various other beings of all kinds of exterior form breeding on their planet.

"Among these productions were also various what are called 'allegorical-beings' which were represented with the head of one form of a being there, with the body of another and with the limbs of a third and so on.

"The learned beings belonging to this group indicated all that was requisite in the lawful inexactitudes derived from what was then called the Law of 'Dimensions.'

"You must know that to all the three-brained beings of the Earth and also of course to the sculptors of that period, it was already known that, in accordance always with the same great Law of Sevenfoldness, the dimensions of any definite part of any whole being are derived from the seven dimensions of other of his secondary parts, which in their turn are derived from seven tertiary parts, and so on and so forth.

"According to this, each large or small part of the whole totality of the planetary body of a being has exactly proportionately increasing and diminishing dimensions in relation to his other parts.

"For a clear understanding of what I have just said, the face of any being can serve as a good example.

"The facial dimensions of every three-centered being in

general and also the facial dimensions of the three-centered beings who please you of the planet Earth are the result of the dimensions of seven different fundamental parts of the whole of his body, and the dimension of each separate part of the face is the result of seven different dimensions of the whole face. For instance, the dimensions of the nose of any being are derived from the dimensions of the other parts of the face, and on this nose in its turn there are actualized seven definite what are called 'surfaces,' and these 'surfaces' also have seven lawful dimensions down to the said atom itself of this face of theirs, which is one of the seven independent dimensions composing the dimensions of the whole planetary body.

"In the deviations from these lawful dimensions, the learned sculptors among the members of the 'Adherents of the Legominism' then in the city of Babylon, indicated all kinds of useful information and fragments of knowledge already known to them which they intended to transmit to the beings of remote generations.

"On Saturdays—the 'Day-of-the-Mysteries,' or the 'day-of-the-theater,' the demonstrations produced by learned members of this group were the most interesting, and, as it is said, the most 'popular.'

"I personally preferred these Saturdays to all the other days of the week and tried not to miss one of them; and I preferred them because the demonstrations arranged on those days by the learned beings of that group, frequently provoked such spontaneous and sincere laughter among all the other terrestrial three-centered beings who were in the given section of the club, that I sometimes forgot among which three-centered beings I was and that being-impulse manifested itself in me which properly arises only in one-natured beings like myself.

"At the outset the learned beings of that group demonstrated before the other members of the club various forms of being-experiences and being-manifestations. Then, later, they collectively selected from all that was demonstrated, what was suitable for the various details for one or another already existing mystery, or for one newly created by themselves; and only after all this did they indicate what they wished, in those being-experiences and manifestations reproduced by them, by means of intentionally allowed deviations from the principles of the law of Sevenfoldness.

"Here it is necessary to notice that although in former epochs, mysteries occasionally containing many instructive conceptions now and again reached some of their generations mechanically, and sometimes passed from generation to generation to beings of very remote generations, yet those mysteries in the contents of which the learned members of the club of the 'Adherents of the Legominism' then intentionally placed various knowledge, calculating that it would reach beings of very remote generations, have almost totally ceased to exist during recent times.

"These mysteries there incorporated in the process of their ordinary existence still centuries earlier already began gradually to disappear soon after the Babylonian period. At first their place was taken by what are called their 'Kesbaadji,' or, as they are now called there on the continent Europe, 'Puppet-shows,' (Petrushka), but, afterwards, they were already finally ousted by their still existing 'theatrical-shows' or 'spectacles' which are there now just one of the forms of that said contemporary Art of theirs which acts particularly perniciously in the process of the progressive shrinking of their psyche.

"These 'theatrical-spectacles' replaced the Mysteries after the beings at the beginning of the contemporary civilization—to whom only 'a-fifth-to-a-tenth' was passed down of the information about how and what these said Babylonian learned mysterists had done—began to think of imitating them in this also and set about doing, as it were, the same.

"From that time on, the other beings there called these imitators of the mysterists, 'Players,' 'Comedians,' 'Actors' and, at the present time, they already call them 'Artists,' of whom, I may say, very many have been bred during recent times.

"And these learned beings of that time belonging to the group of the mysterists indicated various useful information and the knowledge already attained by them, by means of what are called 'currents-of-associative-movements' of the participants in these mysteries.

"Although the three-brained beings of your planet, then already well knew about the laws of the 'currents-of-associative-movements,' yet absolutely no information whatsoever concerning these laws has passed to the contemporary three-brained beings.

"As this said 'current-of-associative-movements' does not proceed in the presences of the three-brained beings who please you, as in general it proceeds in the presences of other three-brained beings, and as quite other bases proper only to them were the causes there of this, I must therefore first of all explain this to you in rather more detail.

"The process is the same as that which also proceeds in us, but it proceeds in us when we are intentionally resting in order to allow the whole functioning of our general presence freely to transform without hindrance by our will, all the varieties of being-energy required for subsequent all-round active existence—whereas in them, these said various being-energies can now arise only during their total inactivity, that is during what they call their 'sleep,' and then, of course, only 'after a fashion.'

"Also consisting, like every other three-brained being of the whole of our great Universe, of three separate independent spiritualized parts, each of which independent spiritualized parts has, as a central place for the concentration of all its functioning, a localization of its own, which they themselves call a 'brain,' all the impressions in their general presence whether coming from without or arising from within, are also perceived independently by each of these 'brains' of theirs, in accordance with the nature of these impressions; and afterwards, it is also proper to proceed in the presences of every kind of being without distinction of brain-system these impressions together with previous impressions, compose the total material and evoke in each of these separate brains, thanks to occasional shocks, and independent association.

"So, my boy, from the time when those favorites of yours completely ceased consciously to actualize in their general presences the 'being-Partkdolg-duty,' only from the results of which both what is called sane 'comparative-thinking' and also the possibility of conscious active manifestation can only arise in beings from various natural associations and furthermore from the time when their separate brains, associating now already quite independently, began producing in one and the same general presence three differently-sourced being-impulses, they then, thanks to this, began gradually, as it were, to acquire three personalities in themselves having nothing in common with each other, in the sense of needs and interests.

"Rather more than half of all the anomalies arising in the general psyche of your favorites, particularly those of recent times, just proceed, because they have in their whole presence a process of three different kinds of independent associations that evoke in them the being-impulses of three localizations of a totally different kind and of different properties; and because there is a connection between these three separate localizations in them as there is also in general in the presences of every kind of three-brained being preassigned by Great Nature for other what are called 'general-presence-functionings'; and because from everything perceived and sensed, that is, as I have already told you, from every kind of shock, associations of three different kinds of impressions proceed in the three said localizations in consequence of which three totally different kinds of being-impulses are evoked in one and the same whole presence: then, on account of all this, a number of experiences are nearly always proceeding in them at one and the same time, and because each of these experiences by itself evokes in the whole being a desire for a corresponding manifestation, a corresponding movement is thus actualized in accordance with separate parts of their total presence.

"Just these said differently-sourced associative experiences proceed in their general presences and are derived one from the other also in accordance with the same Law of Sevenfoldness.

"The learned members of the club of the 'Adherents of the Legominism' belonging to this group then in Babylon, indicated what they wished in the movements and in the actions of the participants in the mysteries in the following way: "For instance, suppose that in order to fulfill the role of some participant in the given mystery some or other definite associations were bound to be evoked in one or another of his brains, by the action of one or other new impressions given to him; and suppose that associations were bound to evoke some or other manifestations or movements of the given participant, then intentionally they produced those manifestations or movements, not as they should have been produced in accordance with the Law of Sevenfoldness, but 'otherwise,' and in these 'otherwises' also they inserted in a certain way what they wished to transmit to distant generations.

"Now hear at which demonstrations I used always to be glad to be present on Saturdays, in order to rest from my intense activities at that time, and how these learned mysterists demonstrated before the other learned members of the club of the 'Adherents of the Legominism' all kinds of being-experiences and manifestations according to flowing associations, from among the number of which fragments for future mysteries were selected.

"For these demonstrations they constructed in one of the large halls of the Club a special raised place which they then called, the 'reflector-of-reality.' Beings of subsequent epochs to whom the information concerning these Babylonian learned mysterists chanced to be transmitted, and who began imitating them and as it were doing the same, called and still call their constructions of a similar kind 'estrada.'

"So, two of the participants would always come upon these 'reflectors-of-reality,' or 'estrada,' first; and then usually one of them stood for a while and, as it were, listened to what his own what is called 'Darthelhlustnian' state, or, as it is sometimes otherwise said, to the state of his own inner 'associative-general-psychic-experiencings.'

"Listening in this way, he would make it clear to his Reason that, for instance, the sum total of his associative experiences emerged in the form of an urgent inclination to hit another being in the face, the sight of whom had always served as the cause for the beginning of the association of a previous series of impressions present in him, just the associations of those impressions which had always evoked in his general psyche disagreeable experiences, offensive to his own self-consciousness.

"Let us suppose that these disagreeable experiencings always proceeded in him when he saw someone who was then called 'Irodohahoon' which professional there is already now called by the contemporary beings a 'policeman.'

"Having then made this 'Darthelhlustnian' psychic state and inclination of his clear to his Reason, but at the same time, being on the one hand well aware that in the existing conditions of external social existence it was impossible for him to gratify his inclination completely, and, on the other hand, being already perfected only in his reason and being well aware of his dependence on the automatic functioning of the other parts of his general presence, he clearly understands that on the gratification of this inclination of his, will depend the fulfillment of some prospective and important being-duty of his, of great importance to those around him; and having thought over everything in this way, he decides to gratify this urgent inclination of his as best he can by at least doing a 'moral injury' to that 'Irodohahoon,' by evoking in him associations that would lead to unpleasant experiencings.

"With this object in view he turns to the other learned being who had come on the 'estrada' with him, and treating him now as an 'Irodohahoon' or a 'policeman,' he would say:

"'Hi! you! Don't you know your duty? Don't you see that there . . . ?' pointing with his hand at that moment in the direction of another small room of the club where the other participants of the demonstrations that day were, 'a couple of citizens of the city,' a 'soldier' and a 'cobbler' are fighting in the street there and disturbing the public peace, and here you are leisurely strolling about imagining yourself God knows who and leering at the passing wives of honest and respectable citizens of the city!!! Just you wait, you scamp! Through my chief, the city's chief physician, I shall report to your chief this negligence of yours and breach of duty!'

"From that moment the learned being who had spoken would be a physician, because he had chanced to call his chief, the head physician of the city, while the second learned being whom the former had called a 'policeman' would assume the role of a policeman. The two other participating learned beings who were then immediately brought from the other room where the one who assumed the role of policeman went for them, assumed one of the role of a 'cobbler' and the other, the role of a 'soldier.'

"And these two latter learned beings assumed and had to manifest themselves in just those roles, namely, one in the role of a 'soldier' and the other in the role of a 'cobbler,' only because the first learned being, who, having himself in accordance with his 'Darthelhlustnian' state assumed the role of a physician and had called them 'soldier' and 'cobbler' respectively.

"Well then, these three learned beings who were thus cast impromptu by the fourth learned being for the fulfillment of every kind of perception and manifestation, which had to flow by law, of types foreign to them, or, as your favorites say, of 'strange roles,' namely of the roles of the 'cobbler,' 'soldier,' and policeman,' further produced their experiences and relaxed manifestations from these said experiences, thanks to the being-property in them called 'Ikriltazkakra'—a property also familiar to the learned beings of the planet Earth of that period, who previously had already the possibilities of perfecting their presences up to the ableness of actualizing it.

"Three-centered beings can acquire this said being-property called 'Ikriltazkakra' only if there is already personally acquired in their presences what is called 'Essoaieritoorassnian-will' which in its turn can be obtained thanks to always the same being 'Partkdolgduty,' that is, to conscious labors and intentional sufferings.

"So it was in this way that the learned members of the group of the Mysteries then in Babylon became players of 'strange-roles' and demonstrated before the other learned mothers of the club, the experiences and the actions derived from them, and which were produced in accordance with the directing of their well-informed Reason.

"And thereafter, as I have already said, they, together with the other learned members of the club of the Adherents of Legominism who were present, selected the corresponding from among the number of being-impulses demonstrated in such a way, and which had to be experienced and manifested in the actions of the beings according to the law of the flowing of differently-sourced associations, and only then did they include those selected in the details of some mystery or other.

"Here it is very important to emphasize that then in Babylon the three-brained learned beings who belonged to the group of the mysterists indeed reproduced in action amazingly well and precisely the subjective particularities of the perceptions and manifestations of various types foreign to them.

"They reproduced them well and precisely not only because as I have already explained, they contained the being-property 'Ikriltazkakra,' but also because the learned beings of the planet Earth of that time were very well aware also of what is called the 'law of type' and that the three-brained beings of their planet were ultimately formed in twenty-seven different types, and also which of them and in which cases what had to be perceived and how it had to be perceived, and how they were bound to manifest themselves.

"Concerning the said being-property, I have just called 'Ikriltazkakra,' I must add further that just this property alone gives beings the possibility of restraining themselves within the limits of all those impulses and promptings which are evoked at any given moment in their general presences by the associations flowing in that brain in which they themselves have consciously given the start for the proceeding of associations of one or another series of impressions already present in them; and it is only thanks to just that property that beings have the possibility of perceiving every kind of detail of the psyche of the type they have already previously well studied, and of manifesting themselves similarly to it, and, so to say, fully impersonating it.

"In my opinion, it is on account of the absence of just that property that the majority of all those anomalies have arisen which have just resulted in the three-brained beings of the planet Earth who please you, becoming possessed of such a strange psyche.

"You must know that both in the presences of the three-brained beings these also of the present time, as well as in the presences of every kind of three-brained being in general, every new impression is accumulated in all their three separate brains in the order of what is called relationship, and afterwards they take part with the impressions already previously registered in the associations evoked in all these three separate brains by every new perception, in accordance with and in dependence upon what are called the 'center-of-gravity-impulses' present at the given moment in their whole presence.

"So, my boy, seeing that there continue to flow in the presences also of your contemporary favorites, three kinds of independent associations which also continue to bring forth totally different kinds of being-impulses, and at the same time they have already entirely ceased the conscious actualization in their presences of every kind of those cosmic results by means of which alone the mentioned being-property can be acquired in three-brained beings, then in consequence of all this the result was just obtained, that the general presence of each and every of your contemporary favorites in the process of his existence consists, as I have already told you, as it were, of three quite separate personalities—three personalities which have and can have nothing in common with each other, either in respect of the nature of their arising or in respect of their manifestations.

"Hence it is that there just proceeds in them that particularity of their general presence which is expressed thus: that with one part of their essence they always intend to wish one thing; at the same time with another part they definitely wish something else; and thanks to the third part, they already do something quite different.

"In short, what happens in their psyche is just what our dear teacher Mullah Nassr Eddin defines by the word a 'mix-up.'

"Concerning the demonstration of the Babylonian learned

beings of that time belonging to the group of the Mysterists; I must add that in the course of the action the number of the participants was gradually supplemented by their other colleagues also dependently on various voluntary associative happenings.

"And besides all this, every participant thus engaged in the fulfillment of the perceptions and accurate automatic manifestations that happened to be connected with him and were proper to a personality of a type quite foreign to him, had at the same time that he was fulfilling that role to give himself time, under some plausible pretext to change into corresponding costume.

"And they changed their costume in order to manifest themselves more clearly and more strikingly in the fulfillment of the role they assumed, and so that the other learned members present of the club of the Adherents of the Legominism who checked and selected the fragments of the future mysteries could more easily and surely collate them and make a better selection of everything they saw.

"On Sundays, namely, on the days consecrated to music and singing, the learned beings belonging to this group first produced on various sound-producing instruments, and also with their voices, every kind of what is called 'melody' and then explained to all the other learned beings how they indicated in these works of theirs whatever they wished.

"They also had it in view to implant these works of theirs in the customs of various what are called peoples, in the calculation that these 'melodies' they created, passing from generation to generation, would reach men of remote generations who, having deciphered them, would discover the knowledge put into them and that had already been attained on the Earth, and would also use it for the benefit of their ordinary existence.

"For your understanding of how the learned beings there

of that group made their indications, in the 'musical and vocal' productions of theirs, I must first explain to you concerning certain special particularities of the perceptive organ of hearing present in the general presences of every kind of being.

"Among the number of these special particularities is the property called 'Vibroechonitanko.'

"You must know that those parts of the brains of beings which objective science calls 'Hlodistomaticules,' and certain of which on your planet the terrestrial, as they are called, 'learned physicians,' call 'nerve-brain-ganglia,' are formed of what are called 'Nirioonossian-crystallized-vibrations,' which in general arise in the fulfilled formation of every being as a result of the process of all kinds of perceptions of their organ of hearing; and later on, these 'Hlodistomaticules,' functioning from the reaction upon them of similar but not yet crystallized vibrations, just bring forth in the corresponding region which is subject to the given brain, the said "Vibroechonitanko' or, as it is sometimes also called, 'Remorse.'

"In accordance with the foresight of Great Nature these said 'Hlodistomaticules' serve in the presences of the beings as real factors for assisting the arising of the processes of association of those moments, when either the promptings arisen within are absent or the shocks coming from without do not reach their brains.

"And the as yet non-crystallized 'Nirioonossian-vibrations' in general arise and later enter into the general presence of the beings, either by means of what are called the vocal cords of every kind of being or by means of certain 'sound producing instruments' which the beings have artificially invented.

"So, just these vibrations arisen from the said sources and entering into the presences of the beings, when they touch the 'Hlodistomaticules' of one or another brain then, according to the general functioning of the whole being, they produce the said process of 'vibroechonitanko.'

"The second particularity consists in this, that in general by the action of vibrations obtained from the sequence of sounds of every kind of melody, the association is usually evoked in the presences of the beings in one or another of the three brains, just in that brain in which at the given moment what is called 'the-momentum-of-what-was-experienced' is increasing more intensively, and the sequence of the impulses evoked for experiencing already usually proceeds in an automatic order.

"The learned musician-singers then in the city of Babylon, combined their melodies in such ways that the sequence of the vibrations of the sounds should evoke in the beings a sequence of associations, and therefore also impulses for experiencings, not in the usual automatic order, that is to say, so that the sequence of the vibrations, on entering into the general presence of the beings, should evoke the 'vibroechonitanko' in the 'Hlodistomaticules,' not of just one brain, as it usually proceeds, namely, in just that brain in which at the given moment the associations predominate—but now in one brain, now in another, and now in the third; thus, for seeing also the quality or, as they say, the numbers of the vibrations of the sounds which would affect one or another brain.

"This latter, namely, from which vibrations, in which brain of the beings, which data are formed, and for which new perceptions these data might serve for what are called 'determinants-of-new-resultants,' they were also already quite familiar with.

"Owing to these sequences of sounds which they combined simultaneously in the presences of beings, different kinds of impulses arose, which evoked various quite opposite sensations, and these sensations in their turn produced unusual experiences in them and reflex movements not proper to them.

"And truly, my boy, the sequences of sounds they combined did indeed affect all the beings, into whose presence they entered, exceedingly strangely.

"Even in me, a being cast, as they would say, in another mould, various impulses were brought forth and were alternated with an unusual sequence.

"It happened in this way because as the sounds of their melodies which they had combined in a definite sequence entered into my general presence, there proceeded 'Djartklom' in them, or as it is otherwise said, the sounds were 'sorted out' and acted equally upon all my three variously caused 'Hlodistomaticules,' with the consequence that the associations proceeding in me in the three independent brains—though simultaneously and with an equal intensity of similar but differently natured series of impressions—produced in my presence three quite different promptings.

"For instance, the localization of my consciousness, or, as your favorites would say, my 'thinking-center,' brought forth in my general presence, let us suppose, the impulse of joy; the second localization in me, or my 'feeling-center brought forth the impulse called 'sorrow,' and the localization of the body itself, as once again your favorites would call it, my 'moving center,' brought forth the impulse of 'religiousness.'

"And it was just in these unusual impulses evoked in the beings by their musical and vocal melodies, that they indicated what they wished.

"And so my boy, after all I have already related about this terrestrial contemporary notorious 'Art,' I imagine you have enough to understand why and how, during the period of my fifth personal stay on your planet, I happened to be a witness of the events of the causes of its arising and in what connection and with what meaning it was pronounced for the first time just then at that period which your contemporary favorites call the 'Babylonian-civilization.'

"So I will now already speak about those facts there, after learning which, you will be able clearly to represent to yourself and approximately to understand how greatly 'logical-mentation' in all these three-brained beings pleasing to you must have deteriorated in so short a time, that without any what is called 'constancy-of-self-individuality,' they have submitted to be made the 'slaves' of those few from among their midst who are called 'wastrels,' and who, in consequence of the final loss of the divine impulse 'conscience,' could for their egoistic aims create from this 'empty-word' Art which chanced to reach them, also such a sure-fire 'factor' in all of them for the final atrophy of all the data for 'conscious-Being' that still survived in them.

"When during the period of my sixth and last personal stay there I heard everywhere about this contemporary 'Art' of theirs and came in contact with its results, and when I made clear to myself just what it was all about, then having recalled about my Babylonian friends of that time and about their good intentions towards their remote descendants, and as opportunities offered, made clear to myself more in detail just which results were obtained from all that of which I happened then to be a witness, and about which I have just been telling you.

"Initiating you now into the process, hidden from strangers and which became fixed in my general presence, of my conscious impressions during my last personal stay there on the surface of this planet of yours concerning this contemporary Art of theirs, then my 'I' must now as a result, with an arisen and profound being-impulse of regret, emphatically state that of all the fragments of knowledge already attained by the beings of the 'Babylonian-civilization'—which fragments, it must be allowed, did also contain a great deal—literally nothing has reached the beings of contemporary civilization for the benefit of their ordinary being-existence, apart from a few 'empty-words' without any inner content.

"Literally nothing whatever has reached them, not only of all the various fragments of general knowledge already then known on the Earth which they indicated in lawful divergences from the sacred Law of Heptaparaparshinokh, or, as they called it, the 'Law of Sevenfoldness,' but in the interval of time between these two civilizations of theirs, their being-rumination has so deteriorated, that they now already do not know nor even suspect the existence of such an all-universal law on their planet.

"And as regards this word Art itself, upon which thanks to the strangeness of their reason, there has been 'piled up' during this time, as they themselves would say, 'devil-knows-what,' I must tell you that my special investigations regarding to this word made it clear to me, that when this word among the other words and separate expressions used by the learned beings of that time, also began automatically passing, generation by generation, and it chanced to get into the vocabulary of certain three-brained beings there, in whose presences on account of various surrounding circumstances, the crystallizations of the consequences of the properties of the organ Kundabuffer had proceeded in just that order and 'mutual-action,' which by chance became of the kind that it predisposed the arising in their general presences of data for the Being of 'Hasnamuss-Individuums,' then this said word for some reason or other happened to please just that kind of three-brained being there, they began using it for their egoistic aims, and gradually they made from it that very 'something' which, although it continues to consist of, as it is said, 'complete vacuity, yet has gradually collected about itself a fairy-like exterior, which now 'blinds' every one of these favorites of yours who keeps his attention on it only a little longer than usual.

"Besides this word, from among the number of other definite words used in their discussions by the learned beings then in Babylon who were members of the club of the Adherents of the Legominism, there also passed automatically from generation to generation quite a number of other words or even several what are called 'foggy-notions' concerning certain definite understandings of that time.

"Among the latter, both in respect of name and pseudo-imitation caricatures, are their contemporary theaters now existing there.

"You remember that I have already told you that both the hall and the demonstrations themselves of the learned beings belonging to the group of the mysterists then at Babylon were still designated by the word 'Theater.'

"If I now explain to you a little more in detail concerning this contemporary theater of theirs, then possibly you will have enough material for the elucidation, first of all, concerning what came of all the good intentions and efforts of the learned beings of the Babylonian period; and secondly, what of all that had already been attained in respect of true knowledge passed from the times of that 'Babylonian-culture' to the beings of this contemporary 'European-culture,' in which the said 'Art' has become mainly covered with the mentioned exterior; and thirdly, you will sense certain aspects of the maleficence of that said contemporary notorious Art of theirs.

"A certain amount of information concerning the activity of the group of the Mysterists, learned members of the club of the Adherents of the Legominism, having also reached, as I have just told you, the beings of the contemporary epoch, the latter thereupon had the wish to imitate them also in this, and for this purpose they began also building special halls and also calling them 'Theaters.'

"The three-brained beings of the contemporary civilization quite frequently assemble in considerable groups in these theaters of theirs and also to observe, and, nominally, to study the various prepared manifestations of their 'artists,' as they have quite recently begun to call them, just as the other learned members of the club of the Adherents of Legominism studied then in Babylon the reproductions of the learned beings of the group of Mysterists.

"These 'Theaters' of theirs came to have a significance of the greatest importance in the ordinary process of existence of your favorites, and on account of this they put up particularly large buildings for this purpose which rank in most of their contemporary cities as the most remarkable constructions.

"It will do no harm, I think, to comment here upon the misunderstanding connected with the word 'artist.'

"I am bound to comment upon this, because this word was also transmitted to your contemporary favorites from the Babylonian epoch, but it was transmitted not like other words, that is, merely as empty words without sense, but just as one single particle of the consonance of a word then used.

"You must know that the learned beings then in Babylon, the members of the club of the Adherents of the Legominism, were called by the other learned beings of that time who were well-disposed towards them, and they also called themselves by a name which your contemporary favorites would write as 'Orpheist.'

"This word is composed from two definite roots of words then in use, which, in contemporary times, would signify 'right' and 'essence.' If someone was called thus, it meant that he 'rightly-sensed-the-essence.'

"After the Babylonian period, this expression also automatically passed from generation to generation with almost the same meaning, but nearly two centuries ago, when the beings of that time began wiseacring with the mentioned data, particularly in connection with that 'empty word 'Art,' and when various what are called 'Schools-of-Art' arose and everybody considered himself a follower of one or another of those schools, well just then, never having understood its genuine sense and chiefly because among the number of the said schools of Art there was also a school of a certain, as the contemporary beings already call him, 'Orpheus,' a figure invented by the ancient Greeks, they then decided to invent a new word defining their 'vocation' more exactly.

"So, instead of the said expression 'Orpheist,' they just invented the word 'artist,' which had to mean 'He-who-is-occupied-with-Art.'

"In order better to represent to yourself all the causes subsequently arising also from that misunderstanding there, you must first of all know that before the second terrestrial 'Transapalnian-catastrophe,' when these favorites of yours still arose and were prepared to become responsible beings normally, they by means of intentionally producing from themselves of corresponding consonants for their what is called speech, that is, for mutual intercourse, had and could make—also like all the three-brained Beings of all the great Universe—consonants up to three hundred and definite as they are called 'letters.'

"But later on, when, thanks as always to the same conditions of ordinary being-existence abnormally established by themselves, every kind of property proper to be possessed in the presences of the three-brained beings gradually deteriorated, this 'being-ableness' also deteriorated in them and at such a tempo that whereas the beings of the Babylonian period could now use for conversational intercourse among themselves, only seventy-seven definite consonants, the deterioration continued at such a tempo after the Babylonian period that after five centuries they could already use at the most only thirty-six definite 'letters,' and the beings of certain communities could not reproduce even this number of separate articulate sounds.

"So, my boy, seeing that information concerning the Babylonian period passed from generation to generation to the succeeding generations not only by means of what is called 'verbal-transmission,' but still also by means of marks on durable materials, that is, as it would be expressed there, by means of 'inscriptions'—and these 'inscriptions' consisted of conventional signs, which then stood for definite 'being-articulate-sounds' or 'letters'—then, when at the beginning of the contemporary civilization certain beings there began to collate them 'from a fifth to a tenth' and reflected that they already could not con-sound or pronounce many of these definite 'letters,' they then just invented what is called a 'written-compromise.'

"This mentioned 'written-compromise' consisted in this, that instead of every kind of sign of 'letter,' the taste of the pronunciation of which although they understood, yet they could not pronounce it, they decided to employ a slightly similar 'letter' contained in their alphabet at the given time, and so that everybody should understand that it was not that letter but quite another, they always wrote by its side the letter of the ancient Romans now already meaningless, but existing, and called in English 'h' and among the contemporary French 'ahsh.'

"From then on, all the rest of your favorites began doing the same, namely to each of these suspicious letters they added this Roman 'inheritance.'

"When this 'written-compromise' was invented, they had about twenty-five of these suspicious 'letters,' but in the course of time, as their 'ableness' to pronounce deteriorated side by side with the increase of their 'wiseacring,' the number of the letters they specially invented for such a 'being-ableness' diminished, and by the time the word 'Artist' was invented, they had already only eight of these letters; and in front of this notorious 'ahsh,' they wrote letters, partly ancient Greek and partly ancient Latin, which they indicated in the following way: 'th,' 'ph,' 'gh,' 'ch,' 'sch,' kh,' 'dh,' and 'oh.'

"The basis they had for the arising of such a misunderstanding there, was the compromising sign 'ph.'

"And it was the basis because it appeared both in the word by which the learned mysterists were designated and also in the word which stood for a personality invented by the ancient Greeks, with whose whole name, as I have already said, one of the 'schools of Art' then existing, had been connected; and the result of this was that the mentioned representatives of this terrestrial Art of that time, with their already now quite bobtailed reason, thought that it was nothing more than the word indicating 'the-followers-of-this-historical-personality'; and as many of them did not regard themselves as his followers, then instead of the mentioned word, they just invented the word 'Artists.'

"As we have seen not every inheritance of the ancient Romans turned out to be maleficent for the beings of subsequent generations, but in the given case, this little letter 'h' of theirs has been even an inspiring factor for the bringing forth of that 'being-ableness' in the presences also of such beings of subsequent generations, to whom it became already definitely proper to have no initiative or ableness of their own, and they wished and succeeded in substituting for the already long-existing definite expression 'Orpheist' the new word 'Artist.'

"Here it is very important in general to inform you concerning a great strangeness there, in respect of the mentioned gradual atrophy in the presences of all three-brained beings of this planet also of such a 'being-ableness' as the capacity to reproduce the 'consonants' required for mutual intercourse.

"You must know that the tempo of the deterioration of this being-capacity in the general presences of the beings does not proceed in everyone in every generation uniformly in the sense of the psychic and organic functioning of their planetary body; but it alternates, as it were, at different times and on different parts of the surface of this planet, affecting at one time more the psychic and at another time the organic part of the functioning of the planetary body.

"A very good elucidating example of what I have just said, is afforded by the sensations of the taste and the capacity to pronounce those two definite consonants or those 'letters' known there at the present time which are used among all the contemporary beings who breed on all parts of the surface of your planet and which passed to them through the ancient Greeks from times long past.

"The said two letters were called by the ancient Greeks 'Theta' and 'Delta.'

"Here it is interesting to notice that your favorites of very ancient times specially used just these two letters for making definite names of two quite opposite meanings.

"Namely, they used the letter 'Theta' in words which expressed ideas relating to the notion of 'good' and the second letter 'Delta' they used in words relating to the notion of 'evil'; as for example, 'Theos,' that is 'God,' and 'Demonos,' that is, 'Demon.'

"The notion and 'taste' of the consonance of both these letters passed to all the beings of the contemporary civilization, but both these different letters, having entirely different essences, they for some reason or other indicated by means of one and the same sign, namely, the sign 'th.'

"For instance, the beings of the contemporary community called 'Russia,' try as they may, already cannot pronounce these said two letters at all. But they already are very definitely aware of their difference, so that whenever they have to use these letters in words with definite notions, then although the letters they pronounce do not correspond at all, they correctly sense their difference and do not use one letter for the other.

"On the other hand, the beings of the contemporary community called 'England,' still pronounce each separate letter almost as the ancient Greeks pronounced it; but while doing so, sense no difference in them, but without the least embarrassment, employ for words of entirely opposite meanings, one and the same conventional sign in the form of their notorious 'th.'

"For instance, when beings of that contemporary England utter their favorite and frequently used expression 'thank you,' you can clearly hear the ancient letter 'Theta'; and when they pronounce the word they like no less, and equally frequently use—the word, 'there'—then you hear distinctly and definitely the ancient letter 'Delta'; but, all the same, without any what is called 'Remorse,' for both these letters they make use of one and the same 'pan-paradoxical' 'th.'

"However, I think I've talked enough about terrestrial philology.

"We had better continue to clear up first the causes why it has been customary just among your contemporary favorites to have such theaters everywhere, and afterwards about what their contemporary artists do in these theaters, and how they manifest themselves there.

"As regards the question why it became quite the custom among them to assemble often in considerable groups—in these theaters of theirs, in my opinion it was because these contemporary theaters of theirs and all that goes in them chanced to turn out to be very congenial with the abnormally formed general presences of the majority of these contemporary three-brained beings, namely with those beings there who had already finally lost the need, proper to three-brained beings, to actualize their own initiative in everything, and who exist only on chance shocks from outside, or by orders of the consequences crystallized in them of one or the other properties of the organ Kundabuffer.

"From the very beginning of the arising of those theaters of theirs, they assembled and they till now assemble in them for the purpose of watching and studying the reproductions of their contemporary 'artists'; no . . . they assemble only for the satisfaction of one of the consequences of the properties of the organ Kundabuffer—a consequence which had been readily crystallized in the general presences of the majority of them, and which was called 'oornel,' and which the contemporary beings now already call 'swaggering.'

"You must know that thanks to the mentioned consequences of the properties of the organ Kundabuffer, the majority of the contemporary beings acquire in their presence a very strange need to evoke the expression in others of the being-impulse called 'Astonishment' regarding themselves, or even simply to see it on the faces of those around.

"The strangeness of this need of theirs lies in this, that they get satisfaction from the manifestation of astonishment on the part of others, regarding just their exterior appearance, which they have precisely in conformity with the demands of what are called their 'fashions'—that is to say, with just that also maleficent customs of theirs, which began there still from the times of the Tikliamishian civilization and which has to the present time become one of those being-factors which already now automatically leaves them neither the time nor the possibility to see or sense reality.

"This custom maleficent for them themselves consists in this, that they periodically change the external form of what is called 'the-covering-of-their-nakedness.'

"Here apropos it is interesting to note that it has gradually become the rule in the general process of the ordinary existence of these three-brained beings who please you, that the changes of the appearance of the mentioned covering are directed by such beings there of both sexes as have already 'become worthy' to become candidates for 'Hasnamuss-Individuums.'

"In this respect, the contemporary theaters turned out to be corresponding to your favorites, because it is very convenient and easy for them to show off, as they like to say, their 'chic' coiffures, or the specially tied knot-of-their-cravat, or the daringly bared, what is called 'Kupaitarian-part-of-their-body,' and so on and so forth, while at the same time they can look at the new manifestations of the 'fashions' already actualized conformably with the up-to-date indication of the same candidates for 'Hasnamuss-individuums.'

"As regards what these contemporary artists do with their 'swaggerings' in these theaters, to get a clear picture of this, you must first hear about this, still another exceedingly strange 'illness' existing there under the name of 'dramatisacring'; the predisposition to which illness arises in the presences of certain of them thanks only to the carelessness of what are called their 'midwives.'

"This criminal carelessness on the part of their 'midwives' consists in most instances of this: before doing her job, she calls on the way at the house of her other clients and drinks there rather more than usual of the 'wine' they offer her, so that while she is doing her job she unconsciously utters words, already fixed in the processes of the ordinary existence of your favorites, like the 'formulae' of what are called their 'magicians,' and the new unfortunate being first takes in at the moment of what they call 'its-appearance-in-God's-world,' the words of this maleficent 'formula.'

"This formula consists of the following words: 'Eh, you, what a mess you've made!' "Well my boy, thanks to that criminal carelessness on the part of the midwife, the unfortunate newly appeared being acquires in his presence just that predisposition to the mentioned strange illness.

"When such a three-brained being there who has acquired at his first appearance the said predisposition to the illness 'dramatisacring' reaches the age of a responsible being, should he by that time know how to write and should wish to write something, then he suddenly gets this strange illness and begins wiseacring on paper, or, as it is said there, to 'composing' varies what are called 'dramas.'

"What usually serve as contents for these works of theirs, are various events which are supposed to have occurred, or which might occur in the future, or finally, events of their own contemporary 'unreality.'

"In addition to this, among the symptoms of this peculiar illness there appear in the general presence of the sick being, seven other very specific particularities.

"The first is this, that when this strange illness arises and already functions in the presence of the given being, particular vibrations are spread around him which act on his environment—as they say—just like the 'smell-of-an-old-goat.'

"The second consists in this: that from the change of the inner functioning in such a being, the exterior form of his planetary body undergoes the following changes: his nose is held aloft; his arms, as it is said—akimbo; his speech is punctuated by a special cough, and so on.

"The third—that such a being always gets fearful of certain perfectly harmless, natural or artificial formations, as for instance, of what are called 'mice,' of 'hands-clenched-in-a-fist,' the 'wife-of-the-chief-stage-manager-of-the-theater,' the 'pimple-on-his-nose,' the 'left-slipper-of-his-own-wife' and still many other formations outside of himself.

"The fourth particularity leads him to this, that he already entirely loses all capacity for understanding the psyche of the surrounding beings similar to himself and of getting clear about it.

"The fifth—consists in this, that both inwardly and in his manifestations, he criticizes all and everything that he hasn't himself.

"The sixth—that the data for the perception of anything objective are more atrophied in him than in all other terrestrial three-brained beings.

"And the seventh and last particularity consists in this, that there arise in his presence what are called, 'Hemorrhoids,' which, by the way, is the sole thing which he carries with modesty.

"It usually then further happens there, that if the sick being had an uncle who is a member of one or other of their 'Parliaments,' or if he himself gets acquainted with the widow of a ' former-businessman,' or if the period of his preparation for becoming a responsible being has for some reason or other passed in such an environment or under such conditions that he has automatically acquired the property called 'slipping-in-without-soap,' then what is called the 'producer,' or, as he is also called, the 'owner-of-lambs,' takes this work of his and orders the mentioned contemporary 'artists' to 'reproduce' it exactly as it was wiseacred by this being who has fallen ill with this strange illness of 'dramatisacring.'

"And already further, these contemporary artists there first reproduce this work themselves alone without strangers, and they reproduce it until it goes among them exactly as the sick being himself had indicated, and the producer has ordered, and when finally the work goes among them without the participation of their own consciousness and feelings, and these contemporary artists themselves are completely transformed into what are called 'living-automatons,' then and then only, with the help of all those among them, who have not yet become entirely 'living-automatons'—for which reason they later acquire the name of 'stage-managers'—they do the same thing with their assistance and under their direction, but already now in the presence of other ordinary beings assembled in these contemporary theaters of theirs.

"Thus you can now, from all I have just said, easily conclude that, besides many definitely maleficent consequences, the expounding of which I shall soon touch upon more in detail, these theaters cannot of course yield anything else for that lofty aim which the Babylonian learned beings then had in view when they created for the first time, such a form of conscious reproduction of perceptions and of the associative reactions to them of other beings similar to themselves.

"All the same, it must be admitted, that they obtained, of course accidentally, from their theaters and from these contemporary artists of theirs, for the processes of their ordinary being-existence, one 'not-bad-result.'

"To understand in what this 'not-bad-result' consists, I have first to explain another particularity which becomes proper to the general presence of beings who arise according to the principle 'Itoklanoz.'

"In accordance with this principle, the elaboration in the presence of such beings of energy necessary for what is called their 'waking-state,' depends on the quality of the associations which proceed in their general presence during their 'complete-passivity,' or as those favorites of yours say, 'during sleep'; or vice versa, that energy necessary for the 'productiveness' of this said 'sleep,' of theirs, is elaborated in its turn also from the associative process proceeding in them during that said 'waking-state' of theirs, which this time is already now dependent on the quality or intensity of their activity.

"And this began to apply also to these terrestrial three-brained beings from the time, when, as I have already once told you, Great Nature was compelled to substitute for the 'Fulasnitamnian' principle previously proper to their presences, the principle 'Itoklanoz.' Thereupon there was acquired and there is up till now in the process of their existence such a particularity, that if, as it is said among them, they 'sleep-well,' then they will also be 'awake-well' and vice versa; if their waking-state is bad, then they will also 'sleep' badly.

"So, my boy, because during recent times they have been existing already abnormally, then in consequence, that established automatic tempo which had more or less previously helped the procedure of the obligatory associations was even changed, and as a result, in recent times they have been sleeping badly and when awake have been even worse than before.

"And why these contemporary theaters of theirs with their contemporary artists have come in useful for improving the quality of their sleep, was due to the following circumstances.

"After the need to actualize the 'being-Partkdolgduty' in them themselves had entirely disappeared from the presences of the majority of them, and in the process of their 'waking-state' every kind of association of unavoidably perceived shocks proceeded only from several already automatized what are called 'series-of-former-imprints' consisting of endlessly repeated what are called 'impressions-experienced-long-ago,' and there began in its turn and has continued up till now, to disappear in them even the instinctive need to perceive every kind of new shock which are the 'daily bread' for the three-brained beings, and which issue from their inner separately spiritualized being parts of from corresponding perceptions coming from without for conscious associations, namely, for just that being-association upon which depends the intensity of transformation of every kind of 'being-energy' in the presences of beings.

"During the latter mentioned three centuries, the process itself of their existence became such, that in the presences of the majority of them during their daily existence, that 'being-comparative-association' almost no longer arises, which usually proceeds in the three-brained beings thanks to every kind of their new perceptions, from which alone in the general presences of the three-brained beings can data be crystallized for their own individuality.

"So, when your favorites existing in such a manner in their 'daily-life' began going to these contemporary theaters and watching the senseless manipulations of these contemporary artists of theirs, and received shocks, one after the other, of every kind of reminiscence, already previously perceived, of not less senseless and absurd notions, then during this waking state of theirs, more or less tolerable being-associations are willy-nilly obtained in them so that when they get home and go to bed—they sleep much better than usual.

"Although indeed these contemporary theaters with all that is done in them chanced to prove in this way—but of course only 'for-today'—an excellent means for the better sleep of your favorites, nevertheless the objectively evil consequences for beings of these theaters, and particularly for the rising generations, are in general incalculable.

"The chief harm for them from these theaters of theirs consists in this, that these theaters served as an additional factor for the final destruction in them of every kind of possibility of ever possessing the need proper to the three-brained beings, called the 'need-of-real-perceptions.'

"It came to be a maleficent factor for this chiefly because of the following circumstances.

"When they go to these theaters of theirs, and sitting quietly, look on at every kind of varied and many-sided, even if senseless, 'manipulations' and manifestations of their contemporary artists, then although they are in their usual waking-state, every kind of association, both 'thinking' and 'feeling' proceeds in their presences, exactly as they must during the periods of their complete passivity, or sleep.

"Namely, when they receive a large number of accidentally corresponding shocks for stimulating shocks already fixed and perceived before and automatized in a series of impressions, and when they reflex these with the functioning of the, what are called, 'organs-of-digestion-and-sex,' then as a consequence, obstacles arise in their presences for the procedure even of those deplorably conscious being-associations which have already somehow become sufficiently automatized to produce in them a more or less regular tempo for the transforming of the required substances for that passive existence of theirs, during which the required substances must be transformed just for their active existence.

"Otherwise speaking, when they happen to be in these theaters of theirs, they are not during these periods, entirely in that passive state in which the proceeding of the transformation of substances required for their already usual waking-state that has some how become sufficiently automatized in them also—with the result that these contemporary theaters of theirs have come to be for them only an additional maleficent factor.

"Among many other aspects of the maleficence of this contemporary 'Art' of theirs, one of the most obviously ignored, but for all the three-brained beings there one of the very harmful in respect of the possibility of acquiring of conscious what is called 'individual-Being,' is the radiation of the representatives of the contemporary 'Art' themselves.

"Although this maleficent radiation gradually becomes there the lot or specific attribute of the representatives of all the branches of their 'Art,' yet my detailed physio-chemical investigations definitely showed me that it is always worst just in those mentioned contemporary 'artists' or 'actors' who mime in these contemporary theaters of theirs.

"The maleficence for all the other of your favorites of those total radiations issuing from them has become distinctly noticeable, particularly in recent times of their present civilization.

"Although certain of the ordinary beings used already long before to become such professionals there, yet in former times, on the one hand, every kind of data for 'Hasnamussian-properties' did not become fulfilledly crystallized in the presences of every one of these professionals, and on the other hand, other of your favorites obviously instinctively felt the maleficent influence issuing from those professionals, and hence were on their guard and behaved towards them in a corresponding manner and very carefully.

"Namely, in former centuries such artists or actors were everywhere relegated to the lowest caste by other beings, and were regarded with contempt. And even at the present time there, in many communities, for instance on the continent Asia, it is unpleasant to shake hands with them, as one almost always does when meeting beings similar to oneself.

"Even up till now in these said communities, it is also considered defiling to sit with such artists at the same table and to eat together with them.

"But the contemporary beings of that continent which has come to be at the present time, the chief place of what is called their 'cultured-existence,' not only put these contemporary artists on a level with themselves in their inner relations, but even largely imitate them in respect of their appearance, and at the present time they imitate them pretty thoroughly.

"The custom of shaving the beard and mustache, now followed by all your favorites, can serve as a very good example for confirming what I have just said.

"I must tell you that these in past epochs terrestrial professionals-artists had always to go with shaved mustaches and beards during the ordinary process of their existence.

"They had to shave these 'expressers' of masculinity and activity of theirs, first of all, because, always playing the roles of other beings, they had often to change their appearance and for this they not only had to put on their faces a corresponding what is called 'paint' but also to wear wigs and false mustaches and beards, and the latter was impracticable if they had their own beards and mustaches; and secondly, because the ordinary beings of all former communities there, considering such artists dirty and a harmful influence, and fearing to fail to recognize them if they chanced to meet them in ordinary conditions of existence and of somehow touching them, then promulgated everywhere a severe law, that the beings of the profession of artists or actors, in order to be unmistakable for other beings, should always shave their mustaches and beards.

"While explaining just now to you the cause of the arising of the custom of shaving mustaches and beards among artists there, I recall a very reasonable and very economic what is called 'measure-of-justice' of the three-brained beings of the epoch of the 'Tikliamishian civilization' connected also with the shaving of the hair, but in this given case with the hair growing on the heads of the beings there.

"A law was then established and strictly enforced that those petty criminals among them who, after trial and sentence by, in their turn, seven elderly beings of the given region, had been ascribed to one of the four already previously established categories of 'immorality' and 'crime'—with which beings all what are called their 'prisons' are now also usually crowded—should for a definite term go about always and everywhere with one of the four corresponding sides of their heads shaved; and furthermore, any such convicted being was obliged to uncover his head whenever he met or spoke with others.

"It is interesting to note that there then also existed a law of the same kind about shaving the head in regard to the immoral behavior of women.

"And namely in regard to women, a sentence existed and was also very strictly enforced—in this instance by seven elderly local women who had earned respect by their previous conduct.

"And the penal measures for women were fitted to the four manifestations which were then considered there, for women, as the greatest laxity and immorality.

"Namely, if all her neighbors noticed, and all the seven mentioned elderly women confirmed it, that the given woman had behaved without due regard and neglectfully towards her family duties, then according to the law, she had for a definite term to appear everywhere with painted lips.

"But if various women noticed that she had begun to manifest towards her children with a weakening of her maternal impulses, then under the same conditions, those around her condemned her to go about everywhere also or a definite term with her face made up and painted white and red, but only the left half.

"And if, following the same procedure, it was established that a woman manifested a disposition to avert the conception in herself of a new being for the purpose of the prolongation of her generation, then she was condemned to appear with her face made up and painted also with white and red, but this time only on the right half.

"And women who attempted to violate their chief what is called 'wifely-duty,' that is, who deceived or who only tried to deceive her legal husband, or who attempted to destroy a new being conceived in her, was obliged by the same procedure to be always and everywhere, also for a definite term, made up and painted with white and red, this time over the whole of her face.'

At this point of the tales, Beelzebub was interrupted by Ahoon with the following words: "Your Right Reverence! All your explanations concerning the terrestrial Art and those three-brained beings there who now practice it and are so to say its representatives, and particularly your elucidations concerning the contemporary 'comedians' there or 'artists' have suggested to me to use all the impressions fixed in my general presence which were perceived during my last stay on the surface of this planet Earth which has pleased our dear Hassein, and to give him a good piece of very practical advice . . . "

Having said this, Ahoon intended to look expectantly at the face of Beelzebub with his usual glance, that is, without blinking for a long time, but as soon as he had noticed his usual, though always grieved yet kind and indulgent smile, he, not expecting the requested permission and being somewhat confused, at once turned this time to Hassein and spoke as follows:

"Who knows? Maybe, our dear Hassein, you indeed will have to be on that planet Earth and to exist among hose peculiar three-brained beings who are pleasing to you . . . "

And this time, again keeping the style and intonations of Beelzebub himself, he continued:

"For just that reason I wish here to initiate you in any case into the results of various impressions which I involuntarily perceived both concerning the resulting type and concerning the particularities of its manifestation just by those said contemporary representatives of Art there.

"You must know that this contemporary Art, adorned with a false halo and also those beings who are assumed to be its adepts, are not only put on their own level by the other three-brained beings there of the contemporary civilization, particularly during the several latter decades and imitated by them in their exterior manifestations, but they are always and everywhere undeservingly encouraged and exalted by them.

"And in these contemporary representatives of Art themselves, who really in point of their genuine essence are almost nonentities, in them there is formed without any of their being-consciousness, on their own part, a false assurance that they are not like all the rest, but, as they entitle themselves, of a 'higher-order,' with the result that in the presences of these types, the crystallization of the consequences of the properties of the organ Kundabuffer proceeds more intensively than in the presences of all the other three-brained beings there.

"Just in regard to such unfortunate three-brained beings, the surrounding abnormal conditions of ordinary being-existence are already so established, that there are bound to be crystallized in their general presences and to become an inseparable part of their general psyche, those of the consequences of the properties of the organ Kundabuffer which they now themselves call 'swagger,' 'pride,' 'self-love,' 'vanity,' 'self-conceit,' 'narcissism,' 'envy,' 'hate,' 'offensiveness,' and so on and so forth.

"These enumerated consequences are particularly conspicuously and strongly crystallized in just those contemporary 'representatives-of-Art' there, who are the 'manipulators' of the contemporary theaters there, and they are particularly strongly crystallized in them because, always performing the roles of beings similar to themselves, whose being-Being and significance in the process of their existence are ordinarily far superior to their own, and as I have already said, being themselves really almost nonentities, they with their already finally automatized reason, gradually acquire a false view of themselves.

"In other words, with such an already quite automatized 'consciousness' and finally 'nonsensical-feelings,' they feel themselves to be immeasurably superior to what they really are.

"I must confess, dear Hassein, that though during our earlier visits to the surface of that planet of yours and also at the beginning of this last stay there, I was in many places, and had various dealings with those three-brained beings pleasing to you, I scarcely ever felt in my general presence a genuine impulse of being-pity—pity, that is, for the infinitely unhappy Fate of every one of these favorites of yours, due to circumstances hardly depending upon themselves at all.

"But when, towards the end of that sixth stay there, certain of them were formed with the kind of inner presence, which is now possessed by all the representatives of almost all the branches of that Art of theirs, and those newly arisen 'types,' among the number of three-brained beings there, taking part in the process of their ordinary being-existence on the basis of equal rights with the rest, began dropping into the field of the perception of my sight with their already now exaggeratedly innerly-abnormal, what is called 'being-self-appreciation'—well, just then, they served as a shock for the beginning of the arising in me of the impulse of pity, not only in respect of them themselves, but also in respect of all these unfortunate favorites of yours in general.

"Try now to give your attention not to all the three-brained beings in general, nor to the other representatives of their contemporary Art, just to those who become and acquire the title of 'artist' or 'actor.'

"Everyone of them really being in respect of genuine essence almost what is called a 'nonentity,' that is, 'something' utterly empty but enveloped in a certain visibility, they have nevertheless gradually acquired such an opinion of themselves, by means of favorite exclamations always and everywhere repeated by them themselves like 'genius,' 'talent,' 'gift,' and still a number of others, each like themselves, void with only an exterior—that it is as if, among the similar beings around them, only they have 'divine origin,' only they are almost 'God.'

"Now listen and try to transubstantiate for use at the proper time in the corresponding parts of your general presence, my truly very practical advice.

"This practical advice of mine consists in this, that if for some reason or other you should have to exist, particularly before very long, among the three-brained beings of that planet Earth pleasing to you—I say before very long, because both the presence of these three-brained beings who please you and all the already fixed exterior conditions of their ordinary being-existence frequently undergo degeneration—and if you should have there some affair or other proper to every conscious three-brained being, just such affairs as have as their basis the aim of attaining some benefit or other for surrounding beings and the fulfillment of which depends also on those same surrounding beings—then in whatever community of the contemporary civilization this may proceed, then if you should have to meet these contemporary terrestrial types, in what are called there the 'circles' you meet in the interests of these affairs of yours, oblige yourself never to fail to be very, very careful and take every kind of requisite measure to keep on good terms with them.

"Why you must be so careful towards just them, and in general, in order that you may better represent to yourself and understand from every angle these terrestrial contemporarily arisen types, I must be sure to explain two further facts definitely formed there.

"The first is this, that on account, as always, of the same conditions of ordinary being-existence abnormally established there, and thanks to the arisen and existing there 'ephemerally-puffed-up' maleficent idea there of their notorious Art, these representatives of Art gradually become crowned with an imaginary halo in the preconceived picturings (representations) and conceptions of other three-brained beings there, and automatically thereby acquire an undeserved authority, in consequence of which all the rest of your favorites always and in everything assume that any opinion they express is authority beyond dispute by anybody.

"And the second springs from this, that these contemporary types newly arisen there, acquire, as they are formed, a corresponding inner presence that permits them to become, quite consciously on their part, just as easily somebody's slave, as they can, thanks merely to chance exterior conditions, become his worst enemy.

"That is just why I advise you to be very careful not to make enemies among them, and by that means to make a lot of trouble for yourself and in the carrying out of your affairs.

"So, our dear Hassein, the very 'Tzimus' of my advice to you is this, that if you should indeed have to exist among the beings of that planet Earth and have dealings with these representatives of contemporary Art, then you must know first of all that you must never tell the truth to their face.

"Let Fate spare you this! "Any kind of truth makes them extremely indignant, and their animosity towards others almost always begins with indignation.

"To such terrestrial types you must always say to their face only such things as my 'tickle' those consequences of the properties of the organ Kundabuffer unfailingly crystallized in them and which I have already enumerated, namely, 'envy,' 'pride,' 'self-love,' 'vanity,' 'lying,' and so on.

"And these means of tickling, infallibly acting on the psyche of these unfortunate favorites of yours are, as I noticed, among other things, during my stay there, the following: "Suppose that the face of one of these representatives of Art resembles the face of a crocodile, then be sure to tell him that he's the spit and image of a bird-of-paradise.

"If one of them is as stupid as a cork, say that he has the mind of a Pythagoras.

"Suppose his conduct in some business is obviously 'lunatic,' tell him that even the great cunning fellow Lucifer couldn't have done better.

"Suppose that in his external appearance, you see signs that he has a number of terrestrial diseases from which he is progressively rotting day by day, then with an expression of astonishment on your face, ask him:

"'Do please tell me, what is your secret for always looking like a youth in his "pink and cream"?' and so on and so forth. Only remember one thing . . . never tell the truth.

"Although you have to behave like this towards all the being in general of that planet, it is particularly necessary towards the representatives of all the branches of contemporary 'Art.'"

Having said this, Ahoon, smirking like a Moscow suburban matchmaker at the marriage of her clients, or the proprietress of a Parisian fashion-workroom in what is called a 'high-life' cafe, began rearranging the folds of his tail.

And Hassein looking at him with his usual sincerely grateful smile, said: "Very many thanks to you, dear Ahoon, both for your advice and, in general, for your elucidation of certain details of the strangeness of the psyche of the three-brained beings of that in all respects ill-treated planet of our great Universe.'

And then he turned to Beelzebub himself with the following words: "Please explain to me, kind grandfather. Is it really possible that nothing has resulted from the intentions and efforts of those Babylonian learned things and that indeed, nothing whatsoever has passed of those fragments of knowledge which were already then known on the Earth, to the contemporary three-brained beings of that strange planet?"

To this question of his grandson Beelzebub said as follows:

"To the great sorrow of everything that exists in the Universe, scarcely anything has survived, my boy, from the results of their labors, and hence nothing has become the property of your contemporary favorites.

"The information they indicated in the said manner passed from generation to generation, only, in all, for a few of their succeeding centuries.

"Soon after the period of the 'Babylonian-Magnificence,' thanks to the same chief particularity of theirs, namely, to the 'periodic-process-of-reciprocal-destruction,' there almost wholly disappeared from amongst the ordinary beings there, not only the Legominisms concerning the keys of the lawful inexactitudes in the Law of Sevenfoldness contained in each of the branches of the 'being-Afalkalna' and 'Soldjinoha,' but, as I have already told you, there gradually also disappeared even the very notion of the Universal Law of the holy Heptaparaparshinokh, which in Babylon they then called the 'Law of Sevenfoldness.'

"Every kind of conscious production of the beings of the Babylonian period were gradually destroyed; partly by themselves decaying with time, and partly, thanks to their processes of 'reciprocal destruction,' that is to say, to that degree of that psychosis of theirs which is called the 'Destruction-of-everything-existing-that-comes-within-the-sphere-of-the-perception-of-visibility.'

"Thanks chiefly to these two causes there little by little disappeared from the surface of that ill-starred planet almost all the consciously actualized results of the learned beings of the Babylonian epoch and at such a tempo that after three of their centuries already scarcely any of them were left.

"It must also be noticed that, thanks to the second mentioned cause there, there also gradually diminished and finally almost entirely ceased, the employment of that new form—which had been begun and established then from Babylonian times—for the transmission of information and various fragments of knowledge to subsequent generations, through the beings they called 'Initiates-of-Art.'

"About the disappearance there of just that practice of certain beings becoming 'Initiates-of-Art,' I know very well, because just before my departure forever from that planet, I had to elucidate this very carefully for another aim of mine.

"And for the purpose of making this clear, I even specially prepared a very good 'Tiklunia' from among the beings there of the female sex and made these elucidations of mine through her.

"'Tiklunias' were formerly called there by the name 'pythias' but the contemporary ones are already called now 'mediums.'

"So then, I made it clear that there in the most recent times, only four of such beings, 'Initiates-of-Art,' still remained, by means of whose, what is called, 'immediate-line-of-inheritance' the keys to the understanding of the ancient Art still continue to be transmitted, and this transmission by inheritance now proceeds there under very complex and arcane conditions.

"Of these four contemporary initiated beings, one comes from among those who are called 'Redskins' who dwell on the continent America; another—from amongst the beings dwelling on what are called the Philippine Islands; the third, from the beings of the continent Asia, from the country called 'The source of the river Pianje'; and the fourth and last, from amongst those who are called 'Eskimos.'

"Now hear why I used the expression 'almost,' when I said that at the end of three of their centuries after the Babylonian period there 'almost' entirely ceased to exist every kind of conscious and automatic reproduction of the 'being-Afalkalna' and 'Soldjinoha.'

"You must know, that two branches of the conscious hand-productions of the beings of the Babylonian period chanced upon favorable conditions and partly consciously and partly automatically on the part of the transmitting beings, some of them passed from generation to generation.

"One of these said two branches recently ceased to exist; but the other has even reached certain beings of contemporary times almost unchanged.

"This branch which reached beings of contemporary times is called there 'sacred-dances.'

"So, thanks to this branch alone, which survived from the period of the Babylonian learned beings, a very limited number of three-brained beings there now have the possibility with certain labors conscious on their part, to decipher and learn the information hidden in it and which is useful for their personal being.

"And the second mentioned branch which recently ceased to exist was that branch of the knowledge of the Babylonian learned beings, which they called the 'Combination-of-different-tonalities-of-color' and which the contemporary beings now call 'Painting.'

"The passing of this branch from generation to generation proceeded almost everywhere, but with the flow of time, gradually disappearing, also everywhere, it proceeded in quite recent times at a still quite regular tempo both consciously and automatically only among the beings of the community called 'Persia.'

"And it was only just before my last departure from that planet of yours when the influence of a similar profession of beings of the contemporary 'European culture' began to become noticeable also there in Persia, and the beings of that profession in the community Persia also began wiseacring, that such a transmission already ceased entirely.

"It must also be noticed that in spite of all this, not a few of the still surviving productions of the Babylonian times reached the beings also of the contemporary civilization, namely chiefly to the beings breeding on the continent Europe.

"But these productions which reached the beings of this contemporary civilization—and not originals but only bad copies made by the copyists of the productions of the Babylonian epoch—who had not finally become what are called 'Plagiarists'—they simply stuffed into what are called their 'Museums,' without suspecting the 'well-of-wisdom' concealed in them and without taking corresponding practicable measures. And there in these museums they gradually were either destroyed or they were partially ruined by frequent copyings from them, made by means of various eroding and oxidizing compositions, as, for instance, 'alabaster,' 'fish-glue,' and so on, only that the copyists might swagger before their friends or cheat their teachers and achieve some other Hasnamussian aim.

"It must in fairness be remarked that now and again certain beings also of the contemporary civilization have suspected that 'something' was concealed in the productions which chanced to reach them in the original, specially created then in Babylon by the members of the Club of the Adherents of the Legominism, or in those copies which were made during their transmission from generation to generation by various conscientious professionals, that is, by such professionals to whom, as I have already said, it was still not quite proper to 'plagiarize,' and who therefore did not resort to the detailed remaking of productions in order to give them out as their own, and thereafter while searching very seriously for this 'something' certain of those inquiring beings of that European civilization even found in them a certain definite 'something or other.'

"For instance, at the beginning of the contemporary European civilization, one of these beings, a certain monk names Ignatius, who had formerly been an architect, attained even to the possibility of deciphering the hidden knowledge and useful information in the productions of almost all the branches of what was already named an ancient Art, which had reached him from the Babylonian epoch.

"But when this monk Ignatius was about to share what is called this said 'discovery' of his with other beings there like himself, namely, with two of his what are called, comrades, monks—together with whom he as a specialist had been sent by his Abbot for the purpose of directing the laying of the what are called 'foundations' of a temple, which later became famous, then, for some trifling reason flowing from the consequences of one of the properties of the organ Kundabuffer crystallized in them, called 'envy,' he was murdered while asleep and his planetary body was thrown into the water-space surrounding that small island on which it was proposed to erect the said temple.

"The said monk Ignatius sprang and was formed for the Being of a responsible being, on the continent Europe; but when he reached the age of a responsible being, then with the aim of enriching himself with information concerning the profession which he had made the aim of his existence, namely, the profession there called 'Architecture,' he left for the continent of Africa. And just he it was who entered as a monk into the 'Fraternity' which existed on that continent Africa under the name the 'Truth-Seekers'; and afterwards when this fraternity migrated to the continent Europe and increased, and when its brethren began to be called 'Benedictines,' he himself was already an 'All-the-Rights-Possessing Brother' of this said brotherhood.

"The temple I referred to exists there even up till now and is called, it seems, 'Mont-Saint-Michel.'

"In this Europe still several other inquiring beings noticed from time to time lawful inexactitudes in the works of various branches of Art which had reached them from ancient times; but no sooner did they find the key to the understanding of these inexactitudes then their existence came to an end.

"Still one other, that is, another being from that continent Europe, also noticed, and continuing to interest himself further and perseveringly to labor, he began fully to decipher the productions of almost all the branches of Art.

"And this wise terrestrial three-brained being was named 'Leonardo-da-Vinci.'

"At the end of my present tale about the terrestrial contemporary Art, there is no harm, I think, in noting still another of the many specific particularities of just those beings of the contemporary civilization who are occupied with the notorious Art.

"This specific particularity of theirs consists in this, that whenever one or other of the mentioned beings, namely, of the beings who notice in various productions which have reached them from ancient times, some very 'lawful-illogicality' and begins to produce the given branch in a quite new manner, perhaps in order to make the said 'lawful-illogicality' practically clear to himself; then the majority of the beings around him, having the profession of the same branch, at once become his followers and begin doing supposedly the same thing but of course without either aim or sense.

"And it is just this said 'specific' psyche of the beings there representatives of contemporary Art, that brings it about that on the one hand, what are called new 'movements of Art' are always arising there among your favorites, and, on the other hand, those which, even if only 'after a fashion' are nevertheless somehow arranged rightly by the preceding generations, are constantly shrinking.

"Although this 'illogicality' proceeds among the representatives of all the branches of contemporary Art, yet for some reason or other it is the beings who are occupied in the branch their called 'painting' who are most susceptible to it.

"Hence it is that at the present time there exists among these contemporary professions a great many 'new movements of painting' which have arisen in this way and have nothing in common among themselves. These new movements of painting are known there under the names of 'Cubism,' 'Futurism,' 'Synthesism,' 'Imagism,' 'Impressionism,' 'Colorism,' 'Formalism,' 'Surrealism' and many other similar 'movements' whose names also end in 'ism.'"

At this place of Beelzebub's tale, the hoofs of all the passengers of the trans-space ship *Karnak* suddenly glowed as if it were radiated from themselves a 'something' phosphorescent. This meant that the ship *Karnak* was nearing the place of her destination, that is, the planet Revozvradendr. Therefore, a bustling movement began among the passengers, for the preparations for descending from the ship. Beelzebub, Hassein and Ahoon ended their conversation and hurriedly began to prepare themselves also. The phosphorescent gleaming of the hoofs was obtained because there was directed from the engine-room to that part of the ship, concentrated together in a particular proportion, the holy parts of the sacred Omnipresent Okidanokh.

BOOK TWO

CHAPTER XXXI

The Sixth And Last Descent Of Beelzebub To Our Planet

BEELZEBUB began as follows:

"I was on that planet for the sixth and last time just before I received my full pardon and permission to leave this solar system, and return to my native country.

"During this sixth descent of mine I spent a considerable time amongst these Earth beings. I was there for a quarter of our year or according to their time calculation fifty years.

"As I have already told you, I used to observe the existence of these beings through my observatory, and, as I have also told you, I was particularly interested in their peculiarity of mutual destruction. After many centuries, and with all my efforts I was still unable to find a completely satisfactory explanation of this phenomenon of the psyche of those beings. Nevertheless, I hoped to understand it sooner or later, and I therefore always very attentively observed these processes of mutual destruction, whenever I happened to be on that planet, as well as from my observatory. At other times when I was a little free, I had for hours together made observations of the particular methods of these processes so that I already knew all the subtleties involved and had psychological explanations in every instance.

"Once, while, as was my custom, I was looking from Mars, through the 'Zuruaga' on one such process of mutual destruction, or, as they say, on their war, I saw what struck me as something entirely new, which nullified all my previous psychological explanations.

"I saw namely that without a being moving from his place, something was done with something, with the result, that a puff of smoke appeared, and immediately after the smoke, a being on the opposite side, fell down quite dead. This method of destruction had not before existed, and it struck me, because the explanation I had already arrived at of how their psyche reaches such a state that they can, or, more correctly, that something in them can, destroy the life of another did not apply in this case. At the same time this method appeared to me the most improbable, as far as the possibility of destroying.

"I already knew that when beginning such actions formerly these beings did not decide to kill others. It was only afterwards, as the slain increased in numbers, that they gradually became excited, and finally completely savage. I had explained this to myself previously; and it was more or less logically intelligible.

"My explanation was in fact, that seeing life so easily destroyed, everybody began to think for his own; and thus gradually the instinct of fear awoke. This feeling, in its turn, aroused the instinct of self-preservation; and with the realization that this preservation depended on others, everybody destroyed as many as possible, in order to increase his own chance of being saved. But those new means of mutual destruction, which I then saw, struck me very forcibly. Logic was quite excluded from the case, since the combatants stood quite a distance from each other, and among their own beings; and it was quite cold-bloodedly and as if from boredom, that by means of a certain something they destroyed the lives of others. Being wholly unable to understand it all, my interest was intensified; and I wished at all cost to discover in detail what could be the cause of this new means of destroying the lives of others. I therefore decided to descend to that planet and to find out on the spot.

"Some days after my decision I again flew down on the ship '*Occasion*.'

"As the phenomenon was just then taking place on the continent Asia in the country called Afghanistan, I made up my mind to descend near the latter country and afterward to send my ship to be moored somewhere near the North Pole of that planet.

"For I must tell you that on this occasion it was difficult to find a mooring place for our ship, because among the beings of that planet, the number of ships had considerably increased on the surface of the waters, and they rushed around the continents in all directions.

"Although we could make our ship invisible to these beings, we could not annihilate its presence so as to enable it to remain safely beyond the chance of collision with other ships. And this was why we flew our ship so far, and where ships do not go.

"While our ship was on its way to the Earth, the war in Afghanistan ended; but I decided nevertheless to remain on the great continent of Asia, and in the country called Turkestan which is not very far from Afghanistan. This peculiarity of theirs manifested itself, from time to time, in the neighboring countries, and Turkestan, being centrally situated geographically, made it convenient for me to set off for any place where this peculiarity could be witnessed.

"I began not only to observe their actions very attentively, but to make every kind of experiment, medical, physicochemical, and even hypnotic, upon the psyche of individual beings; but even then I could not learn the reason of this peculiarity at all.

"I spent thirty of their years on the continent of Asia in these experiments and observations.

"Besides Turkestan I visited during this time many of the countries great and small of that continent. I was in what are called China, India, Persia, Tibet and in many other smaller lands. I was several times also, of course, in the largest social organization of that planet, namely, Russia, which is situated on the northwestern side of the continent Asia, and occupies the eastern portion of another continent called Europe. For this reason Russia is sometimes spoken of as Eurasian.

"My observations during these thirty years, concerning this peculiarity, yielded however no results. But I did then make the discovery in the organization of these beings, of a singularity which not only no beings of other forms on that planet possess, but no beings of any other planet either.

"I discovered, namely, the fact that in these Earth beings there are two consciousnesses.

"Having discovered this singularity in their organization, namely, this duality of their consciousness, these beings began to interest me still more, and I wished to learn the details of their peculiar psyche. I therefore did not return home to the planet Mars, but remained upon Earth in order to be able eventually to elucidate the mystery, perhaps, of the strange embodiment of the souls inhabiting that planet, which had interested me during so many centuries.

"I began to study more of the languages in which the beings of the various social organizations and continents converse, for the purpose of making possible observations of those beings who might prove suitable for my aim, but whose language I did not know.

"The multitude of languages for intercourse among themselves was another of their singularities.

"Everywhere else in the Universe, on every planet containing soul-bearing beings there is one language for everybody, but on that planet Earth, on every bit of land, among every small group however accidentally segregated, there was a different language, with the result that if by chance, one being should find himself in an unusual part of that planet, he could have no dealing with its inhabitants.

"In spite of my perfect knowledge of sixteen of their languages, I was sometimes so placed during my travels that I could not even get food for my horse, though my pockets were full of those objects for which everyone on that planet cheerfully gives you anything you wish.

"For instance, you live in a town, and know all the languages necessary for dealing with all the beings of that place. Suppose that for some reason it is necessary to go to another place, perhaps no more than a hundred miles away, nobody in this latter place would understand a word of what you wish to say, and you would not understand a word of theirs.

"Their numerous languages have moreover nothing in common. Some of them were even formed in such a way that they had no correspondence with the vocal chords provided by nature specially for speaking. Even I, who had unusual possibilities could not pronounce some words correctly. Regarding this idiocy, they eventually realized how awkward it was; and even while I was there the representatives of various social organizations met together to find a means of clearing up the confusion.

"They decided to make a common language for the whole planet Earth. As usual, however, nothing resulted from it owing to the same disharmony which is the cause of the failure of even their reasonable plans. The disagreement this time arose on the choice of a common language. One section wished that the language should be ancient Greek; another Latin, also ancient; while a third insisted on an 'Esperanto,' invented by some absurd being. The result was that nothing was decided and now everything continues in the old way, that is that this small planet with a half dead terra-firma has a thousand gibberishes.

"Of those three languages, two were created long before, among two groups of Asiatic beings who almost simultaneously emigrated from the continent Asia to the neighboring continent Europe.

"The first group consisted of beings who followed the profession of fisherman, and who, on account of their profession, occupied the coasts and islands of the strait separating the continents of Asia and Europe.

"The second group was formed of shepherds and sheep farmers who emigrated to the south coast of the continent Europe, because the nature of that place fully corresponded to their needs.

"Both these groups, fishermen and shepherds, afterwards multiplied and organized, and became strong and powerful social organizations, and their languages for intercourse were preserved and passed down to contemporary beings.

"The representatives of contemporary organizations chose neither of these languages for the universal language. Latin they found poor in vocabulary; and indeed it was not to be expected that shepherds with their limited needs could create a language rich in vocabulary; and though Latin became the language of the large social organization called Rome, the Romans, beyond the special words needed for orgies, introduced nothing into the language to make it suitable for present needs.

"As regards the second language, namely Greek, its vocabulary is greater on account of the fact that from boredom, those fishermen, in ancient times, occupied themselves during bad weather in inventing all sorts of fantastic knowledge and coined a large number of new words which have remained; but the representatives of the chief powerful social organization had no intention of selecting Greek, that language being nowadays spoken only by the present Greeks, who, although the descendants of the former great Greeks, have now neither a large, nor, what is more important, a powerful social organization.

"These representatives, with their self-love and vanity, could not of course, choose Greek, for how could the world be expected to speak the language of such a trifling social organization?

"As regards Esperanto, this language might possibly do for

the cackle of hens, but not for the whole planet. Its inventor must surely have imagined that a language is like contemporary knowledge, which can be made up in a laboratory. He certainly could not have suspected that a language, whatever it may be, can be formed only by life, and during tens of centuries.

"For instance, on that planet there are many languages, which, owing to their being still young, are about as interesting as beetroot soup. In the English language, for example, though it has now existed for several centuries, it is impossible to say or to write anything essential. The impression left by writing would be, instead of New York, with all its objects and buildings, the hut of Robinson Crusoe with the properties of Man Friday.

"While I was studying those languages, I began to think seriously what profession I should adopt as the best means of associating with those beings. This question is a very difficult one on that planet, because caste differences are very strongly developed there. You must belong to their caste to associate with them. For if they belong to a higher caste than your own, you may not approach them; and if to a lower, they are servile to the degree of incredible humiliation. To make the observations I wished was impossible in such conditions.

"I needed to be able to associate with beings of every caste, because as yet I did not know which beings I should find most suitable for my purposes.

"After much reflection I decided upon the profession of a physician. My choice was made for several reasons. In the first place, I had already realized that the peculiarities of these interesting beings do not lie in their external and visible consciousness but in their inner, which can be understood only with the help of the beings themselves. It is necessary, however, that they should be frank; and they can be frank only with priests or physicians. I had no wish to become a priest, since in that profession I should always have to act the hypocrite; and this is not necessary for the physician. And in the second place, under the forms of medical treatment, I could more easily carry out my experiments on beings. And although the caste of physicians is also very popular among many of the other castes, yet nevertheless many of the physicians happen to receive admittance everywhere to all castes.

"But you may not even know what a physician is? Really . . . ! No? . . . Well, a physician in general is one who is obliged to help other beings to discharge their duty, those beings namely, who for some reason or other have some temporary derangement of bodily functioning, and cannot carry on their duty. But among beings of the planet Earth, the name physician is given as well to those beings who make a business of collecting information about methods of healing—for example, those methods which certain beings, such as old women who have become childish, (as it is usual for old women of the planet Earth to become)—have prescribed throughout the ages for healing the sick. These Earth physicians, in their turn, now prescribe these methods for those sick beings who apply to them for treatment. They have many thousands of things, which they use for healing, but the most important and essential, which really effect results, are only three in number: the first, the flower the seeds of which the beings of Goblandia chewed, that is the poppy, or elements obtained from it; the second, castor oil; and the third, quinine, a substance obtained from a certain tree. I shall also tell you about the significance of thousands of other of their remedies. For who knows, you may happen one day to be on that planet yourself, and you will then know how to use them.

"It will be much better, I think, if I give you not my personal opinion, but the explanations which certain beings of that planet gave me regarding the importance of these remedies. He was a very queer fellow who first explained them to me. He was a priest by profession and belonged to what is called the Armenian religion. His name was Termosses.

"I got to know this queer priest fellow in the following way. At the insistence of a being with whom I was a little friendly, I wanted to get hold of a certain ancient Armenian Manuscript; and for this purpose I had to go to the country Transcaucasia, to the town of Alexandropol. This old Armenian priest Termosses was the very being to help me to get hold of this manuscript. He was a remarkably queer fellow compared with the other beings of that planet, and he was very amusing and witty. Of his numerous whims, I need only tell you one, from which you will understand the character of this Termosses.

"Special respect is shown on that planet Earth to those beings belonging, as a rule, to the profession of priest, and especially if they are old. You always bow before them and ask their blessing.

"As this Termosses was an old priest, everybody respected him quite without distinction of creed; and everybody regarded it as an honor to approach him and ask his blessing, and, of course, to kiss his hand. But Termosses himself could not bear this fussing. If anybody dared to come near him, without giving him a chance of beginning, Termosses would say, 'If you have anything important to say, out with it quickly, and if not, be off with you, there's somebody round the corner impatiently waiting to give you a free meal.'*

"This was Termosses all over. In short, he was not like other beings, especially not like priests; yet in spite of this, all the Armenians of the town loved him.

* *Editor's Note:* At this point in The 1931 Manuscript the following sentence appeared in parentheses. However, it does not seem to relate to the text:
(Kelah, in Transcaucasia, is the name given to a dish, which the relatives of a deceased being distribute in honor of the dead soul of the deceased to all who wish it.)

"There were hundreds of other priests in that town, but none of them had such a following as he had. Yet he passed all his spare time in one cafe or other, where usually no priest of any faith is to be found.

"Well then, I became friends with this Termosses, and I always used to visit him while I lived in that town. He had a large family.

"One day his eldest son fell sick of a certain illness. The best known physician of the town was immediately sent for, and after having examined the invalid, made out a very long and complicated prescription. I happened to be in the sick room when the mixture arrived from the chemists, and I noticed that Termosses emptied the whole bottle into a big jug and gave it all at once to his sick son to drink. He then put the bottle back on the table where I was sitting. I glanced at the directions pasted on the bottle and was alarmed to see that a dessert spoon only of this medicine was to be taken three times a day; and here Termosses had given his son the whole of the fairly big bottle at once.

"Being greatly astonished, I expressed my concern to Termosses; he only said laughing: 'Don't be alarmed, my dear fellow, it's nothing serious.'

"Taking a seat beside me he explained as follows: 'The medicines of our physicians are of two kinds. You must always be a little careful with the first kind, because, although it very seldom occurs, and usually only by mistake, yet it does sometimes happen, that something poisonous to the organism is contained in it. Anybody, however, can instantly recognize this dangerous kind of medicine, because there is always a skull and cross-bones on the bottle. As for their other medicines, they are all alike. They have different names, but they are all taken from the same barrel, whatever the disease or the dozens of learned words on the prescriptions; only sometimes, for variety, something harmless is put into them to change the color or taste. At worst, you might get a little stomach ache on taking these medicines of the second kind, that is, a quickened action of the bowels; but a purge, as everybody knows, is absolutely necessary in every case.'

"And, indeed, towards the evening, his son got such a diarrhea from this mixture that he was empty. He was quite well, however, the following day, proving that his illness must have been due to the clogging of the stomach. As the prescription was made, of course, in ignorance of the precise cause of the illness and had nothing to do with the real cause, it was only thanks to the system of this queer fellow Termosses that the young man was so quickly cured and out of bed.

"I was told about these medicines by another being whom I used often to meet for various reasons in one of the capitals of the Russian social organization, where my business often took me during my sixth descent. He was a pharmacist. Beings of this profession keep shops where they sell the numerous varieties of medicines which these Earth physicians prescribe or advise for their patients. This pharmacist was an old acquaintance of mine. He had no whims, but he was a very good sort of being and very kind to everybody about him. By religion he was Jewish. Nobody knows why, but on all the continents of that planet, the profession of pharmacist is followed chiefly by beings of the Jewish faith. When I happened to be in his town, I always used to go to his shop and chat with him at the back, which room he called his laboratory.

"Once when I dropped in as usual, I found him in his laboratory pounding something in a mortar, and I asked him what he was doing. He said he was crushing burnt sugar for a prescription; and he showed me a piece of paper, on which was written the prescription of a certain remedy, very well known on that planet, and called Dover's powder.

"On Earth this powder is used chiefly for coughs, and was invented by English physician named Dover; hence its name.

"I read the prescription he gave to me, and saw that no sugar, and certainly no burnt sugar was included in it. I looked a little puzzled, of course, whereupon he laughingly said:

"'Certainly there is no sugar in the prescription, but a certain percentage of opium instead. But this Dover's powder happens to be our most popular remedy, and it is used by nearly all the peoples of our vast Russia. They use hundreds of thousands of packets every day. But the opium which ought to be in it, is not, as you know, the cheap variety and if real opium were used, the opium alone would cost from six to eight kopeks a packet; and we pharmacists have to sell this powder for three or five kopeks a packet. And again, suppose we could collect all the opium in the world, we should be still in the same fix. There would not be enough for Russia alone. So instead of the prescription of this Doctor Dover we pharmacists have invented another prescription, containing substances which are profitable and easy for everybody to obtain. We make this powder of soda, burnt sugar and a little quinine. These substances are all cheap; though the quinine is a little expensive. But how much of that is necessary? Only one half percent of quinine is used in the composition of these powders.'

"I couldn't help asking him how he managed it. 'Won't anybody discover that you are giving him 'Solianka' and not Dover's powders?'

"'Certainly not,' laughed my amiable acquaintance. 'It could only be discovered by sight or by taste; and we make our Dover's powder exactly as it should be according to the genuine prescription, in color and taste. You can use any magnifying glass you like and you will find our powder of exactly the same color as if it were made with real opium. And as regards the taste, it cannot be distinguished from the real powder chiefly because of the amount of quinine we put in it.'

"'What about the analysis?' I asked him.

"'What is analysis?' he replied sarcastically. 'A thorough analysis of one powder might cost enough to buy hundreds of pounds of this powder. You could probably open a whole pharmacy on it. And nobody would be so silly for the sake of three or five kopeks worth of powder. To tell the truth, moreover, you can nowhere get the analysis you are thinking of. There are, of course, analytic chemists in every town and even every municipality employs such analysts. But what do they amount to? Perhaps you do not know what it is these specialists know and how they are trained and how they come to fill such responsible posts. I will tell you. For instance, there is some Mama's darling, a young man who has a pimpled face, because his Mama being cultured considered it immoral to tell her son about certain things. The young man, not having as yet any consciousness of his own, acts according to what acts in him; with the result that there appear on his face the pimples well known to medicine. He studies at some University or other to become a chemist; and he naturally reads the books manufactured by German savants.

"'By the way these German drones have the habit of compiling books on all the branches of what they call science. As chemical analysis is one of them, these German savants have accumulated an enormous quantity of books on this subject. And most of the European nations, as well as, other countries, refer to them.

"'So, my dear friend, these analyses are made by this young man who has completed his training and therefore, of course, studied these German books containing the composition of various substances and all the fantastic formulae of their elements.

"'The appearance of those substances when they contain all their elements are described in these books, and also their appearance when some of their elements are missing.

"'Though it is all, of course, a long way from the actual

truth several homely methods of recognizing substances are mentioned, as for instance, sight, taste, burning, and in fact those ways which our grandmothers heard from olden times.

"'Having finished his training, our young man is entitled to call himself an analytic chemist; but sometimes, before taking a responsible post, he does some practical work, by which is usually meant that he serves a term at a slaughter house, as assistant to the local chemist. The Mama's darling ascertains with a microscope, by means known only to himself, whether there is trichina in the pork; after which, as soon as a vacancy occurs he is given an official post.

"'Suppose that such an official analytic chemist is given one of our Dover's powders to analyze. Having got it, looked at it, and tasted it, just like any ordinary mortal he at once recognizes it as Dover's powder, or possibly the sender told him. The first thing he must do is to take from his table the pharmaceutical guide, also compiled by Germans, which every official chemist analyst must have; and here he looks for the place where the formulae of powders are given. As Dover's powder is known everywhere, he will certainly find it in the book. Our estimable chemist analyst then takes from the table a form, on which his official title is printed, and writes: 'The powder sent me for analysis, proves to be, from its composition, Dover's powder. During my analysis there were found in it . . . ' and he proceeds to copy the formula from his German Pharmaceutical guide. Of course, he takes care to raise or diminish the figures a trifle, so as not to give himself away altogether.

"'And he does it all this way, firstly, in order to let everybody know that he has written it, not just anyhow, but after a real analysis; and secondly, because the city pharmacist, whatever else he may be, is also an official. I imagine that few people like to make enemies in the town where they live. The completed form is dispatched to the sender of the powder, while the famous chemist analyst himself remains quite calm. He knows that nobody will know that he has made no analysis at all and no one will be able to check him, first, because he is the only official chemist analyst in the town; and secondly, even if the powder were taken to another town, to some other wonderful chemist, nothing terrible would happen. Are there no other Dover's powders in the world? And the particular one he analyzed no longer exists; because he naturally had to destroy it in making his analysis. No, my dear fellow, I don't think you would find anybody who would kick up all that fuss for three kopeks worth of Dover's Powder.

"'Anyhow I have been making these powders according to our prescription for thirty years, and naturally selling them; and so far there has not been a single case of trouble about them.

"'There cannot be, because everybody knows Dover's powders, and that they are very good for colds. And that is quite enough. All that is required of a remedy is that it should be reputed to be a good remedy. As regards its composition and how it should be made—what does it matter what is put into it? In any case, nobody can ever be helped. Faith only can help man; and if this powder is called Dover's, that is enough. You can cure anybody of anything only provided he believes in the remedy, or in whatever it is that is said to be good for his complaint. Besides, all our prescriptions now are really better than the originals, if only because they contain no harmful substance. The prescription of Doctor Dover, for instance, contains a very deleterious substance, namely, opium; and you know the peculiarity of opium. If a man takes it often, even in small doses, his organism will soon be so used to it that if he should stop taking it, he will suffer a good deal. But from the powder made according to our prescription, nothing like this can happen, because it contains neither opium nor any other injurious matter. It can be taken as often as you like without any ill effects.

"'In fact, my dear fellow, everybody, so to speak, ought to shout it on the housetops: "Hurrah! for the new prescription of Dover's powders."'"

CHAPTER XXXII

The Hypnotism

SO, MY dear Hassein, I decided to become a physician; not, however, an ordinary physician, but what they call a physician hypnotist, there being a great demand for such physicians in most of the continents and amongst all classes. Ordinary physicians rarely inspire the confidence and sincerity which I required for my purpose; and besides, I had already had a wide experience in this specialty, having before practiced among Earth-beings as a physician hypnotist.

"Grandfather, dear," said Hassein, "Please explain what hypnotism is."

"Hypnotism," began Beelzebub, "is the name these beings give to that property from which all their peculiarities proceed. This property is the feature which distinguishes their psyche from the psyche of all the other beings of the whole Universe.

"If these beings did not exist, then this property of hypnotism would also not exist in the whole Universe. Their whole life, moreover, moves, as it were, under a spell. The only difference is that in life the hypnotic condition moves slowly and gradually; and only when it is accelerated do the very obvious absurdities called 'hypnotism' arise.

"You can tell or show a being in his hypnotic state, anything you please, he will immediately believe it. He does not arrive at this belief in the usual gradual manner, but he at once becomes convinced for the rest of his life. Suppose, for instance, you show a flea to a being in that state and tell him it is a rhinoceros he will believe that is really a rhinoceros; and not only will this belief and understanding last while he is in that state, but afterwards when it has completely passed. Moreover, whenever they see a flea, it will really seem to them to be a rhinoceros. You can try all you like by ordinary means and logic to convince them otherwise—they will always continue to think that the flea is indeed a rhinoceros, and never doubt it. The more you try to prove the contrary, the more positive and convinced they become. The only other thing of which they will be equally certain is that you are eager to deceive them; and they will probably get offended and angry.

"It is quite possible to bring these beings into this accelerated hypnotic state by artificial means. Indeed having accidentally discovered this property of theirs and also accidentally how to induce this state in each other, they use it as a means of freeing themselves from certain too obvious and transparent absurdities. By chance, they also discovered that anybody in this state can be persuaded of the contrary of anything.

"For inducing this state, which as I have already said, they call 'hypnotism' they, by chance, found a certain means. The counter process of convincing others being called 'suggestion.' And those physicians who know how to induce this state in others, are called 'hypnotists' to distinguish them from ordinary physicians.

"Information regarding this property, its process and significance, has become amongst them, at the present time, a very well known science; and, as about everything else, they have, of course, hundreds of fantastic theories about it. Equally, there are thousands of books written on the subject. So far, however, not one of them knows what kind of property hypnotism really is or how it is produced in them.

"If I explain why this special property is produced amongst these unfortunate beings and what it is, you must try your best to understand it, because, as I have already told you, this particular property is unique in the whole Universe. Well, the chief reason for their possession of this peculiarity is that these unfortunate beings have two kinds of consciousness resulting from the exceptional environmental conditions created on that planet in which they are developed and educated.

These two kinds of consciousness are as follows: first, their real consciousness, common to all the beings in the whole Universe including the beings of all other forms on this same planet, for example, animals, birds, fish and so on; but in addition to this real consciousness, these strange biped beings have yet another, a secondary consciousness, not their own, but derived from outside and formed temporarily in them, an extraneous one, or how shall I say it, a consciousness foreign to them. Even their brains have been gradually adapted by Nature, and now contain independent regions in which are recorded every perception and impression for both these two kinds of consciousness.

"Their real consciousness, as in other beings, belongs to their essence; but the other consciousness is acquired during life. As I have already told you this is due to the established environmental conditions of their development and education. It is as if in the brains of these beings two kinds of thoughts exist—one, their real thoughts, proper to every being, that is, the thoughts of his essence, the other foreign thoughts which have nothing in common with him.

"Finding both these forms of consciousness in themselves, these beings call the first 'consciousness' and the other 'subconsciousness' to distinguish them.

"But what they call their subconsciousness is in reality just their real consciousness; while what they call their consciousness is something quite different, which has nothing in common with their own essence, being merely the totality of the perceptions which they have accidentally and automatically accumulated from their very first birthday. These impressions so collected begin to think the thoughts, not of their real essence, but by and of themselves; which thoughts being foreign, have no connection whatever with their essence nor with any of its real functions. They continue to be formed independently without any connection with their essence; and having been thus independently acquired and being foreign to their real essence, they can be easily displaced or changed by any chance event. This is why these beings acquire an entirely subjective character, independent of their essence, having, according to law, no connection with the common objectivity, that is with the Nature in which they exist. They have, in consequence, not as yet acquired even with their real consciousness, and in all the many centuries since their creation, any will of their own, nor any logical thinking; and even the ability to employ common sense is quite absent in them.

"Hence you tell such a consciousness that it is so; then without either reflection or question, the being will take it on faith, and be firmly convinced that it is not only so but cannot be otherwise.

"Having, as I said," continued Beelzebub, "discovered this peculiarity of theirs, and accidentally found the means of inducing this hypnotic state in each other, they have recently begun to use it for healing; and the beings professionally so engaged, are called 'doctors hypnotists.' I could be a very good Hypnotist, myself, because during my former experiments upon these beings I discovered several methods of which the ordinary practitioners have never even dreamed; although, it is true, they have recently discovered a few new methods, all, however, based on one and the same principle.

"They know only one principle for inducing this state. Their chief method consists in making their patients look fixedly on a shining object; and, in fact, by this method some beings really are cast into this hypnotic states. This happens because as the two kinds of consciousness are formed in these beings, a separate circulation of the blood for each consciousness is established in the organism, that is to say, two modes of blood circulation are formed: one mode, when the center of gravity of the filling up of the blood vessels is in one part of the blood vessels, that is to say, where the filling of the stream is greatest; and the other mode when the center of gravity is in another part of the blood stream. Each form of blood circulation is produced by its particular consciousness, or vice versa, each form produces its own mode of consciousness. One form produces what they call consciousness, and the other, subconsciousness. Strictly speaking these beings are only really conscious when they are subconscious.

"When a being looks fixedly on a shining object, certain muscles are tensed, and if, at the same time, a certain concentration of thought and feeling is brought about, the blood circulation is changed and the former mode passes into another, that is, into that of the waking state, or his customary acquired consciousness. When the form of blood circulation is changed, the being's subconsciousness, as they call it, is manifested, in short, passes into an unusual non-waking state. And since in their consciousness neither criticism nor comparison exists, both being acquired only by the essence of the beings from their former perceptions and impressions; it follows that beings in this state believe everything they are told and take it exactly as given. This state they sometimes call a trance, or it is sometimes otherwise said, the being becomes a 'medium.' He carries out in a waking state all that is suggested to him by beings as well as by inanimate objects.

"The whole trick of such a physician hypnotist lies in the skill with which he consciously or unconsciously changed the forms of the circulation of their blood. By practice I became skillful in changing it simply by stopping the flow of the blood in certain of the vessels. This method of mine is the most uniformly successful. By means of their method, for instance, gazing on a shining object, and others, they do indeed attain concentration of thought and feeling, but they cannot induce the hypnotic state in everybody.

"It cannot be induced, for instance, in those beings called 'hysterical.' But by means of my manipulation of the blood vessels this state can be induced in any biped being you please, and even on certain beings of other forms, quadrupeds, fish etc.

CHAPTER XXXIII

Beelzebub; Professional Hypnotist

I BEGAN my career as a healer in the center of the continent of Asia, in Turkestan. Here, owing to the prevalence of the two very pernicious habits, there was a great demand for physician hypnotists like myself, to whom people could go for treatment.

"These two habits were, smoking of opium, and the chewing of anasha, or, as other places call it hashish. Opium is obtained from the seed of the poppy plant; anasha is derived from the plant, hemp; and likewise from its seeds. When those beings who have acquired the habit of taking this opium and hashish come clearly to realize their bad effect, they decide to cease indulging in them, but after repeated attempts to do so by themselves they ultimately become convinced that they cannot do it alone. If they hear that there is a physician that can cure them of the evil, they apply to him.

"So I decided to make use of my profession for the purpose of visiting likely places for observation and experiments and to associate with various beings on several continents. One of these days I might perhaps understand the strange psyche, which interested me so much, of these beings who populate the planet Earth. For the better direction of my observation, I thought it well to collect special statistics of the psyche of all kinds of beings. As I have already said, I began my healing practice in the center of Turkestan, and gradually moved from town to town in a westerly direction. I very soon became a benefactor of beings of Earth, and many of them even began to call me a savior. Owing to these activities of mine, I soon became known all over the country.

"Moving thus from place to place, I eventually arrived in what is called Russian Turkestan where the first of the pernicious habits, that is the smoking of opium, had almost disappeared. As for the second habit the chewing of Anasha, it was chiefly spread amongst beings of the Boukharin 'Khanstar'; but among the remaining population of Russian Turkestan it existed only among the 'Sarts' and 'Taviks.' For that very reason, however the third evil flourished there, that is, the drinking of Russian vodka, a liquid obtained from potatoes or wheat, which not only makes the already abnormal psyche of the beings quite imbecile, but produces very bad effects on their organism.

"Beings loved me everywhere and looked upon me as a messenger from God Himself, but the local doctors everywhere hated me, since I was a dangerous rival. They had indeed cause for hating me. During my hours of consultation, hundreds of beings came every day; and many could not see me and all the while the doctors might be waiting weeks for paying patients, and nobody came. And on that planet it is almost impossible to live without money.

"I found my profession still more interesting on account of a novel and strange reason, that is, the sincere gratitude, both of those who were saved and their near relatives. I was much affected by their gratitude and could not refuse to help any applicant. I worked very hard; and the incessant work eventually fatigued me and I decided to rest a while. But how to arrange it I did not know. The trouble was that in that country almost everybody knew me personally or had heard of me; and everybody wished to consult me either about himself or his relative in connection with these pernicious habits. I could not remain there and do nothing. I began to wonder where I could take a rest without returning to the planet Mars; and eventually I decided to go to the continent Africa, where, you remember I told you, was a country called 'Nilia,' now called Egypt. Well, it was to Egypt I decided to go. For some unknown reason, beings all over that planet have lately come to regard this country as a good place for resting; and wealthy beings from all continents go there. So I soon started for Egypt.

"Having arrived in Egypt, I stayed in a town called Cairo. And there I soon so arranged things so as to provide the rest which was so necessary for me after so much intensive work. Amongst other things it was a part of my program to walk every morning in the direction of the ancient Sphinx and pyramids. I stayed in Egypt, in this manner, about two weeks, and once during a walk near the pyramids an elderly being approached me and addressed me as 'doctor.' Whether he knew of me before in his native country, or whether he had heard in Cairo, that I was a doctor, I do not know. During my sixth descent on that planet everybody called me doctor. These beings call all physicians, doctors. About this word 'doctor' I will also tell you, because this word is one of those memorable things which remain in my essence like an unpleasant sediment.

"It seems that this word also was invented by Germans, who use it, so to say, for labeling a certain degree of merit among their beings. Now, however, the word has become the common name for physicians everywhere with the result that the causes of confusion have been multiplied. And certainly, this was not necessary; they have plenty without them and, in fact, these causes ought to be diminished. Even I, a being, one might say, cast in a different mold, made an unpardonably stupid mistake on account of this word doctor.

"This misunderstanding arose thus: Towards the end of my stay on that planet, I lived in a certain large European town. In the room adjoining mine, in the hotel where I lived, were a very friendly couple who had been recently married. I happened to become acquainted with this couple and they often invited me to their room, as they say there, for tea. Even without their invitation I used sometimes to call on them in order to shorten the long winter's evenings.

"This couple were expecting their first-born. One day I heard a nervous rapping on the wall between our apartments; and I instantly ran to their door. The husband it seemed was away somewhere for the day; and the wife having fallen ill, she had half unconsciously called for me. When I came she felt a little better, but she urgently begged me to fetch a doctor at once.

Naturally I set off for one at once; and it was only when I had got into the street that I began to wonder where I should go.

Suddenly I remembered that not far from our hotel lived a being whom everybody called doctor. On his door was a metal plate on which the word doctor was engraved below his name. He was dining when I arrived and his maid therefore asked me to wait a little in the drawing room. She explained that dinner would soon be over, and the doctor would then be free. I took a seat in the drawing room, and waited for him, but, of course, with great impatience. I sat as if on burning coals because I was very anxious about my neighbor's condition. Still the doctor did not appear. About twenty minutes passed. I could restrain myself no longer and rang. When the maid entered I asked her to remind the doctor of me and tell him that I was in a great hurry and could wait no longer.

"She went away. Five more minutes passed. Eventually the doctor appeared. I briefly explained what I wanted, at which he began to laugh very heartily. Only when his hysterical laughter finally subsided, was he able to tell me that he regretted that he was not a doctor of medicine, but of philosophy. It was as if for the second time, the judgment of our ENDLESSNESS was passed on me. I immediately ran away from the house of this doctor of philosophy.

"A taxi happened to pass as I came into the street, and as I got into it, I thought, 'Where now?'

I then remembered that in the cafe which I used to frequent, there was nearly always to be found a being whom everybody called doctor. I ordered the driver to hurry to this cafe, but there a waiter I knew told me that this doctor had just been and gone with acquaintances. The waiter had overheard them say that they were off to a certain restaurant, the name of which he told me. Although this restaurant was rather a long way off, I ordered the taxi to take me there, since I knew of no other doctor.

"It took us half an hour to get to this restaurant, where we very soon found the doctor. But on this occasion he turned out to be a 'doctor of jurisprudence.' I was now in a pretty fix. But at last I ventured to speak to the head waiter of the restaurant, and told him just what I wanted. He turned out to be a very good sort; and he not only explained things to me but even accompanied me to a certain doctor—but this time an accoucheur—whom we luckily found at home; and who, moreover, was kind enough to go with me at once. But before we arrived my poor neighbor had already given birth to her first born a son—and with no help had managed to swathe the child and was already sleeping profoundly after her terrible pain.

"Ever since, I cannot bear to hear the word 'doctor'; and I advise everybody to use the word only in anger.

"Well, as I was saying, my dear Hassein, this elderly gentleman called me doctor, as everybody respectfully addressed me, without, of course, knowing how offensive it sounded in my ears, and how much I disliked it. And having addressed me by this odious title, he very amiably said 'perhaps you will allow me to accompany you on your walks?"

"'I have noticed' he continued, 'that you often walk alone in these places in the morning. As I also like walking here in the morning, and am quite lonely here in Egypt, I determined to ask if you would be kind enough to let me walk with you.'

"As this being seemed to be very kind and sympathetic, I

began to take my morning walks with him. He turned out to be a Russian and a very important being in his native land.

"During our walks we chanced to talk mostly about the weak will of the beings on the Earth, and about those harmful vices into which they so readily fall, and which become imperative needs in the organism.

"During one of our walks, he suddenly said to me, 'My dear doctor, in Russia my native land, the passion for alcohol is so strong and has become so widely spread through recent years that, indubitably it will finally destroy the social forms established for centuries; and reduce my dear fatherland back to barbarism. Becoming aware of this, some far seeing Russians met together to consider how best to avert these consequences. And they decided to form a society for the purpose and to call it, 'The Society for preserving Public Sobriety'; and I was elected its President.

"The activities of this society, in organizing methods for combating this stated evil, are just now at their height. A great deal has already been done by the society in the direction of education, and it is hoped to do still more. All the same, my dear doctor, if you ask me my frank opinion of the probable results, I should have to confess that, although I am at the head of this work, there is nothing good to say about it. My only hope personally nowadays is that a miracle may happen.

"The whole trouble, in my opinion, is that this society is public. Its organization and the solution of its problems depend on a number of groups of people, all of which have their own aims and wishes regarding them. The result is that there is a great deal of discussion at the expense of actual work and my fatherland naturally suffers for it.

"There in Russia I naturally thought a good deal about it, but I could get no light on the situation; and here, where I came especially to rest, I cannot escape my gloomy thoughts, neither by day or by night. I consulted many people in Russia and made enquiries where I could find people who knew something on the subject of alcoholism. I heard, in fact, about you during my enquiries, and that you were an authority on the cure of alcoholism and other forms of weakness of will; and I intended to consult you. Having met you by accident, and had many talks with you about the evil habits of men, an idea occurred to me yesterday, which I considered the whole evening and finally decided to put to you today. My idea was to ask whether you would consent to come to my fatherland. I am sure you will not refuse. You have convinced me during your talks of your philanthropy, and I am sure, therefore, that you will come and perhaps save millions of men. You shall go with me and see everything for yourself. Then perhaps your experience will enable us to organize in such a way that our society will accomplish for my fatherland the object for which it was founded.

"After thinking a while I replied to what the friendly being had said, as follows: 'It is quite possible that I may accept your invitation to go to Russia, since Russia may be more suitable for my aim.

"'At the present time,' I continued, 'I have only one aim, that is to know more about the psyche of man, not only of men individually, but of men collectively. And Russia seems to be very favorable since the disease alcoholism is spread amongst almost the whole population, and in such a way as to afford opportunities for experimenting upon men in masses.

"After my talk with this important being, I prepared for my journey, and some days later, we left Egypt together. After a few weeks traveling we arrived in the capital of Russia, the city of St. Petersburg. My new acquaintance at once threw himself into his affairs which during his long absence had greatly accumulated, for, in addition to his other affairs in St. Petersburg, he was busy preparing for the inaugural opening of a big building, now nearly finished, which had been erected by the Society for Combating Alcoholism.

"I decided to use my time to become acquainted with the beings of that town, and also to arrange a chemical laboratory where I could make my chemico-physical experiments on the psyche of these incomprehensible beings. This latter plan of mine could not unfortunately be carried out on account of the idiotic regulations then in force. The trouble on that planet is that you can do anything, and have even a thousand laboratories, but if any proposal could jeopardize the smug social tranquility upon which the quietude of the group of beings exercising power at the moment depends, then it is almost impossible to carry it out.

"At the same time, a laboratory was impossible without official permission, since 'laboratory' also described the rooms in which revolutionaries manufactured bombs against their oppressors, that is, against those in power. Not realizing how difficult it was to get a laboratory of one's own on that planet, and seeing that a laboratory was very necessary for me, I began to take steps to get official sanction.

"I made the great mistake of trying to obtain this permit according to rules as such permits are obtained on all the other planets. Unfortunately I only realized much later that this permit could be obtained not according to the rules, but like everything else done on that planet, that is, without rules. Rules do, of course, exist on that planet, but the psyche of the beings themselves being peculiar, the rules must be obeyed in a peculiar way, and not after the usual fashion. In short, one must act, not according to rule, but according to custom, or according to the manner laid down by some cunning beings for their personal profit.

"My failure to obtain my permit arose in the following way. According to the rules laid down, it was necessary to obtain permission to have a private laboratory, and this permission was given at the discretion of a government department.

I made the mistake of applying to the department, whose business it was to issue such permits. The trouble began when it turned out that nobody in the department knew what the procedure was. Naturally nobody knew, seeing that nobody had ever applied to them; and they had not acquired by practice the routine of the procedure. Yet there were thousands of laboratories in that town; and all of them must certainly have obtained the permit required by law, since the police inspection of permits in that town was organized, and in certain social organizations the sole duties of the police consist in such inspection. I learned afterwards that such a phenomenon is quite in the order of things on that planet even with their own functions, such as thought, feeling, the sexual function and so on.

"It began with this: when I came to this department and applied for this permission, all the clerks looked at each other in bewilderment. They began to rummage in books and to question each other. Eventually the heads of the department requested me to bring them certain information from some other department, upon which began an endless perambulation from one department to another, and from one office to another. For instance, from the police I went to the parish priest, thence almost to the town's midwife, from the police headquarters to the medical department, and so on and so forth. Everywhere it was necessary to answer certain questions and to sign certain papers. In one place I had to answer questions having nothing to do with chemistry and in another I was advised how to handle equipment in a laboratory so as not to poison myself. In a third they tried to dissuade me from setting up a laboratory at all because, during work in laboratories, explosions or something similar always occur. I don't know how the business of getting the permit would have ended if, after having wasted nearly three months of my time I had not given up the whole absurd affair. And I was compelled to do so for a very amusing reason. Owing to the same senseless delay, a certificate from a doctor was required, testifying that my presence in the laboratory would not endanger my personal health, and for this purpose I had to see a doctor. He proposed at once to examine me very thoroughly, and insisted that I should undress, so that he could tap me everywhere with his little hammer. But I could not agree to that for worlds. On no account would I show myself naked, since in that case, I should have revealed the tail which I usually ingeniously concealed in the folds of my dress.

"Had anybody seen my tail they would certainly have concluded that I was not a being of their planet; and I should never have been able to remain amongst them at all to satisfy my curiosity concerning their psyche. So I left the doctor and thenceforward ceased trying to get a permit.

"During all that time my acquaintance, the important Russian used to come to see me, and I was also at his house several times. He always discussed Russian alcoholism and the measures for combating the evil. I also had had time to become well acquainted with the peculiarities of the psyche of the Russian beings, and would often give him my opinion on the organization of the work. He attached great importance to my advice and observations, both on the future as well as on the past, and was very pleased with my comments and with the justice of my remarks. In turn, he reported my suggestions to the general council of the society, by whom they were almost unanimously adopted.

"But the doctors, who also had a voice in the work of carrying out these decisions, opposed the majority of useful measures. More particularly later, when they learned that the initiative in certain cases proceeded from me, a physician not of their association, they persistently organized the opposition to all my suggestions. As I have already told you, it seems that the associative spirit is very strongly developed among them. I was not a Russian physician, that is, one who had the official diploma of the Russian School in his pocket; and hence, I could not belong to their association. However good the advice I might give or the suggestions I might make they meant nothing to them. As I was not a Russian doctor, all my advice was, in their opinion, quackery.

"In spite of the fact that the head of the society was heart and soul devoted to me, and saw hope only in following my advice, he could do nothing. My suggestions were all defeated and nothing was decided in their place. When I was finally convinced that there was no further need for me to remain there, I prepared to leave, much to the regret of my acquaintance, this important Russian, and some other beings who wished their country well.

"During those days they prepared to open the newly built house. This house was named after their Czar, and was called 'The People's House of Nicholas II.' My acquaintance begged me to wait a little so that after the inauguration and formal opening, he would be free to accompany me for a little rest after the worries of the preceding days. For this reason I delayed my departure for several days.

"On the day of the opening, at which the Czar himself was present, my acquaintance spoke to him about me, with the result that it was arranged that I should be presented to the Czar. My acquaintance was particularly delighted with this, because on that planet, a presentation to a sovereign is considered a very great honor. And my acquaintance obviously desired to do me this great favor, as a sop to his conscience, since he considered himself alone responsible for my visit in that capital.

"Some days after the opening of the 'People's House,' on looking out of the window of my apartment one morning, I saw an unusual activity in the street. All the residents were cleaning and sweeping up everywhere and there were many police about. When I asked my servant the cause of it all, he explained that an important general was expected that day; and later in the day, while I was talking to a friend of mine, the concierge came running to me in a very agitated state, to say that this important general wished to see me.

"When this important general entered my room, he sat down, leisurely, and began to talk at first about trifles, as these beings usually do. We discussed the weather, the attitude of a certain king to some question or other, and of course we discussed the nightingales of Kursk. Afterwards, also without haste, he said:

"'You are soon to be presented to the Czar, and as I superintend these affairs, I have come to explain what you must do on that occasion.'

"He then described for me the necessary movements, after which he also informed me that, in the Tsarkoe Selo, he would accompany me everywhere and show me everything in detail on the spot. He over and over again insisted that I should say nothing to the Czar, but what he himself would write. Having explained all this, his super Excellency departed.

"On the day of the presentation, the same important general met me as soon as I stepped out of the train and from that moment, as Mullah Nassr Eddin would say in such a case: 'I began to dance to his tune.'

"Walking by my side the whole time, he instructed me and told me, in every case, what I should do and how I must act; how to move, how to turn, how to speak, ask, and do everything else, and, in short, he entirely took the place of my 'I' in me. Of what happened in the apartment itself, where I had my meeting with the Czar, there is nothing to say. In short, my every step and every word were shown me. Only when at last I got into the train did that important general leave me in peace. I was so busy the whole day performing the innumerable stupid antics demanded of me, that I grew so weary, on account of my age, that I did not even notice how the Czar looked on that day, or how he behaved in the comedy.

"From the station, I naturally went straight home. The next day the fun commenced. The result of my presentation was—how can I tell you—as if I had been reborn and had become another being. My whole external life, as well as my importance, changed for absolutely everybody. I was at once important, clever, remarkable, powerful, extraordinary and so on and so forth. For instance, the proprietor of the shop where I bought my provisions every morning before I went to business, insisted on delivering my purchases for me. All the policemen on duty in the street, and who already knew that I was a foreign physician, saluted me from a distance as if I were a great general.

"When I returned home the same day, one important official brought me, for my unfortunate laboratory, the permit for which I had pined for three months. On the same day I received four more permissions from various ministries and departments, and ultimately, from all the departments to which I had applied during the period of my troubles. The proprietors, shopkeepers, children, and all the neighbors became as attentive to me as if I proposed to leave each of them a fortune. I afterwards discovered, this unfortunate Czar had himself to be prepared whenever he was to meet some strange being; and such meetings occurred almost every day, and sometimes several on the same day. It might be a parade, or an ambassador from some other king, or a delegation in the morning; in the evening, presentations like mine; and then discussions with the representatives of the people and so on and so forth.

"On every occasion he must talk or make a speech. At the same time every word he uttered had to be carefully weighed from every aspect, because the least word of the Czar might have important consequences, not only upon his own subjects but also upon all the subjects of all the other kings of the whole planet. Not having enough facts to go on, and not having a mind capable of dealing with unforeseen cases, these Czars employ beings whose duty it is to instruct them, what and how, they must speak and act. The Czar must certainly remember everything told him; and in order to remember he must practice. The meaning of practice I quite understood when I had to prepare for my own presentation to this Russian Czar.

"But for me, this preparation was only once necessary during the whole of my existence, and I personally have not the slightest desire in the world to stand in the shoes of an Earth king, nor would I wish my worst enemy, or the enemy of my nearest relatives, to be an Earth king under the conditions which now exist, least of all if he has not a mind capable of getting at the truth for himself whenever necessary.

"Soon after my presentation to the Russian Czar, I left St. Petersburg. There was no sense in remaining where the beings had no wish to make the least use of my experience and knowledge concerning the question which interested me for which I had come. On the contrary certain beings began to hate me.

"I returned to Turkestan, and visited some neighboring countries; and only visited St. Petersburg again after several Earth years, but then I went on other affairs."

CHAPTER XXXIV

(Bath) Russia. Old Russia And The Cause Of The New

A LITTLE later Hassein, with a voice expressing pained tenderness, turned to Beelzebub:

"Grandfather! Dear Grandfather! Manifest please aloud those informations which you have in your common presence particularly dear to me, and which you have learned during your long existence and which may serve me as material for the elucidation of that question which has just arisen in my essence, and even for the approximate representation of which I have as yet positively no data for a logical confrontation in any of the spiritualized parts of my common presence.

"This question arising in my essence, the answer to which has already become necessary to the whole of my presence, consists in this: To inquire about the reasons why, namely, if these unfortunate three-brained beings who breed on the planet Earth do not have the possibility, owing to reasons not depending on themselves, of acquiring and having in the period of their responsible existence Divine Objective Reason, why since they arose so long ago and their species has continued to exist such a long time, could not those customs have been gradually formed by now, only thanks to the flow of time, in the process of their ordinary existence even under those abnormal conditions, and those proper 'instinctive-automatic-habits' have been acquired in the presences of every being in general, thanks to which their ordinary existence, both 'egoistically personal' as well as 'collectively general,' might flow more or less tolerably in the sense of objective reality?"

Having said this, our poor Hassein began questioningly to gaze at the Cause of the Cause of his arising.

At the question of his favorite grandson, Beelzebub began to relate the following:

"Why of course . . . my dear boy. In the course of long centuries of their existence, and among them as everywhere on planets where beings arise who spend likewise part of the time of their existence simply in the ordinary process, many customs and also what are called 'moral habits,' at times very good and useful for their ordinary existence, were also gradually formed, and even at the present time are sometimes formed among several of their groupings; but herein lies the evil, that such a being-welfare as becomes fixed in the process of ordinary existence from the flow of time alone, and which improves thanks to transmission from generation to generation, also soon either entirely disappears or is changed to such a direction that these happy achievements of theirs are transformed of their own accord into 'unhappy' ones and increase the number of those small factors maleficent for them, the totality of which year by year 'dilutes,' more and more, both their psyche as well as their very essence.

"If they were even to possess and were to use at least those 'trifles' worthy of the three-brained beings, then this would already be to the good for them, or as they themselves would say, 'would-in-any-case-be-better-than-nothing.'

"Of course, if at least any of these good customs, fixed by them in the process of their existence, and already automatized 'moral habits' could have survived and been transformed by inheritance into the mode of existence of their subsequent generations, then thanks at least to this, their, in the objective sense, 'desolate' existence would have seemed to be, to an outside impartial observer, at least a little reconcilable.

"The causes of the complete destruction and change of even this being-welfare for their tolerable existence achieved by time, both of good customs as well as 'moral usages,' are of course also engendered by these abnormal conditions for the ordinary being-existence around them established by them themselves.

"As a concentrated result flowing from these abnormal conditions around them and which became the basic cause for this evil of theirs, there is a special property which arose not long ago in their psyche which they themselves call 'suggestibility.'

"Thanks to this strange property which had only recently become fixed in their psyche, all the functionings in their common presences began gradually to change, and as a result, each of them, particularly the beings who arose and became responsible during the last centuries of theirs, already began to represent in themselves such a peculiar cosmic formation as has in itself the possibility of acting exclusively only if it were to find itself constantly under the influence of another formation similar to itself.

"And indeed, my boy, at the present time, these three-brained beings who please you, must already as separate persons as well as entire large and small groupings, infallibly 'influence' or find themselves under the 'influence' of others.

"For your better representation and all-round understanding in what way customs and automatic habits useful for their ordinary existence acquired by them during centuries also disappear without a trace, or change for the worst on account of the mentioned property of their strange psyche, we will take as an example just these same terrestrial three-brained beings with their customs whom all other beings of your planet call 'Russians' and who represent the majority of that community named Russia.

"In consequence of the fact that the existence of beings which had been put as a basis of the formation of this large contemporary community there and of their subsequent generations, proceeded in the course of many centuries in the neighborhood of beings who belonged to those Asiatic communities, who, thanks to various events, existed so relatively long a period in consequence of which in the process of their ordinary existence—as this in general happens from a long existence—very many good customs and 'moral habits' were gradually formed by themselves and became fixed in the process of their ordinary existence, then these Russians, after meeting with the beings of these, for terrestrial beings, ancient communities and even at times having friendly mutual relationships with them, gradually adopted and began to use in the process of their ordinary existence, many of the useful customs and 'moral habits.'

"And so, my boy, thanks to the mentioned strange property of the three-brained beings of this planet of yours, which property, as I have already told you, arose and gradually became, soon after the Tikliamishian civilization, fixed in their general psyche—the intensity of the fixing proceeded chiefly in consequence of all the more deteriorating conditions around them of ordinary being-existence established by themselves—and which special psychic property already from the very beginning became obligatorily inherent in the common presences of beings composing this later largest community there, then on account of all this, they all in former centuries found themselves under the influence of beings of one or other of the Asiatic communities, and all the, as it is called, 'external-mode' and 'psychic-associative-form' of their ordinary existence proceeded also under their influence.

"And so, again in consequence of the fact that in the common presences of the three-brained beings of this planet Earth of yours who dwell on that part of the continent Asia which was called, and until now is called Russia, 'being-Partkdolg-duty' also finally ceased to be actualized, on account of which this, for them, most maleficent property of their psyche, namely, 'suggestibility,' began gradually to increase; and in consequence of the fact that they, thanks to changed circumstances which flowed from always the same terrifying process of periodic reciprocal destruction, existing only on that ill-starred planet, were deprived of the former influence and were compelled, not having the possibility of independent existence, to fall under new influences, they this time fell under the influence of beings of European communities, chiefly of the community which exists there under the name 'France.'

"Since the beings of this community France began automatically to influence the psyche of the beings of the community Russia, and these latter began even to strive to imitate the beings of this community France in everything, thus all the good customs among them which were already present in the process of their existence and those moral habits which had become inherent in them, either half-consciously or automatically taken by them from the beings of ancient Asiatic communities, were gradually forgotten, and new ones—French—acquired.

"Among the customs and automatic moral habits useful for the beings of the community Russia, transmitted to them from the beings of old Asiatic communities, there were thousands of indeed very good ones.

"From these thousands of good customs and useful habits, let us take for example at least two: the custom, after using the first being-food, of chewing what is called 'keva'; and the usage of periodically washing oneself in what are called 'hammams.'

"Keva is a certain mastic prepared from various roots which is chewed after eating and which however long it is chewed hardly ever decomposes, but on the contrary becomes still more elastic.

"This mastic was also invented by a certain being with good Reason who belonged to one of the old Asiatic communities.

"The use of chewing this keva consists in this, that by chewing it, much what is called there on Earth 'saliva and also other substances are formed in beings, which are worked out by their planetary bodies so that their first being-food may be the better and more easily transformed in them, or as they themselves say, so that this food may be the better and more easily 'digested and assimilated.'

"Thanks to this keva their teeth are also strengthened and the cavities in their mouths too are cleaned from the remains of the first food; the use of keva is very necessary for your favorites, particularly for this second purpose, as these remains, not decomposing owing to the chewing of keva, do not give off that disagreeable 'odor' from their mouths which has already become proper particularly to the contemporary three-brained beings there.

The second custom, established during centuries, consists of bathing in a special closed room, where not only the surface of the skin is washed, but the dirt, chiefly in the pores of the skin, is dissolved.

"The Earth-beings are organized by nature in such a way, that the air which feeds their blood, passes both through their lungs and through the pores of their skin.

"From time to time these pores become clogged up, not only with dirt from without, but from the internal secretions of perspiration and the like. And from time to time, it is necessary to remove this dirt.

"For this purpose, Asiatic beings invented this particular bath, having been convinced that by ordinary washing, even with hot water, complete cleansing is impossible. The accumulated oily dirt contained in these pores gradually dissolves when it is slowly heated and then exudes. If it is left in the pores and begins to decompose, the beings give off a disagreeable and specific odor. In fact, owing to this dirt, particularly on the European continent, it was very difficult to exist—especially for me, a being with a very acute sense of smell. To sense every bad odor was real torture. Owing to the dirt in their pores, the beings of each social organization have their own special smell, in addition, of course, to the smell peculiar to all beings on that planet.

"For instance, I could, without any difficulty, recognize the social organization to which any particular being belonged; and by their scent alone, distinguish one being from another. Among those beings, these smells are due to time and the quantity of dirt contained in the pores of the skin.

"The smell given off by some beings who never wash away this dirt is intolerable; in others, the smell depends upon the time the dirt has been in their pores and the degree of its decomposition.

"Fortunately for themselves, their scent does not affect them very disagreeably; at first, because their sense of smell is very undeveloped, and secondly, because they gradually get used to them from always living with them.

"The Russians, as I have already told you, took over the custom of vapor baths from the Asiatic beings; but when they fell under the influence of European beings, namely of the French, they gradually began to abandon it.

"Every wealthy Russian family, for instance, used to have its own vapor bath; but when I was recently in their capital, St. Petersburg, with a population of over two million beings, there were no more than seven or eight baths, and only house-porters and beings from villages staying by chance in the capital for a while, attended them.

"The governing class, or the so-called Russian intelligentsia, have ceased to go to these bath; and if from habit one of them should go, he tries to hide the fact from everybody else. . . How could he possibly go to such a bath! It is not 'intelligent,' but indecent. And it is not 'intelligent' because the most intelligent, that is to say, in their opinion, the French, never go. They are unaware that, acting on their own customs quite as well established, these same French not only never bathed, but never even washed themselves for fear of disarranging their artificial exterior which had cost them so much to arrange.

"The other example I mentioned, the custom of chewing 'keva,' has already disappeared in Russia entirely, on the other hand, this same custom is spreading amongst the beings dwelling on the opposite side of the planet, America. There the consumption of keva is developing so rapidly and is assuming such proportions that its manufacture is now a big branch of American industry.

"It is interesting to observe that the bulk of the keva is imported from that part of Russia called Caucasia, and the existing Caucasian beings must surely wonder why these mad Americans import a root which is good for nothing and for nobody. I saw myself a mother beating her son for chewing keva; she shouted at him, that he would grow up an uncouth, that is, an 'unintelligent' being.

"Russia has recently lost a large number of other good customs, and, in fact, about Russians in general, Mullah Nassr Eddin would say: 'One ought to be very cautious with a turkey'; by which wise saying our highly respected teacher advises us what kind of beings to trust and what not. What our Mullah Nassr Eddin calls 'turkey,' is something which is neither this nor that, but something anomalous; and when he said this, he had in mind three birds, a crow, a peacock and a turkey. In her manners and customs Russia should more closely resemble Asiatic beings, because she was under their influence during long centuries; and it might have been said that she had become Asiatic.

"These Asiatic beings, Mullah Nassr Eddin calls 'crows'; but the European beings, whom Russians now emulate, Mullah Nassr Eddin calls 'peacocks.'

"Russia, desiring to become European, in other words, peacock, naturally left the crows and ceased to be crow. But so far she has not yet become peacock. Hence at the present time, Russia is neither crow nor peacock, but only turkey.

"Although a turkey is used by beings for food, and its flesh is considered to be very good, in fact, the bird is very stupid. It always tries to appear courageous, and consequently often becomes puffed up. It tries to appear courageous even when nobody is looking at it. This it does simply from its own imagination and delusion.

"Amongst all the beings populating that planet, this weakness of changing their good customs is so strong that they can be changed as much as you like. Very little is needed for the good customs and habits acquired through centuries to be entirely forgotten. This is why, in spite of the many centuries of their existence, the beings of that planet Earth have never been able to establish mechanical customs, capable of making their disordered existence a little more like the existence of the beings of other planets, that is to say, beings with almost the same possibilities.

"This again is due chiefly, I think, to the property of suggestibility, which these unfortunate beings possess. Owing to this property they are always under the suggestion of somebody or other; they constantly follow the example of the beings under whose suggestion they are; and they follow not only good, but also bad examples.

"For instance, those Russians about whom I have spoken, have followed the example of the French. Why should not a good example be followed? Very reasonable. But, unfortunately, for them, they follow bad examples, and even examples nonexistent amongst the beings under whose suggestion they are. They abandon their own good customs, acquired by centuries, for example, taking vapor baths and chewing keva, only in order to adopt customs that do not exist even among the French.

"They fail to consider that the circumstances of existence in France may have been of such a kind that the French had not yet had time to understand the need for vapor baths and chewing keva after eating. The abandonment of their many good customs merely because they do not exist among the French is indeed 'turkeyness.'

"All the beings of the Earth, however, have this 'turkeyness,' especially the beings of the continent Europe. I clearly understood this when, after leaving the town of St. Petersburg, instead of returning to Turkestan, I visited various European countries and saw everything for myself.

"The mode of existence of European social organizations differs very little from that of the beings of that large social organization, Russia; and the difference is merely the difference between certain customs, existing in the beings of the various social organizations which were formed and strengthened in their psyche, in course of time.

"By the way, the duration of the existence of some of the social organizations really plays a great part in the formation of good customs. Unfortunately, however, no social organization on Earth exists long, owing always to the same peculiarity existing on that unfortunate planet; that is, the existence among them of the property of mutual destruction, or, as I have already told you, war.

"As soon as good conditions for a mechanical existence begin to be established in some social organization, either a war speedily puts an end to the customs acquired during centuries, or the social organization falls under the influence of some other, having nothing in common with its former model. Good customs acquired perhaps during centuries, are thus very soon replaced by others, mostly immature, and good only for a day.

"But the change of influence nearly always depends, as I have remarked, not on the beings of the social organizations themselves, but upon its king. Having himself fallen under somebody's influence, a king tries to copy the customs belonging to him; and the beings of his social organization naturally try to do the same. It can therefore be said that only the king of the social organization is to blame. But why such a king is king depends on the manner of his election.

"In short, on that planet Earth, as the wise Mullah Nassr Eddin says: 'If the mane is pulled the tail will drop, and if the tail is pulled the mane will drop.' The beings of the social organization are as they are because the king is as he is; and the king is as he is, because the beings are as they are.

"From the beginning of these beings' existence, I saw amongst them to my regret, only two methods of electing a king, or as they call it, two forms of state organization, namely—an hereditary monarchy, and an elective republic. There were no other kinds.

"Either of these was replaced by the other with only modifications in detail. In an hereditary monarchy, even if the first emperor happened to be clever, he soon died, owing to the general brevity of existence on Earth, and his place was inherited by his son, or by one of his relations. Even if his first successor happened to be clever, it was all the same, since one of his ultimate successors would be bound to be either stupid or weak. In that case, he would quickly be surrounded by ordinary beings who are egoists to the marrow of their bones; and each would begin to extract from the government of the social organization some profit for himself and his friends. Everybody else, as well would certainly do his best to make this weak or stupid emperor do something profitable to himself or his friends.

"As regards the second method, the case is still worse. In the first form, the smaller mechanism of the government can at least sometimes continue automatically; but in the second form, even this is impossible, because in this kind of state government there appear hosts of petty beings, greedy egoists of smaller degree, who were never accustomed to be even mechanically just towards others.

"The second method is elective; the choice being determined by a majority of votes. Those chosen are well known and well spoken of in their social relations. It is very easy on that planet to become well spoken of, owing to many of the properties of the beings, and to their established customs.

"As I already told you, their duality is very sharply defined. Essence is one thing and mind and conscience quite different. Mind and conscience are inner things that cannot be seen. However bad they may be, they can be hidden very well. They even say that you have to live a long time with a man and eat a hundred pounds of salt with him before you can know him; it is only his exterior that these beings can discern.

"For instance, on their newly discovered continent America, there exists at the present time a republican state organization, the chief of which is called a President, who is elected for four years.

"The last time I was on that planet, I knew of a being there, who was a scoundrel of the deepest dye; his father and grandfather must have been the same since they left him a large fortune. With this fortune, he, being, as I have said, a scoundrel, made another and greater; and at the present time he is considered one of the richest men of this America. The weaknesses and defects of these beings increase or diminish together proportionately, so that with the increase of this being's greed his vanity also increased. Thanks to which he aspired to become the very first man in America, namely, the President. And, as I have already told you, a man is chosen President who is known, and whose 'good' works are much spoken of.

"This being having decided to become famous, he wished that other beings should talk a great deal about him and his works. And having heaps of money he set in motion the machinery which makes beings famous and talked about. Since these beings approve of those engaged in charity, he became charitable. What did it cost him to return a millionth part of his wealth to those from whose sinews he had wrung it? Beings, again, like somebody whose name is often mentioned; and it was a trifle for him to buy several newspapers in which his name and his doings could often appear. These beings prefer also those who are successful in business; so this being began to extend the sphere of his commercial activities, in order to make still more money. What did it cost him? He had not to work or run his business himself. For that very purpose, poor beings exist; perhaps, a thousand times cleverer than he. They will do everything and at least not worse than he himself. Of such beings of every specialty, there are far too many; thousands flock round every wealthy being. All he would have to do would be occasionally to sign some important document.

"When I left that planet the name of this scoundrel was booming throughout all America, and, to a certain extent on the other continents as well. He will, of course, be elected President, sooner or later, whereupon he will govern that land of many millions of beings. The smaller posts under him will naturally be taken by those near to him, egoists and greedy scoundrels like himself, but of a lesser degree. And this cozy little company will govern the destinies of these millions of beings.

"Presidents will change from time to time, until finally a big revolution of the masses will take place; whereupon the form of government itself will be changed, to that of a republic of some peculiarity; or to a monarchy, either of which will last until the next great revolution—and so on without end.

"In that year on the Solar System Ors, the Solioonensius was about to begin; and there on that planet something began to occur like that which occurs during the Solioonensius on all planets.

"The Solioonensius is the same for the embodied souls on all the planets of the Universe, just as Easter is for beings of the Earth; and all incarnated souls await it as impatiently as Earth-beings await their Easter or Bairam. The difference is that on that peculiar planet, revelry and feasting prevail during Easter, whereas on all other planets 'remorse' increases among the beings from the Solioonensius; and from this, the feeling of religiousness and the desire to develop more quickly towards the highest degree of reasonableness also increases.

"But among Earth-beings, although these feelings do appear during the Solioonensius, they take a different form. For instance, they experience a necessity to be free; but free from what, they do not know exactly. And they come to imagine that their liberty depends on their state-organization, or on their elected leaders; and hence almost from the very beginning, great revolts have under various names taken place among them during the years of the Solioonensius; and at the present time such a revolt is called Bolshevism.

"The Solioonensius on the planet Earth arises from the tension of the Sun and this tension in its turn is due to the neighboring solar system of Baleaooto. The solar system Baleaooto includes a very large comet called Solni, whose orbit from time to time approaches very near its Sun Baleaooto. On each such occasion this Sun makes a strong tension for itself in order to maintain its course; and this tension in its turn calls forth the tensions of the suns of its neighboring systems. One of which is the system to which the planet Earth belongs.

"This tension of the planet itself, naturally calls forth a tension in the beings dwelling on it; in the present case, in the beings beloved by you; and this tension manifests itself, how shall I say it, as a kind of nervousness. Instead of the wish to arrive at the highest degree of reasonableness however, a desire appears among them to change the exterior only, that is, to change the state-organizations established during centuries.

"Such tensions on that Solar System occurred under my observation no fewer than forty times. They occur only on that part of the Earth which just then is in maximum tension towards the whole system.

"It happens at this time to be just the place called Russia, about which I have just told you.

"The Solioonensius on that planet certainly manifests itself in a particular way owing to the abnormal psyche formed in these beings, in other words, to the absence in them of objective conscience. Perhaps this is the sole reason why the influence of the Solioonensius assumes these forms.

"From the very beginning, life on that planet arranged itself in the form of social organizations, at the head of which is always one or another group of these beings. Ordinarily this group is composed of favorites or relatives; and it becomes, what they call the governing class. Being without objective conscience, this governing group becomes the very cause of the appearance of the desire for liberty in the beings of these social-organizations during the Solioonensius, that is to say, the desire for deliverance from this governing group itself.

"And this desire appears because this governing group, being without objective conscience, and having the force of arms, compels other beings, that is, those not belonging to the governing class, to bear all the burdens which each being has to bear. When the influence of the Solioonensius manifests in them, the latter begin to feel the injustice of the governing class more intensely; and thus a revolution is ripe.

"But the ultimate cause is that on that planet as well as on many planets, it is necessary to eat to live; and food on that planet as everywhere else does not drop from the skies; it must be earned; and to this end much trouble is necessary. As the beings of the governing class wish to escape this trouble, the non-governing group must endure it for them.

"Although only mechanical mind is to be found on that

planet, it nevertheless sometimes happens in accidentally created circumstances and conditions that in some beings or other, a theoretical understanding is formed concerning the injustice of the existing situation. One being however, does not form an army, but since they have the property of agitating, they begin to agitate about this injustice. On the occasion of the Solioonensius, this agitation affects others, at first a few, and afterwards greater and greater numbers, who in turn begin to agitate and meet, with the result that soon the revolution is ready.

"Owing to the narrowness of their understanding, attitude and ideas, they imagine that what recently they called Bolshevism existed on their planet for the first time. But I personally witnessed beings of the whole planet under the influence of this same Bolshevism. This also is a trait of theirs, to become furious and to suffer in vain. Although that planet is still very young, this phenomenon of Bolshevism took place under my eyes no fewer than forty times.

"The idea of its uniqueness occurred to them, because owing to the brevity of their life, they see only a little. As regards their deductions from monuments and from history, owing to their narrowness, they cannot understand what happened before them. Their limited reflection led them to think that what now exists never existed before; and they still believe that this Bolshevism is due peculiarly to their evolving mind and the attainments of their civilization.

"As a matter of fact, half of these phenomena of Bolshevism took place not far from the contemporary center of these beings, namely on the continent Africa, in the country called Egypt. It is interesting to observe that contemporary beings were supposed to know the whole History of their Egypt. But like everything else among them, it is only empty words without any meaning; they know only a narrow aspect of this History.

"All the beings of that planet, for instance, know that among these ancient Egyptian beings were twenty-four dynasties. Ask any child you please and the reply would be that the Egyptians had twenty-four dynasties, because the History of Egypt is studied in all their schools at the present time. But why just so many dynasties? None of the contemporary beings so much as thinks about this; and if anybody should perhaps think of it and try and picture it to himself, he would imagine something like this:

"Among the Egyptians there were twenty-four dynasties. A dynasty is a name given to a family of kings, reigning according to the monarchic law, that is, by the law of inheritance from father to son. As beings of the same generation bear the same name, there must have been as many dynasties, because there were twenty-four families of kings in Egypt.

"Thus contemporary beings are limited by these reflections and by nothing else. If you ask why there were so many families of kings, then again the picture at best would be something as follows:

"In ancient Egypt was a certain king, Mr. John, who having tired of governing called another Mr. John and addressed him thus:

"'My very honorable and highly respectable Sir John, this social organization over which I am ruling wearies me very much, and I am tired. Loving my son, I have no desire that he should also become tired. I therefore entreat you to be good and kind enough not to refuse my request, namely, to free me and my son and to undertake the government yourself.'

"This second Sir John, being very kind and polite, was unable to refuse the request and from the following day began to rule over that social-organization. As his family name was different, the number of the Egyptian dynasties was increased by one, and so on. The kings of Egypt often becoming tired, often gave up their kingdom to others, which is why in Egypt these dynasties so often changed. In reality however, these dynasties were not changed so simply. On the contrary between one dynasty and the next, there were such upheavals that in comparison with them contemporary Bolshevism is child's play.

"Contemporary beings, for instance, are indignant that Bolsheviks shot a certain Peter Petrovich. If it was surely known that Peter Petrovich had been shot and not somebody else, then it would mean that things had become normal on that planet and that contemporary beings had suddenly become so strong in character that they could act deliberately and justly by their former persecutors.

"In order that you may better understand what was done during such revolts, I will relate two events taken from the History of Egypt, and of which I was a witness. You will perhaps understand the difference between the former phenomena of this kind and those which happen today on Earth, and about which you will learn by the reports of our governor on Mars.

"During one of the intervals between the dynasties, an order was issued by the central committee of the revolutionaries to the population, announcing that in the forthcoming elections for the chiefs of the towns and villages, those contributing the greatest number of kroahns in his sacred cup would be elected.

"In one of the religious customs of that period, during certain ceremonies a cup was placed before every being; and every time certain prayers were uttered some vegetable or fruit, specially designated by the priests for that day was put into it. This ceremony was obviously invented by the priests themselves as a means of living, though it had the appearance of an offering; and these fruits and vegetables were called by the Egyptians 'kroahns.'

"In the order of which I am speaking, the kroahns to be

contributed were the eyes of 'monsters'; and by the latter word was meant those who belonged to the former governing class, not excluding women, children and old men. It was further stated in the proclamation, that the citizen with the greatest number of kroahns in his cup would be appointed as governor of the capital; and that the rest of the governors of other towns and villages would be appointed according to their kroahns. You can imagine what took place.

"On another occasion, I saw the following picture in this same Egypt. You must know that in every town in Egypt, there used to be a big public place, in which every kind of religious and military ceremony was held, and where masses of beings without difference of caste assembled.

"As the humble castes interfered with these ceremonies, a certain Pharaoh ordered a rope to be drawn around those public places, to keep the crowds out. Some of these ropes were broken under the pressure of the people, whereupon the Pharaoh became angry and ordered them to be made of metal; and for greater security the Egyptian priests consecrated them and called them sacred. In the big towns these ropes were sometimes of enormous length, being as much as from six to eight miles long.

"I once witnessed how the crowd spitted on these 'sacred' ropes just like Asiatic 'shashlik' beings of the governing class with out difference of sex or age; and in the evening of the same day, with the help of ten pairs of buffaloes, this peculiar 'Shampour' (spit) was dragged and thrown into the river Nile.

"Many of these acts of summary justice I saw; yet today beings of the whole planet Earth are indignant that a certain Peter Petrovich was shot."

CHAPTER XXXV

A Change in the Appointed Course of the Falling of the Trans-space Ship Karnak*

AT THIS point of Beelzebub's conversation with his kinsmen, he was told that the captain of the ship sought permission to speak with him personally.

Soon after Beelzebub had given his consent, the captain entered and with a respectful salute addressed Beelzebub and said:

"Your Reverence, at the beginning of our journey you condescended to let fall a word which hinted that on the return journey you would perhaps decide to stop on the way at the holy planet Purgatory to see the family of your son Tooilan. If this is indeed your intention, then it will be better if you give me the order to do so now, because we shall soon be passing through the solar system Khalmian, and if having passed this system we do not direct the falling of our ship immediately more to the left, we shall greatly lengthen the path of its falling."

"Yes, please, my dear Captain," Beelzebub replied.

"There is nothing against stopping on the way at this holy planet. No one knows whether there will be another such happy occasion for me to go there and visit the family of my dear son Tooilan."

When the captain saluted and was on the point of going out, Beelzebub suddenly, as if remembering, stopped him and addressed him in the following words:

"Wait, my dear Captain, I want to ask you to accede to yet another of my requests."

And when the captain, drawing nearer, had sat down in his

* ***Editor's Note:*** In the original manuscript this content of this chapter was completely omitted. We have added the whole text here directly from the 1950 publication.

appointed place, Beelzebub continued thus:

"My request to you is that you consent after the visit to the holy planet Purgatory, to give our ship *Karnak* such a course of falling that on the way we may reach the surface of the planet Deskaldino.

"The point is that, in the present period of the flow of time on that planet, the Great Saroonoorishan, my first educator, so to say the fundamental cause of all the spiritualized parts of my genuine common presence, has the place of his permanent existence.

"I should like, as at that first time, before going to the sphere on which I arose, to profit by this occasion and fall once more at the feet of the prime creator of my genuine being, the more so, since just now, returning from my perhaps last conference, the entire satisfactoriness of the present functioning of all the separate spiritualized parts of my common presence was revealed not only to me myself, but also to most of the individuals I met, and in consequence, the being-impulse of gratitude towards that Great Saroonoorishan arose in me and is still inextinguishably maintained.

"I very well know, my dear Captain, that I am giving you no easy task, because I have already been a witness of the difficulties in carrying out this same request of mine, when, returning for the first time after my gracious pardon to the place of my arising on the planet Karatas, I desired before descending onto it, to visit the surface of the planet Deskaldino. On that occasion, when the captain of the intersystem ship *Omnipresent* had agreed to this and directed the falling of the *Omnipresent* in the direction of the atmosphere of that planet and was indeed able to carry out my request, I was able, before my return to my native land, to reach the surface of the planet Deskaldino and I had the happiness of greeting the Great Saroonoorishan, the creator of my genuine being-existence, and to receive from him his 'creator-benediction,' most dear and most precious to me."

To this request of Beelzebub's, the captain of the ship *Karnak* answered:

"Very good, your Reverence, I will think out how it may be possible to carry out your desire. I do not know just what obstacles there were then for the captain of the ship *Omnipresent*, but in the present case, on the direct route between the holy planet Purgatory and the planet Deskaldino, there lies the solar system called Salzmanino, in which there are many of those cosmic concentrations which, for purposes of the general cosmic Trogoautoegocratic process, are predetermined for the transformation and radiation of the substances Zilnotrago; and therefore the direct falling of our ship *Karnak*, unhindered, through this system, will scarcely be possible. In any case, I will try in one way or another to satisfy the desire expressed by your Reverence.'

Having said this the captain rose and, respectfully saluting Beelzebub, went out.

When the captain of the ship had left the place where Beelzebub was sitting with his kinsmen, Hassein ran to his grandfather and again sitting down as usual at his feet, coaxingly asked Beelzebub to continue to relate what had happened to him after his departure from the capital of that large community of the beings of the planet Earth which was called St. Petersburg.

CHAPTER XXXVI

Just A Wee Bit More About The Germans, And France

or

*(Germany and Paris)**

AT THIS point Beelzebub finished his story and put the curl of his tail in order. A little later he turned to old Ahoon and said:

"Eh! Ahoon, are you again sitting with cocked ears listening to me like the prosecution on the planet Earth to the witnesses in a trial? You also now tell our Hassein something."

"How can I do that, your Reverence?" answered Ahoon, "You know yourself how I was all the time very busy there serving your Reverence. And even when I was occasionally free, I was too much interested in the food and drink prepared by those beings. Nowhere on other planets do they spend so much time on it, and nowhere do they serve so many kinds of food and drink as on that planet; especially drinks. I tasted them all everywhere and compared their merits."

"Well then, tell us about food and drink, and on which continents of the planet Earth they were best prepared," said Beelzebub.

Upon this Ahoon smacked his lips with pleasure and answered: "As regards food, the continent Asia is beyond comparison above the other continents. In Asia one can say, the mouth waters at some dishes. But as regards drink, it would be a crime to say a bad word about the continent Europe. As regards . . . beer . . . how is it called? I have forgotten its name . . . Eh! Surely my memory is beginning to get weak from

* ***Editor's Note:*** In the 1931 Manuscript this and the following chapter had not been separated. They were strung together, but denoted as Chapters XXXVI, XXXVII indicating that two chapters were intended. Here we have separated them in conformance with the 1950 publication.

old age. Perhaps your Reverence remembers the name of that social organization which was situated almost in the center of the continent Europe, where pipe smoking was popular?"

"Is it Germany?" asked Beelzebub.

"Yes, yes, your Reverence, just Germany. To say anything bad about the German beer would be a crime."

"Tell us, Ahoon, your opinion about these Germans," persisted Beelzebub.

"What is my opinion worth? These German beings are not so bad when they sit in their beer houses with hot sausages on the table. But one of their passions does not please me at all, that is, their craze for collecting all kinds of rubbish belonging to beings of other social organizations. They collect every sort of thing, stories, proverbs, porcelain and clay objects, carpets, all kinds of drawings, dead butterflies and much other superfluous lumber. They collect, as they persuade everybody, knowledge of some kind or other. As regards their other qualities, it is difficult for me to form an opinion. I think that Hassein can get a pretty complete idea of their psyche if I tell him just this, that when these German beings gather together for feasting or any such purpose they always sing:

'Stumpfsinn, stumpfsinn,
du mein Vergnugen,
Blodsinn, blodsinn,
du mein Lust.'

"By the way, my dear Hassein, note well that many of the words of that song are to be found in no other language, although on that planet there are thousands of languages."

CHAPTER XXXVII

France

WHEN Ahoon finished, Beelzebub continued to relate as follows. He began thus:

"Owing to the turkey-reasoning of the beings of that planet, they form opinions quite contrary to reality. Their understanding of everything is decidedly subjective, and they have no objective understanding. A very good example is the understanding the beings of that planet have of the French, in whose country I finally arrived when I left St. Petersburg to travel in Europe. I told you that present-day Russia is much under the influence of these French, and takes example from them. So although I had never been in that France, and had never seen those French beings, I thought I knew them fairly well from the stories told by other beings who had been among them. Most of these stories I obtained from Asiatic beings and from the beings of the big social organization Russia; and I formed the opinion from them that these French were the most depraved and dishonest beings amongst all the beings inhabiting the continent Europe.

"Quite naturally, therefore, when I arrived on business in France, and began to live in one of their provincial towns, I expected from them nothing but swindling and immorality. You can judge my surprise when they turned out to be not depraved and corrupt, but the most patriarchal, modest, and honest beings of all those populating the continent Europe.

"I wondered how such a deeply rooted, yet false idea had been formed amongst the beings of that planet: But I understood the answer only when I arrived in the capital of France, the city of Paris, and began to make close observations. I went straight to the hotel recommended to me in Russia; and the first thing I noticed was that, although this hotel was in France, the staff spoke only English. I afterwards learned that some years previously the staff had spoken only Russian. I made further inquiries of a Persian, to whom I had an introduction from one of my Persian friends. During the evening my new Persian acquaintance suggested going to the Grand Café on the Boulevard des Capucines, where we sat at one of many tables, occupying half the pavement, as is the custom there.

"Cafes in Europe are very like the chaihanas of Asia, the only difference is that in the chaihanas of Asia they give you a red liquid to drink, the juice of a certain flower, while in European cafes they serve a liquid which is quite black, the origin of which nobody knows, except the proprietor of the cafe.

"The Boulevard des Capucines is situated in the center, not of the city of Paris, no, but of that part of Paris which is now regarded as the center by all the beings of that planet. We began to drink the black liquid called coffee, and I at once observed that the waiters were all Italian.

"In general, in that part of Paris, that is, the foreign quarter of Paris, every business appears to be the specialty of beings of one social organization or other, either of this continent Europe or of other continents of the Earth.

"We began to observe the people who passed on the pavement. They were beings from all the social organizations of the continent Europe as well as from other continents, but chiefly from those social organizations whose turn it was to be rich.

"The beings of America were then predominant; and in Paris they succeeded the beings of the social organization Russia, after the death of the latter. Among the varied crowd were many commercial men who were in Paris for the fashion trade and chiefly for perfumery and ladies' dress. There also were representatives of the governing classes of other social organizations of the continent, who were there for pleasure. There were also young beings of different social organizations who had come to study the fashionable dances and millinery.

"While we were examining this mixed crowd, one of my acquaintances suddenly pointing with his finger, drew my attention to a passing small couple, and said with astonishment:

"'Look, look, they seem to be real French people.'

"I looked and saw indeed that the couple were like the French whom I had seen in their provincial town. When they were lost in the crowd, we began to speculate why they were in this part of the city. After many guesses we unanimously agreed that they probably lived at the end of the real Paris and had been to another part of the city, on the other side, probably to a family feast at the christening of some relative.

"No doubt they had drunk a little more than was good for them, to the health of the new-born, and after the feast they had started for home. Being a little drunk they felt indisposed to go the long way round, so they decided to go by the direct route, which happened to pass the Grand Café. And that explained why there happened to be real French beings in that part of the city.

"Having sat for a little while in this Grand Café, my Persian acquaintance, who became my Paris cicerone, suggested that we should go and see something of French immorality.

"We leisurely went to a licensed house near by, the keeper of which was a Spanish Jew. In the room we entered were women; Poles, and Viennese, Jewesses and Italians, and even two negresses. I wished to see how real Frenchwomen would appear in these surroundings, but I discovered by inquiry there was not a single real Frenchwoman in the whole establishment.

"From there we went out into the street and began to walk on the Boulevard. Everywhere we met a great number of women-beings who pestered us. They were of all the above mentioned nationalities, with the addition of Swedes, English, Dutch, Spaniards and so on, but there was not a single

French woman.

"Some dubious beings stopped us and suggested 'The Grand Duke.' Wishing to learn the meaning of the strange words, it was explained to me that the phrase originated while Russia was flourishing, and while many beings belonging to its governing class were accustomed to go to Paris. As they all passed themselves off as Dukes or Grand Dukes, and, of course, made a point of visiting these suspicious places of Paris, the guides spoke of the 'Tournee de Grand Duc,' or in English, 'The Grand Duke's Tour.' And so it is still called.

"Having taken one of those guides we went to see the wonders of this contemporary Tikliamish. We visited many different places—for instance the cafe frequented by homosexuals and the club of the Lesbians. We also went to many other places where various abnormalities are practiced and imitated from time to time amongst these unfortunate beings in all the centers of that unfortunate planet.

"At last we arrived at what is called Montmartre. This is not on the Montmartre itself, but on the lower slope of the district of that name.

"Here are many dubious establishments and restaurants, catering especially for visitors from other social organizations. The whole district wakes up only at night since during the day foreigners never visit it.

"Most of its restaurants have stages on which are shown marvels supposed to be drawn from other lands of that planet, as for example, the stomach dance of the African beings, Caucasians with their dances, a mulatto with her snakes, in a word, all the so-called special attractions of the season.

"I was much interested to see all there was to be seen in order to understand everything concerning the beings amongst whom I was living. But certainly I had never seen anything like them in the places where I had been, where these marvels were supposed to have originated. And even if I had seen something like them, they had nothing in common with what was shown in these fashionable places.

"In this Montmartre, many Russian restaurants had been recently opened. In these, and in the majority of others, the so-called 'artists' are chiefly Russians, whose fathers had previously in this same Montmartre, lowered human dignity by squandering the money collected by the sweat of peasants. Their children were now, in their turn, being humiliated before other people who had money. In such a case, Mullah Nassr Eddin would say:

"'If fathers will ride sons must drive.'

"While I was sitting in a restaurant with my Persian friend, he was called away by some of his other Persian friends, and I was left alone at a table with champagne, the ordering of which, in Montmartre, was usually obligatory. My solitude aroused in me reflections upon the surprising things done in the world of our ENDLESSNESS.

"Here are souls, apparently the same as on the innumerable other planets of the Universe! Why had such a misfortune befallen the planet Earth that it had been necessary to add to the bodies of the first Earth souls the organ Kundabuffer? Even now, when that Kundabuffer no longer exists and only a few of its consequences remain, those unhappy souls, in spite of the hundreds of centuries which have passed, have still not been able to make the little effort required to be free of those consequences, and to become souls like all the rest of the Universe.

"I looked around and asked myself if there was any difference between the beings sitting and conversing there, and those who existed nearly a hundred centuries before then in Tikliamish, amongst whom also I sat in their 'Kaltaani,' as the restaurants of that day were called in Tikliamish.

"There in front a fat man was sitting with two street girls. Put him in the costume of a Kafirian, and there would be no difference.

"Over there is a squeaky-voiced young man talking with intense conviction about the causes of disorder in some social organization or other. Was he not a Klian?

"And that tall gentleman, sitting alone in a corner, making eyes at the lady who sat at a neighboring table, was he not truly a Veroonk?

"And those waiters, were they not Asklay slaves?

"Many centuries passed after Tikliamish. When those peoples had almost ceased to exist, I was at Babylon. Was it not the same again? Were not the beings the same as the Asklays, Kafirians, Veroonks, Klians and so on and so forth, with only their dresses and names changed to Assyrians, Persians, Jews, Kurds etc.

"Now in their contemporary center, Paris, and after so many centuries is not everything still again the same, the bustle, the noise, the laughter, the quarreling—all just the same as in Babylon and even as in Samlios, their first center on the continent Atlantis?

"Do not the beings meet together to pass the time, as they always did in their center of culture? Not only the people of many of those centers have disappeared, but also the very land on which they dwell, has completely changed or been engulfed as, for instance, the continent of Atlantis.

"After Atlantis, Grabontzi, on the continent of Africa, became their center. Have not its peoples similarly disappeared? At least if the continent itself has not disappeared, yet the place where their center existed, is now covered with sand. The sand of the Sahara, as it is now called, is all that remains of it.

"Once more many centuries passed and their center was formed in Tikliamish. What has remained of it, but deserts of red sand, and perhaps a few descendants of a people, once famous throughout a thousand generations, but now vegetating in obscurity?

"Still more centuries passed and I saw their center Babylon. What has remained of this truly great center of culture? Two stones of its primal grandeur; while the nation, formerly so mighty, still it is true exists, but in subjection and poverty.

"And what will happen to their present center, Paris, and to the people powerful today, who surround it, French, German, English, Dutch, Italians, Americans, and so on? Future centuries will show. As for these unfortunate souls, they always remain the same, the slaves of the properties of Kundabuffer.

"I was absorbed in similar weighty thoughts, when my Persian acquaintance returned.

"We began to discuss where we should go, and we were just about to leave, when some persons present, having overheard where we proposed to go, asked leave to sit at our table, and to go with us afterwards to the place we had in view.

"These new acquaintances of ours were Americans.

"As very soon it became noisy and suffocating in the restaurant, we decided to leave. But our new acquaintances wished to wait a little, as they were expecting an American gentleman.

"One of them, however, wished to wait no longer and went with us to another restaurant. He was a very merry, observant, and loquacious person. All the way there, he talked, remarking at the same time, the comical characteristics of the people we met.

"He was the Director of a school of modern dancing. From what he told me of his business, I gathered that he had in Paris a big school of dancing, the pupils of which were exclusively American, and that they chiefly learned in his school, the most popular American dance, the fox-trot. I further gathered that this dance was entirely of American origin, and is extremely popular there.

"So, after choosing his champagne and having stopped his

chattering, I asked this American:

"'Will you kindly tell me sir, why your school is not in America, instead of here in Paris, so far, not only from your own country, but from the home of the dance itself?'"

"'What, what! What do you mean?' he replied, 'I have a large family and if I had my school in America, not only would my family starve, but there would not be enough to pay the rent of a miserable damp American cellar. But here, thank God, there are plenty who wish to study, and who will pay whatever I charge.'

"'I don't understand,' I replied, 'You tell me that your pupils are exclusively American, yet at the same time you say that in America itself, nobody would attend your school. How am I to understand that?'

"'That is just the point,' answered the American, 'The cause is a little psychological stupidity on the part of our Americans. My school is in Paris, the contemporary Babylon, as clever men say; and Paris has a very great popularity amongst all Americans.

"'So every American must visit this famous world capital. Everybody, who is even fairly well-to-do, considers it his duty to come here.

"'Getting rich in America you perhaps know is not so easy. Dollars do not roll about the streets as they think in Europe. The American has to earn them. He has to get every cent by his own labor and not as in some European countries, where money is paid for fame, an empty title, or some imaginary values.

"'For example, if a painter in Europe happens to paint a good picture that makes him famous, the public will ever afterwards pay him well for any rubbish he likes to turn out.

"'They will say, "This is from his brush."

"'At home in America, things are very different; everything is done for cash, and every work is judged by measure and weight. Fame, talent, genius, and that kind of merchandise, is cheap with us at home, and therefore dollars are acquired with great difficulty; and, as our Americans have other weaknesses, as, for example, sightseeing in Europe, everybody hoards dollars, gradually acquired by hard work, by saving and by going without many necessities, in order to be able to visit Europe, and, of course, the capital of the world, Paris.

"'That is why our Americans are always to be found here. And as Americans have a second great weakness, namely vanity they like it to be said that they have learned the fox-trot, not in a common place like Philadelphia, but in Paris itself, where everything new in fashion, art and good manners, originates for all the Earth.

"'The fox-trot being also a fashion, a fox-trot from Paris is the very latest fashionable novelty for them. Thanks to this stupidity of the Americans, I have always enough Americans to pay me well.'

"I asked him, 'Please tell me, my dear Sir, is it possible that they come here and stay so long only to study this fox-trot of yours?'

"'Why only the fox-trot?' he replied. 'At the same time, they see Paris and round about; and sometimes they even travel far afield; in short, they see Europe.

"'To tell you the truth, they come to Europe from the same vanity; they sightsee not to learn anything, but to be able in conversation, to say that they have been in Europe, and seen this, that, and the other.

"'Do you know how they go sightseeing?'

"'Well, listen! Here in Paris, there is a very convenient establishment for this purpose, called Cook and Son. A dozen or so of our Americans are rounded up like a flock of sheep, and the whole party is put aboard a huge Cook motorbus, which then sets off.

"'On the car, beside the Chauffeur, there is a sleepy person with a weak voice, who talks almost to himself, calling out the names, learned by heart, of places and other sights along the route, which has been mapped out by Cook himself.

"'This sleepy person has a very weak voice and looks consumptive, because he is obviously very tired. It is not easy to live in Paris with a family, and many of these men receive very small wages from Cooks, and certainly have to work at night in another place, in order to make enough to live. But that does not concern our tourists.

"'If you think that the passengers either understand or remember anything, you are mistaken. It is all the same what they see or what it means.

"'They care nothing about that, but what they do want, is to be able to say nonchalantly: 'I was in that place, and saw that thing,' and that is enough for them; they are satisfied, since they can now say, as I have told you with a clear conscience, 'I was there,' whereupon all Americans will know that they are not talking with a nobody, but with somebody who was in Europe and saw the sights.

"'Eh! My dear doctor, do you think that I am the only one who lives on the vanity of my poor compatriots?

"'What am I? I am a little man, only a dancing teacher.

"'But did you notice in the restaurant, a fat man? He is one of the sharks, of which there are many in America; he is an Americanized English Jew, a director of a certain substantial firm with branches in many countries. He is the director of the Paris branch.

"'They make their pile, not just on the stupidity of their compatriots, but by the addition of a little trickery into their business. For example, the branch in Paris has quite a good reputation and is well known by the American beings.

"'Many Americans, owing to this same vanity, and other weaknesses, write for fashionable dresses from this Paris branch, and real Paris models are sent from here all quite straight and above-board.

"'There's no harm in it. But, no, these fellows are not such fools as to divide their profits with other people.

"'The French get a profit out of it, but only what they collect from the postage stamps, which the business and its customers use.

"'How does this firm make its money?

"'Their branch, here, gets an order from America. This order is sent directly to Germany, where this firm has also a branch, and materials and labor are very much cheaper than they are in Paris. The German branch quietly carries out the order, sticks a Paris label on it, and sends it by steamer straight to New York from Hamburg.

"'The customer there, having received her order, is happy and proud that she can wear on the morrow, a dress really made in Paris itself. In short, everybody is apparently satisfied, and everybody is pleased; and, after all, without international exchange, countries could not exist.

"'But what am I but a small dancing teacher?'

"It was late, and having said goodbye to this amusing American, I went home. On the way, I began to think and to ponder the question why such a false idea is formed of the French. It was evident, that beings of other lands, who come to Paris, see and taste, not French life, but a special life for foreigners, organized by foreigners. As all this goes on in French territory and everybody speaks French, everything that is seen and heard is attributed by foreigners to the French beings.

"A foreign being, after having been in Paris, on returning to his country, relates what he has seen as if it were French. And so, little by little, people get an idea of the French, from the stories of these travelers, as false as the opinion I gathered from the beings, mostly Asiatics and Russians, who had seen in Paris only what had been prepared for foreigners."

CHAPTER XXXVIII

Religion Or Jesus Christ

AFTER this fifth descent of mine it was a long time before I was on that planet again, but as before, I watched it very attentively through my observatory. Only just before my departure from that solar system, I was there for the sixth and last time.

"On the occasion of this last descent of mine I stayed amongst its beings a considerable time, a quarter of a year in fact, or according to their time calculation, fifty years.

"In the interval three messengers of our ENDLESSNESS appeared on that planet, but in each case I was advised to be absent from the Earth during their visits, in order not by chance to hinder the course of events.

"All three saints appeared on the continent Asia. The first appeared among the Jews and was called Jesus Christ; the second amongst the Arabs, under the name of Saint Mohammed; and the third, Saint Lama, amongst the people of the most elevated place called Tibet. All three saints left to the beings of the Earth their holy teachings, which exist until the present day.

"As usual, these men-beings soon distorted all the three doctrines and to such a degree, that, at the present time their Saintly authors could certainly not recognize their own teachings. Although the doctrine of the first, that of Jesus Christ, spread quickly on the Earth, and almost a third of all the beings of the planet took up the doctrine, and called themselves Christians, yet unfortunately, with their customary peculiarity, they transformed his doctrine of resplendent love into some jumble. The first thing they did was to split up into different sects, on account of some trifle or other, and to call themselves, not Christians but orthodox, heterodox, and ypsylodox, hamilodox, and other 'doxes'; and next into this doctrine of verity and truth they inserted other doctrines, which had nothing in common with the doctrine of Jesus Christ, and which even contradicted those truths which the Divine Teacher had taught.

"A great deal was taken from the doctrine of Saint Moses. Although it is true that he also was a messenger sent by our CREATOR, yet his teaching was already out of date for that time, it having been created for beings in other epochs and in other conditions of a possible unconscious evolution; and, moreover, other bases then existed, which afforded the sacred nine-fold octave the possibility of flowing on.

"But the chief thing which they inserted into the doctrine of Jesus whether for convenience or for something else I do not know, was the fantastic theory invented by one or another of their half mad 'learned,' the doctrine namely of the Babylonian dualists. The elders of the Church, as they were called in the middle ages, took particular advantage of the Babylonian theory with its Paradise and Hell, in order to frighten the credulous masses and in this manner sell their own wares. And from this theory of pardon by our CREATOR, who suffered for all beings, doctrines are still current concerning His mockery and temptations.

"Who are the Elders of the Church, dear Grandfather?" asked Hassein.

"They call Fathers of the Church those officials of the highest rank who profess some religious doctrine or other," replied Beelzebub, and continued to relate further.

"Only a small group of beings called the Essene Fraternity knew how to apply the doctrine of Jesus Christ to their own life, as well as to the life of their descendants as a means for their deliverance from the consequences of the properties of the organ Kundabuffer, possessed by their ancestors.

"Still later and as the teaching of Jesus Christ became still more widely spread, it was divided into a still greater number of streams. In my opinion, however, there will very soon be an end of this Christianity altogether. I have come to this conclusion after reflecting on recent reports from the planet Mars.

"I do not seem to have told you that I receive everyday from Mars daily reports by etherography of the events occurring on the planets of that solar system, where I passed the greatest part of my existence. I receive more detailed reports of the happenings on the planet Earth, because it is very near, and also because the details can be easily observed from my observatory. These reports are made for me by our governor of the planet Mars.

"You remember that I told you that one of our young countrymen had a disagreeable experience on that planet Earth, for which I descended there, and that afterwards he returned with us to Mars not wishing to remain there any longer. This same young fellow later became governor on Mars, and he is still governor at the present time.

"And so, when I finally left that solar system, I presented him with my observatory, and in gratitude he reports to me all that goes on there, and, knowing my interest in the beings of the planet Earth, he tries to keep me in touch with the events occurring amongst them.

"By the way, in one of his daily reports he informed me that a University for Jewish youth had just been founded in the city of Jerusalem. The opening of this University tells me that Christianity has come to its end.

"Until quite recently," continued Beelzebub, "all the countries of the followers of Christ were engaged in great wars or Crusades on account of this very city of Jerusalem. They wished that this town, in which this holy being, the Divine Teacher, Jesus Christ, lived, suffered, and died, should be wholly Christian. During the struggles towards this end almost half the beings of the planet Earth were destroyed. And now, in this same city of Jerusalem, by these same Christian states, and certainly with their common consent, a University for Jewish youth has been opened.

"Jew is the name given to certain beings who were already in existence when Jesus Christ appeared on that planet; and it was in this city of Jerusalem that they dwelt, those very beings who tortured Him to death, and crucified Him on a cross.

"Although these Jews are not today enemies of Jesus Christ, they all consider Him to have been just a visionary. This is enough to understand what will happen in Jerusalem now that a University has been opened there.

"This establishment—a University—is a stove in which everything acquired by beings of that planet during tens of centuries is burned up and where that day and a half lentil soup is cooked to take its place.

"I can already picture to myself that before many years have passed on that very spot where the body of that Divine Jesus Christ was buried there will be a stand for automobiles—for those machines which are the greatest mechanical locomotive miracle of contemporary civilization. These beings have not only destroyed the divine doctrine of Jesus Christ, but they are now destroying His Memory. This is quite characteristic of the beings of that planet Earth.

"The second doctrine, that of Saint Mohammed—a home of reconciliation and hope, also spread very widely. But, unfortunately, into this also a great deal of the Babylonian doctrine was interwoven, and many pleasant things concerning Paradise were added of which, even Archangel Algamatant, the governor of the planet Purgatory has never dreamed.

"This doctrine, too, was split up into many branches. Its followers were mainly divided into two parties, called the 'Sunnites,' and the 'Shiites.' Their mutual hatred is very intense; and its intensity was further increased at the instigation of certain states, which observing the growing animosity of the two parties, rubbed their hands with glee at the prospect it offered for their own prolonged security, since the reunion in peace and concord between the followers of Saint Mohammed's doctrine, who together form almost half of the population of that planet, would be a menace to the existence of other states.

"As regards the third doctrine, that of Saint Lama, it spread less widely than the rest, owing to the geographical conditions of its origin. For the same reason, however, it more or less entered into the essence of those beings resident there; and for some centuries, it began actually to be realized amongst them, and especially amongst a certain group who were isolated on account of the inaccessibility of their locality, and thus could work without disturbance.

"This group, and their descendants gradually assimilated the objective doctrine of their teacher and began to apply it to the purpose for which it was created, that deliverance from the consequences of the properties of the organ Kundabuffer.

"Some of them attained this deliverance and many were on the path to it. But when the environment necessary for productive work in this direction was arranged, that same singularity of theirs, that is war, again, it seems, completely destroyed what had already been adjusted; and the complete adjustment was delayed for many years owing to this war. I know very well about this war because I happened to be on that planet at that period, and amongst the beings of this very Tibet.

"This peculiarity, war, occurred in the following manner. A certain King from the continent Europe, taking advantage of the civil dissensions of the Indian princes, and owing to a method invented by one of his people gradually conquered India and the neighboring lands.

"One fine day the thought entered his warlike head, why should he not conquer Tibet also. He thereupon assembled troops from his own sate, and from the newly conquered lands and advanced towards that inaccessible place.

"The expedition over awkward routes was very difficult and cost the king a great deal; but eventually after considerable exertions and sacrifices, he succeeded in ascending with his troops.

"The Tibetans knew nothing of this march upon their country. They only learned of it when the king had already arrived with his troops. Having heard of the strange event, however, they became anxious, because they had become accustomed to the idea during centuries that their country was inaccessible to other beings, and they were so certain of this that they had never even been aware of the preparations made to reach their land.

"As this situation was very serious, since the result might be the destruction of all their preparations, the Tibetans became exceedingly anxious and the members of the fraternity of 'those who are delivering themselves' became very sad. They were sad chiefly because they saw that their preparations were in danger. They therefore met to confer and many of those took part in the meeting who had almost delivered themselves from the consequences of the properties of Kundabuffer, and also many of those who had just started on the right path of deliverance.

"Having met and deliberated amongst themselves, they became convinced that it would be impossible by ordinary means of persuasion to induce the king to return home; and they had seriously to consider how to prevent this uninvited entrance into a stranger's house.

"Many methods were suggested, but one method in particular was favored by the majority present at the meeting, namely, to destroy entirely the king with his troops. And this was in fact much the easiest method, the nature of the place where Tibet is situated being such, that one unarmed being could destroy hundreds of enemy beings by dropping stones on them.

"Among the beings present however, some were strongly opposed to this plan, proving that such action would be little a displeasing to our CREATOR, to whom all creatures are dear. They succeeded in convincing the meeting, and the proposal was rejected by the majority. It was decided not to hinder events but to let them take their course. The king, meeting with no resistance, then began to advance further.

"One of the beings who had opposed the suggestion to slaughter the king and his troops, set off to the places where they must pass to persuade the masses to follow the decision of their leaders. In a town through which these troops passed, an accidental or intentional bullet from one of the soldiers killed the being whose intervention had saved many thousands of lives.

"When the king heard of this murder, do you think he felt any remorse?

"No, he only became proud, that owing to his lofty mind and force of arms, no obstacles could stand in his way, and he could go where ever he wished. He reached the interior of Tibet without having met any resistance.

"How it all ended is not important; what is important is, that after the events I mentioned, the core of this doctrine became like all the rest.

"Dear Grandfather please explain to me, how the social organizations were formed amongst them?" asked Hassein.

"At first they had no social organizations" Beelzebub continued to relate. Everybody lived his own life within the life of his family. Afterwards they began to unite; at first several families, and then a greater number. Of these united families, one of the eldest became the chief; and later they chose, to direct their lives, one of the honored members of the newly arrived families. Still later, some of these already united families began to unite with each other; and when dissensions began on account of elections, they made the leadership hereditary, with the condition that the leader's heir should succeed him at death.

"On many occasions attempts at other methods of electing a leader were made, but as they never led to anything, but prolonged quarrels the earlier practice was resumed.

"At the present time there are many united groups on that planet each having its leader. These leaders are chosen in various ways. There are hereditary leaders and elective, some for life and some for a prescribed period. Their social organizations at the beginning, as well as ever since, resembled each other very much. As Mullah Nassr Eddin would say:

"'If you understand even approximately the kind of organization they have in themselves at the present time, you can apply the same understanding to their social organization. Otherwise you have to live a very long time amongst them and perforce have very friendly relations with the police district inspector, the parish priest, the city accoucheur, and the town midwife; then perhaps you will understand their social organization.'

"But as regards their organizing . . .

"In former times it was understandable on account of their special organ Kundabuffer that they should seem strange in comparison with other beings. But now when there is no Kundabuffer, it is impossible to call them merely strange. Nothing in them is as it is amongst beings in general.

"It would be comprehensible if there were any reason for it. But the peculiarity consists just in this that there is no reason. Neither HIS ENDLESSNESS, Nature, nor even the Archangel Looisos, has anything to do with the fact that they are now so strange, and at the same time not such beings as they should be. There must be some misunderstanding. Had the properties of Kundabuffer not existed, they would have been formerly more normal than they are now. Then one could at least understand them. They were what they were.

"But now they are what they should be and yet at the same time they are not.

"Formerly they could be recognized as good, bad, clever or stupid, by their conversation or by their conduct. But by their present conduct it is impossible to recognize them. For instance, when one speaks, you think he is such and such—a very clever being let us say. But when at the same time he does something unconsciously and this manifests himself, he turns out to be quite the opposite, since what is in his essence is not in his manifestations, and what is in his manifestations is not in his essence.

CHAPTER XXXIX

The Holy Planet Purgatory

THE next day, the ship set off for its final destination in the direction of the Planet Karatas, where Beelzebub is now dwelling.

Shortly after the ship had started, Hassein sat down as usual at Beelzebub's feet, and said, "Grandfather, dear grandfather, please explain to me, why, as we have been told, on this holy planet Purgatory, on which we have just been, OUR ALL-COMPREHENSIVE ENDLESSNESS so often appears?"

At this question, Beelzebub thought a little longer than usual and then said: "It is a pity, my dear Hassein, that it is impossible at the moment to reply at length to this question of yours, because we shall soon be arriving on our planet. For a complete understanding, that is, such an understanding as I would like to give you of this holy planet, Purgatory, I should be obliged to talk a very long time. But do not fail to remind me of it, on a more convenient occasion when I may be able to explain it all to you. The understanding of the holy planet Purgatory is the most important thing for your education, and sooner or later, it will become decidedly necessary for every being, of whatever nature or form, to know of it.

"Nevertheless, my dear boy, as we shall not be arriving home at once, in order to shorten the time, I will try my best to reply in brief to your question, "Why our ENDLESSNESS appears so often on that holy planet?"

Then Beelzebub spoke as follows:

"Our ENDLESS CREATOR appears so often on that planet, only because, there dwell the most unfortunate souls from among all the souls existing in the Universe. The souls who are on this planet Purgatory suffer as nothing and nobody suffers in the whole Universe. And for this reason OUR ALL-LOVING BOUNDLESSLY COMPASSIONATE CREATOR, HIS ENDLESSNESS, having no other possibility of helping them with anything, appears often on that planet, to soothe these souls in their terrible inevitable state and grief, by his presence.

"To understand these souls, it is first and absolutely necessary for you to know, in general, what a soul is. But even before you can understand this, you should understand why souls exist in the Universe at all, and why souls, as well as the whole of the Universe, were created by our ALMIGHTY CREATOR.

"So listen attentively and try to assimilate these ideas into yourself.

"Our CREATOR was compelled to create the Universe for the following reason:

"When nothing else as yet was in the World, in the whole of the Universe, only the Sun Absolute existed, and there on this Sun Absolute, Our ALMIGHTY GOD existed with only HIS Cherubim and Seraphim.

"Our ENDLESSNESS, ALMIGHTY GOD, once observed that the Sun Absolute, itself, on which He existed was, owing to Time, diminishing gradually but perceptibly in volume, and HE decided immediately to review all the Laws maintaining the existence of the Sun Absolute.

"In the course of this search, HE discovered that the cause of the diminution of the Sun is the Heropass, that is to say, Time, which gradually diminishes the substance of every force.

"As this question was very serious, HE became thoughtful, and in these Divine reflections of HIS, HE saw clearly, that, if this Heropass should continue to reduce the volume of the Sun Absolute in this way, then sooner or later, it would eventually be to its complete destruction. Our ENDLESSNESS was then compelled to undertake several appropriate measures, so that this destruction of the Sun Absolute from the Heropass should be averted.

"After great labors, HE completely averted the whole of the

threatened danger; and HE accomplished this, in the following way:

"You must know that up till then the Sun Absolute had in itself, for its existence, only the force of the 'Autoegocrat'; that is, an independent force depending on nothing external itself. This same force, in its turn, was formed only of two Laws, namely, the Law of 'Triamazikamno' and the Law of 'Heptaparaparshinokh.'

"To these two Laws, our CREATOR added the third force, called 'Fagologiria,' by means of which the 'Autoegocrat' became the 'Trogoautoegocrat,' that is, a force depending on other forces exterior to itself. Or, as it might be said, after the addition of the Fagologiria, the Laws of Triamazikamno and Heptaparaparshinokh could function only by feeding on the substances and forces coming from without.

"When I shall explain later, pay special attention, and try to understand very clearly these Laws of Triamazikamno and Heptaparaparshinokh, since a complete understanding of these two Laws will enable you to understand completely all other laws, both of the Creation, as well as of the maintenance of the Universe.

"I have already told you that the Sun Absolute formerly existed only owing to these two independent Laws.

"The first of these two laws was just the Triamazikamno, or as it is also called, the law of 'Threefoldness.' This Law of Threefoldness, in its turn consists of three forces, called:

'Surp-Otheos';
'Surp-Skiros'; and
'Surp-Athanatos.'

But, for convenience, mathematics calls these three forces of the Law of Threefoldness, the force 'Plus,' the force 'Minus,' and the force 'Neutralizing'; or 'Pushing,' 'Resisting,' and 'Equilibrium.' On certain planets, these three forces are also called 'God the Father,' 'God the Son' and 'God the Holy

Ghost.'

"The second Law maintaining the Sun Absolute is the law of Heptaparaparshinokh; and this law is a force constantly evolving and involving in itself. The highest physico-chemical knowledge formulates this force as follows:

"'The flowing of the line of a force which constantly deflects according to the law, with its ends meeting again.'

"When our ENDLESSNESS decided to make the existence of the Sun Absolute Trogoautoegocratic, since forces, or substances, coming from outside were necessary for such an existence, HE decided first of all to create the sources whence these forces and substances could come.

"HE created them in the following way:

"HE directed the action of the Laws of Triamazikamno and Heptaparaparshinokh, which had been in the Sun Absolute itself, from within the Sun Absolute to without, and from this resulted what is now called, 'The Word God' or 'Emanation.' From that moment, the Sun Absolute began to emanate from itself the action of the forces of the Triamazikamno and the Heptaparaparshinokh, and this same emanation began to spread everywhere in the Universe.

"It is necessary to tell you, that when our CREATOR directed the forces of the Sun Absolute from within out, the emanations obtained from this had not at first, for a reason which I shall afterwards explain, the possibility of containing all three forces of the Triamazikamno in a vivifying state. Only two of these were vivifying, namely, the Positive Force and the Negative Force. Our ALMIGHTY ENDLESSNESS was therefore obliged to vivify the third force, the Neutralizing Force, during the First Creation by the force of HIS OWN WILL.

"And having concentrated this, HIS force of WILL, HE created from the emanations issuing from the Sun Absolute certain fixed points. And later, at these fixed points, again by the force of HIS WILL, and with the help of the Laws of Triamazikamno and Heptaparaparshinokh, which were already formed in these fixed points, our ENDLESSNESS began to create gradually the 'corresponding,' as the result of which the Suns were formed which exist at the present time.

"After the creation of all that was necessary on these suns, the latter began to emanate also. They became as the Sun Absolute, but as Absolute of the 'Second Grade.'

"The emanations of the Absolutes of the second grade having been established, everything thereafter was created without the WILL of our CREATOR taking part in it. Further creations began to be formed automatically owing only to the Laws of Triamazikamno and Heptaparaparshinokh, chiefly because these laws were now 'fagolished,' that is, could everywhere function only owing to the forces coming from without. From that time forward, the Laws of Triamazikamno and Heptaparaparshinokh began to make their cycles in all their octaves, both inside the suns and outside.

"The automatic creation of the suns proceeded further in the following way: the emanations of the newly-created suns became to each other as positive and negative, and the emanations of the Sun Absolute itself became neutralizing for these emanations of the newly created suns. Owing to this established Law of Triamazikamno, and likewise to the Law of Heptaparaparshinokh, which already began to make its outer chief cycle, there began to concentrate around each newly created sun, further new fixed points, in which and upon which again, owing to the same laws, 'The corresponding' gradually began to be created. As a result, suns again were formed, but suns of the third grade.

"Further, upon these suns of the third grade, on the basis of the chief cycle of the Law of Heptaparaparshinokh, and on the basis of the greatest deflection contained in this law, the smallest likenesses of the Megalocosmos began to be formed;

and, still further, owing to a law, also cosmic, called the 'Accumulation of Similarities,' forms of these smallest similarities of the Megalocosmos were grouped together.

"Having thus accomplished its chief outer cycle, the Law of Heptaparaparshinokh thenceforward entered quite within the cosmoses created on different scales, and began to make its evolutions and involutions in them.

"The part subsequently played by these cosmoses of differing scales, consisted, how shall I tell you, in their becoming something like machines in the Universe, in which machines, owing to these two fagolished laws, that is Triamazikamno and Heptaparaparshinokh, the cosmoses began to convert, or as it is said, to transform all the substance-matters of the Universe of all densities and all rates of vibration; that is to say, those machine-cosmoses began to convert substance-matters from one degree to another degree in the chief octave of the cosmic substances.

"Thus, owing to these machine-cosmoses, all substances began to evolve and involve and from this arose the exchange of substances owing to which a reciprocal feeding resulted in all the cosmoses. In this reciprocal feeding, the Sun Absolute also took part. In this manner Trogoautoegocrat was established in the Universe and all the cosmoses began to maintain the existence of each other by this reciprocal feeding.

"Each cosmos itself began, either to serve as food, or to prepare matters through itself for other cosmoses. And by this Trogoautoegocrat that constant equilibrium was established which now deprives the Heropass of the possibility of doing anything unexpected to our Sun Absolute.

"Names were then given to these cosmoses, and these names exist even to the present day.

"Thus our whole Universe had been called 'Megalocosmos' since then: and this Megalocosmos consists of seven cosmoses, these seven cosmoses are called as follows:

(1) The Sun Absolute itself: 'Protocosmos.'

(2) All the newly created suns together: 'Macrocosmos.'

(3) Each newly-created sun individually: 'Defterocosmos.'

(4) The third grade suns called: 'Mesocosmos.'

(5) Those smallest similarities of the Megalocosmos, which were formed on the Mesocosmoses were called 'Microcosmoses'

(6) Those forms accumulating from these Microcosmoses were called: 'Tritocosmoses.'

"By the way, you must know that the Mesocosmoses are just those points of the Universe, which we now call planets, and Tritocosmoses are just those forms, now called beings, which inhabit the planets.

"Names were given then also to the emanations and radiations of the suns of all three grades. The Emanations of the Sun Absolute were called, 'Ayalogos'; the emanation of the newly-created suns, 'Okidonos'; and the radiations of the planets were called 'Dinamodonis.'

"When all had become regulated in these cosmoses and their harmonious mechanical reciprocal maintenance, through reciprocal feeding had been finally established, then, my dear Hassein, in one of these cosmoses, namely, in the Tritocosmos, owing to the fact that this Tritocosmos had received its form on the surface of the Mesocosmos, that is, of the planets, and owing to the fact that this surface by chance afforded suitable possibilities and conditions, and, of course, also, owing to the fact that this cosmos was a part of the fulfillment of the Trogoautoegocrat, that is, could exist owing to the support of other cosmoses, and in turn served to produce substances for support of other cosmoses—owing to all these reasons, on certain planets, among these Tritocosmoses, the possibility of mechanical movement on the surface of those planets was obtained.

"This mechanical movement was specially helped by the

fact that the need of food of this, as well as of all other cosmoses, was not continuous but periodic.

"When our ENDLESSNESS observed this unforeseen phenomenon, the idea first arose in HIM for the governance of the enlarged Universe, to create for HIMSELF from these Tritocosomoses, a certain help.

"We can clearly see that this idea then first arose in our ENDLESSNESS from the words of the hymns with which our Cherubim and Seraphim still extol the works of our CREATOR, during all the festivals.

"In short, when our CREATOR, HIS ENDLESSNESS, decided to prepare help for HIMSELF, HE first began to organize on certain planets conditions of such possibilities for Tritocosmoses, that, among them, in a certain manner of existence, in their bodies, formed of Microcosmoses, another body could also be formed, of similar shape, but from substances of a higher rate of vibration, namely, from substances of atmosphere already formed around each planet in which such corresponding substances were present; that is, substances formed through the radiations of any solar system, during the action of the Trogoautoegocrat of the chief cycle of the cosmic Heptaparaparshinokh. The forming of this—the second body—was necessary in order that the process of the Triamazikamno should be obtained in these Tritocosmoses, and from the result of the process of the Triamazikamno the possibility of having 'Instinct,' as it is called, is obtained.

"Afterwards when this second body was formed in certain Tritocosmoses, Instinct began to function in them.

"These Tritocosmoses were then named 'beings,' which means 'those who feel.'

"Later on, after these Tritocosmos-beings had become two-bodied and the Instinct began to adapt itself entirely for functioning, a third body, also an exact copy of the first body which was formed of Microcosmoses, gradually began to be formed in this new second body of theirs, from substances still more vivifying.

"These substances were of emanations of almost all the Defterocosmoses, that is, of the Suns-Absolute of the second grade. In these substances, the 'corresponding' entered by means of emanations from the Sun Absolute itself, that is, Our Protocosmos.

"These third bodies of the beings-Tritocosmos began afterwards to be called 'Souls.'

"Owing to this third body, Pure Reason began to be formed among the Tritocosmos from that time. This Pure Reason can also be formed at the present time, but only in those beings, in whom their third body, that is, the soul has been perfected.

"And this forming of the second and third bodies in the beings Tritocosmos was brought about in the following way. Try to understand very well that I am now going to tell you, because at present, our second and third bodies are also formed and improved in the same manner as was done in the first beings. It was as follows:

"When all the seven cosmoses had become machines for our Universe, and through these machines all the substance-matters of the Universe had begun to evolve and involve, that is to say, to pass from one density to another, or as it is said, when the atomic elements began to acquire in themselves the greatest and least vibrations, then in each cosmos, according to the Laws of Triamazikamno and Heptaparaparshinokh, there began to become transformed three kinds of substance matters, which are present in three independent centers of gravity, composing the chief octave of substance-matters present in all our Megalocosmos, that is, in all our Universe.

"By the way, you must absolutely know, that all beings Tritocosmos, then as well as now, besides being independent individuals for the forming and improving of their souls, were and are also machines, through which evolve and involve corresponding cosmic substance-matters for the feeding and maintaining of this, that or the other cosmos. Briefly, they form the existing Trogoautoegocrat of the Universe.

"These beings, being also cosmoses, evolutions and involutions could also begin to proceed through them for the Trogoautoegocrat of the corresponding degree of substance-matters, forming the chief octave of the Triamazikamno and the Heptaparaparshinokh, of the substances of the whole of our Universe.

"And as in every atmosphere of every planet, there are substances derived from all substances emanated or radiated by all the cosmoses of our Megalocosmos, it follows that through these Tritocosmoses, substances of all cosmoses could evolve and involve.

"Generally through every cosmos, three kinds of substances, that is, substances from the three grades of the chief octave of the Triamazikamno of all substances of the Universe, mechanically evolve or involve, according to the law of Triamazikamno. And therefore also through these Tritocosmos-beings, substances of three degrees also evolve and involve.

"The first were substances formed from the radiations of their own planet. The second were substances emanated and radiated, both from their own sun, and from all the other planets of their particular Solar System. And the third matter is that which is formed from the emanation of all the suns of Our Universe, among which, is even our own Sun Absolute.

"Although all the machine-cosmoses of the Megalocosmos in the Universe having nothing in common with each other in regard to size, or by exterior form, nevertheless the processes of the evolution and involution of matter proceed as I have already told you, equally in all cosmoses, according to the Laws of Triamazikamno and Heptaparaparshinokh.

"It will be best, I think, if we take as an example your contemporary beloved beings of the planet Earth.

"In the Universe there are also machine-beings for transmuting substances upwards and downwards; and they also have in themselves the same organization as other cosmoses, that is, they are also similar to the Megalocosmos.

"Although the planet Earth was not yet in existence when the first Tritocosmos-beings appeared, yet the processes of evolution and involution then proceeded through the first Tritocosmos-beings, just as at present, the same evolutions and involutions of cosmic substances proceed through these favorites of yours.

"By the way, you will remember that amongst your beings there is an expression somewhere:

"'That we are made in the image of God.'

"This is quite true, and really they are similar in everything to the Megalocosmos. These words, it seems, are the only thing in which they are not mistaken. But unfortunately these words also, like everything else amongst them, have only the outer form; that is to say, these words are for them only empty, like words learned by heart, meaningless and not understood. For instance, supposing that they should really wish to realize the sense of the words uttered by them that we are in the image of God, they would at best, in order to understand them have to argue as follows:

"'If we are in the image of God, then God must be like us; hence God must have the same appearance as we have; the same mustache, the same nose, the same character; He dresses Himself in the same way,' and so on, and so forth, all in the same manner. Pretty certainly they would represent God with a comb sticking out of His left pocket, for combing His beard. They do, in fact, picture Him to themselves as an old man with a long grey beard and for some reason or other, He has to look like an old Jew.

"These words however, that they are made in the image of God, that is to say, like the Megalocosmos are really very just.

The organization and functions of their bodies are similar to the Megalocosmos in everything, down to the tiniest trifle in every detail. For instance, they have in the head, a brain; by its function this brain exactly corresponds to the role which our Protocosmos, that is, the Sun Absolute, fulfills for the Megalocosmos, and the cells of the brain of the Earth-beings fulfill the same role as the souls who are at present on the Sun Absolute.

"In the marrow of the spine, they have spinal nodes, which are the same fixed points for the brain as the Defterocosmos, are for the Protocosmos. And in the brain, these nodes are similarly resistant in the Law of the Triamazikamno, just as all the Defterocosmoses, that is, the newly created suns of the Universe, are resistant to the Sun Absolute.

"In the trunk, your favorites have certain nervous nodes, which they call the solar plexus. In these nervous nodes there settle to the bottom just those forms of all the results of the strong perceptions and impressions which arise only when, intentionally or accidentally, friction or a struggle takes place between the affirming of the brain and the denying of the spinal marrow, as it always occurs between the Protocosmos and the Defterocosmoses. And the results of these struggles are for their Triamazikamno neutralizing; as for the Triamazikamno of the Megalocosmos, all the creations of the Universe are neutralizing—those creations arising from the positiveness of the Protocosmos and the negativeness of the Defterocosmoses.

"In a word, just as amongst your beings the Triamazikamno is formed by the substances of their head-brain, spinal marrow, and the accumulated results in the nervous nodes of their trunk, so also, for the Megalocosmos, the Triamazikamno is formed by the emanations as follows; the positive are the emanations of the Protocosmos, the negative, the emanations of the Defterocosmoses, and the neutralizing—all the creations of the whole Universe.

"For the maintenance and renewal of the sources of all the three parts of their Triamazikamno, your favorites have also three kinds of food, the substances of which are derived from three different places, having three different densities, corresponding to the three different degrees of the matter of the fundamental octave of substances of the Triamazikamno of our Megalocosmos.

"The substances of the first kind of food of the Earth-beings are those which they obtain through their ordinary food and drink. These are derived from the planet itself, that is to say, they are obtained from substances which are formed from the minerals and 'centrovodi' of their planet, and chiefly during the passing of the substances from one density to another.

"Their second food, they obtain, as they say, by breathing air. This same air, as I have already told you, is composed of substances radiated by their own planet, as well as by the other planets of their system. There are in the same air, substances derived from emanations of all the suns also, and even from the emanations of the Sun Absolute itself; but as yet, these substances cannot be assimilated consciously by your favorites, but enter only as their nature demands, and to serve as the highest neutralizing substances for the possibility of continuing their race, and for the maintenance of the general cosmic harmony of the Trogoautoegocrat.

"They have no necessity, at present, of a conscious assimilation of these substances, because they have also no need to form consciously, and to improve in themselves, the body of the conscience—'Kesdjan' and the body of Pure Reason, namely the body of the soul. On the other hand, for mere existence and the continuation of their race, these same substances automatically enter all the beings without their consciousness and will, and to the degree necessary for the cosmic Trogoautoegocrat. And for this unconscious assimilation, it is not at all necessary for your beings to ruffle and upset their undivine self-complacency.

"The conscious assimilation of these matters is for the beings of that planet at the present time, a quite superfluous luxury. Only at the beginning, for the beings of the continent Atlantis, was the use of this third food considered the most important aim of one's existence. This food was called 'Helkdonis' and the process of nourishment by this food was called, 'Helping God.' But contemporary beings have no name for this third food at all; they neither know nor suspect its existence, or that they assimilate it automatically, and that it is the chief thing for the improvement of beings in general, and also a very necessary food for them.

"Be that as it may, the three kinds of cosmic substances composing the fundamental octave of the Law of Triamazikamno, must also enter into your Earth-beings for transformation. Through ordinary food and drink, negative substances enter into them; through air, positive substances; and through this Helkdonis, the neutralizing; or, as the beings of Atlantis said, these positive and negative substances become deified through the process of 'Helping God.'

"These substances, in general, evolve in beings in the following way. Let us take as an example these negative substances, those namely which enter into beings through ordinary food and drink.

"The evolution of these negative cosmic substances, composing the ordinary food of beings, depends also on the Trogoautoegocrat, and particularly on the Law of Heptaparaparshinokh, exactly as the existence of the Sun Absolute depends upon forces external to itself. In two places, in the path of this evolution according to the Law of Heptaparaparshinokh, help from outside is necessary in the form of substances not their own; and in this case, of substances of the negative kind. And these negative substances can evolve only with the help of these foreign substances, proceeding in the machine-beings in the following way.

"The evolution of the substances proceeds, of course, according to the Laws of Triamazikamno and Heptaparaparshinokh. As I have already told you, all the substances of the Universe are divided into three kinds, composing the fundamental octave of the cosmic Triamazikamno. Each of these substances has its definite density, or, as it is otherwise said, its own definite vibration rate. The food of Earth-beings consists of substances of crystallized definite densities, or definite vibration-rates, peculiar to substances formed among these negative substances and entering into the first food of the machine-beings. In the present case, these substances are formed in the crystallizations; in other words, they are crystallized on the surfaces of the Mesocosmoses, or planets.

"Owing to the Law of Heptaparaparshinokh, every crystallization of substances was formerly derived from the seven highest definite crystallizations; and these latter, in their turn, were formations also of seven, and so on, almost to infinity. According to the same law therefore the crystallizations of the first food of beings were also previously formed during their involution, from the seven definite highest substances with their seven definite densities or vibration-rates. And these substances now occupy the place of the negative substances of the fundamental octave of the Triamazikamno of cosmic substances.

"These crystallizations, then, entering into the machine-beings must evolve from the negative degree, and be transformed into positive cosmic crystallizations.

"When these negative crystallizations enter the Tritocosmos-beings in order to evolve into active cosmic crystallizations they are first decomposed in the Tritocosmoses, that is, they cease to be definite crystallizations, which can generally exist beyond the cosmoses as long as they please.

"I will say here that in the Universe there are three kinds or three classes of crystallized matter only. At the same time, there exist in the Universe, at every moment, substances of hundreds of different densities and vibration-rates, because these latter are part of the process of the Law of Heptaparaparshinokh, and since at every moment they can pass into greater or lesser densities, they cannot exist a long time in this state. Only such crystallized substances as are a part of the fundamental cosmic Triamazikamno can exist for a long time. These same definite crystallizations evolve and involve only through cosmoses which are present in the Universe, among which are just the Tritocosmoses, that is to say, beings. Through the evolutions of the crystallizations of substances of the Universe in these cosmoses, a universal cosmic harmonious Trogoautoegocrat is obtained.

"Thus the negative cosmic crystallization, composing the first food of your Earth-beings is broken down. Each crystallization decomposes again into those seven independent crystallizations of which it consisted before, that is to say, of which it was formed during its former evolutions or involutions, and which were able to be crystallized into their present density.

"Thereupon these former crystallizations, having now entered into the machines of the Tritocosmos beings, must evolve again into the former ones, and become positive cosmic substances.

"Always, in the Tritocosmos-beings, and also in your favorites this evolution as a rule, proceeds in the following manner: The crystallization of substances of which their first food consists, is broken down as I have already told you, or decomposed, the process beginning from their mouth. It is transformed in the stomach into substances having a density or vibration-rate corresponding to the first center of gravity of cosmic active substances, that is, to positive crystallized substances, which exist on the surface of the Mesocosmoses in their radiations, and which generally keep to their circuit, that is to say, they remain around the planets. The evolution of substances in the machine Earth-beings, as well as in all the other beings of the Universe usually proceeds through the mixing of some substances with others.

"And this mixing proceeds in the following way: substances of the first food, introduced into these machine-beings as negative, are mixed with the positive, which have already been acquired and are in the beings. And there enter into this mixture the substances, firstly of 'Abrustdonis' and then 'Helkdonis,' that is to say, in general, neutralizing substances of the fundamental cosmic octave of the Law of Triamazikamno. These substances, by the way, are acquired in your favorites at the present time, chiefly by their voluntary or involuntary, but only acute psychic experiences, which mechanically become in them a means for the perception of this third force, necessary for their machines and for their own Triamazikamno. By means of all this, they fulfill, of course, unconsciously, a part of their duty to Nature. Thus the mixing of substances passing from one center of gravity to the other, finally forms in these machines, crystallizations of positive substances of the fundamental cosmic octave.

"In beings, as also in all the cosmoses, the Law of Heptaparaparshinokh makes its full cycle of this particular octave; that is it transfers substances from one crystallization to another of a higher or lower degree of the octave of the Triamazikamno—in short to such a crystallization, as can exist beyond the cosmoses and have in itself all the properties of both of the chief cosmic laws of Triamazikamno and Heptaparaparshinokh. Here it is very important to notice well in your consciousness that in the Law of Heptaparaparshinokh, during the process of movement from one center of gravity to another, to the final completion of the whole process, there are gaps, or as they are called 'intervals,' in two places, at which intervals there was 'all,' when our ENDLESSNESS made the existing, self-supporting and independent forces for the existence of the Sun Absolute dependent on the foreign forces from without; that is to say, HE transformed the Autoegocrat into the Trogoautoegocrat.

"Well, then, our ENDLESSNESS made, but only in this Law of Heptaparaparshinokh, two gaps or intervals through which forces or substances coming from without should enter. From the time of this change, the Law of Heptaparaparshinokh could no longer completely evolve or involve without foreign help coming through its two intervals. And according to this property of the Law of Heptaparaparshinokh, by means of these two intervals, it now effects the evolution and involution of substances in the beings composing the Tritocosmoses. That is to say, during the transition of substances from one center of gravity to another, substances of the fundamental cosmic Triamazikamno of quite other densities, must, without fail, help in two places. And in those organic machines, such a help proceeds in the following way.

"I have already told you that the substances of the first food of beings, gradually change, beginning from the mouth and are transformed in the stomach into substances corresponding to the first center of gravity of the next higher degree of substances of the fundamental cosmic octave; the substances of this center of gravity are called 'Protoëhary.'

"Proceeding from the stomach, the substances named Protoëhary are mixed in the same manner and pass into the second center of gravity, the central place of which is the twelve-fingered intestine; the densities of substances obtained here are called 'Defteroëhary.' A part of this Defteroëhary is used for the fulfillment of the Law of the local Triamazikamno for the new-coming foods; the other part continues its evolution further.

"The substances named Defteroëhary arising in the twelve-fingered intestine evolve further through various mixings and are transformed into substances of the third center of gravity of the Heptaparaparshinokh. They are called 'Tritoëhary,' and their central place is the liver. And here in this very place of the center of gravity in the Law of Heptaparaparshinokh which exists in beings is the first interval.

"When the substances reach this center of gravity, there is an end for all of them to the possibility of their further evolution, according to the new Law of Heptaparaparshinokh. Other substances having densities of other and higher vibrations, must, without fail, come from outside to help these substances of Tritoëhary to pass into the next center of gravity.

"Now, my dear Hassein, you can very well understand the difference between the forces Autoegocrat and Trogoautoegocrat.

"For instance, if there existed only the old force Autoegocrat maintaining the existence of the Sun Absolute, then by the former Law of Heptaparaparshinokh, when the food of the beings entered into the cosmos-machines and began its evolution, encountering no obstacles, it would assuredly pursue its evolution through successive transformations into higher densities. But owing to the New Law of Heptaparaparshinokh the substances derived from this first food and arising in the third center of gravity of the Law of Heptaparaparshinokh, can no longer continue to evolve independently. They can evolve further only with the aid of help from outside. And this foreign aid for substances of the first food, at this point, is the food which Earth-beings call 'air' and which, as I have already said, is formed from substances radiated from the various Mesocosmoses of the given Solar System.

"These substances derived from air, beginning from the nose of the beings, are also broken down or decomposed. They too are transformed in their lungs into the Protoëhary, but into substances of the first center of gravity of the next class of substances, namely into positive substances of the fundamental cosmic octave of the Triamazikamno; that is, into the crystallizations formed from the radiation of various Mesocosmoses.

"This second Protoëhary of the second Law, having in itself all the possibilities in the cosmoses, mixes without any hindrance with the matters of Tritoëhary of the first food; and both together are transferred higher, that is, are transformed into substances Tetartoëhary.

"These substances Tetartoëhary have their central place in the Earth-beings in both hemispheres of their head brain. And these substances Tetartoëhary thus obtained from the first food, have according to the Law of Heptaparaparshinokh, the possibility of continuing their evolutions further without outside help alone and independently.

"Part of these substances Tetartoëhary is spent as before for the maintenance of the machine itself, while the other part after several admixtures with substances of the same class, already present and previously formed, is finally collected in the cerebellum, as it is called, which is also situated in their head. Substances arising in this place are named 'Piandjoëhary' or as they are still sometimes called, 'The salt of the essence'; the quintessence.

"A part of this 'salt of essence' or Piandjoëhary, in the cerebellum is, once again spent in the corresponding working of the machine itself, while the other part passes through the brain centers of the spinal marrow and through the nervous ganglia of the breast, and is eventually collected in the ovaries as they are called. Here, they come to the second interval of the Law of Heptaparaparshinokh that is to say, they attain here the ultimate possibility of the automatic evolution of substances within the law of Heptaparaparshinokh only; that is, without the aid of the Pure Reason or Pure Will, in the present case, of the beings of your planet themselves. These same substances, collected in the ovaries, are named 'Exioëhary,' or as the Earth-beings call them 'sperma.'

"It will not trouble you if I tell you that in the spinal marrow of your favorites, among the fixed points about which I have told you, there is a certain fixed point, a spinal center, situated at the extreme end of the vertebral column.

"This is that very place, where formerly in their ancestors, the famous organ Kundabuffer, was placed. When this organ was destroyed this very brain center had just been formed in them in this very place; and from that time it began to pass by heredity from generation to generation. Today, they call this spinal center Kundalini, and it now plays a very strange part in their Indian Philosophy as it is called; as if there were in this very organ the lost key to the means of self-development, invented by those Indian Psychopaths.

"It is also interesting to notice that one of the functions of this same spinal center is to act as agent by means of which the tempo of their blood circulation is changed: that is to say, of the filling of the blood vessels about which you remember I recently told you when I said that such filling of blood-vessels induces in the Earth-beings their well known hypnotic state.

"Well, enough about this. Let us continue. We were saying that the substances named Piandjoëhary pass from the cerebellum through the spinal centers of the spinal marrow and the nervous ganglia of the breast, are collected in the ovaries and transformed into the substances Exioëhary or sperma.

"Either owing to the cosmic Triamazikamno for the formation of a new being, or owing to the Pure Reason or Pure Will, for the forming of and perfecting of the second body of being, called 'Kesdjan,' the substances of this sperma or Exioëhary can pass to the next octave.

"But in the absence of either of these two conditions of the matters Exioëhary, they begin to involve and to crystallize into their prime crystallizations, usually in the same order in which they have been evolved.

"The forming and perfecting of the Kesdjan is brought about by means of the substances called 'Helkdonis.'

"Thus owing to the Law of Heptaparaparshinokh in the machine-beings the substances of the first food of the Earth-beings, gradually evolving from their definite crystallizations from one center of gravity to another, are eventually transformed into substances of the final center of gravity of the Law of Heptaparaparshinokh and can be crystallized into permanent active matters and fulfill the cosmic Trogoautoegocrat, that is, serve either for the formation of a new being or for the formation and perfecting of the second body Kesdjan.

"But unless they receive the required help, they begin, on account that same Heptaparaparshinokh, to involve back again and eventually they pass into these negative crystallizations, from which they began their evolutions to the positive ones.

"By the way, you must know that at the present time the substances of the Exioëhary do not serve at all among your favorites for conscious use. Of course without their consciousness and desire, they are used only for the cosmic Trogoautoegocrat, that is, for the formation of new machines which replace them and which are required by Nature for the continuation of their race.

"They are also used as a means of satisfying the consequences of the properties of the organ Kundabuffer, that is to say, for obtaining a certain palpitating self-oblivious pleasure. Latterly indeed during these pleasures, this continuation of the race takes place accidentally among them, and certainly much against their wish, since such a result is for many of them often extremely depressing, as involving in the future, many inconveniences and deprivations of the possibility of satisfying their numerous weaknesses formed from the consequences of the properties of the, for them, fraudulent organ Kundabuffer.

"According to the Law of Triamazikamno, the continuation of their race from this Exioëhary proceeds in the following way. In Earth-beings of the male sex, owing to certain details of mixing, Exioëhary is formed with the properties of positivity, that is, activity; and the Exioëhary formed in beings of the female sex, is, for the same reason, worked out with negative properties, that is passive. If during the mixing of the Exioëhary of the male sex and the Exioëhary of the female sex, there enter into this mixture substances of the third force, that is, of the neutralizing force of the Law of Triamazikamno, conception ensues for a new formation; that is, the result of the union of two opposite consequences, formed from the causes resulting from the former consequences arising during the course of the cosmic Trogoautoegocrat.

"Formerly on this planet, beings also knew that for three-centered beings, besides ordinary coarse food for the stomach, it is also necessary always to feed on a second and a third food; but only the beings of that period when the continent Atlantis still existed arrived at this knowledge, and began to put it into practice. With the destruction of Atlantis there perished forever for the Earth-beings all knowledge and understanding about these two latter foods.

"Although at the present time beings of the Earth also consume all three kinds of food, yet they consume them, especially the two latter, quite automatically, without any desire or understanding.

"They know today only the first food; and they know this only because its necessity and visibility are so obvious that with their best will otherwise, it is impossible for them not to know about it.

"They also know a little about the second food which they simply call 'air.' They know that without this air they cannot exist; but of what it consists and into what its matters are transformed in them, they know absolutely nothing at all.

"But as regards the third food, they not only know nothing about it, but they have never even heard of it.

"The matters of all three foods automatically evolve in contemporary beings to the degree demanded by Nature for the maintenance of their existence and the continuation of their race.

"The beings of the continent Atlantis called the second food 'Abrustdonis' and the third 'Helkdonis.' Regarding these two foods as very important and the productive feeding on them as their most important duty, the evolution of substances of Exioëhary in most of them began to proceed as it proceeds in almost all the three-centered beings on all the planets of our great Megalocosmos.

"Of this knowledge and understanding, that is, concerning the necessity of the second and third foods for beings, something has passed by some means or other from the beings of the continent Atlantis to contemporary beings of the Earth; but unfortunately it has passed to them after the manner described by our eminent Mullah Nassr Eddin:

"'As for seeing him, I saw him; but strange to say, I did not observe his size.'

"In such a case he would also say:

"'I noticed the taste, but only from my throat down.'

"For instance, the knowledge was passed down to contemporary beings, that this Exioëhary is formed in them, and that its substances can serve beings for their perfection. That is true, but unfortunately for them, they did not acquire knowledge of the necessary means. No information reached them regarding the possibility of working out in oneself the substances of Abrustdonis and Helkdonis, which substances alone can help the further evolution of the substances of the Exioëhary to this end.

"On the basis of this same degree of knowledge of Exioëhary, that is, only the truncated remains, many contemporary beings have wished to perfect themselves by means of this Exioëhary. With their peculiarity, they began to 'get clever' with this partial knowledge, and as a result of 'getting clever' they decide that if it is possible to perfect oneself by means of the substances of the Exioëhary, then surely, by abstinence from its ordinary ejection, the perfecting would proceed as a matter of course.

"From that time on, very many of them began to abstain from the ordinary ejection of Exioëhary from themselves. They joined together and formed large communities under various names; and today there exist very many of these sects whose members live together.

"They are called by other beings of the Earth 'monks'; and the places where they dwell are called 'monasteries.'

"It naturally never enters the heads of these monks, that although it is possible to perfect oneself by means of the Exioëhary, yet this perfection can proceed only through the conscious consumption and digestion of the substances of Abrustdonis and Helkdonis, and this is why of course, no effective result has ever been obtained from their abstinence, or will ever be obtained. One very strange result however has arisen.

"As I have already told you, in the process of the complete cycle of transformation of substances from one kind of crystallizations to others, in the Law of Heptaparaparshinokh, the substances in two of their centers of gravity cannot pass independently unless they receive assistance from other matters of higher vibrations. And only the substances of the Abrustdonis and Helkdonis can be of any assistance to the Exioëhary. Without these substances, the substances of the Exioëhary, having no possibility of evolving further, and at the same time being unable to remain in the transitory center of gravity of the Law of Heptaparaparshinokh soon begin to involve in the machine-bodies of these unfortunate monks, back again to their first crystallizations. And this Exioëhary happens to have during its involution the property, that its substances assist the machine-being to deposit what is called superfluous fat.

"This is why nearly all the celibate monks of the planet Earth grow fat, with the result that the consequences of the properties of the organ Kundabuffer, are naturally still further intensified in them.

"One often meets a monk who could give very many points to that form of being which the Earth-beings expressly fatten to increase the fat of their bodies.

"And this form of being, is called 'pig.'

"Here you must be told further that during their involution, the substances of the Exioëhary have still another property sometimes; instead of fat, they deposit other substances, or 'Yadoiounoksir,' as they are called. The monks in whom this Yadoiounoksir is deposited, become not fat, but thin, and furthermore, as a result of these substances their character becomes split and definitely dual, with outer and inner aspects having nothing in common with each other.

"And this Yadoiounoksir is produced in those monk-beings who in childhood have practiced the unpardonable habit from which pimples usually appear on the face, from which time on, certain organs in them, through which the Exioëhary is formed, are already spoiled to such an extent, that these substances are either not produced at all, or are produced in a form, which during the involution of substances of the Exioëhary forms substances of this same Yadoiounoksir. Those monk-beings get thin, and their character gradually divides into two, into the outer, visible to all, and the inner, purely subjective, invisible to others. Outwardly they become hypocrites, as they are called, of the highest order, but inwardly they become cynics, as they are called, also of the highest order.

"And so, my dear boy, in your contemporary beings substances are consciously taken and are transformed in them only from one degree of the fundamental cosmic octave, and as regards the two other kinds of food, they are transformed in them for the cosmic Trogoautoegocrat quite unconsciously, and therefore the beings only automatically help Nature, and not as is done by the beings of other planets with the full consciousness of their duty to the Universe in gratitude of their existence.

"Enough of your beings for the moment. Let us return once more to the beings who were first formed directly from the Tritocosmoses.

"Well then . . . owing to their normal existence and the normal evolution in them of the second food, that is of the Abrustdonis, or as the Earth-beings call it, air, their Exioëhary gradually began to be deposited and to be transmuted in them; and from this process there began to be formed in their first body composed of microcosmoses, a second body. This second body was similar to the first, but formed of finer substances; and it was as if the two bodies, the coarse and the fine were put into each other.

"This second body was and is called 'Kesdjan,' or as it is still sometimes named the 'body of the spirit.' When this second body Kesdjan had in its turn been completely formed in them, it also began gradually to perfect itself in the sense of mechanical reasonableness. This mechanical reasonableness formed itself and at the present time forms itself in both the bodies of the being, namely in the planetary body, or as your Earth-beings call it physical body and in the body Kesdjan. The first beings very quickly acquired this reasonableness because they existed quite normally. Moreover, normal existence was then everywhere quite possible, because on no planet was the idea entertained that any sort of peace could be obtained by means of that complacency, which in general always hinders the beings in their strivings for perfection.

"When this second body was also entirely perfected, well there just began then in this same body Kesdjan, and strictly in the same order, owing to the sacred substances of the Helkdonis a gradual deposit of substances formed from the emanations of the Defterocosmoses. And from these substances there was formed in them, the third body, which later was called 'soul.' These three bodies equal in size and similar in all details are also as if one were put into the other, but they are formed of substances of quite different degrees of the fundamental cosmic octave having totally different properties, and, of course, possibilities.

"Here you won't mind if I tell you further, that this Exioëhary which Nature itself forms in your favorites, without their conscious labors, for the continuation of their race, has long ago been adapted to the service of a vice which has become prevalent among them. Unlike the beings of the whole Universe for whom the use of the substances Exioëhary is considered as the chief sacrament of all their divine cosmic sacraments, your beings employ for themselves the processes of the manifestations of the substances of the Exioëhary, as a means of deriving pleasant thrills, and this habit has now entered into their flesh and blood. At the present day this vice is as indispensable to them, as the nourishment derived from their first food.

"Amongst other beings of our Megalocosmos, the days when the process of this manifestation of the Exioëhary is produced, are the greatest and most solemn days of all; and these days are called 'Days for helping God.'

"These days are celebrated not only on the planet Purgatory but also on nearly all the planets of the Universe, and as I have already told you, they are universally considered the greatest and most solemn days of all the days of the year; and not for three-centered beings only, but for all other rather reasonable beings as well, without distinction of form or place of existence.

"Perhaps you do not yet know the significance of these great days, my dear boy," Beelzebub asked his grandson, upon which Hassein replied in the following words.

"No, my dear grandfather, the details of this I do not yet know. Only I do know, that the helping-God days for beings of our planet Karatas, are considered as holidays, and for these holidays there, all our beings prepare themselves almost from the very end of the previous holiday. A 'lunias' even before the beginning of the holiday, both old as well as young cease to introduce into themselves the first food; they only pray and thank our CREATOR for their existence, I know also that the last two of these solemn days are considered as days for praising our fathers.

"That is why during these days every year, my dear grandfather, we all spoke and thought about you, silently beseeching our ENDLESSNESS to create for you such conditions of existence as might enable you quickly and easily to bring your reasonableness to the required sacred gradation, and to finish more quickly this essential existence of yours."

With these words Beelzebub's grandson very solemnly ended his reply.

"Well now, my dear boy, when we get home, I will explain to you in detail about Exioëhary, and also how these sacred sacraments proceed; but meanwhile, let us go back again to our story of the first Tritocosmos beings. If we spend so much time on digressions we shall be nearing our planet Karatas, and I may be obliged to leave unfinished the tale I have begun concerning the holy planet Purgatory.

"Although we shall not arrive on Karatas so very soon, and I certainly have time to finish my tale completely, yet the fact is, that as we now near home, I wish to have some spare time in which to tell you better about those things about which I decided to tell you at the very beginning when I noticed your interest in beings of the planet Earth; but I will tell you only when we are nearly home.

"Why! Why do your eyes shine like that? Curiosity has already seized you as it does your favorites. Better be patient and you will know all in its due time. At least your patience will prove the difference between your nature and that of the beings of that remote planet of our Megalocosmos, who have aroused your intense interest.

"I can only say, that what I wish to tell you, will be the most interesting for you of all that you have heard from me of the events occurring on that planet.

Having said this Beelzebub resumed the thread of his story concerning the holy planet Purgatory.

"In this manner when in the first Tritocosmos-beings, Pure Reason began to be perfected and had reached a certain degree in their third body, then from that time on, such conscious souls were taken to corresponding places of the Universe for corresponding help to our ENDLESSNESS in HIS Government of the enlarged Universe.

"These reasonable souls happened to be appointed to such duties in the following way:

"When the reasonableness in their souls had reached the corresponding gradations of the sacred scale, they finished their essential existence on the planets, or as it is still said, died. Their spirit, that is, the body of the soul, and the body of the Kesdjan, separated themselves both together from their planetary body. And having left this latter body on the planet, both of these bodies, together, rose to the sphere of substances, from which in general, the body Kesdjan is formed, and there they continued to exist and to perfect themselves further. Just there this spirit died a second time, that is to say, the body of the soul separated itself from the body Kesdjan. And only then did the soul become independent.

"If this particular soul already had a corresponding reasonableness it was taken to the Sun Absolute or to other places where there was a need of such souls, and if its reasonableness had not reached the required gradation, it could then continue its existence as a spirit of this sphere. You must know that in this sphere the spirit cannot continue immortal a very long time, since the body of the Kesdjan has only a definite duration. Hence the spirit might die before attaining its perfection. In these cases, the continuation of the existence of the still unperfected soul proceeded in the following way. While it still has its own Kesdjan, every spirit looked about amongst spirits like itself for another suitable Kesdjan which still had a body of the soul. And if this latter spirit died after its perfection, this soul entered into its body Kesdjan and continued its existence and perfection. Such a transmigration or 'reincarnation' of the soul is called 'Psypohdondr.'

"After the first death of the being, then as well as at the present time, his first planetary body, being formed on planets from microcosmoses and from elements of its planets, gradually decomposes into its original elements, and after the second death of the being, the body Kesdjan also, being formed from the substances of the radiations of planets of the given solar system, gradually decomposes into its original elements, and these substances go to their degree of the octavity of this solar system.

"The body of the soul itself, being formed of substances derived from the emanations of various other suns could not be decomposed in the solar system where it was formed and lived, but continued to exist in the given solar system in definite places, until its final perfection. After this at a certain gradation of reasonableness, this body of the soul became an individual, that is, a force in itself, a unity, no longer subject to decomposition from exterior causes.

"Thereafter this perfected soul was taken, as I have already told you, to that place to which the degree of its reasonableness corresponded. By the way, you should know that during this very period, the Cherubim and Seraphim of our ENDLESSNESS created that sacred scale of Reason which exists even till now. This sacred scale of Reason is nothing but a kind of measure, or line divided into equal parts. On one end of this line is indicated a complete absence of all reason, without even a simple instinct; in short, at this end there is indicated absolute inertia. At the other end, there is indicated absolute reason which is the reasonableness of our INCOMPARABLE ENDLESSNESS.

"This measure of reasonableness is used to determine at the present time the reasonableness of all beings of every form originating on every planet of our great Megalocosmos.

"By the way, it will not trouble you if I here also explain to you about Reason. You must try to understand this as well as you can and also assimilate it in yourself. In our Megalocosmos in all beings without any difference of origin and nature, two kinds of reason can be formed and exist—the first kind, objective, the formation and manifestations of which are equal everywhere in every being of the Universe; but the second kind of reason not only on every planet but in every being is different, or as it is said, it is subjective.

"The objective Pure Reason is material, and its source in all beings is formed from one and the same quality and property of matter; and this matter is nothing but substances formed of that prime emanation of the Sun Absolute.

"You remember that I told you that this emanation had not in the beginning all the three forces of the Law of Triamazikamno. This is why our ALMIGHTY ENDLESSNESS was obliged to replace this third force, namely the neutralizing force, by His Own Force of Will. And then from this first emanation were formed special substances which later on entered into the composition of the Defterocosmoses, in consequence of which the source of Reason is composed only of particles of emanations of these Defterocosmoses. In this emanation one often happens to meet and it is also possible to absorb these residual substances which originated from the satisfaction of the Force of the Will of Our PRIME SOURCE, HIS ENDLESSNESS HIMSELF.

"As regards the second kind of reason, namely, the subjective, it is not material. It is only the result of associations of those subjective ideas which the being has acquired during his existence by means of the mechanical perception of his subjective impressions and information. That is why this reason is called automatic, that is to say, not existing by itself, its existence dependent only on mechanical causes. It is only the totality of all true or false informations coming from without.

"Pure Objective Reason by itself is unchangeable; it can perfect itself only by suffering perceptions of truths; and it has the property of being under the law of attraction, that is, of feeling similar to itself. Automatic reason is, of course, not under the law of attraction. Everyone can judge and understand it subjectively, but only according to the similarly mechanically assimilated reasonings in them.

"Pure Reason can become a function in beings only in that third body of theirs, that is, in the body of their soul. In the two other bodies, namely the planetary body, and in the Kesdjan, there can be only that same automatic reason. But in these two bodies the process of that automatic reason is different.

"For example, the perception of information from the outside, in the first planetary or physical body, is produced only by the sound of the names of the object, or as can be otherwise said, the impressions are recorded and associated with words. In the body Kesdjan, on the other hand, that very process is continued by means of so-called molecular forms, that is to say, in the brain of that body there are formed permanent corresponding form-cells for each idea.

"Thus it comes about, my dear Hassein, that at the present time, of those real souls, formed and perfected in those beings themselves, there are very few on the planets.

"They were formed only in the first beings formed directly of the Microcosmoses, and in the bodies of their true heirs.

"Thus all the real souls have long ago nearly perfected themselves: Already they are helping our ENDLESSNESS in HIS Great Fulfillment.

"Nevertheless at the present time there are on nearly all the planets of the Universe very many beings with souls.

"But these souls are, let us say, souls of the second order. Although similar to real souls, they were not formed in the manner I have just described; and they are formed for quite other reasons.

"These souls of the second order arose in the Universe from the following cause. When on the Sun Absolute, there were collected the necessary great number of those real souls, the following unexpected phenomenon occurred.

"In view of the fact that the atmosphere of the Sun Absolute had in itself its Law of Triamazikamno and that real souls also had such a law of their own, there was soon established between the atmosphere of the Sun Absolute and those souls, what is called Triamazikamnian contact, and from that contact in the atmosphere of the Sun Absolute, there gradually began to be formed a certain particular substance. This substance having a much lighter atomic weight than the rest of the substances of the atmosphere of the Sun Absolute, began to collect above that atmosphere and gradually to form a second atmosphere, as it were, on the Sun Absolute.

"Since the Sun Absolute still continued to emanate, thereafter, together with its emanation which spread themselves through the Universe, that same substance also began to be spread through the whole Universe. And since on certain of the planets a variety of forms of the Microcosmos continued to appear, the following unexpected phenomenon began to show itself. In certain of those Microcosmoses—forms in which localized functions were derived from three sources, or as may be otherwise said, in those forms in which were formed three brains, these forms of the Mesocosmoses began to have the property, after a certain period of development, of receiving this certain substance formed on the Sun Absolute from Triamazikamnian contact between real souls and the atmosphere of Our Own Protocosmos itself and in those forms this substance began gradually to deposit an exactly similar form.

"And thus, my dear boy, since the real souls on the Sun Absolute became from the formation of that certain substance, the active Triamazikamnian source, the forms of the Mesocosmos arising from that substance acquired the property of 'Podoboberossa,' that is, from the souls to those formations heredity passed. Hence those formations not only began to clothe themselves in the same substances with which real souls are clothed, but they even began immediately to exhibit very many of the properties which real souls had then acquired.

"From that time onward, in our Universe many such forms were established, which also began to be called souls. They became, indeed, similar to real souls. But their formation as well as their essence, and also their further perfecting were altogether different. Thus from that time, in the World of Our ENDLESSNESS, there began to exist two kinds of souls, real and similar to real.

"Real souls are those which are formed and perfected by the beings themselves through intentional suffering labors; and 'similar' souls are those which found themselves ready made, thanks to that cosmic lack of foresight. But in spite of all this, these second kind of souls again owing to heredity also had in themselves all the possibilities of attainment of real souls; but the ways to that attainment, as I have already told you, are usually different, and very much more difficult and complicated.

"Thus in the course of time, a few of that second kind of souls acquired on certain planets most of the perfections of Pure Reasonableness, and together with such potentialities as real souls can have; but, of course, all these possibilities depend on many external conditions and events, among which are the circumstances which appear to have been the reason for the origin of that holy planet where we have just been.

"That reason was as follows. Owing to the fact that the soul-bodies of the second order of souls had been formed in an abnormal manner, their further perfecting also continued abnormally on certain planets; that is to say, the perfecting of the body of the soul does not take place in harmony with the perfecting of the Reason of the soul. The perfecting of the Reason of the soul has its own way of proceeding while the perfecting of the body of the soul proceeds in dependence upon many external conditions of the planet in question.

"And the disharmony consists in this, that into the body of the soul of the being during the period of its existence, there enter chemical elements, whose density is not correspondent with the places in which such souls, perfected according to their Reasonableness, must continue to live.

"These non-corresponding chemical substances which enter into the bodies of the souls of the second order, are sometimes called 'involuntary sin'; and the formation of that sin almost entirely depends on the established external conditions existing on the planet where the existence and perfecting of the bearer of such a soul was passed. These conditions of these beings help to deposit those substances involuntarily, that is to say, independently of the reason of any one of the bodies of the being; and in the Universe itself, there exists a universal and invariable rule, especially established from ancient times, to punish ruthlessly all those bearers of Divine Reason who, either voluntarily or involuntarily, appear to be the cause of the creation on the planets of unfavorable conditions for the perfecting of the beings.

"And thus when in those inharmoniously formed souls, their Reasonableness is brought up to the required degree, after which there is no necessity for them to live on the usual planets;—and also moreover, owing to a certain chemical law, existence for them on these planets becomes impossible;—and when again at the same time, owing to those non-corresponding chemical elements in their bodies, they cannot correspond, either to the Sun Absolute, or to any of the places where such reasonable souls may be, then these 'similar' souls become as it were, without a refuge and homeless.

"And it was for just these homeless souls that this same holy planet Purgatory was prepared.

"There on that planet Purgatory, all those homeless souls were gathered from all our Universe; and there they exist while purging themselves from just those undesirable chemical elements which they have had the misfortune to absorb during their life on the planets with unfortunate external conditions established for the essential existence of those souls.

"Solely on account of those chemical substances, such souls have no present access to those places where they belong according to the degree of their attainment in the sense of the Pure Divine Reason.

"That holy planet on which they now live is called Purgatory, just because they there purge themselves from those undesirable chemical elements in their bodies. Their chief misfortune now lies in the fact that having finally reached that holy planet and already knowing and understanding their perfected reason, all the ways in which they might have been useful to our ENDLESSNESS, they cannot at once begin to help HIM in HIS Great Fulfillment for the good of the Universe. They therefore constantly and intensely work on themselves there, in order that they may more quickly purge their bodies from their undesirable chemical elements, and have access to where, as I have already told you, according to their Reasonableness, they have already merited to attain, and be thought worthy to discharge their necessary duties.

"And thus, my dear Hassein, when the phenomenon of that second sort of souls was first noticed by our ALL-COMPREHENSIVENESS, HE being eternally, justly compassionate, could not help paying attention to that regrettable phenomenon. HE immediately chose the best planet of all the planets of the Universe and allotted it to them for their existence, and HE ordered that planet to be arranged in such a way, that these kind of souls might have every possibility of purging themselves of the undesirable elements contained in their bodies.

"Then at HIS own wish, Our All-Quarters-Maintaining Holy Archangel Helkgematios took it upon Himself the organization and chief direction of the planet. He it was who first merited the great Holy Anklad, that is, He was the first who acquired that degree of Reasonableness to which in general, it is possible for beings, whatever their nature, to attain, namely to that Reasonableness, which is the third in degree after the Reason of Our MOST MAGNIFICENT ENDLESSNESS. And He is still the chief administrator of that Incomparable Holy Planet.

"That Holy Planet Purgatory is not only in itself the best of all the planets in the Universe, but on it are collected, by Our Great-All-Quarters-Maintainer, from all the suns and planets, the best they contained. This is why that holy planet Purgatory appears to be at the present time, as much in riches as in beauty, the best point in the Universe, perhaps even better than the Sun Absolute itself.

"You have probably observed, my boy, that on that holy planet, the skies are always turquoise, the atmosphere there is constantly crystal clear, there are perfumes of the most heart-tranquilizing aroma, and of springs alone there are ten-thousand, as authorities on the matter tell us, of mineral as well as fresh water, such as scarcely exist in such limpidity and naturalness on any other planet of our Megalocosmos.

"From all the Universe there are collected on that planet the most beautiful and best songbirds and of these, as the authorities also tell us, there are nearly twelve thousand species; and as for fruits, flowers and berries words cannot describe them.

"On that holy planet it is possible to say with confidence, there are collected every species of flora, fauna, and foscalia from the whole Universe. Besides all this, on that planet everywhere, there are in corresponding gorges various caves, partly made by nature and partly artificial, commanding magnificent views; and these caves are so arranged that everything necessary to a peaceful and comfortable existence is there.

"In those caves, by their own choice live those just and already perfected souls. On that planet there is also for convenience as well as for speed, the best Egolionopty in the Universe, or as they sometimes call it, the omnipresent platform. This omnipresent platform can be moved at discretion in any direction in the atmosphere of the holy planet and at any desired speed, even with the speed with which suns usually fall.

"This Egolionopty was invented especially for that holy planet by the famous Angel now Archangel Herkission, and it moves, it seems, according to the principle of the space ship on which we are now flying.

"In a word, the souls inhabiting that planet Purgatory might have a perfect and quiet existence, with everything uniquely favorable. Nevertheless, for them these external circumstances of quiet and comfort simply do not count at all.

"They are entirely absorbed in the increasing labor of their purgation; and only the hope of one day having the good fortune and the possibility of becoming a part of the Greatness which is fulfilled by our ALL-POSSIBLE ENDLESSNESS for the good of All, appears occasionally to give them peace.

"It will also certainly interest you to know that nearly all the beings in the Universe know of that holy planet. Only your contemporary favorites know absolutely nothing about it. In the whole of our Universe, in fact, those three-centered beings, having souls even of the second order, not only know of the existence of this holy planet, but if they have acquired only a little Reasonableness, they already begin to dream of getting there.

"Owing only to that dream, such beings with great readiness and joy always allow in their lower bodies all the kinds of discomfort which it is natural to them to have. These discomforts they permit, because they understand that their lower bodies, for example, their planetary body, appears to be in their own Law of Triamazikamno, the inevitable source of negative manifestations only and as the negative source, it will always try and must manifest only negatively for its positive source. In other words, the manifestations of the planetary body must necessarily be opposed to those of the body of its soul.

"Every such conscious being well knows that his planetary body inexorably demands what his divine soul-body must not desire; and hence it is that they constantly engage in merciless combat with the desires of their planetary bodies, in order that in the struggle there may be formed in them from the friction substances of the divine Helkdonis, which is necessary and useful to their positive and divine soul-bodies.

"And as regards the desires of Kesdjan, that is, of the second body of the being, all conscious beings having understanding, very well understand that this body of theirs, which appears for their own Law of Triamazikamno to be the neutralizing source, must always remain indifferent in its mechanical manifestations; and as regards its active manifestations, this body, on the basis of the cosmic Law of Urdekhplifata, always strives to desire only those desires of which there are more in one or the other of these two bodies, both opposite in their nature.

"Beings having understanding have no pity on their planetary bodies in order that their second body may perfect itself more quickly, that is to say, the body Kesdjan, as well as their Pantbril body of the soul, or as your favorites call it 'Immortal Body.' And they strive to bring the Reasonableness of this latter body to the degree which gives them the possibility of reaching that very holy planet Purgatory, that planet which is considered by all the beings of the Universe to be, and which is indeed, the heart of all our great Megalocosmos.

"Although I have said that your favorites do not know of this holy planet, this is not altogether so. A certain number there, even of contemporary beings, have heard of this holy planet; but this number is very small and their idea of the holy planet recalls how our highly esteemed Mullah Nassr Eddin described a similar idea. He used only three words, namely:

"'Chihertma provokes sneezing.'

"Other beings, even down to the present, praise as 'great Initiates,' those beings who have heard of it there, though amongst these contemporary 'initiates,' the knowledge of that holy planet is no greater than amongst ordinary beings, who sometimes call themselves 'mortals.' The knowledge of that holy planet, possessed by these unfortunate contemporary 'great initiates' reached them in the following manner. You must know that formerly on the planet Earth, the beings of the continent Atlantis were also well informed about the holy planet Purgatory; and about this information there even existed among them a very detailed and complete Legominism.

"After the destruction of that continent this Legominism survived, in some manner or other, and began to pass from generation to generation through the real 'great initiates' of those times, who indeed did exist in former times on the Earth. But with the final destruction on the Earth of all the results of the Holy Ashiata Shiemash's creation, there also vanished from the race of the Earth the possibility for certain beings of becoming real great initiates, although the rank has continued and exists down to our time. There are many beings of such ranks; but what in their being they represent, it seems, I have already told you.

"The final disappearance from that planet of knowledge concerning that holy planet Purgatory occurred the following way.

"Do you remember I told you that once in Babylon, among the learned beings, it appeared to be a painful necessity to discover at all costs whether the soul exists and whether it is immortal. This illness became so intense, that it afflicted the intellects of the 'Great initiates' of those times, whose minds had already begun to be transformed into mechanisms; though they were not spoiled to such an extent as to change their ideas, as London Phu-Phu-Kle now change their gloves. On the contrary if among beings of that time, an ideal was acquired they strove in spite of everything to attain it. But when the general psychosis began demanding the solution at all costs of the question of the Beyond, their minds already growing weak, could make no resistance but fell under its influence; and, in consequence, additions were made to this Legominism concerning the holy planet, with the result that such a 'Khaboor-Chooboor' was transmitted that the tail of Our Lucifer, from very emotion, permanently took the color of tango.

"In my opinion, the minds of these Babylonian 'Great Initiates' became muddled on account of that beautiful theory of the Babylonian dualists, which spread very widely among the beings of the Earth. Strictly speaking this theory itself was not to blame; but those two words which were used both in this theory as well in the Legominism about the holy planet; namely, the words 'Paradise' and 'Hell.'

"In the Babylonian dualistic theory, it was, by the way, also said, that somewhere up in Heaven, Paradise and Hell existed, and that souls of beings of the Earth, after their death were taken according to their merit, either to this Paradise or to this Hell. And there was much detailed talk about those places, in which Paradise was described as such a wonderful place that only the fantasy of Earth-beings is capable of picturing; and by the word Hell such an abominable place was described as also could only be imagined by this same fantasy.

"These two words were also used in the Legominism about this holy planet. I do not know if these two words were taken from the Legominism or if they were obtained by a chance coincidence.

"But in the Legominism of these very two words, the two following ideas were expressed; that is, the word Paradise determined that splendor and opulence which are on the holy planet, and by the word Hell, that inner state which in reality the souls possess who live on this planet, namely the state of sorrow, affliction and oppression.

"Such an inner state the souls living on that planet Purgatory always have indeed, because after inexpressible, suffering labors, as I have already told you, they, having finally reached this holy planet, and having seen and understood all, and also and so often, are not yet able, owing to the undesirable chemical substances in them, to help HIM in the fulfillment of HIS Holy Problems of the Universe.

"And so, my dear boy, these two words, Paradise and Hell, then become the chief reason of the fact that in the minds of these poor 'great initiates' of that time, their conceptions, which even apart from this, was already muddled, became more so.

"On account of these two words, those unfortunate beings imagined that the fantastic theory of the Babylonian dualists was the same as that mentioned in that Legominism. And they added unconsciously and somewhat consciously certain details of this theory to the Legominism for further transmission, owing to which fact at the present time, the 'great initiates' there on the Earth have such astonishing ideas on the subject of the Beyond, that when the hens of our highly esteemed Mullah Nassr Eddin hear them their cackle produces the very same results as follows from the use of that unique eternally true and beneficent remedy—castor oil."

CHAPTER XL

The History Related By Beelzebub Of How Men Learned And Again Forgot About The Fundamental Universal Law Of "Heptaparaparshinokh"

AS BEELZEBUB was finishing his tale about the planet Purgatory, there entered the place where He was sitting with His grandson Hassein, and His old servant Ahoon, a servant bringing something, who on leaving remarked, addressing everybody, that the reflections from the spheres of the planet Karatas were already visible.

When he had gone Beelzebub rose from His place and suggested to His grandson and to Ahoon to return to the upper glass bell and continue their conversation there while admiring the reflections of the spheres of their beloved fatherland. As soon as they were there, His grandson Hassein turned to Him with a new question.

"My dear and kind grandfather, please help me to clear up one idea which is still confused in me. The trouble is that when you told me in the beginning of your tale about the Holy Planet Purgatory to try to understand very clearly the fundamental cosmic laws of Heptaparaparshinokh and Triamazikamno I really did try very earnestly all the time, and it seems that on the whole I understood them fairly well.

"The Law of Triamazikamno I understood quite well, and although several ideas about insignificant details of the Law of Heptaparaparshinokh have not yet been completely assimilated, yet I hope that if I ponder them a little longer I shall understand them also. But now quite another question interests me. When I tried thoroughly to grasp the ideas of these laws, I clearly realized that they were extremely complicated and in general difficult to be understood. And that is why I was and continue to be much astonished that the beings of the Earth can not only understand these cosmic laws but even realize them, since they have, as I understood from all your tales, only a mechanical reason. To find out such things with an automatic reason is in my opinion quite impossible; and I became quite convinced that it is impossible when I myself tried to realize these cosmic laws; and I am very curious therefore to know how this could happen."

Having said this, Hassein looked questioningly at his at his grandfather with eagerness in his eyes, upon which the latter began at to speak as follows: "Well, my dear boy, I will try to explain this also to you. Since only the reflections of the spheres of our Karatas are as yet visible, then we shall perhaps have time to discuss this matter which you have not understood.

"It seems to me that I once told you that . . .

"Although owing to the abnormal conditions of existence established on that planet, the reason of the majority of the beings as they grow up, almost always becomes quite automatic, yet this does not occur among all of them. It sometimes happens by accident that a few escape the general fate; and instead of this ordinary automatic reason, there is formed in them, as in all the other beings of the Universe, a real objective reason. Although such exceptional cases are extremely rare, nevertheless they do occur, and for the following reasons:

"You must know first of all that there exist in almost all the new-born beings there, all the potentialities in germ for the acquirement of pure objective reason.

"These potentialities exist even in new-born beings today. But the whole trouble is that from the very beginning the abnormal conditions of existence there established begin on the one hand to destroy these germs, while on the other hand not only their reason gradually becomes mechanical, but even several functions of their organism, which have nothing in common with their reason, also gradually acquire the property of responding and reacting only to mechanical shocks coming from outside.

"Certain new-born beings, however, in whom the germs of the potentiality of objective reason are not yet spoiled, find again by accident, such conditions for the process of their formation and perfection that the established conditions fail to destroy these germs before these beings have become responsible, or as they say there, adults. And further, still accidentally, some of these unspoiled adults acquire a certain amount of active objective knowledge.

"So my dear boy, it does sometimes happen that from among those who grow up normally and acquire accurate knowledge, some being is formed with a particularly intense capacity for thinking, and from the phenomena observable on their planet or in the events occurring there, he inwardly realizes several objective cosmic truths which he afterwards communicates to all the other beings of his planet. In this manner all the beings of the Earth learn something of these cosmic truths.

"If only all this proceeded normally on that planet, all its beings would gradually learn what all the beings of the whole Universe know; but the evil lies in the fact that even this process does not take place normally, but in a special and particular manner.

"This abnormality arises from a certain and very strange illness which exists only there and which has long ago taken root in their psyche. This strange illness is called 'Cleverness.'

"Owing to this disease of 'Cleverness,' the other automatic beings there, with their automatic reason, usually very quickly begin to 'get clever' with the cosmic truths discovered by a being having objective reason, with the result that these truths become only material for Arabian Nights.

"This illness of 'Cleverness' is usually contracted by savants and writers and proceeds roughly in the following manner:

"The first symptom to appear is the desire to have a certain sum of money. The victim then runs as if possessed to several of his friends and acquaintances to borrow money 'until tomorrow.' Having thus collected a fair amount of money, he goes importantly into a department of the store of Barefaced-Smith and Co., and there buys:

(1) Wax for the mustache,

(2) Suppositories for hemorrhoids,

(3) Vibratory apparatus for removing wrinkles from the face,

(4) Magic ointment for destroying pimples,

(5) Paper of a special size,

(6) Several pencils and most certainly a very handy penknife.

Only when he has brought all these things home does he sit down on a chair with one of its legs missing and begin to 'get clever.' With words taken from the encyclopedic dictionary compiled by Germans, and most assuredly foaming at the mouth he begins to write in proof or disproof of the validity of those truths which the being with objective reason has discovered. For certain details of these truths he collects from the German encyclopedia several fantastic inventions, by means of which he makes a new theory.

"Such theories or proofs are usually spread very quickly over the whole planet. Particularly quickly are the proofs and theories disseminated of those sick beings who have an aunt with bobtailed dogs, or an uncle who was formerly a speculator on the Exchange.

"In short the effect of most of these theories or proofs is, that all that usually remains of the original truths is scarcely recognizable skin and bone.

"In this fashion, my dear boy, regarding the discoveries of the cosmic truths, centuries pass. Hence it is that at the present time, your favorites only know that if a flea sneezes once, there is a flood on a certain continent of their planet; but if this very same flea sneezes twice, then there will be a universal deluge.

"I think it will be best for you, my dear Hassein, if I tell you historically how the beings of the Earth learned and again forgot this fundamental cosmic law of Heptaparaparshinokh, and into what a state knowledge concerning it has now fallen. These stories will help you to clear up those insignificant details, as you called them, of this law which you have not understood; and again by means of these tales you may learn that occasionally one comes across one of your favorites who is impartial and not a vain savant and whose work for Science might bear good fruit, if the existence of the other beings proceeded normally.

"There can be no discussion, of course, that in the beginning, when the beings of that planet had the organ Kundabuffer in themselves, they could discover nothing whatever of any of these truths. But afterwards when this famous organ was destroyed, and their psyche was freed and became their own—well then, from that time, all sorts of things were possible that might perhaps concern their common sense.

"The history of the knowledge of the cosmic law Heptaparaparshinokh began on the continent Atlantis, at the very time, when, you remember, certain beings there realized that something happened in them which is not 'quite right.' They discovered also that they had certain possibilities of being able to destroy this something not 'quite right' and to become such as they ought to be.

"Well then, at the same time that they were studying these causes in themselves, and seeking every opportunity of freeing themselves from them, a great deal of scientific knowledge became very much perfected there. Among the savants of that place was one very learned savant named Theophany. Whenever this Theophany poured out mastic, which was used when it became hard for chewing after eating, on to a flat marble for drying, and which was prepared from the plant 'Patetook,' from pine resin, and cream from the milk of Khenionian goats famous at that time, he noticed that in whatever manner and however much he poured, the mixture always began to settle on the marble in the same way. When it cooled it always assumed forms, which however multifarious they might be, had always seven different definite forms of surface. This phenomenon interested him so much, that he began to investigate it; and in these investigations, other learned beings of the continent Atlantis also began to take part. As a result, they realized that in many phenomena there existed this same peculiarity of taking and keeping seven aspects.

"The outcome of all their investigations was that on the continent Atlantis, there began to exist a very serious definite knowledge called the 'Law of Sevenfoldness.'

"But when this continent perished, nothing remained of this knowledge, and during many centuries, beings on that planet again knew nothing of this property of cosmic phenomena. So well known had it been on Atlantis that there had not even been made for it such a Legominism as the Atlanteans made for almost all the ideas which they wished should pass unchanged to succeeding generations.

"They did this because they knew very well that ideas transmitted through masses of ordinary beings, are usually gradually changed to the point of non-recognition. Had there existed on Atlantis a Legominism of this, some idea of this knowledge would surely have been preserved through beings who were accidentally saved; since something was preserved of the knowledge for which there were Legominisms.

"Some of the knowledge also would have been preserved through certain beings of this planet who had not yet become entirely victims of the consequences of the damned organ Kundabuffer.

"In short, after the sinking of the continent Atlantis, nothing was known there on the Earth for a very long time about this fundamental cosmic law, and only very many centuries later, it began to be known there again, owing to two savants of the Earth, two brothers named Choon-Kil-Tez and Choon-Tro-Pel, who afterwards became saints, and who at the present time are on that Holy Planet Purgatory, where we recently were.

"You remember that on the continent of Asia in Goblandia there was a king named Konuzion, a descendant of the learned member of the Akhaldan society who went there for observations of Nature. I told you also that this same King Konuzion then invented a religion for his subjects in order to save them from the pernicious habit of chewing the seeds of the poppy flower.

"After his death the monarchy continued, that is to say, the kingdom passed by inheritance to the great-grandson of this King Konuzion after the birth of an heir, who later also became king of Goblandia, there were born two more sons, twins, who being free, devoted themselves to knowledge. They eventually became two impartial and not vain savants and very famous in their day and indeed very good for that planet.

"They were specialists first in medicine, but later they became all-round savants. The elder brother was called, as I have said, Choon-Kil-Tez, and the younger Choon-Tro-Pel, the word 'Choon' in Goblandia meaning 'Prince.'

"When Goblandia began to be covered by sand, both of these brothers were among the number of those refugees, who, you remember, went towards the East. Having crossed the eastern heights of Goblandia, they settled near the banks of a great space of water; and later, there was formed from this group, a definite large group of beings of the Earth, the descendants of which exist to the present time. The place where they now dwell in called China.

"The two brothers continued their studies and investigations in medicine also in this new place; and on one occasion they decided to investigate that substance which has for quite a long time there been called 'opium.'

"You mast know that on that planet there are among plants, minerals, and metals several 'individuums,' as for example, the mushroom called Flykiller, the metal 'sevnonia,' the crystal 'diamond,' and that plant the 'flower of poppy,' from which this opium is obtained, and several other plants, crystals and metals, which are 'polormedekhtic formations,' that is to say, individuums through which for the law of Heptaparaparshinokh all the cosmic crystallizations of substances of any class evolve or involve together. Through ordinary plants, minerals and metals, that is to say, non-polormedekhtic formations, there proceed evolutions and involutions of cosmic substances, but only of one, two or more crystallizations, and not of all the crystallizations.

"You must know that in all the planets of our Megalocosmos there are three kinds of these polormedekhtic individuums.

"Through the first there evolve or involve crystallizations from substances of the planet itself.

"The second kind of polormedekhtic individuums are those through which those crystallizations which exist on the planet effect their evolutions or involutions, and which are crystallized from substances derived from other planets of the same solar system.

"And the third kind of polormedekhtic individuums is that through which there evolve or involve on the given planet, crystallizations formed from substances derived from quite other solar systems.

"The poppy flower, the product of which these great Earth savants investigated, is one of those very polormedekhtic individuums in which the crystallizations formed of substances derived from other solar systems produce their processes of evolution or involution.

"This very opium which the great savants of the Earth, Choon-Tro-Pel and Choon-Kil-Tez, began to investigate, is just a mass of substances, or as the Earth-beings say, active elements, existing on that planet, which effect their Trogo-autoegocrat processes through the terrestrial polormedekhtic formation, which is called the plant 'poppy.'

"Here it is interesting to observe that this very opium which these great savants investigated is formed in that same unlucky flower of the plant poppy, the seeds of which, you remember, were chewed by their ancestors for whom their great-grandfather, King Konuzion, designed that peculiar religion for the purpose of saving his subjects from this destructive habit. There must surely have passed to these great savants by inheritance from their great-grandfather King Konuzion, besides the capacity for clear thinking and impartiality, a passionate interest in the study of this plant which is one of the numerous enemies of the psyche of the Earth-beings.

"At the time when these great savants began to analyze opium, the beings of Goblandia were already using this same mass of substances; and they first called it 'Opium,' a word meaning 'That which makes fantasies.'

"They began their experiments with a medical aim, it having been observed that on the introduction of one kind of this matter into a being every painful feeling was entirely destroyed in him.

"They desired to discover its properties in the hope of finding a means of changing in beings that special form of psychic state then very common amongst the refugees from Goblandia.

"At the very beginning of their investigations they noticed that opium itself consists of seven independent crystallizations or as they said, of seven active independent elements.

"And continuing their investigations, they found that each of these seven active elements consisted, in turn, of seven other independent active elements, and these latter of seven and so on, almost to infinity.

"This both interested them and astonished them and from that time onwards, they devoted themselves to the investigation of this phenomenon, with the consequence that they arrived at results unprecedented among Earth-beings.

"The great variety of active elements in opium is due to the fact that in these polormedekhtic formations, there always assemble and exist all those crystallizations or active elements for which Nature forms the polormedekhtic individuums; and each crystallization, of whatever degree of the fundamental cosmic octave of substances it may be, is generally composed of crystallizations of other degrees, and these in their turn of others. All this happens on account of a law in the Universe called the 'Fusion of Similarities,' according to which substances formed from a certain group of the same density, moving from certain neighboring functionings according to the Law of Triamazikamno, are fused into one.

"These great savants called these seven fundamental active elements of opium as follows:

(1) Erti-Pikan-On
(2) Ori-Pikan-On,
(3) Sami-Pikan-On,
(4) Okthi-Pikan-On,
(5) Khooti-Pikan-On,
(6) Epsi-Pikan-On, and
(7) Shvidi-Pikan-On.

To the secondary active elements composing these fundamental elements they gave the same names but with the addition of a number. For example, the first or fifth secondary element of the first fundamental active element they called simply, Erti-Pikan-On One, or Erti-Pikan-On Five, and so on. And if any active element formed a part of these secondary active elements, they would name it Erti-Pikan-On One and One, or Erti-Pikan-On One and Five and so on. Or again, instead of these terms they might use simply the number of indicating the different atomic weights of the active elements.

"It is very interesting to notice that throughout the ages the learned chemists of your planet have defined the atomic weights of chemicals in the same way; that is to say, they have always taken as the basic unit for defining the weight of every known active element, the atomic weight of our 'Planekurab,' which is there called Hydrogen. Hydrogen on that planet Earth cannot, it is true, be further broken up, but this does not at all mean that this same Hydrogen cannot be divided very many times more in other places of our Megalocosmos. The chemists of the Earth, however, do not even suspect that this is the case and still less that among the cosmic active chemical elements, this Hydrogen occupies a place, by its density and vivifyingness, very far from those active elements which are really basic, that is to say, indivisible, and which are many times less in volume and many times more vivifying than this unfortunate Hydrogen of theirs.

"The learned chemists of your planet certainly do not know that besides this Hydrogen of theirs, there exist on their planet several active elements similar to Hydrogen, which although divisible on the other solar systems, are indivisible in any circumstances on the other planets of their own system, since these active elements belong exclusively to those planets on which they are formed and exist.

"This is due to the fact that any planet of any solar system is a 'Restorial' source of the substances of the octave of that solar system, that is to say, is a center of gravity of the law of Heptaparaparshinokh in that solar system. Thus on this planet Earth, which is one of these 'Restorial' sources of the octave of substance of its solar system, there are certain of these active elements, which can be formed and exist only on this planet.

"Among the active elements existing on this planet and divisible neither upon it nor upon other planets of that solar system is this same Hydrogen, or as we call it 'Planekurab.' Besides this are other active elements which Chemistry calls 'Alillonofarab,' 'Krilnomolnifarab,' 'Talkoprafarab,' 'Khritofalmonofarab,' 'Sirioonorifarab,' 'Klananoizufarab,' 'Idornikellafarab.' The three* latter elements were never known at all by the beings of the Earth.

"The active elements known by contemporary chemists are called by your favorites, Hydrogen, Fluorine, Chlorine, Bromine, Iodine. To the latter three they naturally give no names, since they do not even suspect their existence on their planet nor how extremely necessary they are for their own existence. Although these same active elements cannot be broken up upon any of the planets of that solar system, they can be divided and again divided upon other solar systems down to their real cosmic basic indivisible substance.

"For the determination of the specific gravity of all cosmic chemical substances really learned chemists everywhere take the atom of this substance which is really basic and cannot be divided anywhere in any manner.

"And this substance is nothing else but Our Most Holy Theomertmalogos, or as it is still called, 'The Word of God.'

"So, my boy, after the sinking of the continent Atlantis, the first on that planet to discover the fundamental law of Heptaparaparshinokh were the future Saints Choon-Tro-Pel and Choon-Kil-Tez.

"Not only were they the first who laid the foundation of

* *Editor's Note:* This word "three" was originally "two," both here and in the following paragraph, but we changed it so that the text would be consistent. Alternatively we could have entirely removed 'Idornikellafarab,' the last entry from the list of active elements and left the word as "two."

this knowledge on the Earth, after Atlantis, but they were also the first on the Earth who in general understood, that in this law there are those two gaps to which I referred when I spoke of the first beings of the Mesocosmoses.

"The first gap or interval occurring between the third and the fourth centers of gravity of this law Heptaparaparshinokh and serving for the entrance of the lower forces, they called 'Cato-Ilshiosta'; and the second, occurring between the seventh and the next higher repetition and serving as the place for the entry of higher forces from without, they called 'Ano-Ilshiosta.'

"You must know that in consequence of the discoveries and realizations concerning the chief cosmic law made by these great Earth savants, of the place called China, then still young, there was formed a very important, independent science, called the Science of the Law, not of Sevenfoldness as it was called by the Atlanteans, but of Ninefoldness.

"The Chinese savants thus named it because to the seven multiform manifestations contained in the Law Heptaparaparshinokh, they added the two intervals they had observed. For they clearly saw, as they continued their researches, that just as these seven multiform manifestations are repeated in all phenomena, so also in all phenomena this law manifests in certain places infallibly always with the two properties they had noticed. In these places, all phenomena exhibit a process which the great savants called 'Chaotism'; and having found these special processes of equal importance with the inevitable seven multiform manifestations belonging to this law, they came to the conclusion that this law had not seven multiform manifestations but nine; and hence they gave to it the name of 'Ninefoldness.'

"Later and also in China, this science became very important for certain beings, and it continued to pass from generation to generation. It even reached some of your favorite contemporaries.

"When before long I shall say more of this law, pay special attention to these intervals. With a clear understanding of them, you will also clearly understand the difference between the chief cosmic forces, that is, between the former force Autoegocrat and the present force Trogoautoegocrat, of which I spoke when I was telling you of the creation of the Universe.

"The fact is that it was solely by means of these very intervals that the former sustaining force of the Sun Absolute, the force Autoegocrat, became the force Trogoautoegocrat. It was through these two gaps or intervals, already existing in the Law of Heptaparaparshinokh that foreign forces began to enter from without, from which time this law has been not independent but dependent on forces from outside.

"Strictly speaking, when our ENDLESS CREATOR decided to take measures against the terrible Heropass, HE added to the Law Heptaparaparshinokh which already existed on the Sun Absolute, only those two gaps; that is to say, HE added to the five deflections of the five Dooczako of this law, two further lengthened Dooczako, so that through these lengthened Dooczako the sustaining forces should constantly come from without. And that is why that Law Heptaparaparshinokh was then and is still called Pentaparaparshinokh; that is to say, a line having five deflections. And indeed, both of these lengthened Dooczako have their place; the first between the third and fourth, and the second between the last and the beginning of the next repetition.

"These two lengthened Dooczako of the Law Heptaparaparshinokh are those very properties of this law, which these great savants of the Earth observed and which they called intervals.

"Let us now return to the investigations of opium.

"When these great savants began to investigate the product formed in one of the polormedekhtic individuums called opium, and first observed this phenomenon in it, happening in their further researches to examine a great many other phenomena, they became convinced beyond all doubt that in all the phenomena great and small occurring on their planet there exists this very law of Ninefoldness. Every phenomenon, that is to say, contains and manifests itself in seven aspects, each of which aspect is formed from seven other causes, and so on almost without end. At first they investigated, as I have said, very many phenomena, but later they confined their investigations to three having nothing in common with each other, namely Opium, the White Ray, and Sound.

"Having need for their investigations of every chemical, physical and mechanical experiment, they gradually devised a very complex and interesting apparatus, which they called 'Alla-attapan,' by means of which they clearly saw that in all these three phenomena the same properties exist and that these properties act upon each other in the same manner as the actions which these properties have in themselves. Or as might otherwise be said: As any of the Dooczako belonging to any phenomenon influenced other Dooczako of the same phenomenon, so also these Dooczako influenced in the same manner the Dooczako of other phenomena.

"Many centuries later, I myself saw the apparatus by means of which they made their experiments, and became familiar with its arrangement. This was due to my friend Gornahoor Harharkh of the planet Saturn who by some means or other had learned of it as well. He is, in general the most famous learned being in all our Universe, and interests himself in every apparatus that demonstrates cosmic truths.

"Once when I was on this Saturn, He begged me if I should happen to visit the Earth again, to bring Him one of these Apparatuses 'Alla-attapan.' And when soon afterwards, I again descended upon the planet Earth, I obtained the apparatus and took it to Mars with the intention of sending it on a convenient occasion to the planet Saturn to Gornahoor Harharkh.

"For a long time it happened that our ship *Occasion* did not go to the planet Saturn and hence the apparatus 'Alla-attapan' remained with me on Mars for quite a long time, and I had time to become familiar with all its details. If you like I will tell you how it was arranged," Beelzebub said to His grandson Hassein.

"Yes, dear grandfather, yes, the story of this apparatus will surely be as interesting as your tale about the apparatus 'Lamp' of Gornahoor Harharkh Himself," replied Hassein excitedly.

Beelzebub then began as follows: "This experimental apparatus 'Alla-attapan,' created by the brothers, the future Saints, consisted of three independent parts. The first, the anterior part, was called 'Loosochepana,' the second or the central part was called 'Dzendvokh'; and the third, the posterior, was called 'Riank-Pokhortarz.'

"Each of these three parts consisted in turn of several parts. For example, the first had a special pipe in the form of a cone, the large end of which was hermetically fixed to the sides of the only window of the room where the experiments were carried out; its other end was a very small hole through which could pass the concentrated rays of the daylight entering through the window.

"This white ray, as it is called there, obtained from daylight passed first through a crystal of a special form and by which it was broken up into seven different colored rays, which fell upon a special platform made of ivory and called 'Pirinjiel.'

"This platform Pirinjiel was combined in such a way that these colored rays were reconcentrated in another manner and passed through a second crystal also of a special form. Only then did they finally fall on to another but larger platform also made of ivory called 'Polorishboorda.'

"Opposite this Polorishboorda was a small apparatus

through which, by certain adjustments, any of the colored rays could be directed from this Polorishboorda upon the third part of this entire apparatus, the part which was called 'Riank-Pokhortarz.'

"By the way, may dear Hassein, you must be told here, and perhaps later this fact will also be useful to you, that the knowledge of the arrangement of the first crystal of this part of the apparatus Alla-attapan has reached your contemporary favorites and they now call this crystal a 'Prism.'

"By means of this prism, the contemporary Earth savants also obtain from the white ray its seven colored rays and they now imagine that they can thereby discover certain other phenomena related to it. From these fancies and speculations, however, there can be no real result, since by means of this prism they obtain only the negative colored rays of the white ray. But in order to understand other phenomena, it is absolutely necessary to have the positive colored rays.

"This so happens among them because, concerning the apparatus Alla-attapan of the first great savants, only the knowledge of the arrangement of the first crystal has reached them, while to obtain the positive colored rays two forms of crystal are required and were used by the great savants.

"Through the first crystal they obtained the negative rays; and it was only through the second crystal that they obtained the positive rays.

"Furthermore, these odd contemporaries imagine that the colored rays they obtain issue from their source in that very order in which they are broken up in passing through their single prism.

"Now, enough about these queer Earth fellows. . .

"And so, by means of these two crystals, these great savants obtained the colored rays from the white ray, and then later with the aid of the platform Polorishboorda which was on the Loosochepana, any chosen ray of these colored rays could be directed upon the third main part of the whole apparatus Alla-attapan, namely, upon the part called Riank-Pokhortarz.

"This Riank-Pokhortarz was the chief demonstrating section of this famous apparatus.

"It consisted of an ordinary tripod on which were mounted two balls also made of ivory, in a certain manner, one upon the other, the upper being much larger than the lower.

"On the lower and smaller ball, just opposite the part Loosochepana from which the ray was directed, there was a hollow of a special form, in which opium and its selected active elements were placed for the experiments.

"The ball had a bore drilled horizontally through it.

"In this upper ball and opposite the Loosochepana was drilled a bore of a special form, extending half a diameter, through which the desired colored rays could be directed into the other bore, either directly from the Loosochepana, or by reflection from the hollow of the lower smaller ball.

"Through this bore drilled through the big ball could freely be moved a long bamboo rod, which was considered by the great savants as the most important item for their experiments. They called it 'Itter-tagerlen-estech.' It was a long ordinary bamboo of a definite thinness and was prepared in the following manner.

"Many of these bamboos were soaked for a long time in absolute darkness or in orange-colored-light obtained from the burning of 'Simkalash,' a substance obtained from a kind of clay found on that planet and usually formed in the earth containing accumulations of Salounilovian acids, which acids in their turn are formed from the minerals of 'Mamzolin,' or, as the beings of the Earth call it, from minerals of 'Naphtha.' These bamboos were then steeped in a liquid consisting of

(1) the white of eggs of a certain bird,

(2) the juice of the plant 'Chiloonakh,'

(3) the secretion of a quadruped being named 'Pirmaral,'

and

(4) an amalgam especially prepared from mercury.

"When they had been well soaked in this liquid, they were placed one by one in bamboos the ends of which were then hermetically closed. These last processes, of course, were also conducted in absolute darkness or in the orange colored light of Simkalash.

"Later, when these moistened bamboos were required, one end of the exterior non-moistened bamboo, designed to open in a certain manner, was specially fitted into the hole drilled through the larger ball of the Riank-Pokhortarz, while the interior and moistened bamboo was caught in a special manner by a hook which was fixed to a rod that enabled the moistened bamboo to be moved with any speed one wished.

"The action of the liquid in which these bamboos had been steeped was such, that the part of the bamboo upon which the colored ray coming from the Loosochepana or from the lower small ball fell, instantly became colored forever the color of that ray.

"These bamboos also became colored if there were directed upon them the simple vibrations of sounds produced on the strings contained in the central part of the apparatus, Alla-attapan, the part called 'Dzendvokh.'

"This Dzendvokh was a very firm frame of a special form, made of fine tusks of the Mammoth. Upon this frame were stretched many strings of different lengths and thicknesses, made of twisted gut and hairs of the tails of Earth-beings of various forms."

"Tell me please, my dear grandfather, what is a Mammoth?" asked Hassein.

"A Mammoth," replied Beelzebub, "is a being of a certain kind which formerly existed on that planet.

"Beings of this form became victims of those former pieces of that planet, Moon and Anulios, but chiefly on account of the Moon, the parvenu-planet of that solar system and the chief bringer of Evil to your planet Earth.

"Owing to this Moon those big winds took place of which I told you, and which covered up several parts of the Earth's surface with sand, and the valleys of the northern regions were also covered, but with snow, which then fell in great quantities.

"The beings called Mammoth loved to dwell in these northern regions and thus it happened that during these unprecedented snow-storms they were covered up by snow, and from that time, this form of being has never again been reestablished there.

"Even at the present time, a well-preserved planetary body of one of those Mammoths is sometimes discovered buried deep down beneath a layer of Kashiman, that is, substances usually forming the soil on the planets.

"These planetary bodies of Mammoths were well-preserved for so long a time, because the snow was quickly covered over by this Kashiman, 'isolatsochlanno,' that is to say, hermetically. In consequence, they have not been exposed to decomposition, that is, to the transformation of the active elements of which their planetary body is formed, into their prime crystallizations.

"Well, let us go on, my dear Hassein.

"So this astonishing apparatus Alla-attapan showed that all these three phenomena not only manifest themselves in the same manner, but it also showed that all these three phenomena are formed owing to the same factors.

"By means of this apparatus it was possible to demonstrate and prove, that in three cosmic phenomena having nothing in common, the same processes proceeded, and further, how these processes influenced each other in the same manner according to the Law of Heptaparaparshinokh. This apparatus, in fact, proved the complete affinity of these three phenomena.

"It was further stated that vibrations existing in these three phenomena, involved or evolved with the same properties and in the same successions. For example, corresponding colored rays directed upon any active element of opium transformed it into another active element, the vibrations of which corresponded to the vibrations of this colored ray.

"Again, if instead of this colored ray, there were directed upon this same active element vibrations of the strings of Dzendvokh corresponding to the colored rays, a similar result was obtained.

"Further, if any colored ray was directed through an active element of opium, then this ray in its passage took on a color corresponding by its vibrations to the vibrations of this active element.

"Or if any ray was directed through the vibrations of a corresponding string of the Dzendvokh, then having passed through these vibrations, its color also changed and the ray took on the color corresponding to the vibrations of this string.

"If simultaneously upon any given active element of opium, a given ray and given vibrations of strings were directed, this active element would be transformed either into another corresponding active element or into a quite different substance having nothing in common with any of the active elements of opium, and so forth.

"In short, these three cosmic phenomena, which the great Earth savants investigated by means of this famous apparatus, the phenomena called the white ray, the octave of sound, and the polormedekhtic product formed in the poppy-plant—all having nothing in common—were shown to have not only a complete affinity among themselves in respect of vibrations, but in both their seven fundamental parts as well as the succeeding ones, were shown to be able to help each other and to assist their mutual evolution and involution in spite of the difference in their origin and mode of manifestation. It also showed that the higher vibrations of one phenomenon can always affect the lower vibrations of other phenomena.

"You will certainly be interested to know that the knowledge of the methods of extracting certain active elements from this same opium has reached contemporary beings of the Earth. At the present time these elements are extracted by the beings, a number of whom moreover use them very eagerly to appease and gratify their weaknesses.

"But of course these active elements have now other names.

"A certain being, the contemporary Earth chemist named Mendelejeff, invented names for these active elements and, it seems, classified then according to their atomic weights.

"Although his classification does not correspond at all to reality, nevertheless, according to these atomic weights, one could approximately reestablish the classification made by the Earth-savants of the future China.

"Of the number, about four hundred, of active elements of opium known to these savants, the knowledge of obtaining only forty-two of them has reached the contemporary chemists. They are as follows:

(1) Morphine
(2) Protopine
(3) Lanthopine
(4) Porphiroksine
(5) Opian or narcotine
(6) Paramorphine or thebaine
(7) Phormine or pseudophormine
(8) Metamorphine
(9) Gnoskopine
(10) Oilopine
(11) Atropine
(12) Pirotine

(13) Dephteropine
(14) Tiktoutine
(15) Kolotine
(16) Khaivatine
(17) Zoutine
(18) Trotopine
(19) Laudanine
(20) Laudanosine
(21) Podotorine
(22) Arkhatozine
(23) Tokitozine
(24) Liktonozine
(25) Makanidine
(26) Papaverine
(27) Krintonine
(28) Kodomine
(29) Kolomonine
(30) Koilononine
(31) Katarnine
(32) Hydrokatarnine
(33) Opianine (mekonine)
(34) Mekonoiozine
(35) Pistotorine
(36) Phykhtonozine
(37) Codeine
(38) Nartzeine
(39) Pseudocodeine
(40) Microparaine
(41) Microtebaine
(42) Messaine*

"There also reached the contemporary beings of the Earth,

* ***Editor's Note:*** We have added in this list of 42 substances which we took directly from the 1950 publication. In the original manuscript this list was completely omitted.

the fundamental principle of the arrangement of the strings of the second part of the famous apparatus Alla-attapan, the part which was called Dzendvokh, but in a much changed and reduced form.

"You shall now hear in detail how the knowledge of this arrangement of the octave of vibrations of sound reached your favorites.

"I wish you to know this for several reasons: first of all, because the principles of this arrangement of vibrations were first created on the planet Earth by those great Chinese savants I mentioned; and secondly because the application of these principles has reached your favorites who today, mechanically and without knowledge, use them for many of their sound-producing instruments, which, on our return home, you will be able to see with your own eyes; and thirdly, because all the evolving and involving laws of the vibrations of the great Universe, designed for the beneficent cosmic Trogoautoegocrat, can readily be explained by this.

"Although the arrangement which reached the contemporary beings of the Earth, and which produces the vibrations of strings, is greatly modified and reduced, both the fundamental laws, nevertheless, of the cosmic vibrations as well as the principles of the Great Earth savants—according to which the strings were stretched on the Dzendvokh—can still be clearly explained.

"There are several forms of these sound-producing instruments amongst your favorites, the strings of which are still tuned according to the principles of the Dzendvokh.

"They call these contemporary sound-producing instruments, 'Organ,' 'Grand-piano,' 'Piano,' 'Harmonium,' 'Cymbal' and so on.

"One of the great brothers, Choon-Kil-Tez, happened for some unknown reason to become particularly interested in this Dzendvokh, and he began so investigate it thoroughly, with the result that he arrived at a complete theory called the 'Evolution and Involution of Vibrations.'

"After his death, the theory passed from generation to generation through real initiated beings of the Earth, but only several centuries later did another savant, also in China, and named King-Too-Toz, create on the basis and according to the principles of this theory a special apparatus for the practical study of these vibrations. This apparatus he called 'Lav-Merz-Nokh.'

"It, too, consisted of a very strong frame with very many strings stretched upon it, made also of various gut and hairs from the tails of various forms of beings. One end of each of the strings was fixed to one edge of this frame and the others were fixed to pegs, fitted in the other edge.

"These pegs could be easily turned in their holes and the strings which were fixed to them could be loosened or stretched at will; any string could be stretched to give the required number of vibrations.

"Of strings on the Lav-Merz-Nokh forty-nine mere colored white, they were called 'whole centers of gravity'; at the present time, they are called 'whole notes.'

"And each set of seven strings of these whole notes, then as well as now, was called 'Octave.'

"On the apparatus Lav-Merz-Nokh, there were stretched in this manner, seven octaves of whole notes, which together gave 'Haluiono,' or as the great Earth-savants called it, 'Obschiniriunosisky,' or Universal Sound; and each separate octave of strings gave the vibrations, which, according to the calculations of the great savants, the substances issuing from the seven fundamental universal sources must have and which must exist in the Universe. They are, in fact, such as do really exist in our Megalocosmos.

"And each white string of this Lav-Merz-Nokh made by this Chinese savant, King-Too-Toz, was tuned in such a manner that it gave that average number of vibrations, which according to the calculations of these great savants is the same as in the substances in each center of gravity of the fundamental cosmic octave.

"All the octaves of the whole notes, as well as each whole note, on the Lav-Merz-Nokh had their own names as follows:

'Arachiaplnish,'
'Erkrordiapan,'
'Erordiapan,'
'Chorortdiapan,'
'Piandjiapan,'
'Vetserordiapan,' and
'Okhterordiapan.'

"And the white strings of the center of gravity were also named. The first center in every octave was called 'Adashtanas,'

the second, 'Evotanas,'
the third, 'Govorktanis,'
the fourth, 'Maikitanis,'
the fifth, 'Midotanis,'
the sixth, 'Lookotanas,'
the seventh, 'Sonitanis.'

"Contemporary beings of the Earth name them, Do, Re, Mi, Fa, Sol, La, and Si.

"In every octave between the white strings or whole notes on the Lav-Merz-Nokh were stretched five other strings painted black.

"These strings were called 'Demisakhsakhsa,' or as contemporary Earth-beings call them, half-notes. These half-note strings were stretched only between those whole notes or centers of gravity between which, according to the calculations of these great savants, there are no intervals at all. Between the whole notes where intervals should be, the savant King-Too-Toz then stretched special strings, made of hairs of the tails of beings, called 'Horse' and 'Alogokipos.'

"The vibrations of these hair strings were not always equal; nor did their vibrations-rate depend upon their stretching, as in the other strings, but on three other factors, namely , the vibrations of neighboring strings, the temperature of the air at any given moment, and the radiations of the beings present.

"Between the white, black and hair-strings of the Lav-Merz-Nokh were also stretched in each octave fifteen strings of twisted gut painted red, and called 'Keesookesschoor.' Contemporary beings of the Earth call them 'quarter-notes.' These quarter-note strings, stretched beside the hair-strings, were arranged so that at any moment their vibrations could be changed and regulated by tightening or loosening them. By this means, according to one's hearing, they could be harmonized with the changing vibrations of the hair-strings.

"This arrangement was made because in consequence of the frequent changes in the hair-strings, the vibrations of the red strings acquired such a property, that unless they were harmonized with the vibrations of the hair strings, they affected the beings present very cacophonously and harmfully, even to the point of destroying them. By means of the frequent changing of the stretching of the red strings and the union of their vibrations with the general vibrations arising from the Lav-Merz-Nokh, they succeeded in making these vibrations of the Lav-Merz-Nokh flow harmoniously, with the result that they ceased to produce these harmful effects.

"After the death of the Chinese savant King-Too-Toz, the other beings of China began gradually to change and to forget his invention.

"Many centuries again passed. The sense and significance of the Lav-Merz-Nokh were almost forgotten though its principle continued to pass from generation to generation, through a small number of beings. And apparatuses similar to the Lav-Merz-Nokh but much modified, are still preserved among beings as a curiosity.

"At this same time there was born, also in China, a certain Chai-Yoo, whose invention has reached the contemporary beings of that planet.

"You must know that by the time of Chai-Yoo's birth, there had already begun to enter into the beings of the Earth—during their formation until they became adults—into their brains and muscles, all the consequences of the properties of the organ Kundabuffer. When therefore this Chai-Yoo became a savant, though of a new kind, that is to say, when he had acquired a good deal of dubious information, it happened that he accidentally learned some details of the arrangement of the important apparatus Lav-Merz-Nokh; and he learned them at that period of time, peculiar to all savants of the new kind—that is, when having assured themselves of bread, cigarettes and a rich widow, they begin, out of boredom, to 'get clever.'

"This same Chai-Yoo also began to 'get clever' and with what he learned he modified and simplified the arrangement of the great Lav-Merz-Nokh so that it could be used only to produce sounds of which the beings of the Earth at that time were very fond; and since that time the sounds of the tune of vibrations created by the great savants for the understanding of the laws of vibration, by which the Universe is maintained, began to flow through sound-producing instruments which became gradually altered in appearance. First of all they flowed in their brothels, but at the present time they flow in their 'Dance-Halls.'

"The sound-producing instrument devised by this Chai-Yoo was called King. Chai-Yoo greatly simplified the tune of the vibrations on this King, in order that the instrument might be accessible for the use of all beings. It was made without the red or the hair-strings, that is, without the quarter notes and those hair-strings which produced irregular vibrations. He also reduced the number of the repeated octaves.

Although this King had changed greatly in appearance since that time, yet its tune of strings has remained the same; and it has reached your contemporary favorites, who now employ it on a variety of instruments, some of them heavy to the point of idiocy.

"I have just brought one of these sound-producing instruments from this remarkable planet for some of my proposed experiments, of which you will soon hear. This particular instrument is there called a 'Grand Piano.'

"Although the tune of this Grand Piano has reached the contemporary Earth-beings, they do not even suspect that it was constructed on the principles existing in and maintaining the whole Universe.

"They use this piano quite mechanically with no idea of its significance; nor, of course, does there even exist among them at the present time, any theory concerning the great cosmic laws of vibrations.

"A certain theory concerning vibrations does indeed exist among them, but, strictly speaking, they do not study it with the idea of understanding cosmic laws. No, they study it only in order to have the privilege of being entitled a learned 'physicist,' or a learned 'musician,' that is to say, as one of those representatives of Art, of whom you remember our dear Ahoon spoke.

"Something indeed of the science of vibrations has reached them from ancient China; but it has shared the fate of all the real knowledge handed down from their ancestors. The idea of the resultant jumble our dear Mullah Nassr Eddin expressed when he said with his honeyed lips:

"'Eh! You! You're such a queer fellow, just think a little. Isn't it all the same to you whether you employ a rabbit or a donkey, since they each have four legs?'

"This wisdom can be very well applied to the case mentioned.

"The beings who seem to be a little more serious and conscientious, sweat over this science of vibrations as it exists at the present time, but apart from various absurdities, these poor Earth-beings find nothing.

"In fact, the existing knowledge of vibrations is full of every contradictory idea. In my opinion, all this has happened on the planet Earth for the following reason:

"The knowledge of vibrations reached your contemporary favorites from two independent sources, namely, from those Chinese I mentioned and from the ancient Greeks. You remember I told you that long ago between the continents of Asia and Europe, there was formed from fishermen at first a small and later a large group of beings, afterwards called Greeks; and how, during bad weather, out of boredom, these Greeks would invent various sciences. Among them was this science of vibrations, which passing from generation to generation finally reached your contemporary favorites, almost simultaneously with the Chinese.

"The fundamental misconception underlying all this arose from the fact that in the Chinese science the octave of vibrations of sound had seven whole notes, while in the Greek science the same octave has only five whole notes.

"As both theories were beautifully, and for the Earth beings also logically expounded, they were at a loss to know which to choose. After long reflection they decided to combine them in one and thus to offend nobody.

"A contemporary being named Gaidoropoolo (Greek for Mr. Donkeyson) even invented a very long 'mathematical' explanation of why in one theory the octave is divided into seven whole notes, and in the other into five, and how it happened that such an important contradiction arose.

"His 'mathematical' explanations eventually pacified the contemporary savants of the Earth, who now base all their 'cleverness' concerning vibrations on the explanations of the worthy Gaidoropoolo. In his 'mathematical' explanations, by the way, the worthy Gaidoropoolo, by a method known only to himself, counted the number of vibrations of all the Chinese whole notes; and according to his calculations demonstrated that in the Chinese octave, the notes 'fa' and 'si' are not whole notes at all, but only half notes, since the numbers of their vibrations 'almost' coincide with those of the Greek half-notes, which are found in the Greek octaves just between the Chinese whole notes 'mi' and 'sol' and also between 'la' and 'do'; and the vibrations of which would correspond to the vibrations of those Chinese whole notes, called 'fa' and 'si.'

"He made the further supposition that it was obviously convenient for the Chinese to have the 'Restorial' of the voice, that is to say, its center of gravity, in these half-notes, and hence they did not divide their octave into five whole notes like the Greeks, but into seven; and other suppositions of the same kind.

"The new theory, with, of course, the explanations of Gaidoropoolo, now exists in great comfort on the Earth without corns to trouble it and with plenty of frozen Australian English roast beef; it lives an easy and peaceful life.

"But why in reality has the Chinese octave seven whole notes and the Greek only five? This is due really to a very small reason.

"The basis for the Chinese division is the true law of vibrations existing everywhere in cosmic phenomena as well as in cosmic substances; namely, the laws discovered by those almost unprecedented savants whose like can never again appear on the Earth, the holy brothers Choon-Tro-Pel and Choon-Kil-Tez. Indefatigably pursuing their investigations with their almost Non-human minds, they discovered these great cosmic laws of vibrations, owing only to which our whole Universe exists and is maintained. And on the principles of these laws of vibrations was later based the Chinese octave of whole notes.

"Nothing so important was the basis of the Greek octave. The Greek five note octave was based only on the 'Restorials' existing during the sound of beings, and in particular, of the Greek beings of the period when this theory was composed.

"There are almost as many of these 'Restorials' of sound or as they sometimes say, 'light-soundings' of the voice of the beings of that planet, as there are different social organizations there, for the reason that these 'light-soundings' are formed among them by many outer and inner conditions, not depending on themselves; as, for instance geographical, hereditary, religious and many others.

"Owing to these conditions, the Greeks possessed and produced in their singing only five 'centers of gravity' of sound, all very subjective, with the result that even had they composed their theory of the octave conscientiously and honestly, they still could not have found in it more or fewer than these five whole notes.

"These 'Restorials' in the producing of sounds in the octave by the Greeks of that period, could belong only to their organic 'Restorials.'

"The 'Restorials' in the vibrations of the voice of beings in general, are indicated by the vibrations which they can produce in certain places of the octave for a long time, and at the same time feel calm. In other words, these vibrations harmonize with the other 'functionings' established in them by their environment.

"Owing to differing environments there are usually formed in the beings of every social organization or every locality different positions for the 'Restorials' in the octave of sound. Hence the division of the octave into whole notes differs for each definite locality.

"This quality arising from the nature of beings was not, however, taken into consideration by the Chinese in their division of the octave into whole notes. They took as the basis of their whole science of 'Ninefoldness' as well as their decision of the octaves of vibrations, only those results obtained by the great Earth savants, whose souls later became blessed and attained to the Holy Planet Purgatory. And they became blessed chiefly because their investigations were made only for the sake of Science and not for the sake of their own vanity and gain. As a means of nourishing themselves by the Holy Helkdonis they employed only their persevering disinterested labor, which replaced suffering. Thereby, the reasonableness of their souls could be more quickly perfected and reach the degree considered as worthy for attaining to that holy planet.

"By the way, it will do no harm if I tell you now, that the divine feeling of suffering is at the present time quite unknown among your favorites. Nevertheless there do exist among them certain ideas about suffering.

"They also 'suffer' and this feeling is called by the same word, suffering. But this feeling is aroused only by shocks from without, which accidentally affect certain functions in them arising from the consequences of the properties of the organ Kundabuffer; that is to say, functions called 'pride,' 'self-love,' 'vanity' and so forth.

"Nobody on your planet endeavors to create in himself this unique holy sensation which can give real satisfaction to beings according to their merits.

"During all ages, the 'savants' of that planet have made their investigations only for the sake of their vanity or gain.

"But when these great Earth savants discovered through their labors and impartial physico-chemico-mathematical investigations, those real fundamental cosmic laws, they created that division of the octave for the other beings of their planet to enable them also to understand the great laws of vibrations.

"The Greek five note scale on the other hand is based on one of the numerous 'Restorials' of the vibration of sound of the voices of beings; and there are as many of these being 'Restorials' as there are external conditions of existence.

"There exist, at the present time, various groups of beings who possess the capacity of producing the 'Restorials' in the octaves of sound, not only of five and seven whole notes but even of thirteen and seventeen whole notes. Of course, they also produce this quite unconsciously. There are also localities on that planet where beings do not possess the capacity of producing the organic 'Restorial' of sound, even of the Greek five notes.

"I personally used to like very much to listen to the singing of the beings of a small social organization dwelling on the continent Asia, who produced their songs to the point of rapture. In spite of the fact that they produced vibrations of sound in the octave up to forty distinct notes, they really had only three organic whole notes; and however they might trill, yet their calm and long sustained vibrations were on one of their only three organic notes.

"As this interested me very much, I decided to investigate this rare particularity.

"By the way, I specially ordered three tuning forks for my investigations of these three 'Restorial' whole notes, and I began my experiments with the help of these and of several instruments called 'vibrometers' which had already been very well made for me by my friend Gornahoor Harharkh. At the present time, these latter instruments are not to be found at all on that planet.

"In the course of these investigations I proved that no matter how many vibrations their other notes might have, these three notes in the octave of their voice always had a greater number of vibrations and manifested continuously during their action the properties of arousing the neutralization and echo.

"To my great regret it is not possible to explain by means

of the grand piano the vibrations of all the cosmic substances, as was easily possible on the Chinese Lav-Merz-Nokh. For on this Lav-Merz-Nokh were stretched just as many strings as there are places in the Universe in which during their Trogo-autoegocratic processes, the cosmic substances acquire vibrations of a special kind. And it contained seven octaves each of which had seven whole notes, equal in number to the sources of independent kinds of vibrations, all of which sources taken together compose the fundamental cosmic octave really existing in the whole Universe.

"Nevertheless, with this arrangement of the piano strings the principles of vibrations of any one center of gravity of the fundamental octave can be clearly understood; and from this fact, it is possible to understand roughly the vibrations of all the centers of gravity of the fundamental octave, each center of gravity, in all respects, being similar to the fundamental octave. For in each center of gravity the reciprocal action of the vibrations proceeds exactly as in the fundamental cosmic octave. Having therefore understood the laws of vibrations of any one center of gravity, it is possible to understand also the laws of vibrations of all centers of gravity, subject, of course, to the difference of their scales.

"Owing to its arrangement of the whole notes of this piano as well as of the Dzendvokh and Lav-Merz-Nokh, and even of the King, have the possibility, of course, if its strings are tuned correctly, of vibrating and uniting exactly according to the law of Heptaparaparshinokh.

"The transitions and successive vibrations in the arrangement of this piano in the mathematical sense coincide exactly with this same law. Since any center of gravity or the whole note of the octave can by the law of Heptaparaparshinokh pass into another, it follows that their vibrations can reciprocally help each other to evolve and involve, exactly as happens everywhere in the Universe under this same law; only, I repeat, of course, if the strings of this piano are tuned exactly according to the calculations of these great savants.

"By the way, it is interesting to notice, that the numbers of vibrations indicated in this Chinese Science almost coincide exactly with the numbers existing in the vibrations of the cosmic substances, surrounding most of the planets of the Megalocosmos.

"Their exactitude was due, I think, chiefly to the fact that whereas chemists in general take the atom of the Very Holy Theomertmalogos, as the Earth chemists take the atom of the active element Hydrogen as their unit for defining all cosmic chemical substances, these great savants took the absolute vibrations of the note 'do' as their basic unit of vibration; and the Chinese later took the same absolute vibrations of the note 'do' for their own sound-producing instruments.

"These vibrations, also according, of course, to the indications of the great savants, were, moreover, considered to be the vibrations of a sound produced once or twice a year after certain meteorological disturbances of the atmosphere in the region formerly Goblandia, later called the desert Gobi; and that sound has, in fact, those very vibrations of the Chinese absolute note 'do.' These places were known by the beings of China even before Goblandia was completely covered with sand.

"The grand piano which I brought with me has in each of its octaves the Law of Heptaparaparshinokh as well as seven centers of gravity, which, as I have already told you, are called by them 'whole notes.'

"Like all the former similar Chinese instruments it has also half-notes.

"And here it is interesting to note that the keys of this grand piano, for the whole notes as well as for the half notes, are of the same color as the strings of the great Lav-Merz-Nokh; the keys of the whole notes are white and the keys of the half notes are black.

"Whether this is done intentionally or by coincidence I do not know, but in any case, this coloring of the keys is a great help in showing the intervals in this law.

"A clear idea of the intervals by means of the keys of this grand piano can be formed in this way. A whole series of sounds is divided into octaves and each octave is divided, as in the Law of Heptaparaparshinokh, into seven 'Restorials,' which in the case of sounds are called 'whole notes'; the keys which produce the vibrations of these whole notes are painted white.

"On the piano, there are several successive octaves of whole notes. Between these whole notes in each octave, that is to say, between these seven white keys, there are five keys for producing the vibrations 'Demisakhsakhsa' or half notes; and these are painted black, like the corresponding strings on the Lav-Merz-Nokh.

"These black keys occur between all the white keys of the piano, except between those whole notes corresponding to those 'Dooczako' of the Law of Heptaparaparshinokh, between which are the 'Intervals.' On the piano, they are between those white keys of the whole notes, between 'mi' and 'fa' and between 'si' and 'do' of the following octave.

"Here there are no black keys; and hence the places of the 'Intervals' on this piano are shown by the absence of black keys.

"I repeat that it is a great pity that the grand-piano has not, like the Chinese Lav-Merz-Nokh all the necessary strings and the seven complete octaves to enable me to explain to you, practically, the process of all the cosmic vibrations. However, thanks to its arrangement, it can serve to explain more or less well how the vibrations of the substances evolve and involve in any center of gravity.

"Each of the seven octaves of the Lav-Merz-Nokh gave

those vibrations which indeed exist in the substances issuing from the seven corresponding fundamental cosmic sources.

"For instance, the strings of its highest octave gave the most vivifying vibrations, that is to say, externally, the highest and finest sounds; and the numbers of these vibrations were the same as the numbers of the vibrations of those emanations, which according to the calculations of the great savants, must emanate from the cosmic prime sources, by which they meant our Protocosmos. This highest octave they called 'Arachiaplnish.'

"The strings of the second highest octave called 'Erkrordiapan' gave the vibrations corresponding to the emanations reaching their solar system from all the other suns of our Megalocosmos.

"The strings of the third octave or 'Erordiapan' gave vibrations corresponding to the vibrations reaching their planet from their own sun.

"The fourth octave, 'Chorortdiapan,' gave vibrations reaching their planet from all the other planets of their own solar system, that is to say, those vibrations of their own sun, which are first transformed through these other planets, before reaching their own planet.

"On the Lav-Merz-Nokh this same octave was and still is sometimes called the 'Astral' Octave.

"The fifth octave on the Lav-Merz-Nokh, named Piandjiapan, gave those vibrations belonging to those substances radiated by their own planet. They are always those which come from outside the planet and undergo transformation owing to the active elements already existing in the planet.

"Such transformations take place everywhere owing to the second chief cosmic law, namely the Law 'Triamazikamno'; owing to this law the vibrations are transformed and proceed further.

"The strings of the sixth octave of this astonishing apparatus Lav-Merz-Nokh were called the octave 'Vetserordiapan,' and gave those very vibrations belonging to the radiations arising from the beings themselves.

"These vibrations which come from above, are always the same, and, becoming eventually transformed in their own planet, enter into the machine beings in order to become transformed into vibrations of the last involving center of gravity of the fundamental cosmic octave of the Law of Heptaparaparshinokh.

"That is why the science of vibrations calls the sum total of the beings of that planet, the note 'Evotanas' or the note 're' of the fundamental cosmic octave.

"These vibrations, corresponding to the vibrations of the note 're' are transformed in general through all the three kinds of food, but among your favorites they are transformed for the cosmic Trogoautoegocrat, chiefly as I have already said, through their first food alone.

"Thus my boy, the strings of the Lav-Merz-Nokh of this sixth octave gave those vibrations corresponding to the radiations required in general by nature from all beings for the cosmic Trogoautoegocrat, that is, from beings who have not yet reached the Holy Anklad.

"The seventh and last octave of the strings of the famous Lav-Merz-Nokh called 'Okhterordiapan,' being the 'Restorial' of the fundamental octave Sonitanis, gave vibrations of the last center of gravity, that is, the vibrations of the note of the octave 'do' of the fundamental cosmic octave.

"Although the source of this octave 'do' is everywhere usually found in the very center of the planets, yet owing to that great catastrophe which occurred on your planet at the beginning, this source was found to be not in its center, but on its former pieces called 'Moon' and 'Anulios.'

"In this respect this planet Earth is like our planet Karatas, on which the source of the fundamental cosmic note 'si' is found not in its center, but in the satellite, namely, in our Prnokhpaioch.

"But, as you remember, the causes of the formation of the satellites of the planet Earth and our planet Karatas are quite different.

"By the way, you must know that for this reason, namely, that the latter sources of the centers of gravity of the fundamental cosmic octave are here found not in these planets but in their satellites, the Law of Heptaparaparshinokh for the prolongation of the generation of beings themselves, carries out its process through two beings and not through one.

"Hence on the planet Earth and on the planet Karatas, two sexes exist, male and female, this process there taking place through two beings, and not, as on the majority of planets of the Universe, through one being called Monoenithits, or as your favorites call such beings 'Androgynes' or 'Hermaphrodites.'

"On some future occasion I shall explain this in detail.

"Thus, the strings of the seventh octave on the Lav-Merz-Nokh, called 'Okhterordiapan' had just those vibrations which the Holy Firm* generally gives everywhere in the Universe, that is to say, the very opposite of the emanations of our Sun Absolute, the Protocosmos.

"These vibrations are those which from the last center of gravity or from the octave 'do,' begin through that same Law of Heptaparaparshinokh to evolve up again towards the Protocosmos, in order to produce again by their evolving processes all that is necessary for the great cosmic Trogoautoegocrat.

"In this manner the seven octaves of the great Chinese apparatus Lav-Merz-Nokh created by King-Too-Toz on the basis of the truths discovered by the great Earth savants Choon-Tro-Pel and Choon-Kil-Tez represented the vibra-

* *Editor's Note:* We have added the word "Firm." Originally there was just a place holder here which read "(intext)."

tions proceeding from all the seven fundamental sources of cosmic substances, by means of which functions the Trogoautoegocrat—the savior from our CREATOR's greatest enemy, the unmerciful Heropass—that is to say, our savior from that enemy who at the beginning of the creation of the Universe was the cause of such great trouble to our ALL-LOVING ENDLESSNESS, WHO indeed, as Our Cherubim and Seraphim tell, toiled with extreme intensity without a single moment's rest, until HE had completed the creation of this savior Trogoautoegocrat.

"When these labors were ended our Cherubim and Seraphim composed and sung a whole series of hymns to the glory of our ENDLESSNESS.

"It is said in these hymns, by the way, that when our CREATOR had completed HIS creation and could be at peace, HE said:

"'Let all now circulate and the merciless Heropass wibble-wobble.'

"For the clear understanding of my further explanations of the famous Chinese apparatus Lav-Merz-Nokh, as well as the laws of vibrations, it is essential for you to know first of all how the great Earth savants formulated the 'Adashtanas,' that is, the note 'do.'

"In their explanations about the cosmic vibrations they said that every definite cosmic formation in Adashtanas, that is, every definite formation has vibrations corresponding to the vibrations of the note 'do.'

"They further added that every Adashtanas is a unit but only a relative unit. Every such unit in the Universe of whatever kind, as soon as it acquires within itself any independent existence, immediately becomes Adashtanas, that is, a unit having vibrations of Adashtanas, or as your favorites would say, of the note 'do.'

"They further said that in every vibration of the Adashtanas, there is in its turn a whole octave of vibrations which produce their evolutions and involutions in the same manner, as in the fundamental octave of vibrations, strictly according to the Law of Ninefoldness.

"The great Earth savants erred only in one respect; and how they erred I will explain on some future occasion. Meanwhile, you should know that this error of theirs was only in one small insignificant detail. You need not therefore pay any great attention to it; but try to accept and understand all I have told you and will tell you of this science, as if it were strictly accurate.

"When these great Earth savants said that every unit is only relatively independent, they were right. Indeed, every unit in the Universe is only relatively independent, with the exception, of course, of the Units, the Holy Anklad, who are near our ENDLESSNESS, and all the individuums who have already attained and merited this same Holy Anklad.

"So, my dear Hassein, this Chinese apparatus Lav-Merz-Nokh was admirable for explaining all the laws or cosmic vibrations.

"It was, in fact, so good that at the present time, chiefly owing to my friend Gornahoor Harharkh, it is an indispensable experimental apparatus for all the real savants of the whole Universe; as a means of elucidating the laws of cosmic vibrations.

"On the planet where it was created, however, its strings though tuned according to the original principles are used to produce only sounds to satisfy several 'Hasnamussian' experiences of the beings of that place.

"In order to picture to yourself more clearly how the evolutions and involutions of vibrations in this famous Chinese Lav-Merz-Nokh proceeded, and particularly in that grand piano which I have brought with me and on which I wish to demonstrate to you how the vibrations of its strings proceed, I strongly advise you to compare them with these explanations I gave you of how the crystallizations on the planets produce their evolutions by means of beings through their foods.

"I then took as an example the first food of your favorites and we will take it again.

"I told you that the crystallization composing their first food for the service of the cosmic Trogoautoegocrat must evolve again; and that these evolutions can proceed only according to the Law of Heptaparaparshinokh.

"Although each of your favorites is a note 're' in the fundamental cosmic octave, yet each has also in himself a complete octave of vibrations, that is to say, in every one of them are the very vibrations of a whole octave, proceeding in the same order with all the same details as everywhere else in the Greatest as well as in the Smallest, exactly according to the Law of Heptaparaparshinokh.

"For instance, the first food of the Earth beings contains vibrations corresponding to the 'Adashtanas,' or as the science of vibrations says, the first food of beings sounds like the note 'do.'

"These vibrations of the note 'do' or the crystallizations existing in the first food, must then pass into higher crystallizations; in other words, the vibrations of this note 'do' must evolve in beings into vibrations of the note 'do' of the next higher octave.

"Of course, all evolutions and involutions proceed everywhere according to the Law of Heptaparaparshinokh. Hence the crystallizations of the first food must pass from one center of gravity to the other, in order to be eventually transformed into crystallizations of a higher degree; just as the vibrations of the note 'do' must evolve through all the notes of the octave, namely 're' 'mi' 'sol' 'la' and 'si' in order to be transformed ultimately into vibrations of the note 'do' of the next higher octave.

"Since in the Law of Heptaparaparshinokh, there are those two intervals which do not allow these evolutions and involutions to proceed further independently, so in the evolutions and involutions of these particular vibrations, the same occurs to the first food, representing the substances Protoëhary. Through various mixings with the substances of their own octave these must pass into higher substances, namely, the substances Defteroëhary, exactly as the vibrations of the note 'do' are transformed into vibrations of the note 're' when there are mixed with them other vibrations of the same class and formed chiefly of the vibrations of the notes 're' and 'mi.'

"And again, the vibrations of the note 're' evolve into the note 'mi' just in the same manner as the substances Defteroëhary are transformed into substances Tritoëhary.

"The same occurs with the vibrations of the note 'mi' as with the substances Tritoëhary. Just as the vibrations of the note 'mi' cannot evolve further without help from without, so neither can the substances Tritoëhary evolve further from this center of gravity of the Law of Heptaparaparshinokh without help from without.

"And just as for the substances Tritoëhary this help consists of the substances of the second food of the beings, called air, so also for the vibrations of the note 'mi,' there must come a constant help from without. For the vibrations of the note 'mi' this help usually consists of various noises, rustlings and rappings, also of those 'momentum' vibrations occasionally formed from previous vivifying vibrations, arising naturally or expressly produced, as for example, on that Lav-Merz-Nokh or even on the grand piano.

"That is why, if the vibrations of the note 'mi' are produced in a hermetically closed room, these vibrations either cease instantly or involve back to the note 'do,' and from the note 'do' again to the note 'mi' and so on, until the vivifyingness which exists in them is finished.

"Further just as the substances Tritoëhary, which owing to the help of substances from the air, are transformed into substances Tetartoëhary, evolve further without help into the substance Exioëhary, so also, if the vibrations of the note 'do' pass beyond the note 'mi,' they can evolve further without help until the note 'si' is reached, where occurs the second interval of the Law of Heptaparaparshinokh. And just as for the substances Exioëhary help from without is here required, so also for the vibrations of the note 'si' help from without is necessary, but help of another kind.

"Only when these vibrations of the first note 'do' receive this help can there be obtained vibrations corresponding to the note of the octave 'do.'

"Eh, my dear boy! Willy-nilly I shall have to tell you about the experiments concerning the laws of vibrations which I saw on that planet Earth. I must tell you for several reasons.

"The first reason is that I have already told you very much about the chief cosmic Law of Heptaparaparshinokh; and it will be a pity if for any reason you should not clearly understand this law; so I must describe these experiments, since I am sure that they will give you an exhaustive idea of the great Law of Heptaparaparshinokh.

"The second reason is that among these experiments was one with a sound-producing instrument arranged like this grand-piano.

"Although both instruments are called 'Piano,' yet, they differ in appearance; but the stretching of the strings and the arrangement are quite the same. I shall tell you of the experiments on this piano so that when we return home and I illustrate the laws of vibrations on this piano in a practical manner, you will be able to explain clearly to yourself how the Trogoautoegocrat process proceeds in our Megalocosmos.

"My third reason is that the being who produced them on that planet Earth, was the only one who, during the many centuries of my stay there, discovered my real nature by means of the knowledge he had acquired about vibrations.

"The Chinese science of the Law of Ninefoldness was gradually and completely forgotten even by the beings of China itself; and today almost nothing remains, if we except certain very famous fragments, which pass from generation to generation through an extremely limited number of beings.

"But it seems that only quite recently on that planet Earth, a similar science has been revived, not in China but in the locality called upper Bokhara, also situated on the continent Asia and almost in its very center.

"This happened during my last descent upon that planet.

CHAPTER XLI

The Bokharian Dervish, Hadji-Asvatz-Troov

WHILE travelling in Asia in this region called from its mountainous character Upper Bokhara, I chanced to meet and to become friendly and familiar with a being of that place, called a Bokharian Dervish. His name was Hadji-Zephir-Bogga-Eddin.

"He used to be very fond of discussing with me 'higher matters' as the beings of the Earth say. He once began to talk about the ancient Chinese science, called there, 'Shat-Chai-Mernis'; it is nothing but the ancient Chinese science of the Law of Ninefoldness.

"As I have told you that certain fragments of this science are still preserved and reached a very limited number of beings of the present time. Glory be to our CREATOR, they have not, however, so far gone into the hands of those beings and savants who would surely either completely sweep them off the face of that unfortunate planet or cook them into a scientific porridge, with which to muddle the already sufficiently muddled minds of the beings of the Earth.

"And so, during conversation with this Dervish concerning this Shat-Chai-Mernis, that is, the ancient Chinese science of the Law of Ninefoldness, he suggested I should go with him to see his friend, also a Dervish and a great authority on this ancient Chinese science.

"He said his friend lived in the mountains, far from everybody where he occupied himself with experiments concerning this science. As I had no special business at the moment, and his friend lived in those mountains which I had long intended to examine, I immediately consented.

"The very next day we set off. After traveling three days on foot, we arrived finally high up in the mountains of Upper Bokhara, at a small pass near the entrance to a cave. Here my

Dervish friend, Hadji-Zephir-Bogga-Eddin, gave a signal and suddenly beside the entrance of this cave, an enormous rock moved aside exposing another entrance leading into another cave. After we entered and passed several turnings, we saw coming to meet us, a being who greeted us and led us further. This being was the friend of my Dervish friend Bogga-Eddin.

"He was a thin and very aged being, and was called Dervish Hadji-Asvatz-Troov. While speaking with us, he led us into a small section of the cave where he dwelt.

"We all sat on a felt carpet and while talking we began to eat from a clay vessel, cold Bokharian 'Shila-Plav' which the aged Dervish brought us.

"During the course of the conversation, my friend the Dervish Bogga-Eddin happened to tell him that I was much interested in the science Shat-Chai-Mernis. He repeated briefly what we had been discussing, and the matters I already knew.

"This aged Dervish Asvatz-Troov then himself began to question me; but I replied in that accustomed manner of mine, by means of which I could always hide on the Earth my real nature and knowledge.

"I usually spoke so skillfully there that the beings of the Earth regarded me only as a savant and colleague.

"In further talk with him, I learned that this venerable Hadji had long been interested in that science and during the past ten years he had been studying practically. I learned also that he had attained such results as contemporary Earth-beings can no longer attain.

"Knowing that this science had long ceased to exist in the minds of the beings of the Earth, I was greatly surprised and wished to know how that venerable Hadji had become interested in the science, and whether he had heard anything about it. It was all the more strange, as I know very well it had long been common among the beings of the Earth to be interested in what they ordinarily see or hear, and that such interests suppress in them the rest of their psychic needs, it seeming always clear to them that the thing in which they are interested at the moment is just that which sustains the whole world. In short, when the necessary kind of relations was established between this Hadji-Asvatz-Troov and myself, that is to say, when he began to speak with me normally, without that mask which at the present time all the beings of that planet wear in their relations with others, particularly if they meet these others for the first time, I asked him, of course in an appropriate manner, why and how he became interested in this science.

"Here it will do you no harm to say, that among your favorites there have long existed in each locality, special forms for outward relationship, for the reason that the inner feeling of relationship common to all the beings of the Universe without difference of form or place of existence, has long been destroyed in them.

"Good or bad relations among them are established at the present time only by external manifestations, chiefly by politeness, as it is called, that is to say, by empty words.

"However much one being might inwardly wish another being good, if for some reason or other, he should express himself in the wrong words . . . all would be over. The other being would be quite certain that his real well-wisher only lived to give him trouble.

"It is therefore extremely important to know the customary forms of speech in order to make friends and avoid making enemies.

"It is also interesting to note that the abnormal existence of your favorites has not only spoiled their own psyche, but it has reacted on the psyche of other forms of beings on this same planet.

"Such an inner feeling is entirely atrophied in those forms of beings with which your favorites have a frequent contact, and it has been preserved only among those other forms of beings, whose form of existence is such that they have no contact at all with these biped beings of yours; as for example, those called tigers, lions, bears, hyenas, snakes, phalangas, scorpions and so forth.

"In the psyche of these forms of beings moreover, a very strange peculiarity has been formed. These tigers, lions, bears, hyenas, snakes, phalangas, scorpions and so forth, perceive the inner feeling of fear of other beings as hostility, and hence try to destroy them in self-defense.

"This strange peculiarity in their psyche was also acquired on account of your favorites. Thanks as usual to their abnormal conditions of existence, they gradually became cowards from head to foot; and at the same time, and equally completely the peculiarity of destroying the existence of other beings entered into them.

"Being thus by nature cowards of the highest degree, whenever they set out to kill other forms of beings or accidentally meet any of them, who, physically and in other respects, are much stronger than themselves, they sweat with fear, and long with all their being for a means of killing them. In this manner, in the psyche of beings who have no frequent contact with your favorites, side by side with the real function placed in them by Nature, instinctively to pay respect to those forms of beings, which in the gradation of the sacred reasonableness are higher than themselves, an instinct is gradually acquired and formed, owing to which the feeling of fear in others is perceived as a menace to their own life, which menace they try accordingly to destroy.

"In spite of the difference of their exterior forms, all the beings of this planet lived together at first in peace and concord; and even at the present time, it happens occasionally that one of your favorites so perfects himself that he realizes that all living creatures are alike to our ENDLESSNESS; and then succeeds in completely destroying his fear of other forms of beings. In consequence not only do these other forms of beings not attempt to harm him but they even pay him every respect and render him every service as a being higher in the scale of reasonableness.

"In short, my dear boy, thus arose among your favorites, various forms of politeness and in each locality, these forms differ.

"Although this Dervish being Hadji-Asvatz-Troov was sympathetic, I wished that his attitude towards me should become rather more than friendly in the Earth sense and I therefore began to use very often in conversation with him the local forms of polite address.

"My reason was that I was anxious to learn how he had become interested in that science and how he had arrived at results then unknown on the Earth.

"You must know that excellent relations were immediately established between this venerable Earth-being and myself chiefly because I was a friend of his friend. By the way, the beings of this locality are the only ones remaining on that planet amongst whom really friendly relations exist.

"A friend there is not only a friend, but his friend's friends are also his friends, and his attitude towards them is the same as towards his own friend. Having represented myself as the friend of the Dervish Bogga-Eddin, since the latter was a good friend of this Hadji-Asvatz-Troov, the venerable Hadji-Asvatz-Troov became very friendly towards me.

"In constant talk with him on the science of Shat-Chai-Mernis, he, now and then, referred to the octave of sounds.

"'Not only,' he said, 'has the whole octave of sounds seven centers of gravity, but the vibrations of any of these seven centers, both in fact and in effect, are according to this same law.'

"Continuing to speak about vibrations, he said that he had

become interested in the science Shat-Chai-Mernis chiefly on account of these same laws.

"'Strictly speaking,' he said, 'it was precisely on account of these vibrations that my whole life became devoted to this science. Before my entrance into the brotherhood of the Dervishes I was a very rich man; but I used to like very much to occupy myself as a 'saz-dji'; that is to say, I made various stringed musical instruments called 'sayaz,' 'tar,' 'kiamancha,' 'zimbal' and so forth.

"'After entering the brotherhood, I devoted all my free time to this craft, making instruments for our Dervishes, chiefly.

"'The Sheik of our monastery once called me and said:

"'"Hadji, in the monastery where I was a novice, all the Dervishes used to experience various corresponding feelings from the sacred melodies played during certain mysteries by the Dervish musicians. But during my long and careful observations here, I have never yet noticed any special influence from those sacred melodies in our own Dervishes.

"'"What is the explanation of this? What is the cause? It has for some time been my aim to discover the reason and I have asked you here just now, to discuss it with you. Perhaps as an amateur specialist in making instruments, you can help me to elucidate the question."

"'Following this conversation, we began to consider the problem in all its aspects; and after long deliberation we eventually concluded that the reason must certainly lie in the nature of the vibrations of sound, since it had been established during the conversation that outside the tambourine, only stringed instruments were used in the monastery where our Sheik had been a novice. Here in our monastery, the sacred melodies were played on wind instruments as for instance, on 'gavalls,' 'doodooks,' 'daks,' 'talfans,' and so on.

"'We decided at once to substitute strings for all the wind musical instruments of the monastery; whereupon the very serious difficulty arose, that amongst our Dervishes, we could not find a sufficient number capable of playing on stringed instruments. After a little thought our Sheik said to me:

"'"Hadji, you are already proficient on stringed instruments, see if you can perhaps make stringed musical instruments of such a kind that any unskilled Dervish can produce sounds of the required melody on them just by turning or striking, or some such mechanical action."

"'The suggestion greatly interested me and I immediately undertook with great pleasure to carry it out.

"'After so deciding, I got up, received the blessing of our Sheik and went away.

"'Having returned to my room, I sat down and began to think a very long time. The result of my thought was that I decided to ask Dervish Kerbalai-Azis-Nuaran to devise a system of small hammers, from the strokes of which, the corresponding sounds would be produced. And that same evening I went to this friend of mine.

"'Although the Dervish Kerbalai-Azis-Nuaran was considered to be a very queer fellow, everybody respected and honored him for his learning. He used often to speak of matters that made people think very deeply.

"'Before he had become a Dervish he had been a professional 'Saatchi,' that is, a watchmaker; and he continued to devote all his spare time in the monastery to his beloved craft.

"'By the way, he recently has been much absorbed in another of his queer ideas, namely, how to make a watch which would go perfectly without a spring.

"'He explained and formulated this idea of his very briefly and very simply by saying:

"'"Nothing on the Earth is absolutely at rest, since the Earth itself moves. Only weight is at rest, but, even then, only on half of the place occupied by its volume.

"'"I wish" he said, "to get such an absolute balance of levers that their movement, necessitated by the tempo of the movement of the Earth, will exactly correspond to the movement of the hands necessary for twenty-four hours."

"'When I came to this queer fellow and explained what I wished to do, he also became very interested and promised to help me as much as he could. And on the following day we began to work. The cymbal itself was soon ready; my queer friend continued to work upon the mechanism and I began to tighten the strings and to tune them properly. It was just then that something happened that aroused my interest in experiments I am still continuing today.

"'It happened thus: I knew very well that half a string gives twice as many vibrations as a whole string of the same tension, and according to this principle I began to put the bridges for the strings on the cymbal, and afterwards with the aid of my 'Perambarrsasidaan' or as it is called in Europe, 'tuning-fork,' with the vibrations of the absolute note 'do,' to tighten and tune the strings for a very ancient sacred melody containing one-eighth note sounds.

"'During this tuning I realized clearly for the first time, that this principle, namely, that the length of the string is inversely proportional to the number of its vibrations, is not always exact for obtaining the general united harmonious consonance; it is only sometimes so.

"'This realization interested me so much, that I gave all my attention to the investigation of this phenomenon and ceased entirely to occupy myself with the cymbal.

"'My queer friend also happened to find himself greatly interested in it and together we began to investigate this inaccuracy.

"'It was only some days later that my friend and I noticed that we had neglected our main work, whereupon we decided from that day on to devote half our time to finishing the cymbal and the other half to continuing these investigations.

"'We soon grew to be so expert in carrying on these two tasks of ours, that neither suffered on account of the other.

"'In spite of the delay, we did finish the cymbal we had begun, and it turned out quite satisfactorily. We changed its arrangement several times and eventually it became rather like the new Greek barrel-organ, only much larger and with quarter-tones.

"'It was started by turning and this caused the little hammers to strike on the corresponding strings. The strokes were regulated by bundles of flattened reeds perforated with corresponding holes, which as they passed under the handles made them strike.

"'For each sacred melody we prepared a special bundle of these flattened reeds; and these could be changed according to the melody desired.

"'When we eventually delivered this cymbal of ours to our Sheik and told him frankly what it was that most interested us at that moment, he not only blessed our leave of absence in the pursuit of our interest but contributed a very large sum of money.

"'The more we studied, the more absorbed we became in our work; until at last we came here where we lived apart from our brotherhood.

"'All this time I lived with my dear friend, the Dervish Kerbalai-Azis-Nuaran in full peace and concord. And only recently have I lost this irreplaceable friend forever. Some weeks ago he descended to the banks of the river Amu Darya, to the town X, for various instruments and materials. While leaving the town to return here, a stray bullet from the firing between the Russians and the Afghans struck and killed him. A mutual friend of ours, Kara-Kirgiz, who happened to be nearby, saw the event and immediately informed me of it.

"'Several days later we brought his remains home and buried him there,' he added, pointing to a strange projection in the corner of the cave. And having said this, he rose and after making some gestures of prayer for the repose of his friend, indicated by his head that we were to follow him.

"We did so and found ourselves again in the main passage of the cave. This venerable Earth-being then stopped before a projecting part and pressed. Again a block was moved aside and an entrance was revealed in another section of the cave.

"As I afterwards learned, the movable block on this occasion was not of stone but of thin sheets of felt, oil-cloth and clay.

"The place into which we entered was so remarkable that I should like to describe it to you.

"The walls, the ceiling and even the floor were covered with very thick felt. This was done, I was afterwards told, so that not the smallest vibration of any manifestation, rustle, noise, or even the vibrations of breathing arising from creatures, large and small, present in the neighborhood, should be able to penetrate from without.

"In this extraordinary place were several apparatuses of strange forms, and also a sound-producing instrument, a piano. The latter was without its front board and hence all its strings were visible. To each series of strings each representing a note, was attached in a special manner an independent little apparatus called a 'vibrometer' which, I learned later, counted and measured the vibrations of sound. I was again much astonished by these little apparatuses. For I knew very well that, at the present time, there does not exist on the Earth any such apparatus, capable of counting vibrations. And I wondered how this venerable old being, dwelling amidst almost wild animals, could have come by them.

"Among the other apparatuses in that remarkable room, was one on which there were fixed several objects like masks. They were joined to a place in the roof of the cave by a thick pipe made of the throats of cows. Through this pipe, as I afterwards learned, air for breathing could pass from without. This air was necessary because during the experiments the room was hermetically closed and without fresh air, staying there was out of the question. The beings present wore the masks which were on this apparatus.

"When we were all seated on the floor of this remarkable place, the venerable Hadji continued his talk. He told us, by the way, that he and his friend had had to study very carefully during their researches all the theories of vibrations invented by the great savants of the Earth. He said, 'We examined the Assyrian theory established by the great Malmanash, the Arabian theory of the famous Selneh-eh-Avaz, the theory of the Greek philosopher Pythagoras, and, of course, all the Chinese theories.

"'We made exactly the same apparatuses as those on which all these ancient sages carried out their experiments; and we even added a new feature to one of them. It is the one I now must use.

"'Pythagoras made his experiments in ancient times on this very apparatus. It was then called a 'Monochord,' but having now modified it, I call it a 'Vibrosho.'

"Having said this he pointed to a certain apparatus of a very strange form and remarked that this was the modified 'Monochord.'

"It consisted of a board too meters long, the lower half of which was divided into separate divisions like the finger-board of the sound-producing instrument called 'Guitar.'

"On the upper half were fixed a large number of vibrometers like those which were or the strings of the piano, they were placed just above the divisions of the board.

"On the upper half of the back of this board which was divided like a finger board, was a whole network of various small glass and metal pipes. These were used especially for the measuring of vibrations obtained from certain movements and also from currents of artificially condensed or rarified ordinary air.

"As the venerable Hadji paused to put some pounded tobacco into his mouth, I first asked him the following question:

"'Venerable Hadji,' I said, 'I have hitherto been quite convinced that nowhere on the Earth does there exist any apparatus for the exact measuring of vibrations. Yet I see many such here. How am I to understand this? Where did you get them? All the time I have been here this question has worried me.'

"The Dervish Hadji-Asvatz-Troov replied: 'These apparatuses were made for our experiments by my deceased friend Hadji-Azis-Nuaran, and I am chiefly indebted to them for my attainments in the knowledge concerning the laws of vibrations.

"'Dear friend of my friend,' this great and perhaps the last sage of the Earth continued, 'While Tikliamish flourished, all kinds of these apparatuses once existed, but at the present time, there are no longer to be found any such apparatuses for measuring vibrations, unless, of course, we include that childish plaything by means of which it is said to be possible to count vibrations. In Europe they call this toy a 'siren.' I also used it in the beginning of my experiments.

"'This "siren" was invented two centuries ago by a certain learned physicist Zehbek. In the first half of the last century it was said to have been improved by a certain Cognar de la Tour.

"'Its arrangement is such that a current of condensed air from a pipe is directed upon a revolving disc, perforated around the edge. Each of the holes coincides exactly in size with the opening of the main air pipe, and during the revolving of the disc, the access for the current of air coming from the main pipe alternately opens and closes.

"'As the disc revolves, currents of air pass through its holes in succession; and from these are produced sounds of equal degree. The number of revolutions indicated by a clock mechanism, multiplied by the number of the holes in the disc, is supposed to give the number of vibrations of this sound during a given space of time.

"'Unfortunately for these Europeans, neither the first inventor nor the improver of the siren realized that sound is obtained from vibrations as well as from air currents. As this siren sounded only from air currents and not from vibrations it is quite out of the question. All the same, it is a very interesting fact that sound can be produced from two causes, namely, the vibrations themselves and from the air currents. I shall now demonstrate this to you practically.'

"Having said this the venerable Hadji got up and from the other section of the cave brought a pot containing flowers which he put in the middle of the room. He then sat down near that apparatus, formerly the Monochord of the famous Pythagoras.

"Addressing us he said, 'I shall now produce from these combined little pipes only five different sounds. Fix your attention on this pot of flowers and note the numbers indicated by the hands of the vibrometers. Observe also the watch, please, and notice how many times I reproduce these sounds.'

"With a small pair of bellows he then began to blow into corresponding pipes from which there began to issue a monotonous melody of five notes.

"The melody continued for ten minutes, and we not only remembered the figures indicated on the vibrometers but these five sounds were well impressed on our hearing.

"And when the Hadji had finished his monotonous music, the flowers in the pot were still alive as before. Hadji now sat down at the sound-producing instrument called piano, and drawing our attention again to the hands of the vibrometers, he struck the corresponding keys of the piano and produced the same monotonous melody as before.

"The hands of the vibrometers, moreover indicated the same figures. Two minutes had not yet passed when by a sign of his head the Hadji directed us to look at the pot of flowers. We saw very clearly with our eyes that the flowers in the pot had begun to fade; and when after ten minutes, the venerable Hadji ceased his music, there remained of the former blossoming plants in the pot, only fallen petals and faded stalks.

"After this experiment the Hadji sat down again by our side and said:

"'My investigations during many long years have convinced me that there really exist in the world, as the science Shat-Chai-Mernis says, two kinds of vibrations, namely, vibrations of momentum and creative vibrations. And, by the way, these creative vibrations manifest only in metal strings or strings made of goat-gut. Strings made of other materials have not this quality. They can only produce sounds by means of air currents or by the friction of air; and by these means momentum vibrations are formed.

"'Formerly we made our experiments on this Vibrosho, that is the apparatus I adopted from the Greek philosopher Pythagoras.

"'But once when my friend Hadji-Azis-Nuaran was in the Bokharian town of X on business, he happened to see this piano in a sale of the furniture of some Russian general who was leaving. He bought it and later with great difficulty dragged it up here into the mountains.

"'We then tuned its strings exactly according to the laws of vibrations, indicated in the ancient Chinese science Shat-Chai-Mernis. For this purpose we not only employed the absolute sound of the note 'do' but as this science indicated, we also took into consideration geographical conditions, the pressure of atmosphere, the form and dimensions of the room and the average temperature of the surrounding space as well as the room itself and so on. We even considered the number of people present from whom radiations might arise.

"'Having tuned the piano in this manner really exactly, the vibrations produced by it immediately acquired the properties mentioned by this great science.

"'I will show you what it is possible to do with the knowledge attained by man and with the vibrations proceeding from this ordinary piano.'

"Having said this he again rose from his seat. He then brought from the other room an envelope, paper and pencil, and again sat down by the piano.

"He then wrote something on the paper and put it into the envelope; which he attached to a hook hanging from the ceiling in the middle of the room. Again he sat down at the piano and without speaking began as before to strike different keys from which a monotonous melody was again obtained. But on this occasion two octave sounds were also constantly and equally repeated in the melody.

"I noticed in a little while that it had become inconvenient for my friend, the Dervish Bogga-Eddin, to sit still; he moved his left leg from place to place.

"A little later he began to stroke his left leg and from his grimaces it was plain that this leg pained him a great deal. But the venerable Dervish Hadji-Asvatz-Troov paid no attention to this whatever and continued to strike the same definite keys.

"Having eventually finished he turned towards us and addressing himself to me said:

"'Please get up, take the envelope from the hook and read what is written inside.'

"I got up, took the envelope, opened it and read as follows:

"'From the vibrations of the sounds of this piano there must be formed on the left legs of both of you, two inches below the knee and an inch to the left center, a furuncle, called

"Pendcheeban."'

"The venerable Hadji at the same time begged us to expose these places of our left legs; and when we had bared them, there was found to be a real furuncle on the left leg of the Dervish Bogga-Eddin, exactly on the spot described. But to the great astonishment of the venerable Hadji, there was nothing on any part of my body.

"When he had assured himself that there was no furuncle on my left leg, he leapt up instantly from his place just as if he were young and exclaimed:

"'This is impossible.' Then he stared intently at my left leg with eyes almost like a madman's.

"Nearly five minutes passed in this manner. I confess that for the first time on that planet I was embarrassed and could not immediately devise an escape from the situation that had arisen.

"Finally he approached me and made an effort to speak. But his legs began to shake very violently from agitation, and sitting down, he gave me a sign to do the same. When we were seated he looked at me with very sad eyes and told me as follows:

"'Friend of my friend; In my youth I was very rich, so rich that no fewer than ten of my own caravans with no fewer than a thousand camels in each, were always moving somewhere or other in our great Asia. My harem was considered by the experts, to be the choicest on Earth; and everything else was on a similar scale. In short, I lived in such a style that it might be said, "I could do everything my left foot wished."

"'But all this, that is to say, everything that ordinary life can give, so satisfied me that every night as I went to bed, I thought with horror that on the morrow I must go through the same old daily round called "life."

"'Eventually I found it intolerable to live with such inner emptiness, and having felt that vacuity of ordinary life with particular intensity, I finally and resolutely decided to kill myself, and calmly and very coldly began to prepare everything necessary to carry out this decision, without missing fire or leaving room for misunderstanding.

"'On the last evening as I entered the room where I intended to put my resolution into effect, I suddenly remembered that I had not bade farewell to the one person who had been partly responsible for the creation and shaping of my life.

"'I remembered my mother who was still alive.

"'Remembering her completely changed everything in me.

"'I immediately imagined how she would suffer when she should hear of my death, and when I pictured this to myself, I began to feel so much pity for her, that my sobs almost choked me.

"'In short from that time onward, my mother was the source of my life.

"'Remembering her face, at whatever hour of the day or night it might be, I was filled with new strength, and with the desire to live and to do everything to make her life happy.

"'Ten years thus passed and then after a pitiless sickness, she died, and I was left alone.

"'After her death my inner emptiness again began day by day to torture me more and more.'

"Just at this point of the story, as he happened to look at his friend, the Dervish Bogga-Eddin, the venerable Hadji jumped up from his place, as if stung by a snake, and turning to him said:

"'My dear friend, in the name of our friendship pardon me for having forgotten to remove the sufferings caused by the maleficent vibrations.'

"Having said this, he sat down at the piano and again began to strike various keys. On this occasion, however, he produced the sounds only of two notes, one high and one low, and all the time alternately. Then almost with a shout he exclaimed:

"'Now thanks to the same vibrations of sound, this time beneficent, the sufferings of my good friend will cease.'

"'And indeed five minutes had hardly elapsed before the face of the Dervish Bogga-Eddin brightened up, nor did there remain on his leg even a trace of the enormous malignant furuncle which up to that moment had continued to adorn it.

"The Dervish Hadji-Asvatz-Troov then again sat down near us and having become outwardly, that is, apparently, quite calm, he resumed his tale.

"'The fourth day after the death of my dear mother,' he continued, 'I was sitting in my room and desperately meditating on what would happen, when in the street near the window a wandering Dervish began to sing his sacred hymns.

"'I looked out and seeing that the singing Dervish was old and had a very fine appearance, I suddenly decided to seek his advice and immediately sent my servant to invite him in. When he entered and after the usual welcome, he sat down on the "Mindari" and I spoke to him of my soul state without concealing anything.

"'When I had finished, the old Dervish became deeply buried in thought; and it was only after a long time that he looked at me very steadily. Then rising from his seat he said:

"'"The only way out for you is to devote yourself to religion."

"'Having said this, he departed uttering a prayer as he left my house forever.

"'After he had gone, I also became thoughtful and the very same day, I decided irrevocably to enter one of the "brotherhoods" of Dervishes, though not in my own country but somewhere further.

"'The following day I began to divide and distribute all my wealth amongst my relations and the poor, and two weeks later, I left my country forever, and came here to Bokhara.

"'Here I chose one of the numerous Dervish 'Brotherhoods' and entered it. I selected it because its Dervishes were very well known for the severity of their ordinary life.

"'But unfortunately they soon destroyed all my illusions about themselves; and I therefore entered another "Brotherhood" where the same thing happened. At last I was considered as a Dervish of that "brotherhood," the Sheik of whose monastery gave me the work of the inventing the mechanical stringed musical instrument.

"'As I have told you, I became completely absorbed in the science of vibrations and have occupied myself with it until today.

"'But today just this science has made me undergo the same state which I first experienced the night before the death of my mother, whose love alone had been my hearth and warmth and had for so many years made tolerable a life which had become so empty and so desolate. Even now I cannot recall without a shudder the moment when the doctor told me that my mother would not live beyond the morrow.

"'In that terrible state of mine, the first question that arose in me was, how shall I possibly continue to live?

"'What followed and what happened to me afterwards I have already briefly told you.

"'In short, as I became absorbed in the science of vibrations, I gradually discovered my new divinity. This science replaced my mother during many years and supported me as faithfully and loyally as she had done. By its truths alone I have lived and been inspired until today.

"'Never in a single instance before today have the truths I have discovered concerning vibrations failed to manifest the exact results I expected.

"'But today for the first time the results I expected I have not obtained and my terror is chiefly due to the fact that, today I was more than usually careful in my calculations of the vibrations necessary in this case. I calculated exactly that the furuncle should be formed on that very part of your body named, and nowhere else.

"'And now the unprecedented has happened; not only is it not on the indicated place, but it has not been found at all.

"'The science which has hitherto taken the place of my loyal and faithful mother, has today betrayed me; and now I am wretched beyond words. I can bear this greatest of misfortunes today, but what tomorrow will be I cannot even imagine.

"'I can bear it today only because I remember the words of our ancient great prophet Issi-Noora, who said that an individual is not responsible for his actions when dying.

"'Obviously my science, my divinity, my second mother is dying in agony for having betrayed me today.

"'I also know very well that, after the agony, death is near. And you, dear friend of my friend, have today unwittingly become for me like one of those doctors who, the night before her death told me that my mother would not live through the next day. Today, you inform me in the same way that my new hearth will be cold tomorrow.

"'I again experience the pangs and sensations I felt from the moment I was told my mother would die until she died.

"'But even then and during those feelings and sensations, I had a hope that perhaps she would not die; and there is the same feeling in me now.

"'Friend of my friend, knowing now the state of my soul, I earnestly beg you as my friend's friend to explain, if you can, what supernatural force interfered that the furuncle which should infallibly have been formed on your left leg, was not formed at all.

"'My confidence in the certainty that it would be formed has long been as strong in me as the Tookloonian stone. For nearly forty years, I have studied the great laws of vibrations day and night, until it might be said that my knowledge of them has become second-nature.'

"On uttering these last words the Dervish Hadji-Asvatz-Troov looked expectantly into my eyes.

"Can you imagine my position at that moment? What could I reply?

"On his account, I was thus the second time in a situation from which I did not know how to escape. Besides the strange state I was in on this occasion, I also felt a profound pity for this being. I was sorry chiefly because he was suffering on my account. I knew at the same time that if I should tell him anything, not only would he be at peace from what I should say, but he would understand that by the very fact that a furuncle had not been formed on my left leg, the truth and accuracy of his beloved science had been more completely proved.

"I had moreover, full moral right to tell the truth about myself to this Earth-being, since, by his attainments he had already become a 'Kalmanuior,' to whom, although belonging to that planet, we are not forbidden to be frank. But I could not be frank at that moment. My friend Bogga-Eddin was there, and he was still just an ordinary being, to whom it had long been forbidden by oath and authority that beings of our race should communicate true information in any circumstances whatever.

"This prohibition was laid upon the beings of our race, it seems, on the initiative of the Very Holy Ashiata Shiemash. And it was imposed on us chiefly because information gives only mind knowledge; and mind knowledge tends to reduce the possibility of acquiring knowledge of one's Being.

"And since the sole means remaining on that planet for ultimate deliverance from the consequences of the properties of the organ Kundabuffer is knowledge of one's Being, this command was laid upon our race in respect of the beings of the

Earth. This was why I could not undertake, with my friend, the Dervish Bogga-Eddin, present, to explain to this worthy sage, at the moment, the real cause of his failure.

"But I had to say something, since this Dervish Hadji-Asvatz-Troov who merited the title of sage, continued to await my reply. On that occasion, however, I said no more than this.

"'Venerable Hadji-Asvatz-Troov,' I said, 'if you will defer my reply, I swear to you by the cause of my creation, that I will give you such an answer that you will be fully satisfied that not only is your beloved science that very Truth itself, but you will be convinced that next to those great savants, the Saints Choon-Kil-Tez and Choon-Tro-Pel, you are the greatest savant of all the Earth.'

"At this reply, the Dervish Hadji-Asvatz-Troov simply pressed his right hand over his heart—a gesture meaning, 'I believe and hope without doubt.'

"Then, as if nothing had happened, he turned to the Dervish Bogga-Eddin and resumed his talk of the Science Shat-Chai-Mernis.

"With that same aim in view, of passing over the recent incident, I again addressed myself to this Dervish Hadji-Asvatz-Troov and pointing to a recess in the cave where a great deal of colored silk was hanging in strips, said:

"'Highly respected Hadji, what is that material over there in the recess?'

"'These colored materials,' he replied, 'I used for the experiments that recently enabled me to discover the degree of harm the color vibrations of materials produce on men and animals. If you like I will demonstrate it by an exceedingly interesting experiment.'

"Having said this, he rose and left the room and from the other section of the cave brought in, first of all, three quadruped Earth beings called 'dog,' 'sheep' and 'goat.' Then he fetched several apparatuses of a strange form of bracelets. One of these bracelets he placed on the arm of the Dervish Bogga-Eddin and the other on his own arm; during which process, by the way, he said, addressing me, 'I do not put one on you for very weighty reasons.'

"One by one he put these strange apparatuses on the necks of the goat, the sheep and the dog, like a collar, and then pointing to the vibrometers attached to these strange apparatuses, he asked me to notice and remember the figures indicated by the hands of the vibrometers on all the five beings.

"We looked at all the vibrometers and then noticed what he had told us to remember.

"He then sat down and said that there is a sum of vibrations peculiar to every form of life; it is the sum of the vibrations issuing from all the various definite organs. This total differs in every being at different times, and depends on the intensity of the sources which transform the corresponding vibrations. All these heterogeneous vibrations are invariably assembled in a single general subjective vibration.

"'For example, take my friend Bogga-Eddin and myself' he went on, showing me at the same time the figures which the hand of his vibrometer indicated. 'I have in general a certain number of vibrations but my friend Bogga-Eddin has more. This is because he is much younger than I and some of his functions produce in him many more vibrations than in me.

"'Now look at the figures on the vibrometers of the dog, sheep and goat. The sum of the dog's is three times that of the sheep, and one and a half that of the goat, yet it has a great many times fewer vibrations than my friend and I. Even amongst the inhabitants of the Earth, there are very many beings with fewer vibrations than the dog, owing to the fact that their chief human function, the function of emotion, has become so atrophied, that it scarcely transforms the vibrations at all, or transforms far fewer than the same function when more developed in a dog.'

"The venerable Hadji rose once more and went towards the place where the colored materials were. He then began, color by color, to unroll these materials of Bokharan silk, and to cover with each colored roll the walls, the ceiling and even the floor of this whole section of the cave. Thus all the room was covered with a material of a certain color.

"Every time a new colored material was unrolled we saw that the hands of the vibrometers of the five different beings changed and changed differently. By some colored materials the average figures for the vibrations of these five beings, so different in their individuality, were diminished almost by half or increased almost by a quarter.

"By the way, the Dervish Hadji-Asvatz-Troov remarked that certain vibrations proceeding from certain colors of materials as well as from objects, whether naturally or artificially colored, have particularly harmful effects on the vibrations of people. And these harmful vibrations are among the causes tending century by century to reduce the length of man's life.

"After the experiments with colored materials, this contemporary great Earth savant invited us to follow him. We again reached the main passage of the cave and entered into a small passage on the side, leading elsewhere. The goat, sheep and the dog crawled after us in their improvised collars. We all walked a fairly long way and at last arrived at an enormous section of the cave.

"Here in this subterranean cavity, Dervish Asvatz-Troov approached one of the niches and pointing to a large heap of material of a very strange color said:

"'This material is specially woven from fibers of the plant 'Chaltandr': it has a natural color. The plant from the fibers of which this material is woven, is one of the very few formations on the Earth, the color of which cannot change the vibrations arising from neighboring sources. It follows that the color of this material has absolutely no effect on any kind of vibrations arising from whatever cause.

"'It was for this reason that for my experiments on vibrations not originating from color, I specially ordered this material of which I made for the whole of this large cave something like a very big tent, arranged in such a manner that it could be moved anywhere and given any form.

"'It is with the aid of this strange tent that I carry out the experiments which I call 'architectural,' which show me clearly which and to what degree rooms react harmfully on people.

"'I am convinced that not only the size and form in general of a room have an enormous influence on people, but also the shape, the corners, projections, and the broken portions of wall and many other factors which produce changes of the vibrations of the room, affect the vibrations in people for good or evil.'

"His experiments with this enormous tent eventually convinced me also that not only the forms and the sizes of a room effect to a large extent the beings of the Earth, but I became convinced that vibrations in general affect beings of this planet much more than the other beings of our Universe.

"Later this great sage led us into other small sections where he showed us other experiments. For instance, he explained and showed us experiments demonstrating the effects of vibrations formed from radiations of other beings, from their voices and from other of their habitual actions.

"He also explained and showed us several experiments demonstrating the harmful action on Earth-beings arising from causes which the beings themselves create on a large scale as if expressly for their own harm, from what they call 'productions of art.'

"Amongst these latter are painting, sculpture, and of course, their famous music. But from all the experiments demonstrated by this sage, the most harmful vibrations for Earth-beings, as far as I understood, proved to he those formed from their medical remedies, specially from 'patent-medicines.'

"I was a guest of this most sympathetic Earth-being, the Dervish Asvatz-Troov, for four Earth days and then I left with the Dervish Bogga-Eddin for the town from which I had set out.

"Thus ended my first meeting with the last great savant of the Earth."*

* If anyone is greatly interested in the ideas mentioned in this chapter, then I advise him to read without fail, my book entitled 'The Opiumists,' that is, of course, if I ever write this book, as I intend. Author.

BOOK THREE

CHAPTER XLII

Beelzebub In America

TWO "Dionosks" later, when the intersystem ship "*Karnak*" had resumed its falling, and the confirmed followers of our respected Mullah Nassr Eddin had again sat down in their usual seats, Hassein once more turned to Beelzebub with the following words:

"My dear Grandfather! May I remind you, as you bade me, about . . . the three-brained beings . . . of the planet Earth . . . about those . . . how are they called? . . . about the beings who breed and exist just on the diametrically opposite side of the place where contemporary terrestrial civilization is flourishing . . . about those three-brained beings there, who, as you were saying, are very great devotees of the 'fox-trot.'

"Ah! About those Americans?"

"Yes, that's it, about those Americans," joyously exclaimed Hassein.

"Of course, I remember . . . I did, indeed, promise to tell you a little also about those contemporary queer ducks there."

And Beelzebub began thus:

"I happened to visit that part of the surface of your planet now called 'North-America,' just before my final departure from that solar system.

"I went there from my last place of existence on that planet, namely, from the city of Paris of the continent of Europe.

"From the continent of Europe I sailed there on a steamship, according to the custom of all contemporary what are called 'dollar-holders,' and arrived in the capital of 'North-America,' in the city of 'New York,' or, as it is sometimes called there, the 'city-of-the-melting-pot-of-the-races-of-the-Earth.'

"From the pier I went straight to a hotel called the 'Majestic' which had been recommended to me by one of my Paris acquaintances and which for some reason or other was additionally, though not officially, called 'Jewish.'

"Having settled in this 'Majestic' or 'Jewish' hotel, I went the same day to look up a certain 'Mister' there, who also had been recommended to me by still another of my Paris acquaintances.

"By this word 'Mister' every being of the male sex is called on that continent who does not wear what is called a 'skirt.'

"When I found this Mister,* to whom I had a letter of introduction, he, as is proper to every genuine American business man, was up to his eyes in innumerable, as is said there, 'dollar-businesses.'

"I think I might as well remark now at the very beginning of my elucidations about these Americans, that those three-brained beings there, especially the contemporary ones, who constitute the root population on this part of the surface of your planet, are in general almost all occupied only with these 'dollar-businesses.'

"On the other hand, with the trades and 'profession' indispensable in the process of being-existence, exclusively only those beings are occupied among them, who have gone there from other continents temporarily, and for the purpose as is said, of 'earning-money.'

"Even in this respect, the surrounding conditions of ordinary being existence among your contemporary favorites, chiefly among those breeding on this continent, have been transformed so to say, into 'Tralalalooalalalala,' or, as our respected teacher Mullah Nassr Eddin would define it, 'a-soap-bubble-that-lasts-a-long-time-only-in-a-quiet-medium.'

"Among them there at the present time, these surrounding conditions of ordinary collective existence have already

* ***Editor's Note:*** Here we added the words: ' "every being of the male sex is called on that continent who does not wear what is called a 'skirt.' "When I found this Mister," .' These words, taken from the 1950 publication, had clearly been omitted.

become such, that if, for some reason or other the specialist professionals of all the kinds necessary for their ordinary collective existence should cease to come to them from the other continents to 'earn-money,' then it is safe to say that within a month, the whole established order of their ordinary existence would completely break down, since there would be none among them who could even so much as bake bread.

"The chief cause of the gradual resulting of such an abnormality there among them, is on the one side, the law established by them themselves in respect of the rights of parents over their children, and on the other hand the institution in schools for children of what is called a 'dollar-savings-bank' together with the principle of implanting in children a love of such dollars.

"Thanks to this, and to still various other peculiar external conditions of ordinary existence also established by them themselves, just this love of 'dollar-business' and of dollars themselves, has become, in the common presence of each of the native inhabitants of this continent who reaches responsible age, the predominant urge during his responsible what is called, 'feverish-existence.'

"That is why each one of them is always doing 'dollar-business' and moreover, always several of them at once.

"Although the aforesaid 'Mister' to whom I had a letter of introduction was also very busy with these 'dollar-businesses,' he nevertheless received me very cordially. When he read the letter of introduction I presented to him, a strange process immediately began in him which has already been noticed even by certain of your favorites—it having also become inherent in your contemporary favorites in general—and which they call 'unconscious preening.'

"And this same process proceeded in him because, in the letter I presented, the name of a certain other acquaintance of mine, also a 'Mister,' was mentioned, who in the opinion of many, and of this 'Mister' also, was considered, as they call him behind his back, 'a-damn-clever-fellow,' that is to say, a 'dollar-expert.'

"In spite of his having been entirely seized with this inherency, proper to your contemporary favorites, he nevertheless, as he talked with me, gradually calmed down, and eventually he informed me that he was 'ready-to-place-himself-entirely-at-my-disposal.' Suddenly, however, he remembered something, whereupon he added that to his profound regret, owing to circumstances over which he had absolutely no control, he could not possibly oblige me that day, but not until the following day, because he was extremely busy with important affairs.

"And, indeed, with the best will in the world, he could not have done so, for these unfortunate Americans, who are always governed by these 'dollar-businesses' of theirs, can do what they please only on Sundays, whereas it just happened that the day I went to see him was not a Sunday.

"There on that continent, all dollar and other businesses depend never upon the beings themselves; on the contrary, your favorites there always themselves depend entirely on these 'businesses' of theirs.

"In short, the day not being a Sunday, this genuine American 'Mister' was unable to do as he pleased, namely, go along with me, and introduce me to the people necessary to me, and we had therefore to agree to meet the following morning at a defined place on the famous street there called 'Broadway.'

"This street 'Broadway' is the foremost and principal street not only in this New York, but, as is said there, is the longest street in any of the large contemporary cities of your planet.

"So I set off there on the next day.

"As the 'automobile-taxi' in which I drove to this place happened not to come from one of Mr. Ford's factories, I arrived too soon, and consequently this 'Mister' was not yet there.

"While awaiting him, I began strolling about, but as all the New York what are called 'brokers' take their 'Constitutional' before their famous 'quick-lunch' just in this part of the street 'Broadway,' the jostling in this crowded place became so great, that in order to escape it, I decided to go and sit down somewhere in some spot from where I could see the 'Mister' I was awaiting arrive.

"A suitable spot seemed to be a neighboring typical restaurant there, from the windows of which all the passers-by could be seen.

"I must say, by the way, that there, on all that planet of yours, there are not so many restaurants in the places of existence of any other group of your favorites as there are in that New York.

"They particularly abound in the main sections, and moreover the proprietors of these restaurants there are chiefly 'Armenians,' 'Greeks,' and 'Russian-Jews.'

"Now my boy, in order that you may rest a little from active mentation, I wish for a while to confine myself entirely to the form of mentation of our dear teacher Mullah Nassr Eddin and to talk about a certain in the highest degree original custom which has prevailed during the last few years in these contemporary New York restaurants.

"Inasmuch as the production, importation, and consumption of what are called 'alcoholic-liquids' have recently been strictly prohibited to the ordinary beings by the power-possessing beings of this group, and corresponding injunctions have also been given to those beings there upon whom the power-possessing beings rest their hope for their own welfare, it is now almost impossible for the ordinary beings there to obtain such liquids. At the same time, in these New York restaurants, various 'alcoholic liquids' called 'Arak,' 'Doosico,' 'Scotch-whisky,' 'Benedictine,' 'Vodka,' 'Grand-Marnier,' and many other different liquids, under every possible kind of label, and made exclusively only on what are called 'Old-barges' lying at sea off the shores of that continent, are to be had in any quantity you please.

"The very 'Tzimus' of the said practice lies in this, that if you point your fourth finger, and covering one half of your mouth with your right palm, utter the name of any liquid you fancy, then immediately, without more words, that liquid is served at table—only in a bottle purporting to be lemonade or the famous French 'Vichy.'

"Now try with all your might to exert your will and to actualize in your presence a general mobilization of your 'perceptive-organs,' so that, without missing anything at all, you may absorb and transubstantiate in yourself everything relating to just how these 'alcoholic-liquids' I have enumerated are prepared at sea on 'old-barges' off the shores of that continent.

"I regret very much that I missed making myself thoroughly familiar with all the details of this contemporary terrestrial 'science.'

"All I managed to learn was that into all the recipes for these preparations, the following acids enter—'sulphuric,' 'nitric,' and 'muriatic' acids, and most important of all, the 'incantation' of the famous contemporary German professor Kishmenhof.

"This last ingredient, namely, 'Professor Kishmenhof's incantation' for alcoholic liquids, is delightfully intriguing; and it is concocted, so it is said, as follows:

"First of all, there must be prepared, according to any old recipe, already familiar to specialists in the business, a thousand bottles of liquid. Precisely one thousand bottles must be prepared, because if there should be merely one bottle more or one bottle less, the incantation will not work.

"These thousand bottles must be placed on the floor and then, quietly beside them, a single bottle of any genuine 'alcoholic-liquid' existing anywhere there, must be placed and kept there for a period of ten minutes; at the end of which time, very slowly and quite indispensably, while scratching the right ear with the left hand, one must utter with certain pauses this said alcoholic incantation.

"Upon this, not only are the contents of all the thousand bottles instantly transformed into precisely that alcoholic liquid contained in the said single bottle, but every bottle of the thousand even acquires the same label borne by that one bottle of genuine alcoholic-liquid.

"Among the conjuries of this unprecedented German professor Kishmenhof, there are, as I learned, several indeed most amazing ones.

"This famous German professor, a specialist in this branch, started, as is said, 'inventing' these remarkable 'conjuries' of his quite recently, that is to say, in the early years of the last great general European process of reciprocal destruction there.

"When a food crisis supervened in his fatherland 'Germany,' he, sympathizing with the plight of his compatriots, invented his first conjury, which consisted in the preparation of a very cheap and economical 'chicken-soup.'

"This first conjury of his is called 'German chicken-soup,' and its execution is likewise extremely interesting, namely, as follows:

"Into a very commodious pot, set on the hearth, common water is poured, and then a few very finely chopped leaves of parsley are strewn into it.

"Then both doors of the kitchen must be opened wide, or, if there is only one door, a window must be opened wide, and, while very loudly pronouncing the incantation, a chicken must be chased through the kitchen at full speed.

"Upon this, a most delicious 'chicken-soup' is ready hot in the pot.

"I heard further that during the years of that great process of reciprocal destruction, the beings of Germany made use of this conjury on a colossal scale, this method of preparing chicken soup having proved in practice to be, as it were, good and, at least, extremely economical.

"The reason is that a single chicken could do duty for quite a long time, because it could be chased and chased and chased, until for some reason or other, one chicken all by itself, as is said there, 'went-on-strike' and declined to breathe any longer.

"And in the event that the chicken resisted the infection of hypocrisy, in spite of its having existed among your favorites, and indeed did cease to wish to breathe any longer, then for this eventuality, as I afterwards learned, a common custom was established there among the beings of that group called Germany.

"Namely, when the chicken went on strike, its owners would very solemnly roast it in the oven, and for this solemn occasion would unfailingly, invite all their relatives to dinner.

"It is interesting to notice also, that another professor of theirs, also famous, named Steiner, in the course of his, what are called, 'scientific-investigations-of-supernatural phenomena,' mathematically established that on the occasions when these chickens were served at these 'invitation-dinners,' always their owners would recite the same thing.

"Namely, every hostess, rolling her eyes to Heaven and pointing to the chicken, would say with great feeling, that it was the 'famous-Pamir-pheasant' and that it had been specially sent to them from Pamir by their dear nephew who resided there as consul for their great 'Fatherland.'

"On that planet there exist in general 'conjuries' for every possible kind of purpose.

"These 'conjuries' began multiplying particularly after many of the beings of this peculiar planet had become specialists in supernatural phenomena and came to be called 'occultists,' 'spiritualists,' 'theosophists,' 'violet-magicians,' 'chiromants,' and so forth.

"Besides being able to create 'supernatural-phenomena,' these 'specialists' also knew very well how to make the opaque look transparent.

"This same American prohibition of the consumption of alcohol can serve us, yet again, as an excellently illuminating example for understanding to what degree the possibilities for the crystallization of data for being-reflection are atrophied in these contemporary responsible power-possessing beings, in respect of the fact that such an absurdity is being actually repeated there.

"There on that continent, everybody without exception, thanks to this prohibition, now consumes this same alcohol—even those who in other circumstances would probably never have consumed it.

"There on the continent America, the very same is occurring with the consumption of alcohol as occurred with the chewing of the seeds of the poppy by the beings of the country Maralpleicie.

"The difference is that in the country of Maralpleicie the beings were then addicted to the use of at least genuine poppy-seeds, whereas in America, the beings now consume any liquid that comes their way, provided only that it bears the name of some alcoholic liquid existing somewhere on their planet.

"And another difference is, that in respect of concealing their consumption of the prohibited product from government eyes, the contemporary beings now breeding on this continent America are not by any means so naive as were the beings of the Maralpleicie epoch.

"To what lengths your contemporary favorites have gone in this respect, you can understand very well from the following examples.

"At the present time there in that place, every young man with his 'mother's-milk' scarcely dry on his lips, infallibly carries with him what seems to be a perfectly ordinary harmless 'cigarette' or 'cigar-case'; and, sitting in a restaurant or in one of their famous dance halls, he casually produces this cigarette—or cigar-case from his pocket, and everybody around imagines of course that he is about to smoke.

"But not a bit of it! He Just gives a peculiar little twist to this cigarette—or cigar-case of his, when, presto, a diminutive tumbler appears in his left hand, whereupon with his right hand, he s-l-o-w-l-y and q-u-i-e-t-l-y pours out for himself from this cigarette—or cigar-case into this diminutive tumbler of his, some kind of liquid—probably Scotch whisky, but concocted as I have already told you, on some barge off the American coast.

"During my observations there at that time, I once witnessed still another picture.

"In one of the said restaurants sat two young American women not far from my table.

"An attendant of this restaurant, or, as they say, a 'waiter,' served them with a bottle of some mineral water and a couple of glasses.

"One of the women gave a certain little twist to the handle of her fashionable umbrella, whereupon a liquid, obviously also Scotch whisky or something of the kind, began likewise to flow very q-u-i-e-t-l-y and very s-l-o-w-l-y from the handle into their glasses.

"In short, my boy, the same is being repeated on this continent America as also took place quite recently in the large community called Russia. There the power-possessing responsible beings also prohibited the consumption of the famous 'Russian-vodka,' with the consequence that these beings very soon adapted themselves to consume, instead of this 'Vodka,' the no less famous 'Hanja,' from the effects of which thousands of these unfortunate beings are still dying there daily.

"But in the present case, we must certainly give the contemporary American beings their due. In their skill at concealing their consumption of this famous alcohol from the authorities, they are infinitely more 'civilized' than the beings of the community Russia.

"Well then, my boy, to avoid the bustle of the street, I entered a typical New York restaurant, and having taken a seat at one of the tables there, began gazing out of the window at the crowd.

"As it is the common custom there on your planet, when people sit in a restaurant or any other such public place, always and without fail to pay what they call 'money' for something for the profit of the proprietor of the establishment, I did the same and also ordered for myself a glass of their famous what is called 'orangeade.'

"This famous American drink consists of the juice squeezed from oranges or from the famous what is called there 'grapefruit,' and the beings of that continent drink it always and everywhere in incredible quantities.

"It must be admitted that this famous 'orangeade' of theirs does occasionally refresh them in hot weather, but, on the other hand, in its action upon what are called the 'mucous-membranes' of the stomach and intestines, this drink of theirs is still another of the many factors there, which taken together, are gradually bringing about—although slowly yet inexorably certainly—the destruction of that 'unnecessary' and 'negligible' function called the 'digestive-function-of-the-stomach.'

"Well then, sitting in the said restaurant with this famous 'orangeade' and watching the passers-by in the hope of seeing among them the 'mister' I awaited, I began casually looking around at the objects in the restaurant also.

"On the table at which I was sitting, I saw among other things also what is called the 'menu' of the restaurant.

"'Menu' there on your planet, is the name given to a sheet of paper on which are written the names of all the varieties of food and drink available in the said restaurant.

"Reading the contents of this paper, I found among other things, that no fewer than seventy-eight different dishes could be ordered there that day.

"This staggered me, and I wondered what on earth kind of a stove these Americans must have in their kitchens to be able to prepare seventy-eight dishes on it for just one day.

"I ought to add that I had been on every one of the continents there, and had been the guest of a great many beings of different castes.

"And I had seen food prepared innumerable times, and also in my own house. So I already more or less knew that to prepare a single dish, at least two or three saucepans were required; and I reckoned that as these Americans prepared seventy-eight dishes in one kitchen, they would certainly need about three hundred pots and pans.

"I had the fancy to see for myself how it was possible to accommodate on one stove three hundred saucepans, so I decided to offer what is called there a 'good-tip' to the waiter who served me with the 'orangeade,' to let me see the kitchen of the restaurant with my own eyes.

"The 'waiter' somehow arranged it, and I went into the kitchen.

"When I got there, what do you think? . . . what kind of picture did I see? . . . A stove with a hundred pots and pans?

"Not on your life! ! . . .

"I saw there only a small what is called there 'midget-gas-stove,' such as what are called 'Old-bachelors' and 'man-haters,' that is to say, 'worthless-spinsters' usually have in their rooms.

"By the side of this 'pimple-of-a-stove' sat an extremely fat-necked cook of 'Scotch-origin' reading the newspaper inseparable from every American—he was reading, it seems, the newspaper 'The Times.'

"I looked around in amazement and also at the fat neck of this cook.

"While I was thus looking round in astonishment, a waiter came into the kitchen from the restaurant and, in peculiar English, ordered a certain very elaborate dish from this fat-necked cook.

"I think I may as well tell you that I then also noticed from his accent that the waiter who ordered this dish with a fancy name had only recently arrived there from the continent of Europe, obviously with the dream of filling his pockets there with 'American-dollars'—with that dream in fact about these 'American-dollars' which indeed every European has who has never been to America and which now allows no one in Europe to sleep in peace.

"When this aspirant to an 'American-multimillionairedom' had ordered the said fancy dish from the fat-necked cook, the latter got up from his place without haste and very heavily, and first of all took down from the wall a small what is called there 'bachelor's-frying-pan.'

"Then having lighted his 'dwarf-stove,' he put the frying-pan on it; and still moving ponderously, he then went over to one of the many cupboards, took from it a tin of some canned food, opened it, and emptied its contents into the said frying-pan.

"Then in the same way, he went over to another cupboard, and again took out a tin of some canned food, but this time he only put a little of the contents into the frying-pan, and having stirred the resulting mixture, he put the whole lot with great precision on a plate which he set on the table, and again he sat down in his former place and resumed the interrupted reading of his newspaper.

"The waiter who had ordered this 'fancy-dish' soon recurred to the kitchen bearing a very large what is called 'copper-tray' on which were a vast quantity of hollow metal, what is called, 'fashionable-cutlery,' and having placed the dish with this strange food on the said tray, he carried the whole into the restaurant.

"When I returned and resumed my seat at my table, I saw that at another table quite near, a 'mister' was sitting who was smacking his lips while eating the dish which I had chanced to see prepared in the kitchen.

"Looking again out of the window into the street, I eventually discerned the 'Mister' I expected in the crowd, so, settling my bill at once, I left the restaurant.

"And now, my boy, maintaining the form of mentation of our dear teacher, I might as well tell you also a little about the 'speech' of these American beings.

"You must know that before my arrival on that continent I could already speak the 'tongue' of the beings of that continent, namely, what is called the 'English-tongue.'

"But from the very first day of my arrival in the capital of this 'North-America,' I already experienced great inconvenience in my 'verbal-intercourse' because, as it turned out, although these beings use this 'English tongue' for 'verbal-intercourse' among themselves, this 'English-tongue' of theirs is rather special and in fact quite peculiar.

"So, having felt the inconvenience, I made up my mind to learn this peculiar 'conversational-English' of theirs also.

"On the third day after my arrival there, as I was on my way to my newly-acquainted 'Mister' specially to ask him to recommend me a teacher for this 'English-tongue,' I suddenly saw reflected on the sky by projectors, an 'American-advertisement' with the words:

'SCHOOL OF LANGUAGES BY THE SYSTEM
OF MR. CHATTERLITZ"
13 North 293rd Street.

"The languages and the times when they were taught were set forth and, of the 'American-English-language' in particular, it was stated, among other things, that it could be learned in from five minutes to twenty-four hours.

"At first I could not make head or tail of it, but I decided all the same to go the next morning to the address indicated.

"When the next day I found this 'Mr. Chatterlitz,' he received me himself in person, and when he heard that I wished to learn the 'American-English-language' by his system, he explained to me first of all that this conversational-language could be learned by his system in three forms, each form corresponding to some special requirement.

"'The first form,' he said, 'is the conversational language for a man who is obliged to earn here among us our American dollars.

"'The second form is required for a man who, although not in need of our dollars, nevertheless likes to do 'dollar business' and furthermore, in order that in his social relations with our Americans everybody will think that he is not "just-a-nobody" but a real "gentleman" with an English upbringing.

"'As for the third form of the "English-language," this form is required by anybody who wishes to be able to procure here, there and everywhere and at any hour—"Scotch-whisky."'

"As the time for learning the second form of the English language by this system suited me best, I decided to pay him immediately the dollars he charged in order to know the secret of his system.

"When I had paid him the 'dollars' he charged and he had, seemingly quite casually, but in reality not without that avidity which has also already become proper to all the beings of your planet, placed my dollars in an inside pocket, he explained to me that in order to learn this second form, only five words had to be memorized, namely:

1) Maybe,
2) Perhaps,
3) Tomorrow,
4) Oh, I see,
5) Alright.

"He added that if I had occasion to converse with one or more of their 'misters,' I should only need to utter any one of these five words every now and then.

"'That will be quite enough,' he added, 'to convince everybody that firstly you know the "English-language" very well, and secondly that you are an old hand at doing "dollar-business."'

"Although the system of this highly esteemed Chatterlitz was very original and meritorious, yet I never had occasion to put it into practice.

"And the occasion did not arise, because the next day I met by chance in the street an old acquaintance, an, as he is called, 'editor,' from the continent of Europe who in conversation confided to me an even more ideal secret for the American language.

"When I told him, among other things, that I had been the day before to 'Mister' Chatterlitz about the local language and had told him a little about the system, he replied:

"'Do you know what, my dear doctor? As you are a subscriber to our paper over there, I cannot help revealing to you a certain secret of the language here.'

"And he said further:

"'Knowing several of our European languages, you can by employing this secret of mine, be master of the language here to perfection, and indeed converse about anything you wish—and not simply make others think that you know the English language—for which purpose, I do not deny, the system of this Chatterlitz is indeed excellent.'

"He explained further that if when pronouncing any word

taken from any European language, you imagine that you have a hot potato in your mouth, then some word of the English language is in general bound to result.

"'And if you imagine that this same hot potato is furthermore well sprinkled with ground "red-pepper," then you will already have the pronunciation of the local "American-English-language" to a tee.

"He advised me moreover not to be timid in choosing words from the European languages, since the English language in general consisted of a fortuitous concourse of almost all the European languages, and hence that the language contained several words for every ordinary idea, with the consequence that 'you-almost-always-hit-on-the-right-word.'

"'And suppose that, without knowing it, you use a word entirely absent from this language, no great harm is done; at worse your hearer will only think that he himself is ignorant of it.

"'All you have to do is just to bear in mind the said hot potato and . . . no more 'baloney' about it.

"'I guarantee this secret, and I can safely say that if, on exactly following my advice, your 'language' here does not prove to be ideal, then you may stop your subscription.'

"Several days later, I had to go to the city of Chicago.

"This city is the second in size on that continent and is, as it were, a second capital of 'North America.'

"""On seeing me off for Chicago, that 'Mister,' my New York acquaintance, gave me a letter of introduction to a certain 'Mister' there.

"As soon as I arrived in this city Chicago, I went straight to this said 'Mister.'

"This Chicago 'Mister' turned out to be very amiable and most obliging.

"His name was 'Mister Belly-Button.'

"For the evening of the first day, this amiable and obliging 'Mr. Belly-Button' suggested my accompanying him to the house of some of his friends so that, as he expressed it, I should 'not-be-bored' in a quite strange city.

"I, of course, agreed.

"When we arrived, we found there a fair number of young American beings, guests like ourselves.

"All the guests were exceedingly gay and very 'merry.'

"They were telling 'funny-stories' in turn and the laughter from these stories of theirs lingered in the room like the smoke on a day when the wind is south over the chimneys of the American factories where the American sausages called 'hot-dogs' are prepared.

"As I also find funny stories amusing, that first evening of mine in the city of Chicago, passed very gaily indeed.

"All this would have been quite sensible and very delightful, if it had not been for one 'feature' of the stories told that first evening, which greatly astonished and perplexed me.

"And that is, I was astonished by their what is called 'ambiguity' and 'obscenity.'

"The 'ambiguity' and 'obscenity' of these stories were such that any single one of these American story-tellers could have given a dozen points to 'Boccaccio,' famous there on the planet Earth.

"'Boccaccio' is the name of a certain writer who wrote for the beings of the Earth a very instructive book called the 'Decameron'; it is very widely read there at the present time and is the favorite of contemporary beings breeding on all continents and belonging to almost all communities there.

"The following day, also in the evening, this kind 'Mr. Belly-Button' took me again to some still other friends of his.

"Here also were a large number of young American beings both male and female, sitting in various corners of a very large room conversing quietly and very placidly.

"When we were seated, a pretty young American girl soon

came and sat down beside me, and began chatting with me.

"As is usual there, I took up the conversation, and we chatted about anything and everything, she asking me among other things many questions about the city of Paris.

"In the midst of the conversation, this American, as they say, 'young-lady' suddenly, for no earthly reason at all, began stroking my neck.

"I immediately thought, how kind of her—she must certainly have noticed a 'flea' on my neck and is now stroking the place to allay the irritation.

"But when I soon noticed that all the young American beings present were also stroking each other, I was much astonished and could not understand what it was all about.

"My first supposition concerning the 'fleas' no longer held good, because it was impossible to suppose that everybody had a flea on his neck.

"I began speculating what it was all about, but try as I might I could give myself no explanation whatever.

"Only afterwards, when we had left the house and were in the street, I asked 'Mr. Belly-Button' for an explanation of it all. He immediately burst into unrestrained laughter, and called me 'Simpleton' and a 'hick.' Then, calming down a bit, he said:

"'What a queer guy you are; why we have just been to a "petting-party!"' And still laughing at my naïveté, he explained that the day before we had also been to a party, but to a 'story-party,' and tomorrow, he continued, 'I was planning to take you to a "swimming-party" where young people bathe together but, of course, all dressed in special costumes.'

"When he saw that the same look of perplexed astonishment still remained on my face, he asked, 'But if for some reason or other you don't like such "tame-affairs," we can go to others that are not open to everybody. There are lots of such "parties" here and I am a member of several of them. At these parties which are not open to everybody, we can, if you like, have something more "substantial."'

"But I did not take advantage of this kindness of this 'obliging' and exceedingly 'amiable' Mr. Belly-Button, because the next morning I received a telegram which made it necessary for me to return to New York."

At this point of his tales Beelzebub suddenly became thoughtful and after a rather protracted pause; sighing deeply, he continued to speak thus:

"The next day I did not go by the morning train as I had decided on receiving the telegram, but delayed my departure until the night-train.

"As the cause of the delay of my departure may well illustrate for you the evil resulting from a certain invention of these American beings which is very widely spread over the whole of your planet, and which is one of the chief causes of the continued, so to say, 'dwindling-of-the-psyche' of all the other three-brained beings of your unfortunate planet, I shall tell you about it a little more in detail.

"Just this maleficent invention of the beings of this continent, which I now intend to explain to you, has not only been the cause of the acceleration of the tempo of the still greater 'dwindling' of the psyche of all the three-brained beings breeding on that unfortunate planet of yours, but it was and still is the cause also that in the beings of all the other continents of recent times there is already completely destroyed that being-function which it is proper for all three-brained beings to have, and which was the one single function which even until the last century arose in their presence of its own accord—namely, that being-function which is everywhere called the 'sane-instinct-to-believe-in-reality.'

"In the place of this function, very necessary for every three-brained being, another special very definite function gradually crystallized, whose action induces in its bearer a continuous doubt about everything.

"This maleficent invention of theirs they call 'advertising.'

"Better to understand what follows, I must first tell you that several years before this trip of mine to 'America,' once when traveling on the continent of Europe, I bought myself some books to read in the train to pass away the prospective long and tedious railway journey. In one of these books, written by a very famous writer there, I read an article about this 'America' in which a great deal was said about what is called 'the slaughterhouse' existing in that same city Chicago.

"Slaughterhouse is the name there for a special place where three-brained terrestrial beings carry on the destruction of the existence of those beings of various other forms whose planetary bodies they are addicted to using for their first being-food, again owing to those abnormally established conditions of ordinary being-existence.

"Moreover, executing this manifestation of theirs in these special establishments, they even say and imagine that they do it from necessity and, as it were, in a perfectly what they call 'humane-way.'

"This said terrestrial contemporary very famous writer, the author of this book, rapturously described, as an 'eyewitness,' this in his opinion superlatively well organized slaughterhouse of this same city Chicago.

"He described the perfection of its machines of every possible kind and its marvelous cleanliness. Not only, he wrote, does humaneness to the beings of other forms reach in this slaughterhouse the degree of 'Divinity,' but even the machines are so perfected that it is almost as if a live ox is driven through a door at one end and some ten minutes later, out of a door at the other end you could get if you wished, hot sausages ready to eat. Finally, he specially emphasized that it was all done entirely by the 'perfected' machines alone, without the touch of a human hand, as a consequence of which, as he said, everything was so clean and neat there that nothing could possibly be imagined cleaner and neater.

"Several years after reading that book, I chanced to read again almost the same thing about this 'Chicago-slaughterhouse' in a certain also serious Russian magazine, in which this slaughterhouse was lauded in the same way.

"And thereafter, I heard of this Chicago slaughterhouse from a thousand different beings, many of whom had been, presumably, eyewitnesses to the marvels they described.

"In short, before my arrival in the city of Chicago, I was already fully convinced that a 'marvel,' unprecedented on the Earth, existed there.

"I must mention here that I had always been greatly interested in these establishments of theirs, namely, those places where your favorites destroy the existence of various forms of terrestrial beings; and furthermore, from the time when I began organizing my observatory on the planet Mars, and had to do with various machines for it, I took always and everywhere a great interest in every other sort of machine as well.

"So, when I happened to be in this same city of Chicago, I thought it would be inexcusable on my part not to use the opportunity to see this famous 'Chicago-slaughterhouse.' So, in the morning, on the day of my departure from there, I decided to go, accompanied by one of my new Chicago acquaintances to inspect this rare construction of your favorites.

"Having arrived there, we took as our guide, on the advice of one of the assistants of the chief director, an employee of a branch of some bank there which was connected with this slaughterhouse, and together with him we set off to inspect the place.

"Accompanied by him we first of all went through the places where the unfortunate quadruped beings are driven and where they remain until their slaughter.

"This place was in no way different from that of all establishments of the kind on your planet, except that this particular place was on a considerably larger scale. On the other hand, it was very much dirtier than any of the slaughterhouses I had previously seen in other countries.

"Afterwards we went through several more, what are called, 'annexes.' One of them was the 'cold-storage' for the meat that was ready; in another they destroyed the existence of quadruped beings simply with hammers and also stripped off their hide—again in the manner usual in other slaughterhouses.

"By the way, in passing through this last annex, I remember I then thought; this place here is in all probability for the slaughter of cattle intended especially for the Jews, who, as I already knew, in accordance with the code of their religion, destroy quadruped beings in a special way.

"Walking through the said annexes took rather a long time, and all the while I was waiting for the moment when we should eventually arrive at the section about which I had heard so much, and which I was determined to see without fail.

"But when I expressed my wish to our guide to hasten on to that section, I learned that we had already seen everything there was to see in this 'famous-Chicago-slaughterhouse,' and that no other sections existed.

"I had not, my dear boy, seen there anywhere a single machine, unless one includes the rollers on rails which are in all slaughterhouses for moving the heavy carcasses; and as for the dirt in this Chicago slaughterhouse, you could see as much as you liked.

"In cleanliness and general organization, the slaughterhouse of the city Tiflis, which I had seen two years before, could have given many points to this slaughterhouse of the city Chicago.

"In the Tiflis slaughterhouse, for example, you would not

find anywhere on the floor a single drop of blood, whereas, in the Chicago slaughterhouse, everywhere, at every step, there were pools of it.

"Obviously some company of American businessmen, inevitably resorting to 'advertising' for every business in general, had to 'advertise' the 'Chicago-slaughterhouse' also, in order to spread a false notion about it, totally unrelated to reality, over the whole planet.

"As is in general the rule there, they certainly did not spare their dollars in this case either, and since the sacred being-function of 'conscience' is completely atrophied among contemporary terrestrial what are called 'journalists' and 'reporters,' the result is that in all your favorites breeding on all the continents, there is crystallized just that definite, monstrously exaggerated notion of the slaughterhouse of the city of Chicago.

"And it can be said, indeed, that they did it in true American fashion.

"On the continent America, the three-brained beings have become so expert in this advertising of theirs, that it is quite possible to apply to them the satire of our dear Mullah Nassr Eddin which declares that 'That-man-will-become-a-friend-of-the-cloven-hoofed-who-perfects-himself-to-such-Reason-and-such-Being-that-he-can-make-an-elephant-out-of-a-fly.

"They have indeed become so skillful at 'making-elephants-out-of-flies' and they do it so often, that already at the present time on seeing a genuine American elephant, one has to 'remember-oneself-with-the-whole-of-one's-being' not to get the impression that it is only a fly.

"From Chicago I returned again to New York and as all my projects for the fulfillment of which I had come to this continent were then unexpectedly rapidly and rather successfully actualized, and seeing that the surrounding circumstances and conditions of the ordinary existence of the three-brained beings of that city turned out to be corresponding to what was required for my periodic complete rest which had already become customary for me during my last personal sojourn on the surface of your planet, I decided to stay there longer and exist with the beings there merely according to the being-associations inevitably flowing.

"Existing in the said way in this central point of the beings of this big contemporary group and rubbing shoulders on various occasions with the various typenesses among them, I just then without any premeditation but thanks only to my acquired habit of collating material, so to say, 'by-the-way,' for those statistics of mine, which, as I have already told you, I gathered during the whole of my last personal sojourn among your favorites for the purpose chiefly of comparing the extent to which all the illnesses and all the strange what are called 'being-subjective-vices' existing among the beings of the different groups are spread, I constated a fact which greatly interested me, namely, the fact that in the common presences of almost half of all the three-brained beings I met there, the proceeding functioning of the transformation of the 'first-being-food' is disharmonized, that is, as they themselves would say, their digestive organs are spoiled; and that almost a quarter of them have or are candidates for that form of disease specific to beings there, which they call 'impotence,' thanks just to which disease a great many of the contemporary beings of your planet are forever deprived of the possibility of continuing their species.

"When I chanced to constate this, a great interest in the beings of just this new group arose in me, and I thereupon changed by previously determined mode of existence among them, and allotted half my time from by personal rest to special observation and investigation of the causes of this fact—for me so strange and for them so deplorable. In pursuit of this aim I even took occasion to visit various other provincial points of the beings of this new contemporary group; though I stayed nowhere more than one or two days, with the exception of the city 'Boston,' or, as it is sometimes called, 'the-city-of-the-people-who-escaped-race-degeneration.' There I existed for a whole week.

"And so, as a result of these observations and statistical investigations of mine, it became clear that both these aforesaid diseases, which to a certain extent are prevalent among the contemporary beings in general who breed on all continents, are, on this continent so inordinately widespread, that its proximate consequences were immediately patent to me, namely, that if it continues among them at the present rate, then just the same fate will befall this contemporary large independent group of three-brained beings who have taken your fancy, as recently befell that large community there which was called 'Monarchic-Russia,' that is to say, this group also will be destroyed.

"The difference will be only in the process of the destruction itself. The process of the destruction of the large community 'Monarchic-Russia' proceeded in consequence of the abnormalities of, so to say, the Reason of the 'power-possessing-beings' there, whereas the process of the destruction of this community America will proceed in consequence of organic abnormalities. In other words, the 'death' of the first community came from, as they say, the 'mind,' whereas the death of the second community will come from the 'stomach-and-sex' of its beings.

"The point is, that it has long ago been determined that in general, the possibility of long existence for a three-brained being of your planet depends at the present time exclusively only on the normal action of these two aforementioned being-functions, namely, upon the state of their, as they say, 'digestion' and upon the functioning of their 'sex-organs.'

"But it is precisely these two functionings necessary to

their common presence, which are now both going in the direction of complete atrophy; and moreover, at a highly accelerated tempo.

"This community America is at the present time still quite young; it is still, as they say there on your planet—like an infant, all 'peaches-and-cream.'

"And so, if while still so young its beings have in respect of the two chief motors of their existence thus deviated retrogressively, then, in my opinion, in this case also, as it in general occurs to everything existing in the Megalocosmos—the degree of the further movement for the purpose of blending again with the Infinite, will depend on the direction and degree of the forces obtained from the initial impetus.

"In our Great Megalocosmos, there is even established for all beings with Reason a law, as it were, according to which one must always and in everything guard just against the initial impetus, because, on acquiring momentum, it becomes a force which is the fundamental mover of everything existing in the Universe, and which leads everything back to Prime Being."

In this place of his tales Beelzebub was handed a 'Leitoochanbros' and when he had finished listening to the contents of the communication, he turned again to Hassein and said:

"""I think, my boy, that it will be very useful to you for your more detailed representation and understanding of the strangeness of the psyche in general of these three-brained beings who have taken your fancy and who arise on the planet Earth if I explain to you in somewhat greater detail the causes which in the common presences of these American three-brained beings, produce disharmony in both of these fundamental functionings of theirs.

"For convenience of exposition I shall explain to you separately the causes of the disharmony of each of these two fundamental functionings, and I shall begin with the explanation of the causes of the disharmony in the functioning of the transformation of their 'first-being-food,' or as they themselves would say, with the causes of the 'spoiling-of-their-stomachs.'

"For the disharmony of this function of theirs, there were and now still are several definite causes, comprehensible even to the Reason of ordinary normal three-brained beings, but the chief and fundamental cause is that from the very beginning of the formation of their community, they gradually got accustomed—owing to all kinds of established surrounding conditions and influences proceeding from authority which happened to be formed of itself abnormally—and they are now already thoroughly accustomed, never to use for their first 'being-food' anything fresh whatsoever, but to use exclusively only products already decomposed.

"At the present time the beings of this group almost never consume for their 'first-being-food' any edible product which still retains all those 'active-elements' put into every being by Great Nature Herself as an indispensable requisite for taking in power for normal existence; but they 'preserve,' 'freeze,' beforehand all those products of theirs and use them only when most of these 'active-elements' required for normal existence are already volatilized out of them.

"And this abnormality proceeded in the ordinary process of being-existence of the three-brained beings who have taken your fancy—in this instance, in the case of this new group—and continues to be spread and to be fixed everywhere there, also of course in consequence of the fact that, subsequent to the time, when they—that is to say, when all the three-brained beings in general of that planet of yours had ceased to actualize in themselves the indispensable being-efforts, there was then gradually destroyed in them the possibility for the crystallization in their common presences of those being-data thanks to which, even in the absence of the guidance of true

Knowledge, the maleficence for themselves of any of their manifestations can be sensed instinctively.

"In the present case, if only a few of these unfortunates possessed this instinct proper to three-brained beings, they might then—if only thanks merely to habitual accidental being-associations and confrontations—first, themselves become aware, and afterwards inform all the rest, that as soon as the prime connection with common Nature of any product in general serviceable as a 'first-being-food' is severed, then, no matter if this product be kept completely isolated, that is to say, 'hermetically sealed,' 'frozen,' or 'essensified,' it must like everything else in the Universe change its form and decompose according to the same principle and in the same order in which it was formed.

"Here you should know concerning the active-elements from which all cosmic formations are in general formed by Nature—both those subject to transformation through the Tetartocosmoses and which are the products of the first food of beings as well as in general all other completely spiritualized and half-spiritualized arisings—that, as soon as the corresponding time arrives, these active-elements, in whatever conditions they may be found, obligatorily begin separating in a certain order of succession from those masses in which they were fused during the Trogoautoegocratic process.

"And the same, of course, proceeds with those products, so dear to the American beings, which they preserve in what are called 'hermetically-sealed-cans.'

"However 'hermetically' these cans of products may be sealed, as soon as the time of, so to say, 'disintegration' arrives, the corresponding 'active elements' infallibly begin to separate from the whole mass. And these active elements, thus separated from the whole mass, group themselves as a rule according to their origin in these hermetically sealed cans in the form of 'drops' or small 'bubbles' which, so to say, dissolve immediately the cans are opened for the consumption of these products, and, volatilizing into space, are dispersed to their corresponding places.

"The beings of this continent do sometimes consume fresh fruit; but as for these fruits of theirs—they cannot be said to be fruits, but simply and solely as our dear teacher would say, 'freaks.'

"By means of the fruit trees, existing in abundance on this continent, little by little various scientists of 'new format' have succeeded with their 'wiseacrings' in making of these American fruits at the present time, just, so to say a 'feast-for-the-eye,' and not a form of being-nourishment.

"The fruits there are now already so formed as to have within them scarcely anything of what was fore-ordained by Great Nature to be consumed for the normal being-existence of beings.

"These scientists of 'new-format' there are of course very far from apprehending that when any surplanetary formation is artificially grafted or manipulated in any such fashion, it arrives in a state defined by objective Science as 'Absoizomosa,' in which it absorbs from its surrounding medium, cosmic substances serviceable only for the coating of what is called its 'automatically-self-reproducing-subjective-presence.'

"The point is, that from the very beginning of this latest contemporary civilization of theirs, it somehow so fell out among the beings of all the innumerable separate groups there, that, of the seven aspects of the fundamental commandment given to three-brained beings from Above, namely, 'Strive-to-acquire-inner-and-outer-purity,' the single aspect they selected and in a distorted form have made their ideals is that aspect which is conveyed in the following words: 'Help-everything-around-you-both-the-animate-and-the-still-inanimate-to-acquire-a-beautiful-appearance.'

"And indeed, and especially in the last two centuries there, they have striven simply to attain a 'beautiful exterior'—but, of course only in regard to those various objects external to them themselves, which chanced in the given period to become as they expressed it, 'fashionable.'

"During this said period, it has been of no concern to them whether any object external to them themselves had any substance whatsoever—all that was necessary was that it should have what they call 'a-striking-appearance.'

"As regards the achievements of the contemporary beings of this continent in respect of actualizing the 'external-beauty' of these fruits of theirs, then indeed, my boy, I have nowhere seen, not only on the other continents of the same planet but even on the other planets of that solar system, fruits so beautiful in appearance as those of the present time on this continent America; on the other hand, as regards the inner substance of these fruits, one can only use that favorite expression of our dear Teacher, which consists of the following words:

"'The-greatest-of-all-being-blessings-for-man-is-the-action-of-castor-oil!'

"And to what height they have carried their skill in making their famous preserves out of these fruits—as for this, as is said, 'neither-tongue-can-tell-nor-pen-describe!' You have to see them for yourself to experience in your common presence the degree of the impulse of 'rapture' to which one can be carried on perceiving with the organ of sight, the external beauty of these American fruit preserves.

"Walking down the main streets of the cities of the beings of this continent, especially of the city New York, and seeing the display in any fruit store, it is hard to say at once just what it is the eyes behold. Is it an exhibition of pictures by the futurists of the city Berlin of the continent Europe, or is it a display of the famous perfumery stores for foreigners of the 'world capital,' that is, the city Paris?

"Only after a while, when you have finally managed to take in various details of the appearance of these displays and somehow start reflecting again, can you clearly constate how much greater is the variety of color and shape of the jars in these American displays of fruit preserves than in the mentioned displays of the continent of Europe; and this is evidently due to the fact that, in the common psyche of the beings of this new group, the combination resulting from the intermixture of former independent races, happens to correspond more completely to a better perception and a thorough cognition of the sense and beneficence of the achievements of the Reason both of the beings of the contemporary community of Germany in respect of the chemical substances they have invented, called there 'Aniline' and 'Alisarine,' as well as of the beings of the community France in respect of 'perfumery.'

"I myself when I first saw there such an exhibition could not refrain from entering one of these stores and buying about forty jars of all shapes containing fruit preserves of every shade of color.

"I bought them to please the beings then accompanying me, and who came from the continents of Asia and Europe where fruits so rarely beautiful to look at did not as yet exist. When I brought my purchases home and distributed them, these beings were at first, indeed, not a whit less astonished and delighted than I had been of their appearance, but, afterwards, when they had consumed them for their 'first-being-food,' all that was needed was to see their grimaces and the change of color on their faces to understand what effect these fruits in general have upon the organism of beings.

"The case is still worse on that continent with that product which, for them as well as for almost all the three-brained beings of the Universe, is the most important product for 'first-being-food,' and namely, that product called 'Prosphora' which they themselves name 'bread.'

"Before I describe the fate of this American bread I must tell you that this terra-firma part of the surface of your planet, called 'North-and-South-America' was formed—thanks to various accidental combinations ensuing, firstly, from the second great 'cataclysm-not-according-to-law' which occurred to that ill-fated planet, and secondly, from the position that terra-firma occupies in relation to the process of the 'common-systemic-movement'—having a stratum of what is called 'soil' which was and still is suited for the production of that 'Divine-grain' of which this same 'prosphora' is made. With conscious knowledge of how to use it, the soil-surface of these continents is capable of yielding in a single what is called 'good-season,' the fullness-of-a-complete-process-of-the-sacred 'Heptaparaparshinokh,' or in other words, a 'forty-nine-fold-harvest'; and even by its semiconscious use, as is now the case, the soil there yields of this 'Divine-grain' a considerable abundance in comparison with the other continents.

"Well then, my boy, when the beings of that continent began to have thanks to various fortuitous circumstances many of those objects which, for the strange psyche of the contemporary three-brained beings who have taken your fancy, are a subject for their dreams and are everywhere called there 'dollars,' thanks to which fact, according to long-established usage there, they acquired in their 'picturings' of the beings of all the other continents, what is called a 'sense-of-superiority,' with the result, also now usual among them, that they began to wiseacre with everything to achieve that said contemporary ideal of theirs, then they also began 'wiseacring' with all their might with this 'Divine-grain' out of which 'prosphora' is made.

"They began employing every possible means to, so to say, deform this 'Divine-grain,' in order to give to its product a 'beautiful-and-striking appearance.'

"For this purpose they invented a variety of machines by means of which they 'scrape,' 'comb,' 'smooth' and 'polish' this wheat, which has the misfortune to arise on their continent, until they accomplish the complete destruction of all those 'active-elements' concentrated on the surface of the grains just underneath what is called the 'husk' and precisely which are appointed by Great Nature for renewing in the common presences of beings what they have expended in worthily serving her.

"Hence it is, my boy, that the prosphora or bread now produced there from this wheat which arises in such abundance on this continent, contains nothing useful to the beings who consume it, and from its consumption there is produced in their presences nothing but noxious gases and what are called there, 'worms.'

"However, it must in all fairness be remarked, that if they get for themselves from this wheat nothing that enables them to serve Great Nature better or more consciously, nevertheless, by producing in themselves the said 'worms,' they do unconsciously very very greatly assist their planet in honorable service to the Most Great Common Cosmic Trogoautoegocrat—for are not these 'worms' also beings through whom cosmic substances are also transformed?

"At any rate, the beings breeding on this continent have already achieved by these wiseacrings of theirs with this bread, what they have very greatly desired and striven to obtain, and namely, that the beings of all the other continents should never fail to say of them, as, for instance, in the given case, something as follows:

"Astonishingly smart fellows these Americans! Even their bread is something extraordinary! So 'superb,' so 'white' and simply charming—really the splendor of splendors of contemporary civilization!

"But that from this deformity of wheat, their bread results

in being 'worthless' and, furthermore, constitutes another of the innumerable factors in the spoiling of their stomachs—what is that to them? Are they not also in the front rank of contemporary what is called 'European-civilization'?

"The most curious thing in all this naïveté of theirs is that they give the best and most useful of what Nature forms in this Divine grain for their normal existence, to the pigs, or simply burn it, while for themselves they consume that substance which is formed by Nature in the wheat only for connecting and maintaining those active elements which are localized chiefly, as I have already said, just under the husk of the grain.

"A second and also rather important factor in the disharmonizing of the digestive function of these unfortunate American three-brained beings, is the system which they have recently invented for the elimination from themselves of the waste residue of their 'first-food'; and that is to say, the 'comfortable-seats' of what are called their 'water-closets.'

"In addition to the fact that this maleficent invention was and still is one of the chief factors in the said disharmonization now proceeding in them themselves and also in almost all the beings of the other continents—who, by the way, have already begun in recent times very jealously imitating them in all their peculiar methods of 'assisting' their transformatory functioning— your favorites, thanks to this invention of theirs, now striving to fulfill even this inevitable being function of theirs with the greatest possible sensation of pleasant tranquility, have got, as it were, a new incentive for the jealous service of their god 'Self-calming,' which, as I have already said more than once, has been and still is for them almost the chief evil engendering and evoking all the abnormalities of their psyche as well as of their ordinary being-existence.

"A good example, and even, so to say, an 'illuminatingly-enlightening-picture-for-your-being-representation' of what extraordinary perspectives are opened for the future by just this invention of theirs, is the fact that already certain of these contemporary American beings who have acquired, of course also by a variety of accidents, a quantity of their famous dollars, now arrange in their 'water-closets-with-comfortable-seats,' such accessories as a small table, a telephone and what is called a 'radio-apparatus,' so that when so sitting, they may continue their 'correspondence,' discuss over the telephone with their acquaintances all their 'dollar businesses,' quietly read the newspapers, which have become indispensable to them, or, finally, listen to those musical compositions, the work of various Hasnamusses there which, because they are, as is said, 'fashionable,' every contemporary American 'businessman' is also obliged to know.

"The main harm in the significance of the resulting disharmony in the digestive functioning of all the contemporary three-brained beings of your planet from this American invention is due to the following causes:

"In former times, when more or less normal data for the engendering of objective Reason were still crystallized in the common presences of your favorites, and they themselves could reflect and understand when other similar and already enlightened beings explained the subject to them, they made the said posture as was required; but subsequently, when the said being data had definitely ceased to crystallize in them, and they also began discharging this function of theirs only automatically, then, thanks to the system prevalent before this American invention, the planetary body could of itself, automatically, by virtue only of what is called 'animal-instinct,' adopt the required definite posture. But now that the American beings have invented these 'comfortable-seats' and they have all begun using them for this inevitable function of theirs, their planetary body can no longer possibly adapt itself even instinctively to the required posture, with the consequence that not only have certain what are called 'muscles' which actualize this inevitable being-function, become gradually atrophied in those of your favorites who use these 'American-comfortable-seats,' owing to which what are called 'obstructions' are formed in them, but in addition the causes are engendered of several specifically new diseases which, in the whole of our Great Universe, arise exclusively only in the presences of these strange three-brained beings.

"Among the various primary and secondary causes, the totality of which is gradually bringing about the disharmonization of this fundamental function in the common presences of your contemporary favorites breeding on that continent of 'North-America,' there is still another exceedingly peculiar cause which, although, 'blatantly-obvious' among them, nevertheless, owing to their 'chicken-reflections,' flourishes with an impulse of egoistic satisfaction, under as it were, a 'cap-of-invisibility.'

"This peculiar cause arose and also began slowly and quietly, but infallibly disharmonizing this function in them, thanks simply to the fact that in the strange presences of the beings of this new large group, a 'ruling-passion' prevails, to be as often as possible on the continent of Europe.

"You should also be informed about this peculiar cause, chiefly because you will learn from it of yet another result, harmful for all your favorites, of the 'evil wiseacrings' of their contemporary 'scientists.'

"For your better representation and understanding of this cause of the gradual disharmonizing of this inevitable being-function in the common presences of the American beings, you should first be familiar with a certain detail of just those organs which actualize the said function in their common presences.

"Among their organs for the complete transformation of the 'first-food' is one that exists almost everywhere under the name 'Toospooshokh,' or, as they themselves call it, a 'blind-process' and in their scientific terminology, 'appendix.'

"The action of this organ, as appointed by Great Nature, is that various connective cosmic substances separated by the transformation of the various surplanetary crystallizations which compose the 'First-being-food,' are gathered in it in the form of what are called 'gases,' in order that later, at the time of the elimination from the common presences of the beings of the already waste residue of the said food, these 'gases' should by this pressure assist this act.

"The 'gases' gathered in this organ actualize by their so to say 'discharge,' the mechanical action designed by Nature, independently of the general transformatory functioning proceeding in the beings, and only at definite periods of time established in each being differently according to subjective habit.

"Well then, my boy, thanks to their frequent trips to the continent of Europe, the round trip taking from twelve days to a month, conditions are created for a daily change of time for the fulfillment of this established function, with the consequence that a serious factor results for the gradual engendering of disharmony in the process of their common fundamental transformatory functioning. That is to say, when for a period of many days, on account of the change of the established time, they fail to perform this indispensable function of theirs, and the 'gases' thus collected in this organ, not being utilized by them for the automatic action of the purpose indicated, and not fulfilling the design preconceived by Great Nature, gradually escaping from their presences unproductively into space—the totality of these manifestations of theirs, by the way, making existence on these passenger-ships of theirs almost intolerable for a being with a normally developed organ for perceiving odors—then, as a result of all this, there often occurs in them what is called a 'mechanical obstruction,' which in its turn, also conduces to the said gradual disharmonization of this fundamental transformatory function of theirs.

"When I began to explain to you, my boy, the causes of the disharmony in the presences of these American beings of the function of the transformation of the 'first-being-food' and when I mentioned the 'comfortable-seats' invented by them, I said among other things, that these strange three-brained beings who have taken your fancy and who breed on the planet Earth, were 'again' striving to perform even this indispensable being-function of theirs with the greatest possible sensation of self-satisfaction for themselves. I said 'again' because previously in various periods of the flow of time, these strange three-brained beings there who have taken your fancy had already several times introduced something similar into the usages of their ordinary existence.

"I remember very clearly one of those periods when the beings of that time, who, by the way, according to the notions of your contemporary favorites, were nothing but ancient 'savages,' invented every possible kind of convenience for performing this same although prosaic yet indispensable being-need, on account of which these contemporary Americans, who in their naïveté consider themselves already civilized to the ne-plus-ultra, have invented these comfortable seats in their water-closets.

"This was precisely during the period when the chief center of culture for the whole of your planet was the country Tikliamish and when this country was experiencing the height of its splendor.

"For this being-function, the beings of the country Tikliamish invented something rather like these 'American-comfortable-seats,' and this maleficent invention also spread widely everywhere among all the other beings of that ill-fated planet.

"If the said invention of the beings of the Tikliamishian civilization were compared with the invention of these contemporary Americans, then, according to the expression they sometimes use for comparison, the latter may be called a 'child's-toy.'

"The beings of the Tikliamishian civilization invented a certain kind of 'comfortable-couch-bed' which could be used for sleeping as well as for what is called 'lounging'—so that while lying on this 'wonderful contrivance,' and without manifesting the slightest being-effort whatsoever, they could perform this same inevitable being need for which the contemporary beings of the continent America have invented their 'seats-of-ease.'

"These 'wonder-beds' were so adapted for this purpose that a lever by the side of the bed had only to be touched lightly to enable one instantly, in the bed itself, to perform this same indispensable need freely and of course very 'cozily' and also with the greatest so to say 'chic.'

"It will not be superfluous, my boy, for you to know also, by the way, that these same famous 'beds' had the effect of causing great and momentous events in the process of their ordinary existence.

"So long as the previous relatively normal system still prevailed among the beings there for the said being-functions, everything went along very peacefully and quietly, but as soon as certain what are called 'power-possessing' and 'wealth-possessing' beings of that time had invented for this purpose the mentioned 'comfortable beds' which came to be called 'If-you-wish-to-enjoy-felicity-then-enjoy-it-with-a-bang,' there then began among the ordinary beings of that time, that which led to the said serious and deplorable consequences.

"I must tell you that it was just during those years when the beings of Tikliamish were inventing these 'wonder beds,' that this planet of yours underwent a common cosmic process of 'Chirnooanovo,' that is to say, that, concomitantly with the displacement of the gravity-center movement of this solar system in the movement of the common-cosmic harmony, the center of gravity of this planet itself was also displaced.

"During such years, as you already know, thanks to this cosmic manifestation, there increases everywhere on planets in the psyche of the beings inhabiting any planet undergoing 'Chirnooanovo'—a 'Blagonoorarirnian-sensation,' or as it is otherwise called, 'Remorse-of-Conscience' for one's past deeds against one's own convictions.

"But there on your planet, thanks to the common presences of your favorites having become so odd, from a variety of causes both proceeding from outside of them and arising through their own fault, the result of the action of this common-cosmic actualization does not proceed in them as it proceeds in the presences of three-brained beings arising on other planets during 'Chirnooanovo'; that is to say, instead of this 'Remorse-of-Conscience,' there usually arise there and become widespread certain specific processes, called the 'reciprocal-destruction-of-Microcosmoses-in-the-Tetartocosmos,' which processes, when proceeding in them, they themselves look upon as what are called among them, 'epidemics' and which in ancient times were known by the names 'Kalunom,' 'Morkrokh,' 'Selnoano,' etc., and, in present days by the names 'Black-death,' 'Cholera,' 'Spanish-Influenza' and so on.

"Well then, thanks to the fact that many of these diseases—diseases then called 'Kolbana,' 'Tirdiank,' 'Moyasul,' 'Champarnakh' and so on and called by contemporary beings 'Tabes,' 'Sclerosis-Disseminata,' 'Hemorrhoids,' 'Ishias,' 'Hemiplegia' and so on—were widely prevalent among the majority of those using these exceedingly comfortable 'couch-beds,' those beings from among them in whose common presences the data for Hasnamussian properties had, thanks to the complete absence of the actualization of being-Partkdolg-duty, already previously begun to be crystallized more intensively than usual, and among whom were those called 'revolutionaries,' observing this particularity, decided to take advantage of it for their own purposes; that is to say, types of this kind invented and circulated broadcast among the masses of beings of that time, that all the aforesaid epidemic contagious diseases resulted from the fact that, thanks to the beds 'If-you-wish-to-enjoy-felicity-then-enjoy-it-with-a-mighty-bang,' the 'parasitic-bourgeois' contracted various diseases, which diseases afterwards spread by contagion among the masses.

"Thanks to that peculiar inherency of theirs called 'suggestibility,' which I mentioned before and which had been acquired in their common presences, all the surrounding beings, of course, believed this as they call it 'Propaganda' of theirs, and, there usually being in these cases, a quantity of talk about it, there was gradually crystallized in each of them the periodically arising factor which actualized in their common presences that strange and relatively prolonged 'psychic-state,' which I should call the 'loss-of-sensation-of-self'; in consequence of which, as also usually happens there, they set about destroying everywhere, not only these 'wonder beds,' but also the existence of those beings who used them.

"Although the acute stage of this, so to say, obtuseness in the presences of most of the ordinary beings of that period soon passed, nevertheless the 'raging destruction,' both of these beds themselves and of the beings who used them, continued by momentum during several terrestrial years. Eventually, this maleficent invention went completely out of use, and soon it was even forgotten that such beds had ever existed on the planet.

"At any rate, it can be said with certainty that if the 'civilization' of the beings of the group now breeding on the continent America develops in its present spirit and at its present rate, then they also will unquestionably 'civilize-themselves' to the degree of having 'bed-couches,' as astonishing as were those beds 'If-you-wish-to-enjoy-felicity-then-enjoy-it-with-a-bang.'

"It will not be amiss now, my boy, also to remark, by way of illustration, upon the invention of preserved products for the 'first-being-food' and their application in the process of being-existence by the beings of this contemporary group, who in recent times have chanced to become for the strange Reason of the beings of all the other continents, so to say, 'objects-of-imitation,' chiefly on account simply of the fact that they were supposed to be the first, on their planet, to invent such beneficent and convenient being-usages, namely, in the given case, the device of feeding themselves with preserved products, thanks to which they, as it were, save time.

"The contemporary unfortunate three-brained beings in general who breed on your planet are, of course, not aware; nor, for causes already explained to you, have they in themselves the possibility of reflecting, that their remote ancestors of various past ages, who were much more normally formed into responsible beings, must have 'racked-their-brains,' as is said, 'not-a-little' to discover means for minimizing the time spent on this inevitable being-necessity of feeding themselves with products; and having found such apparently expedient methods, they every time, after a brief trial of them, eventually became convinced that these products, of whatever kind and however they might be preserved, always deteriorated with time and became worthless for their first food; and hence they ceased to employ these methods in the process of their ordinary existence.

"As a parallel to this contemporary means of preserving products for one's first-being-food in hermetically sealed vessels, let us take as an example that means of preserving which I personally have witnessed in the country Maralpleicie.

"It was just at the time when the beings of the locality of Maralpleicie were vying in everything with the beings of the country Tikliamish and were engaged in a fierce rivalry with them that the beings of all other countries should consider their country the first and foremost 'center-of-culture.'

"Just then it was that they invented among other things something similar to these American preserves.

"Those beings of Maralpleicie, however, preserved their edible products sealed hermetically not in 'poison-exuding-tin-cans,' such as the contemporary beings of the continent America use, but in what were then called 'Sikharenenian-vessels.'

"These 'Sikharenenian' vessels in Maralpleicie were prepared from very finely ground, what are called there, 'mother-of-pearl,' 'yokes-of-hen's-eggs' and a glue obtained from the fish named the 'Choozna-sturgeon.'

"These vessels had the appearance and quality of the unpolished glass jars now existing there on your planet.

"In spite of all the obvious advantages of preserving products in such vessels, yet nevertheless, when certain beings with Reason, in the country Maralpleicie, constated that in those beings who habitually used products preserved in this way, there was gradually atrophied what is called 'Organic-shame,' then, having succeeded in widely spreading among the other ordinary beings information about this constatation of theirs, all the other surrounding beings, similar to them, gradually ceased to employ this method, and eventually it was so completely dropped from common use, that even the knowledge that such a method had even existed, failed even to reach the fifth or sixth generation after them.

"On this continent 'Asia' there have existed throughout almost all the ages, all kinds of methods for preserving edible products for a long time, and even now several of these methods exist there which have come down to the contemporary beings from their very remote ancestors.

"But of all there methods not one was so harmful for the beings themselves as this method invented by these contemporary beings of the continent America, namely, the preserving of products in poison-exuding-tin-cans.

"Even this device for preserving products 'hermetically sealed' so that without being exposed to the effects of the atmosphere, they should as it were, escape the process of decomposition, exists among certain contemporary Asiatic groups, but they do not all have recourse for this purpose to the aid of these poison exuding American tin cans.

"At the present time on the continent Asia, only what is called 'sheep's tail-fat' is used for this purpose.

"'Sheep's-tail-fat' is a product which is formed in a large quantity around the tail of a certain form of two-brained quadruped being, named there 'sheep,' breeding everywhere on the continent Asia.

"In this 'sheep's tail-fat' there are no cosmic crystallizations harmful for the common presence of a three-brained being, and it is itself one of the chief products for the first food of the majority of the beings of those several groups on the continent Asia. But as regards the metals from which these contemporary beings of the continent America prepare cans for the preservation of their products, however completely they may be isolated on the inside from the influence of the atmosphere, they also after a definite time, like the contents of the cans, give off from themselves various of their active elements, some of which are very, as they express it, 'poisonous' for the common presences of beings in general.

"These poisonous active elements which issue from tin or similar metals remaining in hermetically closed cans, are unable to volatilize into space, and in time, meeting among the elements of the products within these cans certain elements which correspond to them by what is called 'kinship-of-class-by-number-of-vibrations,' fuse with them according to the cosmic law named 'Fusion' and remain in them; and together with these products, of course, afterwards enter into the common organism of the beings who consume them.

"Besides preserving their products in those 'poison-exuding-tin-cans' so harmful for them, your contemporary favorites grouped on this continent America furthermore preserve them preferably in raw states.

"The beings of the continent Asia always preserve all their food-products roasted or boiled, because according to this custom which reached them from their remote ancestors, products preserved in this way do not decompose so rapidly as when raw.

"The explanation is, that when a product is boiled or roasted, there is induced an artificial what is called 'chemical-fusion' of the several active elements of which the fundamental mass of the given product consists, thanks to which fusion many active elements useful for beings remain in the products for a comparatively much longer time.

"I again advise you to become thoroughly and particularly well acquainted with all the kinds of 'fusion' proceeding in the Megalocosmos, with the chemical as well as with the mechanical.

"Knowledge of this cosmic law will greatly help you, by the way, to represent to yourself and well understand why and how these numerous and varied formations are in general produced in Nature.

"And how what is called a 'permanent-fusion-of-elements' is obtained in products from boiling or roasting, you will clearly understand if, upon reflection, you grasp merely the process which occurs during the artificial preparation of 'Prosphora.'

"'Prosphora' or 'bread' is in general made everywhere by beings who are aware of its sacred significance. Only your contemporary favorites regard its preparation, without any consciousness of its effect, but merely as a practice automatically transmitted to them by inheritance.

"In this bread the crystallization of cosmic substances is also obtained according to the law of 'Triamazikamno,' the substances from the following three relatively independent sources serving as the three holy forces of this sacred law, namely—the holy affirming or active principle is the totality of those cosmic substances composing what your favorites call 'water'; the denying or passive principle is the totality of the substances composing what your favorites call the 'flour' obtained from the Divine wheat-grain; and the holy reconciling or neutralizing principle is the substance issuing or obtained as the result of burning, or, as your favorites say, from 'fire.'

"For a better elucidation of the thought I have expressed concerning the significance of a permanent fusion of diverse-sourced cosmic substances, let us take as an example the said relatively independent totality of substances which in the formation of this 'Prosphora' or 'bread' is the active principle, namely, the relatively independent totality which is called by your favorites 'water.'

"This relatively independent totality of cosmic substances named there on the Earth 'water,' being in itself one might say, a 'natural-mechanical-mixture,' can be preserved exclusively only in conditions of conjunction with common Nature. If the connection of this 'water' with common Nature is cut, that is to say, if a little of this 'water' is taken out of a river and kept separately in a vessel, then after a certain time the 'water' in this vessel inevitably begins to be gradually destroyed, or as it might otherwise be said, to decompose, and this process, to the perceptive organs of beings, usually smells very 'malodorously,' or, as your favorites would say—'this-water-soon-stinks.'

"And the same will proceed with the mixture, as, in the

given case, of this said 'water' and 'flour.' Only a temporary mechanical mixture or what is called 'dough' will be obtained, in which, this water, after lasting also a relatively short time, will inevitably begin to decompose.

"Further, if this 'dough,' that is, water mixed with flour, is baked over a fire, then, thanks to substances issuing from or formed from this 'fire'—substances which in the given case, as I have already said, serve as the third holy neutralizing force of the sacred Law of Triamazikamno—there will result in the given case a 'chemical-fusion,' that is, a 'permanent-fusion-of-substances,' as a result of which the new totality of substances obtained from this water and the flour, namely, the 'prosphora' or 'bread,' will now resist the merciless Heropass, that is to say, it will not decompose for a much longer time.

"The 'bread' made in this way can 'dry,' 'crumble' or even be to all appearances gradually completely destroyed, yet from this process of transformation, the elements of the water will, during the said fairly long time, be no further destroyed but will remain active for the said time among what are called, the 'enduring-prosphora-inactive-elements.'

"And in the given case my boy, I again repeat that if the contemporary beings breeding on the continent of Asia preserve their products exclusively only in a roasted or boiled state, and not when raw, as the contemporary American beings prefer to do, this also occurs there in consequence of the fact that these usages reached the beings of Asia from their ancestors, the term of whose communities was many centuries, and who in consequence had a long practical experience, whereas, the term of the community of those American beings is still, as our wise Teacher would say, 'only-a-day-and-a-half.'

"In order that you may better evaluate the significance of this invention of those contemporary beings breeding on the continent America, and which is, as it were, the real outcome of contemporary civilization, I do not consider it superfluous to inform you also of the methods of preserving several other products for a long time, which methods are now in use among the beings of the continent Asia.

"Such, for instance, is the method of preparing what is called 'Haoorma,' a particularly favorite product of the beings of many groups of the continent Asia.

"This 'Haoorma' on the continent Asia is prepared in a very simple manner; namely, small pieces of well-roasted meat are tightly packed into 'earthenware-jars' or goatskin 'Boordooks.' (A 'Boordook' is the skin stripped in a special manner from the being called 'goat.')

"Melted sheep's tail fat is then poured over these roasted pieces of meat.

"Although the pieces of roasted meat thus covered with fat do also gradually deteriorate with time, yet, over a relatively very long time they do not acquire in themselves any poison.

"The beings of the continent Asia use this 'Haoorma' either cold or heated up.

"In the latter case, it is as if the meat were freshly killed.

"Another very favorite product there preservable for a long time, is what is called 'Yagliyemmish' which consists of nothing else than various fruits.

"For this purpose, fruits freshly gathered from the tree are immediately strung on a cord in the form of what is called a necklace and then thoroughly boiled in water; when these odd necklaces are cooled, they also are dipped several times in melted sheep's-tail fat, and, after all this, they are hung up somewhere, where they are exposed to the effects of a current of air.

"However long fruit prepared in this way may hang, it scarcely ever spoils, and when these odd necklaces are to be used for food, they are put into hot water for a little, whereupon all the fat on them being heated entirely disappears, and the fruit itself is as if it had been freshly picked from the tree.

"Even though fruit preserved in this manner differs very little in taste from fresh fruit and will keep a very long time, nevertheless all the well-to-do beings of the continent Asia prefer the fresh fruit.

"And this is obviously because in most of them as direct descendants of the beings of long-existing ancient communities, thanks to the possibilities which have reached them by inheritance, the crystallizing of data for the instinctive sensing of reality proceeds much more intensively in them than in most of your other contemporary favorites.

"I repeat, my boy, that there on your planet, the beings of past epochs, especially those breeding on this continent of Asia, had already many times attempted to use various methods of preserving products for a long time, and it always ended as follows: first of all, certain persons, thanks to their conscious or accidental observations, discovered the undesirable and harmful consequences of this kind of practice both for themselves and for those near them; and then they communicated this to all the other beings, who, having also made observations with as much impartiality as possible towards themselves, also became convinced of the correctness of these deductions; and ultimately, they all ceased to employ these practices in the process of their existence.

"Even quite recently on this same continent Asia, certain beings again attempted not only to find a method by which it might indeed be possible to preserve their edible products for a long time without deterioration, but they even tried to find some entirely new means for minimizing as much as possible the time spent on this inevitable being-need of feeding on the first food; and this time they were almost on the verge of discovering a very suitable method for this purpose.

"I can give you satisfactory details concerning the interesting results of their new investigations in this sphere, because I not only personally knew the terrestrial three-brained being who, by his conscious labors, discovered the said method, but was even present personally at several elucidatory experiments upon the possibilities of applying this method to beings, conducted by the initiator himself of the, so to say 'new-investigations.'

"His name was Asiman and he was a member of a group of contemporary Asiatic three-brained beings, who, having cognized their slavish dependence upon certain causes within themselves, organized a collective existence for the purpose of working upon themselves to deliver themselves from this inner slavery.

"It is interesting to notice that this group of contemporary terrestrial three-brained beings, one of whom was this Brother Asiman, had previously existed in the country formerly Pearl-land, now called 'Hindustan,' but afterwards when beings from the continent of Europe appeared there and began disturbing them and hindering their peaceful work, they all migrated across what are now called there, the 'Himalayan-Mountains' and settled partly in the country 'Tibet' and partly in what are called the 'Valleys-of-the-Hindu-Kush.'

"Brother Asiman was one of these who settled in the 'Valleys-of-the-Hindu-Kush.'

"As time was precious to the members of this Brotherhood who were working for their self-perfection, and the process of eating robbed them of a great deal of time, this Brother Asiman, being very well versed in the science then called 'Alchemy,' began working very earnestly in the hope of finding what is called a 'chemical-preparation,' on the introduction of which into himself, a being could exist without spending so much time in the preparation and consumption of all kinds of products for his first food.

"After long and intensive work, Brother Asiman found for this purpose a combination of chemical substances in the form of a 'powder,' one small thimbleful of which introduced into a being once in every twenty-four hours, made it possible for him both to exist without consuming anything else except water as food, and to perform all his being-obligations without injury.

"When I chanced to visit this monastery where Brother Asiman existed with the other Brethren of the said small group of your contemporary favorites, this preparation had already been used by all the Brethren for five months, and Brother Asiman with the participation of other of the brethren who were also very familiar with this question was intensely busy with elucidatory experiments on a large scale.

"And these same experiments showed them that this preparation could not ultimately suffice for normal being-existence.

"After this constatation of theirs, they not only entirely ceased the use of this preparation, but even destroyed the very formula for preparing it, which Brother Asiman had found.

"Several months later I again happened to come upon that monastery and acquainted myself personally with the document of these Brethren which had been composed by them on the day when they finally ceased the use of this indeed astonishing preparation.

"This document contained, among other things, several very interesting details about the action of this said preparation of Asiman. It was stated that when this preparation was introduced into the presence of a being, it had besides its nourishing property, a particular action upon what are called the 'wandering-nerves-of-the-stomach'; from which action not only did the need for food immediately cease in beings; but furthermore, every desire to introduce into oneself any other edible product whatsoever entirely disappeared. And if something should be forcibly introduced, it took a long time before the disagreeable sensation and state thus provoked would pass.

"It was also stated that at the outset no change was noticed in the presence of beings who fed on this preparation. Even their weight did not diminish. Only after five months did its harmful effect begin to be evident in the common presence of a being in the gradual weakened functioning of certain perceptive organs and of the manifestations of their so to say ableness and sensitiveness. For example, their voices would grow weaker, and their sight, hearing and so on worse. Furthermore, in several of them from the beginning of the derangement of these being-functions, changes were observed in their common psychic state.

"In the document composed by these Brethren, there was among other things, a lengthy description of the changes in the character of beings after five months' use of this remarkable preparation of Asiman, and, in illustration, some very excellent and apt comparisons were given.

"Although the examples themselves which were given for comparison in this document have not remained in my memory, yet thanks to the so to say 'flavor' of them which I have retained, I shall be able to give you their purport if I use the language of our respected Mullah Nassr Eddin.

"For example; an ordinary good fellow with a character of as they say one of 'God's-Angels,' suddenly became as irritable as those of whom our dear Mullah Nassr Eddin once said:

"'He-is-as-irritable-as-a-man-who-has-just-undergone-full-treatment-by-a-famous-European-nerve-specialist.'

"Or again, beings who one day had been as pacific as the little butter 'lambs' which the pious place on the festal table at their most important religious feasts, would on the next day get as exasperated as a German professor when some Frenchman also a professor, discovers something new in contemporary 'science.'

"Or again, a being whose love resembled that of a contemporary terrestrial suitor for a rich widow—of course before he has received a single penny from her—would turn just as spiteful as one of those malicious persons who, foaming at the mouth, will hate that poor author who is now writing about you and me, in his books entitled 'An-Impartial-Criticism-of-the-Life-of-Man.'

"This poor upstart author, by the way, will be hated both by the 'full-bodied-materialists' and by the 'ninety-six-carat-deists' and even by those of the three-brained beings who have taken your fancy, who, when their stomachs are full and their 'mistresses' are for the moment 'making-no-scenes,' are 'incorrigible-optimists,' but who, quite the contrary, when their stomachs are empty are 'hopeless-pessimists.'

"Now my boy that we have mentioned this 'queer-upstart-writer,' there is nothing for it but to inform you here of a certain perplexity which already long ago arose in me in regard to him, and which has progressively increased, and that is concerning a naïveté of his.

"I must explain that from the very beginning of his responsible existence, he also became, whether by accident or by the will of Fate, I do not know, a follower, and in fact a very devout follower, of our wise and esteemed Mullah Nassr Eddin, and furthermore in the ordinary process of his being-existence he has never lost the smallest opportunity to act entirely according to Mullah Nassr Eddin's unprecedentedly wise and inimitable sayings. And now, according to the information which has reached me by etherogram, all of a sudden he appears to be constantly acting contrary to one of the very serious and exceptionally practical counsels—certainly not accessible to everybody—of this Teacher above all teachers, which is formulated in the following words:

"'Ekh! brother! Here on the Earth, if you speak the truth you're a great fool, whereas if you wriggle with your soul you are only a 'scoundrel,' though also a big one. So it is best of all to do nothing, but just recline on your divan and learn to sing like the sparrow that had not yet turned into an American canary.'

"Now, my boy, absorb carefully the information about the causes of the gradual disharmonization—in the presences of these contemporary beings of the continent of America—of their second fundamental being-function, namely, the function of sex.

"The disharmony of this function in them is due also to several causes of diverse character, but the fundamental cause, in my opinion, is their negligence 'engendered-in-their-essence-and-already-quite-fused-with-their-nature' to keep their sex organs clean.

"Just like the beings of the continent of Europe, the care they give to their faces and their use of what are called 'facial-cosmetics' are only equaled by their neglect of these said organs of theirs; whereas more or less conscious three-brained beings are required to observe the utmost cleanliness in respect to just these organs.

"They cannot however be entirely blamed, because in this respect the beings of the continent of Europe are most at fault with their customs existing in the process of their ordinary being existence.

"The point is that this as yet recently arisen contemporary large group is almost exclusively formed and continues to be supplied with beings from various large and small groups populating the continent of Europe.

"The result is that even if the majority of the three-brained beings now composing this newly-formed large group there, are not themselves emigrants from the continent of Europe, their fathers or grandfathers were, who, migrating to this continent of America, took along with them also all their European customs, among which were those which brought about this uncleanliness in respect of their sex organs.

"So, my boy, when I now tell you how the matter stands as regards the sex question among the Americans, bear in mind that everything I say will also refer to the beings of the continent Europe.

"The results of this uncleanliness of the contemporary three-brained beings of the planet Earth who have taken your fancy and who breed on the continents of Europe and America and are very clearly indicated in my statistics.

"Let us take for example what are called there 'venereal diseases.' These diseases are so widespread on the continent of Europe and on this continent of America, that at the present time you will scarcely ever meet a being who has not one or another form of those diseases.

"There is no harm in your knowing amongst other things, a little more about those interesting and peculiar data, which, in my statistics, indicate in figures, how much more of these diseases there is among the beings of the continents America and Europe, than amongst those of the continent Asia.

"Many of these 'venereal diseases' are entirely absent among the beings of the old communities of the continent of Asia, whereas among the beings populating the continents Europe and America, these diseases are almost epidemical.

"Let us take for example what is called 'clap,' or as scientists there call it 'Gonorrhoea.' On the continent of Europe and America almost all the beings of both male and female sex have this disease in one of its different stages, but on the continent Asia it is met with only on the borders where beings frequently mix with the beings of the continent of Europe.

"A good example of what has just been said are the beings belonging to the group existing there under the name 'Persia' which occupies a relatively large territory on the continent Asia.

"Among the beings dwelling in the central, eastern, southern, and western areas of this relatively large territory, the mentioned diseases are not to be found at all.

"But in the northern part, especially in the locality called

'Azerbaijan,' which comes into direct contact with the large half-European-half-Asiatic community called Russia, the percentage of beings infected with this disease increases more and more in proportion to their proximity to this Russia.

"And exactly the same occurs in other Eastern countries of the continent of Asia—the percentage of this disease increases proportionately to the contact of their beings with the beings of the continent of Europe; for example, in the country called 'India' and partly in China, this disease has in recent times become widespread among the beings there, chiefly in those places where they come into contact with European beings of the community 'England.'

"It can thus be said that the chief disseminators of this disease among the beings of the continent Asia are, from the north-western side, the beings of the large group 'Russia,' and from the Eastern side, the beings of the community England.

"The cause of the absence of this disease as well as of many other evils in the said parts of the continent of Asia is in my opinion, that the majority of the beings of the continent Asia have several very good customs for their everyday existence, which have reached them likewise from their ancient ancestors.

"And these customs are so deeply implanted in their everyday existence by their religion that at the present time, observing them mechanically without any wiseacring, beings are thereby more or less ensured against several evils which owing to the abnormally established conditions of being-existence have been gradually formed and still continue to be formed in uncountable numbers on that ill-fated planet.

"The beings of most of the groups on the continent Asia are safeguarded against many venereal diseases as well as against many other 'sexual-abnormalities' if only, for instance, by such customs known there by the names 'Sooniat' and 'Abdest.'

"The first of these customs, namely 'Sooniat,' or, as it is otherwise called 'circumcision,' not only saves most of the Asiatic beings of responsible age from many venereal diseases there, but also safeguards many of the children and youths of the continents of Europe and America against, namely, that 'scourge' known there under the name 'Onanism.'

"According to this custom, the beings of responsible age in most of the contemporary groups of the continent of Asia usually perform on their 'results'—that is to say, on their children—at a certain age, a ritual which consists in this, that in the case of boys they cut what they call the 'frenum' and 'prepuce' of the 'penis.'

"And today those children of your contemporary favorites who of course automatically are subjects of this custom, are almost completely safeguarded against the inevitable result of several evils already definitely fixed in the process of the existence of your favorites.

"For example, according to my statistics, the said 'scourge,' that is 'children's onanism,' is scarcely met with among the children of those three-brained beings there who observe this custom of circumcision, whereas all the children and youths of the beings who fail to observe this custom are without exception exposed to this same sexual abnormality.

"The second custom I mentioned, namely 'Abdest' which by the way is called differently by the beings of different groups on the continent Asia, is nothing else than the obligatory ablution of the sex organs after every visit to what is called the 'toilet.'

"Thanks chiefly to this second custom, most of your favorites breeding on the continent of Asia are safeguarded against many venereal diseases and other sexual abnormalities there.'

Having said this, Beelzebub became thoughtful, and after a long pause said: "The present theme of our conversation has reminded me of a certain very interesting conversation which I had there during my sojourn in France, with a young sympathetic three-brained being.

"I think that perhaps it would now be best for your understanding of all that has just been said, if I repeat to you that conversation in full, all the more so, as, besides explaining the meaning of the custom 'Abdest' or 'Ablution,' this conversation will enlighten you on many further questions concerning the peculiar psyche of these favorites of yours.

"This same being, my conversation with whom I recall and now intend to repeat to you, was just that young Persian who, you remember, as I have already told you, was at the request of our mutual acquaintances, my 'guide' in the city of Paris, where I happened to be, as I have already told you, just before my departure to this same continent America.

"One day I was waiting for this young Persian in a cafe in the city of Paris—as always the same Grand Café.

"When he arrived I noticed by his eyes that this time he was, as they say there, more 'drunk' than usual.

"In general he always drank more than enough of the 'alcoholic-liquids' existing there; and when we happened to be together in Paris, in the restaurants on Montmartre where it is obligatory to order champagne which I neither liked nor drank, he would always drink it all alone with great pleasure.

"Besides always drinking, he was also, as is said there, a great 'petticoat-chaser.'

"The moment he saw what they call there the 'pretty-face' of a being of the female sex, his whole body and even his breathing suddenly changed.

"When I noticed that he was this time more intoxicated than usual and when, having sat down beside me, he ordered coffee with what is called there an 'aperitif,' I asked him:

"'Explain to me, please, my young friend, why do you always drink this "poison"?'

"To this question of mine he answered:

"'Ekh! My dear doctor!—I drink this 'poison' firstly because I am so accustomed to it that I cannot now stop drinking without suffering, and secondly, I drink it because only thanks to the effect of the alcohol, can I calmly look on at the obscenity which goes on here,' he added, waving his hand around.

"'I began drinking this, as you called it, "poison" because the accidental and for me unlucky and wretched circumstances of my life were so arranged that I had to come and live a long time in this maleficent Europe.'

"'I first began to drink because everybody here whom I met also drank, and, unless you drink, you are called a "woman," a "girl," "dolly," "dearie," "sissy,' "ninny," and similar derisive names. Not wishing my business acquaintances to call me by these offensive names, I also began to drink.

"'And in addition, thanks also to the fact that when I first came over to Europe, conditions of life here in respect of morality and patriarchality were entirely in contrast with those conditions in which I was born and brought up, I, seeing and perceiving all this, used to experience a painful feeling of shame and an unaccountable embarrassment. At the same time I noticed that from the effect of the alcohol I drank, not only was the depression I experienced alleviated, but I could look upon it all quite calmly, and even have the wish to participate in this abnormal life, so contradictory of my nature and my established views.

"'Thus it came about that every time I began to feel the same unpleasant sensation, I began to drink this alcohol even with a feeling of some self-justification and in this way became gradually accustomed to this, as you have quite justly called it, "poison."'

"Having said this with a perceptive impulse of heart-felt grief, he paused a while to puff at his cigarette mixed with

'Tambak' and, taking this opportunity, I asked him as follows:

"'Well, alright . . . Let us assume I have more or less understood your explanation of your inexcusable drunkenness, and can put myself in your position, but what do you say about your other, and, from my point of view, also inexcusable vice, namely, your "petticoat-drooling"?'

"'Why! You run after every petticoat if only it hangs about someone with long hair!'

"At this question of mine, he, sighing deeply, resumed his speaking as follows:

"'It seems to me that I got this habit as well, partly for the reason I mentioned, but I think this weakness of mine can be explained by still another very interesting psychological cause.'

"Of course I expressed the desire to hear him, but first I suggested our going inside that Grand Café into the hall of the restaurant itself, as it was already getting damp out of doors.

"When we were seated in the hall of the restaurant and had ordered their 'famous-champagne,' he continued as follows:

"'When you lived among us in Persia, my dear doctor, you perhaps happened to observe the attitude existing there, very specific for us Persians, of men towards women.

"'Namely, among us in Persia, men have two definite, one can say, "organic-attitudes" towards women, in accordance with which women are, for us men, even unconsciously on our part, very sharply divided into two categories.

"'The first attitude is towards the woman—the present or future mother—and the second, towards the woman-female.

"'This property of the men of our Persia who have in their nature data for these two independent attitudes and for this instinctive feeling, began to be formed only recently, about two and a half centuries ago.

"'According to the explanations once given me by my

'mullah-uncle,' whom those around him called behind his back 'a-mullah-of-the-old-school,' it seems that, two or three centuries ago, owing to causes evidently ensuing from certain higher World-laws, men began to make war on each other everywhere on the Earth, and especially among us in Asia, more intensively than usual, and at the same time, somehow, in most of the men, the feeling of piety began very distinctly to decline and in some of them entirely disappeared.

"'And just at that period a certain form of psychic disease spread among men from which many who were infected by it ultimately either became quite insane or committed suicide.

"'Then certain wise people of various independent groups on the continent of Asia began, with the help of various persons representative of medicine of that time—which, by the way, was then very superior to contemporary medicine—very earnestly to seek the causes of that human misfortune.

"'After long impartial labors they discovered, firstly, that the men who contracted this disease were exclusively those in whose subconsciousness, for some reason or other, there never arose any impulse of faith in anybody or in anything, and secondly, that these adult men, who periodically performed the normal ritual of intercourse with women were not at all subject to this disease.

"'When the news of this conclusion of theirs spread over the continent of Asia, all the rulers and chiefs of the separate Asiatic groups of that time grew alarmed, as almost all the regular troops at their disposal consisted of adult men, and moreover the constant wars permitted none of them to live normally with his family.

"'In view of the fact that at that period all the governments of the separate Asiatic countries needed and wished to have healthy and strong armies, they were compelled to conclude a truce and either themselves assemble or send their representatives to one place, namely to the capital of what was then called the 'Kilmantooshian-Khanate,' in order jointly to find a way out of the situation which had arisen.

"'After serious reflections and deliberations, these rulers of the various independent groups of Asiatic peoples, or their representatives, together of course with the representatives of medicine of that time, then came to the conclusion that it was possible to deal with the situation which had arisen, only if what is called prostitution should be established everywhere on the continent of Asia, as is now the case on the continent of Europe, and only if the power-possessing people should deliberately encourage its development and cooperate in its success.

"'Almost all the chiefs of the governments of than time fully agreed with this conclusion of the representatives of all the peoples of the continent of Asia who had gathered together in the capital of the 'Kilmantooshian-Khanate,' and, without experiencing any remorse of conscience, they began from then on not only to encourage and aid women in general—except indeed just their own daughters—to engage in this occupation so 'abhorrently repulsive' to the nature of every normal person, but also to give, even with a feeling of benevolence, as if this were the most considerate manifestation of man, every possible assistance to women, without distinction of caste or religion, who might wish to leave or to go anywhere for this filthy purpose.

"'Now that we have touched upon this subject, allow me, respected doctor, to digress, and tell you here the reflections, in my view very interesting and wise, of this same Mullah uncle of mine concerning the causes in general of the arising of this evil and scourge of contemporary civilization.

"'Once, on one of the days of Ramadan, when we were conversing as usual while awaiting the call of the Mullah of our district, announcing the meal hour, and we happened to be speaking about this human "scourge," he then, among other things, said:

"'It is wrong and unjust of you to blame and despise all women of this kind.

"'Most of them are not themselves personally to blame for their sad lot; one should blame exclusively only their parents, husbands and guardians.

"'And precisely their parents, husbands, and guardians should be blamed and despised who have allowed the arising in them during their age preparatory to adult being—while as yet they have not their own good-sense—of the property called laziness.

"'Although at this age this laziness is as yet only automatic in them, and young people have not to make very great efforts to overcome it, and are able in consequence, on acquiring their own good-sense, not to allow it to gain complete control of them, yet nevertheless, as regards the organization of women's psyche, the active principle must, owing to results not dependent on our will but ensuing from world laws, unfailingly participate in every initiative and in every good manifestation of theirs.

"'And it is just precisely in the early years of the adult life of these contemporary unfortunate prospective women-mothers, thanks to the various ideas of the people of contemporary civilization concerning "equal-rights-for-women" existing there under the catch-words "equal-rights," "equal-opportunities," etc. . . ideas which are now already widespread everywhere on the Earth, which are naive to the understanding of a man who has lived his life normally, and which are unconsciously accepted also by the majority of contemporary men—that these contemporary not yet completely formed prospective women-mothers, on the one hand, not having around them the law-conformable, requisite sources of the active principle, such as their parents, guardians, and husbands—to whom the responsibility for them passes from the moment of marriage—ought to be, and on the other hand thanks to the intensive process of imagination and enthusiasm which is proper to proceed in then and which is also in this transitional age fore-ordained by Nature according to Law for the purpose of better actualizing the data for the development of their good-sense, they, as it were, gradually absorb the said automatic laziness into their very nature, and this laziness remains in their nature, as a progressive indispensable necessity.

"'A woman with such a nature of course does not wish to fulfill the obligations of a genuine 'woman-mother,' and in view of the fact that being a prostitute enables her just to do nothing and to experience great pleasure, there is gradually formed in her, both in her nature, and in the 'passive-consciousness' proper to her, a factor for the 'irresistible-urge' to be a 'woman-female.'

"'But, in consequence of the fact that in the instinct of each of these women, the data proper to all women for the impulse of 'shame' are not atrophied suddenly and at once, and none of them, with all her mental wishing, can endure to become such a woman in her own native country, every one of them always instinctively and half-consciously tries to get away to some other country where, far from her native land, without any inner discomfort, and also without doing anything, she can abandon herself entirely to this profession personally pleasant for her in almost every respect.

"'And as regards the prevalence everywhere on the Earth at the present time of this human misfortune, the cause of this is in my opinion exclusively only those contemporary men in whom, owing to the same reasons, there arises—as in those young women, future prostitutes—a similar what is called 'Organic-essential-need-to-do-nothing-except-enjoy-oneself,' and one of the forms of satisfying the criminal need of these 'ulcers' among contemporary people consists, in the given case, in enticing and assisting such women to leave their native land for some foreign country.

"'It has already been noticed by many contemporary sensible people, that these two different sexes, victims of the same disease, as a rule consciously and instinctively seek and find each other; and in the given case they exemplify the proverb which has existed from olden times; 'One-fisherman-recognizes-another-from-afar.'"

"'And so, respected doctor! Thanks just to the aforesaid causes wisely understood by my uncle, many women-prostitutes from various other countries then appeared after several years among us in Persia.

"'And owing to the instinctive attitudes which, as I have already said, had been acquired during centuries by the local women of Persia without distinction of religion towards morality and patriarchality in family traditions, these foreign women were unable to mix with the general mass of Persian women, with the consequence that from then on, there began to be among us the two categories of women I have mentioned.

"'Well then, owing to the fact that the majority of these foreign women, living freely among us in Persia and going about everywhere, in the markets and other public places, often became objects for the gaze of our Persian men, there was gradually formed in the latter, of course unconsciously, along with the already existing attitude towards women as mothers, yet another attitude towards women as simply females.

"'The property of having this definite double attitude towards women, being transmitted by inheritance from generation to generation, has even, among us, finally become so rooted that at the present time our men not only distinguish these two categories of women by their appearance as easily as one distinguishes between a man, a sheep, a dog, an ass, etc. but there has even been formed in them a certain something which instinctively prevents them from mistaking a woman of one category for a woman of another.

"'Even I myself could always unmistakedly tell, from a distance, what sort of woman was passing. How I could tell this, whether by their walk or by some other sign, with the best will in the world I could not now explain; but it is a fact that I could tell and was never mistaken, although, as I have already told you, both categories of women wore similar veils.

"'And every normal Persian—normal in the sense of not being under the influence of 'tambak,' 'alcohol,' or 'opium,' the consumption of which has in recent times been unfortunately spreading among us ever more and more—can always unmistakedly tell which woman represents a 'woman-mother' and which a 'woman-female,' that is, a prostitute.

"'To every normal Persian among us, a 'woman-mother,' to whatever religion she may belong and regardless of family and personal relationships, is as his own sister, and a woman of the second category simply an animal who infallibly evokes in him a feeling of aversion.

"'This property of instinctive relationship towards women is very strong in our men and is entirely independent of our consciousness.

"'For example even suppose it should happen somehow or other that the youngest and most beautiful woman of any district should find herself in the same bed with a man of the same district, this Persian man, even with all his willingness, provided, I repeat, that he were not under the influence of 'opium' or 'alcohol,' would be organically unable to treat her as a female.

"'He would treat her as his own sister; and even if she herself should manifest organic actions towards him, he would only pity her the more, and regard her as "possessed-by-an-unclean-power" and would try his best to help her free herself from this misfortune.

"'And the same Persian man will, in a normal condition,

also treat a woman of the second category, that is, a prostitute, as a woman-female, since, however young and beautiful she may be, he will inevitably experience an organic aversion to her; nor could he treat her as a woman unless there had been introduced into his organism the toxic products, maleficent for people, which I have enumerated.

"'And so, respected doctor, I lived until my twentieth year in Persia under these morals and traditions, like every ordinary normal Persian.

"'At twenty, on account of shares I had inherited, I happened to become a partner in a certain large firm which exported Persian dried fruits to various European communities.

"'And my position in this firm, thanks to various circumstances independent of me, was such that I had to be its chief local representative in those countries of the continent of Europe to which these fruits were exported.

"'At first, as I have already told you, I went to Russia, then I went to Germany, Italy and to other European countries, and now, finally, I have lived here in France already seven years.

"'In the life of none of these foreign countries does there exist any such sharply drawn distinction between these two types of women, between the 'woman-mother' and the 'woman-prostitute,' as I saw and felt during the whole of my youth in my native country.

"'Everywhere among them the attitude towards women is purely mental, that is, only thought out, not organic.

"'For instance, a husband here, however unfaithful his wife may be, will never know it, unless he sees or hears of it.

"'But among us in Persia, without any seeing or any gossip, a husband can tell instinctively whether his wife is faithful; and the same thing applied to the women—a woman among us can feel any infidelity on the part of her husband.

"'As to this special instinctive feeling in people, several scientists from the continent of Europe have recently even made among us some very serious special investigations.

"'As I happened by chance to learn, they came to the clear conclusion, that in general where 'polyandry' and 'polygamy' prevail—that is to say, where 'more than one wife' and 'more than one husband' are permitted by the established local morals, there is acquired in people a peculiar "organo-psychic' particularity in their relations as men and women.

"'This organo-psychic particularity exists also in the people of our Persia, in consequence of the fact that, as you know, we, being followers of the Mohammedan religion, have the custom of polygamy, that is to say, each man is permitted by law to have as many as seven wives.

"'And this organo-psychic particularity in our Persian people by the way is that the feeling of the husband's infidelity never arises in any of the lawful wives concerning his other lawful wives.

"'Such a feeling appears in one of the wives only when her husband is unfaithful with a strange woman.

"It is only now, respected doctor, that living here in Europe and seeing all that goes on between husbands and wives, I fully appreciate our custom of polygamy, so extremely sensibly established and so beneficial both for men and for women.

"'Although every man among us is permitted several wives and not simply one, as is the case here in Europe where the Christian religion which allows only one wife is predominant, yet the honesty and conscientiousness of our men towards their wives are beyond compare with the honesty and conscientiousness existing among men here towards their one wife and their family in general.

"'Just look around and see what is going on everywhere here. Glance around merely at these rooms of the Grande Café,' where besides the ordinary professional prostitutes and "gigolos" who are constantly here, hundreds of men and women are always sitting at the little tables gaily conversing.

"'Looking at these men and women now, you would say they were married couples who have come here together, either to see Paris or on some family business.

"'But as a matter of fact it is practically certain that in all the halls of this "Grande Cafe" there is not a single couple among these men and women so gaily chatting and about to go to some hotel together, who are legal man and wife, even though, at the same time, everyone of them may be, on paper, a legal husband or wife.

"'The other 'legal-halves' of the men and women sitting here, who have remained at home in the provinces, are probably now thinking and telling their acquaintances positively, that their "legal-wife" or "legal-husband" has gone to the world-capital Paris to make some very "important" purchases for the family or to meet somebody there very important for the family, or something else of the same sort.

"'But in reality, in order to get here, these birds of passage have had to intrigue for a whole year and cook up every kind of story to convince their "legal-halves" of the necessity of their trip; and now here, in the company of deceivers and intriguers like themselves, in the name of and to the glory of the significance of the "Epithalamium," aided by that fine art which this contemporary civilization has attained, they decorate their stay-at-home "legal-halves" with the largest possible "fine-art-horns.'

"In Europe, thanks to the established order of family life, it has now already come about that if you meet a man and a woman together and notice that while conversing, gay tones are heard in their voices and smiles appear on their faces, you can then be quite sure that very soon, if they have not already done so, they will very effectively and without fail put on some "legal-half" a pair of the largest and most beautiful horns.

"'Hence it is that any one slightly cunning man here may already be accounted a very "honorable-man" and the "patriarchal-father-of-a-family.'

"'To those around him it is of no concern that this "honorable" and "patriarchal-father-of-a-family" has perhaps at the same time—if of course his means permit—as many mistresses as he pleases on the side; on the contrary, those around him here, usually show even more respect for such a man than for one who is unable to have any "mistresses" at all.

"'Here, these "honorable-husbands" who have the means, not only have on the side, in addition to their "one-legal-wife," seven, but sometimes even seven times seven "illegal-wives."

"'And those European husbands who have not the means of supporting several "illegal-wives" in addition to their one "legal-wife," spend almost the whole of their time in what is called "drooling," that is to say, for days on end they stare at and as it were "devour-with-their-eyes" every woman they meet.

"'In other words, in their thoughts or in their feelings, they betray their one "legal-wife" an innumerable number of times.

"'But although among us in Persia, a man can have as many as seven "legal-wives," yet nevertheless all his thoughts and feelings are occupied day and night how he can best arrange both the inner and the outer life of these "legal-wives" of his; and the latter, in their turn, are absorbed in him and try their utmost, also day and night, to aid him in his life duties.

"'Here, the reciprocal inner relationship between husband and wife is the same; just as almost all the inner life of the husband is spent in being unfaithful to his one "legal-wife," so also the inner life of this "one-wife," from the first day of their union, is always straying outside the family.

"'For a European wife, as a rule, as soon as she is married, her husband becomes for her inner life, as they say, her "own-property.'

"'After the first night, being then secure in his ownership, she begins to devote the whole of her inner life to the pursuit of a certain "something," that is, to the pursuit of that indefinable "ideal," which from early childhood is gradually formed in every European girl thanks to that famous "education" which is ever more and more always being invented for them by various contemporary conscienceless writers.

"'During my stay in these European countries, I have observed that there is never formed in the being of a woman here, that "something" which should—in her as in our women—constantly maintain what is called "organic shame" or at least the disposition to it, upon which feeling, in my opinion, what is called "wifely-duty" is based, and which is just what instinctively aids her to refrain from those actions which make a woman immoral.

"'That is why every woman here can very easily, at any favorable opportunity, without either suffering or remorse of conscience, betray her "legal-husband."

"It is in my opinion owing to the absence of this shame in them, that here in Europe the line dividing the "woman-mother" from the "woman-prostitute" has gradually ceased to exist and that these two categories of women have already long ago been merged into one; so that at the present time there is neither in the mind nor in the feelings of the men here, that division of women into two categories which almost every Persian makes.

"'Here one can now distinguish the "woman-mother" from the "woman-female," only if one sees all her manifestations with one's own eyes.

"'In the European conditions of family life, owing to the absence of the beneficent institution off polygamy, an institution which in my opinion should long ago have been introduced here if only for the simple reason that, as statistics show, the women here far outnumber the men—there are thousands of other discomforts and improprieties which need not exist at all.

"'And so respected doctor, the fundamental cause of my second vice was that being born and brought up in traditions of morality entirely opposed to those here, I came here at an age when the animal passions in a man are especially strong. The ensuing evils for me personally arose chiefly from the fact that I came here while still very young and, according to the notions here, handsome; and owing to my genuine southern type, a great many women here, for whom I represented a new and original type of male, began a regular hunt after me.

"'They hunted me like "big-game."

"'And I was "big-game" for them not only on account of my specific type, a genuine southerner, but also on account of my gentleness and courtesy towards women, properties which had been instilled in me from my earliest childhood in my associations with our Persian "women-mothers."

"'When I came here and began meeting the women here, I was, of course, even unconsciously on my part, gentle and courteous towards them also.

"'And so, meeting with the women here and at first only talking with them—chiefly on the subject of contemporary civilization and of the backwardness as it were of our Persia in comparison—I then, of course under the influence of alcohol which I was then already consuming in rather large quantities, fell for the first time, that is to say, I, as a prospective father of a family behaved vilely.

"'Although this cost me at the time much suffering and remorse of conscience, yet the environment together again with the action of this alcohol caused me to fall a second time; and thereafter everything headed so to say down an inclined plane and led to the point where I am now indeed in this respect a most filthy animal.

"'Especially now at times, whenever I happen to be completely free from the influence of alcohol, I suffer moral anguish and loathe myself with the whole of my being, and at such moments I hasten all the more to pour this alcohol into myself again in order to forget myself and thus drown my sufferings.

"'Having lived this ugly life in the countries of Europe I enumerated, I finally settled down here in Paris, in precisely that European city to which women come from every part of Europe and from other continents with the obvious intention of putting "horns" on their other "legal-halves.' And here in Paris I have now become entirely addicted to both these human vices, that is, to alcohol and as you have said, to petticoat-chasing, and I run left and right, without any sane reasoning at all. And now, the satisfaction of both these vices is more necessary to me than the satisfaction of my hunger.

"'That is how it has all gone with me up to the present moment; and what will come next I do not know and do not care to know.

"'I always even try my best and struggle with myself not to think about it.'

"As he said these last words, he sincerely sighed and dejectedly dropped his head. I then asked him:

"'But, tell me please, are you really not afraid of being infected with those terrible diseases which these women usually suffer from, whom a "petticoat-chaser" like you run after?'

"At this question of mine he again sighed deeply and after a short pause told me as follows:

"'Ekh! . . . my esteemed and worthy doctor!

"'In recent years I have thought about this question a great deal. It has even become for me a subject of such interest, that in a certain sense, it has been a blessed means whereby my inner "odious-life" has in spite of everything flowed more or less endurably.

"'As a physician you will I think probably be greatly interested to know how and why this same question interested me so much several years ago, and to what conclusions I arrived after I had, in a relatively normal state, very seriously observed and studied it.

"'About five years ago I had such a fit of depression that even alcohol scarcely had any effect on me nor pacified my psychic state.

"'And it so happened just then that I often met with certain acquaintances and friends who talked a great deal about filthy diseases and how easily one could be infected with them.

"'From these conversations I myself began thinking rather often about myself, and little by little I began fretting about my health almost like a hysterical woman.

"'I used often to reflect that being almost always drunk and constantly having affairs with such infected women, then evidently, even if for some reason or other I had so far no obvious symptom of these diseases, I must nevertheless in all probability be already infected with one of them.

"'After such reflections I first began consulting various specialists, in order to find out what were the early symptoms of whatever disease I already may have had.

"'Although none of the local specialists found anything at all in me, I nevertheless continued to doubt, because, on the one hand my fretting about my health and on the other hand my own common sense continued to assure me that I must certainly already have been infected with one of these terrible diseases.

"'All this brought me to the point that decided at any expense, to have a consultation here in Paris, but this time of the leading specialists from the whole of Europe. I could afford myself this because owing to the world war, when transport had everywhere broken down, and all commodities had gone up in price, our firm, having everywhere very large stocks of dried fruit in storage, had that year made considerable profits, a fairly good portion of which fell to my share.

"'When I had called these European celebrities together, they unanimously pronounced after all kinds of very "detailed" investigations and what are called "chemical analyses" known only to them themselves, that there was not the slightest sign of any venereal disease in my organism.

"'Although this finding of theirs put an end to the chronic fretting about my health, yet it was the cause of the growth in me of such a strong feeling of inquisitiveness and curiosity clear up this question, that from then on it became a sort of mania with me, a kind of "ideé-fixe.'

"'And also from then on, the serious observation and study of everything concerning these diseases animated and justified the sense of what I have called "my-odious-life.'

"'During this period of my life I made these observations and studies of mine at all times with my whole inner real "I" while in a drunken, semi-drunken and also sober state.

"'And then, among other things I also read assiduously every kind of literature existing here in Europe concerning these diseases, and also most of the books on this question in French and German.

"'This I could easily do because, as you see, I have such a command of French that you can scarcely guess that I am not a real French intellectual; and with the German language also I get along very well, because I lived a fairly long time in Germany and always, in my free time studied their language and their literature for want of something to do.

"'So, when I became interested in this question, I was able to become fully acquainted with all the knowledge that exists in contemporary civilization on the subject of venereal disease.

"'In this literature there appeared to be hundreds of theories and hundreds of hypotheses concerning the causes of venereal infection, but I could not discover one convincingly categorical explanation how and why some people are infected with these diseases and others not, and I soon became convinced that I could not clear up this for myself with the knowledge existing on this question at the present time here in Europe.

"'From all this literature—putting aside, of course, and not even mentioning the multitude of those thick "scientific-books" here, whose contents immediately show every more or less normal person that they were written by people who were as is said "complete-ignoramuses" on these questions, that is to say, not specialists in human disease at all—I got the general impression that people were infected and fall ill with venereal diseases, only owing to their own uncleanliness.

"'When I made this categorical deduction, there was nothing left for me but to concentrate all my attention upon finding out in what my personal cleanliness consisted which had so far protected me against infection.

"'I then began to deliberate with myself as follows:

"'I do not dress any more cleanly than everybody else living here in Europe; I wash my hands and face every morning also like everybody else; once a week I make a point of going to a Turkish bath—also, it seems, like everyone; and in this way I turned over many things in my mind, and with the result I found nothing in which, in this respect, I was exceptional; and yet the fact remained that, from my loathsome life, I of course ran more chances of being infected.

"'From then on my thoughts were guided by two definite convictions already fully established in me; firstly, that anyone having relations with such women must inevitably sooner or later be infected; and secondly, that only cleanliness protects one from such infection.

"'In this manner I continued to reflect for a whole week, until I suddenly remembered a certain habit of mine which here in Europe I always scrupulously concealed from my acquaintances; I remembered namely, about that habit of mine which is called among us in Persia 'Abdest.'

"'The custom of "Abdest" which, according to the notions here might be called "ablution," is one of the chief customs among us in Persia.

"'Strictly speaking, every follower of the Mohammedan religion must obey this custom, though it is practiced particularly strictly only by Mohammedans of the Shiite sect; and as almost the whole of Persia is composed of Shiites, the custom is nowhere so widely spread as among us in Persia.

"'This custom is that every adherent of the Shiite sect, male as well as female, must, after every "toilet" unfailingly wash his sex organs. For this purpose, every family has the necessary appurtenances considered among us even as the most important, consisting of a special vessel, a particular kind of bowl called "Ibrkh." And the richer the family the more of these bowls they must have, since such a bowl must at once and without fail be put at the disposal of every newly-arrived guest.

"'I myself was from early childhood also personally accustomed to this habit, and it gradually so entered into my daily life that even when I came here to Europe, where this custom does not exist, I could not live a single day without making this "ablution."

"'For instance it is much easier for me to go without washing my face even after a debauch, than to not wash certain parts of body with cold water after the "toilet."

"'At present, living here in Europe, I not only have to put up with great inconveniences owing to this habit of mine, but I even have to forego some of the modern comfort which I could easily afford.

"'For instance, I now live in Paris, where owing to my means I could well afford to live at the very best hotel with every modern comfort, but, thanks to this habit of mine, I cannot do this but am obliged to live in some dirty hotel situated far from the "center" and from all those places where I have to be almost every day.

"'In the hotel where I now live there are no comforts beyond this single comfort which is very important for me; and this is due to the fact that being of old constriction, this hotel has "water-closets" of the old type and not of the new contemporary American invention, and it is just that old system which is the most convenient and suitable for this habit of mine.

"'It is quite likely that I even half consciously chose France as my chief dwelling place because it is still possible to find everywhere here especially in the provinces "water-closets" of the old system as among us in Persia.

"'In other countries of Europe this, as they now call it, "Asiatic-system" scarcely exists. It has almost everywhere been exchanged for the American system with its comfortable, polished "easy-chairs" upon which I, personally, could only rest and read the book called the "Decameron."

"'And so, my honorable doctor, when I suddenly remembered this habit of mine, I at once understood without any further doubt, that if I had hitherto escaped being infected with some filthy disease, it was solely because I frequently wash my sex organs with cold water.'

"Having said these last words, this sympathetic young Persian extended his arms upwards and with his whole being exclaimed:

"'Blessed forever be the memory of those who created for us that beneficial custom.'

"He said nothing further for a long while but looked pensively at a party of Americans sitting nearby who were discussing at that moment whether women dress better in England or in America; and then he suddenly turned to me with the following words:

"'My highly esteemed and honorable doctor.

"'During my acquaintance with you I have become quite convinced that you are very well educated and as is said very well read.

"'Will you be so kind as to give me your weighty opinion so that I might at last understand and solve one problem which during recent years has aroused my curiosity and which when I am comparatively sober often arises in me and disturbs my thought.

"'The point is, that living here in Europe where people profess the religion whose followers compose almost half the world, I have not up to now come across a single good custom in their ordinary life, whereas among us who profess the Mohammedan religion, there are very many.

"'What is wrong? What is the cause of it? Were there no good ordinances fore-designed by the Founder of that great religion for the ordinary life of people, the followers of this religion?' . . .

"Well, my boy, as this young Persian had become sympathetic to me during our acquaintance, I could not refuse him this request; and I decided to explain the question to him, but also, of course, in such a form the he would not even suspect who I was and what was my genuine nature.

"I told him: 'You say that in the religion which half the world professes, and you probably mean the "Christian-religion" there are not such good customs as in your Mohammedan religion?

"'Are there not? On the contrary; in that religion there were many more good customs than in any of the religions of today; in none of the ancient religious teachings were so many good regulations for ordinary everyday life laid down as in just that teaching on which this same "Christian-religion" was founded.

"'If the followers of this great religion themselves, especially those called the "Elders-of-the-Church" of the Middle Ages, treated this religion, step by step, as "Bluebeard" treated his wives, that is to say, put them into derision and changed all their beauty and charm—that is already quite a different matter.

"'In general you must know that all the great genuine religions which have existed down to the present time, created, as history itself testifies, by men of equal attainment in regard to the perfecting of their Pure Reason, are always based on the same truths. The difference in those religions is only in the definite regulations they lay down for the observance of certain details and of what are called rituals; and this difference is the result of the deliberate adoption by the great Founders of these regulations which suited the degree of mental perfection of the people of the given period.

"'At the root of every new doctrine upon which religions are founded, dogmas are always to be found, which have been taken from earlier religions and which had already been well fixed in the life of the people.

"'And in this case, the saying is fully justified which has existed among people from of old—"There-is-nothing-new-under-the-sun.'

"'The only things new in these religious teachings, as I have said, are the small details, intentionally adapted by the great Founders to the degree of the mental perfection of the people of the given epoch.

"'And so, at the root of this same doctrine upon which the Christian religion is based, there was placed almost the whole of the previously existing great teaching which is now called Judaism, whose followers once also numbered almost, as is said, half the "world.'

"'The great Founders of the "Christian-religion," having taken the Judaic doctrine as their basis, changed only its outer details according to the degree of mental development of the contemporaries of Jesus Christ, and in it they effectively provided for everything necessary for the welfare of people.

"'Provision was made in it as is said both for the soul and for the body; as it even provided all the necessary regulations for a peaceful and happy existence. And this was all surpassingly wisely provided for in such a way, that this religion might be suitable also for people of much later epochs.

"'Had the doctrine of this religion remained unchanged, it might even perhaps have suited these contemporary people, who by the way, our Mullah Nassr Eddin defines by his expression, "He-will-blink-only-if-you-poke-his-eye-with-a-rafter."

"'At its origin there entered into this Christian religion besides those specially established regulations for ordinary existence which met the needs of the contemporaries of Jesus Christ, also many excellent customs which were already in existence and had become well fixed in the life of the people who were followers of the Judaic religion.

"'Even those good customs which now exist among you in the Mohammedan religion were transmitted to you from the Judaic religion. Take, for example, just that custom of "Sooniat" or "Circumcision" which you mentioned. This custom was at first contained in this Christian religion also, and in the beginning was obligatorily and strictly carried out by all its followers. Only subsequently did it very quickly and suddenly entirely disappear from the Christian religion.

"'If you wish, my young friend, I will tell you in detail about the arising of this custom, and you will understand from it why a custom so good for the health and normal life of people was included in the Judaic religion. And since the Judaic doctrine was made the basis of the Christian religion, this custom also could not fail to be taken over and introduced into the process of the ordinary life of the followers of the Christian religion.

"'This custom which you call "Sooniat" was first created and introduced into the Judaic religious doctrine by the Great Moses.

"'And why the Great Moses introduced this custom into the religion of the Judaic people I learned from a very ancient Chaldean manuscript.

"'It was said in this manuscript that when the Great Moses was the leader of the Judaic people and conducted them from the land of Egypt to the land of Canaan he construed the fact during the journey that among the youths and children of the people confided to him from Above, there was very widely spread the disease then called "Moordoorten" which contemporary people call "Onanism.'

"'It was further said in the manuscript that having constated this fact the Great Moses was greatly perturbed and from then on, began observing very closely in order to discover the causes of this evil and some means of uprooting it.

"'These researches of his led this incomparable sage later to write a book under the title of "Tookha-Tes-Nalool-Pan," which in contemporary language means "The-Quintessence-of-my-Reflections."

"'With the contents of this remarkable book I also once became acquainted.

"'At the beginning of the explanation about the disease "Moordoorten," it was said, among other things, that the human organism has been brought by great Nature to such perfection that each and every organ has been provided with a means of defense against every external contingency; and hence that if any organ should function incorrectly in people, it must always be the people themselves who are to blame owing to their own established conditions of everyday life.

"'And concerning the causes themselves of the appearance of "Moordoorten" among children, it was said in Chapter VI, verse XI of this incomparable book, that this disease occurs in children for the following reasons:

"'Among the definite substances elaborated by the human organism and constantly thrown off by it as waste, there is a definite substance called "Kulnabo."

"'This substance is in general elaborated in the organism of beings for the purpose of neutralizing other also definite substances necessary for the functioning of their sex organs, and it is formed and participates in the functioning of the said organs from the very beginning of the arising of the beings of both sexes, that is to say, from their infancy.

"'Great Nature has so arranged it that after its utilization the residue of this substance is discharged from the organism of boys at the place between the "Toolkhtotino" and the "Sarnuonino," and in girls from the places between the "Khartotakhnian-hills.'

"'The parts of the organism of boys located at the end of what is called the "genital-member" and which are named in this incomparable book "Toolkhtotino" and "Sarnuonino" are named by contemporary medicine there "Glans-Penis" and "Prepuce-Penis"; and the "Kartotaknian-hills" covering what is called the "clitoris" of girls, are called "Labia-majora" and "Labia-minora," or as is said in common language, "the-large-and-small-obscene-lips."

"'For the substance "Kulnabo," contemporary medicine has no name at all, this independent substance being entirely unknown to it.

"'Contemporary terrestrial medicine has a name only for the general mass of those substances among which is also the substance "Kulnabo."

"'And this total mass, it calls "Smegma," a composition of entirely heterogeneous substances, secreted by various what are called "glands," which have nothing in common with each other; as for instance, the "grease" gland, the "Cowperian," "Nolniolnian," the "Bartholinian" gland, and others.

"The separation and volatilization of these waste substances should in accordance with the providence of Great Nature be induced for the said places by means of all kinds of chance contacts and by various movements occurring in the atmosphere.

"'But unforeseen by Nature, the clothing which people have invented for themselves prevent the said factors from freely effecting the separation and volatilization of these substances, with the result that this "Kulnabo," remaining for a long time on these places, promotes the arising of perspiration; moreover, as this substance is in general the very best medium for the multiplication of what are called "bacteria," which exist in the atmosphere as well as in what are called the "subjective-spheres" of all kinds of things coming into direct contact with the children, there occurs from this multiplying there on the given parts of the organism of children, a process called "itching."

"'On account of this itching, children begin, unconsciously at first, to rub or scratch these places. Later, as there are concentrated in these parts of the organism all the ends of the nerves created by Nature for the special sensation required for the completion of the sacred process Elmooarno, which normally arises in adult people at the end of what is called copulation, and as, especially at a certain period when according to the providence of Great Nature there proceeds in these organs of children a process of preparation for future sex functionings, they experience from this rubbing or scratching a certain peculiar pleasant sensation, they therefore, begin intentionally—having instinctively realized from which of their actions this pleasant sensation is evoked in them—to rub these places even when there is no itching; and thus the ranks of the little

"Moordoortenists" on the Earth are always increasing by leaps and bounds.

"'As regards just what measures the Great Moses took for eradicating that evil, I learned not from the aforementioned book "Tookha-Tes-Nalool-Pan," but from the contents of an also very ancient papyrus.

"'From the contents of this papyrus it could be clearly seen that the Great Moses gave practical effect to the thoughts set down on this question in the book "Tookha-Tes-Nalool-Pan," by creating for his people those two religious rites, one of which is called "Sikt-ner-chorn" and the other "Tzel-putz-kann.'

"'The sacred "Sikt-ner-chorn" was specially created for boys and the sacred "Tzel-putz-kann" for girls, and they were to be obligatorily performed on all children of both sexes.

"'The rite of "Sikt-ner-chorn," for instance, was identical with your "Sooniat.' But cutting what is called the "Vojiano" or the "Frenum penis" of boys, the connection is severed between the head and the skin covering it, and thus there is obtained the free movement of this skin, or, as it is called "Prepuce-penis.'

"'According to the information which has come down to us from ancient times and also according to our own common sense, it is plain that the Great Moses, who as we learn from another source, was a very great authority on medicine, wished by this means to secure that the totality of substances accumulating in the said places might of itself be mechanically removed owing to all kinds of accidental contact and thus cease to become a factor for the arising of the mentioned maleficent itching.

"'Concerning the vast learning of the Great Moses in the province of medicine, many diverse historical sources agree that he obtained his medical knowledge during his stay in Egypt as a pupil of the Egyptian high-priests to whom this knowledge had come down from their ancestors of the continent Atlantis—the first and last genuinely learned beings of the Earth, the members of the society then called "Akhaldan."

"'The beneficial results of the customs then created by the Great Moses even now continue to be fairly visible in practice.

"'Concerning for instance the custom of "circumcision" in particular, I, being a good diagnostician and able to tell from one glance at a man's face what disharmony he has in his organism, can safely say that this terrible children's-disease of "Onanism" is scarcely ever found among those children upon whom this rite has been performed, whereas the children of those parents who fail to observe this custom are almost all subject to it.

"'The exceptions in this respect are only the children of those parents who are indeed cultured in the full sense of the word, and who clearly understand that the future normal mentation of their children depends exclusively upon whether they do or do not contract this disease in their childhood or youth.

"'Such cultured parents know very well that if even once the sensation of the climax of what is called the "Ooamonvanosinian-process" occurs in what is called the "nervous-system" of their children before they reach majority, they will already never have the full possibility of normal mentation when they become adult; and hence it is that such cultured parents always consider it their first and chief duty towards their children, to educate them in this respect.

"'Unlike most contemporary parents, they do not consider that the education of children consists in badgering them to learn by rote as much poetry as possible, composed by "Moordoortenist-psychopaths," or in teaching them to "click-their-heels-well" before their acquaintances, in which accomplishments according to the notions of people of recent times, the whole education of children unfortunately consists.

"'And so my dear friend—and though very depraved yet nevertheless sympathetic young man.

"'These two rites were created by the Great Moses and introduced then into the ordinary life of the Judaic people, in order to counteract that maleficent invention of clothes, thanks to which those factors were destroyed which were provided by Nature for the protection of these organs from the harmful action of the substances given off by them; and these two rites were transmitted from generation to generation both to the followers of this Judaic religion themselves, as well as to others who took over these useful rites almost unchanged. And it was only after "the-death-of-the-great-King-Solomon" that the rite "Tzel-putz-kann" ceased for some reason or other to be performed even by the followers of this Judaic religion and only the rite "Sikt-ner-chorn" automatically continued to be performed and reached the contemporary representatives of that race.

"'And this custom together with many other ancient Judaic customs also reached the followers of the Christian religion who at first observed it very strictly in their everyday life; but very soon, both this custom itself and even the information about its adoption among them, similarly quickly disappeared from among the followers of this then still new religion.

"'Yes . . . my dear friend. If only the teaching of the Divine Jesus Christ were carried out in full conformity with its original, then the religion unprecedentedly wisely founded on it, would not only be the best of all existing religions, but even of all religions which may arise and exist in the future.

"'Besides the custom of polygamy, there is nothing in the Mohammedan religion which was not also in the Judaic as well as in the Christian teachings.

"'The custom of polygamy, established on the basis of the scientific deductions of the then famous Arabian learned beings Naoolan El Aool, was introduced into the everyday life of people in general after the period of the founding of the Christian religion.

"'Your religion arose much later and its contents were intentionally restricted by its great creators, who had it in mind to lay particular stress on certain everyday customs.

"'They did this because at that time there were clearly manifest both the decline of the Christian religion and the disappearance in ordinary people of the capacity for contemplation, that is, for the state in which alone the truths indicated in the detailedly genuine religious teachings can be understood.

"'Having noticed all this, the great creators of the Mohammedan religion decided on the one hand to simplify the teachings itself, and on the other hand to emphasize certain customs so that the everyday life of the followers of this new teaching—who had lost the capacity for contemplation and consequently the possibility of understanding truths consciously—might at least mechanically flow more or less tolerably.

"'Just at that time, among other customs, they established and laid particular stress on the customs you mentioned of "Sooniat," "Abdest" and "Polygamy," the beneficial results of which we can see even now in practice.

"'For example, as you yourself have justly observed, thanks to "circumcision" and "ablution," one rarely finds among the followers of this "religion," either "onanism" or certain venereal diseases, and thanks to "polygamy" we see among the followers of this religion such a reciprocal so to say "psycho-organic" maintenance of the foundation of family life, as is almost entirely absent among the followers of the Christian religion.

"'Of the useful customs originally contained in the Christian religion and which were introduced by the creators of that religion into the life of its followers for the preservation of health and for the maintenance of the foundations of morality necessary for a happy life, nothing now remains except the custom of periodic fasting, that is, of abstaining at certain times of the year from the consumption of certain edible products.

"'And even this one surviving good custom is either already fading completely out of the ordinary life of the followers of this religion or its observance is so changing year by year that no shock is obtained from it for the fasters, though it was just for that shock that this "fast" was established.

"'The changes now taking place in the process of this Christian custom of fasting are very characteristic and provide an excellent example for understanding how in general all the "good-Christian-customs" have little by little undergone change, until they have finally entirely ceased to exist.

"'A good illustration is the present-day observance of this fast by those called the Russian "orthodox Christians."

"'These Russian "orthodox-Christians" took their religion entirely from those called the "orthodox-Greeks," from whom together with many other Christian customs this same custom of "fasting" also passed to them.

"'Most of the millions of these Russian "orthodox Christians" still continue to fast, as is said "rigorously" in conformity with what is called the "orthodox-code" now existing there.

"'But as to the manner of their fasting—one cannot help recalling the saying of our dear Mullah Nassr Eddin in such cases:

"'Isn't-it-all-the-same-if-I-sing-like-a-donkey-as-long-as-they-call-me-a-nightingale.'

"'The fasting of these Russian "orthodox-Christians" is just a case of this kind.

"'As long as they are called "Christians" and moreover "orthodox"—even though they receive no shock whatever from the fast, is it not all the same?

"'As I have already said, these Russian orthodox Christians even of the present time very strictly observe the seasons and the days of the "fasts" indicated in the aforesaid "codes.'

"'But as to what should and should not be consumed as food during a fast—just in that question "is-buried-the-left-paw-of-the-curly-haired-dog-of-the-ex-Emperor-Wilhelm.'

"'You will clearly understand how these contemporary Russian orthodox Christians fast, if I repeat to you the exact words of one of these genuine Russian orthodox Christians, spoken to me not long ago there in Russia.

"'I used to meet this Russian there on certain business and even became somewhat friendly with him and visited him in his home.

"'He was considered by those around him a very good "Christian" and the "patriarchal" father of a family; he was descended from what they call the "Old-Believers."

"Here my boy you might as well know that certain of the beings who compose this large group Russia are called by the rest 'Old-Believers.'

"'Old-Believers' is the name given to those orthodox Christians whose ancestors several centuries ago declined to accept the new rules then laid down by somebody or other for Russian orthodox Christians but remained faithful followers of the previously existing rules also laid down by somebody or other, only a century or two before the given 'religious-schism' such as usually occurs among them from time to time.

"'And so the said worthy Russian "Old-Believer"'—I continued to the young Persian—'once when we were dining together at his house in the company of several other Russians, also orthodox Christians, turned to me and said:

"'"Eh! old dear"

"By the way, I must tell you that it is common among the beings of this group there, after the second glass of genuine Russian vodka, to call their acquaintances by various pet-names such as 'old dear,' 'my Zapoopoonchik,' 'my-potbellied-beauty,' 'eh-my-little-brown-jug,' and so on and so forth.

"'And so this worthy genuine orthodox Christian addressing me as "old dear" said:

"'"Never mind, old dear! We shall soon be having Lent and then we shall feast together on real Russian dishes.

"'"To tell the truth, here in Russia we almost always eat the same things during the "meat" periods.

"'"But it is quite a different story during the fasts, especially during Lent.

"'"Not a day passes but one is privileged to see some of the most tasty dishes.

"'"You know what, old dear?

"'"I made the other day a remarkably interesting 'discovery' on this subject.

"'"This new 'discovery' of mine is miles above the discovery of that old codger Copernicus, who when he was once lying dead drunk on the ground clearly sensed, it seems, that the Earth goes round.

"'"Ah! What a marvel! What a discovery!

"'"In our own mother Moscow alone, hundreds of thousands of such discoveries are probably made every day.

"'"No! . . . my discovery is a real one and exceedingly instructive and substantial.

"'"This discovery of mine is, that we have all been complete fools and hopeless idiots ever to have imagined and been fairly convinced that for the host of good, varied and most tasty dishes during Lent, we are indebted to the famous art of our chefs and cooks.

"'"On the day, peculiarly blessed for those near to me, when I became worthy to understand this truth, that is to say, when our incomparable Doonyasha finally succeeded in placing within the layers of the pie for the 'gromwell-fish-soup-with-Turbot-livers' a series of secondary layers, I understood with my whole being, that this had been a great mistake on our part.

"'"First I understood this myself, and afterwards I proved it to the whole of my household, that if we have so many varied and most tasty dishes during Lent, we are indebted only to our blessed and glorious fishes alone.

"'"During fasts and especially during Lent, our homes are made happy by the frequent visits of the

Most Honorable "Sturgeon," and the
Estimable "Sterlet," and the
Respected "Dried-Sturgeon," and the
Ever-memorable "Turbot," and
Her Illustrious Highness the "Salmon," and the
Musical "White-Sturgeon," and the
Serenely Plastic "Mackerel," and the
Eternally Angry "Pike," and the
Ever demure "Gwyniad," and the
Leaping Alive "Trout," and the
Beauty "Trioshka," and the
Proud "Shamai," and that
Worthy Personality "Bream," and all our other like benefactors and protectors.

"'"Merely the names alone of these our givers of good and felicity are already for us the greatest gift of God.

"'"When we hear their names, our hearts almost leap within.

"'"These names of theirs are not just names, but real music. Can one really compare the sounds of the music invented there by various Beethovenings and Chopinings, and other fashionable triflers, with the sounds of the names of these blessed fishes?

"'"Every time we hear the names of these glorious creations, a state of bliss flows within us and courses through our veins and nerves.

"'"Eh! Blessed fishes, first created by our CREATOR! Have mercy on us and sustain us also in these "meat-days," Amen.

"'After this prayer, this worthy "orthodox-Russian-Christian" drained a monster glass of genuine "refined" Russian vodka and stared fondly at a little statue of "Venus and Psyche" which stood nearby.

"'And indeed my friend, almost every Russian "orthodox Christian" has a similar idea of fasting and a similar attitude towards it.

"'During these "Christian-fasts" which passed to them from the orthodox Greeks, they all eat the flesh of fish.

"'It is not considered a "sin" among them to eat the flesh of fish, and they eat it heartily as a fast dish.

"'I personally find only one thing incomprehensible—from where did these Russian "sorry-orthodox" get the idea that during the Christian fasts, especially during Lent, the flesh of fish may be eaten?

"'I find it incomprehensible because the orthodox Christians from whom they took this religion, namely the Greeks, neither in the past nor in the present, have ever eaten or do eat the flesh of fish during fasts.

"'Even the Greeks of today eat fish during Lent only on one day, and even then in accordance with the code of the orthodox church in memory of a day associated with the Divine Jesus Christ.

"'The result of a fast permitting the consumption of the flesh of fish not only gives no shock at all to the fasters, but is even directly contrary to what the Divine Jesus Christ himself intended and taught, and for which this custom was established by the great creators of this Christian religion.

"'In confirmation of what I have just told you, you might as well, my young friend, listen to what I once chanced to read about Christian fasting in an ancient Judaic-Essene manuscript.

"'In this ancient Judaic-Essene manuscript it was stated that the custom established for the followers of the teaching of Jesus Christ of fasting at certain times of the year, as instituted long after His death, namely, in the two hundred and fourteenth year after his birth.

"'The custom of fasting was instituted and introduced into the Christian religion by the great secret Kelnuanian council.

"'This secret Kelnuanian council was convened by all the followers of the still new teaching of Jesus Christ in the locality of Kelnuk, lying on the shores of the Dead Sea. Hence, it is known in the history of the Christian religion as the Kelnuanian Council.

"'And it was held in secret because the followers of the teaching of Jesus Christ were then everywhere rigorously persecuted by the '"power-possessing" people.

"'The "power-possessing" people persecuted them because they greatly feared that if people lived according to this teaching, then although they themselves, namely, the "power-possessing" people, could also live very well, yet all the motives for displaying their power would disappear, and thereby those shocks would cease the satisfaction of which evoke the tickling of their inner god named "Self-love.'

"'It was just during that Kelnuanian council, that its members first laid down the rule that the followers of the teaching of Jesus Christ should on certain days abstain from consuming certain edible products for food.

"'And the initial cause of the institution of this fast was the dispute at this Kelnuanian Council between two then famous learned men, namely, the Great Hertoonano and the great Greek Philosopher Veggendiadi.

"'The great Hertoonano was the representative of all the followers of the teaching of Jesus Christ settled on the shores of the Red Sea, while the philosopher Veggendiadi was the representative of all the then followers of that teaching in

Greece.

"'The philosopher Veggendiadi was famous for his learning only in his own country, but Hertoonano was famous all over the Earth. He was considered the greatest authority on the laws of the inner organization of man, and also an authority on the science then called "Alchemy,"—not of course the alchemical science of which contemporary people have a notion and which they express by the same word.

"'The famous dispute between the great Hertoonano and Veggendiadi arose on the following occasion.

"'The philosopher Veggendiadi, it seems, occupied two days in affirming and proving that it was absolutely necessary to spread among all the followers of the teaching of Jesus, the notion that to kill animals for the purpose of consuming their flesh for food was the greatest sin, and moreover that such flesh was very harmful to the health and so on.

"'After the philosopher Veggendiadi, several other representatives ascended the rostrum and spoke for or against his case.

"'Finally, as this manuscript stated, the Great Hertoonano with measured dignity slowly mounted the rostrum and spoke in the manner proper to him, clearly and calmly.

"'According to the text of this manuscript, he then spoke as follows:

"'"I fully concur in all the evidences and arguments set forth here by our Brother in Christ, the philosopher Veggendiadi.

"'"I for my part will even add to all he has said, that to cut short other lives merely to stuff one's own belly is an infamy of infamies such as only man is capable of.

"'"Had I not also been interested in this question for many years and had I not reached certain entirely different definite conclusions, then after all that our Brother in Christ Veggendiadi had said here, I should not hesitate a moment but should urge and conjure you all, not to delay until tomorrow, but without looking behind, to hasten back to your towns, and there in the public squares to cry aloud: 'Stop! Stop! People! Consume no more meat for food! This practice of yours is not only contrary to all the commandments of God, but is the cause of all your diseases.'

"“"As you see, I do not do this now. And I do not do so only because during my long years of unremitting study of this question, I have, as I have already told you, arrived at an entirely different definite conclusion.

"“"Concerning the definite conclusion at which I have arrived, I can now tell you only this, that it will never happen on the Earth that all people will profess one and the same religion. Hence, in addition to our Christian religion, other religions will always exist. And it is not possible to be certain that the followers of these other religions will also abstain from consuming meat.

"“"But if we cannot now be certain that at some time or other all people on Earth will abstain from meat, then we must now, as regards the consumption of meat, take quite other more practicable measures, because if one part of mankind consumes meat and the other part does not, then according to the results of my experimental investigations, the greatest of evils—than which nothing could be worse—would befall the people who did not consume meat.

"“"Namely, as my detailed experiments have shown me, among people who do not consume meat but who nevertheless live among those who do, the formation ceases of what is called 'will-power.'

"“"My experiments proved to me that although when they abstain from meat people's bodily health improves, nevertheless, when such abstainers find themselves mixing with those who consume meat, their psychic state inevitably grows worse, in spite of the fact that the state of their organism may at the same time sometimes improve.

"‘“Thus, a good result for people who abstain from meat can be obtained exclusively only if they live always in complete isolation.

"‘“As regards the people who constantly consume meat, or those products which contain the element called ‘Eknokh,’ although the appearance of the state of their organism undergoes no change, nevertheless their psyche, especially its chief feature which is sometimes designated by the general word the ‘character’ of man, gradually changes in regard to positiveness and morality for the worse, beyond all recognition.

"‘“I must tell you that I made all these deductions from the experiments I was enabled to conduct over a period of many years, thanks to two good philanthropic men, namely, to the rich shepherd Alla Ek Linakh and his money, and to the scientist we all respect El Koona Nassa with his remarkable invention, the apparatus ‘Arostodesokh.’

"‘“By means of this said remarkable apparatus ‘Arostodesokh’ I was enabled for several years to register daily the general state of the organism of all those thousands of people who lived under test conditions at the expense of the good shepherd Alla Ek Linakh.

"‘“May our CREATOR multiply his flocks!

"‘“Well then, when thanks to those experimental researches or mine, I became clearly convinced that if people continue to consume meat for their food, it will be very bad for them and that on the other hand, if only some of them should abstain, no good would come of this either; I thereafter devoted myself entirely for a time to finding out what could nevertheless be done for the future welfare of the majority of the people.

"‘“At the outset I then established for myself two categorical propositions; the first—that people accustomed for so many centuries to consuming meat for their food would never, with their weak wills, be able to make themselves cease consuming it in order to overcome this criminal tendency of theirs; and the second—that even if people should decide not to eat meat and should in fact keep their decision for a certain time, and should even lose the habit of eating meat, they would nevertheless never be able to abstain from eating it for a sufficient length of time to acquire a total aversion to it. They would not be able to do so because never on the Earth will it occur that all people will have the same religion or form a single government, without which condition there can never exist common to all, any suggestive, prohibitive, penal, or other kind of compulsory influence, owing to which alone, people, possessing in general the property of being stimulated by example, aroused by envy and influence magnetically, might be enabled to keep forever a resolution once taken.

"‘"Notwithstanding these two facts incontestably clear in my conviction, I nevertheless, with these facts as the basis of my subsequent researches, persevered in my search for some possible way of escape from the unhappy situation confronting people.

"‘"Of course all my further investigations on a large scale proceeded again with the aid of the inexhaustible wealth of the herdsman Alla Ek Linakh and the wonderful apparatus of the wise El Koona Nassa.

"‘"The results of these last researches of mine made it clear to me that although in general people's psyche does indeed deteriorate from the constant introduction into the organism of the substance 'Eknokh,' yet this substance has a particularly harmful effect only at certain times of the year.

"‘"So, my brethren in Christ . . . from all I have said and chiefly from my experimental observations which I made on people daily during a whole year and which clearly showed me that the intensity of the harmful effect of the substance 'Eknokh' decreases at certain times of the year, I can now confidently express my personal opinion that if the custom would be spread and confirmed among the followers of the teaching of Jesus Christ, of abstaining during at least certain times of the year from the use of these products in the formations of which that substance 'Eknokh' takes a special part, then if such a measure could conceivably be put into effect, it could bring the people a certain amount of benefit.

"'"As my numerous alchemical investigations have shown me, the substance 'Eknokh' participates in the formation of the organisms of all lives without exception breeding on the surface of the Earth as well as within its different spheres, as for instance, within the Earth, in the water, in the atmosphere and so on.

"'"This substance is present also in everything which exists for the formation of the said organisms, as for example, in the vascular fluid of every pregnant female of every kind of life, and in such products as milk, eggs, caviar, etc."

"'The ideas expressed by the great Hertoonano so astounded and agitated all the members of that Kelnuanian Council, that the commotion made it impossible for the Great Hertoonano to continue speaking, and he was compelled to abandon his speech and descend from the rostrum.

"'It was further said in that manuscript that the day's result was a unanimous decision on the part of the members of the Kelnuanian Council to fix, with the help of the Great Hertoonano, those times of the year when the substance "Eknokh" has more harmful effects on people and to spread widely among the followers of Jesus Christ the custom of fasting at these times of the year—that is, of abstaining at certain times of the year from products containing the, for them, harmful substance "Eknokh."

"'With this that Judaic-Essene manuscript ended.

"'As you see from this, the creators of this custom had in view that the followers of that religion should abstain at the fixed times from those products which contain the substance very harmful for their health and particularly to their psyche.

"'But these Russian "sorry-orthodox-Christians" who consider themselves faithful followers of that great religion, also fast, but during their fast, they eat the flesh of fish, that is to say, they eat just those organisms which contain according to the researches of the Great Hertoonano that harmful substance "Eknokh" precisely to guard them against which that wise and salutary custom was created.'

"And with that, my boy, I then concluded my conversation with that sympathetic young Persian.

"Concerning the destruction and transformation by contemporary beings of these good customs which were handed down from the ancient days of their wise ancestors, our incomparable Mullah Nassr Eddin has also a very apt and wise sentence.

"'Ekh! People, people! Why are you people? If only you were not people, you might perhaps be clever.'

"A favorite saying of the American Uncle Sam also does very well to define the same idea.

"It is said that when that Uncle Sam from America happens to have drunk a little more gin than usual, he always says during a pause: 'When nothing's right—only then, all right.'

"But for myself I will only say, in this case, 'Wicked Moon.'

"At any rate, my dear boy, I must admit that certain customs existing there which have reached the contemporary favorites of yours from remote antiquity are exceedingly good for the ordinary existence of the beings of certain communities there.

"These customs are good because they were invented and introduced into the process of the existence of beings by those three-brained beings there, who brought the perfecting of their Reason up to so high a degree as unfortunately none of your contemporary beings there any longer attains.

"The contemporary people-beings are able to create only such customs as make the quality of their psyche still worse.

"For instance they have recently made a practice of always here, there and everywhere dancing a certain dance called the 'Fox-trot.'

"At the present time this 'fox-trot' is indulged in everywhere at all times of the day and night not only by young still unformed beings who do not even begin to be aware of the sense and aim of their arising and existence, but also by those whose faces clearly express—as it can be constated by every normal more or less sensible three-brained beings—that in respect of their duration of existence, as our teacher would say 'not-only-have-they-one-foot-in-the-grave-but-even-both.' The point however is that the process of the experience in a being during the said 'fox-trot' is exactly similar to that which proceeds during that children's disease which the Great Moses called 'Moordoorten.'

"The disease which the Great Moses devoted half his existence to eradicating from among children, a host of your contemporary favorites of responsible age have, almost deliberately, resurrected again and spread not only among children and the general mass of adults, but also even among the aged as well.

"These good customs for ordinary existence reached your contemporary favorites from ancient three-brained beings of your planet, and very many now still exist there among the beings of various communities of the continent Asia.

"Certain of these customs existing there now, appear when first witnessed, as absurdly strange and barbaric, but on a close and impartial investigation of the inner meaning of any of these customs, one can see how skillfully there has been incorporated in them for the people who follow them, one or another moral or hygienic benefit.

"Take, as an example, one of the most seemingly senseless

of the customs there—one existing among a certain tribe of Asiatic beings called 'Kolenian Loors' or 'Kolenian gypsies' dwelling between Persia and Afghanistan, and which other beings there call 'Gypsy-self-fumigation.'

"Exactly the same end is served by this seemingly stupid custom as by the Persian custom of 'Ablution' or 'Abdest.'

"This gypsy tribe is regarded as the lowest and filthiest of all the tribes existing on the Earth; and indeed they are so filthy that their clothes are always swarming with the insects called lice.

"Their custom of 'self-fumigation' also serves by the way to destroy these insects.

"Although the men-beings of that tribe are indeed exceedingly filthy, yet not only do no venereal diseases exist among them, but they do not even know and have never even heard that such diseases can be contracted.

"In my opinion, this is the outcome entirely of that custom of theirs, which some ancient clever being there invented, for the welfare of the people of his epoch, and which passing afterwards from generation to generation, chanced to reach these contemporary filthy beings of the tribe of 'Kolenian gypsies.'

"For this rite of 'self-fumigation' every family of Gypsies has also what is called an 'Ateshkain,' that is a stool of a special form which they regard as sacred; and this whole ritual of theirs they perform with the aid of this sacred stool.

"Every family of these gypsies has also what is called a 'Tandoor,' that is, a special kind of earth pit, such as is found in the houses almost everywhere on the continent of Asia and which serves as a hearth on which they usually bake bread and prepare food.

"In these 'Tandoors' in Asia they burn chiefly what is called 'Keeziak'—a fuel composed of the dung of quadruped animals.

"The rite itself consists in this, that when the family of these gypsies returns home in the evening, they first remove all their clothing and shake them in this 'Tandoor.'

"It is almost always hot in this 'Tandoor,' because the dung burns very slowly and the ashes formed around the Keeziak keep the fire burning for a very long time.

"By the way, it is interesting to remark, that when these gypsies shake their clothes in the 'Tandoor' a highly interesting phenomenon results from this action of theirs; namely, the lice in their clothes crawl out and falling into the fire explode before burning, and the various sounds of the explosion of these lice, large and small, produces altogether a surprising 'musical symphony.'

"From the said explosion of the lice, a hearer sometimes has the impression that somewhere not far off, firing is going on from several dozen of their what are called machine-guns.

"Well then, after these 'worthy-gypsies' have shaken their no less worthy clothing, they proceed with the sacred ritual.

"First of all they solemnly and with a certain ceremony, lower their sacred family-stool into the 'Tandoor' and in turn, according to age, they step into the 'Tandoor' and stand upon it.

"The sacred stool consists simply of a small board to which four iron legs are fixed; and by this means it is possible to stand in the 'Tandoor' without burning one's feet in the hot ashes.

"As each member of the family stands on that sacred stool, all the other members of the family sing their sacred canticle, while the one standing upon this stool slowly and solemnly, bending the knees, lowers and raises himself and at the same time recites prayers. The custom requires that he should do this until every part of his sex organs has been warmed by the Tandoor.

"A second custom, very similar and seemingly just as stupid, I saw, among the people of another small tribe, called 'Toosooly-Kurds,' dwelling in Transcaucasia not far from Mt. Ararat.

"This tribe is not so filthy as the tribe of the 'Kolenian gypsies.' On the contrary, from their daily bathing in the river Arax, and existing mostly in the fresh air—being chiefly shepherds—not only are the people of this tribe very clean but they even do not give off the specific odor which is peculiar to people of almost all the small tribes which populate this great Asia.

"Each family of this tribe has its own what is called 'hut,' which serves as a dwelling and for the reception of guests—as the custom of visiting one another is highly developed among the separate families of this tribe.

"In each 'hut' it is customary for them to have, in the corner of the front section, what is called a 'sacred-Mungull,' that is a hearth on which a fire of smoldering charcoal or of the said 'Keeziak' is constantly kept, and near each such sacred-Mungull there hangs a small wooden box called 'Ktulnotz' which is always kept supplied with the roots of a certain plant.

"The 'rite-of-self-fumigation' consists in this, that every member of the family and every guest of either sex, before going into the principal section of the hut, is obliged to enter this 'sacred-Mungull' in order as they say to purify himself from the influence of those evil spirits by which man is surrounded when he is busy with honest work.

"And this purification is carried out in the following manner:

"Each person going into the hut must approach and take a few roots out of the hanging box and throw them into the fire, and afterwards in the smoke from the burning of these roots, fumigate his sex organs. In the case of a woman, she simply spreads her skirt and stands over the 'Mungull.' If it is a man he either takes off or lets down his trousers and also stands over the said smoke.

"Only after such a purification can they enter the chief room; otherwise, as they affirm, not only will evil influences be brought into the house, but owing to these accumulated influences, a man might contract very evil diseases.

"These sacred Mungulls are usually screened by the very best 'Djedjims,' that is, by a special fabric woven only by the Kurds.

"I repeat, my boy, there exists at the present time on that continent Asia a great many similar customs.

"I personally saw hundreds of them which seemed at first sight no less strange and barbarous, but upon a serious and impartial study of their hidden meaning, always revealed one and the same aim, namely, either the destruction of the noxious carriers of various diseases, or the strengthening of moral shame.

"But on the continent of Europe I scarcely found a single custom specially created either for the purpose of hygiene or for instilling morality among the masses.

"It cannot be denied that various customs also exist on the continent of Europe, even thousands of them, but they are all established only in order that beings may have the possibility of pleasing each other, or to conceal the real state of affairs, that is to say, to disguise the undesirable forms of one's exterior—undesirable of course only according to subjective understanding—and to conceal the nullity of one's own inner significance.

"These customs existing there progressively increase year by year the 'duality' of the personality and mind of the beings there.

"But the principal evil lies in this, that at the present time there, all the 'Oskianotsnel' of the rising generation, or the education of the children, is rendered and reduced only to the adoption of these innumerable customs which exist among them and engender only immorality. Hence it is that year by year, the data crystallized in them by tens of centuries for the Being 'of-an-image-of-God,' and not simply, as they themselves would say, 'of-an-animal,' are on the one hand decrystallized, and on the other hand their psyche is already becoming almost such as our dear teacher defines by the words:

"'There-is-everything-in-him-except-himself.'

"And indeed my boy, owing to the complete absence of good patriarchal customs and to their notorious 'education,' the contemporary beings of that continent have already become completely transformed into what are called 'automatons' or living mechanical puppets.

"At the present time any one of them can become animated and manifest himself outwardly, only when there are accidentally pressed the corresponding what are called 'buttons' of those impressions already present in him, which he mechanically perceived during the whole of his preparatory age.

"But unless these 'buttons' are pressed, the beings there are in themselves only, as again our highly esteemed Mullah Nassr Eddin says, 'pieces-of-pressed-meat.'

"It must without fail be remarked here that one of the principal causes of this state of the beings of contemporary civilization is also that same 'onanism' of theirs, a disease which in recent times has come to be almost epidemic there, and which is in its turn also a consequence again of their education of children, thanks to a certain maleficent idea established among its rulers and which is already, as it were, an inseparable part of the consciousness of everybody, namely, their maleficent idea that 'to-speak-to-children-about-the-sex-question-is-absolutely-improper.'

"And further, I again emphasize, that just this, for their naive reason, trifling idea, the significance of which none of them takes into consideration—considering it simply as what they call a question of 'decency' or 'indecency'—is the chief cause of their having come to this phenomenal so to say 'psychic-mechanicality.'

"In the totality of definite understandings which they call 'education,' there is even a certain section which elucidates and exactly indicates just what is, as they express it, 'decent' and what is 'indecent' to say to children.

"You must know, that at the end of my last sojourn on the surface of your planet, I had to make this maleficent terrestrial question the subject of my special observation and even to study it in great detail.

"To know approximately what results the terrestrial contemporary education of children leads to, I will tell you of just that one occurrence which was the first cause of my subsequent special interest in the question of this terrestrial misunderstanding.

"Although this occurrence took place in the large community of Russia, yet nevertheless this 'story' which I shall now tell you is very characteristic and gives a very good picture in general, of the education of the children of their contemporary civilization.

"It is characteristic because in this large community Russia also, the contemporary responsible beings, especially the beings of what is called the upper 'ruling-class,' educate their children exactly as the contemporary responsible beings of the other communities breeding on the continents of Europe and America educate theirs.

"My account of this occurrence which evoked in me an impulse of interest to acquaint myself specially with the question of the terrestrial education of children, I shall preface with a story of something that occurred just previously to this and which admirably illustrates the significance of this education of theirs and was also, so to say, a 'link' in my gradually becoming interested in this question.

"I happened once to exist continuously for several months in the capital of this community—in the city of St. Petersburg.

"During my stay there I became acquainted with an elderly couple.

"The man was what is called a 'senator' and his wife was a 'society-lady' and a patroness of several 'welfare institutions.'

"I used to visit them often at their home and enjoyed playing chess with this senator—as is customary there among what are called 'respectable-people.'

"This elderly couple had several daughters. All the elder daughters were already settled, that is married; only their youngest daughter, twelve years old, remained at home.

"As this couple had no further care concerning their other daughters, they decided to give this youngest daughter of theirs the very best education according to the notions of that time, and for this purpose they placed her in a special 'boarding-school,' a higher educational establishment called an 'Institute.'

"This youngest daughter of theirs came home only on Sundays and for the chief holidays, and once a week on special days her father or mother used to visit her at the boarding school.

"I was almost always with them during the holidays, and I met this charming as yet unspoiled girl and sometimes even took walks with her in the neighboring what is called 'park.'

"During these walks we either joked or she told me about her lessons and her new impressions.

"During these meetings and conversations, a tie, something like friendship, grew up little by little between us.

"She was very quick in her perceptions and manifestations, or as your favorites themselves define such persons from among themselves, an 'alert-and-thoughtful' girl.

"My acquaintance, this senator, was sent on a certain, as

they say there, 'inspection,' somewhere far off in Siberia.

"His wife decided to accompany him, for the senator was suffering from what is called 'liver-trouble' and constantly needed care; but they could not make this joint trip because of their youngest daughter, since there would be no one to visit her at the institute and to take her home during the holidays.

"So, one morning, the parents—these elderly acquaintances of mine—came to see me at my apartment and asked me if I would agree to take their place with their youngest daughter during their absence, to visit her every week at the institute and to take her home with me for the holidays.

"I, of course, at once agreed to this proposal of theirs, and when very soon after, the senator and his wife left for Siberia, I began punctually to fulfill the obligation taken upon myself in regard to their daughter who had by that time become a pet of mine.

"Upon my first visit to this educational establishment which existed specially for the education of children, I noticed a certain strange thing which also served as one of the causes of my subsequent observations and studies of the consequences of your contemporary favorites of that 'maleficence' invented by them themselves.

"On the day of my visit to this, as they call it, 'genteel-institution,' there were many visitors in the reception room where the meetings of the parents or guardians with their children or wards actually took place.

"One or two parents or guardians had only just come in, others were already talking with their children or foster-children, others were waiting the arrival of their children, and all their attention was fixed on the door through which the pupils of that establishment usually entered. I also, after I had come into this reception room and had explained to the inspectress on duty who it was I wished to see, sat down to wait for my chance foster-child. While waiting I looked around. All the pupils of this 'genteel-establishment' were dressed alike and all wore their hair similarly braided in two braids, the ends of which, tied with ribbons, hung down their backs.

"What struck my eye was a certain peculiarity in these ribbons and braids. On some of the pupils these ribbons simply hung down the back, but on others, although they also hung down the back, yet the ends of these ribbons were tied together in a certain way.

"On the very next holiday, when I took my foster-child home, talking with her over what is called a samovar, I asked her:

"'Tell me Sonia please, why although the pupils of your institute dress alike in everything else, there is that peculiarity in the ends of their braids?' She immediately blushed and without answering this question of mine stared pensively into her tea, and only after a certain time, nervously replied:

"'It's not just a simple thing among us. Although this is our big institute secret, yet I cannot help telling it to you, my friend; as I am quite sure that you will not give away this big institute secret of ours to anybody.'

"She proceeded to tell me frankly as follows:

"'The manner of tying our ribbons was intentionally devised by the pupils so that they could recognize one another; that is, know to which club a pupil belongs, and, at the same time, so that the class-teachers and supervisors and in general anyone not a pupil of the institute, should not know or discover the secret.

"'All the pupils of our institute are divided into two categories, one belongs to what is called the "men's-club" and the other to the "women's-club," and we recognize one another just by the manner of tying these ribbons.'

"After this she explained to me in detail in just what the difference between these two clubs lies.

"She said that as a rule, all new arrivals in the Institute were at first members of the women's club, and only afterwards, if any pupil proved to be daring towards the teachers or in general showed herself very active in some way or other, then by the common consent of all the pupils she was enrolled as a member of the men's-club and from that moment tied the ends of the ribbons of her braids together.

"'We usually make the meeting place of our club, a spare classroom or dormitory, but more often the toilets.

"'The members of the men's club have in general the following privileges; they have the right to choose and to command as many as they like and who they please of the pupils who are members of the women's club; and these latter are obliged always to gratify every wish of the given member of the men's club and do their utmost to make her stay in our boarding school easy for her, as for example: to make her bed in the morning, copy her lessons, share with her the presents sent from home and so on and so forth.

"The chief occupation in the clubs consists of reading together forbidden books procured by one of the pupils. They chiefly read one very rare manuscript, obtained with money raised by a general institute subscription, wherein is expounded in detail, the whole teaching of the famous poetess Sappho.

"I must tell you my boy, that Sappho was the name of a certain Greek poetess who first discovered there on your planet the 'way-to-real-happiness' for many women of the Greek-Roman as well as of the contemporary civilization.

"This great creatress of 'women's-happiness' had her dwelling place on the island of 'Lesbos,' from which word originated the title of those women who have already become worthy to understand and to actualize during the process of their existence the teaching of this remarkable woman, and who at the present time are called 'Lesbians.'

"This foster-child of mine, who had chanced to become

my enlightener upon the subtleties of the psyche of the beings of the female sex of your planet, further explained to me that every pupil of the Institute who was a member of the men's club could choose for herself as many partners as she wished for the common pastime; this of course proceeding in full accordance with the teachings of the poetess Sappho.

"I think that thanks merely to this one fact which I have related to you out of thousands of other observations of mine, you can already clearly picture to yourself that such a phenomenal ugliness could not exist among the rising generation if the notion was not prevalent there that it is exceedingly 'indecent' to talk to children about the 'sex question.'

"This notion of 'decency' came down to contemporary civilization by inheritance from the beings of the epoch called the 'Middle-Ages.'

"These candidates for Hasnamuss of the Middle-Ages, having been among the chief agents in the destruction of the real meaning of the teaching of the Divine Teacher, Christ, then also devised and introduced into everyday existence, as a regulation, this maleficent invention which they called 'bon-ton.' And this maleficent invention then become so strongly fixed in the psyche of the majority that it became organized for them and began to pass by heredity from generation to generation, so that now your contemporary favorites, who have become completely weak-willed are unable, however they may try, to overcome such an abnormal psychic fixation as, in the given case, the notion of the indelicacy of talking to their children about the 'sex-question.'

"What? Talk on one's children about 'Sex'? Is that not indecent?

"At the present time the people of contemporary civilization talk to their children and teach them for their edification only what has been invented or is being invented in the manuals of various candidates for 'Hasnamuss-individuums' under the aforesaid title of 'bon-ton.'

"And since in all these manuals it seems that it is very indecent to talk about the 'sex-question' and in the case of children even immoral, then, even if contemporary people see their favorite son or daughter rotting, they simply cannot and even as I have already told you, with all their mental wish, dare not explain frankly to their children the harm and sin of these criminal habits.

"And so my boy, when my good acquaintances the senator and his wife had returned from Siberia and I was free of the obligation I had taken upon myself in regard to my pet, their youngest daughter, there just then occurred the aforementioned event which served as the beginning of my special observations and studies of this same terrestrial contemporary question, maleficent also to them themselves.

"This sorrowful event occurred there in St. Petersburg itself, in just such another educational institution and consisted in the following. The headmistress of this institution, finding that one of her pupils had behaved contrary to their famous regulations of 'decency' reprimanded her so harshly and so unfairly that as a result the accused and her friend, two growing girls with the germs of data for future normal women-mothers, hanged themselves.

"My investigations into this case elicited the following:

"It appeared that among the pupils of the mentioned educational institution was a certain young girl Elizabeth who had been brought by her parents from a distant estate here to the capital, in order that there in a special higher-educational-institution, she might receive this same contemporary 'education.'

"Here in St. Petersburg in this said boarding-school, it happened that this thirteen year old Elizabeth became great friends with another young girl, Mary, who like herself was not yet developed.

"The same year on the day of the 'spring-holiday' or as it is otherwise called there, 'May-Day,' all the pupils of that higher educational-institution were taken, according to custom, for an excursion into the country, and these two 'bosom-friends' happened to be in different groups which were walking at some distance from each other.

"Out in the fields Elizabeth chanced to see a certain 'quadruped-animal' called there a 'bull,' and very much wishing for some reason or other that her bosom-friend Mary should not miss seeing this dear quadruped animal, she shouted, 'Mary! Mary! Look, there goes a bull!'

"No sooner had she uttered the word 'bull' than all the, as they are called, 'governesses' swarmed round this Elizabeth and flung at her all kinds of cruel preachings.

"How could one utter the word 'bull!!' Does not that quadruped animal occupy itself with what no well-brought-up person would on any account speak of and still less a pupil of such a 'genteel-institution'?

"While the governesses were persecuting this poor Elizabeth, all the pupils of the institute gathered around and the headmistress herself came up, who, having learned what it was all about, began in her turn to reproach Elizabeth.

"'Shame on you!' she said, 'to utter such a word which is considered so very, very "indecent!!"'

"At last Elizabeth could contain herself no longer and she asked amid her tears:

"'What then ought I to have called that quadruped animal if it actually was a "bull"?'

"'The word,' said the headmistress, 'by which you called that animal, any of the scum call it. But you, since you are here in the institute, are not of the scum; so you should always find out how to call indecent things by names which do not sound indecent to the ear.'

"'For instance—when you saw that indecent animal and

wanted your friend to look at it, you might have shouted: Mary, look, there goes a 'beefsteak,' or, Mary look yonder, there goes something that in very good to eat when we are hungry, and so forth.'

"From all this poor Elizabeth became so nervous, especially as this 'reprimanding' took place in the presence of all her friends, that she could not restrain herself and cried out with all her might:

"'Oh you wretched old maids! Striped hobgoblins! Spawn of deepest hell! Because I called a thing by its name, you immediately begin to suck my blood. Be thrice damned!!!!!'

"Having said these last words, she fell as they say there, 'in a-faint,' followed in turn by the fainting of the headmistress herself and of several 'class mistresses' and 'governesses.'

"The 'class-mistresses' and 'governesses' of this 'genteel-institution' who had not fainted, then raised such a 'hubbub' as really only occurs at what is called the market where 'Jewesses' from the town of 'Berdichev' exclusively bargain.

"The result of it all was that when the 'class mistresses' and 'governesses' who had fainted, revived, they then and there held in the field under the presidency of this same headmistress of the institution, what is there called a 'teachers'-council,' by whose sentence it was decided immediately on return to town to telegraph Elizabeth's father to come for his daughter, as she was expelled from the Institute with loss of right to enter any other any institute in the Russian Empire.

"The same day an hour after the pupils were sent home, one of what are called the 'porters' of the institute happened to find in the 'wood-shed' that two as yet undeveloped growing 'future-mothers,' were hanging by ropes fastened to the beams.

"In Mary's pocket was found a note with the contents:

"'Together with my dear Elizabeth, I do not wish to live any longer with such nonentities as you, and I am going with her to a better world.'

"This case then so interested me that I began, of course privately, to investigate psycho-analytically from every aspect the psyche of all the parties in this sad story. I partly elucidated among other things that at the moment of the manifestation of her violent outburst, there was in the psyche of poor Elizabeth what is called there 'chaos.'

"And indeed it would have been astonishing if such a 'chaos' had not been in the psyche of this as yet unselfconscious thirteen year old girl, who before this miserable event had always lived on her father's big estate, where she had always seen and felt the same richness of nature as on that day in the field near the city of St. Petersburg.

"She had been brought to that stifling noisy city of St. Petersburg and been kept for a long time in an improvised box. Suddenly, she had found herself in an environment where every fresh impression evokes all kinds of memories of former pleasantly perceived sensations.

"On your planet, during what is called 'early-spring,' there are indeed sometimes pictures, to the charm of which it is difficult not to yield.

"Picture to yourself the following—afar, cows are seen at pasture; near at one's feet snowdrops shyly peep out from the Earth; close to one's ear, a little bird flies by; to the right is heard the twittering of quite an unknown bird; and on the left, one's sense of smell is quickened by the perfume of some also unknown flower.

"In short, at such moments as these, in the beings there, especially in one so young as Elizabeth, finding themselves after a long period of oppressive existence in a suffocating city in the midst of such a rich abundance of all kinds of unaccustomed impressions—the mental associations evoked by a natural being-joy would naturally arise of themselves from every external thing perceived.

"Elizabeth must have felt this especially strongly, having lived, as I have already said, before the Institute, on her father's large estate which lay far from the already exceedingly abnormal conditions of city vanities.

"Thanks to this, every impression newly perceived by her would naturally call up previous childhood memories, each connected in their turn with various other pleasant incidents.

"So it is not difficult to picture to yourself that the sudden appearance of that quadruped animal called 'bull,' such as she had seen at home on the farm and which had enjoyed there the affection of all the children, who secretly even took it bread from the table, was to this as yet unformed impressionable young girl a shock for the corresponding associations under the influence of which, she, being full of a feeling of sincere happiness still unspoiled by the abnormally established conditions of being-existence, instantly wished to share her happiness with her bosom-friend who was some distance off, and shouted to her to look at that dear 'bull.'

"Now I ask you, how should she have called this quadruped being, since it actually was a 'bull'?

"Really 'Beefsteak'?—as advised by the 'esteemed' headmistress of this 'esteemed-higher-educational-institution' which existed there specially for the 'education-of-children' according to the barbarous system of theirs existing there to their misfortune also at the present time.

"As you see my boy, intending to tell you a little more about the three-brained beings who have interested you and who breed on that continent of North America, I have, by the way, said a great deal in general about the three-brained beings arising and existing on all the continents of this peculiar planet.

"I don't think you will have any grievance against me for this, since you have at the same time managed to learn many more facts elucidating the details of their strange psyche.

"Concerning specially what is called the 'degree-of-degeneration' of the common presences of those who compose this contemporary large group on the continent America in respect of the loss of possibilities for the acquisition of Being nearer to the normal Being of three-brained beings in general, I can tell you something somewhat consoling for them, namely, that in my opinion, there remains among them the largest percentage of beings in whose presences the said possibility is not entirely lost.

"Although this new group is composed of and still continues to be increased by three-brained beings breeding on the continent of Europe, where for such beings with the aforementioned possibilities it is already necessary, particularly in recent times, as our wise teacher Mullah Nassr Eddin says on such occasions, 'To-look-specially-with-the-most-powerful-electric-arc-lamps,' nevertheless, I repeat, in this large group there is a larger percentage of such beings than on the continent of Europe.

"It seems to me that this has happened because there have migrated there and still now migrate from the continent of Europe, beings chiefly from among what are called the 'simple-beings,' who are not, so to say, the 'hereditary offspring' of the European beings belonging to the 'ruling-caste,' in whom thanks to transmission by inheritance from generation to generation during long centuries of predisposition to Hasnamussian Properties, there is at the present time so much of what is called 'inner-swagger,' that it would never permit them to blend with the general mass in order to strive together with common efforts to become such three-brained beings as they should be.

"Thanks only to the fact that among the three-brained beings breeding on that continent there were only very few of the 'offspring-of-the-ruling-caste' and that the general mass of beings was in itself a medium in which it was still possible for 'our-brother' to exist and not be under the influence of those local radiations which are formed owing to surrounding beings and which act harmfully on what are called the 'subjectively-natural-inner-forces' of every being—I was therefore able during my stay among them to rest as I desired.

"Now my boy that I have spent so much of my time explaining the meaning of all the various innovations and all the renewals of former pernicious customs—which had already many times existed on their planet—among the beings of this big new contemporary grouping, and which have already at the present time become, in the objective sense, harmful not only for them themselves, but also for all the other three-brained beings who have interested you and who breed on quite other continents, it is therefore in my opinion already unavoidably necessary for a, so to say 'closing-chord,' to initiate you also into those of my thoughts which began in my mentation on the last day of my sojourn among them in the city of New York and which ended on the steamer as it was moving away from that continent towards the East.

"On that day I was sitting in one of the singular cafes there named 'Child's,' situated at what is called 'Columbus Circle,' awaiting the beings from the continent Europe who had accompanied me to this continent, to go with them to the dock of the outgoing steamer, and I was looking out of the window at the various passing beings from among the inhabitants of that city, who although according to automatized perception were distinguishable on that day in exterior appearance—of course chiefly due to the usage, recently fixed in them more than in any beings of any other continents of becoming 'slaves' to always that same maleficent terrestrial invention which they call 'fashion'—nevertheless somehow seemed to me, in respect of their inner content, particularly alike.

"Observing them, I thought just about the final deduction I had made the day before, that in the present period of the flow of the Heropass in the common Planetary process of the ordinary existence of these in general strange three-brained beings, the source of the intensive manifestation of that already long established particularity of the general totality of their strange psyche, which one of the highest sacred Individuals once characterized by the words, 'the-periodic-fundamental-source-of-the-issuing-of-new-causes-of-abnormality,' is represented just by the beings of this new grouping.

"The shock for the beginning of associations and for my further active meditations this time, was the constatation I happened to make of the fact that everything constituting what is called the 'totality-of-the-subjective-appearance' of each one of them—such as clothes, gestures, manners and in general all the established usages which all three-brained beings acquire in the ordinary process of their collective existence—is a totally exact imitation exclusively only of all that exists among the beings of various other independent groupings breeding on other continents, an imitation of just that which is considered by the free beings of these other groupings, that is to say, by those beings among them who have already experienced and consequently been disappointed in everything the process of ordinary existence can give, as unworthy of manifestation by beings similar to them.

"This accidental constatation of mine at once very much astonished me, chiefly because I was already informed from every aspect and wholly convinced that in the present period everywhere on this planet the beings of almost all the other groupings, those recently formed as well as those which are at a very advanced stage of their community, imitate to the full all the innovations of the beings of this still quite recently formed grouping and enthusiastically adopt these innovations in the process of their ordinary existence, and at the same time all the external manifestations of the beings of this new grouping and consequently the 'inner-subjective-significance' which engenders these external manifestations, consist only of that which, as I have already said, has become to the great grief of the free beings of there other independent groupings fixed and inherent in the common presences of the ordinary beings of these groupings.

"In consequence of this unexpected constatation of mine, there then arose in me a highly intensive impulse of curiosity to make clear to myself the logical causes which had engendered this terrestrial incongruity.

"All that day, while sitting in this 'Child's' awaiting the arrival of the beings from the continent of Europe who had accompanied me, and while riding in the 'motor taxi' and also while on the boat itself, I continued to ponder very actively the solution of this question, of course appearing to strangers as an automatic observer of everything proceeding around me; and in the ability outwardly to appear such, in order to resemble them in this respect, and thus not be, so to say conspicuous, or as they say there, 'not-to-strike-the-eye,' I became there on the Earth ideally, or as they would say 'artistically' expert.

"Sitting on the deck looking at the twinkling of the lights on the shore of this continent gradually growing fainter as the steamer moved away towards the East, and pondering over and logically comparing all the facts ensuing one from the other, I, as a result, made it almost entirely clear to myself just why and how the said incongruity could have arisen on this ill-fated planet.

"At the beginning of these ponderings of mine, I established many facts which had enabled this to arise, but afterwards, when I began successively to exclude those which inevitably ensue—as is done in such cases—then as a result one fact became clear to me, which, though at first glance insignificant, astonished even me and which, as it turned out, was all the time and still is, the originating cause of this abnormality there.

"And that is to say, it turned out, that owing to the consequences of that same famous 'education' of theirs, so many times mentioned by me, there inevitably arise in the common presence of each of them in general, during his age preparatory for responsible existence, to whatever independent group he may belong, data for the definite conviction that in the former epochs on their planets, the beings similar to them had never perfected themselves to that Reason to which their contemporaries have attained and in which they can still continue to perfect themselves.

"When my thoughts were concentrated on this and I began to recall my former impressions concerning this question, those consciously and also those incidentally and automatically perceived during my previous observations of them in general, I gradually established that all your favorites, particularly in the last thirty centuries, had indeed become convinced during all their responsible existence that their contemporary what they call 'civilization' is simply the result of the direct continuation of the development of the Reason which began at the very commencement of the arising of three-brained beings on their planet.

"And so when the beings, their contemporaries of any grouping, owing to the formation in them while still in their preparatory age of data for this false conviction, accidentally became the possessors of something which is accounted in the given period desirable and thereby acquire authority, and at the same time, find out, of course also accidentally, about some idea of the beings of past epochs which has already existed many times, and, giving it out as having been thought of by themselves, spread it around, then the beings of other groupings, through the absence in their common presences, due to wrong education, of the data which it is proper to all three-brained beings of responsible age to have in their presences and which engender what are called, 'an-instinctive-sensing-of-reality' and 'a-broad-outlook,' believe firstly that this idea has arisen on their planet for quite the first time, and secondly that once the practical application of it has been actualized by those who already possess the said 'something-desirable,' then it must indeed be very good, and they forthwith begin to imitate everything really good as well as bad, notwithstanding its complete contrariety to everything there is and to everything well fixed in their ordinary existence, merely in order to possess that which 'for-today' is considered desirable.

"I then even remembered that I had already once long before very seriously reflected on this matter in the period of my fifth personal sojourn on the surface of your planet, when the city of Babylon was considered the center of culture of these strange three-brained beings, and when I had, on account of some similar question, to make a' logical-analysis' of just this strange feature of the psyche of these peculiar three-brained beings.

"I then among other things, also reasoned as follows:

"That they think thus, may perhaps be possibly justified by taking it into consideration that owing to the abnormal conditions of ordinary existence established in past epochs, no exact information has reached them about events which have occurred in the past in the process of the existence of the three-brained beings who existed before them on their planet; but how is it possible to admit that up till now there has not arisen in the mentation of any one of them—in whom it has already been established that even until quite recently there does sometimes proceed a 'something' similar to the process of 'comparative-logic'—at least the following simple and almost, as they themselves would call it, 'childish idea'?

"And namely, if as they themselves say and are even certain, that their planet has already existed many many centuries with their species on it beings similar to them, that is to say, beings who could mentate—and that many many millions of them must have also arisen and existed before them, would there really not have been then, from among these many many millions, at least a few beings who could also have invented for the well-being of their contemporaries all kinds of comforts, as in the given case, these contemporary American beings are now inventing and all the other are uncritically and even rapturously imitating, as for example; 'comfortable seats' in the water-closets, preserves, and so on and so forth?

"This unpardonable lack of thought is all the more strange in that they themselves admit the existence of many, as they now call them, 'ancient-sages,' and also do not deny the great amount of most varied information which has come down to them concerning the many objective truths elucidated by these sages, which information, by the way, certain of your favorites at the present time are, without any remorse of conscience, giving out as having been thought of by themselves and exploiting to the full for their various egoistic aims, without at all suspecting that the totality of the results of these wiseacrings of theirs will inevitably lead their descendants sooner or later to total destruction.

"This particularity of their mentation—very complicated for any 'logical-analysis' undertaken for the purpose of understanding it—engendering in them this false conviction, was during the whole of my observations of them, beginning with the end of the existence of the continent Atlantis, always, so to say, the 'gravity-center-cause' of almost all the more or less major events unfavorable for them in the process of their collective existence.

"Thanks to this false conviction, the result of their strange mentation, and in addition, thanks to the effect on the totality of the functioning of their feelings, of the consequences of the properties of the organ Kundabuffer which inevitably arise in their presences at responsible age and which are called 'envy,' 'greed,' and 'jealousy,' it always happens there, that when the beings of any grouping become the possessors of anything which in the given period is considered desirable, in most cases because of that maleficent practice fixed in their everyday existence, which they express by the words 'not-to-cease-progressing,' there immediately arises in the common presences of all the beings of other groupings, on whatever continents they may breed, as soon as the rumor of this reaches them, the desire to have the same, and from that moment, there arises in each of them, firstly, the need to imitate them, and secondly, the 'indubitable-certainty' that the beings of this other grouping must exist very correctly, since they have been able to acquire just what in the given period is accounted desirable.

"In this connection, the so to say, 'piquancy' of the strangeness of the mentation of your favorites is that there never occurs in their mentation the process called 'to ponder' in order to understand if only approximately the true causes of the possession by others of that on account of which there arise in them 'envy,' 'greed,' 'jealousy' and so on.

"And so my boy, in spite of the fact that as far as the acquisition and hence the possession of the results attained by the conscious labors and intentional sufferings of the three-brained beings of past epochs of their planet are concerned, the beings of their new group have absolutely nothing at all, but consist as to inner content as well as to exterior manifestations, only of everything bad that exists among contemporary beings of other independent groupings—solely because in recent times they have accidentally become the possessors of just that which in the objective sense is most despicable, yet which owing in general to the fixed abnormal conditions of the ordinary existence of these unfortunates is considered desirable—nevertheless the beings of all the other groupings now imitate to the full everything they invent.

"Of all the maleficent inventions of the beings of this contemporary grouping which have accidentally acquired authority, the most harmful for their common presences—in respect of the possibility of rectifying in the future the so to say already actualized maleficences—must be considered the practice they have established of passing a great part of the time of their existences in high houses.

"In order that you may clearly picture to yourself the significance of all the harm from just this invention of theirs, I must first of all explain to you the following:

"Do you remember, when I spoke to you about that 'maleficent-means' existing there at the present time called 'sport,' I said that duration of the existence of these favorites of yours was in the beginning also 'Fulasnitamnian,' that is to say they had to exist until their body 'Kesdjan' was completely coated in them and perfected up to the required gradation of Reason, and that afterwards, when very abnormal conditions of ordinary being-existence began to be established there, Great Nature was constrained to actualize their presences and also the subsequent process of their existence on the principle of 'Itoklanoz,' that is, according to the results of certain surrounding causes.

"Thereafter, one of these causes has also been the 'degree-of-the-density-of-the-vibrations' of their 'second-being-food,' that is, as they themselves would say, the 'degree-of-the-condensation-of-the-air-they-breathe.'

"The point is, that this cosmic formation which serves as the second food for beings, is also composed according to the second fundamental common cosmic law of the sacred Triamazikamno, and is also actualized by means of its three heterogeneous cosmic substances.

"And namely, the first is the emanation of the sun of that system in which this same definite cosmic arising serves as the 'second-food' for beings.

"The second are the substances transformed on that planet itself on which the beings fed by this food exist.

"And the third are those substances which are transformed through the other planets of this system and which come to the given planet through their radiations.

"And so, the process of fusion of all those substances required for the normal formation and existence of beings, which are transformed by the planet itself and which actualize the second holy force of the Sacred Triamazikamno, can proceed in the correspondingly required definite proportion, only within certain limits of the atmosphere from the surface of planets, because owing to the second grade cosmic law called 'Tenikdoa,' or as your favorites would call it 'Law-of-gravity,' these substances cannot penetrate beyond a definite height of the atmosphere.

"In my opinion you can yourself apprehend all the subsequent ensuing consequences of this question which I have just now brought to light, and compose data in yourself for your own opinion of the significance of this invention of theirs.

"I think my boy, that I have now already fully satisfied your curiosity concerning these 'dollar-fox-trotting' followers of what is called 'Christian Science.'

"In the name of Objective Justice it now only remains for me to remark that whatever they may turn into in the future, I had however during my existence among them, the possibility of inwardly resting, and for this I ought now to express to them my sincere thanks.

"And you, just you, my heir, to whom has already been transmitted and will be transmitted by inheritance everything acquired by me during my long existence—of course only in so far as you yourself will deserve it by your own conscientious being-existence and honorable service to the ALL-COMMON FATHER MAINTAINER, OUR ENDLESSNESS—I command you, if you happen for some reason or other to be on the planet Earth, to visit without fail the city of New York, or if by that time this city should no longer exist, then at least to stop at that place where it was situated and to utter aloud:

"'In this place, my beloved grandfather, my just Teacher Beelzebub pleasantly passed a few moments of his existence.'

"I even charge you—of course again as the heir to whom, as is general, will devolve the fulfillment of the obligations which your predecessor took upon himself and which for some reason or other were left unfulfilled—specially to turn your attention to and to elucidate a question which greatly interested me and which I personally was unable to elucidate as it was still premature to do so, that is to say, I charge you to elucidate for yourself into what a 'maleficent-form' for their descendants—if of course by that time their descendants still continue to arise—will the results have become molded of the 'disease' very widespread at that time, which one of their Misters, by name Onanson, called 'writing-itch.'

"And indeed my boy, having then during my stay there, a more or less close relationship with many of them, I very soon found out that almost every one of them either had already written a book, or at that time was writing one, or was getting ready quickly to burst into authorship.

"Although this peculiar 'disease' was then, as I have already said, widespread amongst almost all the beings of this continent, moreover among the beings of both sexes and without distinction of age, yet among the beings at the beginning of responsible age, that is, as they themselves say, among the 'youth,' and particularly among those who had many pimples on their faces and an abundance of liquid streaming from their nostrils, it was for some reason or other, as it is said 'epidemical.'

"I must further remark in just these connections, that there flourished that specific particularity of the strangeness of the common psyche of these peculiar beings who have taken your fancy, which has already long existed in their collective existence and which has been formulated by the following words: 'the-concentration-of-interests-on-an-idea-which-has-accidentally-become-the-question-of-the-day.'

"Here also, many of them who turned out to be a little, as is said there, 'more-cunning,' and in whom the data for the being-impulse called 'instinctively-to-refrain-from-all-manifestations-which-may-lead-surrounding-beings-similar-to-oneself-into-error' were more atrophied, organized various what are called 'schools' and composed all kinds of 'manuals,' in which much attention was given to showing in detail just what the sequence of words should be so that all compositions should be better perceived and assimilated by the reader.

"And thus all those attending these 'schools' and all readers of these 'manuals' being themselves in regard to Being and in regard to information concerning reality exactly such types as our Teacher Mullah Nassr Eddin defined by the words: 'Nullities-with-an-atmosphere-of-unendurable-vibrations' began according to these indications, 'to wiseacre'; and since firstly, thanks to various other abnormalities fixed in the conditions of the ordinary existence of the beings of this new grouping, the process of reading has previously in general become an organic need of theirs, and secondly, that it was possible to appreciate the contents of any composition exclusively only by reading it through, and all the other beings of this continent, seduced, what is more, by all kinds of, as they say there, 'loud' titles, read and read, and parallel with this, it was definitely noticeable how their mentation, which had already, so to say, become 'diluted' without this, continued to become more 'diluted' and still more 'diluted.'"

At this point of Beelzebub's tales, what is called a "cross-current" or "agitation" began in the ether which penetrated the whole of the ship "*Karnak*." This signified that the passengers of the ship "*Karnak*" were summoned to the "Djamdjampal," that is, that "refectory" of the ship in which all the passengers together periodically fed on the "second-and-first-being-foods."

So Beelzebub, Hassein, and Ahoon ceased their conversation and hastily went off to the 'Djamdjampal.'

CHAPTER XLIII

Beelzebub's Survey Of The Process Of The Periodic Destruction Of Men Or Beelzebub's Opinion Of War

ON THE following day, when the trans-solar-system ship *Karnak* set off from the planet 'Deskaldino' in the direction of the planet Karatas, the grandson of Beelzebub, little Hassein, sat as usual at Beelzebub's feet, and turned to him with the following words:

"Dear and wise grandfather of mine, I've never been able to reconcile certain things concerning the beings of the planet Earth; and this question has been worrying me more and more during the last Dionosk. (Dionosk—the word expresses the duration of a certain movement of one of the suns of the first magnitude, that is, it is something like what on the planet Earth is called twenty-four hours).

"From all your tales about these beings, I have definitely understood that although the reason is nearly always automatic among the majority of beings, yet even with this Reason they can quite often think fairly logically, and sometimes discover in the phenomena proceeding on their planet various more or less exact laws of Nature, according to which they invent something or other.

"At the same time that special peculiarity of the beings of that planet, namely, their peculiarity of becoming periodically engaged in mutual destruction has been like a red thread all through your tales.

"I cannot understand why over such a long period they have so far not perceived and become aware that this peculiarity of theirs is the horror of horrors in the whole Universe.

"Is it possible that they never think sufficiently seriously to feel this horror, and that they do not try to find some means of abolishing this awful horror from their planet?

"Why is it?

"There, my dear grandfather, that is what I have wished so much to understand during the last Dionosk. But I can discover nothing by myself in any way whatever.

"Help me, kind grandfather, to understand this as well, why this phenomenal peculiarity has existed on that unfortunate planet for so many long centuries."

In reply to this question of his grandson, Beelzebub related as follows:

He began thus: "Ah! my dear boy! This very peculiarity of theirs is the chief reason why the processes of existence on that planet are always full of every sort of extraordinary absurdity.

"You ask whether it is possible that they never think seriously enough about this question, to see the horror of it?

"Don't they think seriously and don't they see!!!!

"Some of them even very often think seriously; and they both see and understand that their mutual destruction is a hideousness beyond words to describe: but no result of course, is ever obtained from the serious thinking of certain beings of that place.

"No result is ever obtained first of all, because such beings are isolated, and secondly, owing to the conditions of existence abnormally established there, but chiefly from the absence of a general planetary organization on that planet.

"It is impossible to spread there in the consciousness of other beings, any of the clear realizations of individual beings; and hence, from the serious thinking and realizations of such individual beings, no result is ever obtained.

"Owing to the conditions of existence abnormally established on your planet, it has gradually come about that the psyche of every Earth-being is such from childhood that he can think sincerely and see things in their real light exclusively only when his hunger and other needs have been thoroughly satiated.

"And as owing to the conditions abnormally established there not all the beings can satisfy themselves to the degree of satiation, the majority of them for this and still other reasons even with all their mental wishes cannot see and feel reality.

"This sincere thinking and feeling of reality has already long ago become there on your planet a very rare luxury, inaccessible to the majority. Certain beings among them, however, have had, for quite a long time, the means of satisfying themselves to the degree of satiety—the beings namely called 'important' and 'powerful'—those very Earth-beings in fact who could possibly do something towards the abolition of this evil, or at least towards its diminution. But these 'important' and 'powerful' beings who have the means of satiety, and who could possibly do something towards this end, do absolutely nothing at all, for quite other reasons.

"And this is because the beings of your planet, particularly those young beings who later on become 'important' and 'powerful' do not profit at all by the years given to them by Nature, which in general Nature gives to all the beings of our great Universe, to prepare themselves for becoming responsible beings; but on the contrary they spend it entirely, either in 'self-calming' or in acquiring those peculiarities inculcated in their celebrated 'education,' those very peculiarities on account of which most of them ultimately become the individuums called 'Hasnamusses.'

"So when your favorites become responsible beings, or as they themselves say, when they become adult and discharge responsible duties, they have in themselves nothing of which the thinking of beings consists.

"Besides on account of this abnormal education of theirs, nothing is formed in them that enables them to do anything real; and, again, owing to this same abnormal education, very many of those peculiarities formed in their psyche by inheritance, as consequences of the properties of the organ Kundabuffer, gradually materialize and become organic functions.

"Those organic functions which are chiefly formed are called 'egoism,' 'prejudice,' 'vanity,' 'self-love' and so on. Our dear sage Mullah Nassr Eddin very wisely defines similar beings, particularly contemporary 'important' or 'powerful' beings of the Earth in the following words: 'The degree of the importance of men, depends on the number of their corns.'

"Well, whenever those beings of your planet, those very same 'important' and 'powerful' beings who can procure satiety and could possibly do something towards the abolition from their planet of this phenomenal evil peculiarity, are actually satiated, and are reclining in their easy chairs for better digestion, then when it is really possible for them to think sincerely about the horrors proceeding on their planet, they indulge only in that criminal 'self-calming' of theirs instead.

"But as none of the beings of our Universe, including the beings of your planet, can exist without reasoning, your favorites in order to be able to indulge quite freely in their 'self-calming' have in a very masterful fashion gradually accustomed themselves to the condition in which, instead of thinking seriously, 'it' thinks in them quite mechanically, that is to say, entirely without the participation of their own 'I.'

"Justice must be done them; they have brought it to perfection.

"At the present time, their thoughts can flow in all directions without any effort whatsoever on the part of their personalities.

"For instance, when these 'important' and 'powerful' beings of the Earth are reclining in their arm-chairs after satiation, the thoughts in them receiving only shocks from the reflexes of their stomachs and sexual organs, walk about freely in all directions full of pleasure, just as their soul wishes, exactly as if they were strolling in the evening in Paris along the

Boulevard des Capucines.

"In short, when these 'important' and 'powerful' beings of the Earth are reclining in their easy chairs, the following trains of thought unroll in them: as for instance how he can get back on his friend John Smith, who, that day looked at his favorite lady, not with his right eye but just with his left.

"Or such an 'important' Earth-being who is digesting his food thinks: why the horse he had backed for yesterday's race did not win, but some outsider.

"Or he thinks, why did such and such stocks, which in reality are worth nothing, rise on the Stock Exchange higher and higher every day?

"Or intimately he thinks as follows: 'If only I were in the place of John Smith who invented the new method of the culture of flies for making ivory from the bones of their skeletons, I should do this and that with the money and not like that idiot who does not eat himself and won't allow others to eat,' and so on and so forth.

"It does however sometimes also happen that a few 'important' and 'powerful' beings of the Earth think not from the reflexes of their stomachs and sexual organs, but very sincerely and seriously about real things. Strictly speaking this sincerity occurs frequently in most of them chemically on account of external causes.

"And these external causes are as follows:

"When somebody very near to them dies, or when somebody deeply and grievously offends them or when somebody evokes their tenderness by doing for them something very good and quite unexpected; or ultimately when they really feel the approach of the end of their existence, that is of their death.

"Well, my dear boy, if these important and powerful beings of the Earth should by chance for some reason or other, think sincerely in one of these states about this peculiarity of their fellow men, they themselves would become also inwardly very greatly agitated and of course inwardly resolve to begin to do everything necessary, at all costs, that this great evil should never occur again on their planet.

"But as soon as the stomachs of these 'important' and 'powerful' beings who inwardly get greatly agitated begin to feel empty, those beings immediately forget all about their inner resolution, not only this but they themselves unconsciously begin to repeat everything that usually serves as a cause for the outbreak of similar processes between social organizations.

"Very often it also happens there, that these same 'important' and 'powerful' beings themselves deliberately aim at doing everything to ensure not only that the process of reciprocal destruction should subsequently take place but on as large a scale as possible.

"They do this because from their processes they always expect either for themselves personally or for their relatives some material or other advantage.

"And they hope that this process should take place on a larger scale, only because they or their relatives should also gain on a larger scale.

"It also happens there that certain of these 'important' and 'powerful' beings unite and form a society with the aim of abolishing this 'arch-criminal' peculiarity from the Earth.

"Just when I left that solar system and was on that planet for the last time, there was again a great deal of talk about the formation of such a society; it seems that they proposed to call this new society of theirs the 'League of Nations.'

"I say 'again' because there had already frequently been formed such societies which always died in a equally strange manner, that is without a struggle.

"Of course from this new society of beings-men also, nothing practical will result, just as nothing practical resulted on former occasions when similar societies with similar aims arose among Earth beings-men. I very well remember when such a society first arose. It was in the town Samoniks in the land Tikliamish, when this Tikliamish was the main center of culture for beings of the whole of the planet.

"It was then first that 'important' and 'powerful' beings of the majority of the communities of the continent Asia, met together with the wish to arrive at a general agreement, that reciprocal destruction should never again occur amongst communities.

"This society had for its motto: 'God is, where man's blood is not shed.'

"But very soon, owing to their own diverse and pretentious aims, these 'important' and 'powerful' beings of the Earth quarreled amongst themselves and ultimately separated without having accomplished anything.

"A few centuries after Tikliamish, a similar society again arose but in the land then called 'Mongolplanzura,' also on the continent Asia.

"And there it took the motto: 'Love others and God will love you.'

"On this occasion also the results were the same.

"Still later beings-men again formed such a society in the land Egypt, but on this occasion under the text: 'When you know how to create a flea, then only dare to kill.'

"Beings-men of the land Persia had for a similar society of theirs the motto: 'All men are divine, and if even one is murdered all will become nothing.'

"The last such society arose in the town which, it seems was called Mosulopolis, also on the continent Asia.

"And this happened quite recently, only about four or five of their centuries ago. And this society of beings-men took the motto at the time of its formation: 'The Earth must be free for all.'

"But on an early misunderstanding amongst the members

of this society, they gave it another name; and the society ended its existence under the motto: 'The Earth for men only.'

"Beings-men of the society, 'The Earth must be free for all,' might have accomplished something effective because, first of all, they had as the basis of their aims a program which could be realized; and secondly, they were all without exception old and respected beings who had already experienced the planetary existence and in consequence were disillusioned about everything which ordinary planetary existence can generally give. There were therefore among them fewer who were personal, egoistic, vain and had other characteristics, on account of which similar societies usually fail. But the chief reason why something effective might have resulted from this society of beings-men, was that there was scarcely a single 'important' and 'powerful' being amongst its members.

"But all the same on account of their egoistic and pretentious aims, these beings usually dispatch with musical accompaniment, all the attainments sooner or later of any society of an ordinary planetary kind, whatever it may be, and to which they belong, to the famous pig of Mullah Nassr Eddin, which always gorges without any 'drawing-room' ceremonies whatsoever.

"These 'important' and 'powerful' Earth beings do not always frustrate the aims of any society—when, that is, these aims are advantageous to them personally or to beings of their own caste.

"But if some advantage could result for all the beings of the whole planet without difference of caste, then at the first small crisis in the affairs of the particular society, the trouble immediately becomes too fatiguing; at the very mention of these problems, painful grimaces appear on their faces.

"And as regards the society 'The Earth must be free for all,' nothing resulted, as I have already told you, owing to a misunderstanding, although the beings, members of that society had already by that time accomplished a great deal toward their aim. A great deal was accomplished of what it is almost impossible to accomplish there under those conditions which always prevail on that incomparably peculiar planet.

"And what occurred with the beings-men, members of this society which were called 'The Earth must be free for all,' I shall also tell you; your knowledge of the cause of the breaking up of this society of beings-men may be very useful for your better understanding of the psyche of your favorites. But I will tell you about this a little later.

"And meanwhile for your further elucidations know and remember the fact that at the present moment on your planet, beings-men are again forming, or they have already formed, quite a similar society which will be called, or which is already called, 'The League of Nations.'

"The problem of this new society there will also be to find some means of abolishing that terrifying peculiarity of theirs. Of course on this occasion as well, there will be no result. And there will be no result chiefly because this peculiarity has already entered into the flesh and blood of the beings of the Earth; and beings with the kind of Reason that contemporary beings of the Earth have, will of course be unable to accomplish anything decisive at all.

"Nevertheless, those 'gentlemen,' the contemporary 'important' and 'powerful' beings will obtain by means of this society of theirs, a result very important for them.

"Namely, owing to this brand new society of theirs, of which they consent to be members, they will have a further excuse for escaping their wives and mistresses and to pass the time pleasantly amidst the circle of their friends, being similar to themselves—without being under the terrifying silent observations of their 'possessors,' namely, their wives, mothers-in-law, mistresses and so on; that is to say, they will boldly enter into those official 'Five-o'clock-teas,' which no doubt will be frequently arranged for the purpose of the business, presumably connected with the aims of this important official society, called the 'League of Nations.'

"From the stratagems of your contemporary favorites nothing effective will ever result, because if those Earth-beings of former epochs did not attain anything at all—those Earth-beings who, when they became responsible beings were sometimes able to attain, at least, in the sense of Being, to what is called 'Self-remembering'—then the contemporary beings of the Earth who attain, in the sense of Being, only as our wise Mullah Nassr Eddin would say, 'As far as they are already beginning to distinguish Mama from Papa,' can of course never achieve the complete abolition of this peculiarity, which, as I have already told you, has entered into the flesh and blood of the beings of that unfortunate planet.

"Such societies of beings-men arose there usually after one of their big processes of reciprocal destruction, and they usually arose in the following manner.

"During the latest process of their reciprocal destruction, or as they say, during the latest war, it happened that certain 'important' or 'powerful' beings of the Earth, themselves suffered some very serious losses, on account of which, there occurred within them mechanically what the Very Holy Ashiata Shiemash had hoped for all the beings of the Earth.

"And that is to say, the function of Objective Conscience which still remains in their organism, mechanically passes temporarily into their consciousness. And therefore in these 'important' or 'powerful' beings, Conscience begins to speak, and they begin to see this Earth peculiarity in its real light.

"The result of all this is that there appears a genuinely sincere wish in them to do everything possible in order to effect the abolition of that terrifying horror which proceeds on their planet.

"And usually, it so happens there that several of these 'important' and 'powerful' beings with resurrected consciences, unite in order to discover collectively, some means of realizing these sincere wishes of theirs.

"It is thus that such societies are usually begun by beings with resurrected consciences. And then beings might perhaps somehow succeed in affecting something, but there the chief evil is that other ordinary 'important' and 'powerful' beings very quickly as a rule begin to take part in these societies, not because their consciences begin to speak, but only because, according to abnormal conditions of existence which have been established there, they must infallibly, as they are 'important' be in every 'important' society.

"And then as a rule, these same 'important' beings, as I have already told you, with their personal, egoistic, and vainglorious aims, not only very quickly send flying up the chimney all the problems and all that has already been done by beings with resurrected consciences, but very soon put a spoke in the wheels of the first founders of these societies.

"In consequence those societies of beings, formed there for the general planetary welfare, always die very quickly and as I have already told you, even without a struggle. Regarding the effective results of the good undertakings of 'important' beings, there is also a very wise saying by our greatly respected Mullah Nassr Eddin, when he says:

'Past centuries have proved to us, that Karabaghian asses will never sing like nightingales, and will not be willing to restrain their taste for Shooshoonian thistles.'

"Do you know, my boy, during all the many centuries of my very close observations of the beings of this particular planet, I have never once noticed in the societies formed by beings-men of the Earth for the collective search of means for the happy existence of the great masses that there ever participated in these societies, beings with more or less Objective Reason, to which as I have already told you, quite a good number of them have nevertheless already attained, owing to their persevering self-perfecting.

"And beings with Objective Reason do not become members of such societies as these for the following reason.

"Owing always to the same abnormally established conditions of existence, any beings who wish to take part in any society must, without fail, be 'important' and an 'important' being there, again owing to abnormally established conditions of existence, can only be a being who either has a great deal of money, or who becomes famous amongst the other beings of the whole planet, or at least of one of the continents.

"And so, my boy, again owing to the same abnormal conditions, which have gradually come to prevail on that unfortunate planet, only those beings can become rich or famous among whom conscience is absolutely non-existent.

"And as, in general conscience is always connected with Objective Reason, then of course in any being in whom there is Objective Reason there is always conscience also, and consequently, such a being in whom there is conscience, will never be 'important' amongst the ordinary beings of the Earth.

"Thus a being with Objective Reason can never take part in any society of beings-men, composed of beings who are 'important' and 'powerful.'

"And about this same question on your planet, it follows as our dear Mullah Nassr Eddin once said: 'This is a real punishment: pull at the tail and the mane gets stuck: pull at the mane and the tail gets stuck.'

"As regards the discovery of means of abolishing this Earth peculiarity—a peculiarity which is also indeed firmly rooted in their psyches—it is, in my opinion, impossible in any way whatsoever, to effect anything at all by rules and agreements, by which methods the ancient beings of the Earth tried, and without doubt also the contemporary members of The League of Nations will also try to achieve their aim.

"And about this peculiarity of theirs one can only say the same as the Very Holy Ashiata Shiemash once said regarding the consequences of the properties of the organ Kundabuffer in his meditations entitled 'The Terror of the Situation.'

"'If it is possible to save the beings of the Earth, then only Time can do so.'

"So we can now also say the same, that is that if this Earth peculiarity can ever be exterminated, then it can only be done by Time, or by beings with a very highly developed Reason, or by some exceptional cosmic events.

"And these arguments and various temporary agreements by which it was and is wished to attain this end, will never lead any of these societies of Earth-beings to anything at all, except perhaps only to those stratagems of theirs which serve contemporary beings of the Earth as material for instance, for their inevitable newspapers, for salon gossip, and of course, for the speculations of exchange jugglers Hasnamusses.

"In general the present position of affairs in regard to this peculiarity of the Earth-beings is such that if any beings with highly developed Reason, and even beings with ordinary Reason from the planet itself, sincerely wish to do good for all the beings of that unfortunate planet, they must do only what can be useful for beings of the planet in the future.

"If members of this contemporary society The League of Nations would even only do what they could, proportionate to their forces, they would render a very great service to the future beings of their planet.

"As for instance, if at the present time, they ceased to busy themselves in an effort to bring about the complete abolition of this peculiarity from their planet, which is already a far too difficult problem for their reason, and would instead try to do only what is proportionate to their forces, trying, let us say, to bring about the destruction of that Hasnamussian science invented by a number of pimpled Earth-beings.

"These pimpled Hasnamusses indefatigably prove in this science of theirs, that the periodical destruction on the Earth is very, very necessary, and that if it did not exist, the result would be first of all, that there would be a surplus of beings-men on the Earth, to an impossible degree, and secondly, that such terrifying economical horrors would occur on the Earth as that beings-men would begin to eat each other.

"If only the members of this new 'important' society, The League of Nations, would busy themselves trying to effect the destruction of this science, they might perhaps greatly help the beings of the future by preventing these idiotic ideas reaching them—the ideas of which there are already more than enough without these, and which in their totality form in their minds that property, the manifestation of which they call doubt concerning the existence of the soul. The existence of this doubt on the Earth is the chief cause of the existence in them of these properties which three-centered beings really ought not to have.

"Owing chiefly to these same 'doubts' the beings of that planet cannot feel deeply all those truths always felt by all the beings of the Universe and in consequence of which all beings always strive only to perfect themselves more quickly to the sacred degree of the Divine Reason necessary for a three-centered being.

"But these contemporary society beings of the Earth, and namely the members of this new society, the League of Nations, will of course, not concern themselves to try to destroy this Hasnamussian science. They will not do so only because they will consider it beneath their dignity to occupy themselves with such a question.

"What!! Such 'important' members of such 'important' societies, to become suddenly occupied with such a trifling question!

"Besides if they should occupy themselves with this question, first of all, they might offend one of their caste, which God forbid! And secondly, if they should succeed in destroying this science, an unprecedented scandal might occur, since it would be their first attainment for the general welfare, which attainments are usually put forward as problems of societies formed of 'important' and 'powerful' beings of the Earth.

"Such aims have never before been attained there on the Earth and if they should now succeed, it would be very offensive for all former members as well as for future members like themselves.

"And thirdly, they will not do this, because, in general, beings of the Earth habitually occupy themselves with and judge only those matters which are higher than their Reason; they do not like at all to occupy themselves with those matters which are proportionate to their reason and their forces.

"For instance, to be occupied in trying to effect the destruction of this science would seem to them quite unsuitable for such an 'important' society of which they are members, and more too, 'important' and 'powerful' members.

"Owing to such a trait of character, the beings of your planet, have even acquired an organic need always to teach and put on the 'right' path others only and not themselves at all, and in such a way on account of this, this highly interesting disease has begun to exist there called 'the Mote and the Beam.'

"Listen, my dear Hassein, I think it will do you no harm if I also give you some useful advice such as our dear Ahoon was giving you.

"You remember that when our dear Ahoon told you how the contemporary beings of the Earth, understand Art, he, by the way, personally advised you, that if, for some reason or other, you should happen to be on that planet Earth, you should always be very cautious with contemporary representatives of art so as not to offend them and make enemies for yourself.

"He also directed you what to do so that they might admire and be on very good terms with you. Our dear Ahoon then cited all their weaknesses.

"He spoke about their self-love and about their pride, and their vanity, and about many other special peculiarities of theirs. He also then told you in what circumstances, which of these peculiarities one should, without fail, tickle.

"This advice of his, it cannot be denied was very good, and indeed among these types, one must, without fail, tickle these weaknesses of theirs.

"But personally I find this advice unpractical for you and not perfect, because, first of all, not all the beings of the Earth are like these representatives of Art, so that you cannot apply this advice to everyone; and secondly, because it will be difficult for you to remember all these numerous weaknesses of theirs, and every time you will have to think very hard in what circumstances one or other of these numerous weaknesses of theirs should be tickled.

"But I myself propose to tell you about only one weakness which almost all these Earth beings have. If by chance you should have to exist among them, then do everything with the help of this weakness of theirs.

"Owing to this weakness of theirs, about which I wish to tell you, you will not only be on friendly terms with everybody there, but even if you wish, you will be able, owing to the knowledge of this weakness of theirs, to guarantee fully your peaceful existence there, as far as the necessary money is concerned.

"Now listen, owing to the conditions of ordinary existence which were already very abnormally established there long ago, their psyche has taken especially during recent times, such a form, that in all of them without exception both young and old, male and female, after their appearance in the world of HIS ENDLESSNESS, and as soon as they begin to differ according to the difference there is between an Astrakhan herring and a Paris brioche this same peculiar weakness immediately appears in them.

"And namely from that moment on, they cease forever to observe their own faults, and begin to see only the various faults of others, and in consequence there is formed among them from that time on, an organic necessity always to teach others and to put others on the path of 'truth.'

"They even begin to teach these others such things, the ideas of which they have not yet even dreamed of. And if these others do not learn from them, or at least do not pretend that they wish to learn, they not only become offended, but even always become quite genuinely agitated.

"But if some of these others learn from them, or at least pretend that they wish very much to do so, then they will not only love and esteem these others but they themselves will also feel happy and content.

"Here it is interesting to observe that only in cases such as these, can your favorites speak about others without being critical. On the contrary, they will always praise these others who learn from them, and say the best things about them, which they could never possibly know.

"And so, my boy, if for some reason or other, you ever happen to exist among them, then I strongly advise you, always to pretend that you wish to learn from them.

"Do this also with their children and then not only will you be on good terms with all of them but even in every family you will be honored as a special friend.

"Know that every one of them, however insignificant he may be himself in his essence, yet owing to his self-conceit, which is only a product in him of his automatic misunderstanding, always regards the behavior and actions of others haughtily and even with disdain, particularly if this behavior and these actions of others are sharply opposed to his own subjectively established views.

"In such cases your favorites always become very indignant and by the way, this inner rage of theirs is also one of those numerous causes owing to which their ordinary Being-existence proceeds with continuous moral suffering. For instance, this inner rage of theirs later continues for a very long time, to react by momentum on their psyche 'Semzekionally,' or as it can be otherwise said, 'depressionably.' And this inner rage also makes them nervous, as they themselves say, owing to which they also become quite uncontrollable in their daily affairs which have no connection with the original causes of their nervousness.

"In spite of the fact that your favorites are brimful of all other kinds of misfortunes, they make their already abnormal existence quite objectively intolerable, owing to this property of theirs of becoming uselessly indignant on account of the defects of others.

"I repeat, your favorites always become furious because certain others have such and such defects, but they never see their own defects and do not acknowledge them, and in consequence this same organic need develops in them about others on the path of 'truth.'

"Apart from everything else and only owing to this single property of theirs, does the existence of beings on that peculiar planet become super-tragic.

"For instance, at every step one meets there pictures like the following. One of these freaks for instance, who is a slave of others to the point of humiliation, or as they themselves say there, who finds himself as far as his whole inner experience is concerned under somebody's thumb, for instance of his wife or his mistress or someone similar who in some way or other penetrates into his inner significance. In other words, this Earth person has already ceased for the possessor of such an interesting thumb to have that artificial mask, which in general is gradually formed owing to the malevolent method existing there of what is called 'education,' owing to which mask the majority of beings there can indeed very well hide their real inner Being-insignificance from their neighbors.

"But then it sometimes so happens there that this external mask ceases for some reason or other, to affect certain surrounding beings, who, in consequence, automatically acquire this same surprising thumb. In short, those Earth beings who find themselves under somebody else's thumb inwardly rage usually more than others, against all the other beings of that planet; as for instance, against some king or other who for some reason is not capable of dominating tens or hundreds of thousands of beings of his social community organization.

"Besides this, those beings who find themselves under somebody's thumb usually write there various books, in which they prescribe in detail how beings-men should be governed.

"Or further if it should happen that one of the contemporary beings of this peculiar planet on seeing for instance a mouse, his soul from fright drops into his boots, as they say, and this same Earth hero learns that such and such another being was rather afraid on meeting a tiger, then he will inwardly rage very strongly against this other, and will of course speak very critically of him for being afraid of a tiger. On your planet, books about what one must do and what one must not do on meeting tigers are always written by such mouse-valiants.

"Pictures like the following also sometimes appear. One of them in whom there are tens of various chronic illnesses, owing to which first of all, his stomach does not work for weeks at a stretch; and secondly, his whole body is covered with every possible kind of malignant pimple; and thirdly, he suffers day and night from these innumerable illnesses; in short, one of those Earth-beings who for many years has been a walking museum of all the ailments existing on that planet, always inwardly rages more than others when somebody else, through carelessness happens to catch a cold. At the same time he will also teach this other with great authority how to get rid of his cold.

"These Earth-beings, that is to say, these walking museums, also usually do nothing but write various books there relating to every possible kind of illness, and in these books of theirs they explain in great detail what precautions to take and what one must do to get rid of these or other illnesses.

"Cases like the following also occur there. One who does not know at all what an ordinary flea which sometimes bites him really looks like, writes a big book or tries with great fury to prove orally that the flea from whose bite the neck of the historical king Nokhan became swollen had an abnormal pink growth on his left paw.

"And if others do not believe it and should express a doubt to his face, not only will he be offended, but he will inwardly rage very strongly that they are so ignorant that even till then they had not learned about those truths.

"In short, my dear boy, at every step in the existence of your favorites, one meets quite enough pictures for observation, and study to become cultured in every branch of general science.

"At all events, when any of our tribe exists among them and is an eyewitness of such Being-absurd-manifestations, then in spite of the fact that one knows the reason of these absurdities and with all one's essence pities these unfortunates, yet at the same time one cannot help but laugh inwardly, though of course always with an admixture of sorrow.

"Owing to this property of theirs about which I am now telling you, the beings of this planet must have without fail individual victims for their instruction; though certain of these, who become by prolonged habit very brazen, must have many beings for their instructions, or if they cannot have them, suffer.

"You must also remember very well that this same weakness of Earth beings is developed particularly strongly among the beings 'intelligentsia,' as they are called.

"The word 'intelligentsia' there signifies that idea which we define by the words 'Force in oneself.'

"Although the word 'intelligentsia' has there almost the same meaning, yet beings of that place call by this word those beings who are the very opposite of what this word signifies.

"The word 'intelligentsia' is also taken from the ancient Greek language; and among the ancient Greeks the following idea was signified by this word: a being or 'something' who is perfected to such a degree that he has already the possibility of directing his functions with his own will, and not as every action usually takes place in everyone, owing to external causes.

"On your planet one still meets beings who approximately correspond to the real sense of the word, but they are to be found only among these beings who, according to the ideas of your favorites, are regarded as not belonging to the 'intelligentsia.'

"If instead of calling them the 'intelligentsia' one called them the 'mechanogentsia' then it would perhaps be quite correct.

"The 'intelligentsia' beings of your planet not only cannot give direction to their functions at all, according to their own wishes, but any Being-initiative for their ordinary process of daily-Being-existence, established by Nature itself, is even quite absent in them.

"When the 'intelligentsia' beings of your planet become responsible beings, they act and manifest only in response to shocks from without. These external shocks just give them the possibility of becoming animated by unrolling corresponding series of perceptions and experiences, which exist in them.

"Only according to these unrollings do they move automatically and 'it' acts in them automatically, that is 'it' only experiences in them what has already been experienced long before.

"And these experiences proceed in them quite independently of their own wishes and will. And the cause of the external shocks for these experiences are usually animate or inanimate objects, which accidentally come within the range of their retinas, or as it may be the various beings they meet, or the sounds or words which accidentally fall where they happen to be; or the accents accidentally sensed by their sense or smell, or, again, unusual sensations in the processes of their organism, and so on and so forth.

"But their actions and manifestations never proceed according to the wishes of their being 'I.'

"When many of these contemporary Earth 'intelligentsia' become responsible beings, and their ordinarily established forces of inner Being-functions change in them from various causes, the other beings of the Earth already cease to call them 'intelligentsia' but call them by other names, also words from the ancient Greek, such as; Bureaucrat, Plutocrat, Theocrat, Democrat, and also, Aristocrat.

"For instance those 'intelligentsia' beings of the Earth become bureaucrats among whom in their mature years the series of their mechanical inner experiences become very limited, in other words, however varied the shocks from without only one of their series of inner experiences is unrolled.

"By the way, it will do you no harm to tell you that such societies as the society called the League of Nations, consists for the most part of such bureaucrats as these.

"And as regards the caste of Earth-beings whom the other beings of your planet call plutocrats, this caste is also formed from amongst the Earth 'intelligentsia.' To these 'intelligentsia' beings of the Earth who become in mature years plutocrats, one could very well apply the following wisdom of our incomparable Hodja Nassr Eddin. For a similar case he says,

"'The most disagreeable thing for man is if there appears amongst them a somebody with an enormous Asanadian boil in the very middle of his forehead.'

"These Earth 'intelligentsia' get into such an honorable caste in the following manner. Having during their responsible existences, thoroughly and artfully trapped all their honest, that is to say, naive, fellow countrymen they meet, in consequence they become owners of great wealth.

"It would be quite justifiable if other beings called these beings simply 'Hasnamusses,' since many of them ultimately become Hasnamusses.

"I accidentally even happened to become acquainted there with the esoteric side of the origin of this word, namely, the word plutocrat.

"It appears that the story of this word is not very ancient, and that it was formed there only seven or eight centuries ago, though such beings also existed in ancient Greece.

"Then they were called 'Plusiocrats.'

"First of all you must know that on your planet during the last twenty or twenty-five centuries, for some unknown reason, all the suspicious ideas and suspicious things have been given ancient Greek names.

"These and similar ideas, as for instance, Bureaucrat, Aristocrat, Democrat, and so on, were all composed and at the present time are also composed from two ancient Greek words.

"Take for instance, the word Bureaucrat; this word also consists of two ancient Greek words, 'bureau' which means office and 'crat' which means to 'hold' or to 'keep.'

"Both these words together mean—those . . . who direct or take care of the whole office.

"In short, when several Earth centuries ago, there had increased on your planet many of these beings now called Plutocrats, and when it was necessary for other beings of the Earth to name them and entitle them, then certain clever beings of the Earth who settled questions such as these decided to invent an appropriate title. This title was to be composed of two ancient Greek Words.

"Those clever Earth beings who then had to form this word, already understood that these beings for whom such a name is necessary, are rogues of the highest degree, and that they ought to be simply called Hasnamusses.

"But as the word Hasnamuss is considered a very offensive word, so out of fear of making them angry, it was impossible to call them Hasnamuss to their face. There indeed one cannot help being afraid of them because owing to their wealth and to the abnormally established conditions of existence, they had greater influence and more varied possibilities than even the Earth kings themselves. That is why these clever Earth-beings decided to be cunning, and invented a word by which one could entitle them and yet at the same time call them by their real name.

"They did this in the following manner. As all similar names have 'crat' in their second half, then in order that it should strike the eyes of those 'scores' of the Earth, they also left crat in this new word. But they did not take the first half of this word from the ancient Greek language, as is usually done, but from the Russian language; namely they took the word 'plut'; but the word 'plut' in Russian signifies 'rogue' and there was thus obtained 'plutocrat,' that is to say 'Roguecrat.'

"These brilliant fellows of the Earth then achieved this aim of theirs very well; to better it would have been impossible because at the present time there on your planet, these Earth-parasites-Hasnamusses themselves as well as all the other beings of the Earth are quite satisfied with this title. The Earth

Hasnamusses themselves are so pleased with their name, that they swagger about even on week days in silk top hats.

"And the other Earth-beings are satisfied that they can call these monsters by their real name, and the latter not only will not be angry but even strut about like turkeys.

"Next to these Plutocrats, the important caste there is the caste of Theocrats.

"Theocrats are also usually formed from among the Earth 'intelligentsia.'

"And regarding the qualms of conscience of these Earth Intelligentsia who become Theocrats, almost the same occurs with them as occurs to the consciences of beings-intelligentsia of the Earth who become Plutocrats.

"As regards the Theocrats, our esteemed Mullah Nassr Eddin also has a saying in which he defines their significance in the following very strange sentences: "Namely he says:—'Isn't it all the same for the poor flies how they are killed, whether by a kick of the hoofs of horned devils or by the stroke of the beautiful wings of divine angels?'

"The difference between the beings of the caste of Plutocrats and the caste of Theocrats is only that, for the satisfaction of their Hasnamussian needs the Plutocrats play on their fellow-countrymen through the function which is called 'trust,' while the beings Theocrats play on that function which is formed on Earth-beings in the place of one of the three sacred paths for self-perfecting, that is, in the place of the sacred 'Faith.'

"Now I must tell you also about the caste of the Democrats.

"With the objective conscience of those Earth intelligentsia beings who become Democrats, almost the same occurs as with the Plutocrats and Theocrats, but only amongst these Earth types this happens entirely without their conscientiousness, as it is called.

"Such Democrats, for the greatest part, do not become 'intelligentsia' by heredity. Usually before becoming 'intelligentsia' these Democrats are ordinary simple Earth-beings. And therefore when such simple beings become Democrats, and accidentally occupy the place of 'powerful' beings, then, owing to the fact that they have not in themselves the hereditary habit of being able instinctively to direct the existence of beings under their control, a very rare cosmic phenomenon sometimes happens there under their administration, that is, their very corns reincarnate into pedicure doctors.

"And regarding such Earth types, our incomparable sage Mullah Nassr Eddin applies the following sentence. When our dear Mullah delivers this sentence, he usually extends his arms towards Heaven and with fervent devotion says:

"'I thank Thee Oh Great Just CREATOR, that by Thy Great and Just Grace, it is so arranged that cows do not fly like little dicky-birds.'

"And as regards the beings of the caste of the Aristocrats, it is impossible to say anything at all in explanation of these Earth beings either in ordinary language, or in the language of our incomparable Mullah Nassr Eddin.

"Although Mullah Nassr Eddin also has a sentence about them, it scarcely explains anything at all. Our Mullah says:

"'Alas! Queer fellows! Can a barge riveted with that kind of rivet keep on the water a long time?'

"And as regards the existence of these Earth-Beings, one can truly say that it is a sport of Nature, or, as it is still some times said, a freak of Nature.

"Even all the hairs of the tip of the tail of great, cunning Lucifer became quite gray from profound thinking in trying to understand how their existence on the surface of this peculiar planet is made possible.

"I, personally was always astonished how these Earth Aristocrats could exist on the Earth for almost as long a time as the other beings of the Earth.

"One can understand a little, for instance, that beings of the caste Bureaucrat are able to exist on the Earth, because although the series of inner experiences among them are very limited, yet nevertheless there are at least in them inner experiences for all times of the day and night.

"But among these Aristocrats, there are, all in all, only three series of inner experiences, yet they exist by them as long as the other beings.

"These three inner Experiences are as follows: the first about food; the second, memories of the former actions of their sexual organs, and the third, memories about their first nurse.

"Apart from these three series of experiences, there is not among them any Being-Tsarkovskinian, that is, thinking with the help of comparisons.

"It is interesting to notice that various nicknames are sometimes given to these Aristocrats to distinguish them from one another; as for instance, Emir, Count, Khan, Prince, Melik, Baron and so on.

"The sound of these nicknames, for some unknown reason, acts on all your favorites very pleasantly, on their function called vanity, on that very function which remains in your favorites until their death.

"It is also interesting to observe that on your planet there are two kinds of Aristocrats.

"Although each kind of these Earth types has its own name, yet both are quite equal in all respects. One kind is called by this same word, namely, Aristocrat, and the other kind is called Zevrocrat.

"In order that you should understand why these two different names for one and the same type began to exist there, you must first of all know that there on your planet, there gradually exist two kinds of state organizations; one is called

Monarchy, the other, Republic.

"And so, in a monarchic state organization such beings are called Aristocrats, and in republican state organizations they are called Zevrocrats.

"And why this acute difference exists there, in the names of one and the same kind of beings, is due, it seems, to the following reason.

"First of all you must know that your favorites are very fond of arranging sometimes children's-plays, as they are called.

"Your favorites, for some unknown reason, also very much like to have these Aristocrats or Zevrocrats take part in these children-plays of theirs, and therefore they introduce them into these children-plays of theirs.

"And as these Earth beings are quite empty, and in consequence also weak, therefore they must without fail be held up during these children-plays.

"And so the difference in their names was obtained from the different methods of support, that is, by which arms they were held up; namely, in the state organizations where there is a monarchy, they are held up by their right arms, and where there is a Republic, they are held up by their left arms.

"Although I don't know very accurately about the causes of these different kinds of supportings, yet knowing the roots of the words from which both of these names were formed, I think that my supposition will be found quite accurate.

"In any case in both of these state organizations, although the beings have different names, yet in all respects they are strictly equal. As regards a similar difference in the names of Earth-beings, I still recollect a remarkable saying of our wise Mullah Nassr Eddin which he personally once told me.

"And this I heard from him in Ispahan where at that time the worthy Mullah dwelt, and where I happened to be, in order to elucidate on the spot how 'politeness' as it is called, originated on your planet.

"There in Ispahan, I often met the highly esteemed Mullah Nassr Eddin, and together we had many talks in elucidating many matters. Once we spoke about the difference between the procedure during a trial, and the reaching of a verdict by Turkish and Persian 'Kazi' that is, justices of the peace, concerning the equality of their justice, when he said:

"'Ah, me! my dear friend! Is there anywhere among us on the Earth a wise investigation of man's guilt? Everywhere the "Kazis" are alike only their names are different. In Persia they are called Persian and in Turkey, Turkish. It is exactly the same, just as everywhere donkeys are the same, only one calls them by different names.

"'For instance, the race of donkeys which breed in the Caucasus are entitled "Karabaghian" and exactly the same donkeys which breed in Turkestan are called "Khorassanian."'

"And since that time this wise saying of his has been imprinted in my mind, and whenever it was necessary for me during my existence on your planet to make any comparisons about the differences, I always recalled this wise saying of his.

"May his name be extolled forever on the planet where he was formed.

"And so, my dear boy, if you ever happen to be on that planet Earth know that the weakness about which I told you is the most highly developed among these beings of your planet who are called the 'Intelligentsia.'

"Know also and remember well that the societies of beings-men, which are formed for the investigations of the possibilities for the welfare of the great masses of beings, consist for the greater part of Earth 'intelligentsia.'

"This new society which is called the League of Nations, also consists of these 'intelligentsia.'

"That is why, as I have already told you, nothing effective will result from this society. On only one occasion did certain beings of the Earth who were neither from amongst the Intelligentsia, nor from the 'important' beings of the Earth, meet together for this purpose, that is, for the purpose of seeking collectively some means of abolishing from their planet the property of their mutual destruction.

"Well, I promised to tell you about this same society of beings-men, how this society arose and why it fell to pieces. I chanced to learn about the details during my last descent to that planet, namely, during my investigations and studies there of the effects on the beings of this planet of the organization of existence created specially for them by the very holy labors of the Saint Ashiata Shiemash.

"I wish to tell you the history of the formation of this society of beings-men in somewhat greater detail, because owing to this story you will be able to understand very well and to have an answer to your question why this peculiarity of Earth beings constantly occurs on your planet.

"And secondly, owing to this history, you will also learn how those natures of our Megalocosmos, when something unforeseen hinders them to function regularly towards the general cosmic Trogoautoegocrat, adapted themselves in such a manner, that the results could not be disharmonious for this greatest cosmic law.

"This society of beings-men arose, as I have already told you, four or five centuries ago on that same continent Asia. And this occurred in the following manner.

"During that period there proceeded on the continent Asia very many of these processes of reciprocal destruction.

"These processes proceeded partly between different communities, and partly within the communities themselves. The latter processes are there called 'Civil Wars.'

"But the cause of these Civil Wars, and partly of the Wars between communities at this period, was chiefly a religion which had just been founded and which was fantastically based on the teaching of the messenger of our ENDLESSNESS, the Saint Mohammed.

"The foundation of this society which was called 'The Earth must be free for all,' was made by the brothers from the monastery called 'Assembly of those who have seen.'

"And this brotherhood of 'Assembly of those who have seen,' also existed at that time on the continent Asia, and this brotherhood was greatly revered by all the beings of your planet.

"This brotherhood was formed long before this of Earth-beings who had observed in themselves the consequences of the properties of the organ Kundabuffer and worked collectively to deliver themselves from these consequences.

"And indeed many beings of this brotherhood succeeded in delivering themselves, and many succeeded in following the right path of this deliverance.

"And so, when wars and civil wars became more and more frequent on the continent Asia, certain brothers of this society 'Assembly of those who have seen' with the very old brother 'Olmantaboor' at the head, laid the foundation of this society which was later called 'The Earth must be free for all.'

"These brothers then having perceived these processes of reciprocal destruction which had increased to an extraordinary degree, decided to try, if it were somehow possible, to achieve either the complete abolition of that horrible phenomenon from their planet, or at least to diminish a crying evil.

"And from that time on they devoted themselves to the realization of their decision. With this aim in view, they then began to visit various lands of the continent Asia and everywhere to preach against this evil peculiarity of the beings of their planet; in consequence they found many beings who agreed with them, and the result was the formation and existence of this same society of beings-men in this town Mosulopolis with the name, 'The Earth must be free for all.'

"They then succeeded in doing a great deal, chiefly because almost the whole program of this society was very successfully composed for its realization, as far as the conditions which existed on that peculiar planet was concerned.

"The fundamental program of this society, by the way, was the gradual working in the direction of achieving, first of all, the realization of one common religion for all the beings of the continent Asia. And they wished to build such a religion on the teaching of the sect Parsees, as they are called, after having changed it somewhat.

"The second aim was to establish one common language for all, and they wished to make this common language the Turkoman, as it was called which is the most ancient language on the continent Asia, and the roots of which had already entered into very many Asiatic languages.

"And thirdly, there entered into the fundamental program of this society the aim to organize in the center of Asia, namely, in the town of 'Margelan' the capital at that time of the Ferghanian Khanate, the chief and fundamental administration of all countries of Asia without exception, composed of respected beings from all Asiatic communities also without exception, and it was proposed to call this administration 'The council of the saints.'

"This council was named in this manner because only the very oldest beings, who had merited the honor could take part in it, because only such beings can be impartial and just towards beings of the Earth without difference of religion and nationality.

"There in the town Mosulopolis there were already amongst the members of this society beings of almost all the Asiatic social organizations. Amongst them were Mongols, Arabians and Persians, and Kirghizes, and Georgians, and Little Russians, and Tamils, and even amongst them was the personal representative of the conqueror Tamerlane, who was quite famous at that time.

"Owing to their impartial and non-egoistic intense activity, these increasing wars and civil wars then began to diminish on the continent Asia, and a great deal was expected.

"But at that time something occurred which became the cause of the beginning of the breaking up of this society of capable beings-men on that incomparable planet.

"And namely amongst the beings of that society, there appeared the then famous philosopher Atarnakh with his theory called: 'Why wars exist on the Earth.'

"With the appearance of this philosopher and his theories, the ideas of all the members of this society of beings-men became confused. The history of the philosopher Atarnakh himself, I also know very well, as during my studies, always of the consequences of the creation of Ashiata Shiemash, I found it necessary to know in detail about the activity of this philosopher, and of course also about himself.

"The history of the philosopher is as follows: he was born in the same town Mosulopolis in a family of Kurds, as they are called.

"Later on he indeed became a savant, very great for the planet Earth.

"At first this same Kurd Atarnakh studied during very many long Earth years the kinds of questions, which, it seemed to him might give him the answer to the question: 'in what does the reason of man's existence consist.?'

"My investigations about him made it clear to me, that during his studies of such questions, by some means or other, a very ancient but well-preserved Sumerian manuscript fell into his hands. This manuscript was well kept because it was written with the blood of a being named 'Chirman' on the skins of the being called 'Snake Kalianjesh.'

"This ancient manuscript was written by a Salmenyian

savant about his own suppositions. These same suppositions served as the first cause of the origin of the famous theory of the philosopher Atarnakh.

"The Kurd Atarnakh himself, as I afterwards discovered, was immediately struck by the contents of that portion of the manuscript, in which it was said that in all probability there exists in the Universe a certain Law of the Reciprocal Maintaining of the All-Existing. Either our life or our death must surely serve for the maintaining of something great or small in the Universe.

"This same portion of the manuscript of the Salmenyian savant, startled the Kurd Atarnakh; and from that time on, he devoted himself entirely to the study from this aspect alone of the question which interested him.

"The result of his minute investigations during several years, and complicated experimental verifications of his intellectual conclusions was the formation of this plausible theory of his, called as I have already told you, 'Why wars proceed on the Earth.'

"I also became very well acquainted with this theory of his. It was indeed near to reality. All the suppositions of this Kurd Atarnakh were very similar to the great fundamental cosmic Law 'Trogoautoegocrat,' which exists in our Universe, and about which I have already explained to you in more or less detail, when I spoke about the sacred planet Purgatory.

"In this theory, the Kurd Atarnakh proved very conclusively and without any doubt, that there exists in the Universe a law of the Reciprocal Maintaining of the All-existing.

"Further, it was proved that for such a maintaining of 'something,' chemical substances are also used, with the help of which the process is formed of the 'essensification' of beings, or giving life, as it is called.

"Chemical substances, however, go towards the maintaining of this 'something' only after the life of man ceases, that is to say, when he dies.

"In the theory of the famous Kurd Atarnakh it was also proved in detail by hundreds of logical examples that a definite quantity of deaths must, necessarily, proceed on the Earth at certain periods, it being all the same whether these deaths are of men or of other forms of life. In brief, this same unusual Earth-being, the Kurd Atarnakh, who was also chosen as representative of the whole of the population of Kurdestan to be a member of the society 'The Earth must be free for all,' began to come into contact with many members of this great general planetary society, and once they approached him with the request to expound fully his theory at a general meeting.

"Hence it was that at one of the general meetings of the members of this society 'The Earth must be free for all,' he expounded this theory of his in beautiful style and in great detail.

"After his detailed exposition, all the members of this society were so struck that for a long time none of them could move, and only after a fairly considerable time did a terrific uproar and din arise amongst them.

"The result of all their noise and din was that late in the evening of the same day, they unanimously decided to elect from amongst themselves a number of the learned beings who, together, should thoroughly in great detail examine this theory, which had struck them so forcibly, and later make a detailed report to the general meeting.

"From the next day, these elected learned members of the society 'The Earth must be free for all,' began to become acquainted with the details of the theory of the philosopher Atarnakh.

"But as it appeared that certain of these learned members were not yet fully experienced and disillusioned Earth-beings, from that very day onwards, as the examination of this astonishing theory proceeded, they began to get into the state of 'typical' beings of the Earth, that is, they began to forget the extraordinary suppositions which had struck them, and gradually to return to their former, typical, subjective and therefore changeable convictions.

"The result from the very first day was that they divided into two opposing groups.

"Half of them, not fully experienced savants, immediately began without any 'sekmentitilno'; that is, without any logical criticism, to accept with conviction the suppositions put forward in this theory; and the other part of the same not fully experienced savants began to think and speak critically, as is peculiar to the majority of the savants of the Earth, against those who became at once convinced of everything. And this half of the savants eventually became hostile not only to this theory, but even towards the personality of the Kurd Atarnakh himself.

"In short, from the next day, these learned members of the society 'The Earth must be free for all,' everywhere began of course with foam at the mouth to speak for and against this theory; and in consequence, amongst the other members of this great planetary society of beings-men there appeared two opposite views.

"The first was that everything really occurs as was said in the theory of Atarnakh, that is, wars and civil wars must periodically proceed without fail on the Earth quite independently of the consciousness of men.

"And the second view was the one which had already existed before among all the members of this society, that if the program of their society could be realized, then it would be possible to abolish this evil of the reciprocal destruction of existence which proceeded on their planet.

"From that time on, quarrels, disputes and great discord began amongst all the members of this society, but ultimately, nevertheless, the adherents of the theory of the Kurd Atarnakh obtained the upper hand, and at a stormy general meeting they unanimously decided to request this Kurd to help them find a way out of the situation which had arisen.

"Thereafter, when the philosopher Atarnakh agreed to the request of the members of the society of beings-men called 'The Earth must be free for all,' he was unanimously elected as the chief director of all the beings of this society, and the further meetings were held under his direction.

"And after several general meetings under his direction all the members of this society unanimously decided to disband their society forever.

"And this decision was made when the following categorical conclusion was reached at one of their general meetings.

"In accordance with the laws of nature, wars and civil wars must always proceed periodically on the Earth, independently of the consciousness of men, because during certain periods Nature demands a greater number of deaths. Having this in view, we are all compelled to agree inwardly that it is impossible to destroy the events occurring between states and in the states themselves by any intellectual decisions of men, and therefore we unanimously decide to put an end to all that has already been accomplished, and also to all the current affairs of our society, and to separate and go home, and there to go on working for our daily bread.

"And so, my boy, when beings-men of the great general planetary society unanimously acknowledged the uselessness of their society, and definitely decided to put an end to all their devices, only then did the selfish proud Kurd Atarnakh ascend to the platform and speak as follows:

"'My honorable colleagues!! I greatly regret that unwillingly I have become the cause of the termination of that great philanthropic work for which you, the most honored and clever men of all the countries of the Earth, have given during several years so much impartial and non-egoistic toil, such toil as men of the Earth never were, nor will ever be able to do for others to whom they are indifferent.

"'Several years did you toil without rest, in order to obtain the greatest happiness for the masses, and my theory at which I toiled for many years for those same masses is responsible for the destruction of your superhuman goodwill.

"'As I was personally to blame for all this, then let us try and see whether, with my assistance we can make good the failure you experienced.

"'I personally think that if the universal laws, which I happened to learn, are an obstacle for you in obtaining happiness for men of the Earth, then these same laws which I learned may help you towards the same aim of yours, if only they are used otherwise.

"'It is because my investigations have proved that it is important for Nature, that at certain times a certain number of deaths on the Earth occur, and for Nature it is immaterial what kind of deaths they are.

"'And so if the number of these deaths required by Nature should be replaced by the deaths of other forms of life on the Earth, then in my opinion, it is possible to obtain a diminution in the number of deaths of men themselves.

"'And this I am sure will be quite possible if you will continue to work with the same intensity, but only not in order to realize the fundamental program of your society, but in order to restore on the Earth on a larger scale, the ancient custom of offering sacrifices by men to their Gods and saints, by means of the killing of other forms of life.'

"When this proud Kurd had finished his speech a great uproar arose amongst the members of the society 'The Earth must be free for all,' which was not less than when he first expounded his famous theory.

"For three days and three nights after his speech they scarcely ever left the place, and owing to the disputes and the discussions, there was a rumbling noise in the halls which were placed by the citizens of Mosulopolis at the disposal of this all-planetary society of beings-men, and eventually on the fourth day, a general meeting was convened at which a resolution was passed by general agreement to do everything in the future as the great Kurd Atarnakh should advise them.

"On that day the name of the society was changed, and it began to be called 'The Earth must be only for men.'

"Some days later, the members of this new society, already with the name of 'The Earth must be only for men,' began to leave the town Mosulopolis and departed to their native countries; and there, under the general direction of the philosopher Atarnakh, began to work in that direction to spread among the population of the continent Asia the idea of propitiating their Gods and idols by killing beings of various forms.

"And, indeed the members of this new society very soon began to put this new aim of theirs into practice, and the custom of offering sacrifices to their Gods or to imaginary saints by destroying the existence of various weak and stupid quadruped beings began to be restored among all the beings of the continent Asia.

"The members of this new society 'The Earth only for men' accomplished this aim of theirs chiefly through the 'clergy,' as it is called, of a religion, which was widely spread at that period, and which was based on the teaching of the Saint Mohammed.

"On this occasion the custom had spread even more than when, at the request of the Angel Looisos, I decided to fly to that planet in order to try and achieve the abolition of this very custom among the beings there, and it was at that time very undesirable for His Conformity, for certain cosmic phenomena on a large scale.

"At this period, the beings began to destroy beings of other forms, because during this time the number of these three-centered beings of the Earth had increased very much, and the number of people who wished to propitiate their idols also increased there.

"Beings of other forms again began to be destroyed on your planet, not only privately but also in special public places.

"At this period, these special places were already associated, for the greatest part, with the saint Mohammed and those around him.

"For instance, each year, tens of thousands of what are called cows and sheep were destroyed in the native country of the Saint Mohammed, namely in the towns of Mecca and Medina in Arabia.

"The same also took place in the town of Meshed, in the locality called Bagdad, in the environs of Yenikishlak in the region of Turkestan, and in several other places, so that on the largest continent of your planet blood again began to flow like a river.

"This offering of sacrifices took place particularly during the Mohammedan festivals 'Bairam' and 'Goorban,' as they are called.

"And indeed, owing to their labors there, year by year the mortality of your favorites gradually began to diminish in quantity and of course the necessity for the process of reciprocal destruction began to diminish, but, in consequence the number of the beings also year by year, began to increase, and, what is more important, from that moment on the length of their existence became shorter and shorter.

"This all proceeded chiefly because the substances they radiated and which were required by nature deteriorated in quality.

"It thus continued for several centuries.

"I do not know how it would all have finished if the famous Persian dervish Assadulla Ibrahim Ogly had not given it quite another direction.

"The dervish Assadulla Ibrahim Ogly began his activity there only twenty to thirty Earth years ago.

"Being only a fanatic of the Mohammedan religion, without any of the serious knowledge which the Kurd Atarnakh had, he saw in this custom of offering sacrifices only a crying injustice on the part of men towards beings of other forms, and made it his aim at all costs to achieve the extermination on the Earth of the custom of offering sacrifices.

"He began to act chiefly through the same dervishes, like himself, who exist on the continent Asia almost in all social organizations.

"This astute Persian dervish Assadulla Ibrahim Ogly began to go about everywhere and ably to persuade the other dervishes of his idea, and they, in their turn, everywhere persuaded ordinary beings of the continent Asia that the destruction of the existence of beings of other forms is not only undesirable to God, but that for all the sins of these destroyed beings, the destroyers themselves would be obliged to carry to the Beyond, to Hell, punishment in double measure, and so on.

"And of course, owing to preaching of this kind to dervishes regarding the Beyond, authorities on these questions among the beings of Asia, began to diminish year by year, their offering of sacrifices.

"'And in consequence,' as our Mullah would say: 'Grandmother no longer liked to eat beans.'

"In short there the result of all the activities of this 'kind' Persian dervish was the last big process of reciprocal destruction, or as your favorites call it 'the great world war.'

"And so, my boy, the suppositions made in the theory of this extraordinary Kurd Atarnakh, as I have already told you, were quite near reality.

"He was mistaken in only one thing; but before I tell you about this mistake, you should know that radiation from themselves of substances of a certain vibration is required for the great cosmic Law of Trogoautoegocrat from every form of being, also of that planet.

"Besides this, a special radiation is also required from beings of the planet Earth for maintaining its two former pieces, now small planets of this solar system, called Moon and Anulios.

"As on your planet your favorites began to dominate and had in themselves corresponding organizations, that is why during the whole of the time it was so, these vibrations required by Nature were obtained almost through the radiations of your favorites alone. But when Meditation disappeared from among your favorites and the quality of their radiations ceased to correspond to the vibrations required by Nature, then from that time on, Nature began to replace these vibrations with the vibrations from which consists the 'essensification,' as it is called, or life of the three-centered beings-men of the planet Earth.

"And according to the amount of these vibrations required by Nature, do the number of these three-centered beings cease their existence, that is to say, die.

"And really, my boy, for obtaining the required amount of vibrations it is necessary at certain times that a certain quantity of deaths should occur on the planet. I repeat that this does really take place, almost as was said in the famous theory of this unusual Earth being, the philosopher Atarnakh.

"But this proud Kurd was unable to think that vibrations which are formed from substances issuing from men during their existence and at death, are necessary for Nature, in quality and not in quantity.

"Perhaps this extraordinary Kurd Atarnakh would have thought about this too if he had known the details of the results which were obtained when the conditions of existence, which were specially created for the beings of the Earth by the Very Holy Ashiata Shiemash, began to exist on that planet.

"At that period when the state of existence created by the Saint Ashiata Shiemash was established on your planet, not only did the mortality of your favorites begin to diminish, but also the number of births.

"And this was because the beings of this period began to exist more or less normally; and in consequence, the equalizing of vibrations required by Nature was made by the quality of the radiations of normally existing beings of the Earth; that is to say, the beings of that period, owing to their Being-existence began to radiate from themselves the necessary vibrations for the great fundamental cosmic law 'Trogoautoegocrat' and the appropriate vibrations required from them for the Moon and Anulios.

"But regarding these substances or vibrations which are necessary for the maintaining of the Moon and Anulios, I accidentally happened to learn about the details when I had the joy of talking about the planet with His Conformity, the Archangel Looisos, the second time.

"From all that His Conformity then told me, I understood very well that for the maintaining of the former pieces of the planet Earth, vibrations of the sacred Askokin must constantly issue from it, that is, from the fundamental piece and go to the Moon and Anulios.

"And then it appears that this sacred substance Askokin exists in the Universe chiefly combined with the sacred substances Abrustdonis and Helkdonis, and in order that this Askokin could be vivifying, as far as the maintaining of the Moon and Anulios is concerned, this sacred substance must free itself from the sacred substances Helkdonis and Abrustdonis, and these latter substances are those very substances by which the higher bodies are formed and perfected in beings, namely, the body Kesdjan and the body of the soul.

"And so, my boy, in general everywhere on any of the planets, for the formation and perfection of their higher bodies by conscious labors and intentional sufferings, the beings transmute in themselves the sacred Askokin used for such a purpose, as for the maintaining of such little planets as the Moon and Anulios are for this solar system, to which your planet Earth also belongs.

"And so my boy, if your favorites, even from this aspect alone would serve Nature honestly, then in consequence, their being-perfecting first of all, would nevertheless proceed without the participation of their peculiar consciousness and secondly, the poor Nature of this unlucky planet would not have always to adjust and adjust herself to be able to maintain herself in the general cosmic harmony.

"But unfortunately, your favorites do not honestly fulfill their obligations, as far as their service to that Nature is concerned, to which they indeed owe their existence.

"The absence of this honesty among your favorites justified that wise sentence, which our incomparable Mullah Nassr Eddin says in similar cases:

"'It is still possible for men who have conscience, to live peacefully during the pest and cholera, for their effects are at least nobler than human honesty.'

"And so my dear Hassein, when it appeared that from the psyche of your favorites there finally disappeared the instinctive needs to labor consciously and suffer intentionally, in order to consume the sacred substances Abrustdonis and Helkdonis for the maintaining of their former pieces, then great Nature herself was compelled to adapt herself to extract the required sacred substance Askokin by other means. And these other ways are for your favorites very, very disadvantageous.

"Here, it will do you no harm to tell you that after the action of the organ Kundabuffer was destroyed in the first beings of your planet, they very quickly learned that a certain cosmic substance must be transformed through them, and that to help in this transformation is one of their beings duties.

"For instance the beings of the continent Atlantis not only already learned about this but they even invented all kinds of methods in order that this beings duty of theirs should be fulfilled as productively as possible.

"The beings of the continent Atlantis combined two being-duties, namely, the duty to perfect their higher bodies, and the duty of serving the great law Trogoautoegocrat for the maintaining of the two little planets of their solar system.

"And the combining of these duties was organized by them in the following manner. In each locality or in each neighborhood at that time, there had without fail, to be three very large special buildings.

"One, especially for beings of the male sex, which was called 'Agoorokhrostiny.'

"The second one specially for the beings of the female sex and this building was called, 'Gynekokhrostiny.'

"And the third special building . . . this was built for those beings who were then called the intermediate sex and the sacred building was called 'Anoroparionikima.'

"These large buildings were then regarded as sacred by the beings of the continent Atlantis, and these buildings were for them what temples, cathedrals, churches and other sacred places are for the contemporary beings of the Earth.

"When I descended for the first time on that planet and was on the continent Atlantis, I visited certain of these buildings and also became very well acquainted with their significance. In the male temples, namely in these Agoorokhrostinys, the beings of the male sex of any particular locality or neighborhood, performed in turns appropriate 'mysteries' in special states called 'remembering oneself.'

"Among the beings of the continent Atlantis, there was a definite understanding that the beings of the male sex are the sources of the active manifestations, and therefore in their

Agoorokhrostinys they meditated the whole time very actively and consciously and performed these appropriate sacred mysteries, so that owing to such conscious meditation, there should be transmuted in themselves the sacred Abrustdonis and Helkdonis.

"And they did this intentionally and with full awareness, so that this certain sacred substance freed in them and issuing through their radiations should become for its further vivification, an active part of the threefoldness of the sacred cosmic law Triamazikamno.

"And the buildings of Gynekokhrostinys existed for all the beings of the female sex of the particular locality, and all of them were obliged during certain periods of the month as they are called there, to remain in these Gynekokhrostinys, without leaving.

"And also being fully aware that they are passive beings they were obliged to be very passive the whole time, so that the radiations of the vibrations issuing from them should serve for their further vivification, as a passive part of the law of threefoldness.

"And therefore in these Gynekokhrostinys they passed their time in complete passivity, trying not to think about anything consciously.

"And this proceeded among them in the following manner. They lay down very passively in these Gynekokhrostinys during their monthly states, and tried not to have any active experiences. And in order that the passing associative thoughts should not hinder them in their concentration, it was so arranged that they should think the whole time about good wishes for their present and future children.

"By the way, it is interesting to remark, that also among the contemporary beings of the female sex, there also proceeds during these definite periods a certain organic process which your favorites call 'Menstruation.'

"And as regards the third kind of the sacred buildings which were on the continent Atlantis, Anoroparionikima, about the beings for whom these temples Anoroparionikima were built, one could speak perhaps only in the language of our honored Mullah Nassr Eddin. To explain it in ordinary language is impossible.

"As I have already told you, the beings for whom these temples were built were called beings of the intermediate sex. Our Mullah would call them 'misconceptions' or 'men neither this nor that.'

"Amongst these beings of the intermediate sex, there were beings of the male sex and also beings of the female sex.

"They were such as for various reasons had the possibility neither to perfect themselves nor to serve Nature.

"The saying of our dear Mullah Nassr Eddin could also be applied to them. In such cases he says: 'Neither a candle for an angel nor a poker for the devil.'

"The beings of the male sex were those who for various reasons were wholly deprived of the possibility of conscious meditation.

"The beings of the female sex, were those chiefly who had no menstruations, or whose menstruations proceeded abnormally, and there were others whose sex changed during certain periods into 'Knaneomeny,' or as our dear Mullah expresses himself, 'Into a woman, who is a real mare in the spring.'

"And on the continent Atlantis at that time, these beings possessed very peculiar distinguishing signs. The first were when they began to believe in all kinds of 'fiddle-faddle,' and secondly, when a being began to prove to others what he himself did not know at all, or which he knew without being certain, and thirdly, if any being began to teach others about those truths of which he himself understood absolutely nothing at all and fourthly if the being was in the habit of breaking his promise, and of taking an oath in vain, and fifthly beings who had the profession of spy, stock-broker, prostitute, 'Tuksusa,' newspaper reporter, writer, representative of art, physician, lawyer and priest.

"But the most indisputable sign was the appearance among these beings of the property which was called 'Moyasul.'

"By the way, it will do you no harm to tell you also, that this property still exists among your favorites and at the present time they also consider this property as an illness which they call 'Hemorrhoids.'

"In these temples which were called Anoroparionikima, beings of this kind had to stay without leaving during the period indicated by the Earth beings around them. They were not obliged to do anything in these Anoroparionikima but existed how they pleased, only without either meeting or speaking with normal beings of the locality. They were so confined in these temples Anoroparionikima of Atlantis at that time because according to current ideas they greatly hindered the peaceful and regular existence of the other beings of the Earth during certain periods of the month, owing to the radiations caused by their various harmfulnesses.

"Eh, my dear boy, beings of the continent Atlantis already had excellent good customs for normal existence, but the great misfortune of contemporary beings of the Earth, all the good customs they invented and all the knowledge about these customs perished together with the destruction of the continent.

"As regards these good temples, about which I have just told you, it appeared as if, later, they would again be established among the beings of the Earth, but unfortunately, with the death of the restorer all was soon forgotten.

"But nevertheless one of these temples, namely, one similar to the temple Gynekokhrostiny was again restored and existed a long time.

"The necessity of these temples was again understood and they were again established by a certain very wise Hebrew

King, named Solomon.

"He first of all decided to reestablish for beings of the female sex, special buildings where these beings should remain during the period of their menstruation, so that they should not hinder the normal existence of the beings of the male sex.

"This same wise King Solomon then understood also very well that generally during the period of menstruation the character of beings of the female sex becomes for other beings, particularly for their husbands, not only intolerable, but even organically harmful, and he therefore then promulgated a decree for his subjects, that they should build near each populated center, special isolated places where the beings of the female sex should be confined during the whole time of this condition.

"I even happened to read the decree he promulgated:

"In it, by the way, it said, that during their menstruations women are unclean; and not only is it a great sin to touch them during these periods; but for others, particularly their husbands, even to converse with them, is a sacrilege of the highest order.

"If during this time, men, particularly the husbands, touch or talk with them, then first of all, evil spirits will enter into them, and secondly, these men, particularly the husbands, will without fail, quarrel with many other men, with whom they have daily affairs.

"This latter observation of the great Earth sage, King Solomon, still remains there an immutable truth.

"And indeed at the present time, it is also one of those numerous causes, owing to which in the general whole, existence for beings of your planet has now become absurd, in the highest degree.

"Among the contemporary beings of the Earth of the female sex, during these states, their specific property called hysteria still further increases, and owing to this they bring the beings around them, particularly their husbands, to such a condition, that the latter become as our great Mullah Nassr Eddin says in such cases:

"'The most unpardonable carelessness of man in the presence of women is to put a barrel of gunpowder near a Tandoor.'

"And indeed owing to the fact that contemporary beings of the female sex are at liberty during their menstruations, many contemporary beings of the male sex not only cannot have permanent good relations among themselves, but owing to this they also very often become real 'After-repenting-blasphemers' as they are called.

"The custom created by this wise King Solomon existed for a very long time among the Jewish people, and would surely have spread everywhere on Earth.

"But unfortunately, as usually happens there, after the glory of this Jewish people had departed from them and they were persecuted by other communities, this custom ceased to spread and was gradually forgotten, even among the Jewish people themselves.

"At the present time such customs exist there only among a very small social organization dwelling on the mountains of Caucasia called 'Khevsoory,' the problem of whose origin gives many contemporary Earth savants sleepless nights.

"And to speak about the unfortunate nature of this incomparable planet, one must also have recourse to the saying of the wisest of all the wise beings of your planet, who is particularly esteemed by me, Mullah Nassr Eddin.

"About these misfortunes, he first of all says:

"'Ah! Ah! Me! If you are very unlucky, you could get syphilis from your godmother.'

"And sometimes he says, 'Oh you unfortunate creatures. While you were being born, your mother sang Armenian songs.'

"For a similar misfortune even the Russian Kusma Prutkoff has a special saying which is as follows: 'Is there anything more unfortunate than these fir cones, for do not all the Makkars stumble against them?'

"This unfortunate nature of the planet Earth, owing to the beings dwelling on it, must always keep on readapting itself constantly and without respite, and manifest itself always differently and differently to remain within the general cosmic harmony.

"For instance, quite recently during their last big process of mutual destruction, now called by them the Great World War, which proceeded between these superpeculiar beings, whether owing to the German invention of poisonous gases or to the inventions by the English, particularly of quick-firing machine-guns, or to any other of their inventions, I do not know, but the fact remains that during their last process the number of deaths was obviously not foreseen by Nature, and proceeded on a much larger scale than was required by this unfortunate Nature.

"In short, on this occasion the consequences of the deaths of beings-men, was as the Earth commercial Hasnamusses of a particular kind would say, 'Overexpenditure,' and therefore, at the present time, the poor Nature of the planet 'puffs' again and jumps out of its skin in trying to accommodate itself for the future.

"On this last occasion, this unlucky Nature, it seems, is preparing to increase for future times, the numbers of other forms of beings.

"And I can assume this, because when I left that planet forever, in the streets of the towns of Petrograd and Tiflis, in the big social organization of Russia, where there perished the majority of the beings who were destroyed in the world war, there were to be seen those quadruped beings who being usually afraid of the biped ones, never appear where the latter dwell.

"These man-hating quadruped beings are there called 'wolves.'

"There also in Russia the births among what are called rats and mice have very greatly increased. To such a extent did the number of these little quadruped beings increase, that at the present time they eat up all the goods of beings of this community.

"By the way, in one of my etherogram reports from Mars I was informed that beings of this same community Russia have applied to the beings of another European community to undertake the destruction of the existence of these little beings rats and mice, who have multiplied among them, and for which they promise to pay them all the money necessary.

"Although a temporary diminution of the number of these poor rats and mice is possible for various methods exist for this purpose among there specialists in destroying the existence of others, yet maybe, the beings of other communities will not agree to do this for nothing.

"The beings of this Russia will of course, not be able to pay with money as they promised, as these payments will perhaps be much greater than the cost of their last war.

"And as regards the flesh of peasants—everybody knows that in peace time, it costs nothing."

When Beelzebub had finished explaining the extravagant multiplication on the planet Earth of rats and mice, his grandson Hassein, as if speaking to himself exclaimed very sadly in a voice full of despair:

"What will then be? Is it possible that there in no escape and that the unfortunate souls formed on that unfortunate planet must remain eternally imperfected and endlessly embodied in different planetary forms, tormented forever and ever by the consequences of that damned organ Kundabuffer, an organ which for reasons unknown to them was added to the planetary bodies of the first three-centered beings of that unlucky planet?

"Where then is that Pillar upon which it seems that the whole of our Megalocosmos rests and which is called 'Justice'? . . . No . . . This cannot be . . . Here something is not quite right . . . because during the whole duration of my existence, never on a single occasion has doubt crept into me regarding cosmic justice . . . I must really find out and understand what is the matter here . . .

"From this moment on, the aim of my existence shall be to understand clearly, why the souls of these Earth three-centered beings are found in such unprecedented terrible conditions."

Having said this, poor Hassein hung his head and became depressingly thoughtful.

And Beelzebub regarded him with a very strange look. Strange, because in this look his love for Hassein was very clearly visible, and at the same time it was obvious that Beelzebub was greatly pleased that his grandson was experiencing such a depression.

A fairly long time passed in this manner. Finally Beelzebub sighed as if with the whole of his being and turned to his grandson with the following words:

"Yes, my dear Hassein, surely something here is not quite right. If nothing could be done for the beings of that planet by that being who has already at the present time the Reasonableness of the sacred 'Podkoolad,' and is one of the first helpers of our ENDLESSNESS in the government of the Universe, namely, the former Saint Ashiata Shiemash—he could do nothing, what then can we say, beings with reasons of almost ordinary beings?

"You remember the Very Holy Ashiata Shiemash in his deliberations entitled 'The Terror of the Situation' said: 'If it is still possible to save the beings of the Earth, then only Time can do it.'

"At the present time we can only repeat the same regarding that terrible property of theirs, about which we have just spoken, namely, about their periodical process of mutual destruction.

"We can only now say, that if this property of the Earth beings will ever disappear from this unfortunate planet, then perhaps it will be only through Time, owing either to the guidance of some Being of a very highly developed Reason, or to some exceptional cosmic event."*

At this point of Beelzebub's tales, there were diffused all along the intersystem ship *Karnak* artificially produced vibrations which had the property of penetrating into the common presences of all the passengers of the ship and which acted on what are called the "wandering nerves" of the stomach.

This artificially produced manifestation was an announcement to the passengers about their assembling in the common what is called "Djameechoonatra," a kind of terrestrial "monasterial refectory" in which the second being-food is collectively taken.

* *Editor's Note:* We inserted the last two paragraphs of this chapter from the 1950 publication for the sake of continuity. In that book, this is the "moving event" Beelzebub refers to at the start of the following chapter.

CHAPTERS XLIV & XLV

Form & Sequence, Justice Or Good And Evil[*]

AFTER this moving event, Beelzebub, Hassein and Ahoon did not at once go to the place on the ship where they usually passed their time, but retired to their 'Kesshah' to recover.

Kesshah is the name given to the compartments on board a ship which are called cabins on terrestrial steamers. Later when Beelzebub had rested a while he returned to the room on the cosmic ship *Karnak* where their conversations were usually held, and silently entered.

The first thing he saw was his beloved grandson Hassein standing with his face towards the wall, his eyes covered with both his hands. Observing him more attentively, Beelzebub saw that Hassein's shoulders were heaving.

Profoundly moved, Beelzebub approached Hassein and in a tone full of compassion said:

"What is the matter, my dear boy? Are you really weeping?"

Hassein tried to speak, but it was evident that he could not for his sobs. And some time passed before his agitation subsided. Then gazing with sad eyes at his grandfather but with a smile of deep affection he said:

"You must not be concerned about me, my dear grandfather. My present state will soon pass. During the recent Dionosk I certainly thought very intensely, and in all prob-

* ***Editor's Note:*** In the original 1931 Manuscript chapters XLIV, XLV and XLVI had not been broken into separate chapters. The text of ***Form & Sequence*** was so interwoven with the text that told of ***Justice***, that we chose not to try to separate them out, preferring to leave them as they were. However we were able to and did separate out the chapter on Electricity, since this presented no problem.

ability the tempo of my bodily functions was changed by the unusual activity.

"Until the new tempo of my intellection has become harmonized with the established tempos of all the rest of the functions of my body, such abnormalities as my present weeping will undoubtedly occur in me.

"But my weeping today is on account of the state of those same souls forming and perfecting themselves upon that planet Earth, and about whom you have recently told me so much. I remembered and thought of them just when I was myself overflowing with joy from all that has just taken place. I remembered the souls of the unfortunate beings of that remote planet who, owing to the consequences of the properties of that accursed organ Kundabuffer, can never experience the delight and happiness arising in souls and beings from these manifestations from Above, one of which I have just had the joy to witness.

When Hassein had finished speaking, Beelzebub looked long and fixedly at him and then said:

"I also see now that during the recent Dionosk you assuredly did not, as your favorites say, go to sleep, but actively pondered. I am very glad, because by the laws of the great Heropass you are just now on the threshold of responsible being and must be beginning to accustom yourself to what is becoming to responsible beings—to spend half your time in active pondering. And you have begun.

"I am glad for you, chiefly because your active pondering is beginning at the right moment, namely, at the moment when other being functions are developing in you which do not depend upon the reason of the being himself but upon the great cosmic Law of Trogoautoegocrat. All the same, my dear boy, try during several Dionosks not to ponder actively, but let those functions in you rest which participate in active intellection and do not depend upon the essence of the being, but on the harmony of the general cosmic tempo.

"Always know and bear in mind that the planetary body of a being is an independent cosmic formation and only a dependent and unconscious part of the whole being. Hence, as the foundation of that cosmic pillar you called Justice, the conscious part of the being must act justly towards the unconscious part and never demand of it, the planetary body, more than it can give.

"And in order that this auxiliary planetary body may rightly, like everything else in the Megalocosmos, serve its principal part, that is, the essence of the being, this essence must be just towards it and demand only what the body can give.

"This must be done in order that this unconscious part may be able gradually and freely to blend its individual tempos with the tempos of the general Megalocosmos. You must remember without fail that in the Megalocosmos, the blending of tempos is possible only with what is called 'Kaznookizkernian' or as it may be said, by degrees or gradually.

"And so if you wish that your active intellection should proceed rightly and productively during your future existence, if and when such intellection has already begun in you, you must cease for a while and not continue in it however agreeable and interesting it may be, if such inner process had undesirable effects on your body. Otherwise there will result in you 'Dezonakooasanz,' in other words, a part only of your whole being will acquire another tempo, and, in consequence of this, you will become such a being as your favorites call lopsided. The majority of them are precisely of that kind.

"Only if the change of tempo of one part is gradual is it possible to change the whole without risk of injury to the whole.

"You expressed yourself quite correctly, my dear boy, when you said that during the recent Dionosk the tempo of your body certainly did not harmonize with your intellection.

"But you would have been even more correct if you had used, instead of the word body, the word feeling, because this function of feeling is predominant during the active intellection of a being. As I am sure that it is extremely important for you to understand this fully I will repeat a little more in detail the difference between the 'knowledge' and the 'understanding' of which we have just spoken.

"But first of all let us go and sit where we usually do to talk. Ah, here comes at just the right moment our dear Ahoon, the constant partner in our conversations.'

When they were all seated in their usual places Beelzebub continued as follows. He said:

"For a clear understanding of the difference between understanding and knowledge we will again take for our example the peculiar Reason of the beings of your planet and compare it with the Reason of the three-centered beings of the other planets of the Universe.

"We can confidently describe the Reason of the beings of the planet Earth, and particularly of the beings of the present day, as the Reason of Knowledge; while the Reason of all the three-centered beings of our Great Universe can be called the Reason of Understanding. In general, the Reason of Understanding is such that it always becomes an integral and inalienable part of the being, while the Reason of Knowledge is a temporary part—as if it were something strange or alien.

"In order that any knowledge newly acquired should remain in a being having only the Reason of Knowledge it is absolutely necessary for him to repeat it. Otherwise such knowledge will very quickly change or fade completely—an event that cannot happen in the case of knowledge acquired by a being possessing real Reason of Understanding.

"However much a being possessing Reason of Understanding may change in other respects, the knowledge he acquires remains in his essence always accessible and an inalienable part of him forever."

As Beelzebub paused to adjust the curls of his tail, Hassein addressed him thus:

"Your Worthiness, the Sacred Podkoolad of HIS ENDLESSNESS, my dear grandfather. Seeing that you have already told me so much concerning the beings of the planet Earth, you surely will not refuse to give me as well the personal opinion you formed during your prolonged observation of the chief cause of the molding of the psyche of the three-centered beings of that unfortunate planet into such a misshapen form?"

To this question of Hassein's, Beelzebub replied as follows:

"Very well, my dear boy, now I can give you my personal opinion also. To tell the truth if you had asked me this question before, I could not have replied frankly, since I had a definite aim in mind concerning you, in telling you so much about the beings of the planet Earth. But now that I have become convinced that my aim has been attained, I can confidently give you my own frank personal opinion as well. I will even tell you why I could not have given you my frank opinion before, and the more readily because you will also be able clearly to understand from it the difference of which I have just been speaking between knowledge and understanding.

"It is like this, my boy. . .

"You are now at the period of your existence when that form of intellection is formed which is proper to all responsible beings of the Megalocosmos; and hence, when we set off on the *Karnak*, I decided to profit by the time to help you so that the formation of your active intellection might proceed rightly. And when at the outset, I noticed that you became very interested in the beings of the planet Earth, I began to tell you about them, under cover of gratifying your interest, in such a sequence that you yourself by your own intellection with just the facts I gave you, would be bound to arrive at certain conclusions and in consequence the 'Autokolizikner' particularly necessary in your present stage would result in you.

"I told you very many things but just not the most important thing.

"The fact is that the real understanding in the essence of a being is also a material substance of chemical composition; and this substance also is always formed according to the same fundamental cosmic law of the sacred Triamazikamno.

"And the three separate factors in the manifestation of this sacred law are in the present case the formations already present and inalienably proper to the being.

"These already materialized, intellectually corresponding understandings become the positive and negative poles of this great law, and these results, which are called being-Autokolizikner, or, otherwise, the realized endeavors of the individuum, serve as the neutralizing principle of this omnipresent law.

"The process of the great law of Triamazikamno proceeds in the present case in the following way.

"Relative to the knowledge newly entering, certain corresponding understandings already present in the being become his positive part and hence begin to affirm; while certain others, also corresponding understandings—begin to deny these affirmations.

"The 'Autokolizikner' set up between these affirmations and denials produce, what shall we say, Zernofookalnian friction; or as it is sometimes called instincto-terebelnian clash.

"And owing to all this the substantial result is crystallized in the being which becomes uniquely his very own being-understanding.

"By the way, it is indispensable for you to know also, that only understandings formed in this order are precipitated in the being into those series of perceptions which were there before and which are similar to this new understanding.

"But in other beings in which the Reason of Knowledge

alone exists these newly transmuted knowledges are precipitated as information at random and are dependent entirely on the existing general state. These newly acquired perceptions become mixed with others having nothing in common with them. That is why in such consciousnesses there always results what our highly esteemed Mullah Nassr Eddin calls 'Eralash.'

"In order that this 'Autokoliziknerian' friction or 'instinc-to-terebelnian' clash should be produced in the being it is necessary that the being himself should produce consciously from within or there must be produced from without such a new direction that new knowledges shall be perceived in the order 'Tavashtner,' and this can occur only if gradation without violence be strictly followed.

"For instance, had I given you at once what you have just asked me, namely, my opinion for the reasons for the misfortunes of those three-centered beings of the planet Earth and had afterwards related the various things that I have told you concerning them, all those facts I gave you would at once have been clear to you without your own 'Autokoliziknerian' intellection; and the knowledge of these facts would have been for you only information without essential understanding. That in why I told you these things in such an order that this same 'Autokoliziknerian' friction should proceed in you continuously throughout my whole story; I saw clearly just now the results of all this interior process of yours in the manner in which you answered my question, 'Why are you weeping?'

"So my dear boy, now that I am fully convinced that the time I have spent in my stories concerning the beings of this peculiar planet have attained the desired result in you and as we are already nearing our beloved planet Karatas and our journey will soon be over I can now not only confidently and frankly give you my own opinion but I will tell you in detail about that real Objective Reason the details of which I myself unfortunately learned too late.

"I say unfortunately because had I known of it earlier I should not have wasted so many long years of my time in the observation and study of the peculiar psyche of the beings of that unique planet.

"It will be best for you if I tell you only about what, as I have just said, I myself learned too late.

"That you should better understand I must first of all tell you something about certain episodes which have nothing in common with this.

"You remember that I recently told you that when I descended on that planet Earth for the fifth time I stayed there only a short while. I returned to the planet Mars on account of the expected appearance there of one of the Cherubim attendant on our ENDLESSNESS, whom I had been informed bore a certain command concerning me.

"Soon after my arrival on the planet Mars this Cherubim appeared and the command proved to be this, that in response to the prayers of the Angel Looisos in recognition of my success in destroying the custom of sacrifices on your planet, our CREATOR had most graciously reduced my punishment so that punishment for my transgressions should not fall to my posterity.

"That was why from that time my children, that is to say, your father and your uncle Tooilan could return to their native country and enter the service of HIS ENDLESSNESS.

"Being well known for their ability my sons were very soon after their arrival assigned some appropriate employment.

"Your father was appointed 'Zirlikner' of one part of the planet Karatas and later rose to the rank he now holds which is that of Zirlikner in chief of the whole of our planet Karatas.

"Your uncle Tooilan was appointed assistant to the director of the etherogram station of the Holy Planet Purgatory, which then as well as now is in communication with almost all the planets of the Great Universe. He later on attained the position of Director in Chief, which office he still occupies.

"By the way, my dear boy, it is to the purpose that you should know that there was once among the beings of your planet, a duty very similar to the duty of our Zirlikners. The beings who fulfilled this duty were called by your favorites Astrologers.

"Among the duties of your Earth Astrologers, as also among our Zirlikners was the compilation for newly born beings of their 'Oblekioonerish' and on the basis of* these for every being on attaining the age of seven was prescribed a marriage partner. Such an 'Oblekioonerish' is called a horoscope on your planet.

"Justice must be done to the beings of the Earth during the time of these astrologers. Then indeed the directions of these astrologers were strictly carried out and the conjugal unions were made exclusively accordingly to their directions. In consequence during that period on the Earth, marriage partners almost always corresponded to each other according to their type.

"These ancient astrologers made their selections successfully because although they were very far from the knowledge of many cosmic Trogoautoegocratic laws they at least knew very well the laws of the influence upon beings of the different planets of their solar system, namely, the influence of their planets on that planet during conception and birth. And having a many-centuried practice in such knowledge passed from generation to generation among these astrologers, they already knew very well the female types corresponding to the types of the male sex.

"And owing to all this, the couples selected according to their judgment proved to be quite suited and not as at the present time. There on the planet Earth as if by design almost always quite opposite types are united; and hence, during the whole subsequent existence of these couples, half their time is spent only in what our revered Mullah Nassr Eddin expressed in the following words:

"'What a good husband or wife it is if their whole inner life is not always engaged in nagging their other half.'

"In any case, my dear boy, if some astrologers had continued there, then surely from their further practice they would by now have succeeded in making the existence of beings on that unfortunate planet in respect of family relations a little like the existence of the other three-centered beings of our Great Universe.

"But this custom also, like all the rest of their happy attainments, they have sent to the dogs of the revered Mullah Nassr Eddin, not having time to use it as it should be used. As it happens there usually, these Earth astrologers first began to dwindle gradually and finally they were quite evaporated.

"After the final destruction of the function of these astrologers, their place was taken by other specialists, but from among the savants of quite a new order who also proposed to be concerned with those defterocosmoses and tritocosmoses.

"These strange fellows of the new order occupied themselves only with inventing different names for the different suns and planets of the Megalocosmos from among the milliards of suns and planets which have nothing to say to them. But they pretend to measure the distance between those cosmic points which they can sometimes see from their planet, through their children's toys also called telescopes. But how they measure, this is by now one of their professional secrets and known therefore to them alone.

"Please, my dear Hassein, don't be indignant with these contemporary Earth astronomers. Even if they do no good to your favorites, at least they are kept from doing harm. They must be busy with something. It is not without reason that they wear spectacles made in Germany, and nightshirts sewed in England, the more so that they wrack their respectable brains to name and measure just those same suns and planets that luckily for them do not quickly change their paths of falling relatively to their Solar System. Thus they can observe the form of the position of these Solar Systems during a long time, but even then for only several of their centuries. Let them!

"Let them occupy themselves with this! May the CREATOR be with them. Otherwise, like the majority of the rest of these queer Earth fellows they will from boredom occupy themselves either with titillation or with the five-fingered exercise. And as you know, my boy, beings so occupied give off to their surroundings—in this case to your favorites, very harmful emanations.

"Well, my boy! So my sons on their arrival were at once thought fitted for these responsible posts; and why this was so I must also tell you in greater or less detail.

"But first of all you must know that among the exiles with me to this Solar System from the very beginning was one of the 'Zirlikners' of the planet Karatas. He was young at that time, but already very learned. His name is Pooloodjistius. By the way, since the pardon, this Pooloodjistius has already been thought worthy to become junior assistant of the Great Observer of the movement of all points of the universe, His Samokeepness, Arch-Cherub Ksheltarna.

"Well, from the very commencement of our exile, this same Pooloodjistius as a great expert in the position of all the suns and planets of our Universe, offered to become the director in chief of the observatory on Mars which I began to organize shortly after my arrival there. Of course I accepted him with great pleasure; and it was in this way that the great savant Pooloodjistius came to reside in my house on the planet Mars.

"Later on when my sons were born and grew to the appropriate age I asked this great savant Pooloodjistius to undertake the further duty of the education of my children. He agreed to my proposal very willingly, because in the unusual circumstances he could not find employment for his varied knowledge, and my proposal opened up a large field for him.

"From that time, apart from his not very numerous duties, he gave himself entirely to the enlightenment or instruction of the Reason of my sons. They soon became so much attached to him that they did not leave him even while he was engaged in the duties of my observatory. Even during these moments the good Pooloodjistius constantly enlightened their Reason and explained practically the technique of the observation and study of cosmic points. He explained why such and such a point occupies such and such a place, the character of their influence on each other, their peculiarities and everything concerning the great and small sources of the substances of the great Trogoautoegocrat.

"In this way, both my sons, under the direction of this remarkable savant, not only acquired the knowledge necessary for responsible beings, but became also particularly well acquainted with the properties and characteristics of most of the suns and planets of our great Megalocosmos.

"Thus it was that at that time both my sons came to devote themselves to their observations. Your father learned to observe and study the distant suns and planets situated in the sphere of the Prime Source, the self-same Sun Absolute, while your uncle Tooilan loved to observe the planet Earth.

"I was partly the cause of the latter fact because during the periods of my observations of the beings of your planet, I used to charge Tooilan to make a note of the changes taking place there; and little by little he became interested himself in these beings of a very strange psyche.

"Well, my boy, when my sons were prepared to leave the planet Mars, forever, to go to the center, and when they received my final blessings, your uncle Tooilan begged me not to refuse to keep him periodically informed of the results of my observations and studies concerning the peculiar psyche of the biped beings of the Earth.

"Of course I promised Tooilan to do so; and they flew away from there to the center nearer to Our Lord.

"When they arrived there it was soon discovered that they were well-informed concerning the position of cosmic points and knew their properties and characteristics. Your father was at once appointed to the office 'Zirlikner' of one part of the planet Karatas; and my younger son Tooilan was made assistant director of the Etherogram station on the Holy Planet Purgatory.

"Well from that time onwards, I used, according to his request, to send Tooilan every quarter a complete copy of all the notes of our observations and studies of the psyche of the beings of the planet Earth.

"Many years passed from the time I first began to send Tooilan these etherograms; but I personally did not know what happened to them. Only later I learned that the Great Governor of the Holy Planet Purgatory, His All-Quarters-Maintainer the Arch-Cherub Algamatant, having learned by chance that the assistant director of the Etherogram station, Tooilan, periodically received from his father very full etherograms from the Solar System Ors, expressed the wish to be kept acquainted with their contents.

"It proved that these etherograms not only interested him personally, but His All-Quarters-Maintainer even requested your uncle Tooilan to reproduce the contents of these etherograms regularly in the 'Toolookhterzinek,' in case some of the souls dwelling on the Holy Planet should wish for a rest to have the information concerning the peculiar beings dwelling on one of the very remote planets of the Great Megalocosmos. Your uncle Tooilan therefore always did so. When he received the etherogram from me, he always at once reproduced them in the general planetary 'Toolookhterzinek'; and by this means all the blessed souls dwelling on the Holy Planet were able if they wished to be kept informed of all my observations during those long years.

"Here, by the way, it will do no harm to tell you that beings of the planet Earth have now invented something like our 'Toolookhterzinek.' Certainly, however, the likeness is rather remote. They call this invention of theirs it seems radio.

"It further transpired that certain blessed souls dwelling on the Holy Planet Purgatory followed my observations very closely; and began to ponder over the peculiarities of the psyche of those beings. And the result of all their ponderings was that they finally saw that something was wrong with the psyche of the three-centered beings of the planet Earth.

"These same blessed souls noted my etherograms very attentively and began to share their impressions with others and these, in turn, with still others, with the result, as it proved, that many of them finally became seriously indignant at what at first seemed to them such an injustice from above. The number of such indignant blessed souls, moreover, gradually increased, until everywhere in the 'Zarooaries' of that Holy Planet the matter was considered and discussed.

"'Zarooaries' on the Holy Planet are those points of existence which on other planets are called towns and villages.

"The result of it all was that fifty blessed souls of those dwelling on the Holy Planet were chosen to investigate and discover in common with real reason why such an anomaly exists in the psyche of the beings on the planet Earth that hinders them from perfecting themselves.

"The fifty so chosen souls were just those who had been already considered worthy to be candidates for their promotion to the Sun Absolute.

"As soon as these fifty souls were chosen His All-Quarters-Maintainer the Arch-Cherub Algamatant expressed his most gracious wish to assist them in their task.

"These fifty candidates for the Sun Absolute having begun their investigations, it became clear to them after long and complicated research that the fundamental cause of the abnormality of the psyche of the beings of the Earth was the rise and prevalence of a certain idea of Good and Evil, the idea namely, that Good and Evil exist outside of the beings themselves; and as if, as soon as they are formed, for some unknown reasons there is crystallized in the essence of the three-centered beings of the planet Earth the idea that all their good and evil acts proceed not from their own essence but are manifestations induced by external circumstances.

"Having discovered this explanation, the blessed dwellers on the Holy Planet began to ponder what to do. It is said that everywhere in all the 'Zarooaries' conferences began to be held in the hope of arriving at some practical issue. Eventually, after long and continued consideration, the following conclusion was unanimously agreed to by all the blessed souls of all the 'Zarooaries' of the Holy Planet.

"Should the soul of that being who first promulgated this maleficent idea perfect itself to the sacred degree of Reason corresponding to the Holy planet Purgatory this soul shall not be admitted to exist on the planet Purgatory but condemned to dwell for eternity on the planet 'Remorse of Conscience.' Meanwhile all those dwelling on the Holy Planet should lay at the feet of his ENDLESSNESS the petition to send such Reason as could find a means there of uprooting this wicked idea.

"By the way, after this resolution was carried out by these fifty candidates for the Sun Absolute, the question was examined what being or soul it was that instigated this wicked idea on that planet. When it transpired that this soul was called during its planetary existence Makary Kronbernkzion, and that it had not only perfected itself and was now on the Holy Planet, but was ranked as one of the first candidates for the Sun Absolute—why there then occurred something on that planet which even now nobody can recall or speak of calmly. It is said that during that time there was not a righteous soul on the whole Holy Planet who was not smitten with remorse in face of such a terrifying fact.

"For nearly a quarter of their time they discussed this unprecedented scandal back and forth. In every 'Zarooary,' it is also said, every kind of committee and sub-committee was formed; and in the end the following decision was unanimously arrived at; to leave in abeyance, the general planetary sentence concerning the soul of Makary Kronbernkzion; but in regard to its carrying out by the dweller on the Holy Planet to lay at the feet of HIS MOST GRACIOUS ENDLESSNESS the petition to mitigate this terrifying sentence. When on the occasion of HIS next visit this request was laid at HIS feet, the ALL GRACIOUS CREATOR, so it is said, thought for a little while and then was pleased to order that the deserving soul should continue to exist on the Holy Planet until the future results of his misdeeds should be revealed.

"This gracious order was evidently given by our CREATOR on account of the fact that the soul of Makary Kronbernkzion, notwithstanding its being the cause of the inability of all souls on that unlucky planet to perfect themselves, and in spite of the unfavorable external conditions for perfecting Reason established on that planet had succeeded in attaining the required sacred degree of Reason. And, further, surely HIS ENDLESSNESS reckoned that the beings of the Earth themselves might finally come to understand their error and begin to exist as it becomes three-centered beings. And in that case there would be no necessity to punish so terribly the soul that without sparing itself and struggling with its own self-negation had perfected itself to the gradation of the sacred measure of Reason required of the soul. In short, owing to this command of our MOST GRACIOUS, the soul of the poor Makary Kronbernkzion remains to the present day on the Holy

Planet; and his future now depends only upon your favorites.

"Do you happen to know anything in general about the planet bearing the name 'Remorse of Conscience'?" asked Beelzebub of his grandson.

"Yes, dear grandfather," replied Hassein, "I know that the planet 'Remorse of Conscience' is also called sometimes 'The Accursed Planet.' I know further that the Accursed Planet is situated all by itself somewhere on the furthermost edge of the Megalocosmos, and that it is in every sense unique in the whole Universe.

"Quite recently my father explained to me," Hassein continued, "that both on and within this unique planet the fundamental cosmic laws proceed in all reversely; and their succession also they make backward. My dear father told me that the particularity of this planet will continue until in the souls dwelling upon it, owing to their terrible sufferings those substances will entirely disappear that were formed in their bodies by their wicked deeds. That is all I know of that planet" concluded Hassein.

Beelzebub then began to speak of this planet. He said: "Indeed, my boy, this planet called 'Remorse of Conscience' is in every respect unique in the Universe. On this planet 'Remorse of Conscience' only thirty-nine souls exist at the present time. And all the beings of the whole Universe must know their names and on every festival curse them. If the soul of Makary Kronbernkzion were taken to this planet he would be the fortieth from among all the souls of our Great Universe.

"The story of this soul whom all the blessed dwellers on the Holy Planet condemned to exist eternally on the planet 'Remorse of Conscience' is as follows. He began his self-perfection on that planet Earth as a being of the second generation of Earth beings of the Society of the Akhaldans who, as I told you, were already on the continent Atlantis. This unfortunate soul was then first called Makary Kronbernkzion.

"By the way, you may as well know that in general all souls, to whatever gradation of the sacred measure of Reason they attain, bear the name they received on the planets where they began their self-perfection.

"Thus the Earth being named Makary Kronbernkzion perfected his soul to the gradation of the sacred measure of Reason which in general corresponds to that of the Holy Planet; and hence after his death the soul of this Makary Kronbernkzion was taken to the Holy Planet Purgatory.

"Owing to the good and strict directions concerning right existence which obtained in the Akhaldan society of which Makary Kronbernkzion was a member, and being himself a very conscientious worker for self-perfection and having begun at the age of eighteen he had time before his death which occurred in his two hundred and tenth year, reckoning by Earth time, to improve the Reason of his soul in a single form of incarnation.

"This unfortunate soul of Makary Kronbernkzion on the Holy Planet also purified his body by persistent sufferings during very many years until he attained the Reason that made him worthy to be reckoned as a candidate for the Sun Absolute. And it was just there that this terrible misfortune happened to him.

"During my thorough investigation of the case of this unfortunate Makary Kronbernkzion, I convinced myself very clearly that owing to the fact that in the Earth beings of that period the consequences of the properties of the organ Kundabuffer had already begun to be manifest, these Earth-beings gradually transformed the nearly correct idea of the unfortunate Makary Kronbernkzion into an idea maleficent for themselves.

"The personal guilt of the unfortunate Makary Kronbernkzion, it seems to me, consisted only in the fact that after he had become one of the learned members of the Akhaldan society and had clearly realized certain cosmic laws, he decided to share his new ideas with other beings of the Earth; and among his doctrines was this knowledge with the name 'Positive and Negative Influences.'

"And he created this knowledge because it was generally known among the beings of the continent Atlantis that every being in every respect represents in himself an exact likeness of the Megalocosmos, and that both the fundamental cosmic laws, the most sacred Heptaparaparshinokh and the sacred Triamazikamno, proceed in every being strictly in the same order down to the tiniest trifle as it proceeds in the Megalocosmos.

"Well, when the learned Makary Kronbernkzion by means of his persistent labors understood the details of this truth, he created a corresponding knowledge under the name, as I have just said, of 'Positive and Negative Influences.'

"And all the other beings of the Earth, owing to the consequences of the properties of the organ Kundabuffer which were already present in them understood poor Makary Kronbernkzion's doctrine in their own way and converted it into their baleful doctrine. I happened also to learn fully the contents of this same knowledge. I satisfied myself that the chief source of this idea of exterior good and evil in the consciousness of Earth-beings was there where among other things it was said:

"'Like all the unities of the world, we men are formed by and consist of three independent forces.'

"'The first of these is called Positive, the second, Negative, and the third Neutralizing.

"'All our perceptions equally with all our manifestations as well as with our substantiality depend solely on these three universal forces.

"'The first and positive force may also be called descending or good, because it arises in and creates from the prime source.

"'And the second or issuing force is called negative because this force is always and everywhere resistant and everything it meets it repels in the direction of the prime source. Hence this repelling force can also be called evil.

"'As for the third or neutralizing force it can be called the spirit, because it is only the process of the blending of these two descending and issuing forces.'

"Well, my boy, this formulation, I think, just made Earth beings imagine that Good and Evil so-called exist outside themselves; and they came to consider that the reason of their good manifestations, and of course, of their base and unconscionable conduct was not in themselves or their own egoism, but in some exterior and alien influence beyond their control. The consequences of this fancy you can see for yourself today.

"So my boy, thanks only to this wicked idea, your favorites have at the present time absolutely no other foundation for their view of the world than their external conception of Good and Evil. For instance, the conditions of their ordinary existence as beings and all the questions relative to self-perfection are based exclusively on this wicked idea. And even all the philosophy and knowledge existing among them, and of course, the innumerable religions of that place also, are founded solely on this imaginary but maleficent idea, you can safely remark here a most peculiar conjunction of circumstances, which arose solely owing to the fact that beings of our tribe once existed on this disastrous planet. This amusing conjunction was due also partly to the fact that this wicked idea of external Good and Evil existed there. The tragi-comedy originated thus:

"I told you a little while ago that for certain reasons the wish was once expressed from above that as few as possible of our beings should exist on that planet. The majority of our tribe thereupon migrated at once to another planet of the same solar system; but the remainder for some personal reason desired to stay there some time longer. And it was just at this time that the beings of our tribe, existing among the beings of the planet Earth came to be regarded by the latter as 'Beings of the Beyond,' as they expressed it, whether because the beings of our tribe had an immeasurably longer existence than the beings of this planet or were much higher in Reason than those three-centered beings nobody knows. Later when this remnant of our beings also migrated from this planet, the Earth-beings invented a religion for themselves, based on this wicked idea of external Good and Evil. And it is just here that the comedy began.

"It happened that amongst other beings it was affirmed in this religion that the carriers of external Good are certain Angels, and the carriers of external Evil certain Devils. And the result was that certain beings of that planet, chiefly the more naive, became firmly convinced that the beings who had recently existed among them and who had suddenly disappeared were no other than just these very devils who without doubt had decided to become invisible.

"From that time the tradition of the existence of certain invisible devils has been handed down from generation to generation; and even the actual names of our beings that remained in the memories of certain Earth-beings have also reached the contemporary queer fellows.

"To these names every possible fantastic attribute has been ascribed; and according to their imagination these must belong to the rank of beings called devils who are assumed to be specially organized and sent to this planet for their torment.

"Thus a devil for your favorites is an invisible being who, by the order of the CREATOR and for certain purposes, known, by the way, only to certain comics dwelling on the planet Earth, is obliged to suggest by every kind of truth and lie and make them commit the numerous uglinesses done by them.

"But they commit these uglinesses because by living unrighteously they become habitual; and even now, owing to the existence among them of this wicked idea of external Good and Evil, though they continue doing these uglinesses with all their might, they are sure that they do them not because they wish to but because they are compelled by devils sent from above.

"In reality, my boy, these unfortunate beings are always full of all kinds of ugliness chiefly because such abnormal conditions of existence were finally established there and because they do not prepare themselves at the right time to become such real responsible beings as all the three-centered beings everywhere else in the Universe aim to become. Hence the grandmothers' fairy tales told them in their childhood not only direct their whole subsequent existence, but they act as a cover to conceal all those cosmic truths which they encounter on their planet at every step.

"On this account, my boy, thanks to your favorites, nowhere in the Universe are the talents of the incomparable Lucifer so extolled as on that planet."

At this point of Beelzebub's story one of the crew, having something, entered the room of the cosmic ship *Karnak* where this conversation was taking place between Beelzebub, Hassein and Ahoon and addressing everybody, announced joyfully that the reflections of the spheres of the planet Karatas were already visible.

CHAPTER XLVI

Electricity[*]

WHEN the servant left Beelzebub sighed deeply and said:

"Heigh-ho, my dear boy, it would not be half so bad if the abnormal existence of the beings of your planet had these terrible consequences only on the perfection of the souls that already have had the great misfortune to be formed and exist on that unlucky planet. But owing to the abnormal existence of beings on the Earth horrors on an enormous scale are beginning. The abnormal existence of these three-centered beings of the planet Earth has already begun to influence very injuriously the development of beings dwelling on quite another planet, though on another planet of the same Solar System.

"If only the reflections of the spheres of our dear fatherland are yet visible, we have still a considerable time to fly, and perhaps we shall have time to talk a little further about how the abnormal existence of beings of the planet Earth begins to affect injuriously the development of beings of other planets also.

"I learned of this also only just before my final departure from that Solar System.

"As you may find the events and conversations which threw a light for me on the lamentable facts instructive and interesting in the highest degree, I shall tell you about this also in a little more detail.

"First of all you must know that I learned of my full pardon just while I was on the planet Earth. Having learned of

* *Editor's Note:* In the original ***1931 Manuscript*** chapters XLIV, XLV and XLVI had not been separated and the text of ***Form & Sequence*** preceded the text of ***Justice***, and ***Electricity***. So, along with changes to the text that occurred between 1931 and 1949, the order of these chapters was changed from ***Form & Sequence***, ***Justice***, ***Electricity***, to ***Justice***, ***Electricity***, ***Form & Sequence***.

it, I, of course, decided to return to my dear fatherland at the earliest possible moment.

"But for this it was first absolutely necessary that I should ascend to the planet Mars and there make myself ready and prepare myself for the long journey and several days later I left your planet forever.

"On the planet Mars there had already been received the order that all those who wished to return to the fatherland must take the ship '*Occasion*' to the planet Saturn where the Trans-Solar-System Ship '*Omnipresent*' which would take us all to our fatherland was due to arrive.

"I had, however, to stay on Mars for several days in order to settle up my affairs there and give directions concerning the beings of our tribe. And it was just during these days that I was told that the Martian Toof-Nef-Tef very much wished to see me personally.

"Toof-Nef-Tef on the planet Mars is the name given to the head of all the beings of that planet. He corresponds to the beings called on the planet Earth, Emperor.

"This Toof-Nef-Tef I had known from his youth when he was still Plef-Perf-Noof, or as they are otherwise called there 'Tranquillizers!' It will do you no harm, by the way, to tell you that on almost all the planets of this Solar System the heads of the beings of the whole planets are selected on their merits from among such former Plef-Perf-Noof.

"This same Toof-Nef-Tef when we first arrived on this planet where my court began to reside, was then Plef-Perf-Noof for that same district.

"Plef-Perf-Noof or tranquillizers on the planet Mars are beings whose whole lives are consecrated to helping those who for some reason or other temporarily cease or become less able to fulfill their being duties. There are beings like Plef-Perf-Noof on your planet Earth also, and such beings are there called doctors.

"For this purpose it will not harm you to be told that on your planet, doctors understand their duty quite differently. Such Earth doctors are called in when someone in the district in which they are enrolled ceases to be able to carry on his being duties.

"So far so good; they come to the house to which they are called, but they manifest, by their essence, these helps in a manner peculiar in the highest degree. The peculiarity consists in that their desire to help a being in need to whom they are called depends entirely upon the smell of the house. Their inner wish to help the being to whom they are called takes one of two quite opposite forms. For instance, when such a doctor comes to the house where some beings need his help, what happens to his psyche is as follows. If the house to which he has come smells of English pounds he is terribly concerned and wishes terribly to help the being who needs his assistance. In this case, even at the outset there will appear on his face, without his personal will, smugness, and secondly, his tail will curl quite between his legs. But if the house smells of cancelled German marks his wish rises to the maximum to write as quickly as possible for this being needing his help a prescription also invented by Germans and leave the house hastily.

"By the way, it is very interesting to note that when, in the second case, they leave the house of a needy being, these Earth doctors walk in the streets so that the whole of their exterior, even the muscles of their face, empress something as follows: 'I'm not a dog's tail but a real dog who has taken his degree.'

"In brief, this Martian Toof-Nef-Tef existed from that time on Mars in various districts; but when he began to attain the state of the Holy 'Ischmetch' he had the desire to return to the district where his youth had been passed, and this was why he was now near my house again. The emperor of the planet

Mars, Honorable Toof-Nef-Tef, was considered very old even for the planet Mars. By the Martian time calculation he was about twelve thousand years old, which time is very little less than his age would be by the time calculation of the planet Earth.

"I must tell you also that beings on the planet Mars have the same length of life as the three-centered beings of our Universe, excepting, of course, those beings who are the direct heirs of the first Mesocosmoses whose length of existence is almost three times that of ordinary beings.

"Beings of the planet Mars, like the three-centered beings of all the planets of the Megalocosmos attain the sacred 'Ischmetch' that is, that state when the existence of the being depends upon the cosmic Trogoautoegocrat from those substances derived from one prime source only and not as it proceeds in other beings whose existence depends upon substances rising from all the centers of gravity of the fundamental cosmic sacred law of Heptaparaparshinokh.

"When a being of this planet also attained the state of the holy 'Ischmetch' if thereafter the Reason of his soul has been perfected to the necessary degree of the sacred measure of Reason, and when the said being, by his own wish, finishes his planetary existence, then his soul is taken directly to the Holy Planet Purgatory. And if this soul for some reason has not yet had time to perfect himself he continues to perfect himself in the state of the sacred 'Ischmetch.'

"In the case of the Martian Emperor the state of the holy 'Ischmetch' had already begun.

"So, my dear boy, it was communicated to me during my last days on Mars that the Honorable Toof-Nef-Tef himself wished to see me personally.

"This request was transmitted to me through our Ahoon by means of a 'Kelli-E-Ofoo.' Kelli-E-Ofoo on the planet Mars is similar to what your favorites, it seems, call a 'letter.'

The text of this Kelli-E-Ofoo was as follows:

"'I have heard that Your Reverence has become worthy to receive from our GENERAL CREATOR a full pardon for the transgressions of your youth and that you are now leaving my fatherland forever. I, an old man am therefore very desirous to see you personally and to receive your blessing and in order also to thank in your person all the beings of your tribe for their constantly kind relations with the beings of my fatherland during so many years.'

"At the end of this Kelli-E-Ofoo the following was further added:

"'I myself would in person come to your house, but as you know my size does not permit it, and I am compelled therefore to beg you not refuse to come to my 'Fal-Fe-Foof.'

"You must know also that from the very beginning the beings of the planet Mars knew of our real nature and of the real reasons why we were dwelling on their planet and not as in the case of the beings of the planet Earth who never either knew or even suspected who we were or why we dwelt on their planet.

"Having received such an invitation I, of course, immediately went to call on this amiable Emperor of enormous beings. Well after the prescribed ceremonies and courtesies and in the course of conversation the great Toof-Nef-Tef suddenly addressed the following request to me.

"Yes, my boy, this same request of the Emperor of the planet Mars had the effect, furthermore, of making it very clear to me that the abnormal conditions of the beings of the planet Earth had already begun to injuriously affect the development of beings on quite another planet also. And the request of this great Toof-Nef-Tef was as follows:

"You will I think understand better if I tell you in full how he explained his request.

"He spoke as follows:

"'Your Reverence and my oldest friend, owing to the most gracious pardon granted you from above, you can now be what you must be; and now surely you will often be meeting such creatures of our CREATOR IN GENERAL as have already attained a very high degree of Reason. So my request to you consists in this that you should especially remember, when you meet any such being of higher Reason, to learn from him what at the present time is my single wish, namely how to help the beings of the planet Mars who have been entrusted to me from above. And what you learn concerning this, I ask you, in the name of our old friendship, somehow to communicate to me.'

"He said further that it had been noticed during the last two 'Ftofoos' among the beings of the planet that for some unknown reason, the 'Noorfooftafaf'* had year by year increased, and hence that every year the possibility of active intellection had been diminishing.

"'So my old and impartial friend, day and night I am much concerned to know the cause of it in order to direct all the beings of our planet Mars to help me to find a means of dealing with this general planetary misfortune.

"'I already begin to feel happier, my old friend, because the hope has arisen in me, that thanks to Your Reverence, I shall soon learn this.'

"With these words, the Honorable Emperor of the planet Mars concluded his request.

"I, of course, at once promised my oldest friend to enquire concerning this of the first corresponding being I should meet and by some means to communicate the result to him.

"Several days later we left that planet forever and on the ship *Occasion* ascended to the planet Saturn to await the ar-

* 'Noorfooftafaf' is the name given on the planet Mars to "willessnesses" or, as your favorites would say, 'Neurosis.'

rival of the great cosmic ship '*Omnipresent*.' But there on the planet Saturn our local bailiff immediately informed us of the contents of an etherogram which had been received concerning the arrival upon Saturn of the *Omnipresent*.

"It was said in the Etherogram that the '*Omnipresent*' would reach harbor on the planet Saturn precisely at the time of Hre-hree-hra. Hre-hree-hra signifies on Saturn a certain period of time determined by the situation of the planet relatively to its Sun and another planet of the same system, namely, Neptune. They count seven such periods in each year, and each such period has its own name. There was still wanting almost half a Foos until this Hre-hree-hra, that is, about one and one half months by the time calculation of the planet Mars.

"As the time for waiting for the *Omnipresent* was fairly long, the beings of our tribe decided to organize their existence during this time more or less correspondingly and hence they divided themselves into several parties in order to arrange themselves conveniently. One party continued to exist on the ship *Occasion* itself; one party was accommodated in rooms assigned to us by the amiable beings of the planet Saturn. But I decided to go with Ahoon to Rirkh, that is, to that large center of beings of that place where my friend Gornahoor Harharkh was just then existing.

"And so, my dear boy, in the course of my friendly talk with Gornahoor Harharkh on the very first evening I enquired how his scion and my godson, dear Rakhoorkh was. He thanked me and said that my godson and his scion had already became his heir in all respects. He further explained his scion had made the aim of his existence the study of the same substance Okidanokh which was the aim of his own existence also. He added further that in respect of the science of Okidanokh his scion had already surpassed him. The significance of his famous invention, namely, the non-radiating lamp, he had so completely pulverized, that he, Gornahoor Harharkh himself, had not only destroyed it, but he even quite agreed with his scion that it had been the greatest evil for him to have occupied himself so long in this pursuit.

"Just while Gornahoor Harharkh was speaking, there came into the room where our conversation was taking place, Gornahoor Rakhoorkh, his scion himself. Although the new arrival resembled his sire externally, he had the appearance of being very brave and full of exuberant youth. When he had taken his seat on the perch proper to the being of that planet, he welcomed me in a voice angelically musical.

"In his welcome among other things he said: 'Although you are only my godfather, you assuredly since my baptism have fulfilled your divine duty very conscientiously and on this account there has grown in me a feeling towards you such as I have toward my producer, and in consequence I very often remembered you in my thoughts and wished you always to be in such circumstances that could lead to a good future for you.'

"Ah, my dear boy, when I said that Gornahoor Rakhoorkh took his seat on the perch, you surely did not clearly understand me.

"The case is that beings of the planet Saturn feel themselves very well only when, having bowed themselves in a particular way, they carry the whole weight of their body on their legs, and so rest. And as such rest is particularly agreeable when they are elevated, they erect in the rooms where they exist very high rods and stand on the top of them. These sticks are just called perches.

"By the way, it is interesting to notice that they decorate these perches of theirs chiefly with various ornaments or they carve all sorts of figures on them. Your favorites have a similar weakness which they call furniture. After his welcome to me, my dear godson Gornahoor Rakhoorkh began also to join in our general conversation.*

"And so, my boy, when during our general conversation on various topics, I, by the way, became interested to learn from my godson what was the reason which led to the crystallizing in his presence of data for the engendering of the impulse to interest himself seriously in the sphere of the elucidating of the details of the Omnipresent cosmic-substance Okidanokh, thanks to which he also, like his producer, had become worthy to make certain great cosmic discoveries; then after young Rakhoorkh's reply with explanatory details to this question of mine, the fact became clear to me that the abnormal existence of your favorites already began to act harmfully on the normal existence and on the conscious self-perfecting of beings breeding on the planet Mars, and at the same time, thanks to this detailed reply of his, which was based on scientific foundations, I drew also data for the elucidating of that question for the solution of which my old Martian friend, the Great Toof-Nef-Tef had applied to me with his request.

"I will try, my boy, to reproduce to you in our speech all the thoughts of this reply of his, also as exactly as possible.

"After having thought a little at the question which I had put to him, Gornahoor Rakhoorkh replied with deep seriousness:

"'At the beginning of my existence, namely, at the age when I was still preparing to be a responsible being, I—as is proper to all three-brained beings at this age—devoted the greater part of my time to practicing for the potency "to-deliberate-actively-and-long"; and of itself it so happened that during the interval of time for necessary rest, I used to be occupied with the various experimental apparatuses of my producer.

* *Editor's Note:* In the 1931 manuscript this chapter terminates suddenly at this point. So, for the sake of continuity we have added here 6 pages taken from the 1950 publication.

"'And it was just then at that period of my existence that I began to notice more than once, that on certain days the forces and degree of my active mentation grew particularly worse.

"'What I thus constated aroused in me a subjective interest which served as the source for the engendering in my presence of the requisite impulse for the thorough cognizance of the cause of this fact, and from then on I began to pay attention both to myself as well as to what proceeded around me and to seek out the causes for it; and after one "Rkhee" I became convinced beyond doubt that this undesirable state proceeded with me each time, on the day when our large "Lifechakan"* was in action.

"'It was just this fact which I then first constated which was the cause that I have, since then, become seriously interested in this omnipresent cosmic substance and deeply absorbed in the study of its details.

"'As a result, from the very beginning of my subsequent experimental elucidations, I came to possess an immeasurable number of every kind of proof for the elucidation, both for myself and for others, of the fact that the Omnipresent substance Okidanokh is such a particle of the common presence of the atmosphere of our planet, and evidently of the presence of the atmosphere of other planets, as takes part both in the arising of every planetary and surplanetary formation—among which of course there is also the "Hraprkhabeekhrokhnian" part of every being—as well as in the maintenance of their existence.

"'Upon my further experimental elucidations I also became aware, beyond all doubt, that although our solar system like all the other solar systems of the Great Universe has its own Ansanbaluiazar, and each planet with its atmosphere is a special place of concentration of one or another class of cos-

* Lifechakan approximately corresponds to what on Earth is called a "dynamo.'

mic substances of the given "Systematic-Ansanbaluiazar," yet nevertheless the cosmic-substance Okidanokh is an indispensable and predominant part of the presence of each planet.

"'And later, also thanks to my experiments, it became clear to me that this cosmic substance is, owing to the common universal equilibrium, concentrated in every system in a strictly corresponding proportion and is distributed also in a strictly definite proportion between the atmospheres of each planet of the given solar system, and that when this universal substance is used up by accident or design in any one place of atmospheric space, it must without fail be replenished for the equilibrium of its common proportionalness in the atmosphere, and this proceeds by its flowing in from other places, and thereby this balancing transposition of Okidanokh must proceed not only from one space to another in the atmosphere of any planet, but also from the atmosphere of one planet to the atmosphere of another planet, if in this other planet for some reason or other more than its established norm is used up.

"'Finally, I still further very definitely and from every aspect made clear to my reason and proved to others that the Omnipresent cosmic-substance Okidanokh present in our atmosphere and which is constantly being replenished, is for the common presence of our planet not only necessary and most important for every kind of arising and maintaining of existence, but also that the essence of every "relatively independent" intraplanetary and surplanetary formation as well as of the beings of every system of brains and external coating depends on this substance, and likewise that the possibilities for three-brained beings to perfect themselves and ultimately to blend with the Prime Cause of everything existing depend exclusively also on it.

"'I repeat, as a result of all my experimental elucidations, I very definitely cognized for myself and acquired indubitable data for the possibilities of proving from every aspect to all those around me, beings like myself, that the destruction in the presences of the planet and of its atmosphere, of the Omnipresent cosmic-substance Okidanokh is almost equivalent to the conscious destruction of all the labors and results of the First-Sacred-Cause of everything that exists.'

"With these words, captivated by the theme of this exposition, my dear godson, the young highspirited Gornahoor Rakhoorkh, finished his talk.

"In the middle of Gornahoor Rakhoorkh's explanations concerning the mentioned properties of the Omnipresent cosmic-substance Okidanokh and the inevitable consequences of its extraction and destruction from the common presence of your planet, the suspicion arose in me, and in my memory there gradually began to be restored all kinds of general pictures—previously perceived during my personal sojourn among your favorites just during the period of my close observations on their existence from the planet Mars of the impressions from their ordinary being-existence—of how they at different periods repeatedly obtained this substance or its separate parts from the nature of their planet and used them for their different, naively egoistic aims.

"And when during the further explanations of Gornahoor Rakhoorkh, I, by association, remembered the request of the great Toof-Nef-Tef of the planet Mars, I then with all my being became aware without any doubt of all the maleficent consequences of just this manifestation of the three-brained beings of your planet.

"They named the totality or the separate parts of this substance, sacred just for them, differently at different periods, and at the present time they name the result of the blending and the mutual destruction of two parts of this omnipresent substance 'Electricity.'

"And, indeed, although there they had already several times

in earlier epochs found out, of course thanks always to accidentally successive circumstances, how to extract by various means from the nature of their planet, and to use for every kind of their, as I already said, 'naively egoistic' aims, various parts of this omnipresent substance absolutely necessary for normal cosmic processes, yet never have they destroyed so much of it as in recent times.

"So in this way, thanks to the explanations of my 'Kesdjanian-result-outside-of-me,' in the first place it became indubitably clear to me concerning the maleficent action, already begun, of the results of the ordinary abnormal being-existence of the three-brained beings who have taken your fancy; and secondly, the disturbing question of my old friend was solved of itself, namely, why during recent times it had become more and more difficult for the three-brained beings of the planet Mars to perfect themselves.

"As regards the solution in this manner of this question, I might say that it was obtained, just as is said about similar cases, in one rarely used saying of our esteemed Mullah Nassr Eddin, who formulated it in the following words:

"'One can never know who might help you to get out of galoshes.'

"And the solution of this question was thus obtained, because my very old friend had in view individuals with quite other data and possibilities than these Saturn friends of mine possessed, who were only ordinary three-brained beings; my friend probably did not suspect that in most cases concerning these questions, just these ordinary three-brained beings, who acquire information about every kind of genuine cosmic fact exclusively only thanks to their being-Partkdolg-duty, are more competent than any of the Angels or Cherubim with their prepared Being, who, though perfected in

Reason to high gradations, yet as regards practical confrontation may appear to be only such Individuals as our always respected Mullah Nassr Eddin defines in the following words:

"'Never will he understand the sufferings of another who has not experienced them himself though he may have divine Reason and the nature of a genuine Devil.'"

At this point of Beelzebub's tales, there were diffused all along the intersystem ship *Karnak* artificially produced vibrations which had the property of penetrating into the common presences of all the passengers of the ship and which acted on what are called the "wandering nerves" of the stomach.

This artificially produced manifestation was an announcement to the passengers about their assembling in the common what is called "Djameechoonatra," a kind of terrestrial "monasterial refectory" in which the second being-food is collectively taken.

CHAPTER XLVII

The Inevitable Result Of Impartial Mentation.

BEELZEBUB intended to say more but just then everything was lit up with a "pale blue something.' From that moment the falling of the ship began to diminish perceptibly in speed.

All this meant that one of the great Cosmic Egolionopties was about to come alongside the space Ship *Karnak*.

And indeed through the transparent outer parts of the Ship *Karnak* the source of that "pale blue something" soon became visible which lit up not only the whole of the interior of the Ship *Karnak* but also all the space of the Universe surrounding this great cosmic Egolionopty as far as the ordinary vision of Beings could reach.

Of these great Egolionopties there are only four in the Universe and each of them is under the jurisdiction of one of the four All-Great-Maintainers of the Universe.

A hurried and anxious commotion began among all of the beings aboard, and in a short time all the passengers and the crew assembled in the main hall set in the center of the ship.

Each of them bore a branch of myrtle in one hand and a branch of Devd'el Kascho in the other.

When the great cosmic Egolionopty had come alongside the Ship *Karnak*, certain parts of the latter were moved apart in a special way and there passed from the Egolionopty into the main hall of the ship a procession composed of several archangels and a multitude of angels, cherubim and seraphim, and they all bore branches in their hands but of palm.

At the head of this procession walked a venerable archangel and immediately after him two cherubim followed solemnly, bearing a casket from which something also radiated, but this time something orange.

In front of every one in the main hall of the Ship *Karnak*

stood Beelzebub and behind him were ranged his kinsmen and the Captain of the ship and all the others stood behind them in a respectful posture.

When the said procession from the Egolionopty reached the beings of Beelzebub's nature who were assembled in expectation, they halted and all of both forces, differently-natured three-brained beings, joined together in singing the Hymn to our ENDLESSNESS, which Hymn is always sung on such occasions everywhere in the Universe, by beings of all natures and all forms of exterior coating.

This Hymn consisted of the following words:

Thou long patient CREATOR of all that breathes,
Thou about to come of all that exists,
Thou unique VANQUISHER of the merciless Heropass
Now to the sounds of our glorifying
Only rejoice and abide in beatitude

By Thy Unprecedented Labors Thou Hast Given Us The Beginnings Of Our Arisings,
By Thy Vanquishing Of The Heropass Have We Obtained The Possibility
Of Perfecting Ourselves To The Sacred Anklad.
And Now Only Rest, As Merited,
And We, In Gratitude, Will Maintain All That Thou Hast Created
And Always And In All Things Will Extol Thee Forever.

Extol Thee MAKER CREATOR,
Thou, The Beginning Of All Ends,
Thou, Proceeding From Infinity,
Thou, Having The End Of All Things Within Thee,
Thou, Our ENDLESS ENDLESSNESS.

When the Hymn had been sung, the venerable Archangel approached Beelzebub and solemnly proclaimed:

"By the decree of his All-Quarters-Maintainer, the Arch-

Cherub Peshtvogner and bearing His own sacred rod, we appear before you, Your Right Reverence, in order to return to you, in accord with the pardon granted you from Above and for certain of your merits, what you lost during your exile—your horns."

Having said this, the venerable Archangel turned towards the casket borne by the Cherubim and with profound reverence carefully took from it the sacred rod.

Meanwhile all those present knelt down on one knee, while the Angels and Cherubim began to sing the appropriate sacred Canticles.

Taking the sacred rod in his hand, the Archangel turned again towards Beelzebub and spoke thus to the beings of Beelzebub's nature:

"Beings created by our same true being ENDLESSNESS who has pardoned this once erring being Beelzebub, who by the infinite grace of our CREATOR will again exist among you, Beings like Himself . . . .

"As the variety and degrees of Reason of beings of Your nature are defined and manifested by the horns on Your Head, we must with the permission of our All-Quarters-Maintainer, and with Your help, restore the horns lost by Beelzebub.

"Beings created by Our One Common Father, your aid will consist in this, that each of you should consent to renounce for Beelzebub's merited pardon, certain particles of your own horns.

"Whosoever therefore consents and wishes to do so, let him approach the sacred rod and touch its handle, and by the length of time the handle of the sacred rod is held, will depend the amount of active elements passing from your own horns for the formation of the corresponding horns on the pardoned being of your Nature."

Having said this, the Venerable Archangel, holding the chief end of the sacred rod, that is, the ball, over the kneeling

Beelzebub, turned the handle towards those there assembled in such a way that whoever wished might touch it.

As soon as the Venerable Archangel had finished speaking, a very great commotion began among the beings of Beelzebub's nature, each desiring to approach nearer and to be the first to touch the sacred rod with their hands as long as possible.

Order, however, was soon established and each in turn approached and held the handle for as long as was indicated by the Captain of the ship, who had taken upon himself the necessary direction.

During the solemn, sacred action, horns little by little began to grow upon the head of Beelzebub.

At first, while just the bare horns were being formed, only a concentrated quiet gravely prevailed among those assembled. But from the moment that forks began to appear upon the horns a tense interest and rapt attention proceeded among them, because everybody was agitated by the wish to learn how many forks would make their appearance on Beelzebub, since by their number, the gradation of Reason to which Beelzebub had attained according to the sacred measure of Reason would be defined.

First, one fork formed, then another and then a third, and as each fork made its appearance a clearly perceptible thrill of joy and unconcealed satisfaction proceeded among all those present.

As the fourth fork began to be formed on the Horns, the tension among those assembled reached its height, since the formation of the fourth fork on the horns signified that the Reason of Beelzebub had already been perfected to the sacred Ternoonald and hence that there remained for Beelzebub only two gradations before attaining to the sacred Anklad.

When the whole of this unusual circumstance reached its end and before all those assembled had had time to recover from their earlier joyful anticipation, there suddenly and inexplicably appeared on the horns of Beelzebub quite independently a fifth fork of a special form known to them all.

Thereupon all without exception, even the Venerable Archangel himself, fell prostrate before Beelzebub, who had now risen to his feet and stood transfigured with a majestic appearance, owing to the majestic horns which had arisen on His head.

All fell prostrate before Beelzebub because by the fifth fork on His horns, it was indicated that he had attained the Reason of the Sacred Podkoolad, i.e., the last gradation before the Reason of the Sacred Anklad.

The Reason of the Sacred Anklad is the highest to which in general any being can attain, being the third in degree from the Absolute Reason of HIS ENDLESSNESS HIMSELF.

And the Reason of the Sacred Podkoolad, to which Beelzebub had already perfected himself, is also very rare in the Universe, hence even the Venerable Archangel prostrated himself before Beelzebub because His own degree of Reason was as yet only that of the Sacred Degindad, i.e., wanting three degrees to the Reason of the Sacred Anklad.

When all had arisen to their feet, the Venerable Archangel, addressing this time all the assembled beings of various natures, proclaimed:

"Beings Created by Our CREATOR,

"We have all just become worthy to be the first to behold the final formation of the appearance of that which is the dream both of all those present and of the beings in general of the whole of our great Megalocosmos.

"And now let us all together exult and rejoice over such a worthiness, which is for us such a vivifying shock of our ability to struggle against our own denying source, which ability alone can lead us to that Sacred Podkoolad attained by one of the Sons of Our Common Father, who although he first transgressed on account of his youth, yet afterwards was able by his conscious labors and intentional suffering to become worthy with his essence to be one of the very reverend Sacred Individuums of the whole of our great Universe."

After this proclamation of the Archangel all the beings without exception present on the space ship *Karnak* then began to sing the prescribed sacred canticle entitled, "I rejoice."

And when this latter sacred canticle also had been sung, all the Angels and Cherubim, with the Venerable Archangel at their head, returned to the cosmic Egolionopty which then left the ship *Karnak* and disappeared gradually into space, whereupon the passengers and crew began correspondingly to disperse to their places and the *Karnak* resumed its falling towards its destination.

After the termination of the most Great Universal Solemnity just described, Beelzebub with his grandson and his old servant Ahoon, deeply moved like all of the other passengers of the space ship *Karnak* by this inexpressible event, returned to that part of the ship where all their talks proceeded concerning the Men beings arising and existing on the Earth.

When Beelzebub, now with a transformed appearance corresponding to his merits and visible to all, had occupied his usual place, Ahoon, the old servant who had been close to him during almost the whole of his existence, unexpectedly fell prostrate before him and in a sincerely entreating voice began to speak:

"Sacred Podkoolad of our Great Megalocosmos! Have mercy upon me and pardon me, an unfortunate ordinary being, for my past unrespectful manifestations, voluntary and involuntary, towards your Sacred Essence.

"Have mercy and pardon me—just this three-centered being, who, though he has existed a very long time, yet to his misfortune—only because in his preparatory age nobody aided the crystallization in him of the data for the ability of intensely actualizing Being-Partkdolgduty—had until now been so short-sighted that he has been unable to sense the reality present beneath an exterior with which, according to the Common Cosmic Triamazikamno, all those existing and newly arising units of the Mesocosmos are coated, who ought to have in their presence that sacred Something which is called Reason."

Having said this, Ahoon stood as if sunk in a stupid silence of expectation.

And Beelzebub, also in silence, gazed at him with a look which though perceived externally from without, was full of love and forgiveness, yet there could be felt in it also his Essence-grief and inevitable resignation.

During the afore-described scene, Hassein stood apart in the posture everywhere called the Posture-of-the-All-Universal-Hermit, Harnatoolkpararana of the planet Kirmankshana.

And when a little bit later Beelzebub cast his eyes around and perceived his grandson in the said posture, he turned to him and said:

"What my boy! Can it be that the same proceeds in your presence as in our old Ahoon's?"

To this question of Beelzebub's, Hassein, also in an uncertain tone unusual for him, timidly replied:

"Almost . . . yes . . . Sacred Podkoolad of our Great Megalocosmos. Only with this difference—that at this moment the impulse of love both for our Ahoon and for the three-brained beings of the planet Earth now functions still more thoroughly in me.

"This impulse of love thus becomes stronger in me, evidently because, as it seems to me, both Ahoon and the three-brained beings of the Earth have greatly aided me in becoming worthy to be a recent eyewitness of the great Solemnity of him who is the cause of the causes of my arising and whom hitherto I have called my dear Grandfather and who has already visibly become one of the Sacred Podkoolads of our Great Megalocosmos, before whom all will bow and before whom I have at this moment the happiness to stand.'

"Eh-eh-eh!" exclaimed Beelzebub, and having given his features the usual expression he was wont to assume during his sojourn on the Earth, said:

"First of all I wish to remark and in the speech of Mullah Nassr Eddin, whom I particularly honor, to voice the thought which arises by association concerning Ahoon's words which were not peculiar to him and his assumed posture quite unusual for him.

"Our dear teacher in such a case would say, 'Don't shed tears in vain like that crocodile which snapped at the fisherman and missed biting off his lower left half.'

"And now first take your places and then let us talk a little more.

"Although our ship is now entering the spheres of our planet Karatas, yet as usually happens with space ships, in order to exhaust the momentum they have acquired, a fairly long time will elapse before it stops at its destined mooring place.'

Hassein and Ahoon immediately and silently proceeded to follow the suggestion of Beelzebub, though by their movements and the translucency of their psyche, it was evident that there had been a marked change in their attitude towards the person of Beelzebub since the above described Common Universal Event.

When they had taken their places they sat down this time not with the unconstraint they had formerly shown.

Then Beelzebub, turning to Hassein, said, "First of all, my dear boy, I give you my word that when we return home—unless any event from external causes independent of our Essence will prevent this—I shall explain to you everything relating to the three-brained beings who have taken your fancy, concerning that which during this journey of ours on the ship *Karnak* I promised to explain, but which I have for some reason or other left unexplained.

"And meanwhile, if you have any question in mind that now needs explanation, ask.

"I promise, however, that we have not enough time to reply in the manner that has become proper to our talk all this time and hence try to formulate your question in such a way that my answer may also be brief.

"By such a question you can even, apropos, once more show me to what extent your logical mentation has increased during my tales concerning the strange psyche of the three-brained beings arising and existing on the planet Earth."

At this proposition of his grandfather, Hassein deeply thought rather a long time and then in an exalted mood, spoke as follows:

"Sacred Podkoolad and fundamental cause of the causes of my arising!

"Since the solemnity which has just taken place, when your Sacred Essence became coated with a corresponding visible exterior and when thereby the whole of the significance which cannot be perceived nor understood by all three-brained beings became clear and even sensible to me as well as to every other cosmic unit, save yourself, every word spoken by you and every counsel of yours is taken by me as Law.

"I must therefore strive with the whole of my presence to carry out the suggestion you have just made to me and try as well and as briefly as possible to formulate my question.

"Sacred Podkoolad, and cause of the causes of my arising.

"In order that the conviction formed in me during this time, owing to your explanation of the abnormalities proceeding on the Earth may become definitely crystallized in me, I still wish very much to have this time your personal and frank opinion as to the following: How you would reply if, let us suppose, our ALL-EMBRACING-CREATOR-ENDLESSNESS HIMSELF, were to summon you before HIM and ask you this:

"'Beelzebub ! ! ! ! !

"'You, as one of the anticipated, accelerated results of all my actualizations, manifest briefly the sum of your long-continued important observations and studies of the psyche of the three-centered beings arising on the planet Earth and state in words whether it is still possible by some means or other to save them and to direct them into the becoming path?'"

Having said this Hassein arose and standing in a posture of reverence began to look expectantly at Beelzebub. And Ahoon also arose.

Beelzebub, smiling lovingly at this question of Hassein's, first said that he was now quite convinced that his tales had brought Hassein the desired results; and then, in a serious tone he continued that if our ALL-EMBRACING-UNIVERSAL-BODY-CREATOR should indeed summon him before HIM and ask him this, he would answer.

Thereupon Beelzebub suddenly also arose unexpectedly and having stretched his right hand forward and his left hand back, he directed his vision somewhere afar off, and it seemed that with his sight he was, as it were, perceiving the very depths of space.

Simultaneously something pale yellow began little by little to rise round Beelzebub and to envelop him, and it was in no way possible to see nor to discern whence this something issued—whether it issued from Beelzebub himself or proceeded to him from space from sources outside of him.

Finding Himself in these cosmic actualizations incomprehensible for all three-brained beings Beelzebub in a low voice unusual to him very peculiarly intoned the following words:

"THOU ALL of the ALLNESS of my WHOLENESS!

"The sole means now for the saving of the Beings of the planet Earth would be to implant again into their presences a new organ, an organ like Kundabuffer, but this time of such proportion that every one of those unfortunates during the process of existence should constantly sense and be cognizant of the inevitability of his own death as well as of the death of every one upon whom his eyes or attention rests.

"Only such a sensation and such a cognizance can now destroy the egoism completely crystallized in them that has swallowed up the whole of their Essence and also the tendency to hate others which flows from it—the tendency seemingly which engenders all those inimical relationships existing there which serves as the chief cause of all their abnormalities unbecoming to three-brained beings and maleficent for them themselves and for the whole of the Universe.'

From The Author

AFTER six years of work, merciless towards myself and with almost continuously tense meditation, I yesterday at last completed the setting down on paper, in a form, I think, accessible to everybody, the first of the three series of books I had previously thought out and six years ago begun—just those three series in which I planned to actualize by means of the totality of the ideas to be developed, at first in theory and afterwards in practice, also by a means I had foreseen and prepared three essence tasks I had set myself, namely; by means of the first series, to destroy in people everything which, in their false representations, as it were, exists in reality, or in other words "to-corrode-without-mercy-all-the-rubbish-accumulated-during-the-ages-in-human-mentation"; by means of the second series, to prepare so to say "new-constructional material"; and by means of the third, "to-build-a-new-World."

Having now finished the first series of books, and, following the practice already long ago established on the Earth—never to conclude any great, as is said, "undertaking" without what some call an epilogue, others an "afterword," and still others "from-the-author," and so on—I also now propose to write something of the same kind for them.

With this end in view I very attentively read over this morning the "Preface" I wrote six years ago entitled "Warning," in order to take corresponding ideas from it for a corresponding so to say "logical-fusion" of that beginning with this conclusion which I now intend to write.

While I was reading that first chapter, which I wrote only six years ago, but which seems to me by my present sensing to have been written long long ago, a sensing which is now in my common presence obviously because during that time I had to think intensely and even as might be said, to "experience" all the suitable material required for eight thick volumes;—not for nothing is it stated in that branch of genuine science, entitled "the-laws-of-association-of-human-mentation," which has come down from very ancient times and is known to only a few contemporary people—formulated as "the-sensing-of-the-flow-of-time-is-directly-proportional-to-the-quality-and-quantity-of-the-flow-of-thoughts";—well then, while I was reading just that first chapter, about which, as I said, I thought deeply from every aspect and which I experienced under the most exclusive action of my own willed self-mortification, in which moreover, I wrote at a time when the functioning of my entire whole—a functioning which engenders in a man what is called "the-power-to-manifest-by-his-own-initiative," was utterly disharmonized, that is to say, when I was still extremely ill owing to an accident that had not long before occurred to me, and which consisted of a "charge-and-a-crash" with my automobile at full speed into a tree standing silently, like an observer and reckoner of the passage of centuries at a disorderly tempo, on the historic road between the world-capital of Paris and the town of Fontainbleau—a "charge" which according to any sane human understanding, should have put an end to my life—there arose in me from the reading of that chapter a quite definite decision.

Recalling my state during the period of the writing of that first chapter I cannot help adding here—owing to still another certain small weakness in me which consists of my always experiencing an inner satisfaction whenever I see appear on the faces of our estimable contemporary as they are called 'representatives-of-exact-science," that very specific smile peculiar to them alone—that although my body after this accident was, as is said "so-battered-and-everything-in-it-so-mixed-up," that for months it looked like a fragment of a general picture which might be described as "a-bit-of-live-meat-in-a-clean-bed," nevertheless, and for all that, my correctly disciplined what is usually called "spirit," even in that physical state of my body, was not in the least depressed, as it should have been according to their notions, but, on the contrary, its power was even intensified by the heightened excitation which had arisen in it just before the accident owing to my repeated disappointment in people, particularly, in such people as are devoted, as they say to "science," and also to my disappointment in those ideals which until then had been in me, and which had gradually been formed in my common presence, thanks chiefly to the commandment inculcated in me in my childhood, enjoining that "the-highest-aim-and-sense-of-human-life-is-the-striving-to-attain-the-welfare-of-one's-neighbour," and that this is possible exclusively only by the conscious renunciation of one's own.

And so, after I had very attentively read over that opening chapter of the first series, which I had written in the said conditions, and when in my memory by association, there had been recalled the texts of those many succeeding chapters, which, according to my conviction, ought to produce in the consciousness of the readers unusual impressions which in turn always, as is said, "engender-substantial-results," I, or rather, this time, that dominant "something" in my common presence which now represents the sum of the results obtained from the data crystallized during my life, data which engender, among other things, in a man who has in general set himself the aim so to say "to-mentate-actively-impartially" during the process of responsible existence, the ability to penetrate and understand the psyche of people of various types.—I decided, urged by the impulse called "Love-of-Kind" which simultaneously arose in me, not to write in this conclusion anything additional and correspondent to the general aim of this first series, but to confine myself simply to appending the first of a considerable number of lectures, copies of which now are in my possession and which were publicly read during the existence of the institution I had founded under the name of "The-Institute-for-the-Harmonious-Development-of-Man.'

That institution by the way no longer exists, and I find it both necessary and opportune, chiefly for the purpose of pacifying certain types from various countries, to make the categorical declaration here and now that I have liquidated it completely and forever.

I was constrained with an inexpressible impulse of grief and despondency to make this decision to liquidate this institution and everything organized and carefully prepared for the opening the following year of eighteen sections in different countries, in short, of everything I had previously created with almost superhuman labor, chiefly because, soon after the said accident occurred, that is, three months afterwards, when the former usual functioning of my mentation had been more or less reestablished in me—I being still utterly powerless in body I then reflected that the attempt to preserve the existence of this institution, would, in the absence of real people around me and owing to the impossibility of procuring without me the great material means required for it, inevitably lead to a catastrophe the result of which, among other things for me in my old age as well as for numerous others wholly dependent on me, would be, so to say, a "vegetation."

The lecture which I propose to append as a conclusion to this first series, was more than once read by my, as they were then called, "pupils-of-the-first-rank," during the existence of the mentioned institution. Certain of them, by the way, turned out subsequently, to my personal sincere regret, to have in their essence a predisposition to the speedy transformation of their psyche into the psyche called "Hasnamussian,"—a predisposition which appeared and became fully visible and clearly sensible to all more or less normal persons around them, when, at the moment of desperate crisis for everything I had previously actualized, due to the said accident, they, as is said, "quaking-for-their-skins," that is to say, fearing to lose their personal welfare which by the way, I had created for them, deserted the common work and with their tails between their legs took themselves off to their kennels, where, profiting by the crumbs fallen from my so to say "idea-table," they opened their, as I would say, "Shachermacher-workshop-booths," and with a secret feeling of hope and perhaps even joy at their speedy and complete release from my vigilant control, began manufacturing out of various unfortunate naive people, "candidates-for-lunatic-asylums."

I append just this particular lecture, firstly, because, at the very beginning of the dissemination of the ideas I imported into life, it was specially prepared here on the continent of Europe to serve as the introduction, or as it were, threshold for the whole series of subsequent lectures, by no less than the whole sum of which was it possible both to make clear in a form accessible to everybody the necessity and even the inevitability of practical actualization of the immutable truths I have elucidated and established in the course of half a century of day-and-night active work and also to prove the actual possibility of employing those truths for the welfare of people; and secondly I append it here, because, while it was last being publicly read, and I happened myself to be present at that numerous gathering, I made an addition which fully corresponds to the hidden thought introduced by Mr. Beelzebub himself into his, so to say, "concluding-chord," and which at the same time, illuminating once more this most great objective truth, will in my opinion make it possible for the reader properly to perceive and assimilate this truth as befits a being who claims to be an "image of God."

LECTURE NUMBER ONE

THE VARIETY, ACCORDING TO LAW, OF THE MANIFESTATION OF HUMAN INDIVIDUALITY

(Last read in New York in the Neighborhood Playhouse, January 1924.)

According to the investigations of many scientists of past ages and according to the data obtained at the present time by means of the quite exceptionally conducted researches of The-Institute-for-the-Harmonious-Development-of-Man according to the system of Mr. Gurdjieff, the whole individuality of every man according to laws and the conditions of the process of life of people which have from the very beginning become established and gradually fixed on the Earth—of whatever heredity he is the result, and whatever be the accidental surrounding conditions in which he arose and developed, must already at the beginning of his responsible life—as a condition of responding in reality to the sense and predesignation of his existence as a man and not merely an animal—indispensably consist of four definite distinct personalities.

The first of these four independent personalities is nothing else than the totality of that automatic functioning which is proper to man as well as to all animals, the data for which are composed in them firstly of the sum total of the results of impressions previously perceived from all the surrounding reality as well as from everything intentionally artificially implanted in them from outside, and, secondly, from the result of the process also inherent in every animal called "daydreaming." And this totality of automatic functioning most people ignorantly name "consciousness," or, at best, "mentation."

The second of the four personalities functioning in most cases independently of the first consists of the sum of the results of the data deposited and fixed, which have been perceived by the common presence of every animal through its six organs called "receivers-of-the-varied-qualified-vibrations," which organs function in accordance with newly perceived impressions and the sensitiveness of which depends upon transmitted heredity and on the conditions of the preparatory formation of the given individual for responsible existence.

The third independent part of the whole being is the prime functioning of his organism as well as what are called the "motor-reflex-reciprocally-affecting-manifestations-proceeding-in-it," and the quality of these manifestations also depends on those aforesaid results of heredity and of the circumstances during his preparatory formation.

And the fourth, which should also be a separate part of the whole individual, is none other than the manifestation of the totality of the results of the already automatized functioning of all the three enumerated personalities separately formed and independently educated in him, that is to say, it is that which is called in a being, "I.'

In the common presence of a man, and for the spiritualization and manifestation of each of the enumerated three separately formed parts of his entire whole, there is an independent, as it is called, "gravity-center-localization"; and each of these "gravity-center-localizations," each with its own entire system, has, for its general actualization, its own peculiarities and predispositions inherent in it alone. In consequence of this, in order to make possible the rounded perfecting of man, a special corresponding correct education is indispensably necessary for each of these three parts, and not such a treatment as given nowadays and also called "education.'

Only then can the "I" which should be in man, be his own "I."

According to the already indicated seriously instituted experimental investigations carried on over many years, or even according merely to the sane and impartial reflection of even every contemporary man, the common presence of every man—particularly of one in whom for some reason or other there arises, so to say, the pretension to be not just an ordinary average man, but what is called "one-of-the-intelligentsia" in the genuine sense of the word—must inevitably consist not only of all the said four fully determined distinct personalities, but each of them must of necessity be exactly correspondingly developed, to ensure that in his general manifestation during the period of his responsible existence, all the separate parts should harmonize with each other.

For a comprehensive and visible clarification to oneself of the varied sources of the arising and the varied qualities of the manifested personalities in the general organization of man, and also of the difference between what is called that "I" which should be in the common presence of a "man-without-quotation-marks," that is a real man, and, as it can be expressed, the pseudo "I" which people today mistake for it, an analogy can be very well made. Though this analogy, as is said, has been "worn-threadbare" by contemporary what are called spiritualists, occultists, theosophists, and other specialists in "catching-fish-in-muddy-waters," in their cackle about what are called the "mental," "astral" and still other such "bodies" which are supposed to be in man, nevertheless it is well adapted to throw light on the question we are now considering.

A man as a whole with all his separately concentrated and functioning localizations, that is to say, his formed and independently educated "personalities," is almost exactly comparable to that organization for conveying a passenger, which consists of a carriage, a horse, and a coachman.

It must first of all be remarked that the difference between a real man and a pseudo man, that is between one who has his own "I" and one who has not, is indicated in the analogy we have taken by the passenger sitting in the carriage. In the first case, that of the real man, the passenger is the owner of the carriage; and in the second case, he is simply the first chance passerby who like the fare in a "hackney-carriage" is constantly being changed.

The body of a man with all its motor reflex manifestations, corresponds simply to the carriage itself; all the functionings and manifestations of feeling of a man correspond to the horse harnessed to the carriage and drawing it; the coachman sitting on the box and directing the horse corresponds to that in a man which people call consciousness or mentation; and finally, the passenger seated in the carriage and commanding the coachman is that which is called "I.'

The fundamental evil among contemporary people is chiefly that owing to the rooted and widespread abnormal methods of education of the arising generation, this fourth personality which should be present in everybody on reaching responsible age, is entirely missing in them; and almost all of them consist only of the three enumerated parts, which parts moreover, are formed arbitrarily of themselves and anyhow. In other words, almost every contemporary man of responsible age consists of nothing more nor less than simply a "hackney carriage," and one moreover, composed of as follows: a broken down carriage, "which-has-long-ago-seen-its-day," a crock of a horse, and, on the box, a tatterdemalion half-sleepy, half-drunken coachman whose time designated by Mother Nature for self-perfection passes while he waits on a corner, fantastically daydreaming, for any old chance passenger. The first passenger who happens along, hires him and dismisses him just as he pleases, and not only him but also all the parts subordinate to him.

Continuing this analogy between a typical contemporary man, with his thoughts, feelings and body, and a "hackney-carriage, horse and coachman, we can clearly see that in each of the parts composing both organizations, there must have been formed and there must exist its own separate needs, habits, tastes, and so on proper to it alone. From the varied nature of their arising and the diverse conditions of their formation, and according to their varying possibilities in each of them there must inevitably have been formed for instance, its own psyche, its own notions, its own subjective supports, its own viewpoints and so on.

The whole totality of the manifestations of human mentation with all the inherencies proper to this functioning and with all its specific particularities, corresponds almost exactly in every respect to the essence and manifestations of a typical hired coachman.

Like all hired coachman in general, he is a type called "Cabby." He is not entirely illiterate, because owing to the regulations existing in his country for the "general-compulsory-teaching-of-the-three-R's," he was obliged in his childhood to put in an occasional attendance at what is called the "parish-church-school."

Although he himself is from the country and has remained as ignorant as his fellow rustics, yet rubbing shoulders, owing to his profession, with people of various positions and educations, picking up from them, by bits here and bits there, a variety of expressions embodying various notions, he has now come to regard everything smacking of the country with superiority and contempt, indignantly dismissing it all, as "ignorance."

In short, this is a type to whom applies perfectly the definition; "The-crows-he-raced-but-by-peacocks-outpaced."

He considers himself competent even in questions of religion, politics and sociology; with his equals he likes to argue; those whom he regards as his inferiors, he likes to teach; his superiors he flatters, with them he is servile; before them, as is said, "he-stands-cap-in-hand.'

One of his chief weaknesses is to dangle after the neighboring cooks and housemaids, but, best of all, he likes a good hearty tuck-in, and to gulp down another glass or two, and then fully satiated, drowsily to daydream.

To gratify these weaknesses of his, he always steals a part of the money given him by his employer to buy fodder for the horse.

Like every "cabby" he works as is said always "under-the-lash," and if occasionally he does a job without being made, it is only in the hope of receiving tips.

The desire for tips has gradually taught him to be aware of certain weaknesses in the people with whom he has dealings, and to profit himself by them; he has automatically learned to be cunning, to flatter, so to say, to stroke people the right way, and, in general, to lie.

On every convenient occasion and at every free moment he slips into a saloon or to a bar, where over a glass of beer, he daydreams for hours at a time, or talks with a type like himself, or just reads the paper.

He tries to appear imposing, wears a beard, and if he is thin, pads himself out to appear more important.

The totality of the manifestations of the feeling localization in a man and the whole system of its functioning, correspond perfectly to the horse of the "hackney-carriage" in our analogy.

Incidentally, this comparison of the horse with the organization of human feeling will serve to show up particularly clearly the error and one-sidedness of the contemporary education of the rising generation.

The horse as a whole, owing to the negligence of those around it, during its early years, and to its constant solitude, is as if locked up within itself; that is to say, its so to say "inner-life" is driven inside, and for external manifestations it has nothing but inertia.

Thanks to the abnormal conditions around it, the horse has never received any special education, but has been molded exclusively under the influence of constant thrashings and vile abuse.

It has always been kept tied up; and for food, instead of oats and hay, there is given it merely straw which is utterly worthless for its real needs.

Never having seen in any of the manifestations towards it even the least love or friendliness, the horse is now ready to surrender itself completely to anybody who gives it the slightest caress.

The consequence of all this is that all the inclinations of the horse, deprived of all interests and aspirations must inevitably be concentrated on food, drink, and the automatic yearning towards the opposite sex; hence it invariably veers in the direction where it can obtain any of these. If, for example, it catches sight of a place where even once or twice it gratified one of the enumerated needs, it waits the chance to run off in that direction.

It must further be added that although the coachman has a very feeble understanding of his duties, he can nevertheless, even though only a little, think logically, and remembering tomorrow, he either from fear of losing his job or from the desire of receiving a reward, does occasionally evince an interest in doing something or other for his employer without being driven to it; but the horse—in consequence of there not having been formed in it at the proper time, owing to the absence of any special and corresponding education, any data at all for manifesting the aspirations requisite for responsible existence—of course fails to understand (and indeed it cannot be expected that it should understand) why in general it must do anything; its obligations are therefore carried out quite inertly and only from fear of further beatings.

As far as the carriage or cart is concerned, which stands in our analogy for the body without any of the other independently formed parts of the common presence of a man, the situation is even worse.

This cart, like most carts, is made of various materials, and furthermore is of a very complicated construction.

It was designed, as is evident to every sane-thinking man, to carry all kinds of burdens, and not for the purpose for which contemporary people employ it, that is, only for carrying passengers.

The chief cause of the various misunderstandings connected with it springs from the fact that those who made the system of this cart intended it for travel on the byroads, and certain inner details of its general construction were in consequence foreseeingly made to answer to this aim.

For example, the principle of its greasing, one of the chief needs of a construction of such different materials, was so devised that the grease should spread over all the metallic parts from the shaking received from the jolts inevitable on such roads, whereas now, this cart that was designed for traveling on the byroads finds itself stationed on a rank in the city and traveling on smooth, level, asphalted roads. In the absence of any shocks whatsoever while going along such roads, no uniform greasing of all its parts occurs, and some of them consequently must inevitably rust and cease to fulfill the action intended for them.

A cart goes easily as a rule if its moving parts are properly greased. With too little grease, these parts get heated and finally red-hot, and thus the other parts get spoiled; on the other hand, if in some part there is too much grease, the general movement of the cart is impaired, and in either case it becomes more difficult for the horse to draw it.

The contemporary coachman, our "cabby" neither knows nor has any suspicion of the necessity of greasing the cart, and even if he does grease it, he does so without proper knowledge, only on hearsay, blindly following the directions of the first comer.

That is why, when this cart, now adapted more or less for

travel on smooth roads, has for some reason or other to go along a byroad, something always happens to it; either a nut gives way, or a bolt gets bent or something or other gets loose; and after these attempts at traveling along such roads, the journey rarely ends without more or less considerable repairs.

In any case, to make use of this cart for the purposes for which it was made, is already impossible without risk. If repairs are begun, it is necessary to take the cart all to pieces, examine all its parts, and, as is done in such cases, "kerosene" them, clean them and put them together again, and frequently it becomes clearly necessary immediately and without fail to change a part. This is all very well if it happens to be an inexpensive part, but it may turn out to be more costly than a new cart.

And so, all that has been said about the separate parts of that organization of which, taken as a whole, a "hackney-carriage" consists, can be fully applied also to the general organization of the common presence of a man.

Owing to the absence among contemporary people of any knowledge and ability specially to prepare in a corresponding way the rising generation for responsible existence by education all the separate parts composing their common presences, every person of today is a confused and extremely ludicrous "something," that is to say, again using this example we have taken, a "something" resembling the following picture.

A carriage just out of the factory, made on the latest model, polished by genuine German craftsmen from the town of "Barmen" and harnessed to the kind of horse which is called in the locality named "Transcaucasia," a "Dglozidzi.' ("Dzi" is a horse, "Dgloz" is the name of a certain Armenian specialist in buying utterly worthless horses and skinning them.)

On the box of this stylish carriage sits an unshaven, unkempt, sleepy coachman-cabby, dressed in a shabby cloak which he has retrieved from the rubbish heap where it had been thrown as utterly worthless by the kitchen-maid Maggie. On his head reposes a brand new top-hat, an exact replica of Rockerfeller's; and in his button hole there is displayed a giant chrysanthemum.

This picture, however ludicrous, of contemporary man, is an inevitable result, chiefly because from the first day of the arising and formation of a contemporary man, all these three parts formed in him—which parts, although diversely-caused and with properties of diverse-quality, should nevertheless at the period of his responsible existence for pursuing a single aim all together represent his entire whole—begin, so to say, to "live" and to become fixed in their specific manifestations separately one from another, never having been trained either to the requisite automatic reciprocal-maintenance, reciprocal-assistance, or to any, even though only approximate, reciprocal understanding; and thus, when afterwards concerted manifestations are required, these concerted manifestations do not appear.

Thanks to what is called the "system-of-education-of-the-rising-generation" which at the present time has already been completely fixed in the life of man and which consists singly and solely in training the pupils, by means of constant repetition to the point of "madness," to sense various almost empty words and expressions and to recognize only the difference in their consonance, the reality supposed to be signified by these words and expressions, the coachman is still able to explain after a fashion the various desires arising in him, but only to types similar to his own outside of his common presence, and he is sometimes even able approximately to understand others.

This coachman-cabby of ours, gossiping with other coachmen while waiting for a fare, and sometimes, as is said, "flirting" at the gate with the neighbor's maid, even learns various forms of what is called "amiability.'

He also by the way, according to the external conditions of the life of coachmen in general, gradually automatizes himself to distinguish one street from the other and to calculate, for instance, during repairs in some street, how to get to the required street from another direction.

But as for the horse, although the maleficent invention of contemporary people which is called education does not extend over the horse's formation, and in consequence its inherited possibilities are not atrophied, yet owing to the fact that this formation proceeds under the conditions of the abnormally established process of the ordinary existence of people, and that the horse grows up ignored like an orphan by everybody, and moreover an ill-treated orphan, it neither acquires anything corresponding to the established psyche of the coachman nor learns anything of what he knows, and hence is quite ignorant of all the forms of reciprocal relationship which have become usual for the coachman, and no contact is established between them for understanding each other.

It is possible, however, that in her locked-in life the horse does nevertheless learn some form of relationship with the coachman and that even, perhaps, she is familiar with some "language"; but the trouble is, that the coachman does not know this and does not even suspect its possibility.

Apart from the fact that owing to the said abnormal conditions, no data for even an approximate understanding of each other are formed between the horse and the coachman, there are also still other and numerous external causes, independent of them, which fail to give them the possibility of together actualizing that one purpose for which they were both destined.

The point is, that just as the separate independent parts of a "hackney" are connected—namely, the carriage to the horse by the shafts and the horse to the coachman by the reins—so also are the separate parts of the general organization of man connected with each other, namely, the body is connected to the feeling organization by the blood, and the feeling organization is connected to the organization actualizing the functioning of mentation or consciousness, by what is called "Hanbledzoin," that is, by that substance which arises in the common presence of a man from all intentionally made being efforts.

The wrong system of education existing at the present time has led to the coachman's ceasing to have any effect whatever on his horse, unless we allow the fact that he is merely able by means of the reins to engender in the consciousness of the horse just three ideas—Right, Left, and Stop.

Strictly speaking, he cannot always do even this, because the reins in general are made of materials that react to various atmospheric phenomena: for example, during a pouring rain they swell and contract, and in heat, the contrary; thereby changing their effect upon the horse's automatized sensitiveness of perception.

The same proceeds in the general organization of the average man whenever from some impression or other the so to say "density-and-tempo" of the Hanbledzoin changes in him, when his thoughts entirely lose all possibility of affecting his feeling organization.

And so, to resume all that has been said, one must willy-nilly acknowledge that every man should strive to have his own "I"; otherwise he will always represent a "hackney-carriage" in which any fare can sit and which any fare can dispose of just as he pleases.

And here it will not be superfluous to point out that the Institute-for-the-Harmonious-Development-of-Man, organized on the system of Mr. Gurdjieff, has among its fundamental tasks, also the task of on the one hand correspondingly educating in its pupils, each of the enumerated independent personalities separately as well as in their general reciprocal-relationship, and on the other hand, of begetting and fostering in each of its pupils what every bearer of the name of man without quotation-marks should have—his own "I."

For a more exact, so to say, scientific definition of the difference between a genuine man, that is, man as he ought to be, and a man whom we have called "man-in-quotation-marks," that is, such men as almost all contemporary people have become, it is fitting to repeat what was said about this by Mr. Gurdjieff himself in one of his personal "lecture-talks."

It was as follows:

"For the definition of man, considered from our point of view, neither anatomical, nor physiological, nor psychological, contemporary knowledge of his symptoms can assist us, since they are inherent in one degree or another in every man and consequently apply equally to all. Hence they do not enable us to establish the exact difference which we wish to establish between people. This difference can only be formulated in the following terms: "man-is-a-being-who-can-do," and "to do" means to act consciously and by one's own initiative."

And indeed every more or less sane-thinking man who is able to be if only a little impartial, must admit that hitherto there has not been nor can there be a fuller and more exhaustive definition.

Even suppose that we provisionally accept this definition, the question inevitably arises—can a man who is a product of contemporary education and civilization do anything at all himself, consciously and by his own will?

No . . .we answer at the very beginning, to this question.

Why not? . . .

Solely because, as the Institute-for-the-Harmonious-Development-of-Man experimentally proves and from experiments categorically affirms, everything without exception from beginning to end does itself in contemporary man, and there is nothing which a contemporary man himself does.

In personal, family and communal life, politics, science,

art, philosophy and religion, in short, in everything entering into the process of the ordinary life of a contemporary man, everything from beginning to end does itself, and not a single one of these "victims-of-contemporary-civilization" can "do" anything.

This experimentally proven categorical affirmation of the Institute-for-the-Harmonious-Development-of-Man, namely, that the ordinary man can do nothing and that everything does itself in him, coincides with what is said of man by contemporary "exact-positive-science.'

Contemporary "exact-positive-science" says that a man is a very complex organism developed by evolution from the simplest organisms, and who has now become capable of reacting in a very complex manner to external impressions. This capability of reacting in man is so complex, and the responsive movements can appear to be so far removed from the causes evoking them and conditioning them, that the actions of man, or at least a part of them, seem to naive observation quite spontaneous.

But according to the ideas of Mr. Gurdjieff, the average man is indeed incapable of the single smallest independent or spontaneous action or word. All of him is only the result of external effect. Man is a transforming machine, a kind of transmitting-station of forces.

Thus from the point of view of the totality of Gurdjieff's ideas and also according to contemporary "exact-positive-science," man differs from the animals only by the greater complexity of his reactions to external impressions, and by having a more complex construction for perceiving and reacting to them.

And as to that which is attributed to man and named "will," Mr. Gurdjieff completely denies the possibility of its being in the common presence of the average man.

Will is a certain combination obtained from the results of

certain properties specially elaborated in themselves by people who can do.

In the presences of average people what they call Will is exclusively only the resultant of desires.

Real Will is a sign of a very high degree of Being in comparison with the Being of the ordinary man. But only those people who possess such Being can do.

All other people are simply automatons, machines, or mechanical toys set in motion by external forces, acting just in so far as the "spring" placed in them by surrounding accidental conditions acts, and this spring can neither be lengthened nor shortened, nor changed in any way on its own initiative.

And so, while admitting great possibilities in man, we deny him any value as an independent unit as long as he remains such as he is at the present time.

For the purpose of confirming the complete absence in the average man of any will whatsoever, I will add here a passage from another of Mr. Gurdjieff's personal lectures, in which the manifestations of this famous assumed will in men are picturesquely described.

Addressing those present, Mr. Gurdjieff then said:

"You have pots of money, luxurious conditions of existence and universal esteem and respect. At the head of your well established concerns are people absolutely reliable and devoted to you; in a word, your life is a bed of roses.

"You dispose of your time as you please, you are a patron of the arts, you settle world questions over a cup of coffee, and you are even interested in the development of the latent spiritual forces of man. You are not unfamiliar with the needs of the spirit, and are well versed in philosophical matters. You are well educated and widely read. Having a great deal of learning on all kinds of questions, you are reputed to be a clever man, being at home in a variety of fields. You are a model of culture.

"All who know you regard you as a man of great will, and most of them even attribute all your advantages to the results of the manifestations of this will of yours.

"In short, from every point of view, you are fully deserving of imitation, and a man to be envied.

"In the morning you wake up under the impression of some oppressive dream.

"Your slightly depressed state, that dispersed on awakening, has nevertheless left its mark.

"A certain languidness and hesitancy in your movements.

"You go to the mirror to comb your hair and carelessly drop the brush; you have only just picked it up, when you drop it again. You then pick it up with a shade of impatience, and, in consequence, you drop it a third time, you try to catch it as it is falling, but . . . from an unlucky blow of your hand, the brush makes for the mirror; in vain you rush to save it, crack . . . there is a star of cracks on that antique mirror of which you were so proud.

"Damn: Devil take it: And you experience a need to vent your fresh annoyance on some one or other, and not finding the newspaper beside your morning coffee, the servant having forgotten to put it there, the cup of your patience overflows and you decide that you cannot stand the fellow any longer in the house.

"It is time for you to go out. The weather being pleasant and not having far to go, you decide to walk. Behind you glides your new automobile of the latest model.

"The bright sunshine somewhat calms you, and a crowd which has collected at the corner attracts your attention.

"You go nearer, and in the middle of the crowd you see a man lying unconscious on the pavement. A policeman, with the help of some of the, as they are called, "idlers" who have collected, puts the man into a "taxi" to take him to the hospital.

"Thanks merely to the likeness which has just struck you, between the face of the chauffeur and the face of the drunkard you bumped into last year when you were returning somewhat tipsy yourself from a rowdy birthday party you notice that the accident on the street-corner is unaccountably connected in your associations with a meringue you ate at that party.

"Ah, what a meringue that was!

"That servant of yours forgetting your newspaper today, spoiled your morning coffee. Why not make up for it at once?

"Here is a fashionable cafe where you sometimes go with your friends.

"But why did you recall the servant? Had you not almost entirely forgotten the morning's annoyances? But now . . . how very good this meringue tastes with the coffee.

"Look! There are two ladies at the next table. What a charming blonde!"

"You hear her whispering to her companion, glancing at you: 'Now he is the sort of man I like!'

"Do you deny that from these words about you, accidentally overheard and perhaps intentionally said aloud, the whole of you as is said, "inwardly rejoices?"

"Suppose that at this moment you were asked whether it had been worth while getting fussed and losing your temper over the morning's annoyances, you would of course answer in the negative and promise yourself that nothing of the kind should ever occur again.

"Need you be told how your mood was transformed while you were making the acquaintance of the blonde in whom you were interested and who was interested in you, and its state during all the time you spent with her?

"You return home humming some air, and even the sight of the broken mirror only elicits a smile from you. But how about the business on which you had gone out this morning

. . . You only just remember it. Clever . . . Well, never mind, you can telephone.

"You go to the phone and the girl connects you with the wrong number.

"You ring again, and get the same number. Some man informs you that you are bothering him, you tell him that it is not your fault, and what with one word and another, you learn to your surprise that you are a scoundrel and an idiot and that if you ring him up again . . . then . . .

"A rug slipping under your feet provokes a storm of indignation, and you should hear the tone of voice in which you rebuke the servant who is handing you a letter.

"The letter is from a man you esteem and whose good opinion you value highly.

"The contents of the letter are so flattering to you, that as you read, your irritation gradually passes and changes to the 'pleasant-embarrassment' of a man listening to a eulogy of himself. You finish reading the letter in the happiest of moods.

"I could continue this picture of your day—you free man!

"Perhaps you thing I am over drawing?

"No, it is a photographically exact snap-shot from nature."

While speaking of the will of man and of the various aspects of its supposedly self-initiated manifestations, which for contemporary what are called 'enquiring-minds'—but according to our reasoning, 'naive-minds'—are matters for wiseacring and self-adulation, it will do no harm to quote what was said by Mr. Gurdjieff in another 'conversational-lecture,' because the totality of what he then said may well throw light on the illusoriness of that will which every man supposedly has.

Mr. Gurdjieff said:

"A man comes into the world like a clean sheet of paper, which immediately all around him begin vying with each other to dirty and fill up with education, morality, the information we call knowledge, and with all kinds of feelings of duty, honor, conscience, and so on and so forth.

"And each and all claim immutability and infallibility for the methods they employ for grafting these branches into the main trunk, called man's personality.

"The sheet of paper gradually becomes dirty, and the dirtier it becomes, that is to say, the more a man is stuffed with ephemeral information and those notions of duty, honor, and so on which are dinned into him or suggested to him by others, the 'cleverer' and worthier is he considered by those around him.

"And seeing that people look upon his 'dirt' as a merit, he himself inevitably comes to regard this same dirtied sheet of paper in the same light.

"And so you have a model of what we call a man, to which frequently are added such words as 'talent' and 'genius.'

"And the temper of our 'talent' when it wakes up in the morning, is spoiled for the whole day if it does not find its slippers beside the bed.

"The ordinary man is not free in his manifestations, in his life, in his moods.

"He cannot be what he would like to be and what he considers himself to be.

"Man—how mighty it sounds! The very name of 'man' means 'the-acme-of-Creation'; but . . . how does his title fit contemporary man?

"At the same time, man should indeed be the acme of Creation, since he is formed with and has in himself all the possibilities for acquiring all the data exactly similar to the data in the ACTUALIZER of EVERYTHING EXISTING in the Whole of the Universe.

To possess the right to the name of man, one must be one.

And to be such, one must first of all, with an indefatigable persistence and an unquenchable impulse of desire, issuing from all the separate independent parts constituting one's entire common presence, that is to say, with a desire issuing simultaneously from thought, feeling and organic instinct, work on an all-around knowledge of oneself . . . at the same time struggling unceasingly with one's subjective weaknesses . . . and then afterwards, taking one's stand upon the results thus obtained by one's consciousness alone, concerning the defects in one's established subjectivity as well as the elucidated means for the possibility of combating them, strive for their eradication without mercy towards oneself.

Speaking frankly, and wholly without partiality, contemporary man as we know him is nothing more nor less than merely a clockwork mechanism, though of a very complex construction.

About his mechanicality, a man must without fail think deeply from every aspect and with an entire absence of partiality and well understand it, in order fully to appreciate what significance that mechanicality and all its involved consequences and results may have both for his own further life as well as for the justification of the sense and aim of his arising and existence.

For one who desires to study human mechanicality in general and to make it clear to himself, the very best object of study is he himself with his own mechanicality; and to study this practically and to understand it sensibly, with all one's Being, and not "psychopathically," that is, with only one part of one's entire presence, is possible only as a result of correctly conducted self-observation.

And as regards this possibility of correctly conducting self-observation and conducting it without the risk of incurring the maleficent consequences which have more than once been observed from people's attempts to do this without proper knowledge, it is necessary that the warning must be given—in order to avoid the possibility of excessive zeal—that our experience, based on the vast exact information we have, has shown that this is not so simple a thing as at first glance it may appear. This is why we make the study of the mechanicality of contemporary man the groundwork of a correctly conducted self-observation.

Before beginning to study this mechanicality and all the principles for a correctly conducted self-observation, a man firstly, must decide once and forever, that he will be sincere with himself unconditionally, will shut his eyes to nothing, shun no results wherever they may lead him, be afraid of no inferences, and be limited by no previous, self-imposed limits; and secondly, in order that the elucidation of these principles may be properly perceived and transubstantiated in the followers of this new teaching, it is necessary to establish a corresponding form of "language," since we find the established form of language quite unsuitable for such elucidations.

As regards the first condition, it is necessary now at the very outset to give warning, that a man unaccustomed to think and act along lines corresponding to the principles of self-observation, must have great courage to accept sincerely the inferences obtained and not to lose heart, and submitting to them, to continue those principles further with the crescendo of persistence, obligatorily requisite for this.

These inferences may, as is said, "upset" all the convictions and beliefs previously deep-rooted in a man, as well as also the whole order of his ordinary mentation; and, in that event, he might be robbed, perhaps forever, of all the pleasant, as is said "values-dear-to-his-heart," which have hitherto made up his calm and serene life.

Thanks to correctly conducted self-observation, a man will from the first days clearly grasp and indubitably establish his complete powerlessness and helplessness in the face of literally everything around him.

With the entire of his Being he will be convinced that everything governs him, everything directs him. He neither governs nor directs anything at all.

He is attracted and repelled not only by everything animate which has in itself the capacity to influence the arising of some or other association in him, but even by entirely inert and inanimate things.

Without any self-imagination or self-calming impulses which have become inseparable from contemporary men—he will cognize that his whole life is nothing but a blind reacting to the said attractions and repulsions.

He will clearly see how his what are called world-outlooks, views, character, taste and so on are molded—in short, how his individuality was formed and under what influences its details are liable to change.

And as regards the second indispensable condition, that is, the establishment of a correct language, this is necessary because our still recently established language which has procured, so to say, "rights-of-citizenship," and in which we speak, convey our knowledge and notions to others, and write books, has, in our opinion, already become such as to be now quite worthless for any more or less exact exchange of opinions.

The words of which our contemporary language consists, convey owing to the arbitrary thought people put into them indefinite and relative notions, and are therefore perceived by average people "elastically.'

In obtaining just this abnormality in the life of man, a part was played in our opinion, by always that same established abnormal system of education of the rising generation.

And it played a part because, based, as we have already said, chiefly on compelling the young to "learn-by-rote" as many words as possible differentiated one from the other only by the impression received from their consonance and not by the real pith of the meaning put into them, this system of education has resulted in the gradual loss in people of the capacity to ponder and reflect upon what they are talking about and upon what is being said to them.

As a result of the loss of this capacity and in view, at the same time, of the necessity to convey thoughts more or less exactly to others, they are obliged, in spite of the endless number of words already existing in all contemporary languages, either to borrow from other languages or to invent always more and more words; which has finally brought it about that when a contemporary man wishes to express an idea for which he knows many apparently suitable words and expresses this idea in a word which seems, according to his mental reflection, to be fitting, he still instinctively feels uncertain whether his choice is correct, and unconsciously gives this word his own subjective meaning.

Owing on the one hand to this already automatized usage, and on the other hand to the gradual disappearance of the capacity to concentrate his active attention for any length of time, the average man on uttering or hearing any word, involuntarily emphasizes and dwells upon this or that aspect of the notion conveyed by the word, invariably concentrating the whole meaning of the word upon one feature of the notion indicated by it; that is to say, the word signifies for him not all the implications of the given idea, but merely the first chance significance dependent upon the ideas formed in the link of automatic associations flowing in him. Hence, every time that in the course of conversation, the contemporary man hears or speaks one and the same word, he gives it another meaning, at times quite contradictory to the sense conveyed by the given word.

For any man who has become aware of this to some degree, and has learned more or less how to observe, this "tragicomic-feast-of-sound" is particularly sharply constated and made evident when others join the conversation of two contemporary people.

Each of them puts his own subjective sense into all the words that have become gravity center words in the said so to say "symphony-of-words-without-content," and to the ear of this impartial observer it is all perceived only as what is called in the ancient Sinokooloopianian Tales of the "Thousand-and-one-Nights," "cacophonous-fantastic-nonsense.'

Conversing in this fashion, contemporary people nevertheless imagine they understand one another and are certain that they are conveying their thoughts to each other.

We, on the other hand, relying upon a mass of indisputable data confirmed by psycho-physico-chemical experiments, categorically affirm that as long as contemporary people remain as they are, that is to say, "average-people," they will never, whatever they may be talking about among themselves, and particularly if the subject be abstract, understand the same notions by the same words nor will they ever actually comprehend one another.

This is why in the contemporary average man, every inner experience and even every painful experience, which engenders mentation and which has obtained logical results which might in other circumstances be very beneficent to those round about, is not manifested outwardly but is only transformed into so to say an "enslaving-factor" for him himself.

Thanks to this, even the isolation of the inner life of each individual man is increased, and as a consequence what is called the "mutual-instruction" so necessary to people's collective existence is always more and more destroyed.

Owing to the loss of the capacity to ponder and reflect, whenever the contemporary average man hears or employs in conversation any word with which he is familiar only by its consonance, he does not pause to think, nor does there even arise in him any question as to what exactly is meant by this word, he having already decided, once and for all, both that he knows it and that others know it too.

A question, perhaps, does sometimes arise in him when he hears an entirely unfamiliar word the first time; but in this case he is content merely to substitute for the unfamiliar word another suitable word of familiar consonance and then to imagine that he has understood it.

To bring home what has just been said, an excellent example is provide by the word so often used by contemporary man—"world.'

If people knew how to grasp for themselves what passes in their thoughts when they hear or use the word "world," then most of them would have to admit . . . if of course they intended to be sincere . . . that the word carries no exact notion whatever for them. Catching by ear simply the accustomed consonance, the meaning of which they assume that they know, it is as if they say to themselves "Ah, world, I know what this is," and serenely go on thinking.

Should one deliberately arrest their attention on this word and know how to probe them to find just what they understand by it, they will at first be plainly as is said "embarrassed," but quickly pulling themselves together, that is to say, quickly deceiving themselves and recalling the first definition of the word that comes to mind, they will then offer it as their own, although, in fact, they had not thought of it before.

If one has the requisite power and could compel a group of contemporary people even from among these who have received so to say "a-good-education," to state exactly how they each understand the word "world," they would all so "beat-about-the-bush" that involuntarily one would recall even castor oil with a certain tenderness. For instance, one of them who among other things, had read up a few books on astronomy, would say that, the "world" is an enormous number of suns surrounded by planets situated at colossal distances from each other and together forming what we call the

"Milky Way," beyond which, at immeasurable distances and beyond the limits of spaces accessible to our investigation, are presumably other constellations and other worlds.

Another, interested in contemporary physics, would speak of the world as a systematic evolution of matter, beginning with the atom and winding up with the very largest aggregates such as planets and suns; perhaps he would refer to the theory of the similitude of the world of atoms and electrons and the world of suns and planets, and so on in the same strain.

One who, for some reason or other, had made a hobby of philosophy and read all the mishmash on that subject, would say that the world is only the product of our subjective picturings and imaginings, and that our Earth, for example, with its mountains and seas, its vegetable and animal kingdoms, is a world of appearances, an illusory world.

A man acquainted with the latest theories of polydimensional space would say that the world is usually looked upon as an infinite three-dimensional sphere, but that in reality a three-dimensional world as such cannot exist and is only an imagined cross-section of another four-dimensional world out of which comes and into which goes everything proceeding around us.

A man whose world-view is founded on the dogmas of religion would say that the world is everything existing, visible and invisible, created by God and depending on His Will. Our life in the visible world is brief, but in the invisible world, where a man receives reward or punishment for all his acts during his sojourn in the visible world, life is eternal.

One bitten with "spiritualism" would say that, side by side, with the visible world, there exists also another, a world of the "Beyond," and that communication has already been established with the beings populating this world of the "Beyond." A fanatic of theosophy would go still further and say that seven worlds exist interpenetrating each other and composed of more and more rarified matter, and so on.

In short, not a single contemporary man would be able to offer a single definite notion, exact for all acceptances, of the meaning of the word "world.'

The whole psychic inner life of the average man is nothing but an "automatized-contact" of two or three series of associations previously perceived by him of impressions fixed under the action of some impulse then arisen in him in all the three heterogeneous localizations of "brains" contained in him. When the associations begin to act anew, that is to say, when the repetition of corresponding impressions appear, they begin to constate, under the influence of some inner or outer accidental shock, that in another localization, the homogeneous impressions evoked by them begin to be repeated.

All the particularities of the world-view of the ordinary man and the characteristic features of his individuality ensue and depend on the sequence of the impulse proceeding in him at the moment of the perception of new impressions and also on the automatism established for the arising of the process of those impressions.

And it is this that explains the incongruity, always observed even by the average man during his passive state, in the several associations having nothing in common, which simultaneously flow within him.

The said impressions in the common presence of a man are perceived owing to the three, as it were, apparatuses in him—as there are apparatuses in general in the presences of all animals—acting as perceivers for all the seven what are called "planetary-gravity-center-vibrations.'

The structure of these perceptive apparatuses is the same in all the parts of the mechanism.

They consist in adaptations recalling clean wax phonograph-discs; on these discs, or as they might otherwise be called "reels," all the impressions received begin to be recorded from the first days after the appearance of a man in the world, and even before, during the period of his formation in his mother's womb.

And the separate apparatuses constituting this general mechanism possess also a certain automatically acting adaptation, owing to which newly arriving impressions, in addition to being recorded alongside those previously perceived and similar to them, are also recorded.

Thus every impression experienced is inscribed in several places and on several reels, and there, on these reels, it is preserved unchanged.

These impressed perceptions have such a property that from contact with homogeneous vibrations of the same quality, they, so to say, "rouse-themselves," and there is then repeated in them an action similar to the action which evoked their first arising.

And it is this repetition of previously perceived impressions engendering what is called association, and the parts of this repetition which enter the field of a man's attention, that together condition what is termed "memory.'

The memory of the average man, in comparison with the memory of a man harmoniously perfected, is a very very imperfect adaptation for his utilization, during his responsible life, of his previously perceived store of impressions.

With the aid of memory, the average man, from among impressions previously perceived, can make use of and, so to say, keep track of, only a very small part of his whole store of impressions, whereas the memory proper to the real man keeps track of all his impressions without exception, whenever they may have been perceived.

Many experiments have been made, and it has been established with indubitable exactitude, that every man in definite states, as for example in the state of a certain stage of hypnotism, can remember to the most minute particular everything that has ever happened to him; he can remember all the details of the surroundings and the faces and voices of the people around him even those of the first days of his life, when he was still, according to people's notions, an unconscious being.

When a man is in one of these states, it is possible artificially, to make even the reels hidden in the most obscure corners of the mechanism start working; but it often happens that these reels begin to unwind of themselves under the influence of some overt or hidden shock evoked by some experiencing, whereupon, there suddenly rise up before the man, long-forgotten scenes, picturings, faces, and so on.

At this point, I interrupted the lecturer and considered it opportune to make the following addition.

THE ADDITION

Such is the ordinary average man—an unconscious slave of the whole entire service to all-universal purposes, which are alien to his own personal individuality. He may live through all his years as he is, and as such be destroyed forever.

But at the same time Great Nature has given him the possibility of being not merely a blind tool of the whole entire service to these all-universal objective purposes but, while serving Her and actualizing what is foreordained for him—which is the lot of every breathing creature—of working at the same time also for himself, for his own egoistic individuality.

This possibility was given also for service to the common purpose, owing to the fact that for the equilibrium of those objective laws, such relatively liberated people are necessary.

Although the said liberation is possible, nevertheless whether any particular man has the chance to attain it—this is difficult to say.

There are a mass of reasons which do not permit it; and moreover which in most cases depend neither upon us personally nor upon great laws, but only upon the various accidental conditions of our arising and formation, of which the chief are heredity and the conditions under which the process of our "preparatory-age" flows. It is just these uncontrollable conditions which may not permit this liberation.

The chief difficulty in the way of liberation from whole entire slavery consists in this, that it is necessary, with an intention issuing from one's own initiative and persistence, sustained by one's own efforts, that is to say, not by another's will but by one's own, to obtain the eradication from one's presence both of the already fixed consequences of certain properties of that "something" in our forefathers, called the "organ Kundabuffer," as well as of the predisposition to those consequences which might again arise.

In order that you should have at least an approximate understanding of this strange organ with its properties, and also of the manifestations in ourselves of the consequences of these properties, we must dwell a little longer upon this question and speak about it in somewhat greater detail.

Great Nature, in her foresight and for many important reasons, (about which theoretical explanations will be given in later lectures), was constrained to place within the common presences of our remote ancestors, just such an organ thanks to the engendering properties of which, they might be protected from the possibility of seeing and feeling anything as it proceeds in reality.

Although this organ was later "removed" also by Great Nature, from their common presences, yet owing to a cosmic law expressed by the words "the-assimilation-of-the-results-of-oft-repeated-acts,"—according to which law, from the frequent repetition of one and the same act, there arises in every "world-concentration" under certain conditions, a predisposition to produce similar results—this law-conformable predisposition which arose in our fore-fathers was transmitted by heredity from generation to generation, so that when their descendants in the process of their ordinary existence established numerous conditions which proved to be congenial for the said law-conformableness, from that time on the consequences of the various properties of this organ arose in them, and being assimilated owing to transmission by heredity from generation to generation, they ultimately acquired almost the same manifestations as those of their ancestors.

An approximate understanding of the manifestations in ourselves of these consequences may be derived from a further fact, perfectly intelligible to our Reason and beyond any doubt whatever.

All of us, people, are mortal and every man may die at any moment.

Now the question arises, can a man really picture to himself and so to say "experience" in his consciousness, the process of his own death?

No! His own death and the experiencing of this process, a man can never, however he may wish, picture to himself.

A contemporary ordinary man can picture to himself the death of another, though even this not fully.

He can picture to himself, for instance, that a certain Mr. Smith leaves the theater and crossing the street, falls beneath an automobile and is crushed to death.

Or that a signboard blown down by the wind falls on the head of Mr. Jones who happened to be passing and kills him on the spot.

Or that Mr. Brown, having eaten bad crayfish, gets poisoned, and no one being able to save him, dies the next day.

Anyone can easily picture all these. But can the average man contemplate the same possibility for himself, as he admits for Mr. Smith, Mr. Jones and Mr. Brown, and feel and live through all the despair from the fact that those events may happen to him?

Think what would happen to a man who clearly pictured to himself and lives through the inevitability of his own death.

If he seriously ponders and is really able to enter deeply into this and to cognize his own death, what could be more terrifying?

In ordinary life, particularly in recent times, over and above the depressing fact of the inevitability of death which must infallibly occur to them, there are indeed for people a large number of other similar facts, whose real picturing alone of the possibility of experiencing them must evoke in us feelings of inexpressible and intolerable anguish.

Suppose that such contemporary people as have already lost entirely all possibility of having any real objective hope for the future, that is to say, those of them who have never "sown" anything during their responsible life and who in consequence have nothing to "reap" in the future—suppose they should cognize the inevitability of their speedy death, then from only an experiencing in thought alone, would they hang themselves.

The particularity of the action of the consequences of the properties of the said organ on the common psyche of people consists just in this, that thanks to it, there does not arise among most contemporary people—these three-brained beings in whom were placed all the hopes and expectations of our CREATOR, as possible servers of higher purposes—the cognition of any of these genuine terrors, and also that it enables them peacefully to carry on their existence, in unconscious fulfillment of what was foreordained, but in the service only of Nature's nearest immediate aims, they have meanwhile lost, on account of their unbecoming abnormal life, any possibility of serving higher purposes.

Thanks to these consequences, not only does the cognition of these terrors not arise in the psyche of these people, but also for the purpose of self-quieting they even invent all kinds of fantastic explanations plausible to their naive logic for what they really sense and also for what they do not sense at all.

As for instance, suppose that the solution of the question of our inability really to sense various possible genuine terrors, in particular, the terror of one's own death, should become, so to say, a "burning-question-of-the-day" which occurs with certain questions in the contemporary life of people—then in all probability, all contemporary people, ordinary mortals as well as those called the "learned," would categorically offer a solution, which they would not doubt for a moment and, as is said, spluttering at the mouth, would set about to prove that what in fact saves people from being able to experience such terrors is just their own "will."

But if this is admitted, then why does not this same presumed "will" protect us from all the little fears we experience at every step?

In order to sense and understand with your whole being what I am now saying, and not merely to understand with that, so to say "mind-fornication" of yours, which to the misfortune of our descendants has become the dominant inherency of contemporary people, picture to yourself now merely the following.

Today, after the lecture, you return home, undress and get into bed, but just as you are covering yourself with your blanket a mouse jumps out from under the pillow and scuttling across your body pops into the folds of the blanket.

Admit candidly, does not a shiver actually already run through the whole of your body merely at the bare thought of such a possibility?

Is it not so?

Now please try and make an exception and without the participation of any of that, so to say, "subjective emotionalness," whatsoever, which has become fixed in you, think with your mentation alone about such a possible occurrence to you, and you yourself will then be amazed that you react to this in this way.

What is so terrifying in this?

It is only an ordinary house-mouse, the most harmless and inoffensive of beasts.

Now I ask you, how can all that has been said be explained by that Will, which is presumed to be in every man?

How is it possible to reconcile the facts that a man is terrified at a small timid mouse, the most frightened of all creatures, and of thousands of other similar trifles which might never even occur, and yet experience no terror before the inevitability of his own death?

In any case, to explain such an obvious contradiction by the action of the famous human "will"—is impossible.

When this contradiction is considered openly, without any preconceptions, that is to say, without any of the ready-made notions derived from the wiseacring of various what are called "authorities" who in most cases have become such, thanks to the naïveté and "herd-instinct" of people, as well as from the results, depending on abnormal education, which arise in our mentation, then it becomes indubitably evident that all these terrors, from which in man there does not arise the impulse, as we said, to hang himself, are permitted by Nature Herself to the extent in which they are necessary for the process of our ordinary existence.

And indeed without them, without all these, in the objective sense, as is said, "flea-bites," but which appear to us as "unprecedented-terrors," there could not proceed in us any experiencings at all, either of joy, sorrow, hope, disappointment and so on, and we could not have all those cares, stimuli, strivings, and, in general, all kinds of impulses, which constrain us to act, to attain to something and to strive for some aim.

It is just this totality of all these automatic, as they might be called, "childish-experiencings" arising and flowing in the average man, which on the one hand make up and sustain his life and on the other hand, give him neither the possibility nor the time to see and feel reality.

If the average contemporary man were given the possibility to sense or to remember, if only in his thought, that at a definite known date, for instance, tomorrow, a week, or a month, or even a year or two hence, he would die and die for certain, what would then remain, one asks, of all that had until then filled up and constituted his life?

Everything would lose its sense and significance for him. What would be the importance then of the decoration he received yesterday for long service and which had so delighted him, or that glance he recently noticed, so full of promise, from the woman who had long been the object of his constant and unrewarded longing, or the newspaper with his morning coffee, and that deferential greeting from the neighbor on the stairs, and the theater in the evening, and rest and sleep, and all his favorite things—of what account are they all?

They would no longer have that significance which had been given them before, even if a man knew that death would overtake him only in five or six years.

In short, to look his own death, as is said, "in-the-face," the average man cannot and must not—he would then, so to say, "get-out-of-his-depth" and before him, in clear-cut form, the question would arise: "Why then should we live and toil and suffer?"

Precisely that such a question may not arise, Great Nature, having become convinced that in the common presences of most people there have already ceased to be any factors for meritorious manifestations proper to three-centered beings, had providentially wisely protected them, by allowing the arising in them of various consequences of those non-meritorious properties unbecoming to three-centered beings which, in the absence of a proper actualization, conduce to their not perceiving or sensing reality.

And Great Nature was constrained to adapt Herself to such an, in the objective sense, abnormality, in consequence of the fact that thanks to the conditions of their ordinary life established by people themselves the deteriorating quality of their radiations required for Higher Common-Cosmic Purposes, insistently demanded, for the maintenance of equilibrium, an increase of the quantity of the arisings and existing of these lives.

Whereupon it follows that life in general is given to people not for them themselves, but that this life is necessary for the said Higher Cosmic Purposes, in consequence of which Great Nature watches over this life so that it may flow in a more or less tolerable form, and takes care that it should not prematurely cease.

Do not we, people, ourselves also feed, watch over, look after and make the lives of our sheep and pigs as comfortable as possible?

Do we do all this because we value their lives for the sake of their lives?

No! We do all this in order to slaughter them one fine day and to obtain the meat we require, with as much fat as possible.

In the same way Nature takes all measures to ensure that we shall live without seeing the terror, and that we should not hang ourselves, but live long; and then when we are required, She slaughters us.

Under the established conditions of the ordinary life of people, this has now already become an immutable law of Nature.

There is in our life a certain very great purpose and we must all serve this Great Common Purpose—in this, lies the whole sense and predestination of our life.

All people without exception are slaves of this "Greatness," and all are compelled willy-nilly to submit, and to fulfill without condition or compromise, what has been predestined for each of us by his transmitted heredity and his acquired Being.

Now, after all that I have said, returning to the chief theme of the lecture read here today, I wish to refresh your memory about what has several times been referred to in defining man—the expressions "real-man" and a "man-in-quotation-marks" and in conclusion, to say the following.

Although the real man who has already acquired his own "I" and also the man in quotation marks who has not, are equally slaves of the said "Greatness," yet the difference between them, as I have already said, consists in this, that since the attitude of the former to his slavery is conscious, he acquires the possibility, simultaneously with serving the all-universal Actualizing, of applying a part of his manifestations according to the providence of Great Nature, for the purposes of acquiring for himself "imperishable-Being"; whereas the latter, not cognizing his slavery, serves during the flow of the entire process of his existence, exclusively only as a thing, which when no longer needed, disappears forever.

In order to make what I have just said more comprehensible and concrete, it will be useful if we compare human life in general to a large river which rises from various sources and flows on the surface of our planet, and the life of any given man to one of the drops of water composing this river of life.

This river at first flows as a whole along a comparatively level valley, and at that place where Nature has particularly undergone what is called a "cataclysm-not-according-to-law," it is divided into two separate streams, or, as it is also said, there occurs in this river a "dividing-of-the-waters.'

All the water of one stream, soon after passing this place, flows into a still more level valley, and with no surrounding what is called "majestic and picturesque" scenery to hinder it, ultimately flows into the vast ocean.

The second stream continuing its flow over places formed

by the consequences of the said "cataclysm-not-according-to-law," ultimately falls into crevices in the earth, themselves also consequences of the same "cataclysm," and seeps into the very depths of the earth.

Although after the branching of the waters, the waters of both these streams flow further independently and no longer mingle, yet along the whole extent of their further course, they frequently approach so near each other, that all the results engendered from the process of their flowing blend, and even at times during great atmospheric phenomena, such as storms, winds and so on, splashes of water or even separate drops pass from one stream into the other.

Individually the life of every man up to his reaching responsible age, corresponds to a drop of water in the initial flow of the river, and the place where the "dividing-of-the-waters" occurs, corresponds to the time when he attains adulthood.

After this branching, any considerable subsequent movement, according to law, both of this river as well as of any of the small details of this movement for the actualization of the predetermined destination of the whole river, applies equally to every separate drop, just in so far as the given drop is in the general totality of this river.

For the drop itself, all its own displacements, directions, and states caused by the differences of its position, by its various accidentally arisen surrounding conditions and by the accelerated or retarded tempo of its movement, have always a totally accidental character.

For the drops, there is not a separate predetermination of their personal fate—a predetermined fate is for the whole river only.

At the beginning of the flow of the river, the lives of the drops are here one moment, there the next moment, and a moment later they might not at all be as they are, but splashed out of the river and evaporated.

And so, when on account of the unbecoming life of people, Great Nature was constrained to engender the corresponding in their common presences, then from that time on, it was so established for the purposes of the common actualizing of everything existing, that human life in general on the Earth should flow in two streams; and Great Nature foresaw and gradually fixed in the details of Her common actualization such a corresponding law-conformableness, that in the drops of the water of the initial flow of the river of life, which have corresponding inner subjective what are called "struggles-of-one's-own-self-denial," there might arise or not arise that "something," thanks to which certain properties are acquired giving the possibility at the place of the branching of the waters of the river of life, of entering one or the other stream.

This "something" which in the common presence of a drop of water is a factor actualizing in it the property corresponding to one or another of the streams, is in the common presence of each man who attains responsible age, that "I," which was referred to in today's lecture.

A man who has in his common presence his own "I" enters one of the streams of the river of life and the man who has not, enters the other.

The subsequent fate of any drop in the general river of life is determined at the "dividing-of-the-waters," according to the stream the drop happens to enter.

And it is determined, as has already been said, by the fact that one of these two streams ultimately empties itself into the ocean, that is, into that sphere of general Nature which often has what is called repeated "reciprocal-exchange-of-substances-between-various-great-cosmic-concentrations" through the process of what is called "Pokhdalissdjancha," a part of which process, by the way, contemporary people name "cyclone"; in consequence of which this drop of water has the possibility to evolve, as it is, to the next higher concentration.

And at the end of the flow of the other stream, as has already been said, into the crevices of the Earth's "nether-regions," where it participates in the continuous process called "involutionary-construction" which proceeds within the planet, it is transformed into steam and distributed into corresponding spheres of new arisings.

After the branching of the waters, great and small successive law-conformablenesses and details for the outer movement for the purpose of actualizing the predetermined destination of both streams, also ensue from these same cosmic laws, but only the results ensuing from them are so to say "subjectivized" for both streams correspondingly; and although they begin to function independently, yet all the time they mutually assist and sustain each other. These subjectivized second grade results issuing from fundamental cosmic laws, sometimes function side by side, sometimes collide or cross, but never mix. The actions of these subjectivized second grade results can sometimes under certain surrounding conditions spread also over the separate drops.

For us contemporary people, the chief evil is that we—thanks to the various conditions of our ordinary existence established by us ourselves, chiefly in consequence of the abnormal what is called "education"—attaining responsible age and acquiring presences which correspond only to that stream of the river of life which ultimately empties itself into the "nether-regions," enter it and are carried along where and whither it wills, and without pondering about the consequences, we remain passive, and submitting to the flow, drift on and on.

As long as we remain passive, not only shall we have inevitably to serve solely as a means for Nature's "involutionary-construction," but also for the rest of our lives we shall have to submit slavishly to every caprice of all sorts of blind events.

As most of the hearers present have already, as is said, "crossed-over" into responsible age and frankly cognize that until now they have not acquired their own "I," and at the same time, according to the substance of all I have said here, have not pictured for themselves any particularly agreeable perspectives, then, in order that you—just you who cognize this—should not be greatly, as is said, "disheartened" and should not fall into the usual what is called "pessimism" everywhere prevalent in the contemporary abnormal life of people, I say quite frankly, without any arriére-pensée, that, according to my convictions which have been formed thanks to long years of investigations strengthened by numerous quite exceptionally conducted experiments on the results of which are based the "Institute-for-the-Harmonious-Development-of-Man" founded by me—even for you, it is not yet too late.

The point is, that the said investigations and experiments showed me very clearly and very definitely, that in everything under the care of Mother Nature the possibility is foreseen for beings to acquire the kernel of their essence, that is to say, their own "I," even after the beginning of their responsible age also.

The foresight of Just Mother Nature consists in the given case in this, that the possibility is given to us, in certain inner and outer conditions, to cross over from one stream into the other.

The expression which has reached us from ancient times, "The-first-liberation-of-man" refers to just this possibility of crossing from the stream which is predestined to disappear into the "nether-regions" into the stream which empties itself into the vast spaces of the boundless ocean.

To cross into the other stream is not so easy—merely to wish and you cross. For this, it is, first of all, necessary consciously to crystallize in yourselves data for engendering in your common presences a constant unquenchable impulse of desire for such a crossing, and then afterwards, a long corresponding preparation.

For this crossing it is necessary first of all to renounce all the what seem to you "blessings"—but which are, in reality, automatically and slavishly acquired habits—present in this stream of life.

In other words, it is necessary to become dead to what has become for you, your ordinary life.

It is just this death that is spoken of in all religions.

It is defined in the saying which has reached us from remote antiquity, "without-death-no-resurrection," which in ordinary language means, "if-you-do-not-die-you-will-not-be-resurrected."

The death referred to is not the death of the body, since for such a death there is no need of resurrection.

For if there is a soul, and moreover, an immortal soul, it can dispense with a resurrection of the body.

Nor is the necessity of resurrection our appearance before the awful judgment of the Lord God, as we have been taught by the Fathers of the Church.

No! Even Jesus Christ and all the other prophets sent from Above spoke of the death which might occur even during life, that is to say, of the death of that "Tyrant" from whom proceeds our slavery in this life and solely on the liberation from which depends the first chief liberation of man.

Summing up all that has been said, the thoughts set out in the lecture you have heard read, as well as what I have added today that is, about the two categories of contemporary people, who in respect of inner content have nothing in common, and about that grievous fact which has been made clear to a certain degree thanks to the addition I have made, namely, that in the common presences of people in recent times, thanks to progressively deteriorating conditions of ordinary life established by us—particularly owing to the wrong system of education of the rising generation—the various consequences of the organ Kundabuffer have began to arise much more intensely, I consider it necessary to say and even to emphasize still more that all misunderstandings without exception arising in the process of our collective life, particularly in the sense of reciprocal relationship, and all disagreements, disputes, settling-ups and hasty decisions—just these decisions, after the actualization of which in practice, there arises in us the lingering process of "Remorse-of-Conscience"—and even such great events as wars, civil-wars and other similar misfortunes of a general character, proceed simply on account of a property in the common presences of ordinary people who have never specially worked on themselves, which property I this time would call 'The-reflecting-of-reality-in-one's-attention-upside-down.'

Every man, if he can even a little seriously think, so to say 'without-being-identified' with his passions, must agree with this if he takes into account, merely one single fact often repeated in the process of our inner life, namely that all our experiencings, which at first, just at the moment they are still proceeding in us, seem to be stark terrors, appear, after the lapse of only an insignificant time and when these experiencings have been replaced by others and are recalled by chance, and when according to our logical reasoning we are already in another mood, not worth, as is said, 'a-brass-farthing.'

In the average man the results of his mentation and feelings often lead to this, that, as it might be expressed, 'a-fly-becomes-an-elephant-and-an-elephant-a-fly.'

The manifestations in the common presences of the said people of this maleficent property is particularly intensely actualized just during such events as wars, revolutions, civil-wars and so on.

Just during these events, the state, even constated by them is particularly sharply manifested, under the action of which they all with few exceptions fall, and which they call 'mass-psychosis.'

The essence of this state consists in this, that average people receiving in their already feeble mentation which at such times becomes still more feeble, shocks from the maleficent stories of some or another lunatic, and becoming in the full sense of the word victims of these malicious stories, manifest themselves completely automatically.

During the period when they find themselves under the action of such a scourge—a scourge which has already become for contemporary ordinary people their inalienable inherency—there already entirely ceases to exist in their common presences that sacred what is called 'consciousness,' the data for the possibility of the acquisition of which Great Nature endowed them with, as God-like beings in differentiation from mere animals.

Informed people sincerely regret just this inherency in contemporary people, because according to historical data and also to experimental elucidations of numerous genuine learned beings of past epochs, Great Nature has already long ceased to have need for such a phenomenon as mass psychosis for Her equilibrium . . . Rather the contrary, such a periodically arising inherency in people compels Her always to new adaptations, as for instance, increasing the birth-rate, changing the what is called 'tempo-of-the-general-psyche' and so on and so forth.

After all that I have said I consider it necessary to say and even to emphasize further that all the historical data which have reached certain contemporary people and which have chanced to become known also to me, namely, the historical data concerning what really did occur in the past in the life of people, not just those data invented by contemporary what are called 'learned-beings' chiefly from among the Germans, with which "Historics" all the rising generation is stuffed almost everywhere on the Earth—clearly show that people of former epochs did not divide into two streams of life, but that all flowed along in a single river.

The general life of mankind has been divided into two streams since the time of what is called the "Tikliamishian-civilization" which directly preceded the Babylonian civilization.

It was just from then on that there gradually began to be and ultimately was finally established that organization of the life of mankind which, as every sane-thinking man ought to constate, can now flow more or less tolerably only if people are divided into masters and slaves.

Although to be either masters or slaves in a collective existence among children, like ourselves, of the Common Father, is unworthy of man, yet thanks at the present time to the conditions existing which have already been thoroughly fixed in the process of the collective life of people, the source of which lies in remote antiquity, we must be reconciled to it and accept a compromise that, according to impartial reasoning, should both correspond to our own personal welfare, and also at the same time be not contrary to the commandments specially issuing to us people from the "Prime-source-of-everything-existing."

Such a compromise, I think, is possible if certain people consciously set themselves, as the chief aim of their existence, to acquire in their presences all the corresponding data to become masters among those around them similar to themselves.

Proceeding from this and acting according to the wise saying of ancient times affirming that "In-order-to-be-in-reality-a-just-and-good-altruist-it-is-inevitably-required-first-of-all-to-be-an-out-and-out-egoist," and also profiting by and the good sense given us by Great Nature, each one of us must set for his chief aim to become in the process of our collective life a master.

But not a master in that sense and meaning which this

word conveys to contemporary people, namely, one who has many slaves and much money, handed down, in most cases, by inheritance, but in the sense that a given man, thanks to his, in the objective sense, devout acts towards those around him, that is to say, acts manifested by him according to the dictates of his Pure Reason alone, without the participation of those impulses which in him as in all people are engendered from the mentioned consequences of the properties of the malevolent organ Kundabuffer—acquires in himself that "something" which of itself constrains all those about him to bow before him and with reverence to carry out his orders.

I now consider this first series of my writing ended and ended in just such a form that satisfies even myself.

In any case, I give my word that from tomorrow I shall not waste even five minutes of my time on this first series.

And now, before beginning work on the second series of my writings, in order to put them, from my point of view, into a generally accessible form, I intend to rest for a whole month, to write positively nothing and for a stimulus to my organism, fatigued to the extreme limit, s-l-o-w-l-y to drink the still remaining fifteen bottles of "super-most-super-heavenly-nectar" called at the present time on Earth "Old-Calvados.'

This "Old-Calvados," by the way, twenty-seven bottles of it, I was thought worthy to find accidentally, covered over with a mixture of lime, sand and finely chopped straw, several years ago when I was digging a pit for preserving carrots for the winter in one of the cellars of my now chief dwelling-place.

These bottles of this divine liquid were buried in all probability by monks who lived near by, far from worldly temptations, for the salvation of their souls.

It now seems to me for some reason or other that they buried these bottles there, not without some ulterior motive and that thanks to their what is called "intuitive-perspicacity," the data for which particularity of theirs, one must assume was formed in them thanks to their pious lives, they foresaw that the buried divine liquid would fall into hands worthy of understanding the meaning of such things; and now indeed this liquid stimulates the owner of these hands praiseworthily to sustain and assist the better transmission to the next generation of the meaning of the ideals on which the cooperation of these monks was founded.

I wish during this rest of mine, which from any point of view I fully deserve, to drink this splendid liquid, which alone during recent years has given me the possibility of tolerating without suffering the beasts similar to myself around me, and to listen to new anecdotes, and sometimes, for lack of new ones, old ones—of course, if there happen to be competent raconteurs.

It is now still mid-day, and as I have given my word that I would not, beginning only from tomorrow, write anything further for this first series, I still have time and shall not be breaking my word, if I add with a clean conscience that a year or two ago, I had categorically decided to make only the first series of my published writing generally accessible, and as regards the second and third series, to make them not generally accessible, but to organize their distribution in order, among other things, to actualize through them one of the fundamental tasks I have set myself under essence-oath, a task which consists in this—ultimately also to prove, without fail theoretically as well as practically, to all my contemporaries, the absurdity of all their inherent ideas concerning the suppositious existence of a certain "other-world" with its famous and so beautiful "Paradise" and its so repugnant a "Hell" and at the same time prove theoretically and afterwards without fail to show practically, so that even every "complete-victim" of contemporary education should understand without shuddering and know—that "Hell" and "Paradise" do indeed exist, but only not there "In-that-world," but here beside us on Earth.

After the books of the first series have all been published, I intend for the spreading of the contents of the second series, to organize in various large centers simultaneous public readings accessible to all.

And as regards the real indubitably comprehensible genuine objective truths which will be brought to light by me in the third series, I intend to make them accessible exclusively only to those from among the hearers of the second series of my writings who will be selected from specially prepared people according to my considered instructions.

The Appendix

[The text below occurred, disjointedly, at the end of Chapter 34 *Russia*. It duplicates content from earlier in that chapter, and thus seemed superfluous. For the sake of completeness we reproduce it here.]

"Grandfather dear, please tell me whether, even though these Earth-beings have no objective mind, it is not possible that even in the absence of established customs, their common existence has, nevertheless, become more or less tolerable since they have existed for so many centuries," asked Hassein.

"Certainly," replied Beelzebub, "During the centuries it sometimes happens that very good customs are formed by life, but owing to their weakness of will and suggestibility, habits and customs acquired during tens of centuries can be utterly destroyed in half a century. The desire to influence and to be influenced by another as well as by a whole social organization, is strongly developed in them. For instance, whole peoples of an old social-organization on the continent Asia, which had existed for many centuries and had during that time acquired many good customs, have today, owing to new conditions, fallen under the influence of beings belonging to the neighboring continent of Europe. These ancient Asiatic social-organizations, which only six months before had been distinguished by their morality, the fruit of the customs acquired during centuries, had already, when I finally left that planet, fallen under the influence of those European beings. The state of morality amongst them when I was last there was such that they could give ten points start to their European teachers. Those who only the day before lived without locking up their property and who possessed a strong sense of shame—that lever of morality—and other things of a similar nature, had become robbers and phenomenally immoral.

Why so quickly? I think the reason of it chiefly lies in the drink which the beings of Europe had brought them together with their influence. A very good example are those Russians about whom I have just told you, and among whom this Bolshevism occurred. The country where they dwell, is adjacent to those old Asiatic social-organizations, and from constant contact with these, many good customs gradually passed thence to those Russians, customs acquired by those old social organizations during many centuries. Existence among those Russians, was largely influenced by these Asiatic peoples, but during the later centuries, owing to new conditions, the Russians fell under the influence of European beings, chiefly those of the social-organization called France. France began to have a very strong influence on Russia, and Russia aimed at imitating France very precisely.

"Russia, having taken many good customs from the people of Asia, then gradually began to lose these customs, and to acquire the new French ones. Among the customs which Russia had taken from the Asiatic beings were thousands of good ones. As an example, let us take two, namely, the custom of chewing 'keva' and hot air baths; and after eating to chew mastic. This mastic prepared from different roots does not decompose however long it is chewed but on the contrary becomes more elastic. It was invented by a very wise being to aid the digestion. The chewing of this keva produces a great deal of saliva and many other necessary substances which enable the food introduced into the organism to digest more quickly and easily. It also helps very much to clean the teeth and the cavity of the mouth from the remains of the food and does not allow the latter to decompose in the mouth. By this means also the teeth are left clean and strong owing to the friction and exercise.

The Original List of Contents

[We revised the contents list because, in some places, it did not agree with the chapter titles in the text. The original list is given below]

The Indexes

There are a number of different indexes to the text provided here. Most are intended to assist those readers who wish not just to read the book, but to study Gurdjieff's writing in detail. The indexes are as follows:

Substitutions

These are word substitutions made in the original text so that the neologisms and invented names of characters and places would conform with the 1950 publication.

Lists

This index highlights every instance in the text where Gurdjieff provides a list of items.

Quotes

This indexes every instance in the text where Gurdjieff quotes proverbs or pithy sayings.

Phrases

This indexes hyphenated phrases.

References to God

This index includes all references to God, both reverential references and mundane references.

Word Index

This last index is of the kind one might expect to find in a text book or reference book, indexing important words, phrases and concepts.

Index of Substitutions

These are substitutions that the editor made in the original text so that Gurdjieff's neologisms and invented names of characters and places would conform with the 1950 publication. Where there are differences between the two texts—and there are many—it appears mostly to be due to the difficulty of translating sounds from words in the Russian draft or, in quite a few instances, typographical error. However there are a few instances (e.g. Triamazikamno for Triamonia) where Gurdjieff changed his mind and chose differently.

Also included here, for completeness, are corrections to the spelling of foreign names (such as Azerbaijan for Azerbeidjan) which were spelt differently in ***The 1931 Manuscript***.

Index of Lists

This index highlights every instance in the text where Gurdjieff provides a list of items. There are a surprising number of instances of this. Some of the lists are enigmatic while others seem on the surface to be mundane.

List of names for Gurdjieff
Black-Greek, Turkestan-Tiger, Monsieur or Mister Gurdjieff, the nephew of Prince Mukransky, a Teacher-of-Dancing *39*
List of pseudo-teachings
Occultism, Theosophy, Spiritualism, Psychoanalysis *233*
List of German inventions/chemical substances
Satkaine, Aniline, Cocaine, Atropine, Alisarine *402*
List of metalware
locks, razors, mousetraps, revolvers, scythes, machine-guns, saucepans, hinges, guns, penknives, cartridges, pens, mines, needles *408*
List of the days of the week on the continent Atlantis
Adashsikra, Evosikra, Cevorksikra, Midosikra, Maikosikra, Lookosikra, Soniasikra *438*
List of the days of the week
Monday, Tuesday, Wednesday, Thursday, Friday, Saturday, Sunday *439*
List of colored items
carpets, fabrics, chinkrooaries *442*
List of artistic movements
Cubism, Futurism, Synthesism, Imagism, Impressionism, Colorist, Formalism, Surrealism *497*
List of active elements of opium
Morphine, Protopine, Lanthopine, Porphiroksine, Opian or narcotine, Paramorphine or thebaine, Phormine or pseudophormine, Metamorphine, Gnoskopine, Oilopine, Atropine, Pirotine, Dephteropine, Tiktoutine, Kolotine, Khaivatine, Zoutine, Trotopine, Laudanine, Laudanosine, Podotorine, Arkhatozine, Tokitozine, Liktonozine, Makanidine, Papaverine, Krintonine, Kodomine, Kolomonine, Koilononine, Katarnine, Hydrokatarnine, Opianine (mekonine), Mekonoiozine, Pistotorine, Phykhtonozine, Codeine, Nartzeine, Pseudocodeine, Microparaine, Microtebaine, Messaine *647*
List of names of the white strings on the Lav-Merz-Nokh

Adashtanas, Evotanas, Govorktanis, Maikitanis, Midotanis, Lookotanas, Sonitanis *650*

List of the octave names of the whole notes on the Lav-Merz-Nokh
Arachiaplnish, Erkrordiapan, Erordiapan, Chorortdiapan, Piandjiapan, Vetserordiapan, Okhterordiapan *650*

List of alcoholic beverages
Arak, Doosico, Scotch-whisky, Benedictine, Vodka, Grand-Marnier, *703*

List of pseudo-teaching adherents
occultists, spiritualists, theosophists, violet-magicians, chiromants *706*

List of English words (Mr CHATTERLITZ)
Maybe, Perhaps, Tomorrow, Oh, I see, Alright *714*

List of fish (Lent)
Sturgeon, Sterlet, Dried-Sturgeon, Turbot, Salmon, White-Sturgeon, Mackerel, Pike, Gwyniad, Trout, Trioshka, Shamai, Bream *791*

List of types of Aristocrat
Emir, Count, Khan, Prince, Melik, Baron *856*

List of animals inimicable to Man #1
tigers, lions, hyenas *238*

List of animals inimicable to Man #2
tigers, lions, bears, hyenas, snakes, phalangas, scorpions *674*

List of the halogens #1
Planekurab, Alillonofarab, Krilnomolnifarab, Talkoprafarab, Khritofalmonofarab, Sirioonorifarab, Klananoizufarab, Idornikellafarab *636*

List of the halogens #2
Hydrogen, Fluorine, Chlorine, Bromine, Iodine *636*

List of musical instruments #1
Organ, Grand-piano, Piano, Harmonium, Cymbal *648*

List of musical instruments #2
gavalls, doodooks, daks, talfans *676*

List of musical instruments #3
sayaz, tar, kiamancha, zimbal *676*

List of diseases #1
Hemiplegia, Paraplegia, Paralysis progressiva, Paralysis essentialis, tabes-dorsalis, paralysis-agitans, sclerosis-disseminata *417*

List of diseases #2
Kalunom, Morkrokh, Selnoano *739*

List of diseases #3

Index of "Quotes"

This indexes every instance in the text where Gurdjieff quotes proverbs or pithy sayings. The majority of these he attributes to Mullah Nassr Eddin.

Index of Phrases

This indexes hyphenated phrases. It appears that Gurdjieff usually creates these constructions to indicate that a single concept for which there is no single English word is intended. Also included here are a few unhyphenated phrases that Gurdjieff frequently repeats.

— A —

— B —

— C —

— D —

— E —

— F —

— G —

— H —

— I —

— K —

— L —

— M —

— O —

— Q —

— R —

— S —

— T —

— Y —

Index of References to "God"

This index includes references to "God," both reverential references, particularly all capitalized references, and also mundane references to "gods and idols."

Word Index

This index references words and short hyphenated constructs that occur in the text. It includes all of Gurdjieff's neologisms and invented words. It includes some lists of words, but only those that consist entirely of neologisms. In most instances, no distinction is made between capitalized words and uncapitalized words (for example, Ape and ape), although in some instances separate lists of page numbers are given for each. This is provided when we believe that Gurdjieff may have intended a distinction between capitalized and uncapitalized words. There is a similar situation with plurals. Where a word is followed with (s) it indicates that the page numbers listed refer to instances either of the singular or the plural of the word. Separate entries are only provided where it was likely to be more useful to the reader.

— Numeric —

— A —

— B —

— C —

— D —

— E —

— F —

— G —

— H —

— I —

— J —

— K —

— L —

— M —

— N —

— O —

— P —

— Q —

— R —

— S —

— T —

— U —

— V —

— W —

— X —

— Y —

— Z —

To Fathom The Gist Volume I

Approaches to the Writings of G. I. Gurdjieff

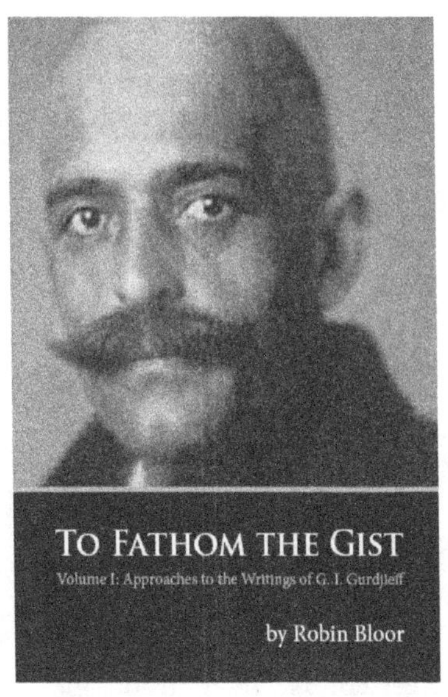

Unheralded and unexpected, **To Fathom The Gist** sparked renewed interest in G. I. Gurdjieff's objective literary masterpiece. Rather than a collection of thoughts or theories on the meaning of **Beelzebub's Tales**, this book is no more nor less than a well written guide on how to read the book productively. It provides a clear and concise description, with abundant examples, of a series of techniques a reader of **The Tales** can employ to make sense of the book. Furnishing explanatory examples it explains: intellectual postures and processes, background research into the content, objective science and how it diverges from modern science, Gurdjieff's language and style, intentional inexactitudes in the text, etymology and Gurdjieff's neologisms, the use of allegory and Gurdjieff's use of egoplastikoori.

The book has been described as: "Insightful and original," "Essential reading for anyone studying Gurdjieff's writings," "A true companion to All and Everything," "Valuable to any student of The Tales," "An ultra-effort" and "Exceptional." It has made a profound impact on many of its readers and has inspired the organization of study groups focussing on Gurdjieff's literature both in North America and Europe.

It is a seminal work, the foremost book written to assist those who wish to fathom the gist of Gurdjieff's on objective literature - and it is likely to remain so for many years.

To Fathom The Gist Volume II

The Arch-Absurd

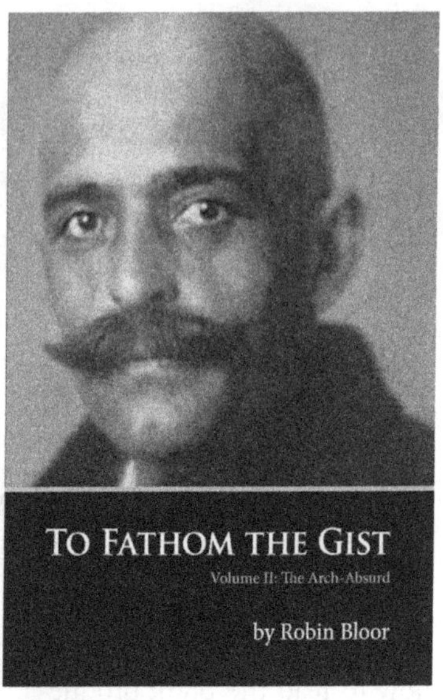

It might be expected that the second volume of **To Fathom The Gist** would continue in the direction forged by the first volume, but go a little further. It does not. Instead the author chose to investigate **The Tales** in a different way. He tried to envisage himself in Mr Gurdjieff's position and investigated **Beelzebub's Tales** from the perspective of the author. In essence, the theory behind this book is: "the more we can find out about how Gurdjieff wrote the book, the better we will be able to understand it."

As with the previous volume in this series, the book is alive with revelations about the meaning of various passages, given *en passant* as examples when the author explains aspects of how he believes the book was written and also, how Gurdjieff intended the book to be read. The book investigates Gurdjieff philology in depth, not through intent, but because wherever the author turned he seemed to barge into it.

At times he was obliged to study both the German and French versions of **The Tales** to identify style and word choice variations between languages. He compared the 1931 private edition to the 1950 edition to identify compositional and editing changes. He conducted a thorough review of the much (and it seems rightly) criticized 1992 version of **The Tales**.

All of this activity leaps from the pages of the book, as the reader moves from chapter to chapter, enticing him or her to try and fathom the gist of Gurdjieff's masterpiece.

CPSIA information can be obtained
at www.ICGtesting.com
Printed in the USA
BVHW041214010320
573389BV00009B/556